E

Poland
a country study

Foreign Area Studies
The American University
Edited by
Harold D. Nelson
Research completed
January 1983

On the cover: Poland's national coat of arms. The white eagle and red shield are also symbolized in the two colors of the national flag.

Second Edition, 1983; First Printing, 1984

Library of Congress Cataloging in Publication Data

Main entry under title:

Poland, a country study.

(Area handbook series)
"Research completed January 1983."
"DA Pam 550-162"—Verso t.p.
Bibliography: p.
Includes index.
1. Poland. I. Nelson, Harold D. II. American University (Washington, D.C.). Foreign Area Studies. III. Series.
DK4040.P57 1983 943.8 83-22431

Headquarters, Department of the Army
DA Pam 550-162

For sale by the Superintendent of Documents, U.S. Government Printing Office
Washington, D.C. 20402

Foreword

This volume is one in a continuing series of books now being prepared by the Federal Research Division of the Library of Congress under the Country Studies—Area Handbook Program. This book, however, is a reprint of a book written by members of the research staff of Foreign Area Studies, The American University. The last page of this book lists the other published studies.

Most books in the series deal with a particular foreign country, describing and analyzing its political, economic, social, and national security systems and institutions, and the interrelationships of those systems and the ways they are shaped by cultural factors. Each study is written by a multidisciplinary team of social scientists. The authors seek to provide a basic understanding of the observed society, striving for a dynamic rather than a static portrayal. Particular attention is devoted to the people who make up the society, their origins, dominant beliefs and values, their common interests and the issues on which they are divided, the nature and extent of their involvement with national institutions, and their attitudes toward each other and toward their social system and political order.

The books represent the analysis of the authors and should not be construed as an expression of an official United States government position, policy, or decision. The authors have sought to adhere to accepted standards of scholarly objectivity. Corrections, additions, and suggestions for changes from readers will be welcomed for use in future editions.

Chief
Federal Research Division
Library of Congress
Washington, D.C. 20540

Acknowledgments

The authors are grateful to those individuals in various United States government agencies and in international and academic organizations who gave of their time, data, special knowledge, and authoritative perspective on Polish affairs. In particular they wish to thank Carl H. McMillan, who wrote "The Council for Mutual Economic Assistance: A Historical Perspective," which appears as Appendix B, and Lawrence T. Caldwell, who wrote "The Warsaw Pact: Continuity and Change," which is included as Appendix C.

Gratitude is also extended to Robert Rinehart, who coordinated the presentation of Chapter 1, and to members of the Foreign Area Studies support staff who contributed directly to the preparation of the book. These persons include Dorothy M. Lohmann, Kathryn R. Stafford, and Andrea T. Merrill, who edited the manuscript; Alison Raphael, who edited Appendix B; and Hariett R. Blood and Farah Ahannavard, who prepared the graphics for the book. The authors appreciate as well the assistance provided by Gilda V. Nimer, librarian; Ernest A. Will, publications manager; Eloise W. Brandt, administrative assistant; and Margaret Quinn, who typed the manuscript.

The aesthetic touches that enhance the book's appearance are the work of Marty Ittner, whose illustrations appear on the cover and the title pages of the chapters. The inclusion of photographs has been made possible in part by the generosity of various individuals and several public and private agencies. Appreciation is expressed particularly to those persons who contributed original photographs not previously published.

Contents

List of Figures

Preface

Poland: A Country Study replaces the *Area Handbook for Poland,* which was researched and written in mid-1972 and published in 1973. During the subsequent decade major social, political, and economic changes have occurred in the country. A mounting economic crisis led to social unrest and a challenge to government authority by the independent labor movement known as Solidarity. The regime of Edward Gierek collapsed and was replaced through action within the ruling communist party. In the aftermath Poles were forced to endure more oppressive restrictions during a year of martial law. In light of these developments, a new examination of Poland is warranted.

Like its predecessor, this study seeks to provide a compact and objective exposition of dominant social, economic, political, and national security aspects of contemporary Polish society. In presenting this new work, the authors have relied primarily on official reports of United States government agencies and international organizations, journals, newspapers, and materials reflecting recent field research by independent scholarly authorities. Detailed data on many aspects of the society were not always readily available, however, and gaps in the information (as well as varied interpretations of certain matters) existed among some of the sources consulted. Where appropriate, such gaps and differences have been noted in the text. Should readers desire greater detail on certain subjects, the authors have noted the availability of amplifying materials in bibliographic statements at the end of each chapter. Full references to these and other sources used or considered are included in the detailed Bibliography.

Polish spelling is used in this study for historical figures whose names are frequently found in English texts in their Latinate forms, e.g., Wladyslaw instead of Ladislas. The spelling of contemporary place-names is generally in keeping with those approved by the United States Board on Geographic Names. Those that have assumed a conventional international usage, however, have been retained in the more familiar form; the reader will find, for example, Warsaw instead of Warszawa. Regions that have significance outside Polish history, e.g., Pomerania and Silesia, also appear in the conventional form. The term *Ruthenia* is used in its historical context to describe Ukrainian and Byelorussian territory included in the erstwhile Polish-Lithuania Commonwealth. The authors have sought to indicate those places that were known in earlier history by German names but that now possess different Polish designations, e.g., Gdansk (Danzig), Wroclaw (Breslau), and Szczecin (Stettin). Former Polish cities in territory annexed by the Soviet Union appear in their current form, e.g., the Lithuanian Vilnius rather than the Polish Wilno and the Russian Lvov rather than the Polish Lwow.

Polish uses the Latin alphabet, adding the following special characters: Ą ą, Ć ć, Ę ę, Ł ł, Ń ń, Ś ś, Ź ź, and Ż ż. Diacritics used in Polish include the inverted cedilla (˛) to indicate nasal sounds, the acute (´) to indicate the palatalization of a consonant, the stroke (/) to indicate that the l is pronounced as w, and the superior dot (˙) to indicate postpalatal sounds. To avoid inaccuracies that often occur in printing Polish words, diacritical marks have not been used.

Because confusion sometimes arises with respect to the terms *socialist* and *communist*, a note of caution is in order concerning their use in this study. Those countries that people in the West refer to as *communist* consistently describe themselves as socialist, making the claim that they are working toward communism, which Lenin described as a higher stage of socialism. In *Poland: A Country Study*, the terms *socialism* and *socialist* are generally used in the context of their treatment in Eastern Europe; that usage should not be confused or in any way equated with the democratic socialism espoused by several countries of Western Europe and elsewhere.

An effort has been made to limit the use of foreign and technical words in the text of this study. When this has not been appropriate, such terms have been defined briefly where they first appear in any chapter, or reference has been made to the Glossary, which is included for the reader's convenience.

All measurements are in metric terms. A conversion table will assist those who may not be familiar with metric equivalents (see table 1, Appendix A).

Table A. Chronology of Important Events

Periods and Dates	Events
Piast Period ca. 850–1370	Piast Dynasty founded (ca. 850). Duke Mieszko converted to Roman Catholicism (966). Archiepiscopal see established at Gniezno (1000). Boleslaw the Brave assumed title of king (1025). Poland divided among appanage princes (1138–1338). Teutonic Knights installed in Mazovia (1226). Tatar invasion countered at Battle of Legnica (1241). Peak of German colonization (ca. 1250 to ca. 1350). Reunification of Poland under Kazimierz III (1338). University of Krakow founded (1364). Death of Kazimierz III the Great and end of Piast Dynasty (1370). Personal union with Hungary during reign of Louis of Anjou (1370–82); concessions granted to Polish nobility.
Jagiellonian Dynasty 1386–1572	Grand Duke Jagiello of Lithuania married Jadwiga of Poland (1386); personal union between Poland and Lithuania. Teutonic Knights defeated at Battle of Grunwald (1410). Statutes of Nieszawa (1454) admitted nobility to full share in government. Legislation enacted requiring tenants to work on landlord's estates (1520); turning point in process of enserfment of peasantry. Publication of Copernicus' treatise on heliocentric universe (1543). Union of Lublin (1569) established formal unification of Polish-Lithuanian Commonwealth. Jagiellonian Dynasty became extinct at death of Zygmunt II August (1572).
The Royal Republic 1573–1795	Henry of Valois first elective king of Poland; religious toleration guaranteed (1573). Reign of Stefan Batory (1575–86).
Vasa Dynasty 1587–1668	Zygmunt Vasa of Sweden elected to Polish throne (1587). Polish candidate put on throne of Muscovy (1609). Cossack wars (1648–67) Muscovite intervention. Swedish-Polish War (1655–60).
Jan Sobieski 1674–96	Jan Sobieski lifted Turkish siege of Vienna (1683).
Saxon Period 1697–1764	August II (elector of Saxony) elected king with Russian support (1697); period of anarchy and decay. Great Northern War (1700–21); Poland occupied by Swedes and Russians. War of the Polish Succession (1733–35).
Reign of Stanislaw Poniatowski 1764–95	Stanislaw Poniatowski elected king through intervention of Catherine II of Russia (1764). Confederation of Bar (1768–72). First partition of Poland (1772). Adoption of May Constitution (1791). Confederation of Targowica and war with Russia (1792). Second partition (1793). National rising led by Tadeusz Koscuiszko (1794). Third partition (1795); elimination of Poland as sovereign state.
Poland Under Foreign Rule 1795–1918	Polish provinces incorporated by partitioning powers: Russia, Prussia, and Austria. Polish Legion formed in

Table A.—Continued

Periods and Dates	Events
	Italy under Napoleon; Polish national anthem composed by legionnaire (1797). Duchy of Warsaw created by Napoleon (1807); Polish army took part in invasion of Russia (1812). Congress of Vienna (1814–15) reconfirmed partition of Poland; Kingdom of Poland (Congress Poland) established in personal union with Russia. Insurrection in Congress Poland (1830–31); autonomy suspended. Republic of Krakow abolished (1846). Revolutionary ferment in Polish lands (1848–49). Armed rising in Russian Poland; emancipation of Polish peasantry by tsar (1863–64). Galicia granted autonomy within Austro-Hungarian Empire (1867). *Kulturkampf* initiated in Prussian Poland (1872). Kingdom of Poland abolished (1874); territory became Russian province. Polish Socialist Party organized in exile (1892). Revolutionary upheaval in Russian Poland (1905).
World War I 1914–18	Outbreak of hostilities (August 1914). Poles engaged on both sides in war between partitioning powers. Russian forces driven from Poland (1915). Polish "kingdom" proclaimed under protection of Germany and Austria-Hungary (November 1916). Provisional Russian government recognized Poland's right to independence (March 1917); Polish National Committee relocated in Paris. Woodrow Wilson enunciated Fourteen Points (January 1918); promise of Polish reunification and independence. Armistice (November 11, 1918).
Independent Poland 1918–45	Poland proclaimed independent republic (November 11, 1918); Jozef Pilsudski named provisional president. A communist party formed in Poland (December 1918). Polish delegates signed Treaty of Versailles (June 28, 1919); Poland recognized by Allies as "associated power." Russo-Polish War (1919–21); Soviets defeated at Battle of Warsaw (August 1920); Treaty of Riga (March 1921). Plebiscite in Upper Silesia (March 1921). Democratic constitution adopted (March 1921); Pilsudski resigned; defensive alliance with France. Economic crisis; institution of zloty (1924). Pilsudski's coup d'etat (May 1926); authoritarian regime introduced. Nonaggression pact with Soviet Union (1932). Nonagression pact with Germany (1934). New constitution introduced presidential system (March 1935). Death of Pilsudski (May 1935). Munich Crisis (September 1938); Poles occupied Cieszyn. Stalin dissolved Communist Party of Poland (official name adopted 1925) in 1938. Anglo-Polish mutual assistance treaty (April 1939); Hitler renounced nonaggression pact with Poland. Hitler-Stalin pact (August 23, 1939).
World War II 1939–45	Germany invaded Poland (September 1, 1939); Soviet Union attacked Poland (September 17, 1939); Poland divided and occupied. Polish government-in-exile set up in Paris (October 1939); transferred to London (June 1940). Polish army and air units served under

Table A.—Continued

Periods and Dates	Events
	British command on several fronts (1940–45); underground resistance organized inside Poland by Home Army. Katyn massacre (April 1940). German invaded Soviet Union (June 21, 1941). Polish-Soviet agreement (July 1941). Polish Workers' Party formed (January 1942); Wladyslaw Gomulka named first secretary (1943). Soviets broke relations with London government-in-exile (April 1943); Polish contingent formed in Red Army. Warsaw ghetto uprising (April 1943). Soviet-backed Lublin government formed (July 22, 1944). Home Army uprising in Warsaw (August-October 1944). Red Army entered Warsaw (January 1945). Yalta Conference acceded to Stalin's bid for Soviet influence over Poland (February 1945). Communist-dominated provisional government signed treaty of friendship and cooperation with Soviet Union (April 1945). Provisional Government of National Unity installed in Warsaw, recognized by Western allies (July 1945). Potsdam Conference (July–August 1945) assigned territory east of Oder-Neisse line to Poland. Eastern territories surrendered to Soviet Union.
The People's Republic 1945–	Sovietization of Poland: Three-Year Plan for Reconstruction (1947–49); nationalization of industry and business; communist "cultural revolution"; attack on church; opposition imprisoned. Transfer of population from eastern to western territories. Establishment of Cominform (September 1947) opposed by Gomulka. Gomulka replaced by Moscow-oriented Boleslaw Bierut as first secretary (September 1948). Polish United Workers' Party (PZPR) formed from merger of Polish Workers' Party and Polish Socialist Party (December 1948). Comecon formed (January 1949). Forced collectivization of agriculture attempted under Six-Year Plan 1950–55. Soviet-style constitution adopted for Polish People's Republic (July 22, 1952). Stalin died (March 1953). Intellectual and political ferment in Poland (1954–55). Polish membership in Warsaw Pact (1955). Bierut died (March 1956).
Gomulka Era 1956–70	Revolt by workers in Poznan (June 1956); Gomulka named first secretary of PZPR, replacing hard-line leadership (October 1956). Celebration of Poland's millennium as Christian country (1966); renewed conflict between church and state. Jews purged from PZPR bureaucracy; universities in "anti-Zionist" campaign (1967–68). Polish response to "Prague Spring"; student revolt (March 1968). Warsaw-Bonn Treaty acknowledged Oder-Neisse line (December 1970).
Gierek Era 1970–80	Revolt of workers in Baltic cities against radical price increases; Gomulka replaced as first secretary by Edward Gierek (December 1970). Constitution amended (January 1976). "June Events": workers protest new price rise; formation of Committee for the Defense of

Table A.—Continued

Periods and Dates	Events
	the Workers (KOR); beginnings of active dissent movement (June 1976). Election of Karol Cardinal Wojtyla, archbishop of Krakow, as Pope John Paul II (October 1978); papal visit to Poland (June 1979). Widespread protests over meat price increases (July–August 1980); 21-point agreement between Gdansk Inter-Factory Strike Committee (forerunner of Solidarity) and PZPR (August 31, 1980).
Kania Interval 1980–81	Gierek replaced by Stanislaw Kania (September 1980); General Wojciech Jaruzelski named prime minister (February 1981). Rural Solidarity recognized by government (May 1981); new Central Committee elected democratically at extraordinary PZPR Congress (July 1981); restructuring of state and economy demanded at National Congress of Solidarity (September–October 1981).
Jaruzelski Era 1981–	Jaruzelski succeeded Kania as first secretary (October 1981). Proclamation of martial law and internment of Solidarity activists (December 1981); Solidarity legally dissolved (October 1982); martial law formally suspended, but political curbs retained (December 1982).

Country Profile

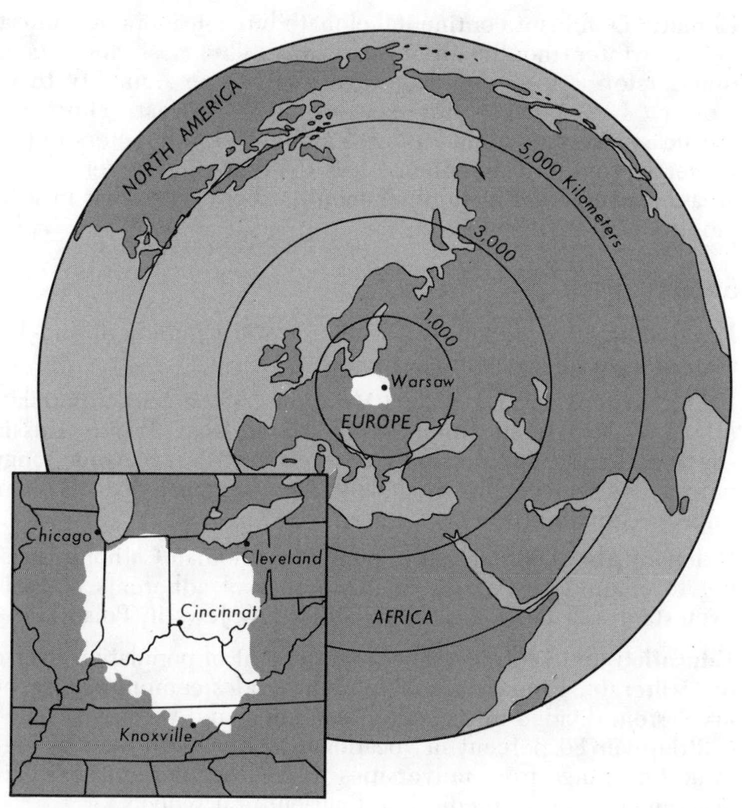

Country

Formal Name: Polish People's Republic.

Short Form: Poland.

Term for Citizens: Pole(s).

Capital: Warsaw.

Flag: Two equal-sized horizontal bands—upper white and lower red.

Geography

Size: 312,683 square kilometers, including inland waters.

Topography: Chiefly vast plain; only significant highlands are Carpathian Mountains in southeast, Sudety Mountains in southwest; no more than 300 square kilometers above 1,000 meters; roughly 90 percent of country below 300 meters.

Climate: Dominant continental climate but considerable snow and fog in winter months from maritime influences. Showers and thunderstorms from June to August but lower humidity than in winter. Longest growing season in southwest, shortest in northeast. Average annual rainfall of 500-650 millimeters in plain, higher in southern mountains, less than 500 millimeters in small areas. Precipitation in summer months about twice that in winter months.

Society:

Population: 35.1 million in 1978 census; 36.1 million in mid-1981, according to official Polish estimate.

Ethnic Groups and Language: More than 98 percent of population ethnic Poles; small numbers of Ukrainians, White Russians (Byelorussians), Germans, others. Polish, a West Slavonic tongue, official and universally used language. Regional dialects do not impede communication.

Religion: About 90 percent of population Roman Catholic, according to common estimate; small number of adherents of various Protestant and Orthodox faiths; still a few Jews in Poland.

Education and Literacy: About 98 percent of population over age of 15 literate. Primary school of eight grades compulsory; secondary system divided into general (academic) and vocational schools, a little over 80 percent in vocational track. Institutions of higher education range from universities to polytechnics and specialized academies, such as medical and agricultural schools.

Health: Free health care available to all Poles except a few in private sector; system extended to peasants in early 1970s. Fairly wide use of medical cooperatives and private practitioners as result of system deficiencies; all physicians work for state but may practice in cooperatives or privately after working hours. Medical facilities' obsolescence and equipment and pharmaceutical shortages generated by lack of capital investment and administrative problems.

Economy

Salient features: Highly centralized planning system generally unable to manage increasingly complex economy efficiently;

persistent overemphasis on development of capital goods industries; labor unrest and periodically large shortages of consumer goods were major economic problems still unresolved in early 1983. Major effort to reform system through more grass-roots autonomy for productive units and introduction of market system features under way.

Agriculture: Divided into large private and much smaller collective and state farm sectors. Agriculture (including livestock raising) provides livelihood for less than 25 percent of population and accounts for roughly 12 percent of national income (see Glossary). Private sector produces about 75 percent of agricultural output. Main crops: grains, potatoes, sugar beets, fodder. Very large livestock population—mostly pigs, cattle.

Manufacturing: Wide range of products, including primary metals, metal products, chemicals, electrical and nonelectrical machinery, data processing equipment, computer hardware, transportation equipment (automobiles, railroad rolling stock, airplanes, ships). Products of much smaller light industries sector include variety of food products, textiles, miscellaneous consumer goods. Level of production in various heavy industries dependent on imported materials. Consumer goods output generally well below domestic demand.

Mining: Major deposits of economically important minerals actively mined, including coal, copper, lead, zinc, sulfur, rock salt. Important deposits of natural gas and petroleum also exploited.

Energy: Major energy sources: domestic coal, natural gas; imported petroleum and natural gas. Wood widely used for fuel but in limited quantities. Installed electricity generating capacity 25,523 megawatts in 1981. About 97 percent of power generated by thermal plants; output affected by availability of domestic coal. Country's hydroelectric potential small.

Foreign Trade: Coal is principal export item; electrical engineering products, wide variety of other machines and equipment account for nearly one-half of total exports by value. Principal imports: petroleum, natural gas, grains, feed grains, electrical engineering products. Roughly 60 percent of exports go to member states of the Council for Mutual Economic Assistance (Comecon)—more than one-half to Soviet Union; some 30 percent to developed Western economies (over half to countries of European Economic Community). In early 1980s import sources and proportions roughly the same as those for exports.

Currency: Zloty (nonconvertible); according to exchange rate in effect in late 1982, US$1 equaled 86 zlotys (see Glossary).

Fiscal Year: Polish government operates on calendar year basis.

Transportation

Railroads: Rail system operated by Polish State Railways consisted in 1981 of 24,356 route kilometers (7,091 kilometers electrified) standard-gauge track and 2,812 route kilometers of narrow gauge; system almost entirely single track. Locomotive power about one-half diesel, one-quarter steam, one-quarter electric.

Roads and Road Transport: State and local road system totaled 254,100 kilometers at end of 1981. About 148,900 kilometers of all-weather roads, of which some 120,000 kilometers paved. Almost 3 million motor vehicles (cars, trucks, buses) in 1980. Since 1981 road transport affected by fuel shortages caused by insufficient foreign exchange for adequate petroleum imports.

Civil Aviation: State-owned Polish Airlines provides domestic service between Warsaw and 11 other cities and operates international routes; all equipment Soviet designed. International airport at Warsaw also serviced by a number of foreign airlines.

Inland Waterways: Over 4,000 kilometers of inland waterways navigable by regular transport services; about 60 percent in Vistula River system, remainder in Oder River basin; two systems interconnected by Kanal Bydgoski in north-central Poland. Inland waterway transportation greatly underutilized, accounting for only small portion of national freight and passenger traffic.

Ports and Shipping: Three large modern ports (Gdansk, Gdynia, Szczecin) on Baltic Sea; over 11,000 ships and 61.2 million tons of cargo handled in 1980. Modern shipyards at ports produce diversified range of vessels. In 1981 merchant fleet of 322 vessels totaled almost 4.6 million deadweight tons; included general cargo ships, bulk carriers, tankers, container, roll-on-roll-off vessels; service to all parts of world.

Pipelines: Comecon Druzhba (Friendship) pipeline transports main supply of petroleum from Soviet Union; extensive gas pipeline network distributes domestic and Soviet-supplied natural gas and domestic manufactured gas to main Polish cities.

Government and Politics

Government: Socialist state based on Soviet Union model. Formal presidential powers exercised by Council of State under chairmanship of Henryk Jablonski. Nonpolicymaking Council of Ministers, headed by prime minister (General Wojciech Jaruzelski since February 1981). Unicameral legislature (Sejm) exercises largely pro forma role enacting government programs. All government bodies subordinate to communist Polish United Workers' Party (Polska Zjednoczona Partia Robotnicza—PZPR); party first secretary (Jaruzelski since October 1981) is country's de facto chief executive.

Politics: Monopoly over policies and programs retained by PZPR. Sejm members drawn from PZPR, two satellite political parties, and three action groups that ostensibly represent Roman Catholic interests; candidates chosen by PZPR-controlled National Unity Front; election results predetermined. PZPR power monopoly contested by independent trade union movement (Solidarity) in 1980–81; Solidarity leaders interned and union dissolved during year of martial law (December 1981 to December 1982). Jaruzelski pledge of reform in consultation with all forces of society belied by conversion of martial law decrees into permanent prohibitions curtailing civil rights, free trade unions, political activity outside sanctioned channels.

Administrative Divisions: Two levels of local government: 49 provinces (voivodships) and more than 2,000 communes, towns, urban districts. Governors (voivods) answerable to central authorities and dominant over people's councils, whose members nominally elected but in fact chosen by National Unity Front.

Foreign Relations: Aligned with Moscow on all major international issues. Allied with Soviet Union and communist countries of Eastern Europe through Warsaw Pact, Comecon, and bilateral treaties. Polish sovereignty over former German territory acknowledged by Federal Republic of Germany (West Germany) in 1970 treaty. Previously good relations with West European countries impaired by martial law and suppression of Solidarity. Dependence on West persists for trade and rescheduling of heavy debts. Polish government angered over United States termination of subsidized grain sales, withdrawal of most-favored-nation tariff treatment, and reduction of other ties in reaction to martial law and outlawing of Solidarity.

National Security

Armed Forces: Ground, air, and naval elements of parent Polish People's Army designated "operational forces"; designed to operate in concert with Soviet and other Warsaw Pact forces. Component National Territorial Defense forces formed for domestic use; no Warsaw Pact responsibilities. In 1982 personnel of operational forces numbered 317,000 (including 207,000 in ground forces, 22,000 in navy, and 88,000 in air and air defense forces). National Territorial Defense forces (excluding National Air Defense Force) numbered 85,000. Conscripts comprised 74 percent of ground forces, 31 percent of air and air defense forces, 27 percent of navy; effective reserves estimated at 605,000.

Military Units: Ground forces (organized along Soviet lines) included eight motorized rifle divisions, five tank divisions, one airborne division, and one amphibious assault division. Air force and National Air Defense Force had about 700 combat aircraft deployed in attack, interceptor, and reconnaissance squadrons. Navy had approximately 150 ships and some 50 combat aircraft; aging equipment limited patrol, attack, and amphibious capabilities. Two Soviet tank divisions and tactical air force equipped with some 400 aircraft stationed in Poland; manned strength of these Soviet forces 25,000 to 35,000.

Equipment: Most military equipment provided by Soviet Union; some ships, armored vehicles, and trainer aircraft designed and produced in Poland; some tanks and combat aircraft produced by Poles under Soviet license.

Internal Security Forces: Ministry of Internal Affairs responsible for all internal security forces, including Security Service (secret police), Citizens' Militia (regular uniformed police), and Motorized Units of the Citizens' Militia (riot police).

Foreign Military Treaties: Member of Warsaw Pact; separate bilateral defense treaty with Soviet Union.

NOTE—Voivodships have the same names as their capitals except for the following:

Voivodship	Capital
Bielsko	Bielsko Biala
Gorzow	Gorzow Wielkopolski
Piotrkow	Piotrkow Trybunalski

Figure 1. Poland: Administrative Divisions, 1982

Introduction

POLAND IS A LAND of anomalies and paradoxes. A communist state since the aftermath of World War II, it exists and operates (by default, many Poles maintain) within the orbit of the Soviet Union and the Warsaw Pact. At the same time, however, a number of its national characteristics and institutions mark the country as different from the other members of Eastern Europe's so-called communist bloc.

Despite the official Marxist-Leninist proclivity for atheism, most Poles have remained staunchly loyal to the Roman Catholic Church, an institution that has exercised great influence on them for centuries. Many observers feel that the church and the Polish nation, in effect, constitute a single entity. This view may represent an overstatement of fact, but a modus vivendi nonetheless does exist between the church and the communist state. Although the government has succeeded in controlling the country's industrial sector, it has been less adept in its attempts to collectivize agriculture, and the vast majority of Polish farms has remained in private hands. In addition, Poles are better informed regarding domestic and foreign affairs than are most of their East European neighbors. This is largely attributable to the absence of any government effort to jam foreign radiobroadcasts, particularly those originated by Radio Free Europe in Munich. (Mobs of Polish people destroyed existing jamming installations in 1956, and the government has not rebuilt them.) Thus the Poles have the shortwave equivalent of a free press.

Even more unusual has been the periodic recurrence of organized protests and popular disorder that have demonstrated the Poles' perennial misgivings regarding the fruits of communism. On three occasions (in 1956, 1970, and 1980–81) widespread dissent and demonstrations forced the replacement of incumbent communist governments—even though those in power had control over the bureaucracy, the internal security institutions, and the armed forces. In other East European countries these pillars of strength—backed by the powerful Soviet sponsor, if necessary—have usually ensured the governments' (and the communist system's) self-perpetuation. Soviet military intervention did not occur in any of Poland's crises, but it was a possibility that concerned Polish authorities, particularly in 1956 and 1980–81.

The trait that most distinguishes Poland from its immediate neighbors is the people's strong sense of nationalism, a cultural heritage forged and reinforced through more than 1,000 years of turbulent history. Many of the problems Poles have encountered throughout those centuries have been the product of certain immutable geographic realities. Polish history amply attests to the difficulty of serving as a buffer between larger, more powerful, and more aggressive neighbors—Prussia and Russia in an earlier age, Germany and the Soviet Union (as these geopolitical entities became known) in modern times (see fig. 1). Changes of dynasties and frontiers, foreign invasions and occupation, loss of political independence, and repeated partitioning of Polish territory—these were the disruptive historical events that have conditioned life in modern Poland.

The borders enclosing Polish territory in 1983 were remarkably similar to those that delimited the first Polish state, which was established in A.D. 966, the same year Poles accepted conversion to Roman Catholicism. Although the configuration of the tenth-century state and its twentieth-century counterpart are similar, the country's size has varied radically during its first millennium. During its "Golden Age" of the late fifteenth and the sixteenth centuries, Poland, in federation with Lithuania, encompassed huge territories that stretched eastward deep into the lands of the Muscovites and even included the ancient Ukrainian city of Kiev. At its nadir, Poland disappeared completely from the map of Europe when, in the late eighteenth century, Austria, Prussia, and Russia partitioned the country and absorbed its land and people. An independent Poland did not reappear until after World War I.

Minor territorial modifications continued during the period between the two world wars, but the most profound changes began with the attack in 1939 by the invading armies of Hitler's Nazi Germany. After the rapid collapse of their own army, which fought valiantly but hopelessly against the invaders, the Poles endured more than five years of occupation, national degradation, and genocidal oppression. In effect, Poland again became partitioned when, two weeks after the Germans invaded from the west, the Soviet Union's Red Army moved in from the east, occupying and absorbing a large area of the country. Frontiers were further altered after the conclusion of World War II as a result of the Yalta and Potsdam agreements between the victorious Great Powers. To pacify Josef Stalin, Poland was recognized as belonging to the Soviet sphere of influence. In the process the Poles lost more territory to their powerful eastern neighbor than they gained from the defeated Germany in the west.

This vast series of territorial transformations and resulting social disruption has had a marked effect on the country's population. As expressed by Leopold Unger, a Pole and managing editor of the Warsaw daily newspaper *Zycie Warszawy* until 1967, "My parents were born and married in Austria, lived and procreated in Poland, were killed in Germany, and were buried in an unmarked grave in the Soviet Union—all this without moving from the same house in the same street in the same city of Lvov (otherwise known as Lviv, Lemberg, etc.)." Similar experiences are shared by many thousands of Poles and, as Unger reports, "have inspired . . . a profound mistrust of all ideological attempts to change the destiny of humanity."

Poles are essentially of Slavic origin, having descended from Western Slavs who had settled in the fertile river valleys of the North European plain sometime before the Christian Era. Other Western Slavic peoples became the Czechs and the Slovaks, who populated Czechoslovakia, and the Sorbs, a tiny minority group currently living in the German Democratic Republic (East Germany). At most points in its history as an independent entity, Poland was multiethnic, owing to the presence of sizable minorities of Germans, Ukrainians, Byelorussians, and Jews. These groups naturally did not share the Polish majority's strong sense of nationhood that had persisted even during the 125 years of partition when their state did not exist.

In 1939 about 70 percent of the country's people claimed Polish ethnic origin, but since then the population pattern has altered from one of great heterogeneity to one of extreme homogeneity. In mid-1981 it was estimated that roughly 98 percent of the 36.1 million inhabitants were Polish in both ethnicity and nationalistic spirit.

For most Poles, World War II looms as the greatest disaster in their long history and, even though most of the population is too young to have personal recollections, the horrors of that war are continually brought to the fore in the mass media, in the theater, in books, and in the schools. During the war 6 million Polish citizens lost their lives, half of them Jews who were systematically exterminated by the Nazis. Some of the concentration camps have been maintained just as they existed at that time and are open as museums, intended to be constant reminders of the calamity known to the world as the Holocaust. Throughout the postwar period Poles have reiterated the slogan "Never again!"

Even before its leaders had gained full control, the Soviet-sponsored postwar regime set about changing the economic, political, and social fabric of the country. The Soviet model was the blueprint on which Polish communists fashioned a reordered state. According to doctrinal formula, the communist party and its hierarchical apparatus would dominate the political system and dictate economic and social policies for the entire society. As the sole authority and the ultimate arbiter on any public question, the party regarded as an act of treason any opposition that might develop.

Building from a small membership at the end of the war, the communist Polish Workers' Party recruited new members and in 1948 merged with the Polish Socialist Party to increase its own rolls and to gain the administrative and technical skills of the co-opted socialists. The reconstituted communist party became known as the Polish United Workers' Party (Polska Zjednoczona

Partia Robotnicza—PZPR). During the early period of building and consolidating its power base, the PZPR undercut the strength of other parties, reducing them to political impotence. The PZPR rapidly gained firm control of the country, owing in large part to the presence of Soviet military forces and security police.

Formalized by a series of agreements—"treaties of friendship and cooperation"—the new Polish government established defense alliances and arranged for economic cooperation with the Soviet Union and the European countries that had been gathered into the Soviet sphere of influence during and since World War II. In the process Poland became a charter member of the Council for Mutual Economic Assistance (Comecon) and the military-oriented Warsaw Pact.

Regarded as communist by Western standards, the Polish government officially calls itself socialist in keeping with Marxist doctrine that defines socialism as an intermediate step on the road to ultimate communism. All the trappings of a constitutional republic remain, including a constitution that officially bequeaths ultimate authority to the country's workers—authority that is expressed through elected bodies such as the Sejm (the unicameral national legislature) and the people's councils at provincial and local levels. In practice, however, political power and control of the economy and virtually all social institutions are manipulated by the PZPR hierarchy. Although its membership totals less than 7 percent of the population, the PZPR controls or sponsors all legally organized activities except the church. In 1983 this self-governing institution operated in accordance with policy established in the Vatican where John Paul II, the first Polish pope, presided. In Warsaw the church was guided by the Polish primate, Jozef Glemp, who in January was elevated to the College of Cardinals.

The social system that had formerly existed in Poland was shattered by the events of World War II. During the hostilities and the occupation, most persons in the existing elites of Polish society were either killed or exiled, and when the war was over, the Communists had sufficient strength to prevent any attempts to reconstruct the former societal pattern.

The social structure designed by the PZPR continues in a state of transition from the old to the new, affected as much or more by industrialization and modernization as by ideological persuasions. The prewar elite, whose status was determined by birth, property, and education, has been replaced by a new elite, the members of which assume their class rank and privilege by reason of their standing in the PZPR. Marxist dogma stresses that a socialist system will in time do away with class structure and bring about egalitarian societies. But the realities of industrialization, modernization, and Polish human nature have militated against egalitarianism and have instead produced social stratification of a new composition.

In communist Poland the new order places the party elite at the top of the social structure, followed by the intelligentsia, i.e., professionals, scholars, and better educated managers and technicians. Below the intelligentsia, in descending order of importance, are white-collar employees, manual workers, peasants, and the private entrepreneurs. In theory, the last group will disappear as the society becomes completely socialized, but the large, privately owned agricultural sector, the thousands of self-employed artisans, and the growing number of informal ("gray") market activities remain indispensable to the functioning of the economy. It seems safe to venture that the disappearance of the private Polish entrepreneur will not occur soon.

Governing—and controlling—Poland has not been an easy task for any of the communist leaders who have tried since 1945. Nor has it been a simple matter for the Kremlin to suggest ideologically acceptable solutions to the problems that have beset the PZPR hierarchy. Poland, after all, does not precisely fit the Soviet Union's mold. After nearly 40 years of living under the monolithic system decreed by Marxist-Leninist doctrine, most Poles reflect a preference for a pluralistic arrangement in which their sense of nationhood and self-reliance can find expression. A case in point has been their continued resistance to the collectivization of agriculture, obligatory elsewhere in socialist systems. As former Radio Free Europe's policy director R.V. Burks suggests, Moscow's failure to insist on total doctrinal conformity probably has resulted in large measure from the Soviets' perception of Poles as "crazy unpredictable [people], traditionally liable to engage in unexpected insurgence even against hopeless odds." Certainly Polish history tends to support this view. As Burks points out, "Communist Poland lurches defiantly from crisis to crisis, now and again achieving a quantum leap toward a pluralistic society."

The Kremlin, the PZPR, and the Polish people well remember that Wladyslaw Gomulka, first secretary of the PZPR, stepped down in the face of serious workers' riots in 1970. Gomulka had been the strong man of Polish communism since 1956, when the preceding government also collapsed in the face of worker discontent. Edward Gierek, who succeeded Gomulka at the pinnacle of the Polish communist hierarchy, was deposed in 1980 (his successor, Stanislaw Kania, met a similar fate a year later) in the continuing climate of worker unrest that had begun with violent demonstrations in 1976 and an increasing threat of economic chaos. In 1980–81, after strikes and industrial plant shutdowns, the authorities were forced to recognize an authentic trade union know as Solidarnosc (Solidarity). Its leader, worker-activist Lech Walesa of Gdansk, rapidly captured the imagination and support of 10 million Poles at home—and the sympathy of all free people abroad—for his courage in defying the country's repressive communist system.

In the crises of 1956, 1970, and 1976 the workers' demands had been strictly economic, and those involved had sought better living and working conditions rather than the overthrow of the system. In 1980–81, however, Solidarity's goals became more expansive, as did the movement's composition and tactics. Whereas earlier manifestations had been spontaneous worker protests, Solidarity's efforts combined the powers and talents of the workers and the intelligentsia. For the first time since the founding of the communist state, the control measures exercised by the privileged PZPR hierarchy acted as a catalyst for pervasive Polish unity.

Although Solidarity's initial goals were economic, its series of confrontations with the communist authorities assumed a political character, and it became increasingly apparent that the existence of a free labor movement was tantamount to the regime's acceptance of an opposition political party that would challenge the PZPR's power monopoly. Such an eventuality, of course, was unacceptable to the Polish regime and the communist hierarchy in the Kremlin. If Solidarity's demands were not contained, similar challenges to communist party dominance in other countries of Eastern Europe might occur. To restore order and preclude the likelihood of Soviet intervention for the purpose of salvaging a faltering and ineffectual regime—a precedent that had already been established in Hungary and Czechoslovakia—Poland's General Wojciech Jaruzelski acted. Exercising his combined powers over the state and party apparatus—and as commander of the Polish People's Army—he placed his country under a state of martial law in December 1981. A year later "suspension" of martial law was announced, but this proved little more than a gesture that failed to moderate the rigors of life in communist Poland.

Prolonged detention of Walesa and continuous harassment of him and his family since his release have only been part of the regime's tactics aimed at destroying the threat Solidarity once posed. Since the year of martial law, the free trade union has been an illegal organization, some of its erstwhile leaders have been arrested and imprisoned, and a few who escaped the police have been driven underground. The repression common during martial law has relaxed to some degree, but the regime's hated riot police (known to Poles as the ZOMO) remain an ever-ready coercive weapon against popular uprisings. Concurrently, Jaruzelski's government has introduced new factory-level trade unions and public associations, ostensibly intended to permit expression by various elements of the Polish society. These government-sponsored bodies, however, have been viewed as an insidious effort to sever the degree of unity that developed among the various social classes during the 16 months that Solidarity sparked the hopes of the Polish People.

Some observers assert that because of Solidarity's failure to bring about reform in Poland, all chances for the revivial of a popular political movement have disappeared. Others see little hope for the future unless social consensus can be achieved. In mid-1983 the country's economic crisis had not yet abated, and the Jaruzelski government still faced problems of major declines in production, large-scale shortages of hard currency, a staggering foreign debt that threatened bankruptcy if Western assistance were withdrawn, and a persistent shortage of consumer necessities that relentlessly lowered living standards. Moreover, Poland was still inhabited by those 36.1 million "unpredictable [people], traditionally liable to engage in unexpected insurgence even against hopeless odds."

May 1983

Harold D. Nelson

Chapter 1. Historical Setting

Clio, the muse of history, from a sculpture in Warsaw's Saxon Gardens

THE PEOPLE OF POLAND celebrated their millennial anniversary as a nation in 1966, tracing their origins not from the founding of a political entity but to their conversion to Christianity under Mieszko, a great war leader who earlier had united under his rule the West Slavic tribes of the Wisla (Vistula) River region. The Poles' sense of nationhood has endured throughout the subsequent thousand years of their history despite invasions, changes of dynasties and frontiers, foreign occupation, loss of political independence, and partition of their country.

The most significant factors in understanding the history of Poland are the central role of Roman Catholicism in the life of the country and its people and the Western orientation of the Polish culture that derives from it. Also of crucial importance to Poland's historical development has been the country's geopolitical position—wedged between Germany and Russia on the great European plain without the protection of natural frontiers. The Poles have an acute historical consciousness, and archetypes from the past have often served as models for action in the present. Martial virtues, for instance, have been traditionally held in great esteem. Typically, the Poles have relied on direction from elite groups and in times of uncertainty have often been attracted by charismatic leadership.

During the first seven centuries of its history, Poland steadily expanded to become one of Europe's largest countries. After the union with Lithuania in the fourteenth century, it was the center of a multiethnic commonwealth, and its political focus shifted in the process to a broad eastern frontier. The Poles conceived of it as their mission to serve as a barrier for the West against hostile intrusions from the East. Polish patriotism, therefore, had more to do with the fulfillment of Poland's historic vocation as a Western and a Catholic nation than it did with allegiance to a ruling dynasty or a political system. The large and privileged Polish-Lithuanian gentry class, whose interests were essentially regional rather than national, came to dominate the country's political and economic life and prevented the growth of a strong and centralized monarchy. Weakened by war and reduced to impotency by political instability that verged on anarchy, Poland fell victim to its powerful neighbors and was dismembered by Prussia, Russia, and Austria in three successive partitions in the late eighteenth century. The last of these, in 1795, marked the disappearance of Poland as a political entity for more than a century.

Although separated politically, the Poles held fast to their cultural unity. The experience of the partitions and the failure of subsequent attempts to throw off foreign rule fostered the image of a martyred Poland, described as the "Christ among the nations," betrayed by the West and sacrificed to expediency in political settlements made by other countries. It was an image that made a deep impression on the best of Poland's creative intellects in the nineteenth century. Often admired at a distance in the West for their heroic impetuosity, the Poles in time demonstrated a parallel aptitude for dogged steadfastness in time of adversity. Through what came to be called "organic work"—setting aside romantic notions and making the best of an unfavorable situation—the partitioned Poles were successful in the face of incredible odds in preserving their national identity without the framework of a nation-state.

Reunited and restored to independence after World War I, the country was able to sustain a parliamentary democracy for only a few years before Marshal Jozef Pilsudski, a figure of heroic proportions in modern Polish history, seized power in 1926 and introduced authoritarian rule. Overwhelmed by Nazi Germany and the Soviet Union in 1939, Poland entered into the darkest period of its long history, suffering the deaths of more than 6 million of its population during World War II.

Poland's postwar fate was determined by the victorious Allies. It was liberated and then occupied by the Soviet Union's Red Army. The country's borders were drastically altered, populations were transferred, and the transformation of Poland into a Soviet satellite was begun. Reorganized as the Polish People's Republic, Poland became a communist state, governed since 1948 under the control of the Polish United Workers' Party (Polska Zjednoczona Partia Robotnicza—PZPR). Although their country has been subjected to enforced integration into the communist system, the Poles' persistent spirit of independence and their enduring quest for greater freedom, strengthened by deep-rooted ties to Roman Catholicism and Western culture, have been major obstacles to the efforts of the party and government to remold Polish society along communist lines. The Polish people have refused to concede the communist regime's legitimacy.

Protests against economic conditions laid to the regime's policies and against violations of human rights, as well as direct challenges to the PZPR's claim to a "leading role" in contemporary Poland, were mounted in the late 1970s by a coalition uniting workers and peasants, the intelligentsia, and the church. World attention was focused on Poland in 1980 and 1981 as the independent trade union movement Solidarnosc (Solidarity) exacted broad concessions from the regime, including its recognition as an organization operating outside the control of the state or party. In December 1981, however, Solidarity was ordered disbanded, and its leaders were arrested when martial rule was imposed by the prime minister and party first secretary, General Wojciech Jaruzelski, who had placed himself at the head of a military government.

The Making of Poland

The early history of Poland was shaped by geopolitical realities. For centuries the West Slavic tribes of the Odra (Oder) and Wisla (Vistula) valleys, ancestors of the modern Poles, had lived in relative isolation, protected by marshes and thick forests and clinging fiercely to their land and to their customs. The basic unit in each tribe was the clan, a close-knit kinship group that held collective title to its ancestral territory. All of the clan's warriors were considered equals, sharing responsibility for the security of their commonly held property and the safety of their kin. A chieftain chosen from a family recognized for its military prowess arbitrated disputes and led the warriors in battle, but he was required to govern the clan in consultation with a council of freemen. A stronghold dominating the tribal territory usually served as a place of assembly and center for the clan's religious cult as well as a refuge in time of adversity.

Under pressure after the seventh century from the Avars and later from the Germans, the weaker tribes consolidated with the stronger, which in turn coalesced under the leadership of the Polanie, a tribe inhabiting the valley of the upper Warta River (see fig. 2). It was not until the year 963, however, that a chronicler made note of the pagan West Slavic tribes who, led by their Polanian duke Mieszko, were resisting German encroachments along the Oder frontier. Although they remained distinctive entities, the allied tribes became known collectively as Poles (Polacy; sing., Polak), and their union under Mieszko's rule marked the formation of the Polish state and nation.

Early Piast Poland

Duke Mieszko (962–92) traced his descent from Piast, the legendary founder of the ruling Polanian dynasty. He, like his predecessors and immediate successors, waged constant war to consolidate his political authority and the territorial integrity of his realm. Tenacious as they were, however, the Poles following Mieszko were defeated by the better organized forces of the German march lords. Responding to the challenge from a more advanced civilization, Mieszko sealed an alliance with neighboring Bohemia by marrying a Czech princess in 966 and, abandoning his pagan religion, accepted Christianity. Missionaries of the Latin church soon arrived from Germany to undertake the task of proselytizing his subjects.

The newly converted Poles identified themselves unreservedly with Roman Catholicism, thereby linking the destiny of their nation with that of Western Europe. Meanwhile, their East Slavic neighbors in Kiev accepted conversion from missionaries of the Greek church, attaching themselves to the competing center of Christian civilization in Constantinople. Mieszko's aims in bringing Poland within Rome's religious orbit were essentially political;

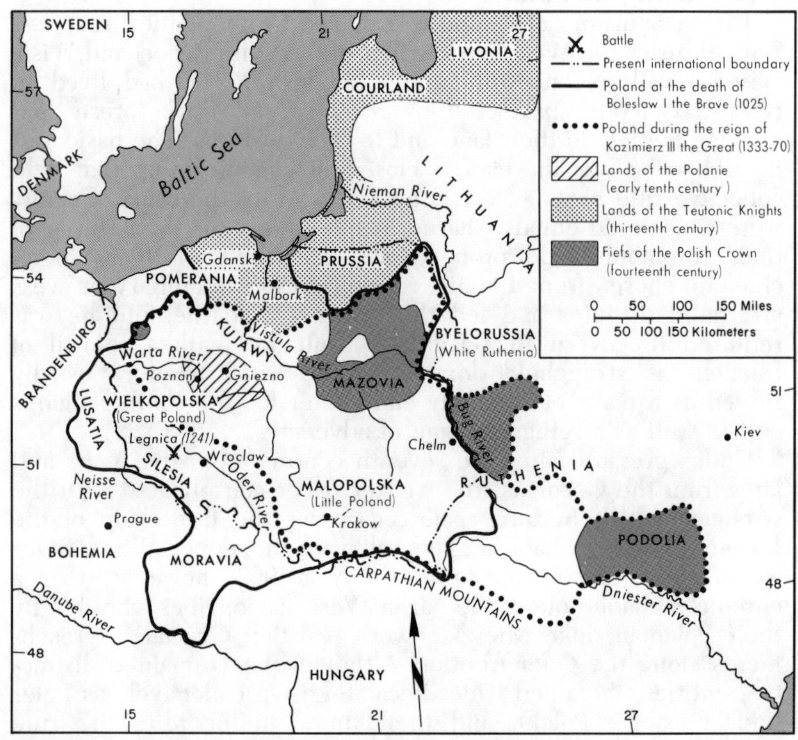

Figure 2. Piast Poland, Tenth to Fourteenth Centuries

Polish membership in the Latin Christian community was conceived of initially as a strategem to stem the eastward-running tide of German colonization and ensure the country's independence. His policies were carried forward by his son and successor, Boleslaw I the Brave (992–1025), an able statesman who in the year 1000 concluded an agreement with the Holy Roman emperor, Otto III, organizing Polish dioceses under the jurisdiction of an archiepiscopal see established at Gniezno. As primate (first in the hierarchy) of the Polish church, the archbishop of Gniezno was responsible directly to Rome for the ecclesiastical authority with which he was vested, removing Poland from the missionary area of German bishops who were recognized as the stalking horses of German expansionism. In a gesture that further emphasized Poland's ties to Rome, Boleslaw, who in 1025 took the title of king, deeded his realm to the pope to be held thereafter by the Piasts as a fief (dependency) of the papacy, an action that gave religious sanction not only to the Piast dynasty but also to Polish nationhood.

Poland's political orientation to Western Europe and its assimilation of the Latin cultural tradition proceeded directly from its Christianization. Monasteries established in Poland by monks from France and Germany in the eleventh century grew in number, size, and importance as Polish clerics were admitted, and by the next century Poland had become the cradle of numerous missionaries working in Pomorze (Pomerania) and Prussia. By the thirteenth century, Poland had emerged as a bulwark of western Christian civilization against hostile forces threatening it from the east, a role that the Poles came to regard as their country's historical mission.

During this formative period in the country's history, the characteristic components of its internal political and social structures began to take shape. From their pre-Christian past, the Poles had inherited three features of social organization: first, a strong clan system that worked against the evolution of the feudal structures typical of many other European societies; second, a tendency toward legal equality among all members of the clan; and, third, the insistence on unanimity in decisions concerning vital issues that pertained to the community as a whole. It was this last characteristic that later degenerated into the institution known as the *liberum veto,* the right of every member of the community to proclaim freely his dissent from decisions of the majority and to enforce the rule of unanimity.

Despite the tradition of legal equality, class differentiation soon began to develop. The heads of clans and their families acquired property and asserted their social superiority over the rest of their kin. The clan chieftains were joined by the dispossessed leaders of tribes that had disintegrated or had been absorbed by stronger tribes as well as by some foreigners and the more able members of their own retinues, who were endowed with land and the labor to work it in return for their military service. These formed the nucleus of Poland's knightly estate, which gradually emerged as a noble class, the *szlachta,* claiming a privileged position as defenders of the country and as the backbone of its society. The process of class formation begun at that level was elaborated on a larger scale in the courts of the Piast dukes.

All members of the noble class were considered socially equal, but a complex system of gradation based on wealth and kinds of wealth developed among them. A few families of extraordinary wealth qualified as magnates (*mozni*; literally, the powerful), and they were deferred to by the gentry, nobles with less extensive holdings, and by landless knights. Because in Poland the principle of primogeniture never took root, all descendants of a nobleman were likewise noble. Consequently, in Poland the nobility were a much more numerous class than in other European countries, composing by the end of the fifteenth century about 10 percent of the entire population. As a class the nobles were referred to as "the nation," and only they enjoyed political rights.

The great mass of Poles were freemen, either independent farmers or tenants on noble estates, but a class of debt slaves evolved, composed of smallholders whose arrears eventually became perpetual rents that transformed them and their families into serfs bound to an estate. The ranks of the latter also included prisoners of war assigned to servitude under a victorious noble.

The Period of Fragmentation

The emperor Otto III's vision of a federation of autonomous Christian princes united by their allegiance to the emperor and the pope, which had lain behind his agreement allowing the establishment of a Polish hierarchy, was rejected by his successors, who embarked on a policy of military conquest and German colonization in the Slavic East. The Poles managed to resist this onslaught—described by the German slogan *Drang nach Osten* (drive to the East)—in part because of the cooperation of the papacy, which was locked in a struggle with the German emperors for control over ecclesiastical administration in the empire. But the task of resisting German expansion was made more difficult by the division of the Piast patrimony into appanages that were parceled out to princes of the ruling Polish dynasty.

The appanage scheme, ingeniously elaborated by King Boleslaw II Crookmouth (1102–38) to prevent a fratricidal struggle for the succession among his heirs, failed to serve its purpose. Quite the contrary, the division of Poland into a series of petty principalities resulted in the progressive fragmentation of the country, attended by political chaos and civil war. As the system developed, the Piast prince at Krakow was recognized as having "seniority," or nominal precedence, over his brother princes, but in practice a focal point of royal authority was lacking. The feuding Piast princes, each of them eager to take Krakow and eventually rule the entire country, seldom cooperated, even to counter outside threats to the country. The German emperors intervened in Poland's domestic affairs and seized the western fringes of the Piast patrimony with impunity. The divided Poles were likewise powerless to check the incursions of the pagan Prussians into the province of Mazovia.

In 1226 Mazovia's Duke Konrad, preoccupied with internal struggles, called in the Teutonic Knights, a military religious order, to assist in the task of subduing his aggressive Baltic neighbors and converting them to Christianity. In exchange the duke promised to grant the order some of the conquered land, while still preserving his sovereignty over it. Disregarding their compact with Konrad, the knights established an autonomous state that eventually comprised the entire region between the mouths of the Vistula and the Nieman rivers. In conjunction with

Fortress of Malbork (also known by its German name, Marienburg), seat of grand masters of the Teutonic Knights in fourteenth and fifteenth centuries
Courtesy Jean R. Tartter

Krakow's main market square, centered by the Sukiennice (Cloth Guildhall), constructed between 1380 and 1400

the Order of the Sword, a German military brotherhood that had previously conquered Courland and Livonia, the Teutonic Knights controlled most of the southeast shore of the Baltic, thus barring both Poland and Lithuania from access to the sea. The Poles and the Lithuanians tried separately to resist the encroachments of the knights, and both were separately defeated.

Meanwhile, another and more devastating calamity was to overcome all Eastern and Central Europe in the early thirteenth century when it was ravaged by the horde of the Tatars, savage Mongol warriors who had ridden out of Central Asia. In 1241 Duke Henry the Pious of Silesia challenged the Tatars at the Battle of Legnica, slowing down their westward advance, but at a high cost. Henry, a potential unifier of Poland, perished in the battle along with a large segment of the Polish nobility.

The Tatars eventually withdrew, and the Poles, unlike the Kievan Slavs, never fell under the Mongol yoke. Nevertheless, the devastation resulting from the Tatar raids had grave consequences in that it opened up the depopulated Polish countryside to mass colonization by German settlers.

German colonization was a mixed blessing for Poland. The settlers, attracted by the favorable conditions offered by the Polish princes, brought with them a more scientific method of land cultivation and a new system of land tenure. But the newcomers also claimed special rights, constituting states within the state on the lands they occupied and founding new towns that were customarily granted an even wider measure of self-government.

During all the years of internal disorder and foreign intervention, the Polish church preserved its unity and became the main integrating force within an otherwise fragmented nation. The unifying role of the church was particularly reflected in the special position of the primate of Poland, who often spoke on behalf of the country as a whole. Later the holder of this ecclesiastical office would act as *inter rex*, or temporary head of state, in the period between royal elections.

Kazimierz III and the Reunification of Poland

The prestige and prosperity of medieval Poland increased after the country's reunification in 1338 by the Piast king on the throne of Krakow, Kazimierz (Casimir) III the Great (1333–70). Kazimierz' success in bringing together most of the fragmented parts of the Piast patrimony under his rule was based on the groundwork laid by the conquests of his father, Wladyslaw I (1313–33), and the support given him by the church. A brilliant administrator, he fostered trade, reformed the currency, codified the law, protected the Jews, and sheltered the peasants from exploitation by the nobles. Kazimierz formed a close alliance with Hungary and sought improved relations with Lithuania, while strengthening the country's defenses by building a network of

Kazimierz Dolny, town on Vistula River, founded in fourteenth century by Kazimierz III the Great
Courtesy Consulate General of Polish People's Republic, New York

fortresses. He was also noted as a builder of churches and monasteries, and in 1364 he founded the University of Krakow, which became one of Central Europe's most important centers of learning. His long reign marked the beginning of a period of prosperity for Polish towns, most of which were inhabited largely by Germans and, as members of the Hanseatic League, shared in its profitable Baltic and Levantine trade.

Kazimierz, who had no male heirs, designated as his successor his nephew and ally, King Louis I of Hungary (1370–82), a strong monarch descended from the French house of Anjou. Together Poland and Hungary comprised a formidable bloc opposing further German expansion in Central Europe. To ensure the support of the Polish magnates for a foreign monarch, Louis granted concessions to the nobility, freeing them from any military and financial obligations to the crown that they did not undertake voluntarily. After an interregnum that followed his death, the magnates chose his ten-year-old daughter Jadwiga (1384–99) as monarch of Poland under their protection and supervision, bearing the title of "king".

The Jagiellonian Dynasty

As positive as its effects had been initially, German colonization provoked a reaction among the Poles that was closely related to Poland's geopolitical position. To the north was the rapidly expanding domain of the Teutonic Knights and to the south, a hostile Bohemia, whose king, John of Luxembourg, had been a pretender to the Krakow throne and laid claim to Silesia. Bohemia also was a menace because of its alliances with the expansionist ecclesiastical state and with the mark of Brandenburg, which had gradually extended its control along the Oder River facing Poland's western frontier. In this situation Kazimierz III had decided on a compromise. Considering the security of Poland's access to the Baltic the priority, he drove a wedge between Bohemia and the Teutonic Knights by paying King John a considerable sum of money and recognizing his sovereignty over Silesia. In exchange Kazimierz gained John's promise of support against the order, as well as his renunciation of claims to the Polish crown. (Kazimierz regarded the cession of Silesia as a temporary, tactical arrangement, but for nearly 600 years the province was lost to Poland. From the house of Luxembourg, Silesia passed to the Habsburgs, who in turn surrendered most of the territory to Prussia in the eighteenth century.)

To the northeast lay Lithuania, still a pagan country. Although equally menaced by the Teutonic Knights, Lithuania was nevertheless antagonistic toward Poland because the southward drive of its warrior rulers clashed with Polish expansion eastward toward the enfeebled Kievan principalities in Ruthenia (see Glossary). Farther to the east lay the Tatars, who posed a constant threat to both the Poles and the Lithuanians.

Despite past hostilities between them, Poland's only potential ally against the Teutonic Knights was the grand duchy of Lithuania, which, as a pagan state, had an even more precarious relationship with the crusading military order than did Poland. The grand duchy was, in fact, a vast heterogeneous empire, overwhelmingly Slavic and Greek Orthodox in its composition, that had been created by the genius of a series of brilliant leaders whose conquests had extended their holdings far beyond the confines of ethnic Lithuania on the Baltic to the territories of the Dnieper Valley (see fig. 3). The Lithuanian aristocracy held great estates in Ruthenia, and while resisting attempts at conversion to Christianity, its members had assimilated Ruthenian customs as well as the East Slavonic language (Byelorussian) spoken in the region.

Polish-Lithuanian Commonwealth

When the Polish magnates learned that the Lithuanians had approached Muscovy as a potential partner in their stand against the Teutonic Knights, they struck upon the daring idea of achiev-

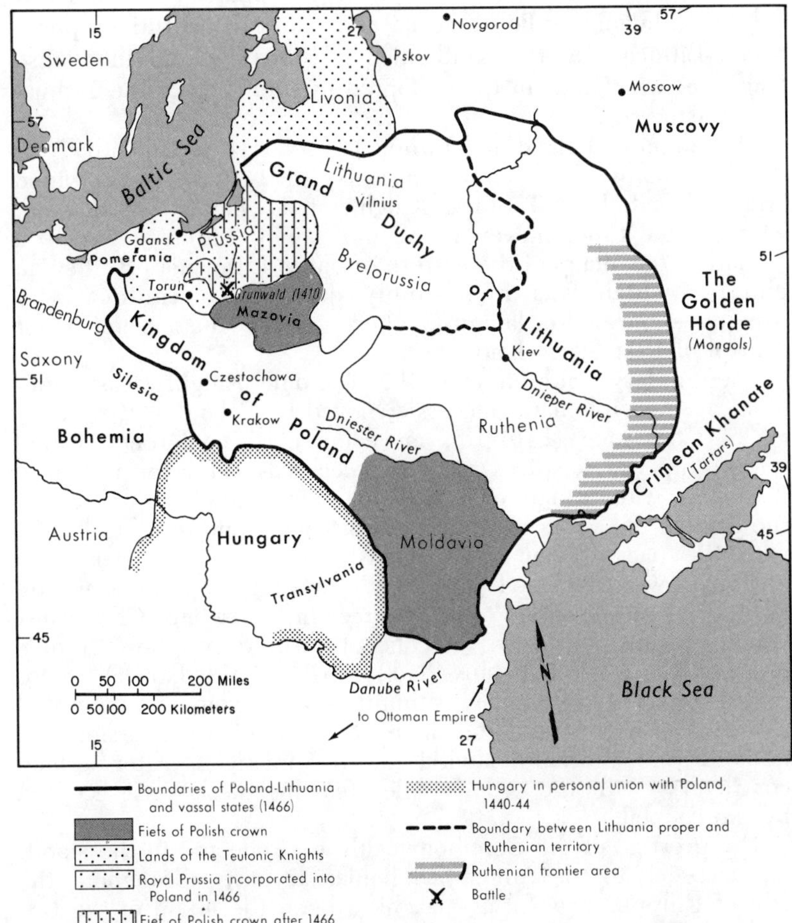

Figure 3. Jagiellonian Poland-Lithuania, Fifteenth Century

ing a dynastic union involving the marriage of Grand Duke Jagiello and Jadwiga, accompanied by the conversion of Lithuania to Roman Catholicism. The alliance between the two countries was sealed in 1386 when Jagiello was baptized and then married the young Polish monarch. Although allied in a dynastic union, Poland and Lithuania remained separate realms with separate crowns, each retaining its own government and distinct aristocracies. The hereditary grand duke in his native Lithuania, Jagiello was king in Poland, ruling jointly there with his wife under his new Christian name, Wladyslaw II (1386–1434). For his part Jagiello pledged to regain the territories lost by both states to the Teutonic Knights. After the gradual acceptance of Catholicism by the Lithuanians, Polish social and political institutions penetrated Lithuania and its Ruthenian provinces, as did the Polish language, which was in time adopted by members of the Lithuanian aristocracy.

The union of Poland and Lithuania—referred to collectively as the Commonwealth—bore fruit when in 1410 their combined armies defeated the Teutonic Knights at the Battle of Grunwald. At the same time, however, the union with Lithuania involved Poland in the affairs of the eastern-oriented Lithuanian-Ruthenian empire, which was increasingly drawn into conflict with Muscovy—the self-ordained "gatherer of the Russian soil"—for control of East Slavic lands.

The military triumph over the Teutonic Knights was paralleled by the diplomatic success achieved by Poland at the Council of Constance (1414–18), an ecumenical conference called under imperial auspices to effect ecclesiastical reform and to discuss a wide range of issues affecting Catholic Europe. At the council the Poles were accused of having entered into league with the pagan Lithuanians against the Christian order. This accusation was connected with a hotly debated proposition: whether it was permissible to use force in spreading Christianity among pagans and Jews, a concept favored by the Teutonic Knights. For Poland, Paulus Vladimiri (Pawel Wlodkowic), rector of the University of Krakow, submitted to the council a memorial in which he formulated the theory that coercive conversion was immoral and therefore should not be practiced. After a long controversy with the order's delegates, his thesis was accepted by the council.

The prestige of the Commonwealth was reflected in the standing accorded to the ruling Jagiellonian Dynasty throughout the rest of Europe. Fruitful as may have been the union of the two realms, the marriage of Wladyslaw II Jagiello and Jadwiga was childless. By a subsequent marriage to a Lithuanian princess, however, the king-grand duke left a son, Wladyslaw III (1434–44), who became king of Poland, inherited the title of grand duke, and in 1440 was also chosen king of Hungary by the estates of that realm. The Polish-Hungarian connection was to serve a double purpose: to spearhead the drive to oust the Turks from Europe and to relieve Constantinople, the besieged Byzantine capital, thereby promoting the reunion of the Latin and Greek churches agreed on in principle by the representatives of both communions at the Council of Florence in 1439. A crusade led by Wladyslaw was launched with papal blessing, but in 1444 at the Battle of Varna in Bulgaria a superior Turkish force defeated the Christian army, and the young king was killed on the field. With his death the dynastic union with Hungary was broken. Constantinople fell to the Turks nine years later, and with it collapsed the union arranged at the Council of Florence.

Meanwhile, the oppressive rule of the Teutonic Knights had precipitated a revolt in Prussia against the order. In 1454 Poland-Lithuania intervened at the request of the rebel landholders and, after a long struggle, inflicted another defeat on the knights. The Treaty of Torun (1466) divided the order's domains between Royal Prussia in the west, which was directly incorporated into Poland, and its eastern territories (later called Ducal Prussia), which were left to the reorganized order as a fief of the Polish crown. The settlement had won for Poland its long-sought direct access to the Baltic, while the port of Gdansk (Danzig) was granted the status of a "free city" under Polish suzerainty.

The Polish monarchy, hitherto a strong and well-functioning institution, paid a heavy price for the triumph over the Teutonic Knights. To secure the military aid of the nobles in the war, King Kazimierz IV (1447–92) was obliged to agree to the Statutes of Nieszawa (1454), regarded as Poland's Magna Charta, in which he pledged to make no laws or binding decisions without consent of the representatives of the nobility, legally admitting them for the first time to a full share of legislation. The effects of this heavy blow to royal authority were not immediately evident, and the prevalent civic spirit prevented the nobility from exploiting their privileges. But in retrospect it is clear that the statutes marked the beginning of a process that rendered the Polish monarchy progressively weaker.

Poland's "Golden Age"

The late fifteenth and the sixteenth centuries have been acclaimed as Poland's "Golden Age," during which the country achieved a high level of cultural development that was stimulated by the new spirit of Renaissance humanism penetrating from Italy and, later, by the intellectual ferment generated by the Reformation. It was during this time in Krakow that Nicolaus Copernicus (Mikolaj Kopernik) first undertook the observations that led him to his epoch-making conception of the heliocentric universe and resulted in his treatise *De revolutionibus orbium celestium* (On the Movement of Heavenly Bodies), published in 1543. Literature in sixteenth-century Poland reached a remarkable level of sophistication that was reflected in numerous perceptive works on political theory. Andrzej Frycz Modrzewski, an enlightened thinker, put forward a scheme for political, social, and educational reform of the Commonwealth in his work *De republica emendanda* (On Improving the Republic), in which he defended the peasants against exploitation and advocated the equality of all citizens before the law. The poet Jan Kochanowski, whose work was admired by Erasmus of Rotterdam, united in his verse the spirits of Christianity and the new humanism. Although Kochanowski wrote mostly in Polish, then considered the colloquial language of the common people, he was also one of Europe's most distinguished Latin poets. The long series of military victories and political successes and Poland's economic prosperity during the period were thereby enhanced by the remarkable artistic and intellectual achievements of Polish society.

The society and the culture it produced were essentially aristocratic in character and accounted for much of the pride and self-confidence exhibited by Poland's ruling elite during the "Golden Age." Since the fourteenth century the regional nobility had met in *sejmiki* (local assemblies, or dietines), each of which the king was obliged to consult in order to obtain approval on taxation and mobilization. The first Sejm (diet) of the "Polish nation" to legislate for all of Poland was convened in 1493 and was composed of deputations from the regional nobility, who voted the king a subsidy provided by taxes levied on the towns and peasants. According to the constitution adopted by the diet in 1505, all legislation thereafter required parliamentary assent. Members of the noble class benefited from a impressive list of rights and privileges confirmed by the diet, including broad freedom of expression and immunity from unauthorized seizure of property and arbitrary arrest. Before the end of the sixteenth century, each nobleman was enfranchised to cast a vote in the election of his king. Because the Polish nobility comprised so large a proportion of the country's population, Poland could be said to have had at that time the most representative government in Europe in terms of the level of participation in political decisionmaking allowed by its system of aristocratic democracy. It was against this background that the Polish nobility viewed absolutist regimes elsewhere in Europe with suspicion and believed their nation to be the freest and most advanced in the world.

The Reformation in Poland

Polish political freedom was paralleled by religious tolerance without equal in Europe. While fierce persecutions and bloody religious wars raged elsewhere, Poland was, in the words of a Polish historian, "a state without stakes" and a recognized "haven for heretics."

The first impulses of the Protestant Reformation were felt in the 1520s in the German towns on the fringes of Poland and in Prussia, but Protestantism made little headway until significant conversions were registered among the patrician class in the Polish cities and among the nobility in the 1540s. Although a minority in the latter group, those who adhered to Protestantism were among the most powerful and influential members of their class. The nobles were especially attracted to Calvinism, whose austere doctrines, unlike those of Lutheranism, seemed to justify their opposition to royal authority and also dispensed with the need for an ecclesiastical hierarchy. Some of the dissidents voiced opposition to payment of the tithes required even of the nobility

Zygmunt Chapel, sixteenth-century Renaissance addition to Wawel Cathedral in Krakow Courtesy Consulate General of Polish People's Republic, New York

or cast covetous eyes on church lands that were vulnerable to seizure. The high tide of the Polish Reformation came in the late 1550s when Protestants gained control of the diet, enacting legislation favorable to the new religious dispensations and penalizing the Catholic hierarchy. Attempts at cooperation among the Calvinists, Lutherans, Unitarians, and various sectaries floundered, however, on the individualism that so typified the Polish nobility. Bad relations among them and the parsimony of the leaders in providing funds for the churches and schools needed in spreading the reformed teachings to a more broadly based congregation severely impeded the growth of Protestantism of all persuasions.

Catholic nobles regained the ascendancy, and in 1564 the diet enforced the decrees of the Council of Trent renewing Roman Catholic institutions. The principle, tacitly recognized in Poland, that no one could be prosecuted—much less persecuted—for religious beliefs was codified in 1573, and religious toleration was made a cardinal legal precept of the Commonwealth. When the last Jagiellonian king, Zygmunt (Sigismund) II August (1548–72), was urged to initiate legislation to curb religious dissenters, he declared in the diet, "I am not the king of your souls."

Protestantism in Poland was always an aristocratic and an urban phenomenon that never touched the mass of the peasantry. By the middle of the seventeenth century, the nobility, with very few exceptions, had returned to Roman Catholicism. The success of the Counter-Reformation in Poland relied on the support given to the Catholic nobles by the papacy, the determination of able bishops, and the presence of the Jesuits, who established schools in dioceses throughout the country.

Religious as well as ethnic toleration was also extended officially to Jews and Muslims. The great influx of Jews had begun in the fourteenth century when persecutions drove thousands from Germany to seek shelter in Poland. Kazimierz III granted them special privileges as "servants of the Treasury" under protection of the crown. In return for acting originally as middlemen in commerce and as estate managers, Jews were given charters of self-government in their own communities, where they were allowed to practice their religion freely. Their numbers grew from some 50,000 in 1500 to about 1.5 million in 1650 as Poland continued to attract Jews from other countries. As a Harvard scholar, Professor Wiktor Weintraub, has explained: "Life was simply more tolerable for Jews in Poland than elsewhere."

The Union of Lublin

When the Teutonic Knights were secularized in 1525 as a result of the Reformation, eastern Prussia had become a hereditary duchy under the last grand master, Albert of Hohenzollern, but the area, known as Ducal Prussia, remained a fief of the Polish crown. In 1562 Courland likewise became a secular fief in the hands of the Protestant former grand master of the Order of the Sword, while the defunct order's territories in Livonia reverted to the Commonwealth. The growing threat posed to the Baltic provinces by Muscovy as well as the constant pressure exerted by the Tatars and Muscovy on Ruthenia, convinced a majority of the Lithuanian boyars that closer ties with Poland were necessary, going beyond the personal union of the two realms under the king-grand duke. They also recognized in the union of the Commonwealth's nobility the means of their own emancipation from the power of the grand duke, whose legal authority in Lithuania was much greater than that which he exercised in Poland as king. The Polish nobles, for their part, saw in the merger an opportunity to acquire estates on the rich lands of Ruthenia.

The protocols agreed on at Lublin in 1569 established the formal union of Poland and Lithuania under the Polish crown, although the king would retain the title of grand duke in Lithuania. Representatives of the Polish and Lithuanian nobility would meet in a common diet to legislate for the whole country and to formulate a common foreign policy. Separate Polish and

Lithuanian civil administrations and armies would be funded, however, from separate treasuries. As part of the agreement, the Lithuanians ceded the largest portion of the Ruthenian provinces (the Ukraine) to Poland, while White Ruthenia (Byelorussia) remained attached to Lithuania proper (see fig. 4).

The Union of Lublin had guaranteed the equality of the Greek Orthodox hierarchy with its Roman Catholic counterpart in the more closely knit Commonwealth, but pressure from the patriarch of Moscow to assert control over the Ruthenian church persuaded Poland's Catholic monarch, Zygmunt III, to promote a union with Rome that would supplement the political federation. At a synod in Brest in 1596, a majority of the Orthodox bishops recognized the supremacy of the pope while retaining for the Ruthenian church its traditional Byzantine liturgy and separate ecclesiastical jurisdiction. The largely Polonized—and increasingly Roman Catholic—aristocracy in Ruthenia supported the bishops in transforming the Ruthenia church into a Greek Catholic community, but the union with Rome was rejected by many of the lower clergy, much of the peasantry, and especially the Dnieper Cossacks.

Social and Economic Developments

The failure of Poland's political institutions in the seventeenth and eighteenth centuries can be traced to the deterioration of socioeconomic conditions in the late fifteenth and sixteenth centuries, during which a privileged nobility grew increasingly powerful on the one end of the spectrum and an oppressed and degraded peasantry and impoverished urban middle class existed on the other. The system of land tenure established at the time of the German settlements, in which land on the great estates was rented on a long-term basis to free peasant tenants, proved advantageous to the Polish gentry as long as there were few markets abroad for agricultural produce; rent-paying settlers were more valuable than land. The closing of the eastern Mediterranean to European commerce after the fall of Constantinople shifted the continent's economic locus to Western and Northern Europe, enhancing the commercial importance of the Baltic Sea. Meanwhile, the introduction of more intensive methods of cultivation turned Poland-Lithuania into a large exporter of agricultural products, as well as of lumber and naval stores from the Baltic provinces.

The opening of the Vistula for grain exports through the port of Gdansk to northern Germany, the Netherlands, and England, where cereal prices were high, introduced new opportunities for Polish estate holders. Land increased in value, and entrepreneurial farming under the landowner's management became profitable. Consequently, the diet, which was composed of noble landowners, enacted legislation that upset the traditional agrarian

Figure 4. Polish-Lithuanian Commonwealth from the Union of Lublin (1569) to 1667

system, gradually converting free tenants on the estates into serfs. First, village self-government was curtailed and then abolished as the squire acted as chief magistrate on his estates. Next, the diet limited the freedom of movement of peasants and tied them to the land that they worked. In 1520 the first law was enacted obligating tenants to work on the squire's demense (land reserved for the landlord's personal use). At the same time, expropriation of the peasant's common land and reversion of tenant holdings to the demense was abetted by the diet in the interests of the landowners.

The enserfment of the peasantry had weighty consequences for the country's economy. Having at their disposal an ample supply of free labor, squires proceeded to set up their own factories to manufacture whatever they could for their own and their subjects' needs. Serfs were forbidden to purchase products not manufactured on their lord's estate. As the large estates became almost self-sufficient in goods, the towns were deprived of a great deal of their trade. In 1493 the nobility had granted itself the right of importing goods for their own consumption without payment of duty. Prices were regulated, favoring landed interests and forcing merchants in the towns to market their wares abroad. In response the diet passed legislation prohibiting the export of any goods manufactured in Polish towns, while reserving for noble landowners a monopoly of the profitable grain trade.

Most Polish cities, subject to the restrictive and oppressive legislation of the diet, declined seriously in the seventeenth century, depriving the once-prosperous and self-governing bourgeoisie of their economic and potential political influence. Only Gdansk, which as a "free city" was exempt from the diet's control, enjoyed great prosperity, flourishing on the booming trade in grain, lumber, and flax. During this period Gdansk became the most important harbor on the Baltic and accounted for nearly half of the region's trade.

The Royal Republic

The Commonwealth in the seventeenth and eighteenth centuries was a federation dominated by the nobility in the diet and in the powerful local dietines, where their primary aims were to enhance the "golden freedom," as the body of aristocratic prerogatives was known, even at the expense of national solidarity and to hobble the authority of an elected monarch whom they had relegated to the role of "crowned president of the Royal Republic." Political initiative lay almost entirely with them, and the corrupting effects of such overwhelming power selfishly exercised in the interests of one group were not slow in appearing. The *liberum veto*, the traditional rule of unanimity, which until the middle of the seventeenth century was interpreted in the sense that a minority had eventually to submit to the will of the majority and join in approving measures before the diet, was applied literally to suit the interests of factions, local interests, or foreign agents, allowing a single dissenting vote to defeat a measure supported by the majority. The legislative process was thereby stymied, and little of positive value was able to be expected from the diet's deliberations. In times of crisis, however, an entire diet, a faction within the diet, or a party of nobles in a region might constitute itself as a "confederation," suspending temporarily the *liberum veto* in order to take concerted action in support of or in opposition to a particular policy.

The civic spirit and martial virtues that had been typical of the nobility in earlier times perished, having atrophied by a precarious prosperity and a false sense of security. Luxury and ostentation knew no bounds among the decadent ranks of the noble class. Drinking, hunting, and gambling vied with politics and the fighting of private wars as the chief occupation of many squires. Often wealthier than the king himself, some magnates kept private armies that numbered in the thousands of men.

Paralleling the internal decay, external problems mounted that ate away at the resources of the Commonwealth. In many ways these difficulties were intertwined with domestic problems. Since the close of the fourteenth century, for instance, the Polish monarch had no power to increase the taxes levied on the nobility. Moreover, the king could not mobilize the nobility for military service beyond the Commonwealth's borders without granting them a substantial indemnity. Owing to the limited funds available to the treasury, the standing army was inadequate for the defense of the country's vast open frontiers, a fact that did not go unnoticed by Poland's neighbors.

The Vasa Dynasty

Several candidates were presented to the electoral convention that met to choose a successor to Zygmunt II August, who died in 1572 without a male heir. The Lithuanian boyars favored the election of Tsar Ivan IV of Muscovy to guarantee the security of the eastern territories. The bishops and the Catholic magnates supported a Habsburg nominee, but his candidacy was vigorously opposed by the Protestant nobles and by a large number of the gentry who were fearful that the centralizing tendencies of Habsburg rule might be imported to Poland. A compromise solution brought a French prince, Henry of Valois (1573–74, later Henry III of France) to the throne, and two years later under similar circumstances he was succeeded by Stefan Batory (1575–86), the prince of Transylvania. The gentry in particular had resisted the reestablishment of the dynastic tradition in Poland, but in 1587 the convention elected as king Zygmunt III Vasa (1587–1632), the heir to the Swedish throne, whose mother was a Jagiellonian princess. The Vasa Dynasty was perpetuated in Poland when Zygmunt was succeeded by his sons, Wladyslaw IV (1632–48) and Jan Kazimierz (1648–68).

In 1596 Zygmunt III moved the seat of royal government from Krakow northward to Warsaw, an important grain market linked to Gdansk by the Vistula, in order to improve his line of communications with Lithuania and Sweden. An ardent Catholic, he was deposed as king of Sweden in 1598 when he attempted to overturn the Reformation in that country. His continuous efforts to recover the Swedish crown drew Poland into a long conflict with Sweden, inviting damaging intervention in the Baltic provinces by that rising military power. Zygmunt also involved Poland—more successfully—in renewed wars with Muscovy,

Castle Square in Warsaw and column with statue of King Zygmunt III Vasa

supporting the claim of pretenders to its disputed throne, and for a short period (1610–12) his son, Wladyslaw, occupied the Kremlin as tsar.

The Cossack Wars

Muscovy's successful attacks on the eastern approaches of the Commonwealth began soon after the fall of Novgorod, an ally of Poland-Lithuania, in 1476 and would continue for three centuries. Muscovite aggression along the upper Dnieper and the Dvina rivers had a long and involved theoretical justification. Poland-Lithuania, according to the Muscovite argument, had annexed the western lands of the old Kievan state after its destruction by the Tatars. The tsars of Moscow, as rightful heirs of the rulers of Kiev, were entitled, therefore, to retrieve the lost parts of the Kievan patrimony. To the dynastic argument was added the religious one that the Muscovites were obliged to free their Greek Orthodox brethren from the Latin yoke and to unite them in one state ruled by a tsar of the same faith. To these arguments the Poles countered that the Dnieper-Dvina lands had become an integral part of the Commonwealth as a result of voluntary unions and peaceful incorporations.

While the eastern approaches were threatened by Muscovy, the southern borderlands of the Commonwealth had become increasingly vulnerable to attack by the forces of the Ottoman Empire. Interconnected with both Muscovite menace and the Turkish peril was the highly explosive problem of the volatile Dnieper Cossacks. The Cossacks were free settlers in military colonies established along the exposed frontier of the Commonwealth to defend it against the Tatars and the Turks. They also formed auxiliary units in the army of the Polish king.

Most of the Dnieper Cossacks were Greek Orthodox Ruthenians, and they came to resent the impositions of the Catholic Polish squires who attempted to enserf them or to use them as cheap labor on the fertile lands of the Ukraine. In 1648 the Cossacks, allied with the Tatars, rose in rebellion against Polish rule. Initially, the objective of their hetman (commander), Bogdan Chmielnicki, was to secure the restoration of Cossack privileges and the return of enserfed Cossacks to the status of free men and soldiers. Unable to reach an acceptable agreement with the Poles, he looked to Muscovy for support and in 1654 recognized the suzerainty of the tsar.

Four years of Muscovite rule were enough to convince the Dnieper Cossacks that it was much sterner than that of the Poles, and in 1658 they were temporarily reconciled with the Polish king. An undertaking, embodied in the Treaty of Hadziacz that same year to organize a separate Ruthenian duchy equal to Poland and Lithuania in a trialist Commonwealth, was frustrated by a lack of resolution on the part of the Poles and by continued Muscovite military intervention. The Cossacks, for their part, were badly divided on the issue of returning to the Commonwealth, and many rejected the pro-Polish leadership. Because a large number of its forces had been diverted to oppose a Swedish invasion of Poland in 1655 and later to quell a rising by rebellious magnates and soldiers, the Commonwealth was unable to concentrate its energies in Ruthenia. It was decided, therefore, to strike a compromise with Muscovy. The Truce of Andrusovo (1667) partitioned the Ukraine between Poland and Muscovy along the Dnieper River, while Kiev on the western bank was turned over to the emerging Muscovite empire.

Years of Crisis

In 1665 Poland—already heavily engaged in Ruthenia—was invaded by Sweden in retaliation for the Polish Vasas' continued claim on the Swedish throne, and Swedish forces soon occupied about half of the country, including the cities of Warsaw and Krakow. Even in the face of aggression of such magnitude, the nobles in the diet were reluctant to approve increased appropriations for the defense of the country on the grounds that a military buildup would strengthen the monarchy. In the three-cornered war that ensued, the Swedes also fought Poland's foe, Muscovy, in Livonia, where they received the cooperation of Polish nobles who had defected to their side in the struggle. Deserted by the nobility, King Jan Kazimierz was compelled to seek temporary refuge in Habsburg Silesia.

In order to deprive the Swedes of their German ally, the Polish king surrendered sovereignty over Ducal Prussia in 1657 to the elector of Brandenburg, head of the Hohenzollern line that had provided dukes in the territory since 1618. Possession of Prussia—later raised to the dignity of a kingdom—laid the foundation for the subsequent expansion of Hohenzollern power in Germany. The Polish military position improved but, as the price of peace with Sweden in 1660, Jan Kazimierz renounced his claim to the Swedish throne and conceded earlier territorial losses in Livonia. In addition to the loss of prestige and territory, Poland was left prostrate materially by the wars with the Swedes and the Muscovites. The best farmland was devastated and the grain trade through Gdansk ruined.

The election of Jan Sobieski (1674–96) as king seemed to augur well for the revival of Poland's fortunes. An outstanding military commander, he dealt the Turks a crushing blow in the Ukraine—without the assistance of the Ruthenian nobles—and during an epic campaign in 1683 he led the Polish army in lifting the Turkish siege of Vienna, thus stemming the tide of Ottoman expansion in Europe.

Jan Sobieski demonstrated that with determined leadership Poland was capable of exerting the military potential of a great power, but the inherent weakness of the Polish political system constantly put the "Royal Republic" at a disadvantage in its relations with the European monarchies. While Poland's neighbors—Muscovy (later Russia) and Brandenburg-Prussia—gained strength under able if often ruthless despots during the second half of the seventeenth century, the Commonwealth—its nobility jealously guarding the "golden freedom"—was plunged into anarchy. This rendered the country vulnerable to foreign intervention, greatly facilitated by opportunities for intrigue provided by the *liberum veto* and the election of kings. Bribery and corruption in government were rife. Of the 44 diets convened during the half-century, 15 were "broken" or dissolved after a single delegate chose to exercise his *liberum veto*. Other diets refused to enact any legislation. Parties were formed around rival pro-French and pro-Austrian nobles through whom their foreign patrons sought to influence royal elections. Local magnates were able to ensure some semblance of order on the regional level through the dietines, which they controlled, but the country as a whole was without fiscal supervision, and as a result Polish currency became devalued. Even Jan Sobieski's efforts to strengthen royal authority were thwarted. Unstable political conditions were magnified in the eighteenth century.

The Era of the Saxon Kings

To succeed Jan Sobieski the electoral convention selected a German prince, the elector of Saxony, who became king of Poland as August II (1697–1733). He was beholden for the crown, however, to the Russian tsar Peter I, soon to be named "the Great," whose backing had been instrumental in his election from a large field of candidates.

Called "the Strong" in recognition of his physical prowess and military exploits before coming to the Polish throne, August II promptly committed Poland to an alliance with Saxony, Russia, and Denmark that initiated hostilities aimed at ousting Sweden from its earlier conquests in Germany and the Baltic provinces. The king-elector sought by means of a successful conclusion to the war to acquire title to Swedish Livonia in his own right, using Saxon troops, and then to bargain with the Polish nobility for its return to Polish sovereignty at the cost of reconstituting the Commonwealth as a hereditary monarchy. But Sweden's young soldier-king, Charles XII, quickly took the offensive in what came to be known as the Great Northern War (1700–21), defeating the Danes, Saxons, and Russians in turn and invading Polish territory. The nobility shifted sides in the war as advantage dictated, but in 1704 the anti-Saxon majority deposed August II and elected in his place one of their own number, Charles XII's nominee, Stanislaw Leszczynski (1704–1709, 1733–34).

Sweden's resources and manpower proved too limited for its king's ambitions, however, and after the Russian victory over the Swedes at Poltava in the Ukraine in 1709, August II was restored to the Polish throne by his patron, Peter the Great. Poland remained a battleground, its territory occupied and pillaged by both sides in the war. By the Treaty of Nystad, which ended the conflict in 1721, Russia was awarded Sweden's holdings in the Baltic provinces, including formerly Polish territory in Livonia, and emerged clearly as the dominant power in the region.

August II had sacrificed Polish interests to those of his dynasty and his Russian protectors. After his death a convention of 12,000 nobles rejected the Saxon connection, turning once again to Stanislaw Leszczynski, whom they resoundingly elected as king after receiving assurances of support from his son-in-law, King Louis XV of France. Russia and Austria soon intervened, however, in favor of the late king's heir, August III (1733–63), when he was named to succeed by a rival Lithuanian-led convention. The Russian invasion of Poland, forcibly supplanting Stanislaw Leszczynski, touched off a general European conflict—the War of the Polish Succession (1733–35)—in which Poland became a sideshow in a larger confrontation that pitted the Bourbon powers, France and Spain, against Habsburg Austria in Lorraine and Italy. The peace, arranged among the great powers, was wholly advantageous to Bourbon dynastic designs in those areas, but it left the Polish throne to August III.

During the reigns of the inept, pleasure-loving Saxon monarchs, state finances, education, and the administration of justice sank to deplorable levels. Meanwhile, the easy living enjoyed by Polish nobles, who consumed the value of their estates, was reflected in the popular saying "Under the Saxon king, loosen your belt, eat, and drink!" Many of the gentry, who had dominated the diet during the previous century, lost political power as well as property to the magnates, who continued to rule the regions according to their own will through the dietines. The central government almost ceased to operate, the diet was incapacitated by the *liberum veto*, and the small royal army cowered in its barracks, overawed by the stronger private armies maintained by the magnates. Rivalries among the magnates were abetted by foreign powers, the Prussians and the Russians sometimes backing the so-called Familia (the Family), a political alliance headed by the powerful Czartoryski family and, as it suited their interests, the Austrians, Prussians, and French supporting the Republicans, led by the Potockis and the Radziwills. The latter, which found a following among the conservative magnates and their clients, gained the reputation of an opposition party concerned with protecting aristocratic liberties, but the division between the two groups had more to do with personal animosities than it did with political differences or loyalty to the dynasty. What recommended the Saxon dynasty to most of the nobility, however, was that it allowed the perpetuation of a state of virtual anarchy in Poland.

The Partitioning of Poland

By means of intrigue, intimidation, and force, Peter the Great had established Russian ascendancy over the decaying Commonwealth, transforming it into a satellite state. Peter meddled in Poland's internal affairs, intervened on behalf of its Orthodox population, stationed troops in its territory, and dictated its foreign policy, but he refrained from pressing his advantage to acquire those parts of the "Kievan patrimony" on the western banks of the Dvina and Dnieper rivers. Russia intended Poland to play a valuable role as a buffer state and potential ally against both Turkey and Sweden. The empress Catherine II, who ascended the Russian throne in 1762, was determined to follow the course set by Peter the Great in dealing with Poland.

When the era of the Saxon kings was brought to a close by the death of August III, Catherine—in concert with Frederick II of Prussia—agreed that the election of one of the Familia, Stanislaw Poniatowski, as successor and the maintainance of the status quo in Poland were in their common interests. Before his installation as Stanislaw II (1764–95), however, Michal Fryderyk Czartoryski, the leader of the Familia, attempted to force through reforms that would have limited the *liberum veto* and introduced a ministerial-type government appointed by the crown. In reaction, opposition nobles, organized in the Confederation of Radom, appealed for Russian intervention to protect their liberties. Backed by Russian troops, Catherine's minister in Warsaw dictated terms to the diet affecting the status of the Orthodox and Protestant minorities that were designed to be unacceptable to the Catholic majority. He arrested Catholic leaders, including several bishops, when they objected to them. Russian-imposed legislation was them enacted by a rump diet that confirmed the *liberum veto* as a fundamental law of the land and ensured against any further attempts to provide Poland with a stronger government.

With French support, patriotic nobles joined together in the Confederation of Bar in 1768 to protest the acquiescence of the king and the diet to Catherine's intimidation and to mount armed resistance to the Russian occupation. One of the confederation's leaders, Kazimierz Pulaski, commanded the defense of the fortified monastery of Jasna Gora at Czestochowa, where Poles had earlier made their stands against Tatar and Swedish invaders. The rising continued for four years before being put down finally by combined Russian, Prussian, and Austrian forces, and it also drew Turkey into a disastrous war with Russia.

The territorial gains made by Russia along the Black Sea coast during the war with Turkey brought demands from its allies, Prussia and Austria, for compensations in Poland. Frederick II, in particular, looked for an excuse to acquire Polish Pomerania and Gdansk in order to bridge the gap between East Prussia and the Brandenburg heartland and thus consolidate his domains. Under

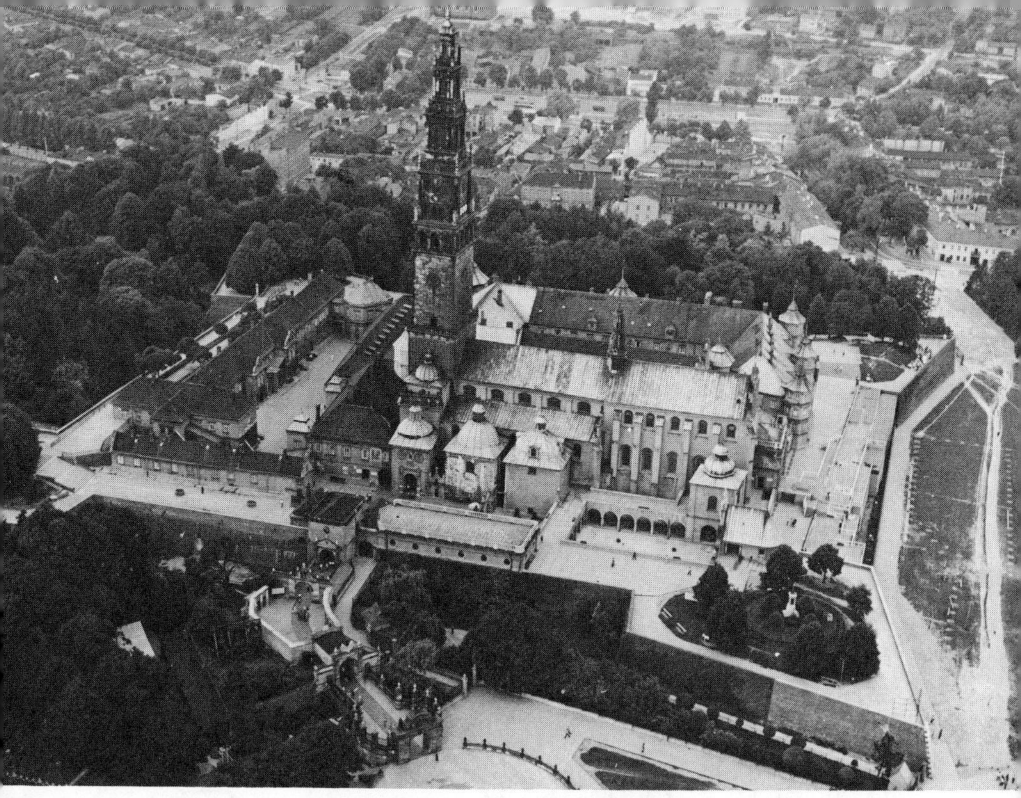

Monastery and basilica of Jasna Gora at Czestochowa, completed in late fifteenth century Courtesy Consulate General of Polish People's Republic, New York

the pretext that the anarchy reigning in Poland was a threat to that country's neighbors, he suggested a deal with Russia and Austria for occupation and annexation of frontier districts by the three powers.

By the first partition, in 1772, Poland was compelled to give up nearly one-third of its territory, almost one-half of its population, and more than one-half of its resources. Prussia obtained most of Polish Pomerania, but because of Catherine's veto, the cities of Gdansk and Torun were denied Frederick. Russia snatched Polish Livonia and all of Byelorussia east of the Dvina River and the valley of the upper Dnieper. Austria appropriated the lion's share, however, taking most of southern Poland, excluding Krakow (see fig. 5).

The partitioning powers also imposed on Poland a new constitution that vested executive authority in a council of the diet elected by the delegates and deprived the king of his prerogative to summon and dismiss the parliamentary assembly. All actions of the Polish government became subject to review by the three

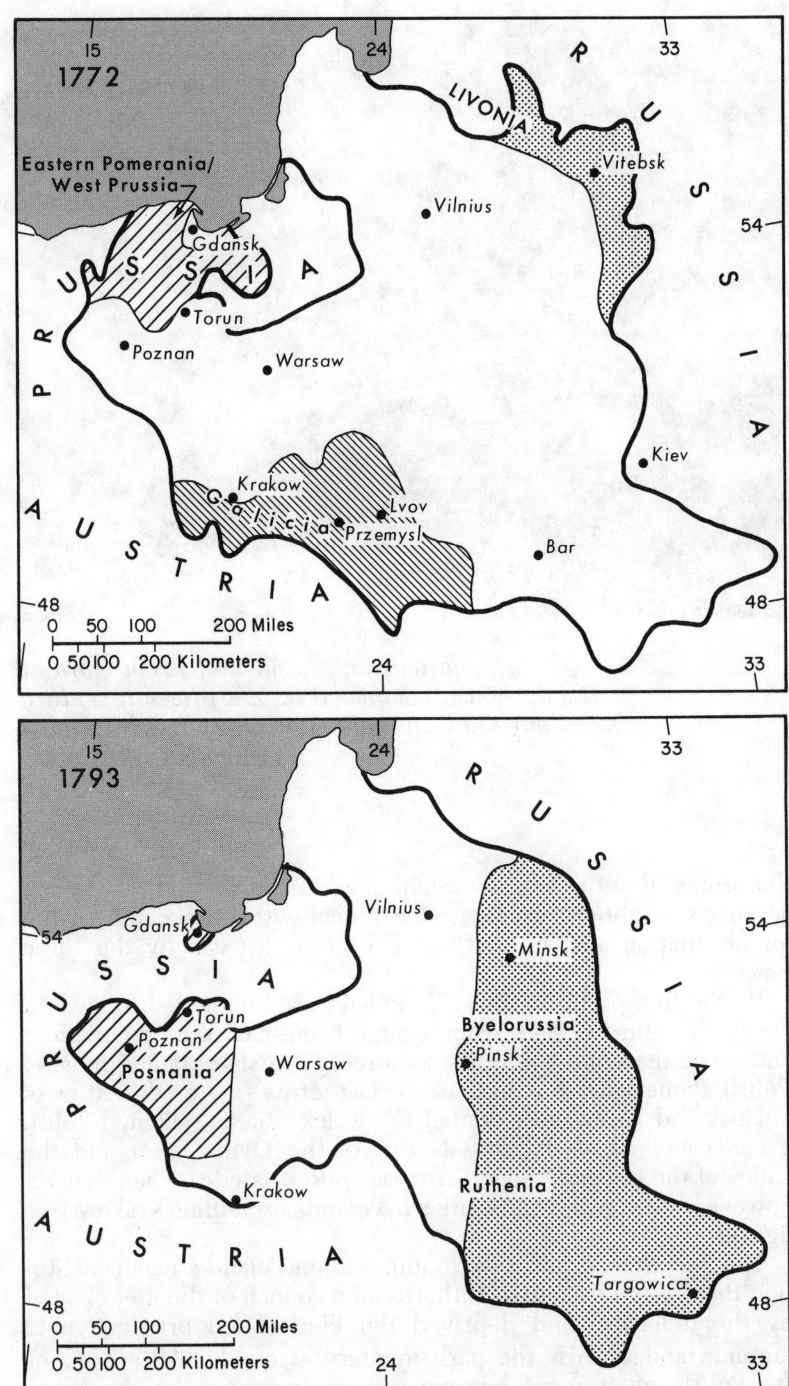

Figure 5. The Partitions of Poland, 1772–95

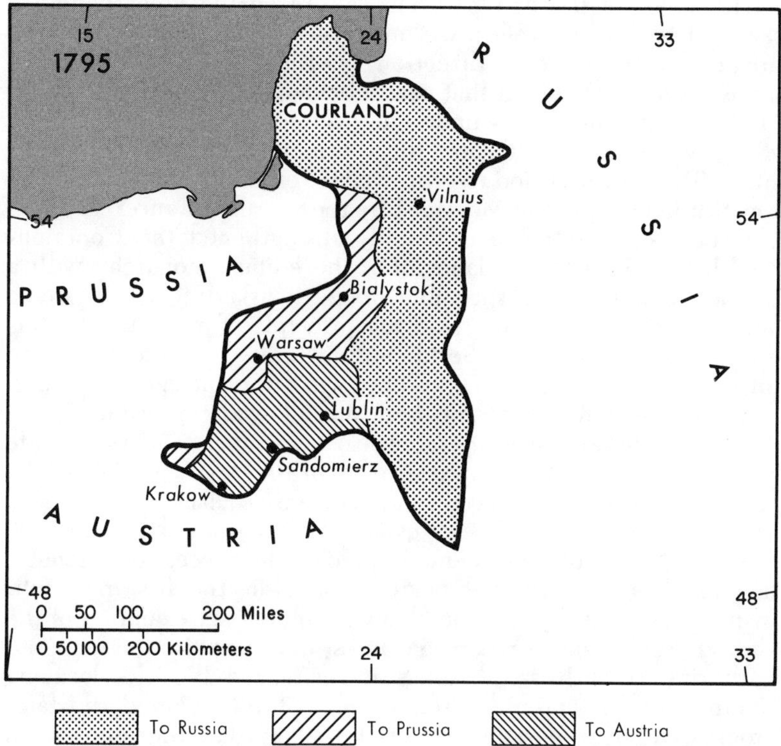

Figure 5. Continued.

powers. Although it reinforced regional autonomy and the *liberum veto*, the new constitution, in defining the role of the central government and providing for ministries to carry out its operations, also introduced an element of stability that had been lacking in the political process before the first partition.

Many patriots fled abroad after the defeat of the Confederation of Bar, among them Pulaski, who made his way to the American colonies where he organized the Continental Army's cavalry early in the War of Independence. The hero of Czestochowa was killed at the Battle of Savannah in 1779. He had been preceded to America by another Polish officer, Tadeusz Kosciuszko, an engineer whose fortifications contributed to the defeat of the British army at Saratoga in 1777. Kosciuszko, who subsequently supervised construction of the fortress at West Point, attained the rank of brigadier general in the Continental Army and was granted United States citizenship.

The shock of the first partition galvanized the Poles behind a series of progressive reforms. A modern secular school system was introduced under the direction of Europe's first education ministry, a development that paralleled a national cultural revival. Modernizing landowners undertook to improve their estates, and efforts were made to restore the commercial vitality of Poland's cities. The post-partition reforms were eventually embodied in the constitution adopted in May 1791 by the so-called Four-Year Diet. The 1791 constitution considerably strengthened the Commonwealth by converting Poland into a hereditary monarchy with a cabinet of ministers responsible to the legislature. The anarchic *liberum veto* was nullified, and the principle of majority rule was introduced in the diet. Serfdom was limited as the first step toward its final abolition. Cities once again became self-governing, and townsmen were enfranchised and allowed representation in the diet. State finances were reorganized, and the royal army was to be brought up to an authorized strength of 100,000 men. Meanwhile, in search of an ally, Poland concluded a defensive alliance with Prussia, which was anxious to dampen Russia's ambitions in Eastern Europe.

The 1791 constitution seemed to crown the process of regeneration and reform that had begun soon after the first partition. Inspired as it was by the liberal and revolutionary examples of the United States and France, Poland's new constitution angered Catherine II of Russia because it revitalized the old decaying Commonwealth and promised to turn it into a modern state, progressive by the standards of the time, that represented an ideological challenge to her absolutist regime in Russia. A resurgent Poland, she reasoned, would be a potential obstacle to Russian expansion westward. Having successfully ended a second Turkish war, Catherine conspired with a small group of Polish magnates who were opposed to the progressive reforms brought about by the new constitution. Epitomizing the worst vices in Poland's past, these reactionary oligarchs formed the Confederation of Targowica, petitioning Catherine for her protection and for Russian aid in restoring the old constitution. With this semblance of legality, Catherine ordered a veteran army of 100,000 men, led by her most seasoned general, Alexander Suvorov, to march into Poland in May 1792.

To counter Russia's aggression the Polish government turned to Prussia, which was bound to give military assistance on the strength of its treaty commitment. But Prussia, bent on getting Gdansk and Torun, had already entered into secret negotiations with Russia and refused to come to Poland's aid. Rebuffed, Poland had to face the Russian invasion alone. After a series of indecisive battles against outnumbered Polish forces commanded by Kosciuszko and Jozef Poniatowski, Suvorov's troops captured Warsaw, forcing the Poles to seek peace. The Targowica confederates, who came into the ascendancy with Russian

Tadeusz Kosciuszko, Polish patriot, army officer, and statesman; famous for his role in the American Revolutionary War and for his leadership of the Polish insurrection of 1794
Courtesy National Portrait Gallery, Smithsonian Institution, Washington, D.C.

backing, repealed the 1791 constitution, reinstating the old regime along with the old form of serfdom.

Russia and Prussia agreed to partition Poland a second time in 1793. By the provisions of the treaty between them, Russia appropriated most of the Byelorussian and Ukrainian territory west of the Dnieper, while Prussia seized the long-coveted cities of Gdansk and Torun and the western province of Posnania. While the first partition in 1772 had left Poland a potentially viable state, the second one dealt a decisive blow to the independence of the Polish nation. Trying to justify the measures they had taken, the governments in St. Petersburg and Berlin stated that the partition was necessary to uproot the spreading evil of "Jacobinism"—the influence of the French Revolution—in Eastern Europe. Thus, in 1772 Poland had been divided on the grounds that it was anarchic and helpless, yet in 1793 the country was despoiled again because it was successfully reforming its institutions and had become a threat to its absolutist neighbors.

A popular uprising was sparked by young army officers in 1794 in reaction to the second partition. Returning from a self-imposed exile, Kosciuszko was granted absolute power with the blessing of the church and proclaimed a state of insurrection in Krakow. Following his lead, insurrectionists also seized control in Warsaw and Vilnius (Polish, Wilno). Kosciuszko's military concepts were influenced by his experience with American militia and by the success of the citizens' army in France. He made his appeal, therefore, to the entire Polish people—serfs as well as nobles—to rally to him. When short of muskets for his rapidly recruited popular army, he successfully led Galician peasants armed with scythes against the Russians. Initially, Polish forces were on the offensive and inflicted several painful defeats on the Russians, but the prospect of a Polish victory caused apprehension in Berlin and pushed Prussia toward direct military intervention. Kosciuszko's efforts to win French support for the Polish cause failed, and the combined Prussian and Russian forces soon proved too much for the insurgents to resist unaided. Warsaw fell after a two-month siege, and Kosciuszko was wounded in another battle and taken prisoner by the Russians.

The crushing of the insurrection was followed in 1795 by the abdication of Stanislaw II and a third partition, which erased Poland from the map of Europe. Austria took the ancient city of Krakow and the region around Lublin and Sandomierz. Prussia obtained a large area in central Poland that included the city of Warsaw. Russia appropriated the duchy of Courland and the remainder of Lithuania and the Ukraine. Its share in the three partitions, which encompassed two-thirds of the territory of the old Polish-Lithuanian Commonwealth and contained nearly 7 million inhabitants, increased the population of the Russian Empire by about 25 percent.

The causes of the rapid degeneration of the once-mighty Commonwealth pose a problem that has challenged the analytical skills of generations of historians. Whatever the universal lessons to be derived from its ultimate downfall, however, the traumatic experience of the three successive partitions deeply engraved in the minds of patriotic Poles one moral imperative—that of regaining Poland's lost independence. This drive has been the main theme of subsequent phases of Polish history.

Poland under Foreign Rule

After the third partition, politically conscious Poles took one of two paths, both directed toward the ultimate goal of securing the reunification of their divided country. Some argued that this could best be achieved through cooperation with one of the partitioning powers; others turned to France for inspiration and for assistance in restoring Poland's independence. Among the first group in Russian Poland was Adam Jerzy Czartoryski, a leading liberal during the period of the 1791 constitution, who became a favorite of the emperor Alexander I and served for a time as his foreign minister. Czartoryski sought to use his influence to promote Polish reunification under Russian auspices.

Other Poles who fled the country after Kosciuszko's defeat found service with France, supporting the republic and later Napoleon Bonaparte through thick and thin because the French had fought against the partitioning powers. The Polish Legion, formed in Italy by exiles and by Polish prisoners of war captured from the Austrian army, saw action beside French forces in Italy, Spain, Egypt, and Haiti. The words of Poland's national anthem—"Poland is not yet lost as long as we live"—were written by an officer of the legion campaigning in Italy, and Napoleon is one of the anthem's heroes. The legionnaires accompanied Napoleon when his army entered Poland in 1806.

The Duchy of Warsaw

After the defeat of the Russian-Prussian coalition by Napoleon, the French and Russian emperors agreed as part of the Treaty of Tilsit in 1807 to the creation of an independent Polish state, designated the duchy of Warsaw, on territory surrendered by Prussia. Galicia was added after Austria's defeat in 1809. Except for Eastern Pomerania, which remained in Prussian hands, and the Bialystok region, which was ceded to Russia, the duchy contained most of the predominantly ethnic Polish areas of the old Commonwealth (see fig. 6).

The title of duke of Warsaw was bestowed on Napoleon's loyal ally, Frederick August I, the king of Saxony. The duchy was administered in his name by a Polish council of state, but its policies were directed by the French minister resident in Warsaw, whose principal concern was the requisitioning of supplies and manpower for Napoleon's war effort. Jozef Poniatowski, the duchy's war minister, fielded a Polish army of 100,000 men under his command for Napoleon's ill-fated Russian campaign in 1812, in which three-fourths of them perished. Despite these losses and the Russian occupation of Warsaw early in 1813, the duchy raised another army, units from which covered Napoleon's retreat all the way to Paris. Poniatowski, who held the rank of marshal of France, fell in the Battle of the Nations at Leipzig. The Poles, who had looked upon Napoleon as a liberator, shared in his defeat.

Congress Poland

The rulers and statesmen who convened the Congress of Vienna (1814–15) to reorder Europe and to bring it stability after a generation of war decided Poland's fate for the next century as a country divided. The incorporation of Lithuania and the eastern territories of the old Commonwealth as Russian provinces was recognized by the congress, where the dominant voices were those of the three partitioning powers and their British ally. Prussia was confirmed in its possession of Pomerania, Posnania, and Gdansk, taken in the first and second partitions, and Austria retained Galicia. Czartoryski, who as a member of the Russian delegation was spokesman for Polish interests at the congress, failed in his long-term effort to have all of Poland reunited under

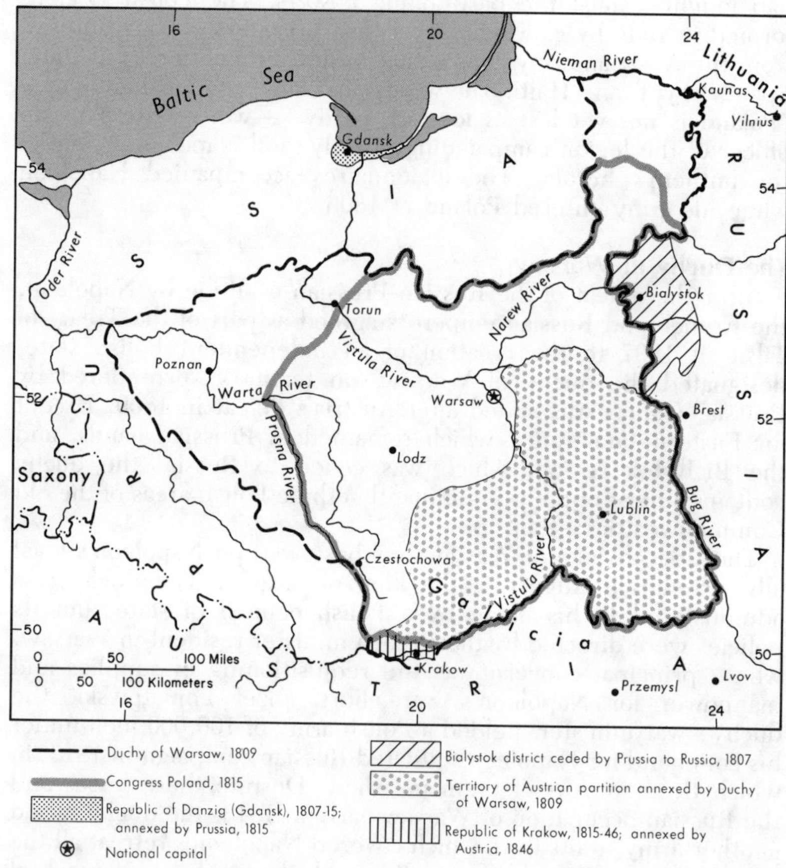

Figure 6. Duchy of Warsaw, 1807–13, and Congress Poland, 1815

one rule. But the congress did agree to the organization of the Kingdom of Poland—referred to as Congress Poland to distinguish it from other parts of the former kingdom—in provinces of the central sector (formerly held by Prussia and Austria) that were transferred to Russia for that purpose. The congress also made the city of Krakow and its environs a free republic.

Congress Poland was a separate political entity, a constitutional monarchy in personal union with an otherwise autocratic Russian emperor who would also be king of Poland. The kingdom's external relations were integrated with those of the Russian Empire, although Poland was excluded from the Russian tariff system. According to the constitution granted by Alexander I, the king-emperor was represented by a governor, who was to be either a Pole or a member of the imperial family and who exercized executive authority through an appointed Polish council of state. The constitution also provided for a bicameral diet with a directly elected lower chamber that was summoned at the discretion of the king-emperor. A 30,000-man Polish army, designated for the defense of Poland only, served under the Polish flag, and the Roman Catholic Church was accorded official status in the kingdom. A Polish judicial system administered a Polish legal code that guaranteed Poles liberties not enjoyed elsewhere in the Russian Empire. Patriotic activities by Poles under Russian rule outside Congress Poland, however, were ruthlessly suppressed.

The grand duke Constantine, the brother of both Alexander I and his successor, Nicholas I, was appointed commander of the Polish army and made his headquarters in Warsaw. He made himself unpopular in the kingdom as a whole because of his autocratic manner and in the ranks of the army in particular when he introduced the Russian code of military discipline. Relations with the diet, which was convened only periodically, went from bad to worse. Students in Warsaw protested the harsh treatment inflicted on their countrymen at the Polish university at Vilnius by Russian authorities. In November 1830 a military insurrection led by junior officers, inspired by the successful liberal revolution in France earlier in the year, broke out in Warsaw and quickly spread to garrisons throughout the kingdom. Constantine was forced to return to Russia, and the diet deposed Nicholas I as king of Poland. The well-equipped Polish army more than doubled its size with recruits to confront the much larger Russian army that marched to restore imperial control in Poland. Entreaties to France and Britain for aid or diplomatic support went unanswered, while Prussia assisted Russia by closing its frontier with Poland. Party strife and indecision within the diet and the civil government undercut the efforts of the army and the masses of the population, particularly among the peasantry, who contributed to the insurrection. The war, which continued until September 1831, ended in a Polish defeat.

In the aftermath of the insurrection, the constitution was amended by the Organic Statute of 1832 to tighten St. Petersburg's grip on Congress Poland. Civil rights were drastically curtailed, Polish units were integrated into the Russian army, and for a time the Polish universities at Warsaw and Vilnius were closed. The hostility of Russian authorities was also directed against the Polish church, which remained the one agency through which patriotic sentiment could be expressed. Defeat and political oppression set off the so-called Great Emigration that saw more than 10,000 Poles—members of the intelligentsia, political and student leaders, and army officers who had participated in the insurrection—leave Poland. Exiles joined a community of Polish expatriates that included the composer Fryderyk Chopin and the poet Adam Mickiewicz, considered Poland's "national bard," who wrote the epic *Pan Tadeusz* in France.

Official Russian policy toward the Poles seemed to soften after the accession of Alexander II in 1855. The Polish council of state, headed by a Polish governor, enacted a number of reforms but aroused the opposition of activist students, many of the gentry, and some of the clergy because of what was interpreted as its overweening subservience to Russian authorities. Student-led demonstrations against the proposed conscription of Poles into the Russian army set the stage for a new insurrection early in 1863.

Lacking the fine army that had defied the Russians in 1830, Polish resistance consisted of uncoordinated, small-scale guerrilla activities, which nonetheless required two years for Russian forces to suppress completely. Again, as in 1830, Western Europe was sympathetic to the Polish cause, and in France Napoleon III promised support, but no help was forthcoming. Also in contrast to the popular uprising of 1830, the 1863 insurrection met with indifference from the Polish peasantry, whose antagonism toward the gentry to whom they were bound had intensified after the abolition of serfdom in Russia in 1861. The gulf between peasants and landowners was widened further when, in the midst of the insurrection, the Russian government instituted agrarian reform in Poland, transferring as freeholds to dependent tenants land that was cut from large estates.

Thousands of Poles were arrested for their part in the insurrection. Some were executed, and many were deported as political prisoners. The constitutional monarchy was abolished, and Congress Poland became a Russian province, administered by a tsarist bureaucracy. Polish was replaced as the language of government, and the process of russification was begun in the educational and legal systems.

The struggle for their own country's independence also involved Poles in revolutionary activities outside Poland. They figured prominently in the ferment that spread from Paris across Europe in 1848–49 and in the Paris Commune of 1871, in which about 1,200 Poles, including two leading Communard generals, were active participants. European socialist movements of all shades were full of Polish followers. According to the Austrian chancellor Klemens von Metternich, the Polish struggle had become the embodiment of "the revolution itself," threatening to "declare war on all existing institutions."

In Poland, however, a deep undercurrent of positivist thinking, which insisted that judgments be based on empirical evidence, manifested itself among the Polish political and intellectual elite in reaction to the successive failures of the armed uprisings against the Russian presence there. Politically conscious groups embarked on a deeply introspective analysis of the national predicament, and many began to reevaluate their political methods and psychological attitudes. The concept of engaging in a permanent struggle for national independence was increasingly questioned by a frustrated and disillusioned younger generation, which had become convinced that hard work in acquiring both wealth and knowledge was the virtue most needed for the survival of the battered country. The advocates of this approach rejected militancy and with it the dreams of the Romantic poets like Mickiewicz who had inspired an earlier generation, urging their countrymen instead to work step-by-step, or "organically," for the rapid modernization of every aspect of Polish life. Rationalization of agriculture and an awareness of the role of industry in improving economic well-being were stressed by the partisans of what came to be known as "organic work."

The intellectual framework for this movement was shaped by a group of journalists and pamphleteers led by Aleksander Swietochowski. In pages of his Warsaw periodical *Prawda* (Truth), Swietochowski formulated a secular program based on a "religion of humanity and gospel of hard work" by which Poland could make tangible, material gains. He worshiped energy, discipline, and progress and regarded the dream of national independence as senseless and unachievable and an excuse for daydreaming and idleness. His more sober and realistic goals were the expansion of education, the development of material resources, and the acquisition of cultural autonomy within the tsarist realm.

This realistic trend toward the acceptance of organic work was encouraged not only by the changing moral and intellectual climate promoted by materialistic positivism after 1864 but also by the rapid industrial development of Russian Poland. Lodz, for example, had developed since early in the century as a textile manufacturing center. When in 1851 Poland was included in the imperial tariff system, its industry gained favored access to a huge Russian market. As additional strides were made in the mining and metallurgical industries, Poland became the most important industrial region in the Russian Empire. Nineteenth-century industrialization accounted in turn for a surge in the growth of Polish cities, accompanied by the emergence of a more prosperous bourgeoisie and a more numerous proletariat. Moreover, Poles began to occupy a number of high managerial positions in the Russian economy. As a result, the attitude of some Poles toward Russia tended to be ambivalent. They resented the political and cultural oppression of the tsarist regime but, at the same time, enjoyed the economic benefits derived from Poland's being a part of the Russian Empire.

Austrian Poland

In the decades immediately following the Congress of Vienna, the administration of Austria's Polish province, Galicia, was tied directly to Vienna and was carried out by an Austrian governor general appointed by the Habsburg emperor. Political and social unrest was rife—incited, Austrian authorities claimed, by revolutionary elements in republican Krakow. A bloody peasant rebellion that swept the province in 1846 gave Austria a pretext for annexing the free republic and incorporating its territory into Galicia. In response to agrarian grievances there and to revolutionary pressures elsewhere in the empire, however, the Austrian government abolished serfdom in 1848. More Poles were introduced into the provincial administration. Count Agenor Geluchowski was named governor general of Galicia in 1850, and provision was made for the seating of local assemblies. after the establishment of the Austro-Hungarian Dual Monarchy in 1867, Galicia received a provincial diet and a government exercising a large measure of autonomy in the region.

At the same time that the positivists were influencing opinion and events in Russian Poland, members of the intelligentsia in Galicia were submitting Poland's past to a critical reappraisal. The granting of provincial autonomy to Galicia had been made possible in large part by the spadework of a group of historians known as the Krakow School. They prepared the minds of their countrymen for acquiescence to the policy of cooperation with Austria, successfully carried out by conservative politicians in exchange for the substantial political and cultural concessions the Habsburg Dynasty granted its Polish subjects. In their rigorous stocktaking of the nation's past, the Krakow historians swept aside the traditional arguments that old Poland had been the innocent victim of three predatory powers. Weak central government, an empty treasury, an impoverished peasantry in bondage, a weakened middle class barred from participation in government, an inadequate standing army—these were, according to the Krakow historians, the main causes of Poland's catastrophe. Enlightened reform had come too late to save the antiquated Commonwealth. Like the advocates of organic work, they argued that the remedy for the mistakes of the past would not be found in more bloody sacrifices but in methodical, well-planned political and socioeconomic development within existing circumstances. A liberalized Austrian state, they continued, offered a favorable framework for Polish national existence. Geluchowski, who after his tenure as governor general (1850–59) held important posts in Vienna, was the political figure most influenced by their arguments. If Poland was ever to regain its independence, he insisted, it could only be done in cooperation with Austria.

After 1867 Galicia was fully integrated into the political life of the Habsburg monarchy. Galician Poles served as governors and cabinet ministers and rose to high positions in the military forces, the diplomatic corps, and the civil bureaucracy. Polish delegates came to exercise a determinant role in the Austrian parliament, where governments could not be formed without the cooperation of their bloc. The expansion of a Polish school system and adult education and the struggle against illiteracy proceeded at a fast pace. The universities at Krakow and Lvov (Polish, Lwow) and numerous cultural institutions contributed to making Galicia a nursery of Polish scholars and artists. By contrast, economic growth was slow, and the conservative landowners who controlled the provincial government did little to encourage industrial development. On the whole, however, self-government in Galicia worked well and allowed for fairly extensive participation in public affairs by the Polish people. Less satisfied were the Ukrainians, who were an underrepresented majority in the eastern, ethnically mixed segment of the province, but even they enjoyed some benefits from Galicia's autonomous status.

Prussian Poland

Eastern Pomerania had been incorporated directly into the Kingdom of Prussia in 1815 as the province of West Prussia, but Posnania was recognized as a semiautonomous grand duchy under Prussian sovereignty. A Polish viceroy, Prince Antoni Radziwill, was appointed to administer the grand duchy as representative of the king of Prussia, Frederick William III, who also bore the title grand duke of Poznan. Polish law was enforced, and a diet, elected by the nobility, met periodically to make recommendations to Berlin. The limited autonomy allowed the Poles was steadily curtailed after 1827, however, and following the revolutionary crisis of 1848 the grand duchy was abolished and Posnania became a Prussian province.

Thus, while the Poles in Galicia were acquiring greater political and cultural autonomy, those in Prussian Poland were made to wage a grim struggle against Germanization. Courts and civil administration were conducted exclusively in the German language. Polish was maintained as a medium of instruction, however, in the large number of schools operated by the church. Otto von Bismarck, architect and first chancellor of the unified German Empire established under Prussian leadership in 1870, regarded the Poles with suspicion. He viewed the presence of a large and coherent ethnic minority in Germany as a threat to the new state, and he found the Poles hateful not only as Slavs but also as ultramontane Roman Catholics who acknowledged an allegiance other than that owed to the state. In 1872 Bismarck formally initiated his campaign—called the *Kulturkampf* (cultural struggle)—against elements within the country that were deemed un-German in outlook. Although Bismarck's policy targeted for attention the activities of the Roman Catholic Church throughout Germany, the *Kulturkampf* was triggered mostly by his fear of an alleged "Polish menace" to the unity and cohesiveness of the German Empire. Polish Catholic schools were closed, cultural organizations were suppressed, and restrictions were placed on the activities of the church and its hierarchy. Poles were subjected to legal discrimination and economic pressures. Polish Catholics responded to the challenge with a redoubling of their religious and national zeal.

In 1886 Bismarck obtained a grant of 100 million marks from the Reichstag (German parliament) for the acquisition of Polish estates on which German colonists were to be settled. Having successfully withstood the *Kulturkampf* and steadily improved their own economic position, the Poles had sufficiently developed both their national consciousness and their material resources to offer stiff resistance to Bismarck's colonization project. The fight was carried on through well-organized self-help institutions, the success of which could be seen in many spheres of activity. A loan bank for Polish farmers was set up in the 1860s, followed by an industrial bank. Polish cooperative societies, which had merged in 1872, were welded into a solid Union of Cooperative Banks in 1886. This was paralleled by the development of the Union of Farmer's Circles, cooperatives that collectively purchased the essential needs of the Polish farmers (such as seeds, fodder, and machinery) while providing them with credit and catering also to their cultural and social needs. The cooperative movement, which by 1914 included nearly 300 local units, spread from Posnania to Pomerania and finally to Silesia, where by the end of the nineteenth century a remarkable Polish national revival was under way.

Despite large expenditures on colonization, Berlin failed to turn these three areas into solid German provinces. German settlers, lured by generous subsidies, always regarded them as colonial lands, while the Poles' resistance to Germanization reinforced their national solidarity. On the economic side of the struggle, Polish society produced its own tough and resourceful bourgeoisie, which was fully a match for its German counterpart.

Political Movements

By the end of the nineteenth century, members of the Polish bourgeoisie, together with an intelligentsia that was largely of gentry origin, had become involved in activating the politically dormant peasant masses and organizing the emerging working class. This increasing political and social involvement on the part of the middle class resulted in the formation of three political movements: socialism, nationalism, and populism. Each movement developed simultaneously in Russian Poland and Galicia, and each eventually took root in the German-controlled area of Poland as well.

The earliest modern Polish political parties were composed of industrial workers led by radical intelligentsia. The first such group of any consequence was a socialist party, Proletariat, founded in 1882 in Warsaw, where the rapid industrialization of Russian Poland had favored such a development. Enterprising

Town Hall, Poznan

capitalists reaped considerable profits, while the lack of social legislation left wide scope for the abuse of workers. As in the rest of the Russian Empire workers in Poland were not allowed to form trade unions or to strike. Party members were arrested by tsarist police, deportations and executions followed, and within a few years Proletariat had ceased to exist. Consequently, in 1892 its successor, the Polish Socialist Party (Polska Partia Socjalistyczna—PPS) was organized in exile. The PPS was the first Marxist group that directly connected the problem of social justice with that of national liberation, and its leaders decided to fight with equal determination for both aims at the same time. The fact that the PPS proclaimed its all-Polish character gave it added strength. The party soon managed to gain allies in similar movements in Galicia, Posnania, and Silesia with its call to the working class for power through a united and independent, socialist and democratic Polish republic.

Opposition to the nationalist aspects of the PPS's program crystallized in 1893 in the founding of a rival socialist party, which later became the Social Democratic Party of the Kingdom of Poland and Lithuania (Socjal Demodracja Krolestwa Polskiego i Litiwy—SDKPiL). The new group rejected the fusion of socialism and nationalism and emphasized close cooperation with the all-Russia socialist movement. The subsequent history of the Polish labor movement was largely that of the conflict between these two rival trends, nationalist and internationalist.

The driving force behind the SDKPiL's struggle against the PPS's hated "social patriotism" was Rosa Luxemburg, an activist who had escaped to Zurich, at that time a rallying point for Russian socialists, in order to avoid imprisonment after the suppression of Proletariat in 1886. She argued that the Polish Marxist movement should reject the idea of national independence because it was only social revolution that could offer hope of better conditions for the Polish working class. The struggle for independence, Luxemburg claimed, diverted attention from the class struggle and was contrary to the goal of proletarian internationalism. Furthermore, in her view, independence would cause the loss of vital Russian markets, which were essential to the existence of Polish industry and therefore essential as well to the welfare of the working class. In this way Luxemburg formulated her theory of the "organic incorporation" of the Polish provinces into the Russian state as a political objective based on economic imperatives. Polish socialists in Germany and Galicia were invited to integrate their activities with those of the SDKPiL.

From the outset the nationalist strain in Polish socialism was stronger than the cosmopolitan one. It was exactly because the party identified the revolution against social injustice with national liberation, for example, that the PPS was able to attract members such as Jozef Pilsudski, who wished to integrate Marxist doctrines with the heroic traditions of the Polish insurrections. Born near Wilno (Vilnius) into a noble family, Pilsudski was drawn early into revolutionary activities and was deported to Siberia for five years because of his alleged involvement in a plot to assassinate the tsar. Returning to Poland, he became the leader of the PPS in 1894, only to be arrested for publishing an illegal party newspaper. Pilsudski subsequently escaped from his Russian prison and made his way to Krakow, where he settled. But the revolution of 1905, part of the general unrest sweeping Russia at that time, found him once again in Russian Poland at the head of the socialist insurrectionists. The failure of the revolution provoked a split in the PPS between the left wing, which dropped its demands for Polish independence, and Pilsudski's intransigent wing. Back in Galicia, Pilsudski drifted away from socialism and devoted himself to organizing detachments of Polish sharpshooters with Austrian assistance for the next round in the fight against Russia.

The late nineteenth century, a period of political activity among the rural masses, witnessed the birth of the peasant, or populist, movement. In its origins this movement owed a great deal to Stanislaw Stojalowski, a Galician parish priest who in 1877 founded the Union of Farmer's Circles on the model of the cooperatives in Posnania. Its program to further the economic interests of smallholders and to promote rural education was modest, but the cooperative was also the first step in the political organization of the hitherto amorphous Galician peasantry.

In 1895 the first populist political party appeared in Galicia. Its purpose was to give peasants the means of participating in political life, thus far monopolized by conservative landowners. Peasant movements in Prussian and Russian Poland soon imitated the example. Several parties were eventually formed that differed from each other as far as their political and socioeconomic goals were concerned, but they shared one primary objective: providing the peasantry with more land by means of a more or less radical agrarian reform that would redistribute among the small farmers the large estates belonging to wealthy landowners, the state, and the church. All branches of the peasant movement, the degree of their radicalism notwithstanding, favored building an independent, united, democratic Polish state. In Galicia it produced several outstanding political leaders, the most significant of whom was Wincenty Witos, a self-educated farmer from the Tarnow region who led his party in the provincial diet and in the Austrian parliament.

Meanwhile, a conservative and more nationalistic trend in Polish politics was being shaped by the work of three intellectuals: Jan Poplawski, Zygmunt Balicki, and Roman Dmowski. Like Swietochowski, they condemned the armed uprisings of the past, but they rejected his aversion to stating definite political objectives. According to Poplawski, organic work was good only as long as it was preparing the nation for eventual reunification and independence which, he contended, was the main task of Polish statesmanship. Drawing heavily on the theory of social Darwinism, Balicki, in a pamphlet entitled *Egoizm narodowy wobec etyiki* (National Egoism and Ethics), published in 1902, elaborated the idea that national survival was the supreme law of politics and a moral imperative.

The political thoughts of Poplawski and Balicki found acceptance in all three segments of the country, and in Russian Poland they provided the ideological underpinning for National Democracy (Narodowa Demokracja—ND), led by Dmowski. The ND stressed the value of grass-roots organization as a precondition of political independence, which Dmowski envisioned a reunified Poland first to be achieved within the context of a pan-Slavic Russian Empire. Poland's enemy, he held, was not Russia but Germany of the *Kulturkampf* and Bismarck's colonization plan.

As a corollary of the ND's anti-German stand, the party also assumed an intransigent attitude toward the Jews and Ukrainians, two groups that Dmowski considered inherently pro-German. The former, he argued, were an alien body incapable of genuine assimilation who, in addition to their Germanophile leanings, were also an obstacle to Polish emancipation because of their dominant position in the country's economic life. Socialism was likewise condemned as an international movement directed by Jews and Germans and therefore a menace to Poland.

In 1903 Dmowski published his programmatic book, *Mysli Nowoczesnego Polaka* (Thoughts of a Modern Pole), in which he subjected his country's traditions and his countrymen's attitudes to bitter criticism. Drawing the logical consequences from Balicki's work, he declared the absolute priority of national interests, elevating patriotism to the rank of religion. If the Poles were to survive as a nation, he argued, they had to cultivate strength and discard what he saw as their traditional softness and passivity. He called for organized, systematic political action by a vigorous middle class, and he set as examples to imitate not only the Poles of Prussian Poland, who had fought stubbornly for their ethnic survival, but also their enemies, the Germans.

Polish delegates played a modest role in the Duma, the deliberative assembly created in imperial Russia as part of reforms following the revolution of 1905. Dmowski tried to win over Russian moderates to the idea of Polish autonomy, but his efforts were in vain. The ND leader feared that a continuation of revolutionary ferment in Poland might increase Russian dependence on Germany and thus weaken the French-Russian alliance on which he had staked his hopes for Poland's future. Consequently, the so-called Polish Circle, a bloc of Polish delegates in the Duma, voted for the military budget, approved conscription, and made numerous declarations supporting a strong Russia as a vital link in the anti-German coalition.

Cultural Life

Political oppression had many debilitating effects on Poland, but the partitioning powers could never extinguish Polish intellectual activity and cultural creativity, which flourished despite numerous obstacles in all parts of Poland as well as abroad. Warsaw-educated Maria Sklodowska won worldwide fame for research on radiation, which led to her discovery of two radioactive elements, polonium (named in honor of her native country) and radium. She and her husband, French scientist Pierre Curie, shared the Nobel Prize for physics in 1903. In 1911 she was awarded a second Nobel Prize for chemistry as a result of research on obtaining pure radium. Another laureate, the author Henryk Sienkiewicz, received the Nobel Prize for literature in 1905 after the publication of his novel *Quo Vadis?* Unable to find a satisfactory outlet for their talents in their own language, the novelist Joseph Conrad (Josef Korzeniowski) and the poet Guillaume Apollinaire (Wilhelm de Kostrowicki) enriched, respectively, English and French literature with their work. Wincenty Lutoslawski taught philosophy at leading European universities, gaining wide recognition at the turn of the century for his innovative interpretation of Plato. Leon Petrazycki, for several years the dean of the law faculty of St. Petersburg University, profoundly affected legal studies with his psychological theory of law and his concept of "social engineering," according to which legislation could be used as an instrument not only for social reform but also of moral improvement. Another Pole, Ignacy Jan Paderewski, achieved acclaim as a pianist and composer. His friendship with President Woodrow Wilson, whose acquaintance Paderewski made while on a concert tour in the United States, was to have a profound bearing on Poland's destiny.

World War I

At the outbreak of World War I, Polish sympathies were split into two camps: one Pro-Russian and the other pro-Austrian. In both cases, Poles gave their partisan support to the great power that seemed most likely to further distinctly Polish interests. Because of the oppressive policies against the Poles pursued in the past by Berlin, Germany had few significant supporters among them.

The single most influential Polish political party in 1914 was Dmowski's ND in Russian Poland. In line with Dmowski's fiercely anti-German and pan-Slavic stance, National Democrats were committed to Russia, convinced that the Entente Powers (Russia and its allies, France and Britain) would defeat the Central Powers (Germany and Austria-Hungary) and reunite all Polish territory under the Romanov Dynasty. Polish reunification was, in fact, one of Russia's stated war aims. This, in turn, according to Dmowski, would lead to the eventual restoration of Poland's independence. Dmowski was responsible for organizing the Polish National Committee (Komitet Narodowy Polski—KNP) to rally broad support for the Entente's war effort.

Austria was recognized as the most benevolent of the partitioning powers and the one that had already granted the greatest degree of autonomy to its Polish subjects. Pro-Austrian sentiment was based on the assumption that the Central Powers' victory over Russia would result in the incorporation of Congress Poland within the liberal Austrian system. Dmowski contradicted this view, pointing out that the Habsburg state was dependent on Germany, a power bent on the destruction of the Polish nation. The Central Powers made the most of anti-Russian feelings among the Poles, however, and the Polish political parties in Galicia set up the Supreme National Committee (Naczelny Komitet Narodowy—NKN) to promote Polish reunification under Austrian auspices. The NKN's military board, headed by Wladyslaw Sikorski, recruited volunteers from Russian Poland for the Polish Legion, which served under Austrian command. Pilsudski was placed in charge of one of the legion's three original brigades.

Pilsudski, however, took advantage of Austrian assistance without identifying himself with the NKN's pro-Austrian stance as his rival, Sikorski, had done. He kept his options open, intimating to close associates that he would switch sides if it served Polish interests. All the while that he cooperated with the Central Powers, "The Commandant"—the brigade commander's title by which Pilsudski was popularly referred to—maintained an underground command intelligence group, the Polish Military Organization, which operated separately from the NKN and the Polish Legion formation.

Poland was one of the war's major battlegrounds. An initial Russian offensive in Galicia in 1914 pushed to within sight of Krakow, and very heavy fighting took place around Gorlice and Przemysl the following spring. Warsaw fell in August 1915 to German forces, which completed the occupation of Russian Poland by the end of the year. Another major Russian offensive was launched in eastern Galicia in 1916. The lot of the civilian population in the war zone was desperate. Retreating Austrian and Russian armies carried out a scorched-earth strategy during their withdrawals. About 1 million Polish refugees fled from the fighting behind Russian lines, and several hundred thousand more Poles were taken to Germany to join the labor force. Polish troops served in the armies of all three belligerents fighting the war on Polish soil. About 1 million Poles were included in the mobilization in 1914, and by 1916 the number in arms on both sides was nearly 2 million. About 450,000 Polish soldiers died in the war.

In an effort to lure Poles to the side of the Central Powers, a "Kingdom of Poland" was reconstituted in occupied Russian Poland late in 1916 under German and Austrian protection. Executive authority in the protectorate was vested in a regency council composed of three Polish conservatives. Pilsudski was appointed to the military board in the new administration, but he made his full cooperation conditional on recognition of Poland's independence and the creation of a separate Polish army. When command of Polish Legion forces was transferred from Austria to Germany in 1917, the majority of the troops followed Pilsudski's example in refusing to take the oath of fealty to the German emperor. As a result, Pilsudski was arrested and imprisoned in Germany; some legionnaires were integrated into the Austrian army and shifted to other fronts.

After the tsarist regime was toppled in March 1917, the provisional Russian government under Alexander Kerensky recognized Poland's independence and urged the Poles in occupied territory to support the Entente against the Central Powers. Some Polish soldiers in the Russian army went over to the Bolsheviks during the October Revolution, while others remained loyal to their officers and formed independent units, organized into three army corps, that defended Polish towns and property in Byelorussia and the Ukraine against the depredations of the Bolsheviks and the Ukrainian nationalists.

The Treaty of Brest-Litovsk in March 1918 ended Russian participation in World War I. A separate peace concluded with the Ukrainian nationalists turned over the Polish province of Chelm to their pro-German provisional government. In protest, the Polish government in the Warsaw protectorate resigned, and legion units commanded by Jozef Haller crossed the line to join Polish units in the Ukraine. Haller's corps was decimated there in heavy fighting against German forces.

As a result of Russia's defection, the Western allies felt free to act on Poland's behalf. Meanwhile, General Haller made his way to France, where he was placed in command of the 100,000-man Polish army raised there under the aegis of the KNP, in Paris, from volunteers from the United States and Canada and from Polish prisoners of war. The Allies recognized the KNP as the legitimate spokesman for Polish interests and Poland as a co-belligerent against the Central Powers. Representatives of the KNP were accredited to Allied capitals, Paderewski being sent by Dmowski to Washington.

Prompted by Paderewski, Woodrow Wilson declared in favor of Polish reunification and independence. On January 8, 1918, the president formally proclaimed his Fourteen Points, of which the thirteenth stated: "An independent Polish state should be erected, which would include the territories inhabited by indisputably Polish populations, which would be assured a free and secure access to the sea, and whose political and economic independence and territorial integrity should be guaranteed by international covenant." Simultaneously, British Prime Minister David Lloyd George declared: "We [the British government] believe that an independent Poland, comprising all those genuinely Polish elements who desire to form part of it, is an urgent necessity for the stability of Western Europe." Similar pronouncements were made by other Allied governments.

Upon the collapse of the government in Vienna and the breakdown of the Austrian army, Polish parliamentarians formed a so-called liquidation committee in October 1918 that assumed complete control of western Galicia and responsibility for its defense. Earlier in the month the regency council in Warsaw had convoked a diet and made contact with the Allied governments.

Independent Poland

Released from internment in Germany, Pilsudski returned to Warsaw on November 10, 1918 (the day before the armistice), and was welcomed as a hero. The regency council and the Galician liquidation committee turned over power to him as provisional president of an independent Polish republic. Meanwhile, in the face of German resistance, a separate provisional government was set up in Poznan by the National Democrats to establish Polish claims in western Poland pending a settlement of the new republic's borders. At Pilsudski's request, Paderewski became prime minister to form a national government that could use his prestige to bring together the rival parties. Elections were held for a constituent assembly to draw up a constitution. The new administration undertook to create a uniform monetary system in a country that had six different currencies in circulation. A national army was formed under Pilsudski's command, incorporating legionnaires, Polish units from the Russian, German, and Austrian armies, and Haller's well-equipped army, which was brought from France in 1919.

The Versailles Settlement and the Plebiscites

The Conference of Paris was convened in January 1919 to negotiate a comprehensive peace settlement. The Polish delegation was officially headed by Paderewski and Dmowski, who in June signed the Treaty of Versailles embodying that settlement. The treaty established Poland's western frontiers, incorporating Posnania and most of Pomerania with Congress Poland and Galicia and allowing Poland access to the Baltic Sea in accordance with Wilson's thirteenth point. The only exception to the largely Slavic character of Pomerania was the German city of Gdansk and its environs. Initially, the Commission for Polish Affairs set up by the conference voted unanimously to restore Gdansk to Poland for strategic as well as for historical and economic reasons. Otherwise, the Polish-German frontier proposed by the commission was based on linguistic criteria of the German census of 1910. Robert H. Lord, a Harvard professor who was an American delegate on the commission, argued that the failure to provide Poland with possession of the mouth of the Vistula would be to favor the interests of 200,000 Germans over that of 20 million Poles. On the insistence of Lloyd George, however, the commission's recommendation was overridden, and Gdansk was declared a free city (Danzig) under the sovereignty of the League of Nations with some special rights reserved for Poland.

Britain also convinced the conference to reconsider the commission's allocations to Poland in Silesia and the Masuria district of East Prussia. It concluded that in both cases, which involved ethnically mixed areas, the question of disposition of territory would be resolved by means of plebiscites. On paper the decision appeared fair enough, but implementation of the plebiscites in the disputed areas, where the oppressive German administration and an intimidating police apparatus were left intact, prevented the free and accurate expression of the will of the resident non-German majorities.

Silesia had passed out of the Polish kingdom in the fourteenth century during the period of fragmentation, and most of the region had been absorbed by Prussia in the eighteenth century. Lower Silesia had become overwhelmingly Germanized, especially its urban centers, and would remain part of Germany. But Upper Silesia was ethnically mixed, and possession of its rich coal-mining and steel-producing areas was considered crucial by the Poles, on the one hand, to the economic development of the new Polish republic and, on the other hand, by the Germans to the postwar recovery of Germany. In the plebiscite conducted in March 1921, 60 percent of the voters, representing a majority in slightly more than half of Upper Silesia's 1,500 communes, chose association with Germany. But their number was supplemented by about 200,000 Germans, born in Upper Silesia but no longer resident there, who were also allowed to participate. On the basis of the plebiscite, Germany claimed all but a small portion of the province. Silesian Poles reacted with a series of armed insurrections, seized control in many areas, and demanded immediate incorporation of the province's Polish-speaking areas into Poland. The question of Upper Silesia was referred to the League of Nations, which awarded to Poland the eastern third of the province, including almost all the communes having a Polish majority and by far the larger share of its heavily industrialized areas. The western part, including the city of Wroclaw (Breslau) and the largely agricultural region of Opole, went to Germany (see fig. 7).

The Cieszyn (Teschen) region on the southern fringes of Silesia was also an ethnically mixed area, having a Polish majority and a Czech minority, that had been part of Habsburg Austria. At the end of the war it was claimed by both Poland and the new state of Czechoslovakia. A compromise was imposed on them by the Allies in 1920 during a crucial phase in the Soviet invasion of Poland when the region had been occupied by Czech troops. As a result of the settlement, Cieszyn Silesia was partitioned, Czechoslovakia obtaining the larger and richer area south of the Olza River in which, according to the 1910 Austrian census, 55 percent of the population had been Polish.

As far as pro-Polish opinion was concerned, the plebiscite in Masuria took place at the worst possible moment—in July 1920 as the Red Army was advancing on Warsaw and the fate of Poland hung in the balance. The Poles made a poor showing—only 40 percent of the eligible electorate turned out for the plebiscite—and Masuria was allotted to Germany by an overwhelming majority. The outcome of the plebiscite was also influenced by the introduction of a large number of new German voters, who accounted for about half of those going to the polls.

The Russo-Polish War

In order to secure its eastern frontier, Poland first had to repulse Soviet Russia's encroachments. As the disarmed German army pulled back from the eastern front, the Soviet Union's Red Army pushed forward, intending to use Poland as the bridge

Figure 7. Independent Poland, 1921–39

across which it would bring the revolution to a chaotic Germany. By the end of 1919, however, the Poles had checked the Soviet attack in heavy fighting.

Pilsudski had been a consistent proponent of the idea that Poland's salvation lay in the establishment of a belt of federated states between it and Soviet Russia and the restoration in a modern and voluntary form of the old Polish-Lithuanian Commonwealth. He also considered the Dnieper Ukraine to be the key to the balance of power in eastern Europe and argued that whoever controlled it would be able to organize and lead the region. This was clearly a role that he had mapped out for Poland to assume.

Soon Pilsudski found a partner in another socialist, Simon Petlyura, the Ukrainian military leader who was the most serious antagonist of the Bolsheviks on the Dnieper. In April 1920 Pilsudski concluded an alliance with him, and within a month their joint forces had entered Kiev and proclaimed an independent Ukrainian government there under Petlyura.

In June the Red Army launched a massive offensive, striking at several points on the long front. The Polish-Ukrainian allies were forced to retreat, and the Soviets pursued them into Poland, within a few weeks reaching the very gates of Warsaw. A Polish communist government was organized at Bialystok, and Josef Stalin (then chief political commissar of the Red Army's southern army) exchanged letters with Soviet leader V.I. Lenin outlining plans for the integration of Eastern Europe into a Soviet confederation. Lenin, for his part, described the expected destruction of the Polish army as a necessary step in Soviet Russia's revolutionary drive to the west. The British government, through its foreign minister, Lord Curzon, proposed an armistice line that essentially traced the eastern boundary of former Congress Poland, but the so-called Curzon Line was rejected by Warsaw because it forfeited to the Soviets areas that had historically been included in the Polish state. In August Polish forces under Pilsudski and Sikorski counterattacked near Warsaw, completely routing the Soviets, but Poland lacked the resources to exploit fully the military victory over the Red Army. Nevertheless, Polish soldiers had turned back the Soviet advance westward and allowed modern Poland to fulfill once again the nation's historic vocation as Europe's bulwark against threats from the east. The compromise peace treaty signed at Riga in March 1921 divided disputed territory in Byelorussia and the western Ukraine between Poland and the Soviet Union. The Soviets also agreed to pay compensation to Poland.

Meanwhile, the Poles reoccupied the region around Vilnius. Polish forces had taken possession of this predominantly Polish-speaking area in Middle Lithuania in 1919 but lost it subsequently to the Soviets, who had in turn ceded it to the newly established republic of Lithuania. Pilsudski tried unsuccessfully to persuade the Lithuanian nationalists to accept a federal union with Poland and thus to share Vilnius, which had been the capital of the old grand duchy. Their refusal effectively put an end to Pilsudski's scheme for an East European federation. The Allies and eventually the League of Nations recognized Poland's claim to the Vilnius region, but for several years a state of war existed between

Poland and Lithuania over the issue, and relations remained throughout the interwar period.

Peoples, Parties, and Regions

Within the frontiers that it had established by 1921, the Polish republic had an area of 390,000 square kilometers. Of its 27 million inhabitants, 70 percent were Poles, 15 percent Ukrainians, 7 percent Jews, 4 percent Byelorussians, and 4 percent Germans. Even among the Polish majority, regional, social, and economic differences were apparent. Western Poland and Silesia, formerly a part of Germany, boasted an efficient capitalist economy that produced a disproportionate share of national income and state revenues. The bourgeois nature of Polish society there contrasted with the aristocratic and peasant outlooks that characterized the rest of the country. Galicia, although economically the most backward region, provided a large corps of bureaucrats trained in the self-administering Austrian province. Krakow, rather than Warsaw, was still regarded as the country's cultural capital. A cleavage existed in the eastern borderlands, including eastern Galicia, between an ethnic Polish minority that predominated in the cities and controlled the landed wealth and a peasant society that was largely Ukrainian and Byelorussian.

In 1921 fully one-quarter of all ethnic Poles lived outside Poland. Throughout the nineteenth century a steady stream of Poles had departed from their homeland for political reasons or to find greater opportunities abroad for their intellectual and artistic talents. By the turn of the century the lack of capital investment and entrepreneurial skill had led to widespread unemployment, and outside Western Poland the economy offered limited prospects for ambitious young Poles. These circumstances stimulated the large-scale migration to Western Europe and to the Americas, particularly to the United States, Canada, Brazil, and Argentina. Between 1850 and 1920 as many as 2.5 million Poles entered the United States. In addition to emigrants, another 1.5 million ethnic Poles remained in Germany, chiefly in border areas not returned to Poland by the plebiscites.

Poland adopted a democratic constitution in March 1921 as proposed by the constituent assembly elected two years earlier. Based on the French model, it installed a parliamentary system in which executive authority was vested in a government responsible to a bicameral legislature. The National Democrats, who were the largest group in the constituent assembly, proposed and obtained a weak presidency in which the head of state's functions were mainly ceremonial, a move that was tailored by Pilsudski's opponents to curb his influence. The parliamentary electoral system encouraged the formation of a multiplicity of political parties that composed right, center, left, and minority blocs in the legislature's lower house (Sejm) and in the Senate. About 30 parties contested elections in the early 1920s, about half that number regularly winning parliamentary seats. Even the larger parties relied on regional bases of support. Parties were often fractured by ideological deviationists or by personalist factions. Inasmuch as no party or bloc of parties received a parliamentary majority, there were frequent changes of government.

Pilsudski, the first head of state under the new constitution, owed his position to his great personal popularity in the nation at large and held power without the backing of a political party. He had an influential following in military circles, however, particularly among former legionnaires and his old socialist comrades. In the early days of the republic he could rely on the PPS, the left wing of the peasant movement, and some ethnic minority groups for parliamentary support. Pilsudski stood for a federal system and decentralized administration that emphasized the role of the minorities in the life of a multiethnic republic. He favored the dominant role of the state in economic planning and a balanced but decidedly anti-Soviet foreign policy.

The main opposition to Pilsudski's policies and to his personal brand of leadership came from Dmowski's ND, the largest party on the right, whose leaders had represented Poland among the Allies during the war and at the Versailles Conference. In contrast with Pilsudski's vision of Poland's future as a federal state, the ND aimed at an integral Polish state with a strong central government that excluded minorities from a full share in the governing process. Anti-German in foreign policy and hostile to the Ukrainians and the Jews, the ND found its strongest following in Western Poland and among Poles in eastern Galicia.

Among the parties in the parliamentary center, the largest was Witos' Piast Party, formally the Polish Peasant Party (Polski Stronnictwo Ludowe—PSL), which had its stronghold in rural Galicia. Controlling about 13 percent of the total vote in the early 1920s, the PSL became the swing party whose support was necessary for forming any viable coalition government. On the democratic left, the PPS was the most important of several socialist groups and had a strong constituency in cities and industrial areas outside Western Poland. It was sometimes allied with—and usually outpolled by—the left-wing peasant parties that opposed Witos' moderate approach to agrarian reform.

A Polish communist party was founded in 1918 as an outgrowth of SDKPiL, adopting the name of Communist Party of Poland (Komunistyczna Partia Polska—KPP) in 1925. Although it won a small number of parliamentary seats, the KPP never developed a significant constituency in the Polish proletariat. Its leadership was largely Jewish and drawn from the radical intelligentsia. In keeping with the heritage of Rosa Luxemburg's Social Democrats, the KPP was internationalist in orientation, placing its loyalty in the Comintern (see Glossary) as distinct from supporting specifically Soviet interests. Banned by the Polish government, its leaders were eliminated in the Stalinist purges of 1936, and the party itself was abolished two years later by order of the Comintern. In contrast with right-wing extremist movements in other European countries during the interwar period, Polish fascist groups were small and politically ineffectual. They made their strongest appeal to university students.

A large bloc of seats in parliament was filled by parties representing the ethnic minorities. These were in turn split ideologically. Jews, for example, might be aligned with one of several parties that were socialist, religious, or Zionist in orientation. Although small as individual parties, some of the minority groupings contested parliamentary elections on a common list of candidates that polled up to 20 percent of the vote. In general, the minority parties supported Pilsudski and his scheme for a federal union, but Ukrainian and Byelorussian nationalists considered the incorporation of their regions into the Polish republic as the forcible imposition of foreign rule. The Polish government regarded recommendations from the Versailles commission on the question of non-Polish nationalities as interference in Poland's internal affairs. Peasants in the eastern borderlands did not share all of the benefits of land reform measures. Polish security forces in those areas were resented by the local non-Polish population. Ambiguous categories in census reports were designed to underrate their numbers. Ukrainian underground groups carried on a low-level insurgency, committing acts of sabotage and assassinating Polish officials. Byelorussians tended to be dismissed as a politically immature peasantry. In other cases, attempts were made at Polonizing parts of the Byelorussian community. Consequently, the Soviet Union made political inroads in Polish Byelorussia, undermining Warsaw's authority there by linking communist ideology with Byelorussian national consciousness and setting as an example the cultural autonomy of its component Byelorussian Soviet Socialist Republic.

The postwar German government assumed responsibility for protecting the interests of the ethnic German minority in western Poland and Upper Silesia, and its representatives reported alleged infringements on them to the League of Nations, which monitored conditions in plebiscite areas. Parties representing the German minority won seats in the Polish parliament. When Adolf Hitler rose to power in Germany, Berlin's demands on behalf of the minority became more strident, and the Nazis gained a significant number of adherents among Germans in Upper Silesia, Posnania, and Pomerania.

Non-Polish ethnic groups played an important role in the interwar Polish economy. For example, the Jews, who by 1931 constituted slightly over 10 percent of the total population, made up almost 60 percent of those involved in commerce and over 20 percent of those cited as engaged in industry. These included among them the proprietors of large and medium-sized enterprises as well as much more numerous small shopkeepers, tradesmen, and artisans. They were prominent in the professions, providing nearly half of the country's physicians and lawyers. This resulted in sharp competition with non-Jewish members of the intelligentsia and members of the rising Polish middle class, one consequence of which was the incidence of anti-Semitism. According to historian Erich Goldhagen, an American Jew, this kind of anti-Semitism represented chiefly a manifestation of hostility "born of a genuine conflict of interests between Jews and their host people" on the economic and professional levels, but a degree of social bias and animosity against Jews was also a fixture among the population as a whole. Discriminatory legislation carried over from the tsarist regime was repealed by the Polish government, although quotas adversely affecting Jewish candidates were enforced in university admissions. Poland during the interwar period had the highest percentage of Jewish population of any country in the world but, despite the tensions and conflicts that did exist between Jews and Poles, neither the intensity nor the scope of anti-Semitism ever reached the proportions that it did in some neighboring countries. The nature of Polish-Jewish relations remained more symbiotic than antagonistic, and in addition to their role in the economy and the professions, Polish Jews occupied positions in politics, the civil administration, and the army and were particularly prominent in the artistic, literary, and intellectual life of the country.

Democratic Poland

The slowness of social change and economic growth and the inability of the parliamentary government to come to grips with Poland's most pressing problems in those areas were serious shortcomings of the democratic regime introduced by the 1921 constitution. Despite continuing emigration, the Polish economy still could not provide regular and decent employment for a large segment of the country's people. The process of industrialization was too sluggish to absorb the large surplus of rural population, and agrarian reform, although introduced, was timidly carried out. Moreover, the relative lack of social mobility perpetuated surviving abuses and economic injustices. Yet, against heavy odds, a considerable measure of material progress was achieved in Poland without major financial aid from abroad or without applying totalitarian methods.

There were also notable cultural accomplishments. Illiteracy, which plagued nearly half the people of former Russian Poland at the time of independence, was drastically reduced during the interwar period. Institutions of higher learning produced graduates of a caliber comparable to that of their counterparts in universities in Western Europe. In the creative field, a Polish writer, W.S. Reymont, won the Nobel Prize for literature in 1924 for his novel *Chlopi* (*The Peasants*). Polish artists were awarded international prizes and were particularly recognized in the field of decorative and graphic arts, especially for their work with posters.

The significance of the period, however, was essentially moral. After more than a century of being divided and under foreign rule, the emergence of the independent Poland with a democratic form of government, whatever its imperfections, restored the self-confidence of the Polish people.

Paderewski had resigned as prime minister of the provisional government after less than a year in office, but his tenure set a pattern for the succession of national coalition cabinets that gave the country direction during the hard months of the Russo-Polish war. The first parliamentary election under the new constitution was conducted in November 1922. The right, spearheaded by the ND, remained the most popular bloc at the polls, its parties garnering 30 percent of the vote, followed by the left bloc with 25 percent, the center with 22 percent, and the ethnic minority parties, which together received 20 percent of the total. Dissatisfied with the role allowed the president under the constitution, Pilsudski chose not to present himself for reelection, although he retained his position as army chief of staff and inspector general with the rank of marshal. His successor, Gabriel Narutowicz, was elected by the newly seated parliament with support of the center, left, and minority parties, but the new president was assassinated after scarcely two weeks in office by a right-wing extremist protesting that Narutowicz had owed his election to non-Polish votes. In the wake of the assassination, Wladyslaw Sikorski was called on to head a "cabinet of pacification," which he formed with the backing of the center and left blocs in parliament. Early in 1923, however, Witos withdrew the PSL from its alliance with the left and joined the conservative ND in forming a center-right coalition government in which he became prime minister. Pilsudski resigned his army posts in a furor and went into retirement on his estate. He was replaced as chief of staff by another of his opponents within the army, General Stanislaw Haller, who proceeded to dismiss high-ranking pro-Pilsudski officers from the service.

The Witos government was confronted by a worsening economic crisis that had been aggravated by the instability of previous governments. The dislocation created by the war and the devastation inflicted on Poland's economic infrastructure had caused massive unemployment, and the incomes of those who were employed could not keep pace with a steeply escalating rate of inflation. Food prices, for example, had increased twelvefold during the two-year period of 1921–22. The country's economy suffered as well from low productivity and severe budget and trade deficits. The value of the Polish mark had plummeted to an exchange rate of about 10 million marks to the United States dollar by the end of 1923 when Witos stepped down and was replaced as prime minister by Wladyslaw Grabski at the head of a nonparty government. Grabski, a politically independent economist, introduced fiscal reforms that led to the creation of the Polish zloty in place of the worthless mark. His government also undertook measures to stimulate production and trade as a means of increasing employment.

After considerable delays, comprehensive land reform legislation was enacted in 1925. The law, first proposed in 1920, had been strenuously opposed in parliament by intransigent landowner delegates, some of whom had walked out on the ND when Dmowski conceded that some kind of land reform was necessary. As enacted, the legislation put an upper limit on the size of landholdings, one that was higher in the eastern borderlands where estates were larger and the need for reform greater than in the rest of Poland. Land was to be redistributed to peasants on easy terms according to an annual quota. Full compensation was to be paid to owners, partly in cash and partly in state bonds. Numerous exceptions were made to the maximum-size rule, however, for estates that were judged to be especially efficient producers. Land reform fell far short of the expectations of the law's sponsors. Implementation by local authorities was haphazard, and quotas for redistribution were not met; but by 1939 more than 3 million hectares—fully 20 percent of the land on estates held by private owners, the church, and the state—had passed to peasant proprietors in over 700,000 small holdings.

Grabski's uninterrupted two years in power provided Poland the stable political conditions needed for sustained economic recovery, but his efforts were dealt a mortal blow by the tariff war with Germany that erupted in mid-1925. When the Polish government refused to accept changes in the trade agreement between the two countries that would have imposed a heavy tariff on most of the Polish coal exported to Germany, the Germans barred the importation of over half of Polish goods coming into their country. The action by Germany, which had been Poland's best customer, affected one-quarter of all Polish trade. A financial panic ensued, forcing Grabski to resign in November 1925.

The Pilsudski Era

The apparent breakdown of the parliamentary process in the face of the continuing economic crisis stoked discontent among Pilsudski's following. In May 1926 Witos formed a new center-right coalition cabinet, Poland's fourteenth government since independence, to replace the previous nonparty regime. The total exclusion of leftist participation brought an immediate reaction from Pilsudski. Confident of his support in the army and among a large part of the population, he mounted a military coup d'etat with sympathetic units and seized control of the country after several days of street fighting in Warsaw against units loyal to the government, forcing the resignation of Witos and his government. The president, Stanislaw Wojciechowski, whose approval Pilsudski had sought to give legitimacy to the coup, resigned rather than sanction the military takeover. Pilsudski, who refused the presidency, established himself nonetheless as the virtual dictator of Poland, but his authoritarian regime operated behind the facade of the democratic constitution under which he resumed his military command, retained the post of minister of war in successive cabinets headed by his loyal lieutenants, and on two occasions served as prime minister. The parliament continued to sit, and despite periodic crackdowns, opposition to the regime was openly expressed by political parties and in the press and the classroom.

Pilsudski refused to consider one-party rule but relied for organized support on a political alliance called the Non-Party Bloc for Cooperation with the Government (Bezpartyjny Blok dla Wspolpracy z Rzadem—BBWR), which offered slates of progovernment candidates at election time. His power base, however, resided in the army and among a large portion of the population that was attracted by Pilsudski's great personal prestige. The trade unions and the political left had initially identified their interests with his coup against a center-right government, during which railroad workers had prevented reinforcements from reaching loyalist units in the capital. Socialist, left-wing peasant, and ethnic minority delegates in the parliament backed the coup. Public opinion was at the time disaffected from the old parties that seemed to put short-term partisan advantage ahead of national interests. Pilsudski, by contrast, called for putting national solidarity ahead of narrow class or regional interests. To accomplish the task of "cleansing" (*sanacja*, a term that became the regime's label) the Polish political system of corruption and indecision, Pilsudski preferred technicians drawn from both military and civilian circles to politicians. His critics alleged that he had no political program beyond introducing more efficient public management and entrenching his followers in power.

In the 1928 parliamentary elections, the BBWR obtained 30 percent of the vote and enough seats to ensure progovernment majorities when combined with expected support from either the left or the minority blocs. But Pilsudski alienated segments of the socialists and left-wing peasants by isolating them from decisionmaking in favor of nonparty technicians. At the same time, he courted the support of business and landowning circles.

The Polish economy experienced a modest recovery in the late

1920s, partly because of improved market conditions and partly as a result of economic development programs initiated or carried to completion by Pilsudski. War damage was repaired, older industries were refurbished, and numerous new ones were introduced. Among the latter was the Polish aircraft industry, which recorded impressive achievements. Pilsudski's economic orientation had always been statist. Under the direction of Eugeniusz Kwiatkowski, the minister of commerce, the government took an active role in stimulating economic growth through public investment, central planning, and state participation in vital industries and services. Public sector involvement was significant in the metallurgical and chemical industries, coal mining, and oil refining, and a near state monopoly existed in railroads, commercial aviation, merchant shipping, utilities, and armaments production.

As a result of Poland's earlier partitions, production and the transportation infrastructure that supported it had been geared in the various regions to supply separate markets in Germany, Russia, and Austria. The tariff war with Germany in 1925 had amply demonstrated the vulnerability of an economy overly dependent on one market. Kwiatkowski undertook to integrate Poland's regional economies into a single national economic unit. Rail lines were constructed that linked production centers to the port of Gdynia. During the decade of the 1920s this once-obscure fishing village northwest of Gdansk was converted into one of the largest and most modern harbors on the Baltic, capable of handling 10 million tons of goods a year. Through Gdynia, Poland was successful in opening large new markets for its exports in Scandinavia.

The impact of the world economic depression on Poland beginning in 1929 was immediate and severe. Agricultural prices fell drastically, particularly affecting small peasant proprietors who had only recently acquired land. Price declines also wiped out many tradesmen and artisans. For lack of orders industrial production was cut back sharply. In four years (1928–32) Poland's industrial output dropped by nearly one-half. Unemployment, which had risen to 12 percent of the work force by the end of 1930, reached more than 20 percent the following year.

The Polish government fell back on deflationary measures to deal with the crisis. Labor unrest mounted throughout 1930, and hard-pressed farmers, demanding better prices for their produce, imposed stoppages on food deliveries to the cities. Economic grievances soon combined with minority discontent and popular protests against the authoritarian nature of the regime. A new wave of sabotage and other acts of terrorism sweeping eastern Galicia were conducted by militant Ukrainian nationalists with German support. A tough military crackdown in the region suppressed the insurrection but discredited the moderate Ukrainian spokesmen in the eyes of their radical constituents.

Meanwhile, the regime was confronted by renewed parliamentary resistance to its policies. Center and left bloc parties agreed to combine their opposition in a formal coalition (Centrolew), which with the support of the conservative ND succeeded in voting down the government of the day in the Sejm and forcing its resignation. Pilsudski dismissed the challenge to his regime. "My fundamental disgust for the way in which all parliaments—and in particular our Sejm—function," he remarked, "is well known." A new government was formed to lay the regime's legislative program before the parliament.

When parliamentary measures failed to convince the regime of the depth of opposition to its policies, Centrolew turned to mass demonstrations and prepared a common slate of candidates for elections to be held late in 1930. In reaction important party leaders, many members of parliament, and several thousand political activists were arrested and detained. Strict censorship was enforced before the election, and curbs were imposed on civil rights. In this atmosphere of constraint, BBWR candidates campaigned on a platform calling for constitutional reforms to overcome the deadlock between the government and the parliament. The progovernment group received 47 percent of the vote and a large majority of the seats, but it fell far short of the two-thirds majority required to amend the constitution. Its alteration, however, remained a priority of Pilsudski and the BBWR. When the opposition staged a walkout in the Sejm in December 1934, the government (whose supporters numbered more than two-thirds of those remaining) introduced legislation that led to the promulgation of a new constitution the following March.

The main feature of the 1935 constitution was the shift of executive authority from the parliament to the presidency. The government became responsible to a strong president, who was himself responsible only "to God and to history." The army also came under his direct command and was independent of civilian control. The new constitution gave statutory form to the position that Pilsudski, the national hero, had already molded for himself, creating an office considered fit for someone of his stature to occupy. It also was designed to preserve his near dictatorial powers in the hands of his successor. When Pilsudski died in May at the age of 67, however, there was no potential successor who could lay claim to his great personal prestige.

The 1935 constitution had reduced the size of parliament and had restricted suffrage. New electoral laws that were intended to deemphasize the importance of party affiliation gave responsibility for choosing candidates to nominating committees in each constituency. The effect of this change was to limit the influence of party leaders in parliamentary elections and to increase the government's control over the electoral process, enhancing its opportunities for manipulating the results. The parliamentary election held later in the year was boycotted by more than half of the eligible voters and was widely understood as a popular rejection of the constitution.

Conflict existed within the regime between civilian and military elements. In the scramble for succession after Pilsudski's death, Ignacy Moscicki, president since 1926, remained in that office, but real power in the regime devolved on Pilsudski's protégé, army chief General (later Marshal) Edward Rydz-Smigly. The BBWR was dissolved after the 1935 election, in which its candidates captured a parliamentary majority. It was replaced the next year by Rydz-Smigly with a new progovernment party, the Camp of National Unification (Oboz Zjednoczenia Narodowego—OZON), which had a decidedly more right-wing cast to it. Dubbed the "Colonels' Party," the OZON was formally committed to continuing Pilsudski's policies. The actions of the government under its prime minister, General Felicjan Slawoj-Skladkowski, grew more arbitrary, but no attempt was made to suppress opposing political parties. Since the events of 1930, Polish politics had become radicalized, both to the left and to the right, and infected by a more virulent strain of anti-Semitism than had surfaced earlier. The army was divided politically into rival cliques, opponents of the regime rallying around Sikorski and Josef Haller. Formal opposition was led by old-line party leaders like Witos and Dmowski.

In 1938 the OZON won a decisive victory in parliamentary elections, taking 80 percent of the seats in voting that was conducted in some areas under questionable circumstances. Among the positive achievements of the post-Pilsudski regime was the opening in 1936 of the Central Industrial Region along the Vistula River, conceived of as the foundation of a new industrial area in one of the neglected parts of the country. Still under construction in 1939, it was an example of the sort of long-term coordinated planning that Pilsudski had always urged upon Poland's economy.

Foreign Relations

The cornerstone of Polish foreign policy in its formative years was the political and military alliance in 1921 with France, guaranteeing Poland's independence and territorial integrity. This was supplemented by a bilateral agreement with Romania, another ally of France, pledging military assistance in the event of an attack on either party. At one point Poland considered proposing a multilateral pact that would include the Scandinavian countries and create a neutral Nordic-Baltic bloc between Germany and the Soviet Union.

During the 1920s Poland repeatedly applied to join the Little Entente, a French-sponsored alliance linking Czechoslovakia,

Romania, and Yugoslavia in a mutual guarantee of their frontiers. But the mistrustful Czechs, influenced decisively by their foreign minister, Eduard Benes, rejected all Polish offers of cooperation. Relations between the two countries remained troubled as a result of the Cieszyn controversy. Polish membership in the Little Entente, it was argued in Prague, would shift the alliance's focus from opposition to Hungarian revanchism to defense against Germany. Poland, which traditionally had cordial ties with Hungary, countered that Germany, with which Czechoslovakia cultivated good relations, represented a more genuine threat to the countries of Central Europe. After Hitler came to power in Germany in 1933, the Polish foreign minister, Colonel Jozef Beck, went so far as to offer Czechoslovakia a straightforward military alliance. Benes replied that it was not desirable for Czechoslovakia to align itself with the country that, in his opinion, was destined to be the first victim of German aggression in the event of a new European war. He confided to Sir John Simon, the British foreign secretary, that "it would be dangerous to give Germany clear cause for fearing encirclement."

The main thrust of Pilsudski's foreign policy after 1926 had been to maintain a balance in relations with Poland's two powerful neighbors and potential adversaries, Germany and the Soviet Union. In an effort to achieve that balance, Poland signed a nonaggression pact with the Soviet Union in 1932 and two years later concluded a similar agreement with Germany. The purpose of the latter pact was to keep Hitler from pressing revisionist claims on the Polish-German frontier. Beck explained to France's foreign minister Pierre Laval, that both geography and history were of decisive importance in understanding Poland's relations with Germany and the Soviet Union. These dictated, first, that Poland never become dependent on one or the other of them and, second, that Poland avoid putting itself in a position that would encourage them to take concerted action against it. In such a situation, Beck concluded, no friendly power—not even France—or any alliance would come to Poland's aid. Beck, who was left with a free hand in conducting Poland's foreign affairs after the marshal's death in 1935, continued to adhere closely to Pilsudski's line.

The most serious shortcomings in Polish foreign policy during the interwar period were the early failure of Pilsudski's grand scheme to make Poland the center of an East European federation and Poland's subsequent inability to enlarge the Little Entente. These left the country overly dependent on its alliance with France and lulled many Poles into a false sense of security at a time when their ally was showing a reluctance to assert its influence in Eastern Europe. As a cosigner of the Locarno Pact with Britain and Germany in 1925, France normalized relations with its former enemy without eliciting a German guarantee of

Poland's western frontier. After Locarno the alliance was gradually eroded by French irritation at Poland's refusal to make accommodations that Paris believed were necessary to improve Polish relations with Germany, and it deteriorated rapidly when France disregarded a Polish recommendation for collective action to prevent Hitler's assuming power. In 1936, however, Poland reassured France of its willingness to fulfill its treaty obligations if the French chose to act against the German remilitarization of the Rhineland.

Poland also used the threat of military force to further its foreign policy interests. Frustrated in its attempts to achieve a political settlement to the Vilnius dispute, Poland served Lithuania with an ultimatum in March 1938, demanding and winning the opening of the border between the two countries and the establishment of normal diplomatic relations. Later that year Beck informed Benes that, in the event Germany pressed its claims to the Sudetenland, Poland would be obliged to act to ensure the security of Poles in Cieszyn Silesia. When the Czech government conceded to German territorial demands during the Munich crisis in September, Poland occupied the disputed territory.

After Nazi Germany took over the rest of Czechoslovakia in March 1939, Poland was flanked on the south as well as on the north and would clearly be the next target of German attack. The previous October, Hitler had put forward territorial claims only thinly veiled by a complex scheme that provided for the construction of "extra-territorial highways" across the so-called Polish Corridor in Pomerania to connect East Prussia with the rest of Germany. The Polish government had refused to consider it but declared a readiness to negotiate a settlement that would be acceptable to Berlin. Germany only stepped up its pressure, demanding in addition to the highway scheme the return of Gdansk and extraordinary privileges for Poland's German minority. Mindful of the fate of Czechoslovakia and reinforced by an Anglo-French guarantee, Poland again rejected the German demands as constituting a threat to its existence as a sovereign state.

In April 1939 Britain and Poland signed a mutual assistance treaty to which Hitler reacted by renouncing the 1934 nonaggression pact. Germany began preparing for war with Poland, deliberately provoking incidents along the frontier or involving the German minority. On August 23 Hitler and Stalin abandoned their proclaimed hostility toward one another and through their respective foreign ministers, Joachim von Ribbentrop and V.I. Molotov, concluded a nonaggression pact in Moscow that, in effect, divided Poland and the rest of Eastern Europe into two hegemonical spheres. The pact assured Germany of the Soviet Union's benevolent neutrality in case of war and gave Hitler a green light to attack Poland. Two days later agreement was reached in London on a formal Anglo-Polish military alliance.

World War II

Early in the morning of September 1, 1939, Germany invaded Poland. In fulfillment of their guarantees to Poland, Britain and France declared war on Germany on September 3, but the Allies were not ready to take offensive action to relieve the pressure of the German onslaught on Polish forces. Sixty German divisions drove deep into Polish territory and by the middle of the month had encircled Warsaw. On September 17 the Soviet Union attacked Poland from the east on the pretext of liberating the Ukrainians and Byelorussians from the "Polish yoke." The Poles, fully mobilized at 800,000 men, resisted stubbornly—especially in the besieged capital—but the superiority of the invaders in men, armor, and aircraft was crushing. Warsaw, subjected to heavy aerial bombardment, was surrendered to the Germans on September 27. The last Polish units in the field capitulated on October 6. Some troops escaped to Romania and Lithuania; others buried their weapons and returned to their homes, but most were made prisoners of war.

On September 28 representatives of Hitler and Stalin had reached an agreement dividing the spoils of Poland between them. Western Poland was annexed directly by Germany, and a German occupation authority, the General-Government, was established in the central region that included Warsaw and Krakow. A larger area in the east was annexed by the Soviet Union, which moved its western frontier forward approximately to the once-proposed Curzon Line (see fig. 8).

The period from 1939 to 1945 was the most trying and tragic in the millennial history of Poland. In those years 6 million Poles died—more than 15 percent of the total prewar population. More than 700,000 people (about 100,000 of them combatants) were killed in war-related actions and reprisals. Tens of thousands perished from starvation or other hardships. Hitler's genocidal policies marked Poland's entire Jewish community for extermination. Jews were initially consigned to ghettos in Polish cities to await shipment to concentration camps—like those at Oswiecim (Auschwitz), Treblinka, and Majdanek—where more than 3 million of them were systematically murdered. Some, driven to desperation, preferred to die fighting rather than at the hands of Nazi executioners. This was the case of the Jews of the Warsaw ghetto who, when threatened with final deportation to the extermination camps, rose up in April 1943 and held out against the Germans for 42 days.

From the start, German occupation authorities used violence to transform Poland into a submissive colony. "From now on," said the Nazi governor of Poland, Hans Frank, "the political role of the Polish nation is ended. It is our aim that the very concept *Polak*

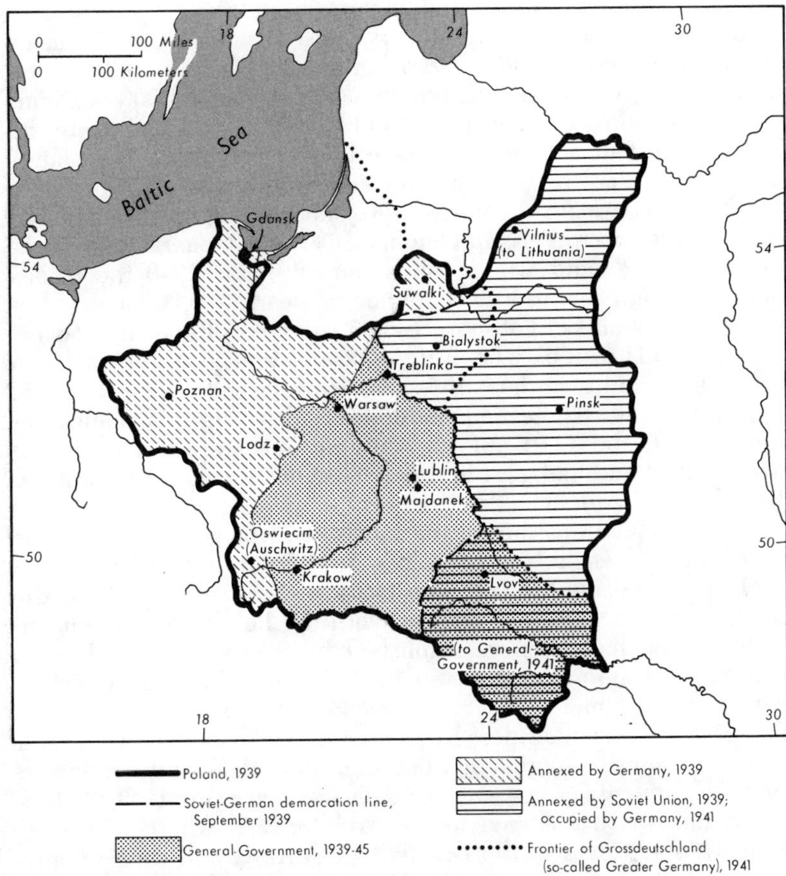

Figure 8. Occupied Poland in World War II

be erased for centuries to come . . .Poles will become slaves of the German empire." His master, Hitler, regarded Poland as "a reservation, a vast Polish labor camp." By means of forced deportations more than 1 million Poles were removed from the regions incorporated into Germany, and German settlers were brought in to replace them. Another 2.5 million Poles were recruited for forced labor in Germany. As a group the educated stratum of Poles was treated almost as cruelly as were the Jews, and nearly half of that class—including teachers, professionals, writers, and clergy—was lost to the country during the occupation.

Before the German invasion of the Soviet Union in June 1941, Soviet authorities had scattered 1.5 million inhabitants of eastern Poland in labor camps throughout that vast country, while many other Poles—particularly those involved in politics or public administration—were executed or thrown into prisons, where they died. About 15,000 reserve officers, most of them professionals or academics in civilian life, disappeared some months after being captured by the Soviets. The bodies of more than 4,000 of them, who had been shot in April 1940 and buried in a mass grave in the Katyn Forest near Smolensk, were later found by the Germans.

Before the fall of Warsaw, the Polish government had fled to Romania, where its members were interned. A government-in-exile was set up in Paris in October 1939 with General Sikorski as prime minister and army commander. By June 1940 the troops under his command in France numbered nearly 100,000 men, composed of remnants of Polish forces and volunteers from among overseas Poles. They took part in the Battle of France and, along with Polish naval units, in the Norwegian campaign. Sikorski was able to regroup about 20,000 men under the Polish flag in Britain after the fall of France. Other Polish ground units were formed in the Middle East and took part in the defense of Tobruk in Libya under British command in early 1941. Polish pilots manned six Royal Air Force squadrons during the Battle of Britain, from which one unit emerged as the record holder in terms of enemy kills.

Within weeks of the German invasion of the Soviet Union, the Kremlin had opened negotiations with the Polish government-in-exile, which had been reestablished by Sikorski in London, to organize Polish forces for service on the eastern front. Six divisions with a complement of 75,000 men were soon formed under General Wladyslaw Anders from inmates in Soviet prisoner of war and labor camps. Cooperation between these Poles and the Soviets proved impossible, however, and in the spring of 1942 Anders' command was transferred to the Middle East, where it was reformed as II Corps in the British Eighth Army and subsequently served with distinction in North Africa and Italy. In May 1944 the Poles captured the fiercely contested German stronghold at Monte Cassino, over which they hoisted the Polish flag. United States Army General George S. Patton noted that they were "the best looking troops" he had ever seen. Armored units of the Polish I Corps, which had been equipped in Britain, took part in the Normandy campaign, playing a vital role in the battle at Falaise. The Polish airborne brigade was dropped at Arnhem in the Netherlands during the unsuccessful Allied attempt to open a bridgehead over the Rhine in the autumn of 1944.

In the meantime, relations between Sikorski and Stalin had gone from bad to worse, and in April 1943 the Soviets broke contact with the London government-in-exile in reaction to questions that had been raised about reports of the Katyn massacre. The Kremlin formed a front group, the Union of Polish Patriots, led by Polish communists and others in the Soviet Union, as a Moscow-based alternative to the London group. Polish military units, recruited under its jurisdiction, grew by 1944 from divi-

Remains of Pawiak Prison in former ghetto area of Warsaw, used by German Gestapo during World War II to house captured Polish resistance members before transporting them to concentration camps
Courtesy Jean R. Tartter

sional to field army strength and under the command of General Zygmunt Berling fought on the eastern front alongside the Red Army. These Polish troops participated in driving the German army from Poland and, ultimately, in winning the Battle of Berlin.

By 1945 the Poles constituted the fourth largest Allied contingent in Europe after those of the Soviet Union, the United States, and Britain. One of the most significant contributions to the Allied victory, however, lay in the area of military intelligence. Polish intelligence had secured classified drawings of the top secret German code machine called "Enigma." With the aid of reconstructed models, a team of Polish cryptanalysts had broken the German military code during the 1930s, and the pertinent information was passed to their French and British allies when war became imminent. The British intelligence service subsequently advanced the deciphering of the "Enigma" code with the cooperation of escaped Polish code experts, thus enabling the Allies to read the orders Hitler sent to his field commanders.

Resistance by the Polish underground began almost immediately after the German occupation. In addition, Poles were later active in underground movements in France and other occupied countries. The Home Army (Armia Krajowa—AK), into which by

1942 the activities of the noncommunist resistance had been coordinated, conducted sabotage, clandestine operations, and guerrilla activities under the direction of the London government-in-exile, which operated in Poland through the underground Home Council. Sikorski was killed in an air crash in July 1943 and was replaced as head of the government-in-exile by Stanislaw Mikolajczyk, a leader of the PSL in prewar Poland. After Germany invaded the Soviet Union in June 1941, communist resistance groups also made their appearance. In January 1942 a small group of surviving communists formed the underground Polish Workers' Party (Polska Partia Robotnicza—PPR) in German-occupied Poland at Moscow's initiation. The following year the PPR organized the People's Guard, later renamed the People's Army (Armia Ludowa—AL), as its military arm. By 1944 the AK claimed to be able to call on as many as 400,000 effectives and the AL, at most, 10,000. There was little cooperation between the two groups.

By the summer of 1944 the Soviet military offensive had advanced well into Polish territory. In August, as the Red Army approached Warsaw, the AK began an uprising in anticipation of liberating the city before the arrival of Soviet forces, which were within the suburbs of the capital lying across the Vistula River. The Soviets, however, did not move to relieve the embattled city, and AK units there were virtually wiped out in fighting with the Germans that lasted over two months. The elimination of the Warsaw AK command undermined the further effectiveness of the noncommunist resistance movement and paved the way for Soviet-sponsored groups to consolidate and assume control of the liberated areas. When the Red Army finally entered Warsaw in January 1945, the Polish capital, whose population in 1939 had numbered over 1 million, was all but uninhabited, and 90 percent of it lay in ruins.

The People's Republic

The Red Army brought a communist-dominated provisional government to Poland in its baggage trains. Prefabricated in Moscow, the Polish Committee of National Liberation (Polski Komitet Wyzwolenia Narodowego—PKWN), successor to the Union of Polish Patriots, was ensconced at Lublin soon after the city's liberation in July 1944 and proclaimed itself the sole legal authority in liberated areas. Meanwhile, the PPR continued to operate underground in German-occupied territory. Wladyslaw Gomulka had been named its first secretary by his Polish comrades in 1943, at a time when contact between the small Polish party and Moscow had broken down. Its political arm, the National Council of the Homeland (Krajowa Rada Narodowa—KRN), was set up early in 1944 under the chairmanship of Boleslaw Bierut, a Polish communist dispatched from Moscow.

Warsaw's Old Town Square was almost totally destroyed during World War II; buildings have been reconstructed to reflect style of originals.

Bierut had been a member of the Soviet security apparatus and owed his escape from the Kremlin's purge of exiled Polish communists in the late 1930s to his obscurity at that time. The KRN, composed of Communists and allied left-wing socialist and peasant leaders, posed as an alternative to the more widely accepted, London-directed Home Council.

In January 1945 the Soviet Union officially recognized the PKWN as the "provisional Government of Liberated Democratic Poland" and moved its seat of operations to the ruins of Warsaw after Soviet forces had resumed the offensive and taken the Polish capital. By this time the AL, formerly the military arm of the PPR, had been incorporated into Berling's Polish First Army (serving with the Red Army) as the PKWN extended its control in the wake of the rapid westward advance of Soviet forces. The provisional government was headed by a noncommunist, left-wing socialist Edward Osobka-Morawski, while Gomulka was installed as deputy premier. All the elements of the Soviet-sponsored central authority were thereby prepared to function as a de facto government for postwar Poland.

The United States and Britain protested these unilateral Soviet actions and initially refused to recognize the provisional government. But at the Yalta Conference in February 1945, the Western powers, confronted with a fait accompli, accepted Soviet claims to eastern Poland approximately along the Curzon Line in return for Soviet agreement to broaden the provisional government. This permitted the establishment of the so-called Provisional Government of National Unity by the addition of noncommunist leaders to include those from the government-in-exile in London. This new government was also bound to hold free parliamentary elections as soon as possible.

The Postwar Settlement

The Poland that emerged from the war was a different country physically as well as politically. In accordance with decisions made by the Allies at Yalta and confirmed at the Potsdam Conference in August 1945, Poland's new western frontier would lie along a line formed by the Oder and Neisse rivers, adding former German territories that included the rest of Silesia and Pomerania and the southern portion of East Prussia that contained Masuria. Poland acquired over 100,000 square kilometers from Germany, incorporating important industrial and maritime areas as compensations for the 180,000 square kilometers (including Vilnius and Lvov) that were surrendered to the Soviet Union. The part of Cieszyn Silesia seized by Poland in 1938 was returned to Czechoslovakia (see fig. 9).

As a result of the territorial adjustments, Poland's physical center was transplanted westward, and the transfer of territory was accompanied by the large-scale movement of population. Some 3 million Poles were removed from their homes in the eastern territories to the newly acquired western lands, from which about 2.5 million Germans were in turn ousted between 1946 and 1949. Because of losses attributable to the war and to territorial changes, the population of Poland fell from 35 million in 1939 to only 25 million in 1950. These losses included all but a small fragment of Poland's large prewar Jewish community. In 1939 about 30 percent of Poland's population had been comprised of ethnic minorities; in 1950 the country was 96 percent ethnic Polish, of whom more than 90 percent were Roman Catholics.

The Provisional Government of National Unity

In July 1945 a new coalition government, which had been enlarged as the Provisional Government of National Unity to include a limited number of noncommunist members, was installed in Warsaw. Osobka-Morawski remained as head of government, and Gomulka was retained as a deputy premier. A second deputy premiership was created for Mikolajczyk, the PSL leader who had succeeded Sikorski in 1943 as head of the London

Figure 9. Polish People's Republic: Postwar Territorial Adjustments

government-in-exile. The United States and Britain extended formal recognition to the Warsaw coalition as the legitimate government of Poland and simultaneously withdrew recognition from the exile government remaining in London, which had refused to follow Mikolajczyk in joining the Provisional Government of National Unity.

The July Manifesto, issued by the new Polish authority, converted the KRN into a provisional parliament and declared the PKWN, which came to function as the KRN presidium, to be the sole provisional executive organ. Bierut was named president of the PKWN; Stanislaw Grabski, an old National Democrat and brother of the one-time prime minister, and the dying Wincenty Witos became its noncommunist vice presidents. The manifesto confirmed that the principles of the 1921 constitution would be the basis for establishing a government after free elections. The actions of the provisional government, however, gave little heed to the democratic framework of the 1921 document.

Many AK units had remained underground after the Soviet occupation, hostile to the Red Army and to the communist apparatus that had come with it to Poland. At the end of the war an amnesty was accepted by about two-thirds of its estimated 70,000 effectives, but resistance to the Soviet-sponsored provisional government continued for many months. Many surviving AK officers, members of the Home Council, and exiles who had returned from London were arrested, and some served long prison terms.

The provisional government, although officially a broad coalition, was heavily weighted in favor of the Soviet-sponsored groups. Of the 20 cabinet positions that were created, 16 were held by the PKWN. These included the key ministries of defense, public security, food, trade, and industry. The Ministry of Recovered Territories, which was formed after the Potsdam decision to place all former German territory east of the Oder-Neisse line under Polish administration, was assigned to Gomulka, the deputy premier and party first secretary.

Lacking popular support, the PPR set up trade unions, mass organizations, and front groups through which it could increase its influence. Under police and army protection, the party also organized people's councils for local civil administration, initiated a thinly disguised party patronage system for the distribution of land, and began to maneuver for control of Poland's well-developed consumer-cooperative network. In the former German territories, population shifts, rehabilitation programs, and economic integration projects were accomplished on a highly selective basis in order to achieve the maximum of party control over the area.

Simultaneously, the PPR also brought strong pressure to bear on all political groups within the coalition government in order to create a communist-led bloc that would produce a single list of approved candidates in the forthcoming elections. Communists infiltrated the other parties and through intimidation and coercion neutralized the anticommunist elements and replaced the leadership with leftist sympathizers who favored cooperation with the Soviet Union and the establishment of a socialist system in the country. The communist tactics were so successful within the formerly anticommunist PSL that its leader Mikolajczyk, in September 1945, formed a new peasant party in order to dissociate himself and his followers from the procommunist policies of the old organization.

By mid-1946 the Communists considered themselves sufficiently entrenched to proceed with setting up a permanent government, making use of democratic processes in an attempt to lend it legitimacy. As a first step the regime held a national referendum asking for and winning approval of its policies of nationalization and land reform and for the changing of parliament from a bicameral to a unicameral body, the Sejm. Under the controlled conditions prevailing (and with little opportunity for opposition groups to be heard), the results of the referendum were favorable to the regime. The regime then scheduled nationwide parliamentary elections for January 1947.

For the elections the regime offered a single list of candidates representing the progovernment Democratic Bloc, which included the PPR, PPS, left-wing peasants, and the liberal Democratic Party (Stronnictwo Demokratyczne—SD). The only party permitted to offer an independent list of candidates was Mikolajczyk's PSL, but its meetings were broken up, and many of its candidates were arrested and forced to resign while in prison. The elections were rigged to favor the regime and its candidates. The final tabulation of votes, conducted exclusively by government-appointed election officials, gave 80 percent of the vote and 417 seats to the regime's candidates against 27 seats to the opposition. The PPR emerged as the strongest single party, giving the Communists legal control of a government that was subsequently transformed into a one-party totalitarian state mechanism.

The Sovietization of Poland

A new government took office after the general elections. Bierut was chosen president of the people's republic, and Joseph Cyrankiewicz, leader of the left-wing PPS, which favored close collaboration with the Communists, was appointed premier. In addition to Gomulka, two other members of the Political Bureau (Politburo) of the PPR were installed as deputy premiers. Within the cabinet, all key posts other than that of premier were assigned to the PPR, the lesser portfolios being held by trusted collaborators from the bloc parties. Mikolajczyk was dropped from his position of deputy premier and within a few months was forced to flee the country to escape arrest under trumped-up charges of illegal activities against the state.

The legal basis for the new government was contained in the constitutional act of 1947 passed by the Sejm as an interim measure until a suitable new constitution could be prepared. The framework of governmental institutions authorized in this so-called Little Constitution was a virtual detailed listing of those institutions and activities that had been established by the Communists since 1944. Under this law, authority over essential matters was theoretically retained by parliament, but in practice this was merely a formality. Most legislation was proclaimed by decree, a power granted to the president that quickly became the primary means of translating party policies into law (see The Constitution, ch. 4).

Firmly in control of a legal government, the Communists then turned their attention to consolidating their hold over the parties with which they still formally shared political power. After Mikolajczyk was forced out of the country, the PSL was no longer a major factor in Polish politics. Some members joined with the procommunist peasant group from which they had earlier split, and in 1948 the new body, the United Peasant Party (Zjednoczone Stronnictwo Ludowe), was formed. The major target remaining was the PPS, which had wide appeal for workers and which, despite its collaborationist leaders, still included a large membership of independent democratic socialists. After a lengthy and careful screening process, the party was merged late the same year with the communist PPR into a single organization, the Polish United Workers' Party (Polska Zjednoczona Partia Robotnicza—PZPR), the leadership of which remained firmly in communist hands.

The remaining political elements, consisting chiefly of non-Marxist intellectuals, professionals, and white-collar workers, were merged into the Democratic Party (Stronnictwo Demokratyczne), whose leaders had already demonstrated their willingness to cooperate with the Communists. By 1951 these cooperating political parties had been grouped into the PZPR-led National Front, later renamed the National Unity Front (Front Jednosci Narodu), along with various mass organizations to form a broad political base that could be manipulated for the support of PZPR programs. Among these nonparty groups was Pax, which attempted to co-opt the support of "progressive Catholics" to the communist regime (see Polish United Workers' Party; Other Political Organizations, ch. 4).

After the creation of the Communist Information Bureau (Cominform) by the Soviets in September 1947, Soviet control increased in Poland as it did in other satellite countries. Conflict developed within the Polish party between the pro-Soviet Bierut and Gomulka, who as an advocate of the "Polish way" to socialism had opposed forced collectivization and had refused to join in the condemnation of the Yugoslav communist party. In September 1948 Gomulka, in a move directed by Moscow, was denounced for his "nationalist tendencies" and replaced as party first secretary by Bierut. Many of Gomulka's associates in the PZPR, army, and civil administration were also purged. Thereafter, the Polish government assumed the role of a willing instrument of Soviet policy.

In 1949 Poland became a member of the Council for Mutual Economic Assistance (Comecon), an agency for the economic integration of East European countries within the Soviet sphere (see Appendix B). In exchange for "Soviet fraternal aid" during the war and in its reconstruction, Poland's communist regime made generous trade concessions to the Soviet Union, while Western economic contracts were discouraged. Coal was shipped to the

Soviet Union at below the world price until 1954. In return, the Soviets sold oil and grain to the Poles at a discount. Soviet officials occupied positions in the party and civil administration, as well as in the management of the economy.

Soviet officials were assigned to commands in the Polish armed forces and the police, often to posts vacated by Polish officers who had been purged. In 1949 Marshal Konstantin Rokossovsky, a Polish-born Red Army officer, was appointed as Poland's minister of defense and commander in chief of the Polish People's Army. Under his guidance, the Polish armed forces were thoroughly reorganized along Soviet lines, equipped through extensive Soviet military aid, and trained by Soviet advisers. In 1955 Poland was host to the founding session of the Warsaw Treaty Organization (Warsaw Pact), the East European military alliance of which it became a charter member (see Appendix C).

The process of Sovietization—the imposition of the Soviet model on the country's political, economic, and cultural life—was carried on at a slower pace and with relatively less violence in Poland, however, than in other East European countries. The fear of popular resistance persuaded the PZPR to proceed very cautiously as, for example, in the implementation of agrarian reform. Under the land reform programs introduced by the Lublin government in September 1944, arable land over a 50-hectare maximum and total holdings of more than 100 hectares were to be confiscated from private owners without compensation, netting a total of 2.3 million hectares for potential distribution to landless peasants. Some large estates were to be kept intact as state farms. An additional 3.7 million hectares was soon expropriated from German owners in the newly acquired western lands for allotment to Polish settlers from the lost eastern territories. The PZPR took great care to disclaim any intention of setting up collective farms of the Soviet style as the prevailing mode of farming. Nevertheless, the agrarian reform was conducted from the very beginning with an eye to eventual collectivization. The parcels of land were, on the whole, too small to provide a decent income, and the necessary credits, implements, and livestock were not always provided to individual peasants. This method, which neutralized the peasant masses during the crucial stages of the communist takeover, was intended to demonstrate the alleged absurdity of individual farming. At the same time, propaganda boasted the superiority of "socialist farming." In 1950 the regime inaugurated centralized economic planning under the Six-Year Plan 1950-55, which not only called for accelerated development of heavy industry but also provided for forced collectivization of agriculture, which had previously been voluntary. The net results, however, were meager because of peasant resistance. By 1953 collectives and state farms amounted to only about 20 percent of land under cultivation in Poland (as compared, for instance, with

43 percent in neighboring Czechoslovakia), despite "administrative pressures" that included a punitive tax structure and state subsidies for the collective farms.

Simultaneous with the agrarian reform, all banks, credit and insurance companies, as well as large industrial and commercial enterprises, were taken over by the state. Only the small service and artisan shops—usually family businesses—were left in private hands as a vestigial, barely tolerated form of private ownership. The proprietors were constantly harassed by taxes, state inspections, and other "administrative pressures." A third set of state reforms was the attempt to alter the cultural patterns of Poland. The policies of the new regime emphasized atheistic education, and "socialist realism" became the prescribed norm for artistic creation. Folklore, which was said to embody "people's art," was to be stressed in contrast with the "decadent Westernized art" of the bourgeoisie. Intimate cultural relations were established with the Soviet Union, the so-called Rome of the Proletariat.

Although refraining from open intervention with freedom of worship, the regime sought to exploit latent anticlerical feelings. The church hierarchy, while trying to avoid a direct confrontation with the regime, repeatedly denounced "the atheistic and materialistic philosophy of communism." Pastoral letters from the bishops were the only remaining public form of criticism to be heard in Poland after 1945. Speakers, addressing the 1948 party congress at which the PZPR was formed, decried the hierarchy's critical attitude and attacked the Vatican.

In July 1949 a Vatican decree was issued excommunicating Catholics who belonged to the PZPR. Warsaw replied by passing a law providing prison sentences of up to five years for clergy who refused the sacraments to citizens because of their political opinions. All religious orders and associations were required to register within three months. The Vatican was castigated for not having recognized the Oder-Neisse frontier. The regime began sponsoring groups (such as Pax) composed of so-called patriotic priests and laymen who, while not rejecting the Catholic dogma, tried to reconcile Christianity and Marxism. In 1950 the church's largest welfare institution, Caritas, was placed under state control, and in March church estates in excess of 100 hectares were confiscated. Bishops were variously accused of warmongering, spying, and acts of sabotage. By the beginning of 1954, nine bishops, including the primate, Stefan Cardinal Wyszynski, and several hundred priests had been arrested and were held in prison.

Internal Politics, 1951-56

By 1951 the Polish government was functioning in the Soviet-approved style of a "people's democracy." The constituent parliament, seated in 1947, undertook to draft a new constitution, which was officially adopted in 1952 after the formality of a public debate. Under this frame of government, which was based on the 1936 Soviet Constitution, the office of president was replaced by a collective executive, the Council of State. Bierut, the first premier under the new constitution, resigned as head of government in 1954 when he was made first secretary of the PZPR. In whatever state or party office he held, Bierut had been entrenched as Poland's communist strongman, favored by the Kremlin, since Gomulka was deposed in 1948. Gomulka, the personality around whom opponents of Bierut's hard-line policies continued to rally, was arrested in 1951 and remained in confinement for three years.

Despite Bierut's ascendancy, a split remained within the PZPR between the "Muscovites" (the hard-liners who were behind Bierut) and the so-called nationalists who had supported Gomulka. The former were typically Moscow-trained operatives who had lived for a long period in the Soviet Union, had been attached to the Lublin government, or had served with the Polish First Army or in the Soviet security service during the war. The nationalists, often dubbed "revisionists" by the Muscovites, were usually home-bred communists who had spent the war in the underground movement. The strain between the two tendencies also reflected a conflict between the deep-seated Polish tradition of pluralism and the totalitarian impulse inherent in communism. It was to some extent comparable to the fissure that developed between the Pilsudski and Luxemburg factions in the early days of the PPS. It also involved the confrontation of rival ambitions that were manifested in different approaches to economic problems and different perspectives of Poland's relationship with the Soviet Union.

From a small group of less than 20,000 in 1945, the communist party in Poland by the mid-1950s numbered over 1 million members. many of them gained from the PPS. On the one hand. the fast expansion of the PZPR also brought in numerous opportunistic elements whose joining had little to do with a commitment to communism. On the other hand, the merger with the PPS, which had been the main exponent of native Polish radicalism, introduced into the ranks of the PZPR a large number of patriotic individuals who had decided to accept the inevitable but who did not alter their true convictions. These former socialists tried to preserve their ties with the broad masses of the people, frequently sharing their complaints and even their anti-Soviet sentiments. Although the party leadership stuck to a rigidly dogmatic policy line and used tyrannical methods modeled after those of Stalin, disappointment with Sovietization was growing at the lower levels of the PZPR.

The first wave of popular discontent surfaced soon after Stalin's death in March 1953 as an expression of resistance to

Sovietization. The demise of the Soviet dictator coincided with an acute crisis within the PZPR. In eight years of near-absolute power, the communist elite had become thoroughly corrupted by the plethora of privileges that the ruling party had arrogated to itself: special shops, exclusive villas, servants, and other accoutrements of the "new class." All of this took place amid the vicious persecution of actual and imagined political enemies and their condemnation in show trials.

The struggle for Stalin's mantle between the first secretary of the Communist Party of the Soviet Union (CPSU), Nikita Khrushchev, and Lavrenti Beria, chief of the Soviet secret police, revealed profound disarray among the Soviet leadership. The liquidation of Beria in July 1953 disoriented the Soviet secret police, with which the Polish police apparatus was closely linked. His execution was followed by a reduction in the influence of the Polish security police and the release of some prisoners from forced-labor camps. Khrushchev's visit to Belgrade in 1955 and his efforts to achieve a Soviet reconciliation with Yugoslavia's President Josip Broz Tito was of special importance to Poland in view of what were perceived as similarities between Gomulka's and Tito's "national" approach to communism. Khrushchev's speech the next year at the Twentieth Party Congress of the CPSU, in which he attacked Stalin's cult of personality and his vicious practices, including the liquidation of Polish communists in 1938, compromised the Stalinist clique then ruling Poland. The congress was perhaps more meaningful to the PZPR than to any other communist party outside the Soviet Union. It had not only debunked Stalin but had also rehabilitated the spiritual parents of the PZPR. For the great majority of Poles, however, the discrediting of Stalin meant repudiation of communism, because for them Stalinism and communism were one and the same.

The death of Bierut in March 1956 accentuated the split within the PZPR. Criticism of government policies became more vocal, and in June serious rioting broke out in Poznan when workers there called a strike to protest rising food prices and work quotas. Calling for "bread and freedom," the strikers' demands were soon extended to include free elections. Units of the Polish army were deployed to suppress the uprising, leaving 54 dead and several hundred wounded in the fighting that ensued. The Poznan revolt represented a palpable challenge to the regime and underscored the need for a new leader who could restore unity to the PZPR and gain some measure of popular support for government policies.

To cope with the challenge, the frightened PZPR agreed to reinstate the only credible leader, Gomulka, as first secretary. This was done despite vigorous protests from Khrushchev, who descended on Warsaw with his Kremlin entourage in October to veto the party's choice. For a moment Poland and the Soviet

Memorial in Poznan honoring workers killed during general strike of June 1956
Courtesy Committee in Support of Solidarity, New York

Union seemed to be on a collision course. But once Khrushchev was reassured that Golmulka did not intend either to alter the basic foundations of the communist regime in Poland or to break the country's ties with the Warsaw Pact and Comecon, Khrushchev relented and accepted his election.

The Gomulka Era

Initially, Gomulka's return to power was widely hailed by the Polish people. They realized that, given the existing geopolitical conditions, Poland was condemned to remain in the Soviet sphere and had to be ruled by the communists. Among the PZPR leaders, Gomulka was more acceptable than the others: he had a good record of underground work during the Nazi occupation, he had stood up to Stalin, and he had been imprisoned by the Stalinists. Moreover, Gomulka persuaded the Polish people that the PZPR, reformed under his leadership, was the only sure guarantee of continuing good Polish-Soviet relations, thus safeguarding Poland's existence as a nation. In a speech delivered on the eve of elections for the Sejm in January 1957, Gomulka warned his countrymen that a failure to support him and the ruling party would result in Poland's disappearance from the map. He tried to establish the PZPR in a dual role: as keeper of communist ideological values, which made it indispensable to the Kremlin, but also as the guardian of national independence, which made it acceptable to the Polish people. Although voters had only one list of candidates to choose from, a heavy turnout and the approval it gave to the National Unity Front were interpreted as an endorsement for Gomulka.

The opening phase of Gomulka's rule was auspicious. He curbed the power of the secret police, explaining that this step represented a "return to socialist legality." Rokossovsky was replaced, and Polish military officers were reinstated in command positions. Most of the 10,600 collective farms disappeared as farmers left the land, some of which was sold to private proprietors through a process officially described as the "return to the principle of voluntary establishment of rural cooperatives" (see Structure of Agriculture, ch. 3). Censorship was relaxed and greater freedom allowed for artistic expression. Political prisoners, including members of the clergy, were released from prison. A modus vivendi was arranged with the church, whose value in promoting peace and avoiding violence Gomulka understood. Nonparty political organizations were recognized, among them Znak, an independent Catholic "parliamentary circle" whose influence as an institutionalized opposition group went beyond the presence of a few of its delegates in the Sejm (see Other Political Organizations, ch. 4). Gomulka also promised a return to "inner party democracy" and pledged to reform the economy by decentralizing its planning and management, including the introduction of workers' self-management. The upheaval of 1956 had caused no less than a revolution within the communist framework. For the first time in the history of any communist party, the pressure of public opinion had brought about political party reform and a change of government.

The shock of the Poznan uprising gradually began to wear off and, after paying lip service for a few years to the principles of political democratization and economic decentralization, Gomulka gradually returned to the former ways. Repeatedly he rejected reforms that would have liberalized the Polish economic system. Underneath his legalistic and technical arguments was the fear that decentralization of the economy would weaken the PZPR's hold over the country and result in gradual dismantling of its leading role.

Against the warnings of technical experts that economic decentralization was a necessity and that Poland needed a more balanced economy, Gomulka returned to the policy of strict centralized planning, pursuing the goal of rapid industrial growth and increasingly focusing on capital goods production. But this proved impossible to achieve without the tightening of political controls. Despite renewed "administrative pressures" and a noisy ideological offensive, efforts to improve the economy's performance produced very meager results.

Throughout the Czechoslovak crisis of 1968, by acting consistently along parallel lines with Moscow, Gomulka tried to reverse one of the endemic patterns of East European history: that of Russo-Polish rivalry. This was the key to Poland's participation in the suppression of the "Prague Spring" by the Warsaw Pact troops in August. By supporting the Soviet intervention, Gomulka tried to convince the Kremlin that it was possible to cooperate with the Poles as Moscow's most loyal allies.

Gomulka encountered his stiffest opposition within the PZPR from the so-called Partisans, who occupied the right wing of the nationalist faction of which the first secretary stood in the center. Led by Mieczyslaw Moczar, since 1964 the minister of internal affairs, they advocated tighter central control over the party apparatus than Gomulka was willing to use and a broader party membership. A skillful but ruthless political infighter, Moczar appealed to latent anti-Semitism among the worker and peasant constituency that he courted. But most Poles—especially Polish students—were more inspired by the "Prague Spring," which seemed to hold out the promise of "socialism with a human face." Student demonstrations in Polish cities in 1968, protesting the loss of academic and cultural freedom, were dispersed by police, participants beaten, and many student leaders arrested. Moczar, who recognized in the disturbances a means of weakening Gomulka's hold on the party, blamed them on a "Zionist plot" and charged that Jews—of whom there were fewer than 30,000 in

Poland—had used their high positions in the PZPR and government to undermine the authority of the state. Many of those accused were Gomulka's close associates. Under pressure, Gomulka initiated a purge of Jews from the PZPR, press, professions, and universities, encouraging them to leave the country.

Popular dissatisfaction with Gomulka reached its highest point in December 1970 during the bloody workers' uprising that began as a strike in the Lenin Shipyard at Gdansk and quickly spread to the other Baltic ports. The immediate cause of the strike was a sharp, government-dictated increase in food prices (up to 30 percent on some items) and the introduction of a new wage scale ordered by Gomulka just before Christmas, traditionally a festive season in Catholic Poland. The protest soon took up demands for worker control of trade unions. Official organs ascribed the price hikes to poor harvests and the need to reduce domestic consumption of foodstuffs. The move, although explained by economic realities, revealed Gomulka's unresponsiveness to public opinion and the growing gap that existed between the PZPR and the Polish people. When workers refused to vacate the shipyard facilities, heavily armed troops were moved in to disperse them at the cost, according to official publications, of 45 killed and nearly 1,200 injured.

Gierek's Rise and Economic Policy

Although the strikers had been crushed, their revolt toppled Gomulka, who was forced to resign as first secretary by the Politburo. Leadership passed to Edward Gierek, who came from the post of party secretary at Katowice in Silesia. Gierek was a technician who had worked his way systematically through the party hierarchy. He had contacts in various party factions and in the army, and he had avoided making personal enemies. Gomulka's group left office with him, and Gierek slowly eased Moczar and the Partisans out of positions of importance. But in January 1971 the workers in Szczecin and Gdansk threatened another strike, this time compelling Gierek and other top party and government officials to come in person from Warsaw to hear their long-term grievances and to negotiate with them in an open dialogue. Gierek put the entire blame for the crisis on Gomulka and his policies. Coming away from the meetings with the workers, the PZPR's new first secretary rescinded price increases and boosted the minimum pay rates, allowances, and pensions. When unrest persisted, Gierek gave in on another of their demands and allowed for the formation of workers' committees.

Economic reforms were proposed to make the system more flexible. Western credits and technology were supposed to lead to a rapid expansion of modern consumer goods to appease a restless population. Production bottlenecks, however, meant that available goods did not offset the higher personal incomes, leading to inflationary pressures. Gierek's "strategic maneuver," as he labeled the new economic policy, was based, however, on heavy borrowing from the West to buy Western technology, which was to be utilized in turning out goods for export. The sale of products from the newly created Polish industries in Western markets was expected to pay the bill when the foreign loans came due.

Gierek's stratagem prompted a short-term boom, but one that was eventually upset by a variety of internal and external factors. Shortages of essential consumer items continued, while the rise in the cost of living nullified gains made by wage increases. During the mid-1970s the Soviet Union, Poland's main supplier of petroleum, increased the price of its guaranteed consignment of oil, while imports from other oil-producing countries, purchased at world market prices, were necessary to meet increased demands for energy. The rise in the cost of oil made Polish products more expensive than had been originally calculated. Because of this factor and the worldwide recession that either closed many foreign markets or made competition for them much more difficult, the Poles found themselves with reduced receipts from traditional exports (coal, copper, meat, and textiles) as well as with a surplus of unsold manufactured products—for instance, golf carts and color television sets—for which costly imported resources had been allocated. These expensively produced goods faced severe obstacles in competing for sales in Western markets. Poland's foreign debt skyrocketed. At the time of Gomulka's overthrow in late 1970 it had amounted to US$700 million. By 1980 it had exceeded US$20 billion, and Warsaw was faced with increasing difficulties in servicing the debt, let alone repaying it.

Other vital factors also contributed to bringing the Polish economy to near-collapse in the late 1970s. While personal incomes rose, food supplies (especially of meat) fell short of demand, owing in large part to unsound agricultural policies that were dogmatically imposed by successive communist leaders. The large quantities of grain that had to be imported to compensate for inadequate levels of domestic production added further to Poland's debt.

Meanwhile, Moscow increased its pressure on Poland to speed up the integration of its economy with the rest of the Soviet camp through the instrumentality of Comecon. In 1971, at the Comecon session in Budapest, the Polish delegation abandoned Gomulka's stiff opposition to the closer economic integration of Eastern Europe. New, often long-term agreements were signed with the Soviet Union and other Comecon members that committed Warsaw to a series of joint projects up to 1990. Polish capital, know-how, and labor were to be invested in expensive projects in distant parts of the Soviet Union, involving, for example, the exploitation of asbestos mines or natural gas deposits in Siberia. While such projects assured Poland needed raw materials, they also served to involve Polish industries in close cooperation with their Soviet counterparts. The Soviet Union, however, was a useful market for lower quality Polish goods. In many cases, Polish deliveries included components that had to be imported from the West and paid for in hard currency. In return, Poland received compensation from the Soviet Union in nonconvertible "transfer rubles."

After 1975, deliveries to the Soviet Union were greatly increased from Polish shipyards, which by the end of the decade supplied more than one-third of the Soviet merchant vessels. Large quantities of locomotives and rolling stock were also sent eastward, while Polish railroads suffered from a critical shortage of both items. Much of Poland's computer production appeared in offices and factories east of the border. The same was the case with equipment for housing construction, while most Polish families waited an average of 10 years for new apartments.

Although the regime had abandoned forced collectivization and returned most of the land to private farmers, the PZPR never completely jettisoned its objective of driving the fiercely individualistic Polish peasants into what was euphemistically termed "agricultural cooperatives." Unable to attack the individual farmers frontally, the PZPR adopted an indirect approach: it tried to prove that private farming did not pay and that individual farmers should join either collectives or state farms. Agricultural incomes declined further in relation to the much higher wages earned by other categories of workers. One result of this was that the exodus from the countryside to the cities increased, leaving only elderly people in many villages. Meanwhile, the value of the agricultural land decreased steadily. As a consequence, large tracts were sold at low prices or were surrendered to the state by elderly private farmers in return for pension benefits. Furthermore, the regime channeled most of its technical assistance to the state farms, which were supposed to be models of "the highest form of socialist farming." Although constituting only about 20 percent of the land, they received 70 percent of budget investments usually allotted to agriculture. Despite this, the state farms were from 20 to 30 percent less productive per unit than those owned by individual proprietors (see Structure of Agriculture; Crop Production, ch. 3).

The food crisis of 1976 forced Gierek to announce a new policy of encouraging the more productive private farms to enlarge their holdings at the expense of inefficient small plots. Wary farmers did not react quickly to the new incentives. Increases in grain and livestock production were mainly achieved in the socialized farm sector. To cut down politically motivated food subsidies and to increase food exports, a desperate Gierek tried in June 1976 to raise food prices, as Gomulka had done in 1970. In reaction, a series of violent demonstrations broke out near Warsaw and in Radom and threatened to spread to the rest of the country.

Although the force required to restore order in 1976 was not on the same massive scale as had been necessary in 1970–71, even its limited application caused widespread indignation and discredited a regime already shaken by the setbacks of its economic policy. Only the prompt cancellation of the price hikes and the release of most of those arrested prevented nationwide demonstrations.

Dissent and Constitutional Change in the 1970s

The expression of dissent against the regime flowed from three sources: the intelligentsia, the workers, and the church. But their priorities often differed, they were sometimes at odds, and cooperation was not always easy. Student demands in 1968 for greater freedom of expression held little appeal for workers concerned with bread-and-butter issues of pay, prices, and working conditions. The workers refused to support student demonstrations, explaining that as a privileged group they had acted rashly. Likewise, the students spurned the workers' appeals for support for economic demands during the 1970–71 strikes. Meanwhile the church, whose primary aim was to defend its status as an autonomous institution, supported the goals of the other two groups but without actually endorsing their protests (see Class Culture and Consciousness, ch. 2).

A remarkable convergence of interests and methods occurred in the mid-1970s, however, as a common front was formed in opposition to the regime's policies and to proposed constitutional changes that were recognized as infringements on human rights. Already in the late 1960s, after the anti-Semitic campaign in Poland and the suppression of the reform movement in Czechoslovakia, a number of prominent Polish Marxist intellectuals had despaired of attempts to humanize communism or to effect change within the "socialist system." Outstanding figures like the philosophers Leszek Kolakowski and Adam Schaff issued calls for greater pluralism in Polish society. They and others insisted on the "self-organization" of society as a goal to counter the party-state. Catholic intellectuals in particular hearkened back to the idea of organic work, citing the need for creative opposition to the regime that allowed for cooperation without collaboration.

Dissent broke into open confrontation in 1975 when the regime proposed a series of amendments to the Constitution. Protests by the church and the intelligentsia centered on plans to enshrine the leading role of the PZPR as part of the Constitution, to refer to "unshakeable bonds with the Soviet Union," and to make civil rights contingent on the fulfillment of duties to the state (see The Constitution, ch. 4). The state was persuaded to modify these objectionable amendments, but pressures continued to mount for genuine human rights as detailed in the 1975 Helsinki Agreement and for freedom of workers to organize and to strike.

The strikes of June 1976 inspired the formation of the Committee for the Defense of the Workers (Komitet Obrony Robotnikow—KOR) by a group of intellectuals that included Jacek Kuron and Adam Michnik. The committee's purpose was to investigate independently charges of police brutality during the strikes and to provide legal aid for arrested workers as well as assistance for their families. It was largely as a result of KOR's efforts that Gierek granted a conditional amnesty to those arrested (see Popular Political Expression, ch. 4). After September 1977 KOR was known as the Committee for Social Self-Defense-Committee for the Defense of the Workers (Komitet Samoobrony Spolecznej-Komitet Obrony Robotnikow—KSS-KOR).

It was the university-based Committee for Student Solidarity that offered the first alternative to a party-sponsored organization. In cooperation with the KOR, the student committee organized the "flying university," a lecture program intended to break the state's monopoly on education (see Education and Political Controversy, ch. 2). Numerous hitherto clandestine publications began to circulate openly, challenging the monopoly on information claimed by the regime.

Unrest, sparked by rising prices and inadequate wages, grew among workers in the summer of 1980. Work stoppages and plant occupations were called by spontaneously organized strike committees first in Gdansk and, by the end of August, in industrial areas throughout the country. The strike committees were advised by KSS-KOR, which acted as a clearinghouse for information about strikes and negotiations and maintained liaison among the numerous committees and their leaders. Striking workers also received backing from the church hierarchy, which organized a support system for their families. Representatives of the regional committees met in Gdansk in September to form a decentralized independent trade union, known as Solidarnosc (Solidarity). It took for its symbols the Polish flag, the cross, and the banner "Workers of All Enterprises Unite" (see Solidarity, ch. 4).

Solidarity and the Gdansk Agreement

By the summer of 1980 food shortages had become so acute that in July, Gierek made another attempt to impose price increases without adequately preparing the public for such a move. Once again, the first Poles to protest were workers at the Lenin Shipyard in Gdansk, who in mid-August conducted a carefully prepared sit-down strike. The shipyard's gates were closed, and 16,000 workers refused to leave the facility until 21 specific demands were met by the government in Warsaw. The example was imitated by numerous other enterprises, first on the Baltic coast and then throughout the country.

One of the secrets of the eventual triumph of these strikes, which were to last for over two weeks, was an impressive code of

Lech Walesa addressing the First National Congress of Solidarity in Gdansk, September 1981
Courtesy Committee in Support of Solidarity, New York

disciplined behavior imposed by their leaders, whose first rule was the absolute exclusion of any form of violence in order not to provide the authorities a pretext to intervene. The second rule was the strict prohibition against the consumption of alcohol by strikers. The third rule was the firm solidarity of all strike participants—not only manual workers but also middle-level employees, engineers, and management in the shipyards and other industrial and commercial enterprises. The Gdansk workers' demands were supported by workers throughout the country and eventually by university students and intellectuals.

The central figure in this impressive spontaneous movement was Lech Walesa, a 38-year-old Gdansk electrician. Walesa, who had been involved in the 1970 demonstration, was repeatedly dismissed from work by the authorities because of his involvement in politics, only to reemerge as the leader of the striking workers at the Lenin Shipyard in 1980, the spokesman for Solidarity, and a symbol of the protest movement throughout Poland. Inspired by the successful resistance in Gdansk, workers at other industrial plants imitated the example, and eventually the country was covered by a net of similar strikes. Gierek was forced to give in and on August 31, 1980, conceded to the workers' demands, enumerated in the Gdansk Agreement (see Appendix D). Its provisions included pay increases to offset price hikes and the establishment of a five-day workweek, the right to strike and, most important, the right to form an autonomous trade union free from state and party control. The workers also exacted concessions relaxing censorship and permitting the broadcasting of religious services. The regime also consented to allow the construction of a monument in Gdansk honoring the workers killed during the 1970 strike. Once the agreement had been reached, Gierek collapsed both physically and mentally. On September 6 he was removed as first secretary and replaced by Stanislaw Kania, a PZPR Politburo member previously in charge of internal security and the ruling party's relations with the church.

For the third time, a workers' revolt had toppled Poland's top communist official and on this occasion had done so by nonviolent means. The peaceful victory under Walesa's inspired leadership was possible because Solidarity had the support of the vast majority of Polish people. For the first time in Poland's history, unity and cooperation between the workers and the intelligentsia was not merely a programmatic slogan but a living, everyday reality. Economists, lawyers, journalists, and university professors stepped forward to give verbal support to the workers' demands, but they also volunteered their expertise to elaborate the demands, to negotiate them with the authorities, and to lay down the theoretical as well as organizational foundation of the free trade union movement.

Another factor in Solidarity's success was the support that came to it from the church. In October 1978 the archbishop of Krakow, Karol Cardinal Wojtyla, was elected pope, taking the name John Paul II. The election of a Polish pope and his subsequent visit to his native country in June 1979 bolstered the morale of the Polish people and inspired them with greater self-confidence. The orderly crowds who greeted him—in some places numbering over 1 million people—not only gave witness to their attachment to Catholicism and to their patriotism but also gave the Polish people a pretext to defy communist authorities, who had only reluctantly agreed to the papal visit and had tried unsuccessfully to limit its scope and significance. The papal visit of 1979 became, in a sense, a dress rehearsal for the demonstrations of 1980 and 1981. For many Poles the charismatic figure of Cardinal Wyszynski also symbolized defiance to the communist regime. Under his leadership, the church hierarchy and clergy gave both moral and material support to Solidarity in many critical instances.

Solidarity's influence spread from industrial centers to the countryside, where farmers emulated the example of their urban comrades and proclaimed the formation of Rural Solidarity. Through this parallel movement they pressured the regime to reverse policies that neglected the private agricultural sector, insisting that the state should declare the peasant family farm as the fundamental unit of Poland's agrarian economy. At their peak in 1981 Solidarity and its rural counterpart numbered more than 12 million members, representing with their families the great

John Paul II, the first Polish pope
Courtesy Apostolic Delegation, Washington, D.C.

majority of Poland's population of some 35 million.

The PZPR's recognition of Solidarity and Rural Solidarity had great significance not only for the communist regime in Poland but also for those in other East European countries. For the first time, a ruling communist party had accepted the existence of organizations independent of the regime and outside the ruling party. Also for the first time, a communist party in power had to accept the fact that the overwhelming majority of the working class was loyal to a democratically elected leadership fundamentally opposed to everything the party stood for. In short, its "leading role" and monopoly on power had been rejected by the class that it pretended to represent.

Divisions developed within Solidarity. A moderate wing of the movement, following Walesa's lead and supported by Cardinal Wyszynski, reasoned in geopolitical terms that the Kremlin, for strategic considerations, would never allow a Warsaw Pact member to be governed by any group except trusted Communists. Consequently, they stressed from the very beginning the nonpolitical character of the movement. Its aim, they argued, was not to replace the "socialist system" in Poland represented by the PZPR but to humanize and democratize it.

Solidarity's cooperation with the PZPR was necessary to ensure that the reforms were carried out as agreed and also to avoid giving the Soviets a pretext for military intervention in Poland. This cautious attitude was increasingly rejected by the more militant wing of Solidarity. Defying the moderating advice of the church hierarchy, they pressed for confrontation with the communist authorities in wildcat strikes and demonstrations that would destabilize the regime.

The PZPR reluctantly accepted the existence of independent unions to which some 30 percent of its own members belonged. Moderates within the PZPR urged partial compromise and limited cooperation with Solidarity. They sought to induce the Soviet Union to accept such a modus vivendi as a better guarantee of political and strategic stability than sustained conflict between the PZPR and the Polish people. The hard-liners, however, were determined to discredit Solidarity and sabotage the national consensus achieved through the Gdansk Agreement. They advocated stern repression of recurring strikes and arrest of opposition leaders. As the debates continued among the party factions on the one hand and the Solidarity leaders on the other hand, the country plunged deeper into acute economic depression. It was made worse as much by official mismanagement and corruption as by the strikes that continued to paralyze various sectors of the economy.

Jaruzelski and the Military Government

Although Kania had been reelected as PZPR first secretary at a special congress in July 1981, he was replaced in October by General Wojciech Jaruzelski, commander of the Polish armed forces, who since February had also held the post of prime minister. Kania was perceived by both the Soviets and the newly elected Central Committee as being unable to maintain control over an increasingly turbulent political situation. Jaruzelski, by contrast, was viewed by party leaders as a tough-minded soldier who had not been compromised by the PZPR's factional struggles and could restore stability. He also projected the image of a Polish patriot, reflecting the prestige of the army within Polish society (see The Military and the Communist State, 1945–46, ch. 5).

At dawn on December 13, 1981, martial law (technically a "state of war") was declared throughout the country, and Jaruzelski assumed virtual dictatorial power at the head of a military junta. Personal freedoms were drastically curtailed, universities were closed, activities of all organizations (including Solidarity) were suspended, and over 5,000 activists—among them Walesa—were interned. Addressing the nation, Jaruzelski made Polish patriotism the focus of his appeal for cooperation and, in veiled language, justified the crackdown as having been necessary to forestall Soviet intervention. A sullen quiet was imposed on the country. But the record of Poland's long and colorful past suggested that the aspirations of the Polish people could not be permanently repressed nor could their voices be effectively stilled.

* * *

A concise treatment of Polish history, published in Poland, is contained in *History of Poland* by Aleksander Gieysztor et al. A more traditional and comprehensive approach is taken by the authors of the two-volume *The Cambridge History of Poland,* edited by W.F. Reddaway et al., which details the country's history to 1935. Norman Davies presents a broad panorama in his two-volume *God's Playground: A History of Poland,* published in 1982.

The story of Poland's reappearance as an independent state after World War I is told by Tytus Komarnicki in *The Rebirth of the Polish Republic.* Norman Davies' *White Eagle, Red Star* is a history of the Russo-Polish War. Ferdynand Zweig's *Poland Between Two Wars* provides a broad outline and Antony Polonsky's *Politics in Independent Poland, 1921–1939* a detailed treatment of Poland's domestic development during the interwar period. Roman Debicki's *Foreign Policy of Poland, 1919–1950* offers valuable data on international relations, important aspects of which M.K. Dziewanowski explains in *Joseph Pilsudski: A European Federalist, 1918–1922.* Adam Bromke, in *Poland's Politics,* focuses on two major trends in the country's political development: romanticism and realism.

Various aspects of Poland's participation in World War II are described in Nicholas Bethell's *The War That Hitler Won,* John Kimche's *The Unfought Battle,* and Jozef Garlinski's *Intercept: The Enigma War.* The underground struggle against the Nazi invaders is chronicled in Tadeusz Bor-Komorowski's *The Secret Army* and Stefan Korbonski's *Fighting Warsaw.* Poland's fate after the war is described in Arthur Bliss-Lane's *I Saw Poland Betrayed* and Stanislaw Mikolajczyk's *The Rape of Poland.* The country's place in the Soviet system is analyzed in Zbigniew Brzezinski's *The Soviet Bloc: Unity and Conflict.*

Postwar political developments are contained in M.K. Dziewanowski's *Poland in the Twentieth Century* and *The Communist Party of Poland* (second edition), Jan B. de Weydenthal's *The Communists of Poland,* and Nicholas Bethell's *Gomulka.* The events of 1980–81 are dealt with by Neal Ascherson in *The Polish August.*

Polish cultural history is traced in Roman Dyboski's *Poland in World Civilization* and *The History of Polish Literature* by Nobel-laureate Czeslaw Milosz. The controversial subject of Polish-Jewish relations is addressed in Bernard D. Weinryb's *The Jews of Poland* and in Wladyslaw Bartoszewski's *The Blood Shed Unites Us*. Piotr S. Wandycz's *The United States and Poland* offers a comprehensive treatment of Polish-American relations. (For further information and complete citations, see Bibliography.)

Chapter 2. The Society and Its Environment

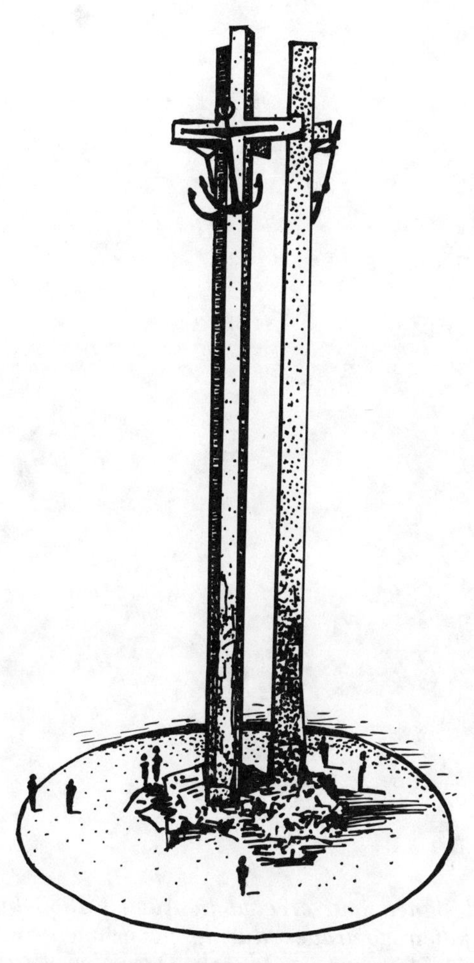

Monument designed and erected in August 1980 by workers in memory of fallen comrades during government suppression of strike at Lenin Shipyard in Gdansk, December 1970

IN THE INTERVAL between World War I and World War II, Poland, an independent state for the first time in more than a century, was ethnically and religiously heterogeneous. Only a little more than two-thirds of its people were ethnically Polish, and less than two-thirds were Roman Catholic. Interwar Poland was also a predominantly rural society. The destruction wrought by World War II and the Holocaust and the relocation of population made necessary by boundary changes led to ethnic homogeneity soon after the war. Membership in the Roman Catholic Church, closely related to Polish ethnicity, became even more significant than it had been in the interwar era.

It took a little longer for a largely rural society to become chiefly urban, but by the late 1970s most of the country's working population were either skilled or unskilled manual workers (about 40 percent) or white-collar workers: low and mid-level white-collar functionaries, technicians, and service workers (about 25 percent). Most were employed directly by the state or in the state-owned economic enterprises. Of those who remained in agriculture—less than one-fourth of the population—most were self-employed. Also self-employed was a very small group of entrepreneurs and artisans, much reduced from the not very large petty bourgeoisie of interwar Poland. Gone as a class were the once-dominant gentry and the small group of wealthy industrialists, merchants, and financiers. Atop the social pyramid was the elite (or new intelligentsia), more heterogeneous in function, origin, and outlook than the largely gentry-dominated intelligentsia of the nineteenth century and the first four decades of the twentieth.

The heterogeneity of the new elite extends to their power and political outlook. Until the institution of martial law in December 1981, power lay with the top ranks of the Polish United Workers' Party (Polska Zjednoczona Partia Robotnicza—PZPR). Other members of the elite might be more highly regarded and as well (or even better) paid on the official salary scale than the party-government elite, but they lacked power. Some of the professional and technical elite and a portion of the so-called creative intelligentsia (writers, academics, journalists, and the like) made their peace with the regime as a matter of career-oriented adaptation or fear (by the mid-1970s rarely out of conviction). Some of the elite, however, particularly a section of the creative intelligentsia, provided an articulate opposition to the regime and until the rise of Solidarnosc (the Solidarity movement) were the only ones to do so, with the exception of the Roman Catholic Church.

The social mobility that flowed from the rapid industrialization and urbanization of Poland in the first two decades after World

War II gave many Poles a sense that their lives had been bettered despite their dislike of the regime. Many of the sons and daughters of peasants became manual workers, and the expansion of the educational system and the growth of the need for functionaries and technicians allowed a fair number of peasants' and workers' children to become white-collar workers and even part of the new intelligentsia.

But the limits of the Polish economy and the failures of the communist system made the situation of the wage worker increasingly difficult, especially to a people who had at first experienced some improvement and hoped for more. Moreover, mobility slowed as economic growth faltered. Particularly galling was the sense—widespread among ordinary Poles—that status and privilege accrued to those who best accommodated to party rule.

The PZPR has never enjoyed popular acceptance in Poland. By the mid- and late 1970s it and the political order it had imposed certainly lacked legitimacy. A common way of dealing with the illegitimate order was to work around it and to ignore it, often by acting in a technically illegal way with the sympathy and understanding of one's friends and colleagues. Above all, individuals tended to their own interests and those of family and close friends and turned an apathetic eye to public issues. The other way of dealing with illegitimacy was to organize to change the order. Until 1980, however, the thinking and unity between various dissenting elements, particularly the working class and the intelligentsia, that would permit a large-scale coherent effort were not present. The repetitive experience of disappointment and frustration and the recognition that dissenters of different perspective and social origin had enough in common to unite led to the emergence and spread of the Solidarity movement. Whether a sense of common fate would survive the suppression of Solidarity could not be foreseen in early 1983.

In the nearly four decades since World War II and the imposition of the communist regime, the Roman Catholic church—long identified with Poles' self-perception as a nation—has remained an alternative to the regime. Despite the efforts of the communist government to end or at least to diminish the role of the church, Roman Catholicism has remained a significant factor in all aspects of Polish life. Its role has in fact broadened the perspective of the church without causing it to lose the loyalty of the faithful. The commitment of the roughly 90 percent of Poles who consider themselves believers is not uniform in intensity or detail, but there is no question that their outlook is shaped by their Catholicism.

Physical Setting

A relief map of Europe depicts Poland as an unbroken plain extending from the Baltic shore to the Carpathian Mountains in the south. Close study, however, reveals greater variety and complexity. Differences in climate and terrain occur, with some local deviations, in bands that extend east to west across the country, accounting for the wide variations in land utilization and population density. The coastal area lacks natural harbors except those at Gdansk-Gdynia and Szczecin. The coast and the adjoining lake district have fewer natural resources, fertile soils, and people than areas to the south. The vast plains south of the lake district have more fertile soils, a longer growing season, and a denser population than the northern regions. The southern foothills and mountains contain most of the country's mineral wealth and much of the most fertile soils and have attracted the greatest concentrations of industry and people.

Most of Poland lies in the North European plain that extends from the North Sea coast of the Netherlands to the Ural Mountains in the Soviet Union. In the far south and southwest are small highland areas in the Carpathian and Sudeten (Sudety) mountains, shared with Czechoslovakia. The country extends for 689 kilometers from east to west and 649 kilometers from north to south, encompassing an area (including inland waters) of 312,683 square kilometers.

Topography

Poland's average elevation is 173 meters; more than 90 percent of its area lies below 300 meters, and only 3 percent, chiefly in the south, rises above 500 meters (see fig. 10). Rysy, the highest peak at 2,499 meters, is on the Czechoslovak border about 95 kilometers south of Krakow in the Tatry range of the Carpathians. Six other peaks on the Polish side of the Tatry Mountains reach 1,900 meters or more. The Sudety Mountains are lower, only one peak exceeding 1,600 meters. In both ranges a total of about 300 square kilometers rises about 1,000 meters. The lower land is found just south of the Gulf of Danzig, where approximately 60 square kilometers lie below sea level.

Geographers usually divide the country into five topographic zones, each extending from west to east. The largest, accounting for three-fourths of Poland's territory, is the great central lowlands area. It is narrow in the west but expands to both the north and the south as it extends eastward. At the eastern border it includes everything from near the northeastern tip of the country to about 200 kilometers from the southeastern corner.

To the south of the central lowlands, extending across the country parallel to the southern border in a belt roughly 90 to 120 kilometers wide, is an area of foothills of the two mountain ranges. The foothills blend into the mountains in the extreme south and in the southwestern corner of the country. Neither range is rugged enough over large areas to limit habitation, and in only a few isolated places is the population density below the country

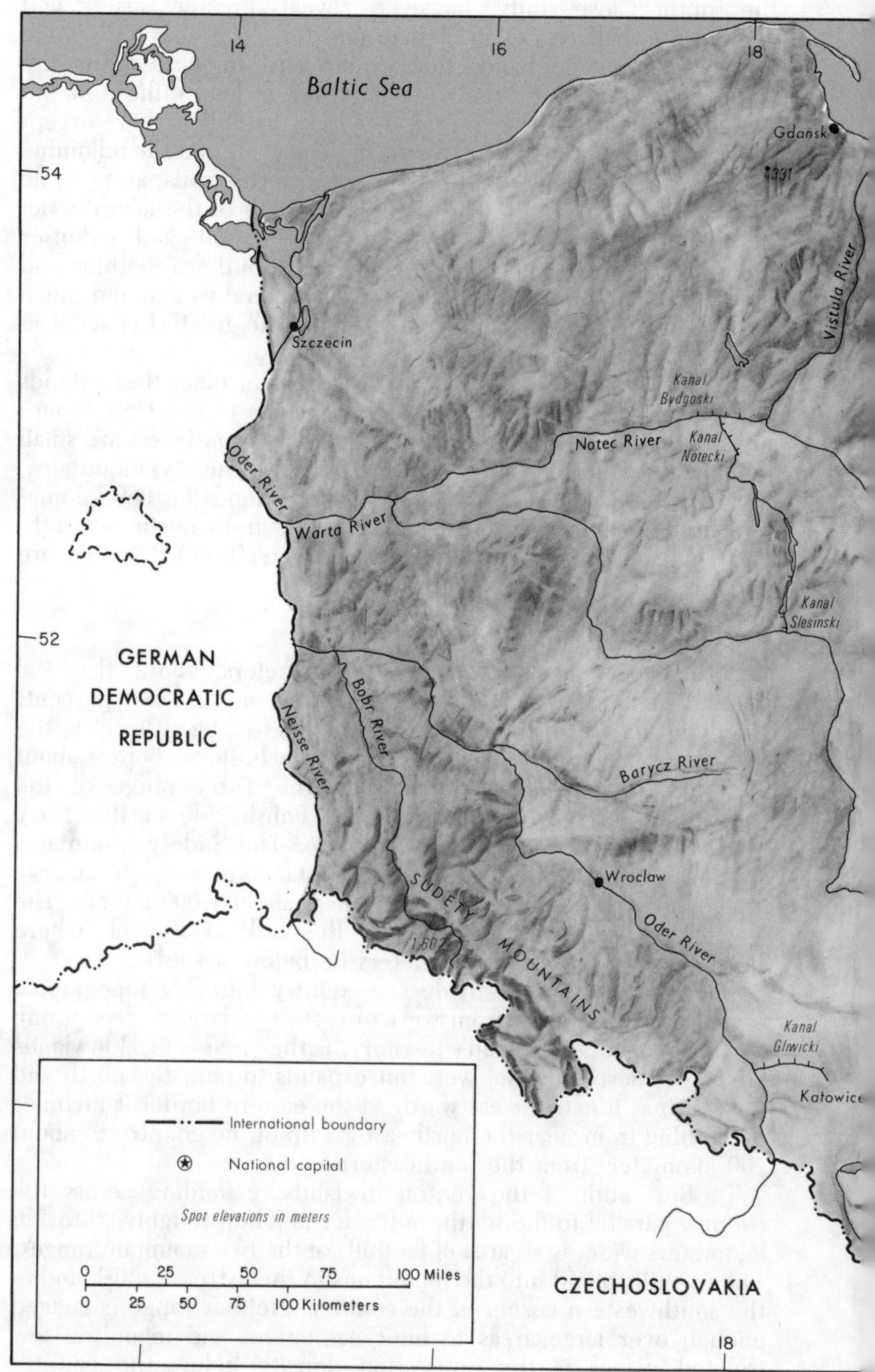

Figure 10. Terrain and Drainage

SOVIET UNION
lf of
nzig
Lyna River
Kanal
Elblaski
AKE
DISTRICT
309
Kanal
Augustowski
54
Narew River
Wkra River
193
LOWLANDS
ENTRAL
Kanal Zeranski
Warsaw
Bzura River
52
Lodz
Kanal
Wieprz-
Krzna
Wieprz River
Bug River
Pilica River
610
N
SOUTHERN
UPLANDS
Vistula River
San River
50
Krakow
CARPATHIAN MOUNTAINS
SOVIET
UNION
Boundary representation
not necessarily authoritative
TATRY MOUNTAINS
2,499
20
22
24

average. Most of the more rugged slopes are in the Tatry Mountains; many slopes in the Sudety range are gentle and can be cultivated or used as meadows and pastures on dairy farms.

North of the central lowlands are the hills, forests, and lakes created by the recession of the most recent glacier millennia ago. The area is usually referred to as the lake district. The effects of glaciation are the most prominent features of the terrain for 200 kilometers or more inland from the Baltic Sea in the western part of the country but for a much shorter distance in the east. The earth and stone carried by glaciers embossed what would have been a nearly flat area. Glacial action led to the formation of many lakes and low hills. Much of the land is forested. The sea is the primary influence over a narrow band of the coastline that distinguishes it from interior regions.

Drainage

By far the greatest portion of the country drains northwestward to the Baltic Sea by way of the Wisla (Vistula) and Odra (Oder) rivers. Most other rivers join the Vistula and Oder systems, but a few streams in the northeastern region reach the sea through Soviet territory.

The Vistula and its tributaries drain the country's largest basin, an area almost double the Polish portion of the Oder basin. The Vistula basin includes practically all of the southeastern and east-central regions and much of the northeast. The Vistula rises in the Tatry range of the Carpathians and exits at the Gulf of Danzig. Most of its tributaries flow to it from the east, rising in the Soviet Union or near the Soviet border. One of them, the Bug, forms about 280 kilometers of the Polish-Soviet border.

The Oder, which with the Nysa (Neisse) River forms most of the border between Poland and the German Democratic Republic (East Germany), is fed by several other rivers and streams, including the Warta, which drains a large section of central and western Poland. The Oder reaches the Baltic Sea through the harbors and bays north of Szczecin.

Much inland area that comprises the lake district and extends across the entire country is poorly drained. Its many lakes add beauty and value to the region, but its swampland has been difficult to reclaim. Most of the lakes are small and shallow, the two largest having areas of little more than 100 square kilometers each; and nearly a dozen, including some very small ones, have depths of 50 meters or more.

Climate

Throughout much of the year the climate over most of the country is continental, dominated by high-pressure polar air masses that bring Poland dry, cool air. But the area is within range of Western Europe's maritime weather, which moderates its

View of Warsaw across the Vistula River, Poland's major inland waterway Courtesy Consulate General of Polish People's Republic, New York

Town of Grudziadz on the Vistula in Torun voivodship Courtesy Consulate General of Polish People's Republic, New York

temperatures and brings the country sufficient precipitation.

Maritime weather influences are more frequent in winter than in summer, and there are long overcast periods of fog, frequent precipitation (usually snowfall), and high humidity. It is less humid when the polar high-pressure systems are dominant, but it can be extremely cold at such times. Nighttime temperatures as low as –40°C are occasionally endured. In mountainous regions during periods of nearly calm winds, cold air sinks to the valley floors, making them oppressively cold—much less pleasant than the sunny higher elevations.

The summer season, from June through August, has frequent showers and thunderstorms. Humidity is generally lower than in winter. When winds are from the south and southeast, it is warm and dry. Weather varies widely during both spring and autumn. Winter relinquishes its hold on the land reluctantly, and pleasant weather may not replace it until mid-April. Early autumn is usually bright, clear, and crisp. By November, weather conditions may turn unpleasantly rainy and cold, although the total precipitation during the season is not great.

Mean temperatures, with few exceptions, range between 6°C and 8°C, but there is much seasonal variation by region. The Baltic coastal areas, particularly in the west, have warmer winters and cooler summers than interior regions. The greatest differences between average winter and summer temperatures occur in the southeast, on the border with the Ukraine. Although winter temperatures average about 4.5°C colder than in the western part of the country, the annual mean is nearly the same because the warmer summer temperatures compensate. The growing season is approximately 40 days longer in the southwest (where spring arrives early and autumn is late) than in the northeast (where springtime is delayed and autumn arrives early).

Precipitation averages between 500 and 650 millimeters annually over most of the plains, a little higher in the southern uplands, and up to 1,300 millimeters at isolated places in the mountains. Only in small areas does it drop below an annual average of 500 millimeters. The largest of these is an area about 80 kilometers in width that follows the Vistula from just northwest of Warsaw to its mouth. The city of Szczecin, a small area to its north, and an equally small area on the border with the Ukraine also receive less than 500 millimeters annually. Throughout the country, summer precipitation is approximately double that of winter and almost always provides adequate water for crops.

Soils

The glacial moraine of the lake district tends to have either dense clay or loose sand. The clays are not necessarily infertile, although they usually need lime, but they do not drain and are difficult to till. Sandy soils of the area drain so quickly that they hold neither water nor the nutrients required by shallow-rooted annual crops. In places where the clay is porous and somewhat less dense, pale, layered soils (podzols) have developed. These have a top layer of humus, but its nutrients leach through the porous clay to lower levels. Such soils are prevalent in the lake district and in the steeper mountainous areas of the far south.

The richer southern upland soils are the black earths (chernozem) and the brown forest soils, both of which have been improved in wide areas by deposits of fine, light loess. These soils drain well, till easily, and are rich in plant food. The bulk of the plains have a mixture of black earth and layered clays. The resultant soil is generally of a slightly poorer quality than the soils of the majority of Europe's arable land, but it is adequate to provide acceptable crop yields.

Demography

The census of December 7, 1978, enumerated a population of slightly more than 35 million, a figure that had been reached in 1939 before the devastation of World War II and the ensuing radical changes in Poland's boundaries and in the composition of its population (see The People's Republic, ch. 1). The consequence of the war and its aftermath was a diminished and more homogeneous population. A more gradual process converted a largely rural population to a largely urban one by the early 1980s. In mid-1981 the official Polish estimate put the population at 36.1 million.

Population Composition

Population losses during the war totaled roughly 6 million people. A very substantial proportion of prewar Poland's large Jewish population was destroyed in extermination camps and elsewhere. A great many Poles and members of other ethnic groups died in combat, of other war-related causes, and in camps. As a consequence of decisions made by the Great Powers at Yalta in 1945, Poland lost more than 90,000 square kilometers, having to relinquish more territory to the Soviet Union in the east than it gained from Germany in the west. The boundary changes led to the loss of large numbers of persons of other ethnic groups who had lived in prewar Poland. The territory ceded to the Soviet Union contained Byelorussians, Ukrainians, and Lithuanians. In the west not only did Germans who had lived in the territory taken over by Poland leave it for various parts of occupied Germany, but many Germans who had lived within the boundaries of prewar Poland also departed. Of the few remaining Jews, many emigrated to Israel or elsewhere. (Many of those who remained left after strong manifestations of official anti-Semitism in 1968.) In this period, roughly 1945 to 1948 but continuing for several years thereafter, Poles who had been living in the east were moved en masse to the west.

The war and ensuing events thus led to a marked change in the ethnic and religious composition of Poland's people. Before the war less than 70 percent of the population consisted of ethnic Poles, and a somewhat smaller proportion were Roman Catholics. By 1950 more than 98 percent were Poles, and more than 90 percent had been baptized in the Roman Catholic faith (see Religious Life, this ch.).

Polish, the language of all but a very few nationals, is one of several West Slavonic tongues (the two others of importance are Czech and Slovak). West Slavonic and two other groups—East Slavonic and South Slavonic—constitute the great Slavonic language family. Polish and other West Slavonic languages, unlike some other Slavonic languages, e.g., Russian, use a Latin alphabet, a consequence of the influence of the Roman Catholic Church rather than that of the Eastern Orthodox Church, which introduced the Greek-derived Cyrillic alphabet farther east.

Population Growth and Structure

The population of Poland was drastically reduced between 1939, when it was estimated at more than 35 million, and early 1946, when the first postwar census enumerated not quite 24 million persons within the country's new boundaries. By the 1950s the population had risen to more than 25 million. The departure of persons of other ethnic groups had continued, but had been more than offset by the repatriation of Poles who had been outside the country as forced laborers and soldiers and by a considerable upsurge in the birth rate, which had been at a low ebb before and during the war.

The rise in the annual rate of growth that began just after the war continued for some years thereafter, reaching a peak of 1.95 percent in 1953 and averaging about 1.7 percent annually from 1955 to 1960. In the next five years the rate decreased to an average of 1.1 percent. After 1965 it diminished to between 0.8 and 0.9 percent. It was estimated to have risen slightly to 1.0 percent in the early 1980s, higher than the estimated rates for all West European countries except Albania, Ireland, and Iceland.

The early surge in the growth rate was principally a result of a rise in the birth rate; as that slackened by the mid-1950s, the death rate began to fall, thus maintaining the growth rate at a fairly high level. By the late 1950s, however, the birth rate was declining more rapidly and continued to diminish more quickly than the death rate until the late 1960s. By the early 1970s both rates had begun to rise again as women born in the mid-1950s began to bear children and as the aged formed a larger portion of the population. Hopes and fears generated by political and economic conditions may have had minor effects on the birth rate, but the basic elements affecting the overall growth rate are an aging population and the relatively small numbers of women of childbearing age. In these circumstances low annual growth rates are likely to persist.

Given the low birth rates—under 20 live births per 1,000 population—of the two decades since 1962 and the gradual extension of life expectancy, Poland's population pyramid, like most of those in industrialized countries, is characterized by a relatively narrow base of young people and a relatively broad apex of those beyond the age of 60 (see fig. 11). The bulge of those between the ages of roughly 20 and 33 reflects the post-World War II rise in the birth rate.

Official Polish sources define the population of working age to include males between 18 and 64 and females between 18 and 59. In 1981 such persons were estimated to constitute more than 59 percent of the roughly 36 million total. That definition gives males a slight edge in absolute numbers in the working-age category. Men and women over the working age made up just under 12 percent, and young persons under 18 constituted roughly 29 percent of Poland's population. Urban-rural differences were of some importance: nearly 63 percent of the urban population was of working age, whereas only 55 percent of the rural population fell into that category. By contrast the older population constituted a greater proportion of the rural total (between 13 and 14 percent) and a smaller proportion of the urban total (between 10 and 11 percent). Persons under the age of 18 also made up a larger portion of the rural population (more than 31 percent) and a smaller part of the urban one (slightly more than 26 percent).

Density, Distribution, and Urbanization

Aside from the events that led to postwar Poland's becoming ethnically homogeneous, the most important postwar demographic trend was the urbanization of the population. The last prewar census (1931) showed that 72.6 percent of the population was rural and that 59.6 percent relied directly on agriculture for a livelihood. In 1950 about 63.4 percent were still rural, and 47.1 percent depended directly on agriculture as their sole or chief source of income. By 1978 the rural population had diminished to 42.5 percent of the total, and only 22.5 percent relied directly on agriculture for a livelihood. In the early 1980s it was estimated that roughly 60 percent of the population was urban, and it is probable that no more than 20 percent was engaged in agriculture. It is likely that Poland would have moved from its agricultural and rural character to a predominantly urban one, no matter what its political order, but the communist regime's insistence on industrialization may have speeded the process.

Cities of over 100,000 inhabitants may be found in most parts of Poland (see table 2, Appendix A). Of particular interests is a cluster of industrial towns near Katowice in the voivodship (see

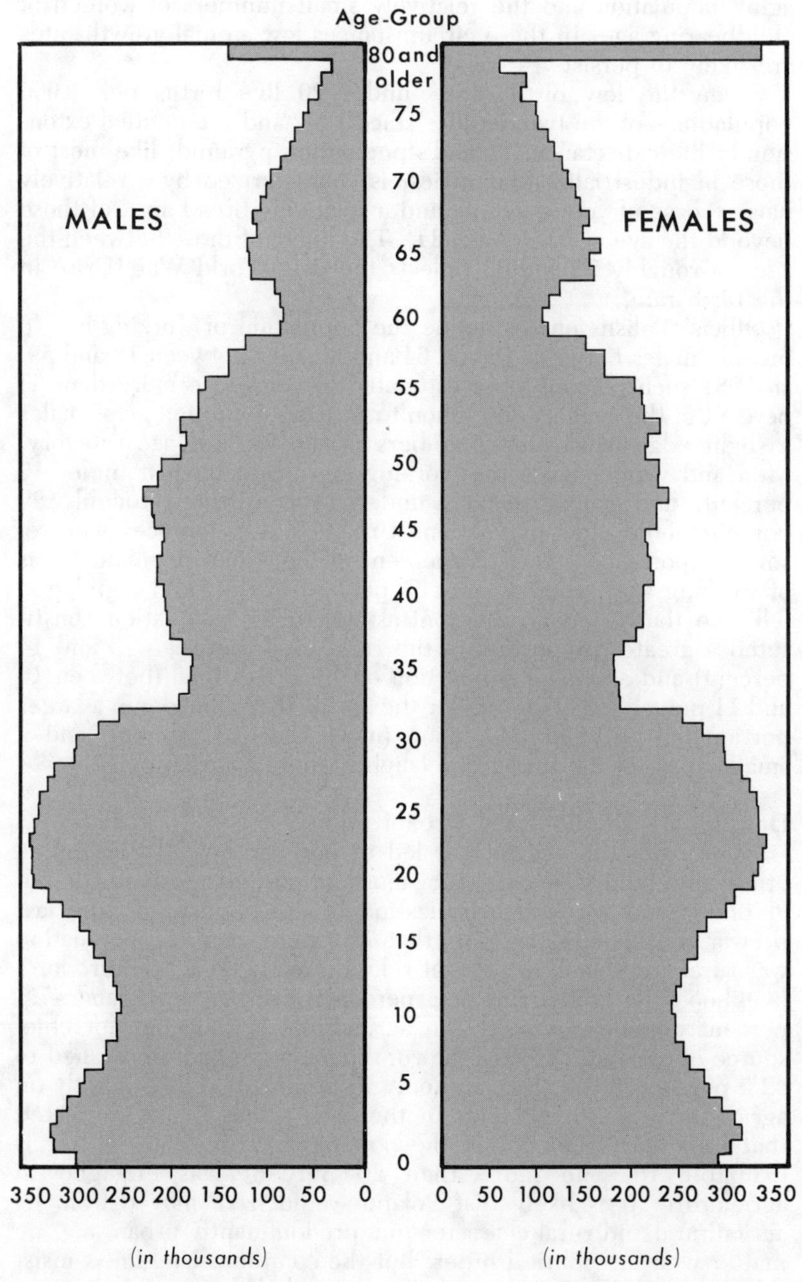

Source: Based on information from Poland, Glowny Urzad Statystyczny (Central Statistical Office), *Narodowy Spis Powszechny Zdnia 7XII 1978*, Warsaw, 1980.

Figure 11. Age and Sex Structure of Polish Population, 1978

Glossary) of that name. None is very large, but together they constitute one of the most intensely urban areas in Poland. In addition to these 38 cities and larger towns, there were in 1981 another 135 towns having populations ranging between 20,000 and 100,000. In these 173 cities and towns lived about 80 percent of Poland's urban population.

Overall population density in 1978 was 112 persons per square kilometer (115 per square kilometer according to the official 1981 estimate); there was, however, some regional variation (see fig. 12). In good part, that variation reflected the degree of urbanization of a voivodship, but it also indicated the carrying capacity of rural land.

Poland's urban areas include 19,559 square kilometers, a little more than 6 percent of its total area. In 1978 these zones had an average density of 1,030 persons per square kilometer, nearly twice that in 1950. But population density ranged from under 500 per square kilometer in the towns of some voivodships (Nowy, Sacz, Lomza, Czestochowa, and Tarnobrzeg) to more than 3,000 per square kilometer in the towns (chiefly Lodz) in the voivodship of Lodz. The urban density in the voivodship of Warsaw (which includes several towns in addition to the capital city) was next highest at just under 2,000 persons per square kilometer.

The country's rural areas (almost 94 percent of the total land area) had an average density of 51 persons per square kilometer, only slightly higher than the 47 per square kilometer registered by the l950 census. A few rural areas were well above the mean, i.e., they carried 80 or more persons per square kilometer; included were the areas in the voivodships of Warsaw, Bielsko, Biala Podlaska, Katowice, Krakow, Lodz, Nowy Sacz, Rzeszow, and Tarnow. These were either near major urban area where farmers practiced relatively small-scale but more intensive agriculture to feed the urban population, or they were in the southern highlands and the foothills just north of them where the good soil quality and adequate rainfall permit smaller scale cultivation to support a larger population (see Agriculture, ch. 3). Less densely settled rural areas, i.e., under 40 persons per square kilometer, were to be found chiefly in the east and north where poor sandy or clayey soils and limited rainfall can support only a sparser population.

The Social Order

The destruction wrought during World War II opened Poland's prewar social order to the possibility of substantial change. Significant sections of the old order's budding industrial and commercial middle classes were wiped out, and its intelligentsia (including the medical and legal professions) was decimated by the Nazis and Soviets. In these circumstances the industrialization and urbanization that followed the war led to the emergence of a social order different from that of prewar Poland. The imposition of a commu-

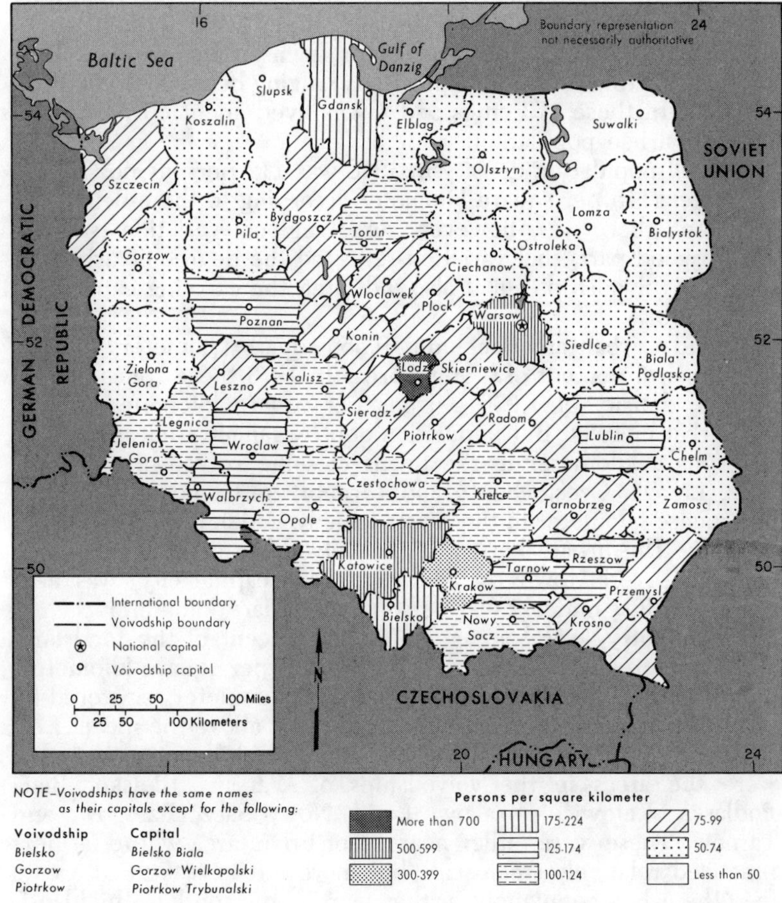

Source: Based on information from Poland, Glowny Urzad Statystyczny (Central Statistical Office), *Narodowy Spis Powszechny Zdnia 7XII 1978*, Warsaw, 1980, Table 1, 2-5.

Figure 12. Population Density by Voivodship, 1978

nist regime gave a specific direction to the change.

The regime pressed industrialization and urbanization, thus rapidly altering the character of the Polish population from a numerically dominant peasantry to a numerically dominant working class (manual and nonmanual). This structural change had the apparent effect of maximizing social mobility. But the rapid social mobility of the first decade or so after the war gave way to a much slower rate. That and the economic order's failures of production and distribution led to recurrent and cumulative frustrations of hopes and expectations.

Modern metropolitan Warsaw, near the intersection of two main thoroughfares, Marszalkowska and Jerozolimskie, site of city's most modern hotel
Courtesy Consulate General of Polish People's Republic, New York

Perhaps more important to the structure of the new social order (and the conflicts within it) was the dominance of the communist party in its Polish form—the Polish United Worker's Party (Polska Zjednoczona Partia Robotnicza—PZPR). The PZPR put a new class at the highest levels of power and income, one that had no significant ties to the older dominant classes, namely, the gentry and the prewar intelligentsia, the latter stemming largely from the gentry.

The arrogation of all significant power to the PZPR—or more precisely to its leading members—soon led to a sharp disjunction among the hierarchies of status (or prestige), income, and power. In no complex and changing social order is there complete congruity of these three dimensions of stratification, but what has been called status incongruity has been marked in East European society and perhaps particularly so in Polish society. Status or prestige is a matter of subjective evaluation of an individual's attributes—in a modern society usually some combination of occupation, education, and life-style—and Poles do not rate party (and government) officials highly. In good part, this reflects the lack of legitimacy of the regime, but it also reflects the widespread perception that the PZPR's decisionmakers at the central and local levels have been typically corrupt and inept.

There is in Poland a good deal of disagreement about the kinds of work that are socially more valuable and should therefore be better paid. Among the significant grievances that gave rise to the Solidarity movement were matters of just compensation and benefits and dislike of privileges and perquisites accruing to those in power. Except for a few, however, equality of income has not been a goal of Poles generally or of the PZPR. Like other ruling parties in Eastern Europe, the PZPR has stressed the allocation of rewards in terms of its conceptions of socially valuable work and of the meritocratic principle. But the Solidarity movement was not solely concerned with the issue of material rewards. The sense of lack of power and therefore of dignity of the working class seems to have been an important element in the rise of the movement.

Social Categories in the Interwar Era

According to the 1931 census, 52 percent of the population of interwar Poland consisted of peasants. Two-thirds of them owned less than five hectares of land and were often constrained to eke out a living by laboring on nearby estates. The remainder were more prosperous, but even these ranged from the peasant who owned only five hectares to the small minority who had as many as 50 hectares. Not quite 10 percent of the population consisted of landless rural laborers. At the other end of the status, power, and income scales in the rural areas (although many had urban homes as well) were the landowners holding at least 50 hectares of land. Members of this category, representing a portion of Poland's traditional aristocracy, constituted less than 1 percent of the population but owned about 27 percent of Poland's land.

The remaining social categories, constituting a little more than one-third of the population, were largely urban, although a significant portion of the artisan and shopkeeper category lived in very small towns. Of these categories, the largest (about 20 percent of the population) consisted of manual wage workers, but the range of income and status in this category was wide. A relatively small number—called the worker aristocracy by some analysts—were skilled workers, employed mainly in mining and heavy industry; a much larger proportion worked in other industries, and a substantial minority, mostly women, were domestics. The next largest category—about 11 percent of the total—consisted of artisans and small shopkeepers (in European terminology, the petty bourgeoisie), either working on their own account, with a few family members, or employing a small number of wage earners. In that period a substantial proportion of shopkeepers were Jews. Families of wealthy industrialists, merchants, and financiers made up no more than 2 percent of the population. Many of this upper bourgeoisie were Germans and Jews. It was only toward the latter half of the nineteenth century and to a greater extent after World War I and the establishment of the Polish state that the landed aristocracy—the magnates and the gentry—considered it suitable to invest in industry and commerce.

About 6 percent of the prewar population were classified as intelligentsia, a category peculiar to Eastern Europe and, in the twentieth century, marked by considerable heterogeneity. The leading segment—perhaps 1 to 2 percent of the category—consisted of creative intellectuals (literary and artistic figures), scholars, scientists, and journalists. Many important political figures in the interwar period came from this category or the next one—professionals with a university education (physicians, lawyers, engineers, and the like). The professional group constituted about 7 to 8 percent of the intelligentsia. It was not uncommon for professionals and higher bureaucrats to devote some of their time to literary pursuits, thus overlapping in their interests and outlook with the creative intelligentsia. Between 35 and 40 percent of the category had a secondary or higher education and held posts as teachers, managers in public and private organizations, and in cultural activities. Included in the intelligentsia—about half of the total—were low- and mid-level white-collar workers in government and private offices. Special status was accorded them because they were functionally literate while many Poles were not. Their jobs, no matter how routine, called for higher incomes than all but the most skilled manual workers. The tradition of ascribing status to the literate was to have some effect in the era after World War II, but it weakened as the incidence of literacy rose substantially.

In the late nineteenth and early twentieth centuries, well over half of those in the upper reaches of the intelligentsia (at that time chiefly writers) had their origin in the gentry who, in the face of earlier political upheaval and economic exigencies, had come to the cities. Nearly one-fourth came from families that had been of the very small earlier intelligentsia. Only 20 percent had their origins in the upper bourgeoisie, the petty bourgeoisie, and the peasantry (in that order). The gentry set the tone of social life, generally taking their standards from their backgrounds in the landed aristocracy. Although the intelligentsia expanded substantially after World War I when Poland was reconstituted as an independent state, the social influence of its gentry component remained important. Members of this group, despite their cultural and social remoteness from most Poles, played a considerable role in keeping Polish culture and aspirations for political independence alive before the war, and many were immediately involved in the politics of the new state after the war, either directly in government or as ideologists for various parties. Despite their largely common social origin, their ideological commitments varied over much of the political spectrum.

To be of the intelligentsia even at the lower level was to have a clean job in a society in which working with one's hands implied a dirty job. A clean job and mental work, no matter how routine, conferred a degree of status—not enough to make a bookkeeper the equal of a gentry-derived higher official or a journalist, but enough to be thought somehow better than a highly skilled manual worker, at least by those who had emerged from the ranks of peasants and workers and those they had left behind. These values reflected the attitudes of the gentry who had for so long scorned not only manual labor but also the contamination of commerce.

Social Categories under the Communist Regime

Polish sociologists have developed slightly varying sets of social categories and subcategories intended to order the socioeconomic status of the members of Polish society in the so-called socialist era. The primary criterion for the establishment of these categories is occupation, but implied in their construction is the level of education, which has substantially affected an individual's chances to have one kind of job rather than another. The categories have their roots in interwar Poland, but some of the earlier ones are no longer relevant, and the composition of others has changed, partly owing to industrialization, partly as a direct result of regime policy.

Two categories, the landed gentry and the upper bourgeoisie—socially, politically, and economically significant but small in numbers—were in effect abolished by the regime when they were deprived of their base—landed estates in the one case and financial and business enterprises in the other. In fact, many members of these two categories were killed during the war or were out of the country and in effect became exiles after the war. The petty bourgeoisie was subjected to changing policies in the postwar period; its heavily Jewish shopkeeper segment had been destroyed, and its artisan component was in part incorporated into the wage-earning skilled industrial force. Official ideology looks askance at this category but has permitted it to exist in the interstices of the economy. In 1975 those deriving their incomes from private ownership of small-scale businesses (in production, distribution, or the provision of artisanal services) constituted 1.7 percent of the population, a sharp drop from the interwar period when it made up as much as 11 percent of the total.

Another interwar social category that has virtually disappeared is that of the rural (landless) laborer. A very small number still work for wages on state-owned farms, but landless laborers either acquired some land from the sequestered estates of the gentry or joined other rural people in the trek to the cities and towns.

By the mid-1950s four general socioeconomic categories had been established and retained their relevance into the 1980s, although their proportions of the population have changed as have the constituent subcategories. The largest comprises the manual workers and their dependents—in the 1970s perhaps 40 to 45 percent of the population. The next largest category includes the peasantry, but that is less than half the size of the largely urban working class, and a substantial portion of this group, although rural, is heavily dependent on wages earned in industry in nearby towns. Most of the once numerically dominant peasantry have gone to make up the manual working class.

The category formerly labeled intelligentsia tends in Poland (and elsewhere in Eastern Europe) to be divided into the intelligentsia proper (sometimes referred to as the elite) and white-collar workers and others, referred to by sociologist Walter D. Connor as "routine nonmanuals." The latter category, which may have included as much as 25 percent of the population in the mid- and late 1970s, has grown with the expanding state and industrial bureaucracy as the demand for services and technicians has increased. The elite in its varied forms comes to no more than 10 percent of the total.

A first approximation to the ordering of the three dimensions of income, status (or prestige), and power of the four significant social categories would place the intelligentsia at the top, followed by the routine nonmanuals, urban (manual) workers, and the peasantry; but the ordering is ambiguous in several respects. For example, not all in the routine nonmanual category are above those in the lower categories even with respect to the most objective and easily ranked of these dimensions—income. Further, those at a given position on the income ladder are not necessarily at the same place with respect to the other two dimensions. To describe the nature of the ambiguity requires some attention to significant subcategories.

Polish sociologists have offered a number of classes and subclasses for the description and analysis of Polish society. The simplest of these and the most consonant with the four social categories noted is that of Jan Szczepanski, a respected sociologist, in his *Polish Society*. Leaving aside his "routine white-collar functionaries" and at least a segment of his "technical specialists" who fall into a separate category, there are in the intelligentsia highly educated professionals (physicians, academics, and engineers), political officials (including party and government people), senior civil servants, and persons at the highest levels of economic management. A subcategory called the creative intelligentsia (or intellectuals) includes writers of various kinds—senior journalists, academics, and other high-level researchers, filmmakers, and the like. Here the term "creative" refers to presumed function rather than to actual performance. In all of these occupations (except perhaps among party officials but frequently there too) education beyond the secondary level is almost universal.

The routine nonmanual category is also differentiated but not so sharply into actual or potential interest groups and culturally distinctive social circles as is the intelligentsia. A great many routine nonmanuals are office or clerical workers; often, as Szczepanski notes, their work requires them to interact with the public, the mass of which is made up of the working class. They are ranked into the specific bureaus or enterprises for which they work and are paid accordingly. Some have a degree of supervisory responsibility. All, of course, are literate, but few have educations beyond the secondary level. Another large subcategory includes those engaged in distribution—salespersons and the like.

Two subcategories are on the borderline between the intelligentsia and the routine nonmanuals: primary- and secondary-school teachers and technical workers. In interwar Poland the place of primary- and particularly secondary-school teachers in the intelligentsia was clear. The spread of education and literacy, the fact that most primary-school teachers have lost the leadership role in their small communities, and comparatively low pay suggest that teachers may be more accurately placed among the routine nonmanuals even if many Poles still accord them much more prestige than they do office functionaries. The subcategory of technicians includes persons with a specialized secondary education ranging from accountants to paramedics. They are more highly paid than office clerks and salespeople, but the kind of education they have received and their life-styles put them closer to routine nonmanuals than to any segment of the intelligentsia.

The range of difference within the category of manual labor with respect to income, prestige, and education is substantial. The standard distinction between skilled and unskilled workers is complicated further by the emphasis the regime has placed on the social and economic value (reflected in wage scales) of heavy and extractive industry. Miners and skilled workers in heavy industry have earned more than skilled manual workers in light industry, e.g., textiles, and their work is seen as more prestigious not only by the PZPR and the government but also by most Poles. Distinctions are also drawn among the unskilled depending on the kind of activity in which they are engaged.

Most persons in the first three categories are either directly employed in state organizations (governmental or economic) or count on the state for support in various forms. There are exceptions among writers and other creative intellectuals, and a small number of people work in manual or other capacities for private entrepreneurs.

Only the farmers constitute a significant category not employed by the state. Within this category there is a range of variation

Farmstead of a rural Polish smallholder, near Lodz
Courtesy Jean R. Tartter

between relatively well-off farmers and poorer ones, but there is also an overlapping distinction between the decreasing numbers who still rely entirely on farming and the growing number (at least 35 percent in the early 1980s) who may identify themselves as farmers and live on small farms but earn at least a part of their income in wages, in local industry, in services, or in what has been termed the alternative, or parallel, economy. Quite different from both these subcategories are the relatively few full-time farm laborers, workers on state farms, and participants in the small number of collectives. Together they constitute a very small proportion of persons engaged in agriculture. Despite the differences between self-employed farmers and wage workers on state farms, they share a rural outlook that differs substantially from that of industrial workers.

Stratification by Income

Official sources and analyses based on these sources and on independent surveys do not group occupations in the same way or provide all the relevant data; determining the allocation of income in relation to the four major social categories is therefore problematic. Nevertheless, it is possible to indicate the general outlines of income ranking and to point to certain tendencies and issues.

Connor, basing part of his analysis on data from state industry only (and thereby excluding party and government officials, the creative intellectuals, peasants, and workers in nonindustrial but urban enterprises), shows clearly that the intelligentsia (represented by engineers, other high-level technicians, and managers) were in 1960 much better paid than workers and routine nonmanuals and continued to be so in 1973, although the gap had narrowed slightly. The gap between manual workers (skilled and unskilled taken together) and routine nonmanuals, whose average pay had been slightly higher, also narrowed to near equality. In this case, the routine nonmanuals were represented by administrative and clerical personnel, not by more highly paid technicians. In 1973, given an index of 100 for manual workers, routine nonmanuals were at 100.1 and intelligentsia at 144.3

A more differentiated breakdown of occupations and their average income (limited to male household heads, thus ignoring the large number of women in the labor force) is available for three Polish cities in 1964 and 1965 (and for one of them, Lodz, in 1967). Here unskilled workers were assigned an index of 100. Depending on the city, the index for the intelligentsia ranged from 163.3 to 206.4 (the latter in Lodz, which probably has a greater number of very high-level professionals and bureaucrats than the other two smaller centers). In these studies differences within major categories were discernible. Thus, among routine nonmanuals, technicians earned higher salaries than clericals, and the average pay of the latter was slightly less than that of foremen in industry. Skilled workers were paid better than the semiskilled and unskilled; but at that time they earned less than clericals, and the amount varied from city to city.

In Poland as elsewhere in the western world (including Eastern Europe), the units of stratification is the nuclear family, not the individual, although the situation of the (usually) male head of household may be decisive with respect to income and status. The same data analyzed to show household per capita incomes change the picture somewhat. The gap narrows between the intelligentsia and the routine nonmanuals, particularly the clericals. It widens between clericals and skilled workers. Here the living patterns of the different strata play a part. In the mid-1960s the wives of routine nonmanuals were more likely to work than were the wives of the intelligentsia and the skilled workers who remained out of the labor market for different reasons. Moreover, if the wives of skilled workers earned some income, it was probably less than that earned by the wives of clericals and technicians. It was also likely that clericals and technicians had fewer children on the average than skilled workers, thus contributing to a higher per capita income.

A national survey in 1975 of the country's economically active population provided somewhat more recent data, but the differentiation of subcategories was more limited, and the measure used—average disposable household income—ignored per capita income. It was not, then, strictly comparable to earlier data. The intelligentsia (here labeled professionals and managers but not limited apparently to roles in industry) remained at the top, but not as far above the unskilled workers as earlier. Technical and office workers were lumped together and maintained a higher pay status than skilled workers, who remained well above unskilled workers in the overall picture; but there was a much smaller gap between skilled and unskilled workers in urban areas and particularly in cities having a population of 100,000 or more. This may have reflected the fact that unskilled labor (in the form of peasant-workers) was more readily available and therefore cheaper in the nonurban areas that have been the locus of a good deal of industrialization since 1960.

Not separately included in the analyses of earlier data but included in the 1975 data was the subcategory of service workers, apparently including nonindustrial, nonmanual workers in trade, transportation, and communication (and perhaps others) and therefore falling into the major category of routine nonmanuals. In 1975 workers in the subcategory were, on the average, better paid than skilled workers in Poland generally and in urban areas of all sizes. They were, however, less well paid than technicians and office workers taken together.

In 1975 the category of peasants showed a slightly higher average disposable income than unskilled workers but a much lower one than skilled workers. It is not clear whether peasant-workers were included; but full-time peasants and peasant-workers were distinguished in another context, and their average disposable income was not markedly different, full-time peasants ranking slightly higher. There was a narrow range of variation among peasant-workers, but it was chiefly regional. Income differences among full-time farmers were apparently much greater, and some farmers were quite well-off, particularly market gardeners in the vicinity of the larger cities.

Finally, another very small group of persons outside the state system consists of craftsmen and self-employed workers (not included are shopkeepers and owners of small production facilities). In 1975 the disposable income of this category was less than that of service workers and slightly higher than that of skilled workers. The self-employed are heavily taxed on the income earned in the official economy.

Not captured in surveys, whether carried out by the state or by sociologists, are the total incomes of those private entrepreneurs who derive varying proportions of their incomes from untaxed operations in the alternative economy. Some observers think such entrepreneurs are among the wealthiest persons in Poland.

The income of two relatively small but socially and politically significant segments of the intelligentsia—party and government officials and the creative intelligentsia—is problematic for quite different reasons. The salaries and other official sources of income of high party and government people have been quite good, but they have often been no higher than those of some creative intellectuals whose output has been well received and of professionals who have been well paid for their expertise. The question is whether the party elite have had regular access to housing, shops, recreational facilities, medical treatment, and the like, which has given them a higher level of living than their salaries alone would indicate. There has been some of that, although it appears not to have been as pervasive as in the Soviet Union. Szczepanski, writing in a text for American publication in 1970, seems to have gone out of his way to deny that "the higher ranks of the political apparatus . . . profiting from the concentration of political power in their hands, have also secured for themselves economic privileges and the highest income." Other observers, writing a decade or more later, argue that the PZPR elite and other elites who have been nominated for their important positions, e.g., as directors of state industries, by the PZPR under the *nomenklatura* (see Glossary) system enjoy a wide range of economic benefits beyond their official salaries.

A different issue is the extent to which particular individuals in power or deriving influence from their connections with the party elite have made what Poles, in and out of the PZPR, would consider corrupt use of their positions. The problem of corruption seems to have been pervasive enough that the PZPR and government have been constrained from time to time to purge and even to prosecute party members. Many of the cited instances of corruption refer not to the highest party officials at the national level but rather to those in lesser regional positions of power and to others at levels below the top. Even if the highest officials have not been accused of corruption, many Poles feel that they have tolerated a good deal of it and have failed to deal with it until it has become a major issue that can no longer be avoided.

The income of creative intellectuals varies greatly, depending on several factors—whether in addition to their creative work as novelists, poets, or essayists they have regular positions as editors, academics, journalists, or broadcasters; the extent to which the regime, through various agencies, provides grants and other subventions; and the degree to which there is a market for their work. Among those in this category whose incomes may be very high are filmmakers. Positions and grants may be withheld from specific persons—as happened in the late 1960s after a major dispute between writers and the PZPR over issues of intellectual freedom—and works that might be popular have not reached the market owing to censorship. The relations between creative intellectuals and the PZPR have strongly affected income. The conflict in the late 1970s and the early 1980s between the ruling party and those intellectuals who supported or were part of the Solidarity movement and the Committee for the Defense of the Workers (Komitet Obrony Robotnikow—KOR; after September 1977 the name changed to Committee for Social Self-Defense-Committee for the Defense of the Workers [Komitet Samoobrony Spolecznej-Komitet Obrony Robotnikow—KSS-KOR]), or who participated in the Society for Academic Courses and its "flying university," led to economic sanctions against the dissident intellectuals (see Education and Political Controversy, this ch.).

The Issue of Power and Influence in Stratification

Power—the capacity to get members of the entire society or a community to do what they may be otherwise reluctant to do or, more broadly, to make policies and decisions and have them followed—has a restricted distribution in Poland. The minority that had power in early 1983 consisted of a small group of high party officials. Some others in the PZPR or outside of it made policy or decided issues applicable to a locality or an enterprise, but they had no independent base for their power and were understood to act either as agents of the PZPR or with its implicit or explicit permission, which could be withdrawn.

The power held by party leaders is ultimately based on coercion and, because the PZPR controls the economy, by the allocation of economic rewards and punishments. These leaders, however, have lacked what most holders of power must have if they are not to resort constantly to force or the threat of force—legitimacy, i.e., the acknowledgment of those who bow to power that its wielders have the right to exercise it, even if particular policies or decisions are disliked. In Poland the legitimacy of the regime has been problematic from the onset of communist rule, although some intellectuals were attracted to it initially. The intensity with which the illegitimacy of the regime has been felt and confronted by different segments of the society has varied over the nearly four decades in which the PZPR has been in power. Acceptance of its right to rule has never been more than minimal.

The restriction of real power to party leaders does not imply monolithic power; there has always been political infighting and interest brokerage within the PZPR. Moreover, from time to time and within limits, the party elite have been constrained to take account of individuals or groups thought to have influence among segments of the Polish population. Such accommodation to those who had no power in the strict sense was a consequence of the need of the party leaders to maintain their own power without excessive and frequent recourse to force.

Individuals or institutions lacking power have been able to exercise influence; that is, significant segments of the population have looked to them for leadership in a variety of situations, most of them involving the expression of opposition to the regime. Such influence has been gained by specific persons, e.g., Lech Walesa, whose qualities and actions have been consonant with the dispositions and concerns of a substantial segment of the Polish people. Membership in a social category or formal status in an institution has not automatically conferred the power to persuade. The traditional prestige of the intelligentsia, particularly that of the creative intellectuals, had in some respects carried over into the communist era, but it was not necessarily recognized by other Poles until the mid-1970s. The Roman Catholic Church has been the major institutional counterweight to the regime, but priests have not always been influential outside the strictly religious sphere. The most obvious example of a great influence over a long period was Stefan Cardinal Wyszynski, former primate of Poland. His status gave him an opportunity to exercise influence over Poles, but in reality only his personal characteristics and actions affected them. The same principle applies to other influential persons, clerical or lay.

In the highly politicized atmosphere of modern Poland, power and influence are not distributed in a stable way that correlates with the major social categories or even with subcategories. Power inheres in the party leaders, but because it inheres only in them, influence on ordinary Poles is exercised by those whose expression of opposition sparks or represents their views.

Social Status

By far the most problematic, because the most subjective, of the dimensions of stratification in any modern society is status or prestige. The Polish people do not necessarily agree on the criteria by which some categories of individuals (or families) are to be regarded as worthy of deference and others are not. The recognition of the worth of socially recognized attributes in terms of which individuals are ranked depends on the values of the Polish people, but these values have changed and vary from one segment of the society to another. The party regime quickly changed the distribution of income and power, but it could not so easily do away with the historical values, sometimes very strong, pertaining to status. Moreover, the PZPR's approach to status was not altogether consistent. As a Marxist party it theoretically ascribed maximum value to the working class, which it tended to define as consisting of manual workers; as a Leninist party it ascribed value to itself as the vanguard of the working class, but its leaders, regardless of their origins, were of the elite. Finally, because the creative and the technical intelligentsia were useful, the PZPR ascribed special value to them as well.

Polish sociologists, following a widespread practice in Western sociology, have focused on the rating of occupational prestige as a major indicator of status. Presumably, those whose occupations have been highly rated by a cross section of Polish society have met a primary criterion for having their status recognized by Poles in general. Studies of occupational prestige have been conducted in Poland since the 1960s and, depending on the sample and the time of research, there have been minor changes in the rank ordering of occupations, but the basic outlines have remained the same, and they are comparable to occupational rankings in industrialized countries elsewhere. There have been some interesting differences, however.

In the latest available of these surveys of occupational prestige carried out in 1975, 30 professions covering occupations in all four of the major social categories were ranked (see table B). The occupations rated significantly higher in Poland than internationally were miner (+25.5), cleaning woman (+14.6), unskilled construction laborer (+13.8), teacher (+9.0), and state farm supervisor (+8.4). Those rated significantly lower were lawyer (–14.0), office clerk (–11.4), typist (–9.7), accountant (–9.6), and minister of the national government (–8.0).

Most of these deviations from the international scale, positive or negative, can be understood either in relation to traditional values or as responses to recent Polish experience. Miners in Poland have a long tradition as independent, highly paid, skilled workers whose production contributes substantially to foreign trade and the domestic economy. The great emphasis placed on construction in a country where housing has long been a problem may account for the higher score of unskilled construction workers. A supervisor, even on a state farm, is seen as a skilled person doing a fairly important job, and supervisory roles are in general held in high regard. Despite some changes in the role of teachers, the esteem in which the occupation has long been held persists. Not comprehensible on the basis of available material is the score and comparative ranking of cleaning women.

The comparatively low score for lawyers may be attributed in part to their less significant roles in the socialist legal system and to the fact that the lawyers with whom most Poles are familiar are public prosecutors who, in Szczepanski's words, "not only prosecute criminals, but are the custodians of the rule of law in state administration, of socialized property, and of the rights of citizens." Except in the last instance, lawyers are most often seen as prosecutors on behalf of a disliked regime, and it is not clear that they have ever actively pursued the last of their tasks. The occupation of minister of the national government is the closest approximation to the occupation of a high party official, which was not assessed in the survey. Its deviation from the international

Table B. Occupational Prestige Ranking in Poland, 1975, Compared with International Scores and Ranking

Occupational Title	Polish Score	International Score
University professor	72.1	74.1
Physician	70.1	74.1
Minister of national government	67.7	75.7
Teacher	64.2	55.2
Factory manager	62.8	67.7
Engineer	60.8	64.0
Journalist	59.3	53.8
Miner	58.5	33.0
Agronomist	57.4	56.2
Priest	56.4	58.4
Army officer	54.0	61.1
Lawyer	54.0	68.0
Nurse	50.0	52.4
State farm supervisor	49.1	40.7
Office supervisor	48.6	53.3
Factory foreman	44.2	40.4
Accountant	44.2	53.8
Lathe operator	42.7	38.7
Electrical technician	40.7	46.3
Small farmer	40.7	38.4
Locksmith with own workshop	37.8	41.2
Tailor with own workshop	36.8	40.4
Truck driver	36.8	34.2
Sales clerk	35.8	35.2
Shopkeeper	35.3	42.7
Cleaning woman	34.4	19.8
Unskilled construction laborer	33.9	20.1
Unskilled laborer on state farm	32.9	25.7
Typist	32.4	42.1
Office clerk	31.9	43.3

Source: Based on information from Matti Alestalo, Kazimierz M. Slomczynski, and Wlodzimierz Wesolowski. "Patterns of Social Stratification" in Erik Allardt and Wlodzimierz Wesolowski (eds.), *Social Structure and Change: Finland and Poland Comparative Perspective*, Warsaw, 1978, Table 7, 138.

scoring and the fact it ranked third highest in Poland rather than first reflects the regime's relative lack of legitimacy. That it remains as highly ranked as it does may be attributed to Polish recognition of sheer power and perhaps to awareness of the historical significance of government ministers even if the regime is disliked. The low scoring and ranking of the three white-collar jobs—accountant, office worker, and typist—may be attributed in part to their employment in what is perceived as an unproductive and unresponsive bureaucracy. The training required and the responsibilities of an accountant do not appear to be as great in Poland as in systems marked by private enterprise. The other two occupations are at the lowest routine nonmanual level. Moreover, they are typically filled by women, and it has been suggested by some analysts that in Poland, as elsewhere, so-called feminized jobs are, for that reason, not highly regarded.

According to Finnish and Polish analysts of their body of data, several factors account for the relatively high status of skilled factory workers and farmers. One is the improvement in income, standard of living, and education of both over the years. Skilled workers, for example, often reach higher levels of formal education—even if their education has a different content—than low-level white-collar workers. Further, whether as a matter of ideology or as a consequence of industrialization, manual workers are perceived as making a more significant contribution to the economy than routine nonmanuals. There clearly has been a change in the way manual work is perceived. Other analysts make the point that the status of farmers may reflect the fact that they retain a degree of freedom. The same freedom does not, however, increase the occupational prestige of shopkeepers and self-employed artisans. Commerce, not highly esteemed in presocialist times, still lacks prestige. Moreover, shopkeepers and self-employed artisans, operating as they do in a free market to provide a very limited supply of goods and services that are even more limited or nonexistent in state-operated enterprises, may be perceived as exploitive by many Poles.

Complicating the analysis of occupational prestige is the issue of the extent to which the domination of an occupation by women tends to diminish its prestige. In any case, such jobs seem to be less well paid than others. The relation between the "feminization" of occupations and lowered prestige and income is not simple, however. Some occupations in light industry, e.g., skilled work in textiles, and some white-collar jobs, e.g., typists and clerks, have been seen as women's work for a long time, which may account in part for their lower pay and prestige. But other considerations enter the picture: both the PZPR and the people see heavy industry as more important for reasons other than the sex of the majority of the workers; low-level office jobs involve limited skills that are not in short supply. Indeed, a common notion among Poles that government and industrial bureaucracies are overstaffed with clerks who do relatively little work may contribute to the low regard in which they are held.

The status of physicians provides an interesting case. In the occupational prestige hierarchy the profession ranked second, just below that of university professor, compared with the international scale, where the two tied for first place. The difference may not be significant, but it is noteworthy that by the mid-1970s more than half of the physicians in Poland were women, which may account for the profession's slight drop in prestige. The more prestigious and remunerative specialities were still largely in the hands of men, as were supervisory positions and significant academic posts.

Generally, in the last quarter of the twentieth century, despite the significance of women in the labor force (nearly half in 1980), most Poles see women as secondary earners whose primary responsibility lies in coping with family and household matters. The jobs they typically have outside the home are perceived as ancillary to the primary function and may for this reason be downgraded in the prestige hierarchy.

Detailed information on the way different segments of Polish society see the occupational prestige hierarchy and evaluate their own positions dates from 1961. It seems that the intelligentsia and skilled urban manuals do not perceive the occupations of most routine nonmanuals as worthy of the esteem to which such nonmanuals would lay claim. Peasants, however, still influenced by the old distinction between manual and nonmanual work, may consider nonmanual positions of greater value. Entering into the self-evaluation of routine nonmanuals vis-à-vis manual workers are differences in life-style. For example, the routine nonmanuals are more likely to be consumers of culture than are manual workers even if the differences in their levels of formal education are not great. Further, routine nonmanuals are likely to be more ambitious for their children and to be aware of the somewhat better chances their offspring will have (for various reasons) of acquiring higher education. At any rate, nonmanuals who have achieved that status are reluctant to become manual workers even when the latter's incomes may be higher.

Although the responses to formal questionnaires on occupational prestige provide an important indication of the ways in which Poles allot high and low status to individuals, they do not adequately convey the complexity of the allocation status. Sociologist Stefan Nowak doubts that the status hierarchy is unidimensional and thinks that there are qualitatively different kinds of prestige. He cites two examples of the complexity involved. The teaching profession, he notes, has earned great prestige, "although everyone knows that teachers are poorly paid, poorly qualified, and altogether for many reasons a socially unattractive group." He also notes the low prestige accorded private entrepreneurs in responses to questionnaires but remarks that "anyone observing the social contacts of the owner of a Mercedes and a private villa with his social environment would have to reach the conclusion that he enjoys enormous prestige of a certain kind."

Social Mobility

Except for certain aspects of regime policy and practice in the early postwar years, structural changes induced by industrialization and related developments were far more important than socialist ideology in generating the social mobility that has characterized Polish society. Among the practices that did have some effect was the placing of manual workers, who often lacked education and experience, in positions of authority in governmental and economic organizations. But that came to an end with the onset of what has been called the Stalinist period in Poland (1947–56). In principle, competence and efficiency became the criteria for appointment to important posts; in the more technically demanding jobs, if not in government, higher education and experience presumably provided the bases for competence. In fact, proven competence, whatever its sources, was not enough to fill economic and technical positions of substantial authority, let alone significant government posts. Positions of authority in government and in the economy have long been on the *nomenklatura*, a putatively secret list, the existence if not the details of which has been long known. The party has appointed persons to posts in the *nomenklatura* on the basis of political reliability, and competence has often been a secondary issue.

In the late 1940s and early 1950s the regime also gave preferential treatment to working-class youth seeking higher education in an effort to break the hold of the old intelligentsia and the upper bourgeoisie on opportunities for entrance to the universities. In the mid-1950s roughly half of the student body was of working-class origin. Although the regime continued to encourage the higher education of working-class youth, preferential treatment came to an end. Moreover, the intelligentsia and the routine nonmanual categories had grown, and their members were more likely than working-class parents to provide the material and psychological encouragement, the bureaucratic know-how, and the cultural background that contributed to the likelihood of their children's admission to the universities. By 1968 only one-fourth of the students in higher education (still high compared with many countries) were of working-class origin, and that proportion has subsequently diminished.

Analysts distinguish two varieties of social mobility—structural mobility and exchange. Structural mobility refers to movement that occurs when new jobs open up because of major expansion in the economic and other domains, such as government, and it accounts for the great upsurge in mobility (for example, from peasant to worker) in Poland from the mid-1940s to the early 1970s. The second form, exchange or circulation, refers to the extent to which individuals or, more likely, their children move up or down from their original occupations or social categories. The extent to which it occurs is more significant when the expansion (or contraction) of the demand for new kinds of work is not extraordinary, and it serves as a measure of the degree of openness of a relatively stable system. In the first two decades or so of the communist era, the expansion of industry, development of technology, growth of government bureaucracy and services, and proliferation of cultural activities required the recruitment of various kinds of labor from social categories that had not hitherto furnished them. By the 1970s expansion had slowed down, and the several categories, e.g., intelligentsia and routine nonmanuals, were large enough that their ranks could, at least in part, be replenished by their own children.

As each of the social categories, except for the peasantry, grew in numbers and the range of occupations included within them broadened, they initially gained their members from other categories. There was also a certain amount of intra-category movement, for example, from unskilled to skilled manual workers. For the most part the large numbers of peasants in the prewar era provided the pool for movement into the urban working class, which was ultimately to become the largest single category. Some peasants' children moved into routine nonmanual and intelligentsia categories, but it was unusual if only because, despite the expansion of the educational system, peasants were less likely to have or demand access to education beyond the primary level, and the teaching staff tended to be weakest in the rural areas.

In 1972 a study of the social origins of persons in a range of occupations showed the degree of mobility of the four major social categories. In that year only 14 percent of the elite had elite parents (usually fathers); about 12 percent had routine nonmanual parents; 44 percent had manual worker parents; and 29 percent had peasant parents. This did not mean, however, that large percentages of persons of manual worker and peasant origin entered the elite category. The manual worker and peasant categories were so large and the elite category so small that even the small proportion of persons of manual workers and peasant origin who became elite constituted nearly three-fourths of that category.

In many ways the category of routine nonmanuals was the most open, i.e., many children born of parents in that category moved either up to the elite or down to the category of manual workers. At the same time, roughly one-fourth of the children of elite parents moved down to the routine nonmanual category. That seems particularly to have been the case with women. Many men and women whose parents were manual workers or peasants had the qualifications to enter routine nonmanual work and became white-collar workers or technicians.

More than half the persons in the category of manual workers had parents in that category. Most of the remainder—nearly 44 percent of all manual workers—were of peasant origin. A fairly large proportion of the children of routine nonmanuals and even of the elite entered the category of manual workers; but their absolute numbers were relatively small, and together they made up only about 6 percent of all manual workers.

In the years between 1945 and 1972 the peasantry was the only category that diminished in size, contributing nearly half its offspring to other categories, chiefly the manual workers. The remainder—slightly more than half—constituted more than 90 percent of the shrinking peasant group. A very few from other categories entered the peasantry. Some who became market gardeners, an often lucrative activity, might be better thought of as self-employed entrepreneurs than as peasants.

The degree of social mobility shown in the period of massive structural change in the economy probably will not continue. The basic shift from agricultural to industrial and service occupations and the concomitant rural-urban transformation had largely taken place by the early 1970s. The proportions of the population included within each of the four major categories were not likely to change significantly.

Class Culture and Consciousness

In the prewar era social categories were marked by cultural differences and by a consciousness of class distinctions. That consciousness arose in part from a sense of disparate and perhaps conflicting material interests, but it also had roots in the distinctive ways of life, values, perspectives on the word, and manners of the several classes. Peasants differed from the small urban working class, and both were markedly different from the gentry and the largely gentry-derived and gentry-influenced old intelligentsia. All differed from the often non-Polish upper and petty bourgeoisie. This diversity and the awareness of it made for fairly sharp boundaries between the several social categories, but it did not necessarily generate a highly politicized class consciousness. There were socialist and peasant parties and proto-parties in the late nineteenth and early twentieth centuries when there was a Polish people but no Poland, and they persisted into the interwar independence period. Perhaps because of the lack of independence before 1918, the potential for class conflict was mitigated by the focus on nationalism and was in part diluted by issues of ethnicity.

Under these conditions, both before and during the period of independence, the intelligentsia—small, culturally distinctive, and very conscious of their role as creators and custodians of Polish culture—provided ideologies and rationales for a wide range of political groups and positions. At the same time, they looked down on and were often contemptuous of all other classes except the gentry from which the majority of them stemmed. According to sociologist Maria Hirszowicz, their "status symbols manifested themselves in etiquette, in the proliferation of titles, in dignified garments and in emphasis on social skills and arts, which were part of upbringing." In this context, minorities, e.g., Jews who were intelligentsia by virtue of their educations and professions, rarely had access to the social circles of the Polish intelligentsia.

The spread of urbanization and education has to some extent diminished the cultural distance between social categories in the postwar era, and social boundaries are no longer as firm as they once were. Some forms of behavior, once peculiar to the gentry and the intelligentsia, have become widespread, such as the hand-kissing courtliness and the use of the terms for sir or madam (*pan* and *pani*) that were formerly restricted to the upper classes and were used by the lower orders only when addressing them. The terms "citizen" or "comrade," encouraged by the regime, are very rarely used.

Despite the diminution of cultural and even social distance, differences in class cultural orientation exist. Some of these reflect traditional views; others have arisen in response to the postwar social and economic environment. These differences are supported or affirmed by the tendency, by no means uniform but still strong, to marry persons of the same category and to find one's friends there.

In a general way differences in behavior and social life are not unlike those in the noncommunist world and follow corresponding social categories, but there are subcategorical variations as well, often associated with differences in education. Thus, persons in the two nonmanual categories are more likely than those in the working class to lead an active social life, i.e., cultivating friendships, whereas the social activity of the working class—especially at home—is likely to be restricted to kin. The better educated routine nonmanuals lead social lives similar to the intelligentsia, but those having less education may not be as socially active as are reasonably well-educated skilled workers. Unskilled workers fall well below the others in this respect. Broadly, the better educated tend to make common interests the criterion of friendship, whereas the less well educated find their friends among kin and neighbors.

Except for television, which seems to attract persons in all categories and at all levels of education, the nature of cultural consumption varies broadly with category and more precisely with educational level. The reading of books and periodicals and the

Musicians and dancer in traditional costumes of Krakow area perform before medieval Sukiennice (Cloth Guildhall) in Krakow's main market square.
Courtesy Consulate General of Polish People's Republic, New York

acquisition of a personal or family library is more characteristic of the intelligentsia and the better educated routine nonmanuals.

Within the working class there appears to be a difference between those families that stem from an old urban working-class tradition and those who are perhaps only one generation removed from the peasantry. Some of these old-line workers (or their fathers) are likely to have been socialists of one kind or another in the interwar period or at least staunch unionists. Some may have become members of the PZPR after the war as a natural move from their previous commitments. At the same time, they are conscious of themselves as workers and have been prepared to see their bosses, often party-appointed, as the opposition. Many workers of peasant background are more likely to have seen their mobility as a step up and to take a longer time to acquire a kind of class consciousness vis-à-vis the economic bureaucracy.

The intelligentsia or elite has been sharply divided in several ways. After the war the category's growth and the inclusion in it of a wide range of high-level political, economic, and technical functionaries made it heterogeneous. Moreover, the residue of gentry-derived or gentry-connected intelligentsia had become a very small part of a category whose members stemmed chiefly from the working class and the peasantry. Sheer size and the heterogeneity of function and origin made it impossible for most of those commonly lumped in this category to know each other and to participate in the same or overlapping social circles as they formerly did, even when they espoused somewhat different political viewpoints.

Unlike the situation in earlier times, most of the elite owe their livelihoods to the regime, directly as employees or indirectly as recipients of awards, grants, and opportunities of various kinds. In the former case, which applies to the great majority, some combination of (usually higher) education, actual performance, political reliability and personal loyalty have become the criteria for climbing bureaucratic and other ladders. Most persons are oriented to success within the system—good incomes, a modicum of power, prestige (if not among the people at large, then among those who have accommodated to the system), the symbols of status, e.g., titles. Nevertheless, despite the fact that they have accommodated to the system, the more competent among them have some regard for expertise; they like to work at what interests them and do a good job of it. Any criticism they have of the system arises out of their self-regard as knowledgeable professionals. They may prefer that their expertise rather than party-political considerations play a larger part in decisionmaking at all levels. At the same time, they must confront the fact that they owe their positions and promotions to the PZPR.

Members of the intelligentsia who are genuinely alienated from the system are to be found even in the subcategory of administrative and technical professionals, in part motivated by a simple distaste for the regime, in part—as in the case of active Roman Catholics—frustrated by the barriers to positions for which they may be highly qualified. But the alienated and the critical are more likely to be part of the relatively small group of creative intellectuals. Alienation and a critical stance took some time to develop, but it was clearly manifest by the late 1960s. A segment of the category, however, has remained at the beck and call of the party, ready to accede to and even implement the shifting rules of censorship and the party line on literature and other creative work. Even among those who have had a basic argument with the political, social, and political orders, there was a split between Roman Catholic intellectuals—laity rather than clergy—and secular intellectuals. By the mid-1970 that gap had begun to narrow, and in the era of Solidarity (1980–81) it almost disappeared. By 1978 many intellectuals still in the party were so disappointed and frustrated that they participated in a discussion group called Experience and the Future, which produced a report quite critical of developments in Poland to that point.

The comparative cohesiveness of the creative intellectual community in the last half of the 1970s and the early 1980s may not be able to withstand the imposition of martial law and the imprisonment of some of its most active people. Perhaps more important, the stamina of the antiregime intellectuals may not be able to survive a growth of distrust between themselves and the workers and a lack of cooperation with the latter. Until 1976, when the Committee for the Defense of the Workers (Komitet Obrony Robotnikow—KOR) was established to help the workers who had suffered the regime's hostility, relations between worker groups and the intelligentsia had been minimal and at times unfriendly. From the perspective of the workers, the intellectuals were a part of the elite who benefited from the system, and they did not distinguish between intellectuals sympathetic to them and those who propagandized for, justified, or rationalized the regime. In particular, university students—the intelligentsia of the future—were perceived as concerned only with their own privileges and perquisites. Although many of the intelligentsia may have stemmed from the working class and the peasantry, they had lost touch with them and were little prepared to understand the nature of working-class and peasant grievances. In the enthusiasm and exuberance of the Solidarity days, the workers and at least a portion of the intelligentsia seemed to draw together. If the workers reject the intellectuals in the difficult post-Solidarity period for reasons of strategy, tactics, or distaste, the latter would have difficulty in standing alone and would have lost some of the rationale for their own solidarity. The working class in turn would be confronted with the expertise of the party intelligentsia but would lack specialists on their side who understood the way the party thought and worked.

Social Values

In the years since World War II, research on the social values of Poles has shown that these values have persisted over decades and that Poles tend to agree on what is valuable. Many of these values have been held despite the extent to which the political order has limited their realization. Polish sociologist Stefan Nowak, who has summarized this research, has suggested that these values have retained their potency and generated the demands for changes in social institutions that were put forward during the Solidarity era. Some values, however, particularly those connected with an emphasis on privatization (turning inward to family and individual satisfactions), appear to reflect a degree of apathy arising out of the perceived difficulty of doing anything in the public sphere. A distinction between private and public morality has also been noted, and that too may stem from the same sense of despair. Nowak comments further that, although Poles tend to have the same social values, these values are not necessarily consistent with one another, i.e., they do not appear to be shaped by a coherent ideological vision.

In questionnaires administered to high school students and their parents in Kielce in 1972 and in Warsaw in 1973 and to students in institutions of higher education in Warsaw in 1978, participants were asked to select from a list of 16 items no more than five features that they thought essential to a "good social system" and no more than five that they thought detrimental to such a system (see table C). The attribute chosen by substantial proportions of all respondents was "equality of life opportunities regardless of social origin" reflecting a position encouraged in principle by the regime and realized to some extent in the social mobility characteristic of Poland in the lifetime of the respondents. The politics of the early 1980s may indicate a widespread sense that equality of opportunity has been diminishing. The only other characteristic of a good social system that was chosen by more than half of all categories of respondents was "assurance of a proper standard of living for all citizens." The content of a "proper standard" was not dealt with, but other research indicates that different social categories have varying views on the issue. The choice of this attribute suggests that Poles expect the society (or the state) to guarantee a minimum level of living for all. Although both of these attributes were chosen by high proportions of the respondents, those who picked one did not regularly choose the other, raising the possibility that they were seen as alternatives rather than as separate but ideologically consistent characteristics of a good society.

No other single attribute commanded more than half the choices of all categories of respondents, but more than one-third to more than one-half of each of the five categories chose three: freedom of speech, influence of all citizens on the way the society is

Table C. Results of Surveys on Polish Social Vaues in the 1970s (responses in percentage)

Survey Question: "Which of the following features should a good social system have (+) or not have (–)? Choose no more than 5 positive and 5 negative features."	Warsaw (1973)[1]		Kielce (1972)[1]		Warsaw Students[2] (1978)
	Parents	Youth	Parents	Youth	
1. Equality of life opportunities regardless of social origin	+77 –1	+79 –2	+71 –1	+84 –1	+83 –1
2. Assurance of a proper standard of living for all citizens	+61 –1	+58 –2	+62 –1	+62 –2	+54 –1
3. Freedom of speech; conditions under which differing views can be freely expressed	+46 –2	+57 –3	+39 –3	+59 –3	+59 –2
4. Influence of all citizens on the way the society is governed	+38 –7	+49 –6	+35 –5	+47 –11	+56 –7
5. Economic efficiency	+43 –1	+44 –0	+34 –1	+35 –1	+50 –1
6. Approximately equal incomes for all citizens	+20 –28	+25 –20	+32 –17	+22 –15	+12 –35
7. Obedience of citizens to the decisions of authorities	+22 –5	+11 –14	+32 –4	+14 –12	+8 –13
8. Nationalized industry	+29 –5	+33 –7	+28 –2	+46 –4	+37 –3
9. A large measure of independence for various experts and specialists	+30 –4	+22 –11	+24 –6	+15 –21	+14 –12
10. Strong apparatus of central power deciding all important issues	+15 –28	+12 –36	+19 –22	+18 –28	+8 –41
11. Equality of life opportunities regardless of the views or opinions held by an individual	+25 –5	+35 – 4	+19 –4	+27 –7	+42 –3
12. Conditions allowing the exercise of influence and initiative by all citizens	+23 –3	+23 –12	+18 –5	+11 –22	+32 –7
13. Fairly strongly differentiated incomes, depending on an individual's qualifications	+21 –22	+13 –40	+17 –29	+10 –50	+17 –32
14. Broad development of various forms of self-government	+9 –9	+8 –22	+10 –8	+5 –32	+15 –10
15. Limitation of freedom of action for adversaries of the political system	+5 –30	+8 –33	+6 –24	+9 –34	+3 –44
16. Absence of greater differentiation of views and opinions among citizens	+3 –24	+6 –38	+4 –16	+6 –30	+5 –40

[1]Response by high school students and their parents.
[2]Response by students at institutions of higher education.

Source: Based on information from Stefan Nowak, "Values and Attitudes of the Polish People," *Scientific American*, 245, No. 1, July 1981, 46.

governed, and economic efficiency. The first two of these values have been limited under the communist regime, but they have persisted and surfaced in various ways in the Solidarity era. Few of those who chose "freedom of speech" also chose "influence of all citizens on the way society is governed," which suggests that either they saw these attributes as expressing the same underlying idea (in which case the choice of both would be redundant) or the idea of influence was perceived as unrelated to freedom of speech. As much as 11 percent of the youth surveyed in Kielce saw "influence of all citizens on the way the society is governed" as a negative characteristic. Lesser but still not insignificant percentages of other respondents had the same view, but which citizens they would exclude from influence was not clear.

There was considerable agreement on the value of "economic efficiency," and very few thought it detrimental to a good society. The interesting aspect of this choice is its positive and negative correlation with other choices. Many of the parents in Kielce (but not in other categories) also chose "assurance of a proper standard of living for all citizens" with some frequency. Many of the youth of Warsaw, however, who chose "economic efficiency" also chose "fairly strongly differentiated incomes, depending on an individual's qualifications," and many of the parents of both Warsaw and Kielce who opted for "economic efficiency" also chose "absence of greater differentiation of views and opinions among citizens" (a feature that was more negatively than positively viewed). It may be argued that the parents of Kielce saw economic efficiency as a means to an adequate standard of living, that the youth of Warsaw saw differential payment as, among other things, a spur to economic efficiency, and that those who also chose "absence of greater differentiation of views" thought of efficiency as requiring unanimity of views. Many who chose "economic efficiency" saw as negative values "equality of opportunities regardless of social origin" and "freedom of speech," which suggests that they considered these social attributes obstacles to efficiency.

Of the remaining qualities of a good social system, only "nationalized industry" was the choice of any substantial number (28 to 46 percent) of respondents. Apparently this aspect of socialism is taken for granted and has little opposition based on a principled preference for private enterprise. Poles may, however, have misgivings about how nationalized industries have been run, and there is no strong indication that they would like to extend nationalization to agriculture.

None of the attributes that were negatively valued, that is, seen as detrimental to a good social order, were chosen by more than half the respondents in any category, although 50 percent of Kielce's youth were opposed to "fairly strongly differentiated incomes, depending on an individual's qualifications" (as were 40 percent of Warsaw's youth, 32 percent of university students, and lesser proportions of parents). Substantial numbers of respondents also opposed "approximately equal incomes for all citizens," although this was offset by similar proportions who considered equal incomes desirable. University students in particular seemed to be strongly divided—35 percent opposed equal incomes, understandable in light of the fact that such students had a good chance at filling well-paying positions. Even so, 32 percent opposed fairly strong differentiation of incomes. Nowak interprets the distribution of choices with respect to issues of income as indicating that Poles are not thoroughgoing egalitarians but that they are unwilling to accept a great range of incomes.

The other features disvalued by large proportions of all categories were "limitation of freedom of action for adversaries of the political system," "absence of greater differentiation of views and opinions among citizens," and "strong apparatus of central power deciding all important issues." These negative evaluations are consistent with the positive evaluations of "freedom of speech," "the influence of all citizens on the way the society is governed," "conditions allowing the exercise of influence and initiative by citizens," and "equality of life opportunities regardless of the views or opinions held by an individual."

Although all categories seem to value and disvalue the same characteristics, there is a real difference of degree between university students and others on matters pertaining to freedom. A greater proportion of the former than of the latter chose social patterns that make for greater freedom of views and disvalued patterns that curtail such freedoms. Only one other category—that of skilled manual workers—approached university students in their apparent commitment to free speech. Although not many respondents chose as necessary for good social order such items as "obedience of citizens to the decisions of authority," "strong apparatus of central power deciding on all important issues," and "limitation of freedom of action for adversaries of the political system," the comparatively few who did tended to opt for two or more of these attributes. The persons who value these authoritarian characteristics may represent a convinced core of party members, but it is possible that they are simply persons marked by a more generalized authoritarianism.

The orientation to private life and the apathy toward public matters noted by many Polish observers is given support by the same studies of Warsaw and Kielce parents and youth that dealt with social values. Not unexpectedly, from 92 to 97 percent of all four categories said they felt strong bonds with their families. A lesser but still high proportion—from 60 to 79 percent in the four categories noted—said they felt strong bonds with friends, close colleagues, and acquaintances. The respondents were also asked whether they felt strong ties with people who thought as they do, people of the same age-group, people of the same religion, and members of the same political organization; but such bonds were less frequently considered important. High school students (but not their parents) did assert that they felt strong bonds with people who thought as they did. The sense of strong bonds with "the Polish nation" was felt by 35 to 43 percent of the four categories of respondents. That these bonds may be even stronger is suggested by the responses of university students in Warsaw in 1958 and 1978; in both inquiries 82 percent thought that "one should risk one's life in defense of country." To risk one's life in the defense of human life was given a higher ranking, but it declined (from 94 to 89 percent) over the 20 intervening years, as did risking one's life for one's family (from 83 to 73 percent). The idea of risking one's life for remoter institutions (religion or abstract values, e.g., truth and human dignity), never higher than 73 percent, declined very sharply in the 20-year interval. Further evidence of privatization is provided by observations throughout the 1970s that Poles evinced less interest in public issues, that their attitudes toward them were marked by apathy and cynicism, and that the focus of conversation tended to be on private wants and concerns.

Independently of these surveys, Nowak and other Polish sociologists have noted a widespread tendency to consider norms of behavior that are applied in one's relations with kin and friends as being inapplicable in relation to institutions. Thus, in Nowak's words, a "decent person" may be a "useless worker," that is, he may feel no obligation to do his job; he may take something from the institution for which he is working (usually state-run) and not think of himself as a thief or be considered one by his friends. "Numerous moral compromises are practiced, excused, even approved by the majority in the name of circumstances generally recognized as higher necessity. The existence of higher necessity brings forth a remarkable softening of judgment, even of absolution."

Absolution does not apply to high party and government officials or to others at higher levels. "A normal Pole, who does not consider himself bound by moral norms in his dealings with official institutions, will judge with the utmost severity anyone high up on the institutional ladder who fails to meet the same norms." The same disjunction that applies to taking property applies to the question of truth-telling. According to Nowak the difference between what Poles will say privately and their public pronouncements is great, but they criticize what they consider the mendacity of public officials and media. He claims that Poles have been able to live with this discrepancy of moral judgment on the grounds of "higher necessity" without feeling that they have lost personal dignity by doing so.

In his article, written before the emergence of Solidarity, Nowak is explicitly critical of the disjunction between private and public morality and seems not to take account of the possibility that corruption in high places and the suppression of freedom have played some part in driving Poles to this position. What seems to have been a flowering of public truth-telling in the Solidarity era indicates that the lifting of repressive forces may alter the moral perspective of Poles.

The responses to the several surveys and observations made independently of them support Nowak's contention that there was in the 1970s a social vacuum between family and friends on the one hand and the largest entity, the nation, on the other. Intermediate groupings, such as unions, professional associations, and other entities that might represent the material or cultural interests of segments of the population, roused little loyalty and, except for patriotism, ideals that suggested a link between human beings who were not kin or friends, e.g., the willingness to risk life for human dignity, had declined. At the same time, Poles continued to hold certain social values. The frustration of ideals and aspirations had led to privatization and by the late 1970s, in Nowak's words, "to political irritation and social apathy at the same time. The combination turned out a few years later to be explosive." He sees the rise and expansion of the Solidarity movement as "[testifying] . . . to the degree of frustration, in the social vacuum of the preceding period, of the need felt by so many people to belong and to feel the support of others," In his view the free trade unions, although instruments for accomplishing certain ends, were also "communities with their own self-fulfilling emotional value." The imposition of martial law and the suppression of Solidarity and the social and political euphoria that had accompanied its emergence and growth may force Poles once again to retreat to private concerns because it is difficult to sustain enthusiasm for free public life in the face of overwhelming power. Nevertheless, the developments of Solidarity suggest that privatization may be a form of retreat rather than a fundamental feature of Polish values.

Religious Life

The great majority of Poles are Roman Catholic, and for most of them Catholicism is an essential attribute of Polishness. This is in part a consequence of the long stretch of time when, lacking an independent state and subject to Russian Orthodox and German Protestant rulers, Poles identified their national aspirations with their Roman Catholic faith. The Poles' attachment to their religion was reinforced after World War II when the new regime attempted a direct assault on it. That assault failed, and the state and the church developed a shifting and tension-filled modus vivendi. For most Poles, including many who were not devout, Roman Catholicism became an important alternative to a regime they did not like. It has not been, however, simply a focus of political identity in religious guise. For many Poles the rites and symbols of the church are charged with meaning and emotions of a more specifically religious kind.

Religious Affiliations and Institutions

Estimates vary regarding the proportion of Poles who are effectively members of the Roman Catholic Church in the sense that they are consciously Catholics, even if they attend church irregularly. Church sources indicate that in 1979 more than 93 percent had been baptized as Catholics, but a portion of those had rejected or lost the faith and no longer thought of themselves as Catholics (or as attached to any other organized religion). In the early 1980s the lowest estimate for the population at large indicated that about 80 percent were Roman Catholics, but a more common estimate was 90 percent.

By the end of World War II the death and the debilitation (in concentration camps) of priests and the destruction of churches left the Roman Catholic Church in a difficult position. During the war the seminaries had been closed, and priests (among them Karol Wojtyla, who later became Pope John Paul II) could be trained only clandestinely. At that time not quite 23 million Poles, largely Roman Catholics, were served by 9,000 to 10,000 priests. By 1980 there were nearly 20,000 priests (including almost 4,500 members of religious orders) and 80 bishops serving the 80 to 90 percent of a population of 35 million that were Roman Catholics. There was also a substantial number of nuns and monks in convents and monasteries. In 1980 nearly 6,300 students were enrolled in Poland's 46 seminaries. In analyst Jan Nowak's words, "one may claim that the Catholic Church exudes greater dynamism in Poland than in any other Catholic country in the world, not to speak of the other East European countries in the Soviet Bloc." Certainly, the difficulties in attracting potential Catholic clergy, widely noted elsewhere, do not beset the Polish church.

The episcopate, the ruling body of the Polish Roman Catholic Church, consists of the 80 bishops in Poland's 27 dioceses. Its president, called the primate of Poland, is named by the pope as archbishop of Poland's oldest see, at Gniezno, and thereby becomes primate. In principle, he was no more than first among equals in prewar Poland. But the primate in the World War II era, August Cardinal Hlond, was granted considerable administrative power by Pope Pius XII in 1945 when Poland came under communist domination, and his successor, Stefan Cardinal Wyszynski, retained and augmented that power by virtue of his personal characteristics. By the time of Wyszynski's death, he was clearly the leader of the episcopate and directly represented the pope. The position of Wyszynski's successor (Archbishop Jozef Glemp, appointed by the first pope of Polish origin, John Paul II), although in theory the same as that of his predecessor, is a little uncertain, given the pope's direct interest in and first-hand knowledge of Polish matters.

Each of Poland's 7,600 parishes serves, on the average, somewhat more than 4,000 parishioners. Many parishes have the buildings necessary to house the full range of religious activities from the Mass to religious education, but many do not, and catechism classes and other activities are held in private homes and ad hoc facilities. Parishioners have often found ways to build churches when the regime has withheld the necessary materials. The most famous example is that of Nowa Huta, a working-class industrial community built near Krakow in the 1950s. The authorities had not provided for a church, but a lay organization put steady pressure on the government until they were permitted to build one.

Less than 5 percent of the population are adherents of the dozen or so non-Roman Catholic churches in Poland. Several of them tend to be identified with the country's small ethnic minorities. For example, the largest, the Polish Autocephalous Orthodox Church, has roughly 500,000 members (less than 1.5 percent of the population) and is linked with the Byelorussian minority. Like the Russian Orthodox Church, its liturgical language is Old Church Slavonic. The next largest, having perhaps 100,000 members, is the Lutheran Church of the Augsburg Confession, identified in part with the German minority but using Polish in its services. There are a number of small groups that emerged either as a consequence of minor splits with the Roman Catholic Church, e.g., the Polish Catholic Church and the Old Catholic Church of the Mariavites, or as a result of Protestant activity after the Reformation. Such, for example, are the Polish Christian Baptist Church and the Methodist Church, the latter founded after World War I.

A number of these churches are joined in the Polish Ecumenical Council. Included are Orthodox and Lutheran churches, the Baptist and Methodist churches, the Reformed Church (Calvinist), the United Evangelical Church (a group comprising several formerly independent churches, including Pentecostalists), the Polish Catholic Church, and the Old Catholic Mariavites. The Christian Theological Academy, the state college that trains clergy for non-Roman Catholic denominations, is also part of the council. A number of small missionary groups, such as the Seventh Day Adventists, are not members. A small group of Jews are organized in the Jewish Religious Association in Poland, and there is even a residue of Muslims in Bialystok.

Polish Catholicism

Polish Catholicism has been described as emotional, traditional, and unintellectual, and Poles have been considered the most devout of European Catholics. It is particularly difficult to distinguish the religious devotion of Polish Catholics in the modern era from their attachment to the church in its sociopolitical role as a bulwark against the regime. It has been suggested that attacks on the church and on religious belief in the early postwar years tended to drive persons of marginal religious devotion closer to the church, thus countering what might have been the secularizing effect of urbanization and the spread of ordinary secular education.

Jan Szczepanski emphasizes the religious involvement of the masses, noting that in the late 1960s customs and activities in rural areas and among the less educated urban population were still permeated with religious elements and that church attendance is higher than that in Western urban societies. In his view this religious outlook was being transformed only slowly.

It is generally agreed that the church is pervasive in the life of the peasantry and that priests have higher status in the countryside than elsewhere. There is, however, some variation in the commitment of rural people to participation in religious activity. The variation, noted in a survey of a sample of villages in four different areas conducted in 1972 by political scientist Donald Pienkos, is related to differences in political participation, age, sex and education. The measures of religious involvement at that time were self-perception, participation in religious activity, e.g., attending Mass and receiving the sacraments, and responses to statements about aspects of Roman Catholic teaching. The factors that had the greatest bearing on diminished religious involvement were membership in the PZPR and the socialist youth groups. The research seemed to show that members of these groups were somewhat better educated than were their fellow villagers and, wishing to exercise political influence, saw participation in them as the sole practical avenue. In many instances the member of the PZPR were among the wealthier farmers in the community and treated their membership as an instrument to accomplish what they wished to achieve.

The scores in the sample showed slightly lower religious involvement for males than for females; younger people scored a little lower than did older ones, and the better educated, somewhat lower than the less educated. These differences were relatively small, however, and did not approach the appreciable differences between the very small numbers who were members of the PZPR and socialist youth groups and the much larger group who were either nonpolitical or members of the United Peasant Party. Even the scores of the political activists in the regime-sponsored groups were not extraordinarily low, and those of the mass of peasants in the survey supported the general perception of peasant religiousness.

Over the years data on the religious self-assessment of urban Poles have been more fragmentary and to some extent conflicting. In 1961 an opinion poll of urban dwellers indicated that 82

New churches continue to be erected to meet the needs of Poland's predominantly Roman Catholic population.
Courtesy Consulate General of Polish People's Republic, New York

percent of unskilled workers and 75 percent of skilled workers considered themselves believers. (Roman Catholic estimates tended to run higher.) A later (mid-1970s) survey of industrial workers in four new industrial centers (Pulawy, Kazimierz, Plock, and Nowa Huta) showed still higher percentages of believers. The lowest proportion identifying themselves as believers was found in Nowa Huta, but even that came to 82.4 percent; the highest, in Kazimierz, came to 93.7 percent. Portions of each group of industrial workers (from 10.6 percent in Nowa Huta to 32.8 percent in Kazimierz) declared themselves to be "deeply religious." Observations in the early 1960s indicated that working-class church attendance was higher in those communities populated by people recently arrived from the rural areas than it was in communities of workers rooted in urban centers for a generation or more. The mid-1970s data do not seem to bear out the implications of the early data that fully urbanized workers gradually lose their attachment to Roman Catholicism. The cumulative frustrations and disappointments of life in Poland may in fact be conducive to continuing adherence to the church.

Whatever the meaning of responses to surveys, the workers who have demonstrated against the government and developed the Solidarity movement have often made use of Christian symbols in their public meetings, and prayer has been a common feature of their public and private gatherings. One of Solidarity's demands was that Sunday Mass be broadcast by radio. That may be, in part, a recognition of the historic role of the church in its relation to Polish patriotism and in its specific actions vis-à-vis the regime, but it also suggests an acknowledgment of the Catholicism of most workers. Cardinal Wyszynski's moral support of Solidarity in its early days apparently meant a good deal to the workers. But even so devoted a Catholic as Lech Walesa acknowledged the different concerns of church and union and pointed out that many in Solidarity were not believers.

The commitment of ordinary white-collar workers (routine nonmanuals) to Roman Catholicism has not received systematic attention. In the 1961 survey of religious beliefs 66 percent of a category labeled "all intelligentsia" considered themselves believers. Within that category, a little more than 60 percent of those with a higher education declared themselves believers. On the assumption that the remainder of the category consisted of routine nonmanuals, it is probable that the believers among them accounted for more than the 66 percent indicated for the category as a whole. Later data are not available.

As indicated by the 1961 data, members of the educated elite are least likely to declare themselves believers. Nevertheless, more than 60 percent did so. Surveys of university students in Warsaw in 1958 and 1978 show a very slight diminution of belief. (The question was general, but most believers were presumably Roman Catholics.) In 1958 roughly 60 percent said they were believers, and another 9 percent claimed to believe strongly. In 1978 the number of those who said they believed strongly had in fact risen slightly to 10 percent, but the proportion who simply claimed belief had fallen to 54 percent. In both the earlier and later surveys the proportions that worshiped either regularly (21 percent in 1978) or irregularly (31 percent in 1978) were much smaller, but the conditions of university work and residence are rarely conducive to regular religious practice.

Members of the intelligentsia who are Catholics apparently derive considerable emotional and aesthetic satisfaction from the rites and traditions of the church, but they do not feel bound by its doctrine and practice to the same extent as peasants and workers. Acknowledging a deep faith in God, they may nevertheless be lax about religious obligations, such as attending Mass. Further, they may question the authority of the church and interpret some aspects of doctrine differently from the clergy. There is no indication of the anticlericalism that occurs among some West European Catholic intellectuals perhaps because they share with the church hierarchy and the clergy a sense of embattlement in relation to the regime. Nevertheless, some groups of Catholic intellectuals have found themselves in disagreement with the hierarchy on issues relating to government, and they have also been more likely than the hierarchy or the ordinary clergy to contemplate the philosophical basis of their faith and its relation to daily life.

Knowledgeable persons characterizing Polish Catholicism from several vantage points seem to agree on its general features. Szczepanski has remarked that it is more mystical and less intellectual than it is generally in the West. Cardinal Wyszynski, interviewed in 1969, considered the chief features of Polish Catholicism to be the Marian cult, emotionality, the emphasis on tradition, and massive displays of religious feelings. Jerzy Turowicz, active in the movement of Catholic intellectuals, has noted that Catholicism in Poland has produced few theologians or philosophers. He also has commented on its traditionalism but suggested in the early 1970s that there were signs of change.

A major focus of Polish Catholic devotion is the Virgin Mary, a pattern that has a long history. In the early eighteenth century the Polish diet (parliament) enthroned Mary as queen of Poland. The most significant locus of pilgrimage is the monastery of Jasna Gora in Czestochowa, site of the shrine of the Black Madonna (an image of the Virgin painted in black on a cypress board) which is believed to have delivered the monastery (and ultimately Poland) from the Tatars in the fifteenth century and from a Swedish onslaught in 1655. Some leaders of the Solidarity movement wear the Czestochowa icon as a badge.

Szczepanski's reference to the mystical and Wyszynski's to emotionality allude to the direct belief in God and in the intercession of Mary uncomplicated by detailed examination of the meaning of belief and ritual that is generally characteristic of the Catholicism of the Polish people. An exception is noted among Catholic intellectuals, who are more inclined to ask just what is implied by their beliefs and what their religion may demand of them in addition to the traditional requirements.

Like the Roman Catholic Church in other countries, the Polish church was affected by the changes wrought by the Second Vatican Council. Polish became the language of the liturgy with little argument. Nevertheless, in the early 1970s Turowicz, writing six years after Vatican II, concluded that "the Polish church may appear to be one of the most pre-conciliar churches." He ascribes this in good part to the precarious status of the church in Poland, which seems to require that internal disputes not be stressed for fear of weakening the church in the face of a hostile state. There is, however, according to Turowicz and some other commentators, a certain tension between some Polish lay Catholics and younger clergy on the one hand and more conservative and traditional groups in the laity, older clergy, and the hierarchy on the other. The tension does not arise with every change or proposal for change: young pilgrims from Warsaw play guitars on their way to Czestochowa, recite their own prayers, and sing their own songs, and their behavior is noted by older people but not castigated. Matters such as birth control and the celibacy of the priesthood had been raised as of the early 1970s but had not led to sharp controversy. In Turowicz's view, one of the chief issues was the extent to which laity and the lower clergy will have a voice in the church's decisions and responsibility for them. He was writing almost a decade before the rise of Solidarity, however, when the church stood almost alone as an alternative to the state. In its brief life Solidarity and the groups it generated provided other outlets for decisionmaking and responsibility. If the church again becomes the sole alternative, it may at the same time undergo internal pressure to change.

Education

Looking to its goals of industrialization and the radical restructuring of the society, the communist regime emphasized the reconstruction and expansion of the educational system when it came to power after World War II. A central concern in the regime's development of a new system was the opening of secondary and higher education to the mass of Poles who had little or no access to high schools and universities in the era between the two world wars. The stress on changing the social composition of the student body reflected the PZPR's theoretical orientation to the working class as its base. Moreover, the party was reluctant to rely for long on the remnants of the prewar gentry-based intelligentsia and the upper bourgeoisie for high-level professional and technical skills. From the perspective of most Poles, the new educational opportunities in postprimary education provided avenues to social mobility in a changing economic structure. The regime's interest in modernization and the desires of most Poles for mobility were largely complementary, although various elements in the PZPR and government and in the population have differed over the years on the school structure and curricula that would best achieve their ends.

The use of education to orient new generations to the values that the regime preferred has been more controversial. Specifically, the emphasis on the Soviet Union and on Russian language and literature has not been attractive to most Poles. Moreover, the Polish people have not cared for the teaching of Polish history from a Marxist or Russophile perspective. Opponents of official history, however, have not necessarily agreed on the way in which history should be taught in the schools.

A major obstacle to the effective teaching of any curriculum at the primary and secondary levels has been the lack of school

Icon of Our Lady of Czestochowa (the "Black Madonna"), Poland's most significant religious relic and symbol
Courtesy Reverend Edward Mroczynski, S.Ch.

buildings and other equipment. Like other social infrastructure (such as health care), education has suffered from relatively low capital investment, and schools have often been used for two and sometimes three shifts.

From the beginning the regime has stressed the training of adequate numbers of teachers, although it has not generally provided incentives in the form of good salaries to those entering the profession. Nevertheless, the body of teachers was large enough by the early 1970s to allow the government to insist that all teachers except those in kindergarten be educated beyond the secondary level. This was possible in part because the primary schools drew heavily on women who, by the mid-1970s, held as much as 90 percent of the teaching positions in the primary schools. There has been a shortage of teachers in the rural schools, however, largely because of the lack of housing. A housing allowance (or the provision of housing) has been among the benefits given teachers, but many rural communities have simply had no housing available at a level considered suitable for teachers.

The rise of the Solidarity movement in 1980 and 1981 and the subsequent imposition of martial law have affected the availability of teachers who were acceptable to the regime. Many teachers had been sympathetic to the movement or were members of it. When the school year opened in the fall of 1982, the Ministry of Education and Upbringing was forced to assign to teaching posts many persons who did not meet the standards of training established in the early 1970s.

Primary and Secondary Schools

When Poland's independence was restored after World War I, the new government decreed compulsory education for all children aged seven to 14, but the seven-year primary-school system was not established until 1932. In the last years of interwar Poland, 10 percent or more of the children did not attend school at all. A much higher percentage, mainly in the rural areas that then contained the bulk of Poland's population, received an average of four years of elementary schooling in generally inadequate schools from teachers not educated beyond the secondary level themselves. With a few exceptions secondary schools were financed privately, and few scholarships were available. The six-year secondary program was divided into a four-year gymnasium offering a broader general education and a two-year lyceum, essentially a college preparatory school. There were also a small number of vocational schools that could be entered either from the primary school or the gymnasium. The costs of attending secondary schools and the limited elementary education received by rural children and many in the smaller urban working class effectively barred all but a very small proportion of these children from high schools.

In 1945 the basic outline of the system of primary and secondary schools was established. Despite some early retreats from the goals then set out and efforts in the early and mid-1970s to change the system, the structure outlined in the immediate postwar years remained in place in the early 1980s. The fundamental component of the system has been the eight-year primary school, normally begun at the age of seven (see fig. 13). In principle, eight years of elementary education are compulsory, but many children, particularly in the rural areas, do not complete a primary education. Until 1961 the lack of facilities and teachers made it necessary to limit the primary schools to seven years, but the eight-year pattern has been in effect since that time. Preceding the primary schools are nursery schools and kindergartens, much used in a country where most women work outside the home. In part to ensure that children are accustomed to a school atmosphere before they begin formal study, attendance at senior kindergarten, i.e. in the year from age six to age seven, has been mandatory since 1977.

Beyond the primary schools are secondary schools of several sorts. Initially the general secondary schools, which provided an academic curriculum, offered four-year programs. In the late 1960s they briefly became three-year schools but reverted to the

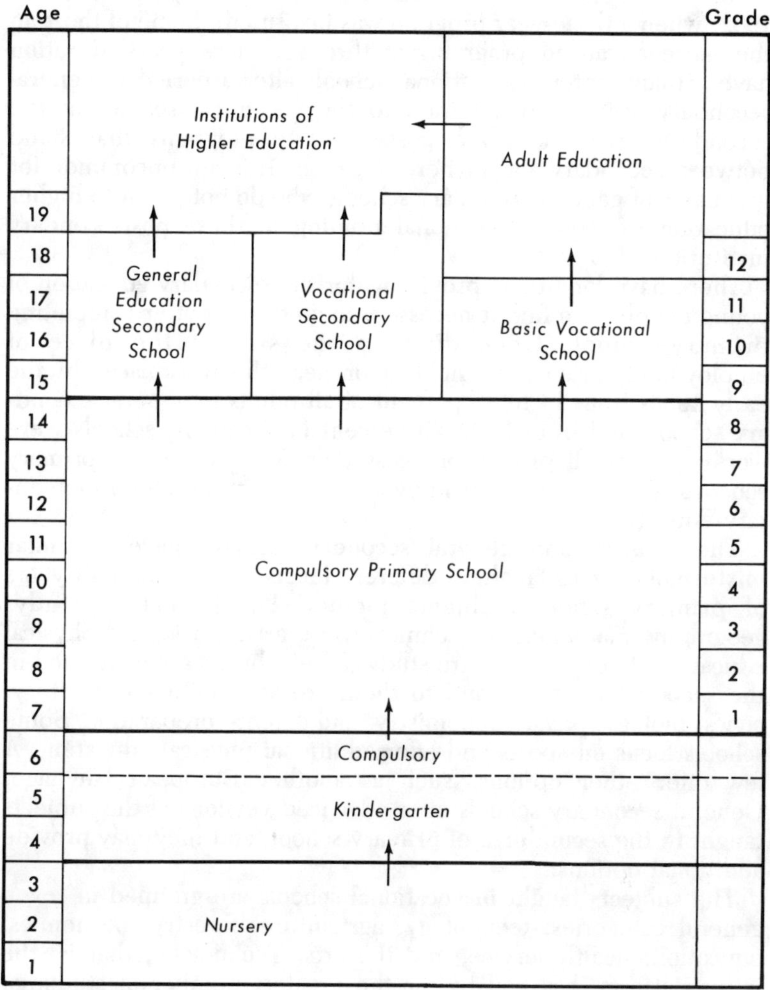

Source: Based on information from Eugene K. Keefe et al., *Area Handbook for Poland*, Washington, 1973; and *International Yearbook of Education*, XXXII, Paris, 1980, 166.

Figure 13. Structure of Educational System, 1982

four-year system in the early 1970s. Most students who complete primary schools go on to vocational schools, which offer programs of varying duration ranging from two to five years. In the early 1980s a little more than 80 percent of all students in secondary schools were attending vocational schools, and a little less than half of the vocational students were attending so-called incomplete or basic schools, i.e., those offering a two-year program (until 1982, when a three-year program was instituted). Some of those in the more advanced programs of three or more years' duration have actually entered vocational schools after a period in general secondary schools. In addition to the vocational schools at the secondary level there are postsecondary programs that stand between secondary and higher education. It is not uncommon for graduates of general secondary schools who do not go on to higher education to acquire vocational training in these postsecondary institutions.

There have long been provisions for the secondary education of young people who find it necessary to go to work after completing primary school. Depending on the size of the place of employment, classes are held at or near the workplace. In the early 1980s from 14 to 17 percent of all pupils in general secondary schools and from 17 to 20 percent in vocational schools were working. A small proportion—less than 3 percent of all primary school students—were attending classes to complete their elementary education.

The primary and general secondary schools have a similar mixture of courses taught at different levels. In the first four years of primary school, subjects include Polish, nature study, geography, mathematics, technical work, arts, music, and physical education. Except for nature study these subjects are continued in the second four years, and to them are added Russian, history, civics, biology, physics, chemistry, and defense preparation. Some schools focus on sports and offer additional physical education. A few offer other options, such as another European language. General secondary schools offer advanced versions of the subjects taught in the second half of primary school, and they may provide additional options.

The subjects taught in vocational schools are grouped in seven general categories: technology, agriculture, forestry, economics, education, health service, and the arts. Technology, that is, the industrial arts, has had by far the greatest number of students. Economics, which has averaged from one-fourth to one-third the numbers in technology, has been the second most popular program. It includes aspects of management, accounting, and related subjects designed to prepare students for middle levels in the government bureaucracy and the economy. Agriculture has been the third most popular program. The vocational schools offering courses in the remaining categories have been well below the top three programs in the numbers of students they attract. Schools of the arts offer music and dance, and their students have often begun their work in special primary schools offering programs in the same subjects.

In 1973 the regime proposed a fundamental change in the school system that was to be completed over a period of 10 years.

The established eight-year primary and two- to five-year vocational or general secondary schools were to be replaced by a uniform and mandatory 10-year program for all students. Presumably, advanced vocational or college preparatory education would have followed for a small proportion of the student population, but that was not elaborated at the time. In any case, very little progress in implementing the reform had been made by the early 1980s. As time went on, parents, teachers, and others had shown substantial opposition to the change on several grounds. They had claimed that the financial and organizational burden and the need to retrain teachers would preclude the effective functioning of the new system. Many who opposed the change also argued that reducing secondary education from four or five years to two years would substantially lower educational standards. Opposition had been voiced from the beginning but became vociferous during the Solidarity era, and the martial law government announced the definitive withdrawal of the change in July 1982, preceding the opening of the 1982–83 school year.

Another complaint voiced in the early 1980s and included in Solidarity's demands had to do with the absence of history courses in the curriculum of the basic vocational schools. Rudimentary history has been taught in the primary schools, but it has not been enough to give young entrants to the class of manual workers and low-level nonmanuals a knowledge of the history of their own country. The government has acceded to that demand and has lengthened basic vocational schooling to three years in order to accommodate the new subject matter.

Higher Education

There is a long tradition of university education in Poland reaching back to the foundation of the University of Krakow (Jagiellonian University) in 1364, the second university to be established in Central Europe. For the most part, advanced institutions founded before World War II offered programs in the liberal arts and sciences. After World War II, however, the new regime emphasized the establishment of institutions specializing in technical subjects.

In the early 1980s the polytechnics (sometimes referred to as technological universities or colleges of technology) numbered 18, and the universities (offering degrees and diplomas in the liberal arts and the pure sciences), only 10; however, the students at universities slightly outnumbered those at polytechnics. A number of disciplines were taught at specialized institutions with smaller total enrollments (see table 3, Appendix A). In addition to the state-operated higher school, the Roman Catholic Church operated and controlled the Lublin Catholic University, the only institution of its kind in communist-dominated Central and Eastern Europe. The decrease in numbers in most kinds of institutions in 1980–81 and 1981–82 after a steady rise in previous years reflected the political turmoil that strongly affected universities and other higher schools in those years.

The 91 institutions of higher education are located in many of the cities and larger towns of Poland. However, in Warsaw there are 13 such schools and 70,700 students (of the total of 423,500 in the 1981–82 school year), and in the ancient university city of Krakow, 11 higher schools (and 55,900 students in 1981–82); together they are the sites of more than 26 percent of the university-level institutions and nearly 30 percent of the students. In several of the towns the only higher institutions are essentially schools for the upgrading of teachers.

More than 30 percent of the students taking courses in higher schools attended evening and extramural or extension courses in the early 1980s, and many of them were already working. This pattern is a consequence of either the students' inability to qualify for full-time entrance immediately after being graduated from secondary school or their lack of the economic resources to study without working for an income. In principle, tuition is free, and the other costs can be met by scholarships, but such scholarships are given only to the best students who aspire to a university education or who are available from industries for education at technical schools. Employers are not always ready to grant scholarships on the grounds that students disrupt the work routine of their enterprises. Increases in costs for room and board in 1982, to which parents or students must contribute, were likely to diminish the number of students who could attend the universities and other higher institutions.

Entrance to any of the higher schools requires the passing of an examination. Typically, those who have higher scores are admitted to the higher schools in the major cities; those who do not fare so well find that they must go to institutions in provincial towns. In an effort to ensure that students from the families of manual workers and peasants would have access to higher education, the government in its early years gave priority to such students and set up special courses to prepare them for entrance to the universities and higher technical schools. These preparatory schools were abandoned in the mid-1950s. In 1965 students of manual worker or peasant origin who took entrance examinations were granted a limited number of additional points in order to enhance the likelihood that they would qualify. As of the early 1970s roughly 55 percent of all graduates of higher schools came from worker or peasant families. This did not, however, match the combined manual worker-peasant proportion of the population in that era, which ranged from 70 to 80 percent. In the late 1970s and early 1980s, although students of worker and peasant background were still granted points when they took entrance examinations, only one in roughly 80 peasant children went on to higher education. Children of working-class families were in a better position—one in 15 to 20 entered higher institutions. By contrast one in three to five of the children of the intelligentsia continued their educations beyond secondary schools.

Having entered an institution of higher learning, a student either gains a diploma indicating a level of accomplishment in a specialized field (usually after three years of study) or goes on for an additional two years and earns a master's degree. Some programs, medicine, for example, automatically require a five-year program. Beyond the master's degree for some students lies the doctorate, which may be granted after three to four years of additional study either by the universities and some of the other higher schools or by the Polish Academy of Science, a research institution.

In the late 1970s and early 1980s about half the students in schools of higher education were women. A decade earlier the proportion of women had been roughly 40 percent, and it had been a good deal less even earlier. Women were more heavily represented in some disciplines, e.g., medicine, education, and the humanities, than in others, such as technology, law, and administration. Data available for the early 1970s indicated that in the polytechnics and academies of economics, women were more likely to be found in the economics of transportation, chemistry, and textiles, but far smaller numbers were studying the technology of transportation, mechanics, electronics, and mining. Engineering was then still considered a man's profession. There have been some increases in the proportion of female students in technology since that time, but males have continued to predominate.

Education and Political Controversy

The PZPR has insisted on using the educational system as a major channel of indoctrination and has been unwilling to permit institutions of higher learning a great degree of self-governance and freedom of inquiry. This has led to an endemic conflict between the regime on the one hand and many parents, academics, and students (especially in higher institutions but also in the secondary schools) on the other hand. Even many academics who have found it convenient to join the PZPR have disliked the heavy hand of the PZPR on the universities. From time to time this conflict has erupted into public complaint and discussion. By 1980 substantial numbers of teachers at the primary and secondary levels, faculty in the higher schools, and students were prepared to join the Solidarity movement or other groups that were pressing for an expansion of the educational system. In response to complaints and demands, the PZPR seemed to give way and tentatively instituted a number of changes in 1981, but the imposition of martial law led either to the dismantling of these reforms or to the promulgation of new laws or policies that effectively left control over educational content and personnel firmly in the hands of the regime. In any case, the manifestation of overt discontent and discussion has been squelched, as have the new organizations that arose during the Solidarity era.

At the primary and secondary levels the use of history and social studies courses, e.g., civics, as instruments of indoctrination was particularly irritating to parents and students. Whatever effects these attempts at indoctrination may have had in the first decade or so of the PZPR's domination, by the 1970s and early 1980s they seemed to lead only to a kind of cynicism on the part of students. Contributing to the cynicism of secondary students was their sense that admission to the universities and other higher institutions was manipulated to benefit those willing to join officially sponsored youth groups. A related complaint, voiced not so much by students as by their parents and others in the unions that were formed as part of the Solidarity movement, was that the basic vocational schools failed to teach history to those who were soon to enter the ranks of manual workers. The demand for history courses has been met by the government, but it is questionable whether their content will be that hoped for by the Solidarity movement.

In an effort to deal with the limitations of the contents of university courses, a number of academics and other intellectuals instituted an informal entity in early 1978 called the Society for Academic Courses. The society's activities—lectures and seminars in private homes and other nonpublic sites—came to be called the "flying university" in reference to a nineteenth-century program carried on by intelligentsia in preindependence Poland. The work of the society was intended "to meet the existing demand for wider, richer and more complete knowledge . . . especially in the field of social studies and humanities." Despite the obstacles put in their way by the regime—raids, harassment, and beatings—these lectures and seminars apparently had considerable success. A good many university students had in effect been prepared to support Solidarity and form their own groups when the movement made its public appearance in 1980.

By 1981, before the imposition of martial law, various elements in the higher schools called upon the government to change the law controlling higher education, to democratize the election of rectors (the highest administrative post in a university or other higher institution), and to give centers of higher education and their components (senior and junior faculty and students) much more autonomy in matters of self-government and the organization and content of educational programs. Some changes were in fact made in 1981; for example, many rectors were democratically elected. After the imposition of martial law, however, academics who had been very active in support of Solidarity and other organizations found themselves in difficulty, independent student organizations were disbanded, and some of their leaders were interned. The official union of Polish students was reinstituted but had failed as of the end of 1982 to gain support among students, many of whom had gone into what the Poles call "internal emigration"—noncooperation with officialdom and all its works.

On September 1, 1982, the new Higher Education Law came into effect. Exactly how the new law would affect the operation of higher education could not be determined in early 1983. In some respects it appeared to be relatively moderate. For example, it called for academic qualifications rather than political attitudes to be the criteria for appointment to teaching posts. It also provided for a range of decisionmaking bodies within each university community and for the academic community as a whole. At the highest level was an elected chief council of higher learning and education. Each institution was to have a faculty senate and a student self-governing group. Before the law came into effect, however, some of the academics who were most obstreperous from the regime's point of view had been purged. That fewer were forced out than had been anticipated reflected the defense put up in their behalf by faculty senates and rectors who had been elected in the premartial law period. Gradually, however, a number of these rectors had been forced to resign or found themselves unable to continue under constant pressure from the regime. The new law, in short, came into effect after some of the more vigorous opponents of the regime had already been dealt with. Perhaps more important in the long run was the fact that the apparent autonomy of the academic community granted by the new law could be overridden by the government, which retained a veto on decisions of the chief council and of decisionmaking bodies of individual institutions.

Health

Beginning in the late 1960s and continuing into the early 1980s, physicians, workers, the intelligentsia, and others in and out of the PZPR and government have subjected Poland's health delivery and maintenance systems to substantial criticism for its manifold shortcomings. Critics have acknowledged that for the first two decades or so after World War II, the health of Poland's people improved as measured by indexes, such as the incidence of certain diseases, infant mortality, and life expectancy. That improvement was in part a consequence of the postwar availability of antibiotics, a rise in the standard of living, and an increase in the numbers of physicians and other health workers. But the rate of improvement was not as high as it might have been. Moreover, it began to level off by the early 1970s, and by the early 1980s some indexes indicated a decline in the health of the population. Obstacles to improvements in health care include a low rate of capital investment in curative facilities, consequent crowding of existing facilities, a lack of many of the tools of modern medicine, and hygienic deficiencies. The structure of the medical profession limits the availability of much-needed general practitioners, and there is marked inattention to preventive and environmental medicine. The system suffers from administrative inefficiency, and economic difficulties leave a substantial proportion of the population at a level of poverty that is not conducive to good health. A special problem, increasingly acute in Poland, is alcoholism.

In the interwar era Poland's health facilities and personnel were largely urban despite the dominantly rural character of the population. During World War II many hospitals and other health facilities were destroyed or badly damaged, and nearly 50 percent of the relatively small number of professional medical personnel (of whom half had been Jews) were lost. In the immediate postwar period the rebuilding of the health care system was largely uncoordinated and depended on local activity. By the mid-1950s a program of health insurance and centralized administration under the Ministry of Health and Social Welfare had been instituted, but the degree of coordination was only marginally improved. Local facilities reported to the ministry, and outpatient and inpatient facilities (mainly hospitals) were separately administered, leading to many inefficiencies. Above all, beginning in the Stalinist era (1947–56) and continuing for all practical purposes thereafter, health care was given little priority in the state budget. In addition, the Ministry of Health and Social Welfare was one of the weaker ministries in the government. It was assumed that health would have to wait for the growth of productive industry, and the ministry had little bargaining power.

The one aspect of the health care system that was given high priority was the education of sufficient numbers of health care workers (see table 4, Appendix A). In Poland such personnel include physicians, dentists, and pharmacists (who require a university-level education) and middle-medical workers, including nurses, laboratory technicians, X-ray technicians, midwives, dieticians, health educators, and school hygienists. In the early 1970s a program for university-level nursing training was established, but most nurses (although fully trained) do not acquire their education at medical academies where physicians, dentists, and pharmacists are trained. There are assistant nurses (roughly equivalent to the American licensed practical nurse), but their qualifications and pay are so low that their numbers have been decreasing. A second-level physician called a *feldsher* (trained on the Soviet model) provided medical care in the early postwar years when there was a dire shortage of fully trained doctors. The training of *feldshers* was terminated in the mid-1960s when the medical academies were turning out physicians in adequate numbers. By the mid-1970s their numbers had declined drastically, and their assignments changed.

The ratio of physicians to population in Poland was fairly high (18 per 10,000) in the early 1980s—nearly double that in 1960—but that of other health care personnel was somewhat lower. In particular, the ratio of dentists to population was only 4.7 per 10,000 and had not risen appreciably for a decade. The ratio of pharmacists (4.3 per 10,000) in the early 1980s had also grown very little in proportion to the population. The ratio of nurses (45 per 10,000) was more than double that in 1960. But there was still a considerable shortage, in part because of low pay (despite a sizable raise in the early 1970s) and in part because fully trained nurses often performed tasks that were done elsewhere by assistant nurses, licensed practical nurses, or hospital attendants.

In general the pay of health personnel of all kinds has tended to be low. Physicians (and to a lesser extent dentists) can legally supplement their incomes, sometimes substantially, either by working extra hours in a medical cooperative or in private practice. By and large, nurses and other health care workers cannot do so.

The Polish health service was established by law in 1948 as a social insurance program. Until 1973 entitlement to medical services for oneself and one's dependents was gained by virtue of employment in a state organization or enterprise. Others paid the health service for each use or were members of a cooperative (usually rural) that hired its own physicians and other health workers to furnish medical care to its members. Health care was also provided by medical cooperatives organized by physicians who were employed by the state but were permitted to provide service in their own clinics for fees set by the Ministry of Health and Social Welfare. State-employed physicians have been required to work a seven-hour day and may put in no more than two hours a day in the cooperative clinic, but even in so short a period and taking in state-regulated fees, they have been able to earn more than their state salaries. Laboratory tests and X-rays have been provided by the cooperative for additional fees, but prescriptions may be filled at public pharmacies for the same cost as those written at state clinics. If a patient must be hospitalized, only a state hospital is available. Roughly 7 percent of the Polish population used medical cooperatives in the mid-1970s, including an unknown number who were eligible to use the public health service. Less heavily regulated as to hours and fees but more heavily taxed are state-employed physicians who engage in private practice, which they must undertake in their own or patient's homes. Moreover, their patients must pay full price for prescriptions. Only state facilities are available if hospitalization is required. The reorganization in the early and mid-1970s of the public health system notwithstanding, medical cooperatives and private practice were permitted to continue and were still in effect in the early 1980s.

The criticisms of the late 1960s and early 1970s led to the rethinking of the goals and the organization of the public health care system. Some of the reforms formulated by the Ministry of Health and Social Welfare and others were put into effect when the government of Wladyslaw Gomulka gave way to that of Edward Gierek in 1970 after the massive strike in Gdansk in that year. (A few changes had been experimentally introduced earlier.) Among the most important of these changes was the inclusion of the peasants and their dependents in the national health insurance system. Their inclusion put a considerable burden on available facilities, however. Although peasants had made some use of the system as paying patrons, their eligibility for free treatment stretched the already sparse rural facilities and personnel.

The other major change was the reorganization of the health care system. Because medical specialization has been more prestigious than general (or family) practice, primary clinics were often staffed by specialists rather than by physicians who knew their patients well and were concerned with prevention and health maintenance rather than dealing with specific pathologies. Further, there was a separate administrative chain for outpatient and inpatient facilities, which led to a great deal of inefficiency and duplication despite the scarcity of resources. Thus, a person who had undergone a series of diagnostic procedures as an outpatient was likely to undergo the same set of procedures if transferred to a hospital.

The goals of the reorganization were to provide curative and preventive services for all; the disparities in services between urban and rural areas and between regions were to be eliminated. The family doctor at the local clinic rather than the specialist was to be the fundamental figure in health care, treating the whole individual and providing continuity of care. Such general practitioners, living in the community, were to take the initiative in preventive medicine. The relationship between community physicians and specialists and access to and use of medical technology were to be made more efficient. Further, the health service was to focus on the fight against infectious diseases (such as tuberculosis and venereal disease) and the degenerative illnesses (such as cancer and cardiovascular disease), which were all persisting or increasing problems (see table 5, Appendix A).

To achieve these goals most facilities were subordinated to a number of area health communities (*zespol opieki zdrowotnej*—ZOZ). A ZOZ was to serve from 30,000 to 150,000 persons—in many instances they served more—in an area containing either a number of rural communes and one or more towns or the whole or a part of a larger urban area. Included in a ZOZ were a number of primary care clinics (each serving from 3,000 to 6,000 persons), a general hospital, and one or more polyclinics that provided specialized services outside the hospital. Primary care has been defined to include general medicine, obstetrics, gynecology, pediatrics, and dentistry. In addition to community ZOZs there were industrial ZOZs attached to large industrial complexes, and they included industrial medicine as a part of primary care. But the dependents of workers used community ZOZs as did the workers themselves after hours.

Although the ZOZ system has continued into the 1980s, the hoped-for improvement in efficiency, completeness, and quality of health care has not materialized. The ZOZ system was planned and developed in relation to the then existing organization of civil administration consisting of 22 voivodships and several hundred counties (*powiaty*). General direction of the ZOZs was lodged at the level of the voivodship as were several kinds of special facilities, and the ZOZs and links between them were organized with reference to the counties. In 1975, however, the number of voivodships was raised to 49, and the counties were eliminated (see Regional and Local Government, ch. 4). The result was administrative confusion for the ZOZs, some of which were split among voivodships, and some uncertainty about the nature of the health services to be provided at the next level above the ZOZs in the new, much smaller voivodships. In the early 1980s there was still considerable variation in the nature of the services provided at this second level of the health care system.

Even after the complications of administrative restructuring had been smoothed over, the health service continued to perform inadequately. Clinics and hospitals remained overcrowded, medical (and to a greater extent, dental) technology and pharmaceuticals were in chronic short supply. The recruitment of health personnel remained problematic: status and income considerations still oriented physicians toward specializations that left general medicine understaffed and overtaxed; nurses and others in the health service, despite an occasional rise in salaries, did not consider themselves adequately paid and were in fact at the lower end of the wage scale.

In 1980 the Central Committee of the PZPR held a special session on health issues at which Stanislaw Kania (later party first secretary) detailed the major problems of the health service. Among the most important demands of the Gdansk strike committee and the subsequent Solidarity movement were improvements in the health service and in the working conditions and wages of its workers. The publication *Poland Today: The State of the Republic* and other material resulting from the work of the discussion group Experience and the Future were also very critical of the health service.

Poland Today also made explicit one of the chief complaints of many Poles: "Irregularities and deficiencies in health care have meant that medical treatment now requires . . . quite a bit of money, as well as connections and pull . . . If one does not bribe the nursing staff, one does not get decent attention and if one does not bribe the doctor, his care will be marginal . . . Gradually the public is being divided into two categories: those who can afford proper medical care and those who cannot." In addition to differences in health care determined by bribery, there has always been a two-tiered system based on officially determined power and status. Certain facilities and treatment have been available only to the most senior party and government officials, and they are luxurious compared to the facilities open to ordinary Poles.

Both the fairly extensive legitimate use of medical cooperatives and private practitioners on the one hand and the occurrence of bribery on the other hand were traceable in good part to the crowded conditions of public facilities—particularly the hospitals— that in turn were a consequence of the low level of capital investment in physical plant. The amount allocated to the construction of facilities has fluctuated over the years, but it has been estimated by the Committee for Health and Physical Culture of the parliament (Sejm) that only 23 percent of all general and clinical beds and 15 percent of all psychiatric beds were located in hospital buildings constructed since World War II and that 60 percent or more of all beds were located in prewar buildings. The average age of general, clinical, and psychiatric hospitals was more than 60 years in 1980–81. The heavy overuse of hospitals, leading to beds in corridors and inadequate sanitation, also generated what was said to be a high incidence of hospital-induced infection. Contributing to this problem was a shortage of disposable syringes and the consequent use of unsterile equipment.

The shortage of space, equipment, and pharmaceuticals has been ascribed by all observers to the low priority given health care by the regime, which has been reflected in the comparative lack of capital investment both in buildings and in equipment. Criticism has led to official reassessment of the situation, as it did in the late 1960s and early 1970s and again a decade later. In the early Gierek years a higher level of investment was promised, but by the mid-1970s the general economic improvement that would support such increased expenditures had not been realized, and as economic conditions worsened, actual expenditures on health care did not match planned investment. The criticisms of the late 1970s and early 1980s arose in part out of that failure but were even more vigorous than the earlier ones. The imposition of martial law in December 1981 and subsequent censorship precluded a continuation of criticism. The difficult economic situation of Poland in the early 1980s—and for the foreseeable future—probably meant that the health care system would continue to suffer from a low level of investment.

* * *

Polish sociologists have published a good deal of material on their own society in varying theoretical perspectives ranging from modified Marxism to frameworks typical of European and American social science. In the circumstances in which they have done their research and writing, the Poles have shied away from explicit description and analysis of some issues, e.g., the distribution of power, but their work is nevertheless useful. Much of it has been translated into English, and European and American social scientists have used works in Polish in the course of their own analyses. George Mink's "La Sociologie polonaise: histoire et tendances," treats the merits and limitations of Polish sociology.

A basic introduction, somewhat outdated but providing good background data, is Jan Szcsepanski's *Polish Society*, published in the United States in 1970. Walter D. Connor, in his comparative study *Socialism, Politics, and Equality*, deals with the development of social stratification in post-World War II Poland, making extensive use of Polish sources. The nature of social strata in modern Poland has been the primary focus of Polish research. Some of the results may be found in articles in such works as *Social Structure and Change: Finland and Poland Comparative Perspective*, edited by Erik Allardt and Wlodzimierz Wesolowski, and in *Class Structure and Social Mobility in Poland*, edited by Kazimierz Slomczynski and Tadeusz Krauze. The matter of relations between social strata and particularly of conflict between them has not been treated systematically but has emerged in articles dealing with Solidarity and related movements, such as Jadwiga Staniszkis' "Polish Peaceful Revolution: An Anatomy of Polarization" and "The Evolution of Forms of Working-Class Protest in Poland: Sociological Reflections on Gdansk-Szczecin Case, August 1980."

Some Polish sociologists have turned to the systematic study of values. Notable is Stefan Nowak, whose "Values and Attitudes of the Polish People," published in *Scientific American*, summarizes his research and that of his colleagues. His "A Polish Self-Portrait" (1981) deals with related matters in a more speculative and interpretative fashion. H. Malewska-Peyre's "Les Recherches sur les modes de pensée égalitaire en Pologne" furnishes an interesting analysis of research on the range of egalitarian views among various segments of the Polish population. Many aspects of Polish society and culture in the post-Solidarity era are described and given preliminary analyses in the situation and background reports published by Radio Free Europe Research.

Much of the published work on the Roman Catholic Church has focused on its political role, and there is little detailed examination of the religious significance of Catholicism for Poles of various social categories. A limited view of the religious situation can be pieced together from articles by Jan Nowak, Jerzy Turowicz, Stanislaw Staron, and Anna Kaminska. (For further information and complete citations, see Bibliography.)

Chapter 3. The Economy

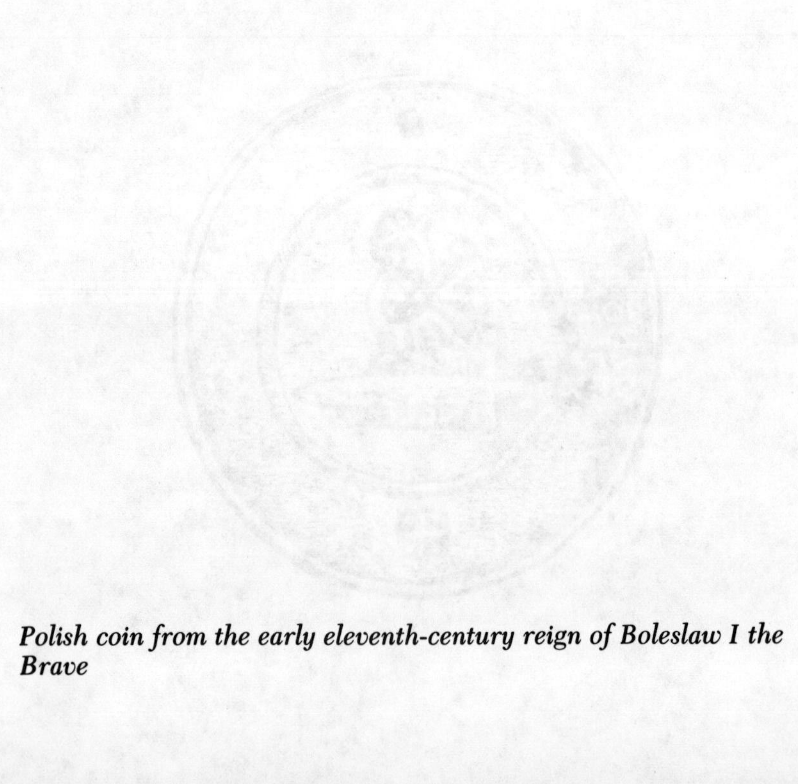

Polish coin from the early eleventh-century reign of Boleslaw I the Brave

IN 1983 THE GOVERNMENT was struggling desperately to revitalize an economy that for more than two years had been in a continuing crisis characterized by major declines in production, large-scale shortages of consumer and capital goods, and the threat of financial collapse owing to the state's inability to meet payments on an enormous foreign debt. Fundamentally, the crisis was but the latest—although the most severe—manifestation of the lack of success by the ruling communist party and the government during three decades of effort to attain, through the mechanism of centralized planning based on the Soviet model, national self-sufficiency and independence. Entering into the failure were serious basic economic misjudgements. Especially serious was the ignoring from the start of the potentially constraining effects on development of the difference between the significant, but overall moderate, resources of the Polish state and the relatively vast resources of the Soviet Union that gave the latter greater flexibility in meeting economic problems. Equally important was the failure to take into consideration the significant differences in the cultural and social outlook of the Polish people. A notable consequence of the latter was seen early in the government's inability to collectivize agriculture, an inability that remained; private farming still constituted the major part of the agricultural sector in 1983.

A persistent priority accorded the development of heavy industry beginning in the 1950s has succeeded in making Poland one of the world's 12 most industrialized nations. However, this was achieved at the expense of greatly reduced investment in agriculture and the light, consumer goods industrial sector. Serious shortages that arose from this policy resulted in major economic crises in 1956 and 1970 and demands for a reform of the planning system. Changes were made, or promised, in each instance. Within a comparatively short time after 1956, however, strong centralized control had been reestablished, and the emphasis on heavy industry continued.

The reforms of the early 1970s included some liberalization of economic activities and a new approach to development that involved greatly increased investment for the modernization of industry. Large amounts of Western machinery and technology, including more than 200 licenses to update and improve production, were imported to implement this scheme, primarily financed from Western loans that were to be repaid through export receipts. Under the new policy the economy showed considerable improvement in the first years of the decade. But by the mid-1970s a disequilibrium had developed, in some degree stemming from the effects of increases in the price of oil and of raw materials imported for processing and in part because of the necessity to import larger and larger quantities of grain. The government had generally continued to ignore the development of agriculture throughout this time. Also a factor was the slowdown in productive investment that had occurred as a substantial proportion of new Western credits were used to purchase consumer goods. Moreover, the planning bureaucracy had managed by then to reimpose the highly inflexible centralized system of direct control from the top throughout the state economic sector. The vast scale of the required coordination of economic activities for the proper functioning of the system reached a stage described by a panel of the Polish Economic Society as probably impossible to carry out even using the most advanced computers.

By the end of the 1970s shortages were appearing in all categories of goods. The situation worsened in 1980, and the following year the cumulative effects of worker actions in the Solidarity movement and a general malfunctioning of the distribution system led to a sharp decline in industrial production; the government's inability to obtain Western credits for essential imports was also contributory. Intensive efforts were undertaken by the regime to develop reforms that would make the economy workable. In 1982 new principles for the operation of state enterprises became effective, under which operating enterprises were to become autonomous, self-planning, self-financing units no longer subject to direct centralized control (which was terminated by law in February 1982). A partially free market and increases in producer prices for certain controlled items were introduced to create production incentives. Implementation of the reforms in 1982 was mixed, however, and much of the economy remained under central direction. At the beginning of 1983 a government spokesman estimated that up to three years would be required before the reforms could be working as planned. What prospects the reforms had for success could not be assessed in early 1983; in the past, other seemingly well-designed reforms had foundered because of failure to pursue them with consistency.

Planning and Management of the Economy

Since World War II, Poland has had an economy that has been largely socialized in the centrally planned, Marxist-Leninist sense of state and cooperative ownership and operation. However, socialization (in effect, nationalization) has not been achieved in a large part of the agricultural sector, nor have handicrafts and small industrial activities been brought fully into the state sector. Small private sector manufacturing—in early 1983 of undeterminable dimensions—continued to exist. Under foreign investment laws there was also the possibility for the establishment of foreign-owned businesses by individuals, particularly of Polish extraction (some 360 private companies had reportedly been established by 1982), and for joint foreign (capitalist) ventures with enterprises in the socialized sector. In all cases, stipulated restrictions limited operations to a relatively small scale, and key industries were excluded. In effect, no private or joint enterprise could participate in the basic industries sectors.

In 1945 restarting of industrial production was urgent. The opportunity for socialization was already present in the disorganized state of the economy. In the industrial sectors—manufacturing, mining, and energy—there appears to have been little opposition. Prewar independent Poland had had a tradition of state participation in the productive sectors, and most of the railroads were state owned. In the newly acquired western territories, ownership was in the hands of the defeated Germans. In 1946 the government explained that nationalization was essential for reconstruction, economic independence, and improvement of living conditions, and industrial operations (except those of small size owned by Poles), all communications facilities, and all banking, insurance, and trading enterprises were taken over. No compensation was given for those holdings belonging to Germans or individuals labeled as collaborators. Continued private ownership of enterprises not covered by the nationalization law (and for certain new enterprises) was also guaranteed. As it then appeared, the economy was to be of a mixed character, and private enterprise was to play an important subsidiary role. As Poland's communist party became more sure of its position, however, indirect methods to limit the private industrial sector were introduced, and by 1953 the sector's contribution to total production had become of comparatively minor significance (see The Sovietization of Poland, ch. 1).

In agriculture a socialized sector was established early, largely based on former government and confiscated land (see Agriculture; Structure of Agriculture, this ch.). The direct effort to socialize the remaining much larger part of agriculture failed. But indirectly, private farming was brought into the state's central planning system through the use of various mechanisms, such as the provision of seeds and fertilizers at lower prices to cooperating farmers, tax rebates on certain food deliveries to state purchasing agencies, commodity price adjustments, and other devices. Although Poland's private farmers have considered themselves to be acting independently, actually their activities have been manipulated to bring them generally into line with the state's central plan objectives.

Central planning began in late 1945 when the first state planning unit was established. The unit was headed by a socialist official rather than a communist. His handling of the national economic plan had come under strong criticism by 1948 from Polish communists because of an alleged lack of understanding and practice of Marxist economic principles. In early 1949 the unit was replaced by a new planning commission, and detailed instructions were issued by the government covering the elaboration, coordination, and supervision and control of the plan and planning process. Fundamental to the plan were the economic policies and goals set out by the country's dominant communist party, the Polish United Workers' Party (Polska Zjednoczona Partia Robotnicza—PZPR). The socialist-directed first national plan (Three-Year Plan for Reconstruction 1947–49) had concentrated on reconstruction and the raising of industrial output. Although it was also characterized by the slighting of investment in agriculture (a feature that continued in succeeding plans), there was no emphasis on restructuring industry—the main feature of the later plans.

The change in the central planning apparatus in 1949 ended the socialist concepts that had characterized the 1947–49 plan: relative decentralization, an increase in consumption during the course of the plan to provide a better standard of living parallel with development, and moderate investment to create the productive facilities needed for economic expansion. These concepts were replaced by a centralized planning system based on the Soviet model. This included state control by command directives of the socialized economy and various forms of intervention in both private farming (which according to Marxist-Leninist doctrine was then in the course of fading away) and the collectives, which were considered a temporary phase on the way to full socialization. A high rate of investment in productive capacity became an integral part of the planning process. A salient feature of the system was the arbitrary allocation of resources rather than reliance on market forces to maintain coordination and balance in the economy. In line with this predominantly Stalinist approach, the Six-Year Plan 1950–55 emphasized the development of the so-called bases of socialism: heavy industry, mining, and power. This redirection was accompanied by the setting (at Soviet insistence) of unduly high plan targets.

From its inception the scope of planning extended from broad, long-range objectives—the fundamental proportions of future economic development—down to the operation of the individual state-sector enterprise. The actual transformation of the economy was through the medium-range plan, which was drawn up from 1956 covering five-year periods. Current production goals were then established through an annual operational plan, known as the National Economic (or Socioeconomic) Plan. From the early 1950s the successive plans became more and more elaborate and detailed. The practical impossibility of balancing in advance supplies and requirements throughout the economy produced frequent inconsistencies and revisions in the annual plans. As a result, no five-year plan has ever been completed as originally projected. After both the failure of the Six-Year Plan 1950–55 to satisfy consumer needs and the riots of 1956 occasioned by economic conditions, the new government headed by Wladyslaw Gomulka initiated changes in the planning process (see The Gomulka Era, ch. 1). Attempts were made to rationalize central planning controls by giving greater freedom of action to the enterprises and by the limited introduction of market features. The rate of investment was reduced, and some shift to agriculture and consumer goods production was made. By the early 1960s, however, there was a return to the emphasis on heavy industry and to the old system of command directives. The efforts at reform failed to face the real underlying issue, i.e., the inherent inefficiency of the command system, and by the middle of the decade stagnation in the economy was mounting.

In 1970 the shortage of consumer goods had reached crisis proportions. As in 1956, popular discontent reached a bursting point and produced another political upheaval. The government of Edward Gierek, who had replaced Gomulka as party leader in December 1970, instituted a new approach to economic development based on a plan to modernize industry (see Gierek's Rise and Economic Policy, ch. 1). In 1973 major economic reforms were undertaken that included formation of the so-called large economic unit system, which was expected to increase efficiency of operations, and the tying of wage increases to net increases in the values of outputs. The large unit system was not fully implemented and by 1976 had become bogged down by regulations and restrictions imposed by the central planning apparatus and had virtually ceased to function. The inefficiency of economic operations increased, and by 1979 the national income (see Glossary) was characterized by negative growth.

The annual plan for 1980 was prepared at the end of 1979 on the basis of numerous assumptions rather than on a realistic analysis of facts. But it had become apparent that any real improvement in the economy would require extensive reforms. The developing economic crisis in 1980 had already generated broad discussions about such reforms. Prominent in these was the Polish Economic Society, which in June had established a team of over 100 experts having practical backgrounds in economic matters to formulate proposals. The rise of the labor movement Solidarnosc (Solidarity) and the labor union actions of August and September 1980 added a new dimension to the question of reform (see Solidarity, ch. 4). In September Gierek was replaced by Stanislaw Kania, who promised to institute economic stabilization and recovery measures and to develop a set of reform proposals. The society's report, published in November in the economic journal *Zycie Gospodarcze*, noted that the grass-roots level of the economy no longer wanted to work within the existing system of centrally controlled management; moreover, at the top level there was a growing feeling that the system could not be used effectively. Whereas earlier calls for reform (during the Gomulka and Gierek eras) had been primarily from economists, based on a studied analysis of economic requirements and the rational implementation of reform, the current broad call for reform was fundamentally a political demand. The opportunity to carry out reforms through the former method, which had been successfully demonstrated in the economic changes effected in Hungary in the late 1960s, no longer existed in Poland. Reforms had become an immediate political necessity, and their shape and form had to take this fact into consideration.

In September 1980 the PZPR's Political Bureau (Politburo) and the Council of State had jointly appointed the Commission for Economic Reform, comprising some 500 members. The society presented to this body a report that was highly critical of the command directive system and outlined in detail proposals for radical reforms. In January 1981 the commission issued its own *Directions of Economic Reform: A Proposal,* a considerably watered down version of the society's proposals. Strong criticism arose, including that of the society, and in July a revision was published. Conservative elements in the PZPR and the bureaucracy had sought to delay implementation of any major reform until economic stability was restored. In the face of the continuing crisis—economic and political—they were overridden, and at the PZPR Ninth Party Congress in July Prime Minister Wojciech Jaruzelski declared that corrective action would be introduced quickly.

The reforms were accepted by the government in late 1981, and a number of laws and decrees were issued that dealt with workers' self-management, activities of state enterprises, and financial management by the state enterprises. These measures were initiated in January 1982. In February 1982 a detailed law on economic planning was passed by the Sejm that defined the responsibilities and limits of the various levels of planning. At that time, laws were also enacted as part of the reforms that concerned prices, taxation, banking, and foreign trade. Under the reforms, the role of the PZPR was specified as making policy and formulating economic strategy. Party organs were neither to interfere in day-to-day management nor to assume the functions of state agencies. Specifically, self-management activities and management of enterprises were prohibited. The productive enterprise, the fundamental unit of the socialized economy, was given the right to draw up plans independently. Such plans were to set the scale and direction of operations and development in accordance with the unit's self-determined needs taking into account the targets of the central and regional plans. The enterprise was given financial responsibility. The direct control exercised by the central planning mechanism through the command directive was formally removed, and indirect instruments—prices, taxes, interest rates, and others—were introduced to influence economic activities.

Labor Force, Employment, Wages, and Prices

At the end of 1981 the country's labor force, consisting of males between the ages of 18 and 64 and females between 18 and 59, comprised more than 21.4 million people, or roughly 60 percent of the total population. Since 1960 the labor force had increased in numbers by over 5.1 million and in proportion to the population by almost 5 percent, the latter being the result of changes in the population age-group growth rates (see Population Growth and Structure, ch. 2). In 1981 roughly 16.5 million people (almost 77 percent of the labor force) were employed, compared with 12.4 million (or approximately 76 percent) in 1960. The share of those employed in the socialized economy rose substantially during the two decades, from 58 percent in 1960 to about 77 percent in 1981. This was accounted for largely by the diminution of the portion of the population engaged in agriculture.

The industrial sector, which according to Polish classification includes manufacturing, mining, power, and marine fisheries, has had the largest number of employees since the mid-1970s, when it surpassed agriculture (see table 6, Appendix A). In 1970 industry accounted for 29.3 percent of employees; construction, 7.1 percent; and agriculture and forestry, 35.5 percent (to which forestry—in Poland classified as a separate sector—contributed 1.2 percent). Together they provided 72 percent of total employment. Industrial employment had increased rapidly during the first half of the 1970s as the modernization program of the Gierek regime was implemented. But it stagnated thereafter as the economy faltered and in absolute numbers showed only a marginal gain through 1981, when the sector accounted for 31.7 percent of employment (compared with 31 percent in 1975). A significant decline occurred in agricultural employment between 1970 and 1975 as large numbers of private sector farmers left for jobs in the industrial centers, a migration that had started with the beginning of major industrialization efforts in the 1960s. The outward movement of job seekers from the rural areas declined late in the decade. After January 1978, however, a retirement pension plan for elderly private farmers resulted in a drop in agricultural employment, but this appears to have been offset to some extent by increased employment in the state agricultural sector. In 1980 and 1981 the number of agricultural workers remained relatively constant, and the sector accounted for about 26 percent of total employment in both years.

The reforms initiated in January 1982 granting autonomy in operations to socialized enterprises—accompanied by the proscription that they become profitable—had been expected to result in an overall substantial reduction in jobs as various enterprises sought to improve operational efficiency. Other factors, such as the difficulty of factories in obtaining needed materials for processing, had also been expected to have an impact on jobs. A

Council of Ministers resolution in December 1981, which officially set the level of employment in the central economic plan for 1982, envisaged during the year a decline in industrial employment of some 350,000 persons and in construction, of 150,000. A report comparing employment at the end of October 1981 and 1982 showed an employment drop during that period of 252,000 in industry, 86,000 in construction, 49,000 in transport and communications, and 18,000 in domestic trade. In July 1982 an article in the Warsaw daily *Zycie Warszawy* about the job situation at midyear declared that, in contrast with the beginning of the year when there had been a general worker fear of unemployment, the usually positive attitude toward work had obviously changed drastically. This was evidenced by the large number of requests—556,000 by the end of June—for early retirement compared with only 168,000 the previous year. (The possible relationship of the large number of retirements to the martial law situation was not discussed.) Some 477,000 of the requests, including many from experienced craftsmen, reportedly had been granted. At the same time, overall productivity in industry and construction had declined further—the third year in a row—and there was a demand for more workers to meet production objectives. Thus, instead of developing large-scale unemployment, shortages of workers to fill jobs had appeared in most socialized employment categories.

The sum and disposition of wages in the socialized economy, like other components of the state sector, were determined on an annual basis by the central planning apparatus. The amount, known as the wage fund, included a number of separate subfunds, of which the largest (constituting over 92 percent of the total from the mid-1970s to 1981) was the personal wage fund. This comprised cash payments and the value of payments in kind to employees for certain regular categories of work. Other subfunds covered payments for commission work, bonuses, certain creative activities, and so forth. The total wage fund in turn was broken down into constituent parts covering the individual sectors of the socialized economy. A separate wage fund was also calculated for the private sector economy, excluding agriculture. This was included in the overall national wage fund amount. Its estimated contribution, however, was relatively small; in 1981 it made up only 1.7 percent of the national wage fund.

The economic reforms begun in 1982 directed a change in responsibility for the wage fund of the individual enterprises. The enterprises were given authority to decide on their own the amount of remuneration for employees—based on the enterprises' own criteria—and how to pay it: as regular pay, bonuses, or other kinds of awards. These matters were no longer to be the prerogative of the central planning apparatus. By 1982 large wage increases had been granted by many firms on their own initiative.

Meanwhile, the Ministry of Labor, Wages, and Social Affairs had continued to maintain that formulation of basic wage policy should remain in its hands. This would include such powers as the establishment of maximum and minimum wage rates (the tables for which would be binding on all enterprises), the development of guidelines for wage categories, and the determination of mandatory measures to restrict the growth rate of wages. A ministry directive already in effect continued the use of the guaranteed wage system in enterprises.

The government from its central planning position had attempted to regulate wage growth and increases in the cost of living by trying to balance the purchasing power in the hands of the population with a matching supply of goods and services. During the first years of the 1971–79 period, limited success was achieved, and this was accompanied by a real increase in wages. But the situation deteriorated thereafter as economic stagnation set in and shortages brought increases in the cost of living. The rate of growth in real wages declined and at the end of the decade was lower than in 1971. As a result of pressures from the Solidarity labor movement in the latter half of 1980, wages were raised substantially. Prices were also officially increased, but inadequate supplies of goods resulted in a large and mounting surplus of buying power. In 1981 the average monthly wage again rose (by almost 25 percent), and there was an accompanying increase in the cost of living (also of 25 percent). In September prices were again raised but the increases were partly offset by the introduction of compensatory pay, the amount of which was related to wage levels.

Again in February 1982 a further large increase in prices was made in an attempt to dampen demand. Additional compensatory relief was given, but many lower income families found it necessary to use savings to make ends meet. A survey of family budgets during the first six months of 1982 by the Central Statistical Office found a considerable drop in living standards. Most affected were families in the lower income group—mainly supported by pensions—because of higher food prices that had raised expenditures to some 50 percent of income compared with under 35 percent a year earlier. In December 1982 a report to the Sejm on economic prospects for 1983 stated that additional official increases in retail food prices would be made during the year, but they were not expected to exceed 9 to 10 percent (compared with up to 400 percent in earlier increases). A rise in incomes sufficient to prevent a drop in average real wages in the socialized economy was also envisioned.

Agriculture

The agricultural sector, which in Poland encompasses the two major subsectors of crop production and livestock raising (forestry and marine fishing are not included in the agricultural sector) is characterized by socialized and private peasant farming subdivisions. Socialized farming includes three categories of farming operations: state farms, which operate like an industrial enterprise using wage labor; collectives, referred to in Poland as agricultural cooperatives; and agricultural associations, or circles, which were formed originally as private cooperative undertakings but subsequently appear to have had a large degree of state control imposed on them. Private farming plays a much more substantial role than it does in other East European communist countries. In 1983, however, agriculture provided the principal source of livelihood for less than one-quarter of the population, compared with some 60 percent before World War II. A marked decline had also taken place in its relative share of the national income—from 58 percent in 1946 to an average of about 12 percent in the late 1970s and early 1980s. However, in terms of gross national product (GNP—see Glossary) as used by Western economists, a study headed by economist Thad P. Alton determined that in 1977 agriculture had accounted for somewhat more than 25.6 percent of total GNP at factor cost. The government's concentration of investment in industrialization, especially since the 1960s, and its failure to give any sustained substantial support to private farming appear to have been main contributing factors to the dimension of the changes (see Density, Distribution, and Urbanization, ch. 2).

Agriculture has been at the heart of Poland's economic problems in the post-World War II period. During this time the prewar ability to meet food needs disappeared, and a constant deficit developed, requiring the regular importation of large quantities of foodstuffs. The expansion of the state farm system and agricultural collectives was accompanied, contrary to communist doctrine, by a decline in agricultural productivity. The reforms adopted in 1981 represented a major attempt to correct this situation in the socialized sector.

The government's agricultural policies had led many private farmers to seek additional work outside farming (in the late 1970s they were estimated to number about 1.5 million). A large proportion owned small farms of less than two hectares (in 1981 about 30 percent of all private farms were within this size), and farming had become a secondary occupation to furnish food mainly for the family. The Gierek liberalization policies of the early 1970s had benefited some private farmers, but fundamental changes had not occurred. Disillusioned private farmers found their efforts unrewarded, and by the middle of the decade the motivation to produce appears to have been seriously lessened. Socialization of all agriculture remained the underlying goal, and most of the investment in agriculture went into the state sector. However, in 1981 the government in agreements with Rural Solidarity acknowledged the importance of private farming and accepted its continuance as a permanent part of the economy (see Mass Associations and Interest Groups, ch. 4). Legal guarantees of the rights of private agricultural property were strengthened. But reports from farm areas through late 1982 indicated widespread skepticism among private farmers about the practical value of the new measures.

Land Use

In 1981 about 62 percent of Poland's land area (roughly 18.9 million hectares, or 189,100 square kilometers) was classified as agricultural land. Of this, cropland made up 77 percent (about 14.6 million hectares). Meadows and pastures (4.1 million hectares) accounted for about 21.5 percent, and orchards (276,000 hectares) made up the remaining 1.5 percent. Forests (about 8.7 million hectares) covered 28.5 percent of the country. Another some 2.8 million hectares, or roughly 9.3 percent, was occupied chiefly by man-made features (buildings, streets, roads, railroad rights of way, and a miscellany of smaller products of human activity). The largest area of cropland lay in a broad east-west zone in central Poland, the country's historical heartland. Extensive areas were also found in Silesia, where agriculture utilized large expanses of loess-enriched soils, and in the southwest. In these three regions cropland occupied from 50 percent to well over 60 percent of the land area. Meadows, usable for livestock raising, occurred in less well-drained areas in the broad river valleys and in the northeastern part of the country, where drainage was poor. Upland areas where soils cannot be farmed profitably were commonly used as pastures.

Structure of Agriculture

Small private farms have long constituted the major form of agricultural organization. At the end of 1981 they still occupied three-quarters of the country's agricultural land despite direct and indirect efforts by the government since the late 1940s to bring agriculture into the socialized sector. There was a long tradition of individual peasant ownership of agricultural land, and at independence in 1918 demand arose for redistribution of the large landed estates of the gentry, as well as land belonging to the state and church. Opposition was strong, but by 1938 desultory efforts at land reform had nonetheless expanded peasant holdings by some 734,000 new farms (see Democratic Poland, ch. 1). In 1946 the Provisional Government of National Unity provided land to peasants in the former German territory in the west and ordered distribution of land elsewhere from holdings of more than 100 hectares. These actions added another 814,000 new farms. State farms and collectives were also set up. In 1948 the government adopted a basic agricultural policy that called for full collectivization. Strong steps were taken to enforce the policy, including imposing progressive taxes on private holdings and requiring food deliveries to the state. Pressures were particularly heavy in the former German lands, where many of the new peasant farmers were very poor and inexperienced in farm management. By 1955 there were over 10,000 collectives throughout Poland. Peasant opposition to collectivization was particularly strong in the older Polish areas, and this became a major factor in the political upheaval in 1956 that led to the assumption of party and government control by Gomulka and the introduction of more liberal policies.

Subsequently, participation in the collectives was made voluntary. Peasant farmers withdrew en masse, and the number of collectives was reduced to under 2,000. Acquisition of land for the state sector continued, however, although at a greatly reduced rate. This was carried out through the State Land Fund, which had been originally established in 1944 to take over the expropriated holdings of Germans, collaborators, and individuals in certain other categories, as well as excess land taken from large estates and church holdings. Later acquisitions had been mainly through attrition involving private farms that could not be passed on because of the lack of an heir who would farm it (as required by law) and especially from 1978 through voluntary relinquishments by aged farmers in exchange for a state pension. This land was made available by the fund to the state farms and collectives, but a substantial amount was also sold or leased to private farmers for the purpose of increasing farm sizes to more economically productive units, i.e., 10 hectares and above. According to government figures the number of private farms declined between 1960 and 1981 from about 3.6 million to roughly 2.9 million and the area of private agricultural land from about 17.7 million hectares to some 14.2 million hectares. Legislation in mid-1980 included provisions for the private farmer to pass on property to an heir regardless of the latter's status and to receive a pension that was not tied to the donating of property to the state. In late 1980 it was reported that only about 10 percent of farmland was being transferred to the state compared with 20 to 25 percent earlier. There was considerable complaint among the farm population against the apparently rather widespread arbitrary takeovers of farms by local administrations based on a 1968 Ministry of Agriculture (later the Ministry of Agriculture and Food Economy) order concerning low levels of productivity. Some return of, or restitution for, property taken in earlier years was reported in mid-1982, and there was evidence that more positive action by the government to resolve cases—many of long standing—was under way. But according to a member of the Polish Academy of Science, only a small beginning had been made to an extensive and complex undertaking.

Harvest time on a small privately owned Polish farm

The state farm system was initiated in the mid-1940s when the State Land Fund allocated some 3.7 million hectares of confiscated land to the state sector for use in setting up collectives and state farms. Aside from the ideological aspect, formation of the state farms was viewed as a means of reshaping the production of crops and livestock along commercial lines. In the course of development the state farm system also became for the entire agricultural sector the major supplier of seeds—in the late 1970s state farms accounted for about 90 percent of national seed production—and an important provider of pedigreed animals for breeding. Additionally, the system has been variously used for conducting propaganda campaigns, for promoting improved agricultural practices, and for training in such practices. In mid-1981 state holdings under the Ministry of Agriculture and Food Economy numbered 2,776. Their total area was almost 4.2 million hectares, of which agricultural land accounted for nearly 3.5 million hectares. During the 1970s the number of holdings had been reduced by roughly one-half (from 5,356), chiefly through consolidation. Meanwhile, the area of agricultural land in state farms had increased by almost one-quarter. Notably, the state farm system has been unable to handle all the land in its possession, and varying amounts have been regularly leased to private farmers for cultivation.

Although there were exceptions, most farms in the state system were considered by many Polish economists and some government officials as inefficient. There also appeared to be a widespread belief that many individual farms were run to benefit first of all their managers and workers. The press over time had cited numerous examples that included state farm production costs for grain and meat that were considerably higher than those on private farms, where operations were technically far less advanced. The production cost of milk was three times higher on state farms than the state procurement price—which had led some farms to buy milk at retail to lower their own costs and then add the milk to output figures to show a successful surpassing of delivery quotas. Also reported was the use of fictitious figures on the purchase and sale of animals, paper creations that increased the apparent economic results from the farm and brought higher bonuses to the employees, and so forth. Much of the blame for this situation was attributed to the highly centralized direction of all aspects of operations that left almost no decisionmaking powers to the farm management staff, thus essentially relieving them of responsibility for their work. A significant outcome was the general ignoring of cost accounting principles by farm operators, an attitude that was abetted by the regular provision of subsidies to cover losses. In the late 1970s and early 1980s, such subsidies amounted on the average to about 20 billion zlotys (for value of the zloty—see Glossary) a year.

The worsening situation in agriculture, evident since the late 1970s in particular, had resulted in the introduction of major reforms in the state farm system effective from July 1981. The reforms were founded on the newly accepted principle that state agriculture would be treated the same as private agriculture and that its success would be judged basically by its profitability. Centralized direction from the top was abolished, and the farms were given autonomy, especially with respect to financial matters. The management and staff of each farm were to plan and organize production in a way they considered best. To aid the reform, state procurement prices for purchases from the state farms were raised substantially in April and again in July and set at the same level as for the private sector. In the government's assessment of the situation at the time, the new prices would enable the state farms to operate profitably; the efficiency of their operations would be judged by financial performance, i.e., whether they made a profit.

State influence on the process was to be indirect: through timely updating of procurement prices, changes in the prices of capital goods and materials, and tax measures. Subsidies were to be eliminated, except for certain activities of concern to agriculture as a whole, such as seed production, raising pedigreed stock, the provision of training, and the like. Investment was to be covered out of profits or, if necessary, through bank loans on which interest would be paid from gross receipts. A factor in the anticipated success of the reforms was the material interest of farm employees who would share in profits. This interest was expected

Plowing with modern equipment at state-owned Kilbacz Experimental Station near Szczecin

to be enhanced by tying the size of total remuneration to the farm's financial performance. To counter possible efforts to limit desirable expenditures—thereby increasing profits—the state expected to keep procurement prices high for products requiring larger outlays, thus permitting high profitability. Potentially profitable intensive farming was to be encouraged through incentives, such as greater depreciation allowances, favorable taxes, and the like. Certain farms that had regularly experienced losses had three years in which to reorganize and develop a profitable pattern; they would be aided during that time by bank loans that would cover their losses. If unsuccessful, they would be shut down or undergo further changes, presumably under new management.

As of early 1983, reports on the progress of the reforms were meager. A problem faced by many state farms at the beginning of the reform—the size of outstanding debts contracted earlier—appeared to have been generally resolved by partial cancellation and the establishment of more convenient repayment terms. Evaluations of the new system indicated the need to educate management staff in cost accounting concepts. It was suggested that the work incentive mechanism might be improved by changing the system of paying bonuses from the standard yearly period to one based on current work results and also by establishing a more direct relationship between wages paid and work effectiveness. There were reports of some continuing interference in farm operations by state and local administrations. There were also managers of state farms, apparently overwhelmed by the responsibilities of independent judgment, who hoped for a restoration of subsidization. Despite the shortcomings of the new system, there were some reported signs of improvement in farming operations, e.g., profit-motivated shifts in crops and from cattle raising to pig raising.

The collective held a significant but much smaller position in the state agricultural sector. After the great surge of government-enforced collectivization in the post-World War II period to 1955 and the subsequent breakup of most collectives between 1956 and 1960, the movement stagnated. This has been attributed mainly to the lack of peasant farmer interest, but another factor considered partially contributory was the government's failure to furnish adequate investment funds, which were mainly directed in the 1960s into industry. The agricultural reforms undertaken by the Gierek regime in the early 1970s (the ending of required food deliveries to the state by private farmers and termination of the progressive land tax) also tended to favor private farming. Investment subsidies for infrastructure development were also provided to collectives, but the effect on further collectivization was relatively minor.

This situation continued until the late 1970s when new agricultural policies (including the donation of land to the state in return for a pension) led to the voluntary transfer of comparatively large amounts of private farm land to the State Land Fund. Distribution of part of the donated land was then used as an incentive for the formation of new collectives. According to official data, the number of collectives rose from 1,092 in 1975 to 2,350 in 1981; the number of associated families operating collectives increased during that time from 41,000 to 130,000. In 1981 total collective holdings amounted to 857,000 hectares, of which 780,000 hectares were agricultural land (roughly 4.1 percent of the country's total). On the basis of production data, the collectives overall appeared to be functioning relatively successfully, although occasional articles in the printed media had raised questions of their real effectiveness. The collectives were also included in the agricultural reforms of 1981, but the latter were not applicable to the collectives until the beginning of 1982. Expected to act as a strong incentive for increased production was the removal of limitations on the distribution of income to collective members, which under the new regulations was henceforth to be determined by the collective itself without need for higher approval. Reports on the new independence granted in economic planning indicated the introduction of more profit-oriented operations. As in the case of the state farms, subsidies were generally terminated, although limited assistance was continued to help maintain the services of certain skilled workers, such as those engaged in housing construction. Collectives appeared relatively strong financially. Some weak, generally newly established collectives were temporarily provided with credit at concessionary rates.

The collapse of the collective movement in 1956 was followed in 1957 by government promotion of the agricultural association, or agricultural circle. The circle (encompassing one or two villages) was represented as a revival of the voluntary village agricultural cooperative organizations that had been first founded before the mid-1800s for self-help action (mainly the procurement for mutual use of farm equipment). Such organizations had persisted through the 1918–39 interwar period, when their activities had become even more widespread. The circle basically represented a new effort by government planners to modernize agricultural practices on private farms as a means to increase productivity. At the same time, the circle appears to have been seen by government and party leaders as an initial step toward collectivization, but one that would not arouse immediate farmer opposition. Its creation also appears to have been an answer of sorts to pressure from other East European states that were disturbed by the slowness of the country's progress toward collectivization.

In 1959 an incentive to join the movement was given when the purchase of tractors and combines for communal use was promised for groups organizing themselves into circles. The purchases were made through the Agricultural Development Fund, set up from part of the receipts from the obligatory food deliveries by private farmers. The equipment was used to service land belonging to individual members of the circles and also for cooperative farming ventures by the circles. However, in 1965 the tractors, combines, and other equipment were assigned to newly established service centers. The centers soon became business operations that were interested more in profitable undertakings—services for larger private holdings, collectives, and state farms and for roadbuilding and the like—than in uneconomical operations on the small and scattered holdings of private farmers. The centers lost their village roots, and the alienation increased in 1972 when the government formed the so-called cooperatives of agricultural associations from groups of the private cooperatives (circles) and the equipment service centers. There were reportedly 1,884 of these cooperatives in 1975 and 1,882 in 1981. The new organizations operated within the scope of the national plan as part of the state sector, but legal distinctions existed between them and the collectives, and they were considered more acceptable to the peasantry. The ordinary farmer, however, in contrast to his position in the circle, had little to say about their management. The 1981 agricultural reforms applied also to these cooperatives effective January 1982. Official figures showed some 35,000 circles in existence in the late 1970s, having about 2.6 million members in roughly 90 percent of the country's villages. These figures have been questioned by foreign observers, because many circles had become inactive or were merely formal bodies having little support from the peasantry.

(Official data for 1981 listed 30,000 circles and 2.2 million members.) The discontent of the private farmers and a desire for more effective representation were major factors in the widespread backing given Rural Solidarity in 1980 and 1981 (see Mass Associations and Interest Groups, ch. 4).

Crop Production

A temperate climate, moderate temperature range, and adequate amounts of rainfall permit the cultivation of most temperate-zone crops, including rye, wheat, barley, and oats (commonly referred to in Poland as the four cereals), pulses, potatoes, several major industrial crops (sugar beets, oilseeds, flax, and hemp), tobacco, and various fodder crops. Conditions are also favorable for fruits requiring dormant periods of cooler weather, particularly apples, cherries, pears, and plums. Regional variations in soils and length of growing seasons are important factors in crop distribution (see Climate; Soils, ch. 2). Among the grains, rye grows well in the light, sandy soils of the central plains, where it is sown on about 40 percent of cultivated land, and in the northern parts of the country. It is the principal market and feed grain, and its production is the largest of the four cereals (see table 7, Appendix A). Wheat is grown more widely in the southern areas, where better soils and a somewhat warmer climate favor cultivation. Oats are raised mainly on the poor soils of the northern lake region, and barley (much of it used to brew beer) is grown on better soils in the central and southeastern areas. Maize, an important grain crop in many temperate-zone countries, produces grain well only in the warmer, more sunny southern part of the country. Much of the maize crop is cut green for silage and contributes materially to fodder supplies.

Poland is the world's third largest producer of potatoes (after the Soviet Union and China), and the country's annual output has usually been almost as large as the total production of Western Europe. Potatoes are a principal staple in the rural diet and a major fodder for hogs. They are grown throughout the country, and in most areas some 10 to 30 percent of cultivated land is devoted to growing them. Legumes (peas and beans) have usually been treated by farmers as relatively minor crops because of economic considerations, including the greater amount of labor required for their cultivation and the lack of government subsidies. The chief oilseed is rape, but production in the early 1980s met only about two-thirds of a growing household and food industry demand for edible vegetable oils. Soybean production was relatively negligible. Some cultivation occurred in southern areas, but climatic conditions in Poland are generally unsuitable for the standard soybean varieties.

The most important industrial crop is the sugar beet. In addition to its use for sugar production, beet tops and pulp are also a

Owner of small private farm surveys new tire provided for his aging tractor by United States relief agency CARE.
Courtesy CARE Photo/Brian Wolff

major fodder for cattle. In 1981 the area sown to beets (470,000 hectares) was the fourth largest in Europe, but in yield per hectare Poland ranked seventeenth. Traditionally, sugar beets were grown chiefly in the western part of the country in a zone extending roughly from Gdansk southward through Bydgoszcz and Poznan to Wroclaw, but cultivation has been actively promoted in the Lublin area and southeastern Poland. In 1982 sugar was produced in 79 factories, only four of which had been built since 1945. Many plants were very old (22 of them more than 100 years old) and, although modernization had been carried out in the older plants, it was reported to be only the minimum necessary to keep the factories operational. At least three of the new plants appeared to have been constructed in locations where beets were not grown traditionally, and raw materials had to be transported to them; local cultivation had been initiated but was still not adequate in early 1983. The reason that emerged in answer to strong criticism of this situation was that the decision to locate plants in such areas had been essentially political, engineered by the local voivodship (see Glossary) administrations.

Between 1975 and 1982 beet sugar production was between 1.6 million and 1.7 million tons (the 1980 total of under 1.1 million tons resulted primarily from disastrous weather conditions). Sugar has been rationed since 1976; individuals were entitled to 1.6 kilograms a month (children and pregnant mothers, two kilograms) in early 1983. About 2 million tons of sugar were considered necessary to meet demand fully. Two or three large new factories were needed to make this possible, utilizing the existing beet output level. These plants would permit an overall reduction in the time required by the industry to process harvest from well over 100 days in the late 1970s and early 1980s to about 85 days (after which time the sugar content of the beet drops steadily). In early 1983, however, investment funds for the plants were reported as unavailable; in that respect, the Polish media pointed out that Poland between 1952 and 1979 had exported more than 60 complete sugar factories.

Grain production has not been adequate to meet the country's needs for food and livestock feed. At the beginning of the 1970s imports of grain—mainly wheat and barley—totaled about 2.5 million tons a year. The agricultural policies of the Gierek government stimulated output in the early part of the decade, but failure to provide sufficient investment funds and agricultural inputs to the private sector, as well as inadequate producer prices, resulted in a decline in output of the four cereals from an average of 19.6 million tons between 1971 and 1975 to under 17.6 million tons in the period 1976–80. Poor weather played some part in the latter decline, however. Imports for consumption and feed amounted to 3.6 million tons in 1975. They had risen to 7.1 million tons (including 2.5 million tons of maize, much of it for feed) in 1981.

The private farming sector accounted for the major proportion of crop production. Official data showed that the sector in 1981 produced 79 percent of the four cereals, 93 percent of the potatoes, and 81 percent of the sugar beets. During the year it farmed 76 percent of the land actually sown to crops. A comparison of grain yields per hectare showed that the private sector was more productive than the state sector (combined state farm, collective, and agricultural circle outputs). In the case of potatoes and sugar beets, private farms produced substantially larger quantities per hectare. Frequent references have been made in Poland to the archaic nature of peasant farming as an important cause of the shortages of farm products. A senior member of the Agricultural Academy in Warsaw, in a study that became available in 1980, refuted this, pointing out that in reality during the period 1970–79, calculated in terms of output per hectare of arable land, private farm production grew at almost the same rate as that of the state sector. At the same time, the private sector received much less investment aid, fertilizers, pesticides, use of farm equipment, and the like. The state sector, although occupying only about 25 percent of the country's arable land, had consumed almost half of total agricultural inputs in 1979. Yet, according to the study, the net final output per hectare of private farming was still some 20 percent higher than in the state sector.

Livestock

In the period 1975–80 animal production accounted (in current prices) for an average of about 45 percent of the value of overall agricultural output. The Polish diet includes a substantial quantity of meat. As personal incomes rose during the 1970s, the average annual consumption of meat increased rapidly (from 53 kilograms in 1970 to 70 kilograms in 1975). Thereafter, the rate slowed but by the beginning of the 1980s had risen to 74 kilograms. Animal numbers had increased markedly in the early 1970s, stimulated by favorable measures taken by the government to increase food supplies. Pigs, which constitute the largest animal stock—pork and pork products are the major meat items—increased in number from over 13.4 million in 1970 to 21.3 million in 1975. The number of cattle increased from 10.8 million to almost 13.3 million. Sheep, raised mainly for wool and skins, remained relatively stable in number during those years at about 3.2 million. Poultry (mainly chickens, but including considerable numbers of geese, ducks, and turkeys), whose meat became increasingly important in the 1970s, multiplied from 76.7 million to 88.8 million in the period 1970–75. The production of pigs and cattle changed little from 1975 through 1980. A campaign to increase the number of sheep during this time brought a significant rise to 4.2 million. The stagnation in the output of pigs and cattle appears to have been due to two principal factors: inadequate producer prices and the quantity of feed, which increased at a much lower rate from 1971 than the rate of animal increase.

As the decade progressed, it became necessary to import increasingly larger amounts of grains for fodder (see Foreign Trade and Foreign Debt, this ch.). This situation was worsened by the disastrously small 1980 feed crop, owing to poor weather conditions. The major results of the shortage were felt in 1981 when the number of pigs declined to 18.5 million and cattle to 11.8 million; the number of sheep dropped to 3.9 million. The poultry industry, in particular the production of broilers, experienced a drastic decline to 65.5 million. According to Polish sources, the domestic feed supply had improved in 1982, but overall animal production had further deteriorated as the result of the suspension of government-sponsored agricultural assistance to Poland by the United States and countries of the European Economic Community (EEC—also known as the Common Market) after the imposition of martial law in December 1981. Commercial poultry production, largely carried on by state farms and collectives and almost entirely dependent on imported feed (mostly maize from the United States), was said to have been devastated. Commercial production of poultry meat was down from some 505,000 tons in 1981 to an estimated 170,000 tons in 1982, and the commercial egg output dropped from 3.5 billion to 1.7 billion. The result was a considerable decline in meat and egg availability in urban areas. Most private farms had a few chickens, as did collectives and state farms, which provided meat and eggs for their own use. The poor meat situation for the nonfarm populace had resulted in the introduction of rationing in late 1980. In early 1983 most Polish individuals covered by the ration program were entitled to 2.5 kilograms of meat a month, although certain categories of workers and some others received more.

Horses are a common sight in the countryside. Numbering over 1.7 million in 1981, they were used mostly by farmers in the private sector for plowing and local hauling.

Forestry

Before the advent of cultivation, most of the area of present-day Poland was covered by forests. In early 1983, however, less than 29 percent (about 8.7 million hectares) was forested, and only a few areas contained primeval forest, the most notable being in the northeast. Deciduous trees predominated in the south, the central plains, and the lake district, whereas conifers were the main forms in the northern glacial moraine region and in the far northeast. They also occurred at the upper elevations of the higher mountains of the south. Some 82 percent of the forests (about 7.1 million hectares) were state owned—of which 6.8 million hectares were under the Ministry of Forestry and Timber Industry. The remaining 18 percent (some 1.6 million hectares) were held by individual farmers and by farming groups, either communally by village members or by agricultural collectives and circles.

Forest production met about 70 percent of domestic needs. Timber cutting in the early 1980s, however, according to the forestry minister, was exceeding replacement. Reduction of cutting by 1 million cubic meters had been effected in 1980 (to 22.3 million cubic meters). Reduction by the same amount was planned for 1981, which would have brought the cutting level down to the yearly wood increment rate, but the goal was only partially achieved because of continuing heavy pressure for forest products. An active program of reforestation and afforestation had increased the total forested area by 1.8 million hectares since World War II. The eventual goal was to increase forest cover to 30 percent of the land area, the optimum amount considered feasible in light of the country's existing economic geography pattern.

Fisheries

Fish have become a significant source of protein in the Polish diet only since World War II. The marine fishing industry, which in 1983 supplied a large part of the fish available in the domestic market, began in a very small way after World War I in operations carried on by the newly acquired fishing villages on the Baltic Sea coast. During the next two decades, however, production remained small, and most of the limited quantities of fish consumed by Poles (principally salted herring) were imported. The industry expanded slowly after World War II and remained largely confined to the Baltic, but by 1960 production had reached 168,000 tons. In the mid-1960s the government decided to give greater emphasis to fishing as a cheap source of protein, and operations were expanded to ocean fishing. A deep-sea fleet was built by the country's shipyards; in 1982 it consisted of 101 trawler-factory ships totaling more than 200,000 gross registered tons and an auxiliary fleet of 10 supply and cargo transshipment vessels.

In the early 1970s Polish deep-sea trawlers operated in the continental shelf fishing areas of the North Atlantic Ocean. Subsequently, the imposition by many maritime countries of 200-nautical-mile exclusive economic zones and limitations on catches within the zones forced extension of Polish fishing activities to other areas. By 1980 these included the west coast of Africa, the east coast of South America, and areas off Peru and Alaska in the Pacific Ocean; fishing was also to have started in seas near Australia and New Zealand during 1982 or 1983. In 1982 Poland also had fishing agreements with Canada, France, and Norway, and others were being sought on a joint operational basis with several African and South American countries. An agreement with the United States, due for renewal in April 1982, was abrogated by the United States after the imposition of martial law in Poland, and Polish vessels were prohibited from fishing in waters off the Atlantic and Pacific coasts of the United States, including Alaska. Annual catches from those areas—amounting to about 250,000 tons—usually made up about 50 percent of the deep-sea total, according to Polish sources.

The need to widen deep-sea fishing operations had greatly increased costs; distances to fishing areas had lengthened from an average of 2,700 nautical miles to almost 6,700 nautical miles. Fuel costs in particular had increased drastically; this had caused major problems in 1981 when fishing boasts were laid up—often for long periods—in foreign ports, unable to purchase oil or to have repairs made because of the Polish government's shortage of foreign exchange. This had been partly resolved by selling fish to foreign countries, but at the loss of supplies for Poland. Some oil had also been delivered to operating fishing fleets by Soviet tankers; the Soviet Union ordinarily supplied about half the marine fishing industry's total requirement, and the remainder was acquired with foreign exchange.

Fishing in the Baltic Sea, accounting for close to 25 percent of the marine catch, was carried out by a fleet of state enterprise-owned cutters and by boats belonging to fishing collectives and private fishermen. Poland established a Baltic Sea exclusive economic zone off its coast in 1977. Limitations existed, however, on the catch of certain fish (herring, lingcod, and anchovies) in this zone under a conservation agreement with the other Baltic states; a combined catch of 172,000 tons was authorized for 1982. Fishing for these species usually did not last more than four months because of their migratory nature. Such a short harvesting period had resulted in problems and wastage because of inadequate storage facilities and a chronic shortage of processing needs, such as cans, oil, seasonings, and the like. Boxes for shipping fresh fish inland were also usually insufficient. In 1982 in an effort to alleviate this situation, ten large deep-sea fish factory ships had been diverted to freeze or carry out preliminary preparation of part of the catch.

The marine fish catch (deep-sea and Baltic operations) increased substantially during the 1970s from over 451,000 tons at the beginning of the decade to 791,000 tons in 1980. In 1981, however, the total declined to 644,400, largely because of periods of inactivity by units of the deep-sea fleet, enforced by the oil shortage problems. In 1980 about 265,000 tons of dressed and processed fish were supplied to the domestic market, and another 50,000 tons were exported. About 60,000 tons of fish meal and roughly 20,000 tons of other products were also produced. The distribution of fish throughout the country was hampered by a lack of adequate refrigerated transportation and storage facilities for fresh fish; therefore, little if any was available outside the larger urban centers.

The freshwater catch—from lakes, reservoirs, rivers, and fish ponds—averaged somewhat over 26,000 tons in the late 1970s and early 1980s. The total catch was much higher than the 21,500 tons taken in 1970 but represented a considerable decline from an average of over 30,000 tons in the middle of the decade. A major part of this decline was attributed to deterioration of fish ponds, which ordinarily accounted for a good part of the total catch, because of poor maintenance and the poor condition of the fry stock. Pollution in rivers, reservoirs, and lakes was reported to be an important cause of declining catches.

Industry

In 1918 the new Polish state inherited separate industrial establishments—factories, mines, and power facilities—from the three former occupying powers. Industries had been developed to serve the political and economic aims of those powers and from the standpoint of the national interests of the Polish republic were completely uncoordinated. Included were the large textile industry in the Lodz-Lublin region of Russian Poland, as well as some iron and steel plants in the Russian territory, oil wells in Austro-Hungarian Galicia, coal mines and metal industries in that part of Upper Silesia acquired from Germany, and food processing plants in other German territory taken from West Prussia. The government sought to fit these and other scattered industrial enterprises into the general requirements of its national economy and also gradually added a few new plants, among them electrical engineering works, radio assembly facilities, and a few others. In the early 1920s this effort was adversely affected by a major economic crisis that, with the subsequent measures taken to resolve it, had a highly detrimental impact on industry (see The Pilsudski Era, ch. 1). Foreign investment funds for industrial development, sought mainly from the West, were generally unavailable; existing manufacturing enterprises remained technically inferior, and their products were unable to compete in foreign markets. This situation was further compounded by the devastating effects of the Great Depression of the early 1930s. As a result, during the years between World War I and World War II, Poland was little more than a supplier of primary and semifinished goods and materials: agricultural products, sugar, livestock, coal, and timber. In the late 1930s the relatively weak position of manufacturing was particularly evident in its employment pattern; almost 70 percent of the work force was employed by a very small number of large enterprises constituting no more than 4 percent of manufacturing operations. The remaining 30 percent of workers were widely spread in a great number of small artisanal shops and plants.

After World War II the westward shift of Poland's borders resulted in relatively small losses of industrial enterprises to the Soviet Union. A substantial new resource of manufacturing plants, mines, and some power facilities was acquired from Germany. The first few postwar years were devoted by the communist government mainly to reconstruction of existing plant, but from the 1950s industrialization, with emphasis on heavy industry, became the dominant theme in line with the socialist precept that industrialization was essential to the development of a modern state. The result was, according to official data, a growth in the contribution of industry to the national income from 26.3 percent in 1950—compared with 51.7 percent by agricultural production—to 50.4 percent in 1975 and 53.9 percent in 1980. By the late 1970s growth had slowed perceptibly as production problems multiplied because of the numerous failures to receive the planned materials and schedules for construction and equipment installation were not maintained. Also significant to the slowdown was an overall shortage of investment funds that resulted in disruptive cutbacks in expansions and new programmed projects.

The major economic crisis in 1981, accentuated by labor unrest and foreign debt factors, was accompanied by a sharp decline in industrial output and a drop in industry's share of the national income to 47.3 percent. Independent analyses by western economists in terms of GNP confirm the dominant economic position attained by industry. In a study presented to the Joint Economic Committee of the United States 97th Congress, economist Thad P. Alton estimated industry's contribution to GNP at about 39 percent in 1977.

Manufacturing

The variety of goods produced by the manufacturing sector has been greatly broadened since 1945, in part through the addition of new processes in older plants but mainly by the construction of new facilities. In 1983 the range of semifinished and finished goods derived from Poland's heavy industry included iron, steel, copper, lead, zinc (and related products), chemicals, transportation equipment (automobiles, trucks, buses, vans, smaller motorized vehicles, railroad rolling stock, aircraft, and ships), a wide variety of electrical and nonelectrical machinery and accessories, and precision equipment, including electronic, automation, and data processing equipment, computer hardware, and others. The principal light industry subsector, textiles, had been greatly enlarged through the acquisition in 1946 of German plants in Silesia and the construction of new facilities, the latter intentionally widely dispersed through the country. Lodz, however, remained the principal center, producing roughly half of the total textile output. The range of goods had been considerably increased and included many items made from artificial fibers. Varying amounts—in some cases substantial—of manufactured products were exported, and some industries were geared largely to the export market.

The iron and steel industry, considered by the government as basic to economic development, produced about 12 million tons of pig iron and 19.5 million tons of steel annually in the late 1970s and in 1980. The totals dropped to 9.4 million tons and 15.7 million tons, respectively, in 1981, reportedly in large part because of the economic crisis and consequently inadequate coal supplies. In the pre-1981 period the output of steel ranked about eighth in the world and in the Council for Mutual Economic Assistance (Comecon—see Appendix B) was second only to that of the Soviet Union. Although domestic coking coal and limestone generally met industry needs, there was still a very high dependence on imported iron ore (see Mining, this ch.). The industry comprised some 27 plants, mostly in Upper Silesia, but only two had been built since World War II; some dated from the early

Chemical plant at Police (near Szczecin) produces fertilizers.
Courtesy Consulate General of Polish People's Republic, New York

Cement plant at Rejowiec
Courtesy Consulate General of Polish People's Republic, New York

nineteenth century. The most modern facility was the Katowice Iron and Steel Plant, which started operations at the end of 1976. Built with extensive Soviet technical and material assistance, the plant had an original design capacity of 4.5 million tons of steel; it produced about 12 million tons in its first three and one-half years. Construction to double the plant's capacity to 9 million tons had been under way, but in late 1980 the effort was discontinued by the government because of the country's economic problems. The largest steel works, the Lenin Iron and Steel Plant at Nowa Huta, which turned out about 6 million tons of steel a year in the late 1970s, began operations in 1954. The plant was built under an economic agreement with the Soviet Union signed in 1948 as part of the post-World War II drive to industrialize the Polish economy.

Some modernization of older plants has been carried out. This included the Bierut Iron and Steel Plant at Czestochowa, which reopened in 1952 after extensive expansion; the plant had a reported output of about 1 million tons a year. Among others was the conversion of a plant in the Warsaw area to produce high-grade special steels. Most of the older plants, however, were characterized by low productivity and poor working conditions. Moreover, their products were not always up to standard. There was also considerable complaint concerning the adverse effect on the environment of their operations, the pollutant emission levels being much greater than for the new plants.

In 1982 the chemical industry, which accounted for about 10 percent of the value to total industrial output, was one of the best developed in Comecon. The industry was based largely on domestic raw materials, and large-scale production was concentrated on less complex chemicals, including sulfuric and nitric acids, sodium hydroxide, calcined soda, carbon disulfide, carbide, and fertilizers. Also produced were plastics and synthetic fibers, but these subsectors were relatively weak in comparison with the basic chemicals. Much of the industry was in the southern part of the country, particularly in Upper Silesia, where raw materials were abundant. The principal petrochemical facility, however, was at Plock in the central area on the oil pipeline from the Soviet Union. A major plant for phosphatic fertilizers, which have been manufactured in considerable part using imported materials, was situated at the port of Szczecin. Although some important facilities were acquired from Germany in 1946, e.g., a plant at Oswiecim in Upper Silesia producing chemicals from coal, the industry's main development was based on large-scale investment by the government during the period 1946–75. Additional funds were programmed, but Polish sources have reported that expansion slowed measurably in the late 1970s when long delays occurred in construction because of underfulfillment of contracts to build or add new facilities. Examples cited in early 1981 included an epoxy resin plant (two years behind schedule), a plant to provide semifinished materials for rayon (21 months behind), a styrofoam unit (over four years late), and various other cases. The loss of production was expected to have a detrimental effect on the foreign trade balance because of the continued need to import these materials.

The motor vehicle industry has developed significantly since the early 1970s. Small numbers of passenger cars (Fiats) and trucks had been assembled at plants near Warsaw before World War II, but these facilities were completely destroyed during the war. The production of passenger cars in small numbers began again in 1951 in the Warsaw area. The government had sought to renew its prewar license with Fiat, but reportedly at Soviet insistence Poland began assembling a Soviet model that was locally labeled the Warszawa. Several years later the Polish-designed Syrena was added (later models were still being produced in early 1983). In the mid-1960s the state factory began assembling the Polski Fiat under license, replacing the Warszawa model. In 1972 the government reached an agreement with Fiat to produce also a smaller, economy "people's" car, the parts for which were manufactured at Bielsko Biala in Upper Silesia. In 1978 the Warsaw plant also began manufacturing a new standard-size Polish-designed car, the Polonez. The production of all models surpassed the 300,000 mark in the late 1970s and reached a high of 350,000 in 1980. Almost half of the annual production was exported, and a further substantial number of vehicles were allocated to a priority list of users, leaving in 1980 roughly 100,000 vehicles for the general public (see Roads and Road Transport, this ch.). The industry also produced a variety of trucks, vans, buses, and special vehicles, such as tank trucks, ambulances, and the like; considerable numbers of them were exported. A majority of these exports went to the Soviet Union and other Comecon countries.

Shipbuilding, which began in 1938, has become a major Polish industry. The principal shipyards at Gdansk, Gdynia, and Szczecin produced a diversified range of vessels, from general and bulk cargo ships to roll-on-roll-off vessels, container and semicontainer ships, tankers, and specialized ships (refrigerated, etc.). The Northern Shipyard, also located at Gdansk, specialized in the construction of large fishing vessels, and a shipyard at Ustka produced small fishing boats. Although the industry has continued to build ships for the domestic merchant marine and fishing fleet, its growth has been based on sales to foreign buyers . Until the late 1960s the main purchaser was the Soviet Union, but during the early 1970s aggressive marketing had greatly expanded the list of foreign clients. However, Soviet orders still constituted a significant backlog of work. Figures available for 1979 showed deliveries of 21 ships totaling almost 218,000 gross registered tons to non-Comecon countries and 22 ships of 182,500 overall gross registered tons to the Soviet Union. The vessels for non-Comecon buyers in that year were registered in Brazil, Britain, Burma, Ecuador, France, India, Iraq, Norway, and the Federal Republic of Germany (West Germany) At the beginning of the 1980s Polish-built vessels were sailing under some 25 to 30 different foreign flags. The industry reached a production peak of over 1 million deadweight tons in 1975, double the output of 1970. Construction declined thereafter as orders decreased worldwide and new competitors appeared, and in 1979 the ships built totaled only 601,000 deadweight tons. The growing economic crisis in 1980 had a serious impact on the industry, particularly because of the failure of domestic suppliers to make planned deliveries. This was further affected by labor unrest and lack of foreign exchange for imported materials. Productivity also dropped, and only 392,000 deadweight tons were reported to have been completed in 1980 and 322,000 deadweight tons in 1981. In 1982 there was also a shortage of people willing to work in the shipyards. During the year, 1,300 workers took early retirement at the main Lenin Shipyard in Gdansk, as did 1,000 more at both the Gdynia and the Szczecin shipyards.

Light aircraft have been manufactured since 1960 based mainly on Soviet models and containing a substantial proportion of materials and semifinished parts from the Soviet Union. In 1982 some airplanes and parts were also being made under Western licenses, but imports from the hard currency countries were relatively negligible. The aircraft ranged from light multipurpose airplanes for local air services (passenger, cargo, executive, and other) to airplanes for agricultural use (pesticide and fertilizer application) and trainers. Among the latter was a jet trainer manufactured for the military. Helicopters designed for a wide variety of uses have also been turned out since 1965. Available data indicated that well over 10,000 airplanes and more than 5,000 helicopters had been manufactured since production began in the 1960s. An unknown number of both versions had been exported. Exports also included engines of various kinds, of which more than 40,000 were reported to have been manufactured by the end of 1981. Planes were fabricated at Warsaw and Mielec (Rzeszow voivodship), helicopters at Swidnik, near Lublin.

Mining

Poland has a variety of minerals, including a number that have major economic importance. Among the latter is coal, which is found in extensive deposits and mined on a large scale. Petroleum and natural gas are also available but have made a much smaller contribution to the economy (see Energy Sources and Use, this ch.; table 8, Appendix A). The metallic minerals of major importance are copper, lead, and zinc. Copper has been mined for many years in Lower Silesia, but in comparatively small amounts

Norwegian vessel in dry dock for repairs at Komuna Paryskie (Paris Commune) Shipyard, Gdynia
Courtesy Consulate General of Polish People's Republic, New York

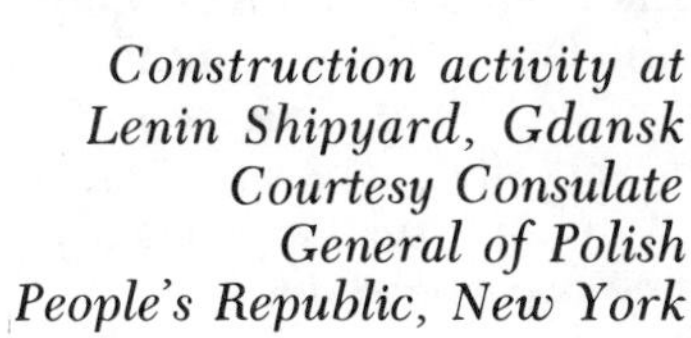

Construction activity at Lenin Shipyard, Gdansk
Courtesy Consulate General of Polish People's Republic, New York

until 1957, when one of the largest known deposits in Europe was discovered in the general area of the earlier workings. Mines were opened at the new location in 1963 and 1968 and a third one in 1974. To process the ores, an existing copper mill at Legnica was expanded, and a second facility was built at Glogow. Ore output, which had been 1.8 million tons in 1960, increased to 6.6 million tons in 1970 and quadrupled further to 26.6 million tons in 1980. The production of electrolytic copper rose from 21,700 tons in 1960 to 357,000 tons in 1980, and Poland became a substantial exporter of the metal. In 1981, however, ore production dropped to 22.8 million tons and electrolytic copper to 327,000 tons. The decline in mining output was attributed principally to the introduction of a five-day workweek during that year (rather than one of seven days) as the result of Solidarity union action.

Poland's deposits of zinc and lead (the two ores occur in association) are ranked about fifth in size in the world. They lie generally along the northern edge of the Upper Silesian coalfields; the main operating mines are in the vicinity of Olkosz. The estimated metal content of zinc ore mined in the late 1970s was about 190,000 tons a year, and that of lead was about 64,000 tons. Total refined metal in both cases was roughly 20 to 25 percent greater because of the inclusion of varying quantities of secondary (resmelted) metal.

Other metallic minerals include iron ore, of which deposits of considerable size are found in several places. The iron content is only moderate, and the ores are enriched before use. The main area mined is in Czestochowa voivodship, where output accounts for about four-fifths of domestic production. Until the late 1970s, when output dropped precipitously, the Czestochowa mines had usually met about 10 percent of total domestic demand; the remainder was imported, mostly from the Soviet Union, Sweden, and Brazil. In the early 1980s preparatory action was reported under way to exploit a deposit of high-grade magnetite discovered during the 1970s in Suwalki voivodship in northeastern Poland. Financing for this development was in part based on foreign loans. The ore was said to contain considerable amounts of titanium and vanadium. There is bauxite in Poland, but aluminum is produced mostly from imported alumina. In the late 1970s aluminum output averaged about 100,000 tons a year, including some reprocessed metal. Small amounts of cadmium and silver are also produced, the former as a by-product of zinc smelting, the latter mainly as a by-product of copper, lead, and zinc ore processing.

Nonmetallic minerals include barite, gypsum, limestone, rock salt, and sulfur. Economically exploitable glass sands are found in several parts of the country, and clays are widespread, ranging in quality from those usable mainly for bricks to those used in the manufacture of ceramics. From the standpoint of export earnings, sulfur has been the most important nonmetallic mineral. Large deposits were first discovered in 1953 near the confluence of the Vistula and San rivers in Tarnobrzeg voivodship. Strip-mining began in 1958, but subsequently two additional mines went into operation (the first in 1969), extracting sulfur through an underground hot water smelting process. Almost 56 million tons of ore had been mined in all by the end of 1981, of which almost 80 percent was exported, either in the form of ore or as processed sulfuric acid. Poland has long been among the world's top producers of native sulfur and at the beginning of the 1980s also ranked about seventh in production of sulfuric acid, a substantial part of which is shipped to the Soviet Union. According to Polish sources, there appeared to be some question whether the annual production of over 5 million tons of sulfur in 1979 and 1980 and about 4.8 million tons in 1981 could be maintained beyond the middle of the decade unless the long-planned investment in existing mines and the opening of several new ones were carried out.

Vast deposits of rock salt underlie various parts of Poland, containing reserves estimated as high as 43.5 billion tons. Salt was an active trade item in the area during the Middle Ages. The first regular mines appear to have been opened in the thirteenth century in the area of Wieliczka and Bochnia, near Krakow in southern Poland. One mine in the Wieliczka area, which started producing in the fourteenth century, has remained in operation, although in the early 1980s it was more a tourist attraction. The greater part of the present-day salt output comes from mines exploiting a large deposit that runs roughly from Lodz in central Poland northwestward to Inowroclaw. Salt is recovered both through standard mining practices and by dissolving it below ground for extraction as brine with pumps. In the late 1970s and early 1980s annual production averaged about 4.3 to 4.4 million tons, of which approximately one-third was in the form of rock salt.

Energy Sources and Use

Poland's predominant domestic energy resource in 1982 was coal, consisting of both bituminous (locally know as hard coal) and lignite (brown coal) varieties. Deposits were large, and mined coal supplied an estimated 75 to 80 percent of the total energy used annually. A substantial amount of coal was used to generate electricity. Known petroleum resources are small, and large-scale imports have been necessary to meet requirements, mainly for a steadily growing motor vehicle fleet. Together domestic and imported petroleum and petroleum products furnish about 15 percent of the country's total energy requirement. Natural gas exists in moderately large quantity, but domestic production has failed to satisfy demand, and annual imports are large. In the early 1980s the combined supply accounted for roughly 8 percent of all energy used. Peat occurs rather extensively, especially in the more northerly area of the country, and is used locally as fuel by the peasantry. Wood is widely used for fuel, but only in very limited quantities. In 1982 neither peat nor wood was significant as a source of energy, accounting together for an estimated 1 to 2 percent of total annual energy consumption. The country has some hydroelectric potential but, according to government sources, economically exploitable hydropower resources are comparatively small. In the late 1970s hydroelectricity provided less than 1 percent of the overall energy supply. Uranium ores, the source of fuel for nuclear power generation, had not been reported in useful amounts as of early 1983.

Coal

Poland's coal resources are among the world's largest. In a report in the late 1970s to the international World Coal Study in which Poland was a participant, the country's documented minable reserves (at a depth of 1,000 meters or less) of hard coal were placed at 58.5 billion tons, and the total had risen to 62 billion tons in 1980. Prospective reserves (to a depth of 1,500 meters), totaled more than an additional 130 billion tons. Brown coal reserves amounted to 8.8 billion tons and prospective reserves to 7.6 billion tons. About three-quarters of the minable hard coal was in Silesia in southwestern Poland and the remainder in the Lublin region in eastern Poland. Major brown coal deposits were located in Zielona Gora voivodship in western Poland and in areas of Konin and Piotrkow voivodships in the central part of the country.

The first record of hard-coal mining in Poland dates from the 1300s, when a mine was open in the area of Walbrzych in Lower Silesia. Mining still continued in this basin in 1982, but production was relatively small, and reserves amounted to less than 1 percent of the country's total. Coal seams in the basin are greatly folded, difficult to work, and occur in a narrow zone only. In 1751 mining began in the Upper Silesian coalfields of which an area of some 4,500 square kilometers lies in present-day Poland. Seams around the rim of the basin are easily minable, and moderate folding of strata within the basin has brought economically even more valuable coal to within working distance of the surface. At the beginning of the 1980s Upper Silesia produced about 97 percent of the country's total hard-coal output. Exploitation of hard coal in the Lublin basin was not undertaken until the mid-1970s, when it was considered essential to raise coal production to meet planned industrial expansion and export goals. Coal seams in eastern and southeastern Poland were estimated to cover about 14,000 square kilometers and the Lublin coal basin itself covered about 8,000 square kilometers. A pilot mine started in Lublin in 1975 was reportedly to produce its first coal in 1981.

Hard-coal output grew steadily after World War II from 44.3

million tons in 1946 to a peak of 201 million tons in 1979. In the late 1970s about 35 to 36 percent of the total was officially allocated for industrial purposes, some 28 or 29 percent for the production of electricity by power plants (most heavy industry operated on power from those plants), and more than 20 percent was exported. About 3 percent was used for fuel by urban areas and another 12 percent by rural communities. During the first half of the 1970s the supply had been generally adequate, and user purchases had not been limited. In 1976 coal availability was found considerably short of needs; as a result, rationing was introduced, and a conservation campaign was begun. Overtime work by miners was widely employed (including work on Sundays and holidays) to meet the requirements for coal demanded by the national economic plan. The demand continued to rise, and the coal mining industry was expected to meet the established goals. Through 1979 regular yearly increases were reported, but Polish domestic sources have questioned the accuracy of the total as well as the coal (calorific) content of the reported amounts, charging the managers, in an effort to meet fixed targets, had counted impurities in their production figures. Major complaints involving production and the fulfilling of plan targets were that mining was conducted without regard for worker safety and that coal was extracted in a highly wasteful way, in many instances utilizing only the easily worked coal faces and leaving substantial quantities of minable coal that would be uneconomical to mine later.

For 1980 the national plan called for 207 million tons of hard coal to be produced. Actual production was 193 million tons, and in 1981 the total dropped to 163 million tons. Various reasons were given for the decline, the government maintaining that the principal causes were strikes in the coalfields and the reductions in work time that had been forced on the industry by the Solidarity movement (see Popular Political Expression, ch. 4). Economists and analysts in Poland, however, also cite as major causes unrealistic production goals, incompetent management, and poorly used investment funds. In late 1980 the minister of mining and power industry pointed out that the government's long-range coal production increase plan, calling for an annual output of 300 million tons by the year 2000, was unrealistic and attainable only by the reckless exploitation of labor and the country's natural resources. Reasonable output, even under improved conditions, was estimated at about 195 million to 200 million tons a year. Implicit for the future health of the economy was the need to adjust development to the domestic potential or to secure energy from other sources to meet expansionary needs. After the imposition of martial law in December 1981 the coal mines were "militarized," and a four-shift, six-day workweek was enforced. Coal production in 1982 reportedly totaled 189.3 million tons.

In 1982 brown coal was used primarily to generate electric

power at thermal stations located at the deposit sites. The greatest production was from the Turoszow basin in western Poland, an area acquired from Germany after World War II when the boundary of Polish administration was moved to the Nysa (Neisse) and Odra (Oder) rivers. These deposits had not been developed to any extent by the Germans and in 1937 produced only 20,000 tons. Large-scale mining in the area under Polish rule began in 1956. In the meantime, development of a major deposit in Konin voivodship was started, and by 1960 the country's total brown coal production had risen to over 9 million tons. It continued to expand, reaching almost 33 million tons in 1970 and 41 million tons in 1978. About 60 percent of the output came from the Turoszow basin. In the early 1980s overall production had dropped (also affected by labor unrest), and in 1981 output was only 36 million tons. A third major brown coal deposit, discovered in 1960, was located near Belchatow in Piotrkow voivodship. During the mid-1970s work began in the area on the development of an industrial complex based on power to be generated at the deposit. All brown coal has been strip-mined. The overburden at Belchatow averaged about 140 meters in thickness, and its removal apparently was still in process in 1982.

Petroleum and Natural Gas

In 1982 the principal known deposits of petroleum were located in southeastern Poland in the Carpathian Mountains and their foothills, an area lying roughly between Nowy Sacz and the Soviet border. (The eastern part of the oil fields in the region had been taken by the Soviet Union in the transfer of territory after World War II.) A second, considerably less important area of deposits was situated in the western part of the country in the lowlands generally south-southwest of Poznan. Petroleum production, according to official statistics, had risen from 194,000 tons in 1960 to 553,000 tons in 1975. Output declined in the late 1970s, however, and in the early 1980s averaged under 350,000 tons annually. Shortages of spare parts and equipment were given as partial explanation for the decline, but a major factor appeared to be the failure to discover new reserves to replace those being exhausted. Exploration was reported to be under way in the Carpathians and the lowlands and also in the Pomorze region of northern Poland, but significant finds had not been reported through early 1983.

At the beginning of the 1970s domestic crude oil accounted for only about 5 percent of the total amount available to the economy. Imports of some 7 million tons in 1970 increased to about 17 million tons in the late 1970s, and the share of domestic petroleum declined to some 2 to 3 percent. Through 1980 roughly four-fifths of the imports were from the Soviet Union and the

Striking coal miners in the Katowice area, November 1981
Courtesy Committee in Support of Solidarity, New York

remaining one-fifth mostly from Middle East oil-producing states (mainly Iran, Iraq, and Libya). Refined petroleum products and synthetic fuels were also imported (2.4 million tons in 1970 and 4.4 million tons in 1980), mostly from the Soviet Union. In 1981 crude oil imports dropped precipitously to 13.5 million tons (all from the Soviet Union) as Poland's balance of payments position with the hard currency countries deteriorated seriously, making it virtually impossible to obtain supplies elsewhere (see Foreign Trade and Foreign Debt, this ch.). Official statistics also reported imports of over 3.9 million tons of refined products during 1981, although early that year the annual Soviet-Polish contract for petroleum deliveries by the Soviet Union had provided for 2.9 million tons. Whether the total had been increased, additional supplies had been obtained from other sources, or a reporting error had occurred that still awaited clarification at the beginning of 1983 was uncertain.

Soviet oil is delivered to Poland through the Druzhba (Friendship) pipeline, a joint Comecon project. The pipeline, completed in 1966, enters Poland near Brest and continues to the German Democratic Republic (East Germany). The major Polish offtake point is at Plock, northwest of Warsaw, where a large refinery was completed in the 1960s. A second major refinery built to process oil from the Middle East went into operation in the early 1970s at a special oil port near Gdansk. The great increase in world oil prices that began in 1973 had not been anticipated, however, and the refinery reportedly has generally operated below capacity. Seven or eight other small refineries in the area of the oilfields process domestic petroleum. Overall refinery output rose from 7.5 million tons in 1970 to a peak of almost 17 million tons in 1978.

The largest known natural gas deposits in 1982 were in the Carpathian foothills (about two-thirds of all reserves), and most of the remainder was in the lowlands region. Domestic production has accounted for a considerably larger share of total consumption than has oil. In 1970 domestic output amounted to almost 5.2 billion cubic meters (84 percent), as against 1 billion imported via pipeline from the Soviet Union. During the decade, imports gradually increased and in 1981 totaled about 5.3 billion cubic meters, but domestic production of 6.2 billion cubic meters still accounted for the greater share (54 percent). Active exploration has occurred in the same areas as for oil, but lack of equipment had hampered the program in 1982.

Electricity

Electric power generation increased tremendously in the post-World War II period from 5.2 billion kilowatt-hours in 1946 to 121.9 billion in 1980; the total dropped to 115 billion kilowatt-hours in 1981 largely as a result of coal shortages and lower demand because of industrial unrest that occurred during the year. The country's installed generating capacity during this same period rose from 2,350 megawatts to 25,292 megawatts and increased further in 1981 to 25,523 megawatts. About 70 percent of the power was generated by thermal plants using hard coal and roughly 27 percent by brown-coal-fired plants; the remaining 3 percent was produced by hydroelectric stations. The amount of electricity produced utilizing oil and gas was negligible.

At the end of 1981 there were 57 thermal plants generating power for general use and 230 others that produced electricity for specific industrial enterprises. The largest plants (some using hard coal, other brown coal) had installed capacities ranging from 1,600 megawatts to 2,600 megawatts. Two additional large plants designed to use hard coal from Upper Silesia were under construction in that region in 1982. One was almost completed, and the other was to have its last units installed near the end of the decade. Existing hard-coal plants, some expansions, and the two new plants reportedly constituted the maximum utilizable capacity based on the amount of coal available from Upper Silesia in the near future. Further plans for expansion of hard-coal-fired generators were based on development of the Lublin coal basin. For the 1980s a new emphasis was being placed on the establishment of power plants at the sites of major brown coal deposits. Construction was reportedly under way in 1982 on a large plant at the new Belchatow coalfield. If plans are eventually implemented as projected in 1982, this will be Poland's largest power plant, having an installed capacity of 4,320 megawatts. Work had also been started on a plant of 720 megawatts near the Turow brown coal mine in western Poland, but questions of when adequate fuel would be available had apparently delayed progress on it. One of the features of thermal generating plants located near large urban areas was the associated production of hot water and steam for heating residential housing blocks; steam was also produced for local industry. In Warsaw, for instance, over 85 percent of officially constructed housing and the city's industrial enterprises were thus served.

At the end of 1981 there were 117 hydroelectric plants in the country, but with the exception of a handful, all were quite small. Total output at the beginning of the 1980s was about 3 billion kilowatt-hours annually. The larger plants included one of 144 megawatts on the San River in southeast Poland and one of 160 megawatts on the Vistula River near Wloclawek. A third plant, of 150-megawatt capacity at Zydowo in Koszalin voivodship, utilized the difference in level between two lakes and the pump storage of water to generate power. Another plant (500-megawatt capacity) using the pump storage principle was reported completed, and one of 68 megawatts was approaching completion in late 1982.

Electricity is distributed through a national grid. Poland is also a member of the Comecon Unified Power Grid and is linked by a number of 220-volt and six (in 1981) 400-volt lines with neighboring countries. The first interstate connection in the system was between Poland and East Germany in 1960, followed shortly by a connection with Czechoslovakia. The dispatching board for the interstate grid is in Prague.

Throughout the 1970s socialized industry (including construction) was the largest user of electricity. Consumption, however, declined during the decade from over 68 percent in 1970 to under 63 percent in 1980. In 1981, largely affected by labor unrest and reduced operations, it dropped further to under 61 percent of total consumption. Households accounted for the next largest amount used—8.8 percent in 1980 as against 6.4 percent in 1970. Use by communal services, of which somewhat less than half was for urban transport and street lighting, stood at 2.8 percent in 1980, little changed from a decade earlier. Power for railroad traction (at 3.4 percent in 1980) also showed little change. Consumption by agriculture almost doubled, from 2.3 percent in 1970 to 4.4. percent in 1980, but the availability of electricity in rural areas remained very limited, and a large number of villages were not connected to power sources. Losses, which averaged about 9 percent, and unspecified uses amounting to about 8 percent accounted for the remaining electricity consumed.

The electric power supply appears to have been generally adequate until the mid-1970s, when rapidly growing industrial requirements began exceeding output. After 1976 it became necessary to ration the supply. This also affected the general population and was reflected in darkened streets in urban centers and power cutoffs in rural areas. To meet growing requirements, the Council of Ministers set the construction goal for new generating capacity at 9,050 megawatts during the period of the Five-Year Plan 1976–80. However, when detailed plan specifications were drawn up, the total had been reduced to 8,100 megawatts, and actual installations amounted only to 5,500 megawatts. This was attributed in considerable part to the reallocation of materials and technical personnel to projects in other industries, many of which were energy intensive. During much of the plan period the electric power situation was worsened by efforts to maintain output at the cost of repairs and delays owing to the lack of spare parts; another significant factor was the delivery to power plants of poor quality coal. Overall efficiency of operations deteriorated, and actual (as against potential) generation declined.

The shortage of electrical energy in 1978 was reported at about 4 billion kilowatt-hours, and the following year a peak shortfall of 5 billion kilowatt-hours occurred. In 1980 and 1981 power shortages were also large; in the fourth quarter of 1981 power to industry frequently had to be cut back, and short blackouts of residential areas occurred. But by early 1982 repairs to many power plants had been completed, and new generating capacity had also gone into operation. In February power output exceeded the needs of the country's reduced industrial activities. Electricity rates were increased at the beginning of the year but, according to Polish observers, they appeared to have had little effect on demand (except by households); industries simply passed on to consumers the higher production costs of their products in a seller's market. The excess supply of power continued through 1982. But it was apparent that in order to avoid a repetition of the power crisis of the 1976–81 period, there would have to be continued improvement in efficiency of operations, broad conservation efforts, stronger action to complete power projects, and an adjustment of the overall plan to the realities of the Polish economy.

Nuclear Power Generation

In August 1971 the government had announced its intention to begin construction of nuclear power generating facilities. A principal reason given was that conventional fuels available to the economy could be better used for industrial purposes than for electric power generation. The first nuclear plant was to be located at Zarnowiec in Gdansk voivodship, and completion was anticipated during the period 1980–82. In the decade that followed the announcement, little if any actual work on the project appeared to have been carried out. On several occasions work was reported to have started, only to be followed later by statements that the undertaking had been postponed. In January 1982 the martial law regime, apparently spurred in large part by the persistent power shortages, decided to go ahead with the nuclear project; by midyear several hundred people were said to be engaged in preparatory work at the site. The first unit at the plant, a 480-megawatt generator, was expected to go into operation about 1989 or 1990. Reports on the eventual size of the Zarnowiec facility have varied, some indicating an eventual installed capacity of 1,760 megawatts provided by four 440-megawatt units; other sources stated that the facility would have two 440-megawatt generators and one of 1,000 megawatts. Equipment for the facility was to be produced partly in Poland and partly in other Comecon countries under the terms of a 1979 production specialization agreement among members of the council. Nuclear fuel for the reactors was to be imported.

Transportation

Rail lines and modern roads provide extensive facilities in the western and southern parts of present-day Poland, but the transportation infrastructure is considerably less developed in the east-northeastern areas of the country (see fig. 14). This disparity has been related in part to economic development but basically stemmed from the politico-economic policies pursued earlier by Russia and Germany (initially Prussia)

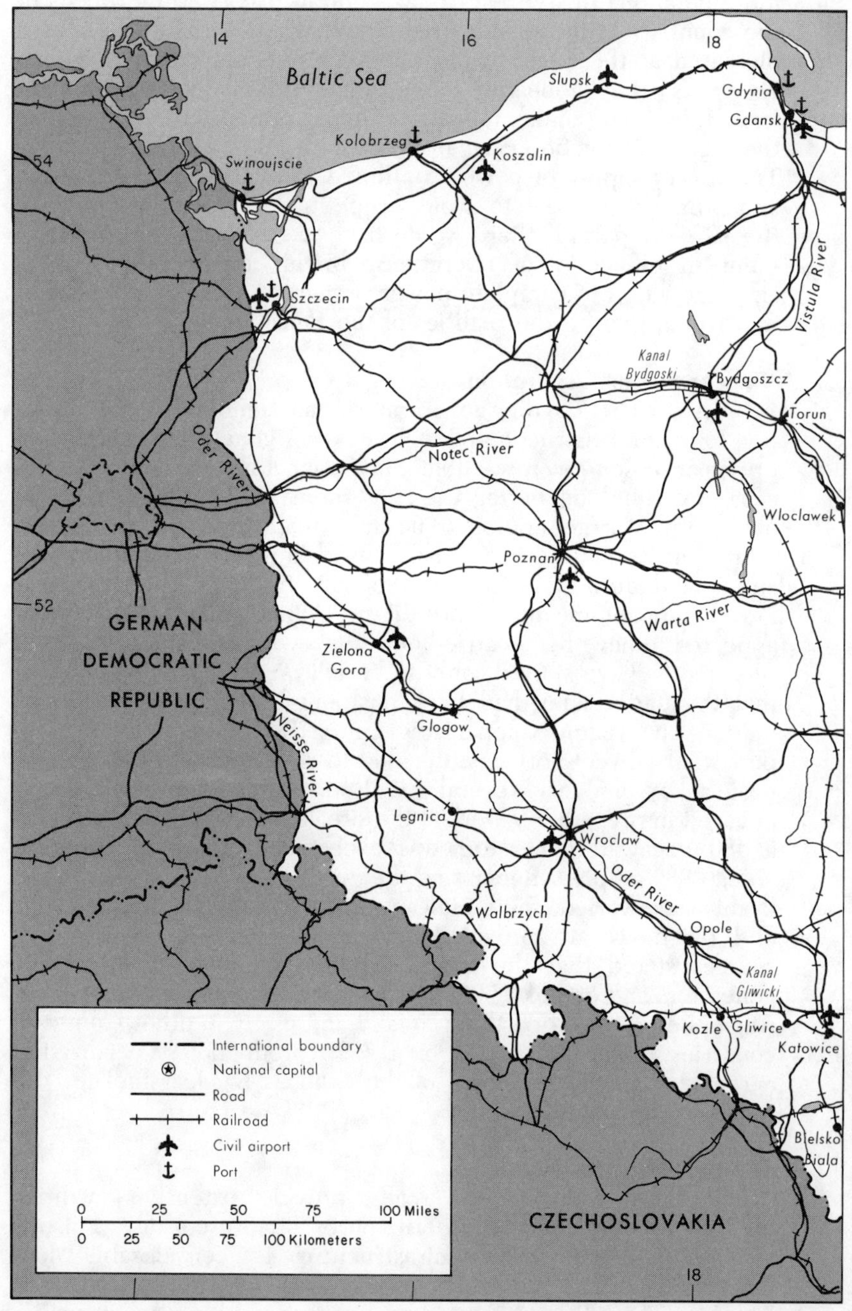

Figure 14. Transportation System, 1982

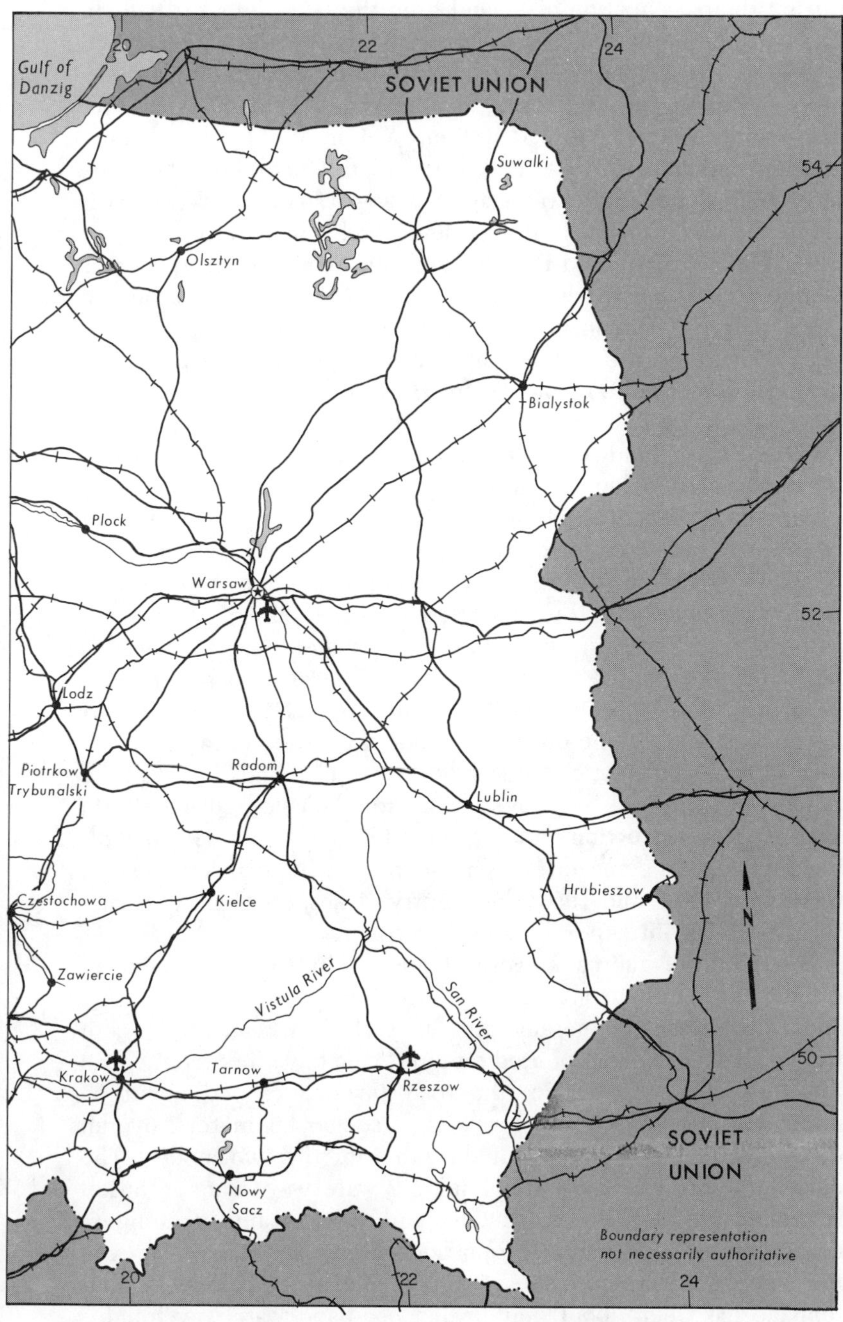

Source: Based on information from Poland, Central Statistical Office, *Concise Statistical Yearbook of Poland, 1982,* Warsaw, 1982, 6.

during their occupation of Poland from the late 1700s to 1918. In the west an industrially developing Germany treated occupied Polish territory as an integral part of its empire and built transportation infrastructures adequate for the area's economic expansion. This well-developed railroad system was inherited by newly independent Poland in 1918 and was greatly enlarged when the international boundary was extended westward after World War II. In the east, however, Russia developed transportation only to the extent that it served Russian domestic economic needs or was of potential value to the Russian army. No effort was made to develop transportation locally, and in fact such development was discouraged because of concerns that it might facilitate rebellion, or that it might aid possible Austro-Hungarian or German military action against Russia.

After 1918 Poland began integrating these separate systems and the sparsely developed transportation net in the area formerly occupied by the Austro-Hungarian Empire. This work had still not been fully completed at the time of the German invasion in 1939. New construction during this period expanded the system somewhat, chiefly in the central area of the country. The major addition was a rail line from the main coalfields in the south to ports on the Baltic Sea, necessitated in large part by Nazi Germany's uncooperative attitude with respect to Polish export needs. Little was done during this time, however, to improve the road network because of the lack of investment funds. Most of the rail and road net was destroyed or greatly damaged during World War II. Reconstruction and rehabilitation began in 1946, including the heavily damaged system in the newly acquired western territory. By the mid-1950s the country's transportation infrastructure was again in generally good condition.

In 1982 the railroads were dominant in the movement of freight. Although in absolute tonnage they usually carried only about 20 percent of the amount transported by road services, in ton-kilometers they accounted for approximately 75 percent of the total. In passenger traffic, the road services carried about 65 percent of the total; but in terms of passenger kilometers, overall distances traveled were about the same for the two modes. The country's large potential for inland waterway transportation remained greatly underutilized, and freight and passengers accounted for only a small proportion of national totals. Good use has been made of pipelines to move petroleum products, and tonnage has been about double that of inland waterway freight. Excellent facilities for foreign trade have been provided by three major ports on the Baltic Sea. About half of this trade has been

Warsaw's new Central Railroad Station; in background, Palace of Science and Culture, a gift from the Soviet Union, completed in 1955
Courtesy Consulate General of Polish People's Republic, New York

carried by the national merchant marine, which in 1982 ranked twentieth in size in the world. A national airline handled both domestic and international traffic.

Railroads

In the early 1980s the rail system, operated by the Polish State Railways (Polskie Koleje Panstwowe—PKP), was third in size in Europe (after France and West Germany and excluding the Soviet system). Its total route length at the end of 1981 was 27,168 kilometers, mostly single track. Of this, 24,356 kilometers were of standard 1.435-meter gauge. The remainder was narrow gauge of varied widths that ranged from 0.6 meter to 1 meter. The standard-gauge track was common to all Comecon countries except the Soviet Union and to the main rail systems of Western Europe. Track in the old Russian system in eastern Poland had been of broad gauge but was converted during the interwar period to standard gauge. After the Soviet reoccupation of eastern Poland in 1939 and as their troops later advanced across the western part of the country, Soviet military forces changed or rebuilt the main east-west lines to their own broad gauge. After the war these lines were used as communication links with their forces in East Germany. Apparently, strong Polish feelings that the gauge was a symbol of domination resulted in Soviet acquiescence to reconversion to standard gauge. The difference in gauges at the Polish-Soviet border had created a major transshipment problem. To resolve it in part, construction of a 400-kilometer broad-gauge line was begun in the late 1970s from Zawiercie in the Katowice region to Hrubieszow on the border to provide a continuous facility for the movement of iron ore from the Soviet Union to the Katowice iron and steel complex and to move coal, other minerals, and manufactured goods to the Soviet Union. Work on some sections of the line appeared to be still in progress in late 1982.

Early transport planning after World War II envisioned the construction of a considerable length of new track in both short- and long-distance projects. Some of these undertakings have been completed, for instance, the major new line connecting the Upper Silesian industrial region with that around Warsaw. But the great emphasis on the country's industrialization reduced available funds, and improvement of the road network obviated some of the need for new construction. As a result, railroad development emphasized modernization of existing facilities, especially electrification. The latter received new support after the increase in oil prices in the 1970s because of the effect on the cost of diesel locomotion, which had been introduced in the 1950s. By 1975 electrified track totaled 5,588 kilometers, or roughly one-quarter of the standard-gauge system. Material shortages and other problems reduced the electrification rate between 1976 and 1981, but 7,091 kilometers (29 percent of the total) had been electrified at the end of 1981. Included were lines radiating mainly east, west, and south from Warsaw and the line from Upper Silesia to Gdansk and Gdynia. Replacement of steam traction by diesel units continued, however. Diesel units rose to one-half of the locomotive stock in 1981, compared with about one-fourth for steam units and the same amount for electric locomotives. A significant factor supporting continued electrification in the 1980s was the domestic production of electric locomotives, whereas high-power diesels still had to be imported.

The railroads functioned reasonably well during the 1960s and 1970s, as evidenced in part by the degree of industrialization of the economy, which could not have been accomplished without adequate transportation. Serious problems existed in early 1983, however. Damage to rolling stock, both by users in loading and unloading operations and by the carelessness of railroad employees, resulted in numerous cars being out of operation at any time. The situation appeared to have deteriorated during 1980 and 1981, and in February 1982 some 56,000 freight cars of all

Main highway leading from Warsaw across new Lazienkowski Bridge toward suburbs on east bank of Vistula River
Courtesy Consulate General of Polish People's Republic, New York

categories (about one-fourth of all cars) were reportedly in this condition. Moreover, pressure on operations was increasing in the early 1980s because of the need to retire railroad cars at a much higher rate than the domestic transport manufacturing industry was replacing them. For 1982 the delivery of only about 3,000 new freight cars seemed to be relatively certain. This compared with and annual average of 12,000 to 15,000 in the late 1970s. A serious blow to normal operations also occurred in late 1981 and early 1982 when some 30,000 experienced railroad employees retired; the railroads had an average of 382,000 employees in 1981. The following year there were about 4,000 to 5,000 fewer workers than were required by rolling stock repair facilities alone.

Roads and Road Transport

The state and local road network, excluding roads in built-up urban areas, totaled 254,100 kilometers at the end of 1981. About 60 percent (148,900 kilometers) were all-weather roads, and of these some 120,000 kilometers were paved with asphalt or concrete. The all-weather road net in the voivodships adjacent to the Soviet border was relatively much sparser than in other parts of the country, a factor that impeded economic development in those areas. Superhighways at the beginning of 1981 amounted to somewhat over 300 kilometers in total length. A long-range program to increase superhighway length substantially in the 1980s reportedly had been seriously affected by the adverse economic situation that began developing in 1980. The state road administration hoped that about 1,000 kilometers might still be built through 1985, but these would encompass only sections of existing highly congested routes of special importance to the economy. It was assumed that general plans to increase or improve state and local roads would also be cut back because of restricted funds.

Major improvement of the national road system began in earnest only in the 1970s. During the preceding two decades, after the basic postwar reconstruction had been completed, investment in the roads had been relatively limited. This was in large part because of the government's premise that the railroads would be developed as the country's principal transport mode. There was little pressure from the road transport sector because of the small number of passenger cars and trucks using the roads. Motor vehicles (regular passenger cars, trucks, and buses) totaled only some 100,000 in the mid-1950s and a decade later a mere 429,000. This situation changed, requiring greatly increased investment in road improvements, when the Gierek regime in the 1970s decided to launch a major expansion of automobile production as an instrument to aid the administration economically and politically. It was reasoned that increased car sales would sop up a great amount of money held by the public at a time of very short supply of a large number of consumer goods. Further, the policy would increase the availability of the automobile—Poland's most highly desired consumer item—and thereby enhance the regime's image. This urge to own an automobile apparently has remained paramount in the public's mind, as evidenced by a mid-1982 report that 1,358,000 people had paid for vehicles in advance of delivery dates scheduled as late as the early 1990s. In 1982 the martial law regime also resorted to using car sales for economic advantage to acquire foreign exchange. Prospective buyers were promised that, on payment of a stipulated amount of United States dollars plus a zloty amount, they would receive a car ahead of other waiting customers. During the Gierek period the number of registered vehicles had almost quadrupled—from 786,000 at the beginning of the decade to nearly 3 million in 1980. In this time the length of paved roads increased by 55 percent, from about 76,100 to 117,700 kilometers. Work on road maintenance, however, appeared to be insufficient to offset the intensified use occasioned by the large-scale economic development of the 1970s; at the beginning of the 1980s over 30 percent of all-weather roads were reportedly in need of repair.

Civil Aviation

The domestic air service is operated by the state-owned Polish Airlines (Polskie Linie Lotnicze, commonly known as LOT). Originally established in 1929, virtually destroyed in World War II, and reconstituted after the war, LOT also provides international service. In the early 1980s domestic operations were based at Okecie International Airport outside Warsaw from which scheduled flights were made to 11 cities (Gdansk, Koszalin, Slupsk, Szczecin, Poznan, Bydgoszcz, Zielona Gora, Wroclaw, Krakow, Katowice, and Rzeszow). Service was interrupted after the seizure of power by the martial law regime in December 1981 but had been resumed to all cities except Bydgoszcz by mid-1982. A number of cities relatively near Warsaw have never had air service; government economists have felt that in these areas travelers' needs are best served by the railroad.

Until December 1981 international flights were made on a regular basis to some 40 cities in over 30 countries in Europe, North Africa, the Middle East, Asia, and North America. Additionally, charter flights had been made; in 1980 they included almost 40 to Chicago and 15 to Japan. About 20 international airlines also provided service to Warsaw. Martial law restrictions disrupted LOT's international flights, and it was not until the early months of 1982 that they resumed. A number of flights, however, were not expected to start again until sometime in 1983, including those to Damascus, Dubai, Bombay, and Bangkok. The regular service instituted in 1973 to the United States (New York) had been terminated by Washington after the imposition of martial law in Poland and had not been resumed as of early 1983. The disruption of international service has had some major impacts on LOT operations; for example, in July 1982 only one weekly flight was made to Frankfurt compared with one daily flight before mid-December 1981.

In 1980 LOT had 45 aircraft—all Soviet models—that included 19 jets used in medium- and long-range flights and 26 turboprop airplanes employed chiefly in the domestic service. The jets were not competitive with the wide-body aircraft flown by Western carriers, and most airplanes were old; three-fifths had an average age of over 10 years. In 1981, however, two Soviet wide-body Il-86s were acquired for scheduled service in 1982. LOT also had a contract in effect with the Soviet Union under which the latter was purchasing older LOT aircraft. Six airplanes, all jets, had been sold by mid-1982, leaving a total of 41 in the LOT fleet. The funds received were to be used to buy new aircraft. Domestic operations have usually suffered a financial loss and are subsidized by the national budget. International service, on the other hand, had generally been profitable to 1981, although the airline's financial position had been increasingly affected by growing numbers of Poles traveling out of the country and paying for their tickets in zlotys.

Inland Waterways

Over 4,000 kilometers of inland waterways—rivers, canals, and lakes—were navigable by regular transport services in 1981. About 60 percent of the total was contained in the Vistula River system, and the remainder was in the Oder River basin. The two systems were connected in north-central Poland by the Kanal Bydgoski, which had been constructed by Prussia during its occupation of the region. The Vistula River was navigable from its mouth at the Baltic Sea to its confluence with the San River in southeastern Poland and technically upstream as far as Krakow. Much of the river was affected, however, by changing water levels during the year and shifting sandbars. In 1978 the government announced plans to improve navigation on the river; but large investments were necessary to carry out channelization and construct dams to control water flow, and little seemed to have been done by 1982. The Oder River was navigable to Kozle in Upper Silesia, where it was connected to the industrial area of the Katowice region by the Kanal Gliwicki, built by the Polish government in 1938. The river had been channelized by Germany and was capable of handling large barges.

The state transport fleet in the early 1980s included a variety of tugs and barges. On the Vistula River, barges of up to 400 tons were used, but the larger ones were generally limited to the river downstream from Warsaw. On the Oder River most were of 500 tons. Cargo was largely bulk goods—mainly coal, mineral ores, stone and gravel, fertilizers, and grain. Passenger ships also plied both rivers. Polish sources indicated that much of the equipment was old but continued to be used intensively. Repairs were being delayed by shortages of spare parts. Plans for acquisition of new equipment existed, but any measurable success appeared to be dependent on expansion of domestic production, on securing of sufficient foreign exchange to import certain equipment, and on whether domestic sources actually delivered projected items.

Ports and Shipping

Despite a maritime tradition that has developed only since World War I, Poland in early 1983 had a substantial, well-developed merchant marine that provided regular and tramp steamer services worldwide. Historically, Polish interest in maritime activity had been minimal. In the period before the country's extinction as an independent state in the late 1700s, exports had been significant through the port of Gdansk; however, that trade had been dominated by Dutch, English, and French shipping.

Modern Poland's exiled leaders of the early 1900s were convinced that when independence was restored, trade with the West would be an essential factor in maintaining freedom, and access to the sea was vital for this. After World War I independent Poland was given a strip of territory between the main part of Germany and East Prussia, but the short 140-kilometer coast contained only minor fishing ports. Although Gdansk was also made a free city, it remained for all intents and purposes under German control. As a result, construction of a major Polish port at Gdynia was begun in 1920. Development of a merchant fleet was also undertaken, and by the time of the German invasion in 1939 it included over 70 vessels.

The territorial acquisitions after World War II greatly lengthened the coastline and, more importantly, gave Poland the major ports of Gdansk and Szczecin. There were several smaller ports, of which Swinoujscie and Kolobrzeg were the most important (the former subsequently became part of the Szczecin port complex). Gdansk, Szczecin, and Gdynia have since been greatly improved and expanded, but most of this work was carried out only after the late 1960s when a realignment of the country's development investment policies made adequate funds available. An impetus to this development was the marked growth in trade with the West in the early 1970s (see Foreign Trade and Foreign Debt, this ch.). The new North Port, constructed at Gdansk, provided bulk cargo handling facilities for coal, petroleum, and petroleum products. In the early 1980s this port could accommodate ships up to 150,000 deadweight tons, about the maximum size of vessels that enter the Baltic Sea. At Gdansk new facilities were installed to handle sulfur (a major export) and fertilizer raw materials. Major new coal export facilities were among additions at Swinoujscie, where the roadstead was also deepened to take ships of 60,000 deadweight tons. A large container terminal was added at Gdynia. Almost 61.2 million tons of cargo passed through the three ports in 1980; this figure dropped to 37.3 million in 1981, owing to foreign exchange shortages, labor unrest, and other factors. Some 11,200 vessels entered the ports (including Kolobrzeg) in 1980 (about the same number as in 1970), but their total of 17 million net registered tons was almost three times the 1970 figure. About half the tonnage in 1980 was under Polish registry, compared with one-third a decade earlier.

In 1981 the Polish merchant fleet had 322 vessels totaling almost 4.6 million deadweight tons. This compared with 259 ships totaling some 1.9 million deadweight tons in 1970. About two-thirds of the vessels were less than 10 years old. Until mid-1982 this fleet was owned and operated by three state enterprises and a joint Polish-Chinese company. Polish Ocean Lines (Polskie Linie Oceaniczne—PLO) provided regular services to most parts of the world. Its fleet consisted of 166 vessels, mostly general cargo carriers, some semicontainers, a roll-on-roll-off vessel, and the country's only passenger liner, the *Stefan Batory*. The Polish Steamship Company (Polska Zeluga Morska—PZM) had 125 vessels that included large tankers and bulk cargo ships that provided worldwide tramp steamer services. The other state enterprise was the Polish Baltic Shipping Company (Polska Zeluga Baltycka—PZB), which operated 19 smaller ships mainly in the Baltic coastal service. It also ran ferries to Scandinavian points, Finland, West Germany, and Britain. The 12 Polish-owned ships of the Chinese-Polish Shipping Company were general cargo carriers that operated between Poland and China. In May 1982 two joint-stock companies registered in Poland acquired most of the assets of PLO and PZM. The purchased vessels were immediately leased back to the original owners on a bareboat charter basis. Various reasons were given for the transactions, including the possibility of securing additional capital through foreign stock participation. About one-half of all cargo carried by the lines was for foreign countries. There was also speculation—strongly refuted in Poland—that the step was taken to prevent possible attachment of vessels if Poland defaulted on its international debts.

Pipelines

Poland has two major pipelines that handle petroleum and petroleum products. The main line (part of the Comecon Druzhba [Friendship] pipeline) carries oil from the Soviet Union to the Plock refinery northwest of Warsaw and on to East Germany. A second major line transports refined products from the refinery at Gdansk to the petrochemical complex at Plock, supplementing supplies from the Plock refinery. The total length of operating oil pipelines at the end of 1981, including branch lines of other refineries, was 1,975 kilometers. An extensive system of gas pipelines was also in use. The main line transported natural gas from the Soviet Union into southeastern Poland where it was fed into pipelines carrying domestic gas produced in the area. From there, pipelines ran northward to Warsaw, Olsztyn, and Gdansk and westward to Krakow, Katowice, and Poznan; a major branch connected Wroclaw and Szczecin. Branch lines from natural gas fields south of Poznan were tied into this line. A manufactured gas pipeline also connected Warsaw, Krakow, Katowice, and Wroclaw; from Wroclaw the line proceeded westward into East Germany. In northeast Poland, Bialystok was supplied with natural gas by a separate pipeline from the Soviet Union.

Foreign Trade and Foreign Debt

The economic reforms of 1981 and 1982 also legislated important changes in foreign trade operations. After World War II foreign trade, which in the prewar period had been carried out almost entirely by private companies (mainly foreign-owned or foreign-controlled), was nationalized and became a state monopoly. By the end of the 1940s trade was conducted completely in conformity with a detailed central plan. The operational units were a number of state foreign trade organizations responsible directly to the Ministry of Foreign Trade. Each unit was responsible for a certain category of goods, e.g., chemicals, machine tools, and so forth. Both export and import prices were arbitrarily set at fixed domestic rates that bore no relationship to the prices paid or obtained abroad by the trading unit. As a result, there was little incentive for the producing enterprise to improve its efficiency, modernize, or economize on raw materials. In 1966 a system of export efficiency bonuses was introduced for manufactured exports, which made up about 60 percent of total exports. The bonuses were not directly related to the financial results of the companies but were based on export profits determined by a contrived system of calculation.

The major economic policy changes introduced in the early 1970s by the Gierek administration gave producers a greater role in foreign trade. A large number of the foreign trade units were placed under industrial branch ministries and controlling organizations that were more directly involved with manufacturing or other economic activities; a small number of large manufacturing operations were authorized to conduct foreign trade activities independently. But all foreign trade organizations, of which there were about 60 in 1980, had to obtain export licenses from the Ministry of Foreign Trade. Under regulations in effect in early 1982, the ministry had no obligation to grant a license, and, despite persistent efforts on the part of a foreign trade agency or enterprise, the license might not be secured. Polish sources stated that the granting of a license was actually regarded as a favor by the ministry, an attitude that seriously impeded rational foreign trade activities. This situation was altered by the reform legislation passed by the Sejm in February 1982 that established new basic principles for foreign trade operations. Under the new measures any enterprise in the socialized economy, any social organization involved in economic activities, or any authorized person in the private sector engaged in production, service, or trade functions could obtain permission to conduct foreign trade. A decision on the application for authorization had to be made by the ministry within three months.

The reforms introduced a major change in import financing procedures. Earlier, foreign exchange availability had been based ultimately on allocations decided by the ministry. The size of the allocation appears frequently to have been dependent on political factors often employing, according to Polish sources, "well-known methods." The exchange secured had to be used in a stipulated year or was lost. The enterprises expending the exchange appear to have had little feeling of ownership, resulting in uneconomical management that was heightened by the expenditure time limitation. An effort to improve foreign exchange use procedures in the Gierek era produced few results. The 1982 legislation established what has been referred to as the foreign exchange retention quota system. This permitted enterprises to keep a share (quota) of their foreign exchange earnings for use in importing materials, spare parts, items for modernization, and the like, needed to produce further export goods. The quota was based on the enterprise's exports and imports of the previous three years. The foreign exchange thus available was deposited in a bank account established by the enterprise. The funds were usable by the latter at its discretion and could be carried forward and expended over an extended period. The new system was expected to improve export performance substantially, inasmuch as the amount of foreign exchange available was linked to earnings. At the same time, because the exchange belonged to the enterprise, it presumably would be used economically to the best interests of the owner. Reports through November 1982 stated that 1,315 enterprises had opened accounts into which US$312 million had been deposited. Less than one-third of that amount had been expended, however. The government had announced that in 1983 Polish enterprises would be allowed to retain a combined total of approximately US$1 billion.

Foreign trade was conducted with nearly 100 countries in all parts of the world. During the interwar period extensive trade existed between Poland and the West. Trade links were also established with Germany and the countries that emerged from the breakup of the Austro-Hungarian Empire, but until after World War II very little trade was carried on with the Soviet Union, mainly for political reasons. In the period 1945–49 imports (except for a small amount from less developed countries) were divided almost equally between the East European socialist states and the developed Western market economies; the latter, however, took a slightly larger share of Poland's exports. After consolidation of communist control in Poland in the late 1940s, the share of the socialist states (mainly Comecon) in Polish imports became substantially higher, accounting until the end of the 1960s for about two-thirds of total imports, compared with 25 to 30 percent supplied by the Western industrialized countries. Beginning in 1972, however, purchases from the West increased substantially (stimulated by the Gierek modernization program). Through the mid-1970s the West's share rose to over 45 percent, compared with less than 50 percent for the socialist countries. The proportion accounted for by the latter again rose in the late 1970s and increased sharply at the beginning of the 1980s as Poland experienced foreign exchange shortages and reduced its purchases from the West (see table 9, Appendix A).

The export pattern has remained relatively constant since 1950, over 60 percent of exports going to socialist, mainly East European markets and about 30 percent to the developed Western economies. Reported exports to the Soviet Union usually accounted for well over one-half of the exports to socialist states and almost one-third of total Polish exports. Imports from the Soviet Union during most of the 1970s were roughly 30 percent of total trade; they rose to 42 percent in 1982 (see table 10, Appendix A).

During the 1960s and through 1971 Poland's trade with the industrialized West was roughly in balance. In the latter year its hard currency debt amounted to only US$764 million; the debt service amounted to 15 percent of export earnings. After 1971 implementation of the ambitious Gierek industrial modernization program and parallel efforts to raise urban worker living standards (as an incentive for increased productivity) included the importation of massive quantities of machinery, equipment, and materials to which was soon added large unanticipated grain imports because of domestic shortfalls. By 1975 imports from the hard currency area totaling US$5 billion were over six times greater in value than in 1971. Exports to the West also increased but at a lower rate than for imports, and against a trade surplus in 1971 of US$260 million, in 1975 there was a trade deficit of more than US$2.2 billion. The net hard currency external debt in 1975 (nearly US$7.4 billion) was four times that of 1971.

Government planners in 1971 had anticipated that loans available from the hard currency area to finance the modernization program would be repaid with export receipts from sales in the area. In part because of factors beyond the government's control and in part because of major policy mistakes and faults in the centralized planning and management system, the expected results did not materialize. Significant noncontrollable factors included the recession in the West beginning in late 1974, the introduction of Western trade barriers including quotas (especially by the EEC), competition in Western markets from new industries in several other East European countries, and the effects of poor weather on domestic agricultural production. Among policy errors, the reaction to the unfavorable effects of the Western recession was too slow both in the reduction of imports from the West and in cutting back on domestic development plans.

There was also an important failure to restrain wage increases and to adjust food prices to control the rise in consumption. This led to a drop in exports (by necessitating diversions to the domestic market) and to an increase in imports of cereals and feed grains. The scope of export diversification was also too broad, and insufficient allowance was made for the import of materials needed for the expanded production facilities.

By 1976 the foreign trade situation forced recognition that the targets of the Five-Year Plan 1976–80 to attain a trade balance with the West by 1979 were unrealistic. As a result of this and the need to alter plans because of the serious domestic economic situation, growth targets for both exports and imports were lowered. Import targets continued to be exceeded because of the need to import large quantities of grain and fodder, which had to be financed by additional foreign loans. However, the severe cuts in other import areas, although they had an adverse effect on industrial production, resulted in lower trade deficits after 1977. In 1979 the deficit totaled US$1.5 billion, and in 1980 it had been reduced to US$900 million. The labor unrest and economic problems of 1981 resulted in a 20 percent decrease in exports and a 29 percent drop in imports from the West; the trade deficit declined to US$60 million.

Increasing debt service payments were added to the hard currency borrowings required to finance the negative balance of trade. In 1971 Poland's debt service ratio (repayments of principal and interest as a percent of export earnings) was comparable to that of most other Comecon countries. From 1972 to 1976 Poland's hard currency loans grew at an average annual rate of 60 percent, and in 1976 when the total external hard currency debt reached US$11.5 billion, the debt service ratio had risen to 30 percent. The debt's rate of growth declined between 1977 and 1979 to less than 25 percent, but repayments in 1979 amount to 92 percent of hard currency exports, and the ratio rose to 101 percent in 1980. At the end of the 1970s the high debt service costs were having a strongly negative effect on development; in 1979 debt servicing alone required 85 percent of currency borrowings. In that year the gross outstanding debt was approximately US$20.5 billion; about 75 percent (US$15.4 billion) was owed to commercial institutions (some 10 percent to United States banks). The remainder (US$5.1 billion) represented official government—backed debts, and nearly 20 percent was owed to United States government agencies. The debt reportedly had risen to about US$27 billion by mid-1982; some US$16 billion of it was owned to private banks.

During the 1970s Poland had little difficulty in securing Western hard currency loans, although from about 1976 United States banks tended to be quite cautious compared with those in Western Europe. The latter, however, were reportedly under pressure by their governments toward the end of the decade to continue lending because of trade factors. By 1979 the precariousness of the Polish economy was already evident, and new requests in 1981 for funds were only partially met. In 1980, however, Poland managed to secure additional hard currency from Comecon (mostly from the Soviet Union) together with some commodities. In 1981 principal and interest payments of about US$9 million were due, but further requests for loans were turned down.

In March 1982 Poland announced that it could not make payment and asked for rescheduling action. An agreement with

Processing canned hams at a Polish meat-packing plant for export to the United States

Western governments was reached in April on official loans. The United States and other governments rescheduled 90 percent of the principal and interest due between May and December 1981. Payments were to begin after four years and would be completed four years later. Rescheduling agreements with some 500 Western banks were signed in April 1982 that covered 95 percent of the principal due in 1981 and were to be paid over four years. Some of the remaining 5 percent and interest were paid before the signing. Further rescheduling of government-backed loans had been frozen in December 1981 when martial law was imposed. Private banks continued negotiations on 1982 payments, and a further agreement was reached in November to extend payment of 95 percent of the principal over three and one-half years following a four-year grace period. The remaining amount and interest were to be repaid during the remainder of 1982 and in 1983. Poland was also granted US$550 million in credits by the banks to finance imports needed to turn out export goods that would produce revenues for servicing payments.

* * *

Much of the current economic information has been derived from the numerous translations of Polish sources available in the continuing series *East Europe Report: Economic and Industrial Affairs*, published by the Joint Publications Research Service. Statistics have come largely from the *Concise Statistical Yearbook of Poland*, published in English by Poland's Central Statistical Office. Useful articles and analyses of the economy are carried regularly in publications of Radio Free Europe Research. The occasional publications on the same subject by the Library of Congress Congressional Research Service are also useful. Thad Alton's *Polish Postwar Economy*, an appraisal of early economic planning, provides valuable background to the subsequent evolution of Poland's centralized planning system. (For further information and complete citations, see Bibliography.)

Chapter 4. Government and Politics

Twelfth-century coronation sword of the Polish kings, the so-called Szczerbiec

THE FORMAL STRUCTURE of the government of Poland was established by the Constitution of 1952. According to the Constitution authority is vested in the working people, expressed through their representatives elected to the unicameral national legislature (Sejm) and the people's councils of the provinces (voivodships) and local districts. The Sejm, in theory, defines the activities of the state and exercises supervision over the executive and administrative organs of government.

In practice, however, the communist party, known as the Polish United Workers' Party (Polska Zjednoczona Partia Robotnicza—PZPR), is superior to all of the constitutional organs of power. It is mandated by the Constitution as the guiding political force of society in building socialism. Instruments of government at both the national and the local levels function as executors of policies and programs determined by the PZPR. The ruling party, nominally directed by a national congress held at five-year intervals, is in reality controlled by its Political Bureau (Politburo) and by the Secretariat of the Central Committee.

The Constitution does not prescribe a separation of powers between the branches of government; legislative, executive, and judicial functions are closely intertwined. The Council of State, a form of collective presidency, is ostensibly responsible to the Sejm in carrying out the state's executive functions and is empowered to issue laws by decree when the Sejm is not in session. The Council of Ministers, which corresponds to a cabinet, is the nation's highest administrative body and is constitutionally responsible to the Sejm and the Council of State. The judiciary enjoys a degree of independence, and court proceedings are generally conducted with a view to reaching a just verdict. In politically tinged cases, however, judges are obligated to act in the interest of the political system and to contribute to the fulfillment of party policies.

In the Sejm and other constitutional bodies, pro forma representation is accorded other political parties and groupings accredited as supporting the existing political order. In August 1980, faced with a dangerous economic crisis and an increasingly rebellious work force, the government reluctantly conceded legal status to an independent labor federation, Solidarnosc (Solidarity). After monopolizing power for 35 years without real sanction from Polish society, the PZPR found itself in contention with an alternative source of power having valid claim to represent the working people. Limited concessions were extracted by Solidarity under pressure of strike threats. With the regime and ruling party paralyzed by their inability to control the popular movement, Solidarity was encouraged to demand broader reforms across the political and social spectrum.

After drawing up secret plans, the government declared a state of martial law on December 13, 1981, suppressing all political activity. The commander of the Polish armed forces, General Wojciech Jaruzelski, who had been named prime minister in February of that year and first secretary of the PZPR in October, assumed supreme powers as chairman of the Military Council of National Salvation, a body superimposed on the constitutional organs of government. Thousands of Solidarity activists were rounded up, and the organization itself was outlawed. During the year that followed, the government embarked on a program to reverse the liberalization of the Solidarity period and suppress institutions and forms of behavior incompatible with state control.

The Constitution

The drafting of a permanent constitution for Poland after World War II was entrusted to a commission established by the Sejm in 1951. The commission's work closely followed party guidelines based on preparatory work carried out in the higher echelons of the PZPR. The draft constitution essentially summarized the existing governmental structure that had already been shaped along communist lines by the party-controlled regime. The document was officially adopted by the Sejm on July 22, 1952, after its circulation among the public for discussion.

Although modeled closely on its 1936 Soviet counterpart, the 1952 Constitution described Poland as a "state of people's democracy." This was revised in 1976 to portray the country as a socialist state, having completed the transition from a people's democracy. The Soviet Union is credited in the preamble with liberating Polish soil from fascism and, as the first state of workers and peasants, of establishing a model for Poland. In its foreign policy the people's republic is committed by the Constitution to friendship with the Soviet Union and other socialist states; its relations with other nations are to be based on the principles of peaceful coexistence.

The Constitution declares that power belongs to the working people of the country acting through their representatives in the Sejm and in the people's councils (voivodship and local legislative bodies) on the basis of universal suffrage and secret ballot. It states that development is to proceed on the basis of a planned economy and the socialization of the means of production. Protection and assistance to individual farmers are guaranteed by the state; collective farms and state farms are to be developed and strengthened.

More than a quarter of the Constitution is devoted to stipulations concerning citizens' fundamental rights and duties. Guarantees are extended for work, rest, leisure, health care, and education. Equal rights are assured all citizens regardless of nationality, race, religion, sex, education, or social origin and

General Wojciech Jaruzelski, commander of the Polish armed forces, Poland's prime minister, and first secretary of the country's ruling communist party
Courtesy United Press International

status. Freedom of religion, speech, the press, assembly, and association are also constitutionally safeguarded. Rights for women are set forth in detail: equal pay for equal work, paid absences from work before and after giving birth, and day-care programs for children. The Constitution prohibits the "spreading of hatred or contempt, the provocation of strife or the humiliation of man on account of national, racial, or religious differences." Inviolability of the person is guaranteed and extends to the home and to the privacy of correspondence.

These individual rights are balanced against the obligations of the citizen to the state. The Constitution calls upon each citizen to "maintain socialist work discipline, to respect the principles of community life, and to do his duty toward the state conscientiously." Among these duties are the safeguarding of "socialist property" and the obligation to perform military service.

Except during a few brief intervals, the record of the government over the years has been one of habitual failure to respect the elementary rights of Polish citizens, belying the freedoms decreed so unequivocally in the Constitution. The realities of the limits on free expression in Polish life were addressed by a group of 57 writers, lawyers, priests, and academicians in a memorandum to the Sejm objecting to the amendments to the Constitution introduced by the government in 1975. They declared that there was no freedom of religion or conscience when people professing a different philosophy from the official one were denied access to leading offices in social life and institutions in the economy. They asserted that there was no freedom to work when the state was the sole employer and when trade unions were subordinate to the ruling party, which virtually ran the state. They insisted further that there was no freedom of expression and information when all publications were subject to censorship, when the state controlled the mass media, when the citizens had insufficient information to judge actions taken by the state, and when the state had little information on the attitudes of its citizens.

Amendments to the Constitution require a two-thirds vote of the Sejm, provided that at least half of the deputies are present. Ten amendments were enacted between 1952 and 1973 dealing for the most part with the organization and function of central and local government bodies. In 1976 a comprehensive revision was promulgated after nearly four years of work on a draft law by a constitutional commission created by the Sejm. The tenor of the changes had been established by the Sixth Congress of the PZPR in December 1971. More than one-third of the original 91 articles were amended. The new text, composed of 106 articles, expanded somewhat the duties of the Sejm, effected several changes in responsibilities of leading government bodies, and amended the procedures for appointing judges. Many articles of the sections dealing with rights and duties of citizens were modified. The paragraphs concerning youth and women were extended. New goals were introduced for improvement of the environment and housing for families.

The PZPR, not mentioned in the 1952 Constitution, was to be defined as having the leading role in the state. The articles dealing with individual rights were to be supplemented with the statement: "The rights of citizens are inseparably linked with the thorough and conscientious fulfilling of duties to the fatherland." The section on foreign policy was to include a new phrase committing Poland to "unshakeable bonds with the Soviet Union."

These proposed amendments stirred widespread protest among prominent intellectuals, students, and the clergy. The Roman Catholic primate of Poland, Stefan Cardinal Wyszynski, denounced in a sermon the assignment of a leading role to the PZPR, asserting that this would result in further division between party members and nonparty Catholics. He and other protestors objected to the apparent effort to intimidate dissenters from party policy by implying that their civil liberties might be withheld. After a quiet mediation of differences, the Polish authorities moderated the language concerning the role of the ruling party with the clause amended to indicate that the PZPR would be "the guiding political force of society in building socialism." The threat of selective application of civil rights was removed by changing the clause to read: "It shall be the duty of the citizens to the Polish

People's Republic to perform conscientiously their duties toward the country and contribute to its development."

Although it was widely recognized that Poland was bound to associate itself closely with the Soviet Union in foreign affairs, the statement proposed by the government was regarded as objectionable because it would have embedded in the Constitution a further limitation on the nation's sovereignty. The language finally adopted declared that Poland will "consolidate friendship and cooperation" with the Soviet Union and other socialist states. This formulation was milder than corresponding language in the constitutions of other states of Eastern Europe except that of Romania, which does not include a direct reference to the Soviet Union.

Government Institutions

The governing apparatus as defined by the Constitution is unitary; the Sejm is at the apex, the source from which the other organs of government derive their power. The Council of State is the executive committee of the Sejm and is nominally accountable to it in carrying out a variety of functions stipulated in the Constitution. The supreme administrative organ of the state is the Council of Ministers. Its members direct and supervise through ministries and other agencies all activities of the government at the national and local levels. The chairman of the Council of Ministers, or prime minister, is appointed by the Sejm, which must also endorse the composition of the council selected by the prime minister (see fig. 15).

Surmounting the formal government hierarchy are the extra-constitutional but powerful organs of the PZPR, the Politburo and the Secretariat of the Central Committee. Policy decisions, administrative directives, and political nominations flow from these high party bodies to guide the actions of the Council of Ministers and other central government institutions. Provincial and local party committees similarly influence and monitor operations at lower government levels (see Polish United Workers' Party, this ch.).

The Sejm

As the highest organ of state authority under the Constitution, the Sejm passes laws and resolutions and, at least in theory, exercises control over the work of other organs of government. Among its functions are the adoption of the annual state budget and the approval of multi-year socioeconomic plans as well as the review of annual plans adopted by the Council of Ministers.

The Sejm consists of 460 deputies elected for a term of four years. During its sessions the Sejm is presided over by a marshal (speaker), assisted by three vice marshals. It is noteworthy that the marshal elected in 1976 and reelected in 1980 was Stanislaw Gucwa of the United Peasant Party (Zjednoczone Stronnictwo

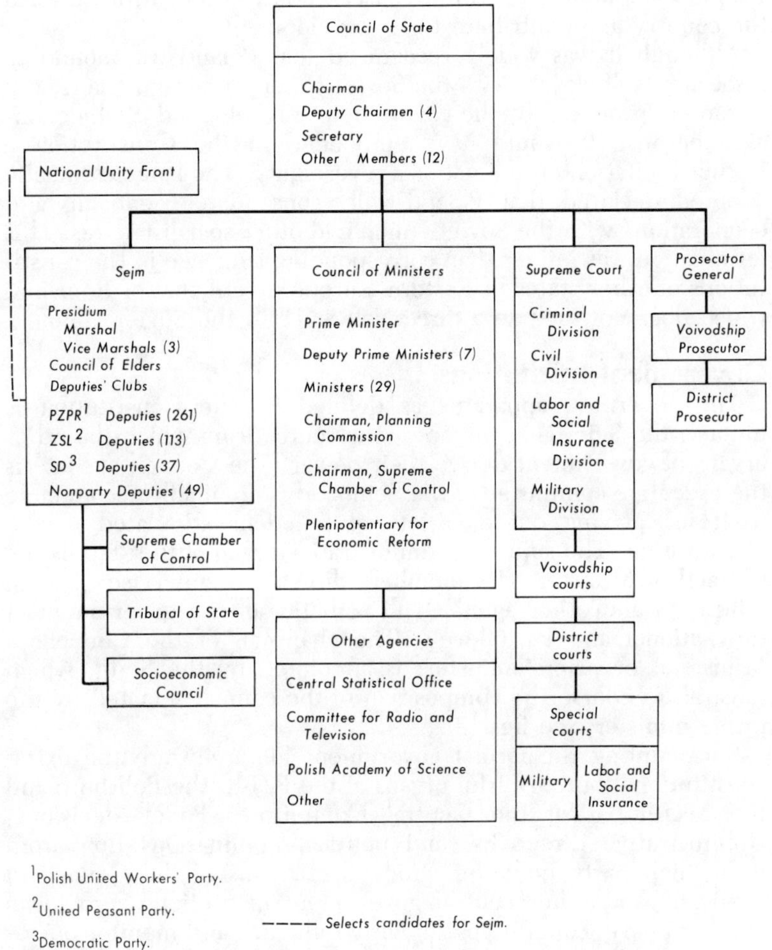

Figure 15. Structure of Polish Government, January 1983

Ludowe—ZSL) rather than a senior member of the PZPR. The three vice marshals included a member of the PZPR Politburo, a prominent member of the Democratic Party (Stronnictwo Demokratyczne—SD), and a nonparty member from a Catholic group. The marshal and vice marshals constitute the Presidium, which supervises the conduct of business in the Sejm, applies its rules, and represents it in dealing with other bodies. The Council of Elders, an advisory group composed of members of the Presidium and chairmen of the deputies' clubs, discusses the composition, agendas, and times for individual sessions and elections to various committees.

Although always subordinate to the party and state administrative organs, the responsibilities of the Sejm were augmented at two stages—the first during the relatively relaxed period after Wladyslaw Gomulka's ascendancy to power in 1956, and the second in 1971 after Gomulka had been succeeded by Edward Gierek. For a short interval between August 1980 and the imposition of martial law in December 1981, debates in the Sejm had a more spontaneous tone, and some latitude was permitted in the framing of legislation proposed by the authorities.

The effort to revitalize the Sejm after 1971 included a strengthening of the committee system. The number of committees was increased to 22, corresponding roughly to the ministerial divisions. The Committee for Legislative Work was added to review the legal soundness of actions taken by other committees. The use of interpellations (inquiries addressed to ministers or government agencies) was expanded, and the right of individual deputies to table questions requiring information on specific facts was introduced. The Sejm was called into session more frequently. During its seventh term (1977–80) the Sejm met in 28 plenary sessions, usually lasting one or two days each, and 1,000 meetings of its committees were conducted. It passed 42 laws and four decrees, adopted 410 resolutions, and addressed 280 proposals to the government in the form of opinions or desiderata.

Virtually all legislation is introduced by the government, although groups of 15 or more deputies may also introduce bills. Each bill undergoes two readings, the first consisting of a report on the principles of the bill by its sponsor, a general discussion, and referral to the proper committee. At the second reading the committee reports to the complete Sejm whereupon another discussion ensues and a vote is taken. Plenary sessions of the Sejm are conducted in public; committee sessions, where detailed review of proposed legislation is conducted, are held in private. If a committee is unwilling to approve a bill, it may be returned through the Presidium for redrafting along lines suggested by the committee.

In mid-1982 a new advisory and consultative body, the Socioeconomic Council, was announced. Composed of over 100 people from all walks of life, the council's purpose was to provide the Sejm with an opinion on draft bills. Intended to underscore the military regime's pledge to act on the basis of public consensus rather than party policies alone, the council was still viewed in early 1983 as an experiment rather than a permanent institution.

It is said that over the years the Sejm has performed a useful purpose in blocking the passage of bills that would be socially harmful, but little comes to light about its role in the lawmaking process, because any real discussion takes place in closed committee sessions. This also means that the public is uninformed about the issues being discussed, and they have no way to express themselves on new legislative proposals.

Some of the most important government measures are rushed through the Sejm without real debate or are implemented by decrees of the Council of State when the Sejm is not in session and subsequently are given pro forma Sejm approval. It has also been observed that laws passed by the Sejm are framed in broad terms and that the body is not equipped to exercise its theoretical supremacy over the flood of administrative orders and ministerial regulations through which the government gives effect to new laws.

The relative unimportance of the Sejm in restraining major government initiatives was revealed when it rubber-stamped the constitutional amendments of 1976, an action the government was later forced to modify when confronted by determined opposition from the Roman Catholic Church and dissident intellectuals. Had the Sejm been adequately consulted before the government imposed major food price increases leading to the riots of June 1976, it might have been able to warn the government of the protests that would ensue.

During the relaxation of party control in 1981, the Sejm passed a worker self-management law incorporating a compromise text as proposed by the Solidarity leadership in place of the language of the government bill. The Sejm deputies failed to enact an emergency powers law demanded by Jaruzelski in early November. After martial law was imposed in December, the Sejm's independence was again curtailed. The unpopular law to abolish Solidarity and other trade unions was approved in the course of a single day in October 1982. During seven hours of debate dominated by proponents of the measure, two speakers ventured to raise objections. Ten deputies voted against it, nine abstained, and about 100 were absent.

Council of State

The Council of State may be regarded as a collective presidency, its chairman acting as titular head of state. The Constitution provides that at its first session after an election, the Sejm shall elect the Council of State from its own members. As of January 1983, the council was made up of the chairman, four deputy chairmen, a secretary, and 12 other members (see table 11, Appendix A). In order to preserve its distinctive character, members of the Presidium of the Sejm may not be elected to the Council of State, nor is it the practice for its members to serve simultaneously in government posts. Leading members of the three political parties and of other important groups represented in the Sejm are elected to the council. Henryk Jablonski has been chairman of the Council of State since 1972. He is not regarded as a major political figure, having been removed from the Politburo in 1971.

The Council of State is endowed with certain executive functions in addition to its authority to issue decrees having the force of law when the Sejm is not in session. The council convenes the Sejm, determines the date for elections, and exercises ultimate supervision over administrative subdivisions (see Regional and Local Government, this ch.). The Council of State has the right to annul resolutions of local people's councils and even to dissolve them in extreme circumstances. The council also ratifies international agreements, appoints ambassadors, and accepts the credentials of other countries' envoys in Poland. Appointments to certain high domestic civilian and military posts are made in the name of the council, as are reviews of death sentences handed down by the courts. All judges are appointed by the council.

Under the Constitution a state of war may be declared by the Sejm (or by the Council of State when the Sejm is not in session) in the event of armed aggression against Poland or when, in conformity with international agreements, joint defense against aggression is necessary. The Council of State may in addition proclaim martial law and partial or general mobilization for considerations of defense or the security of the state. This provision was cited in the proclamation of December 13, 1981, announcing that the council had introduced martial law. It is generally assumed that all material matters acted on in the name of the council are in reality based on decisions taken by the party and government leadership. It is, accordingly, not considered surprising that in spite of a wholesale turnover of party and ministerial posts during 1981, few changes occurred in the Council of State.

Council of Ministers

Referred to in the Constitution as "the Government," the Council of Ministers is defined as the supreme executive and administrative organ of state authority. Appointed by and theoretically responsible to the Sejm (and, when the Sejm is not in session, to the Council of State), the Council of Ministers is composed of the prime minister, deputy prime ministers, ministers, and the heads of certain high boards and offices (see table 11, Appendix A). Members of the council are frequently deputies of the Sejm, but this is not a prerequisite for appointment.

The number of deputy prime ministers is not fixed; seven were in office as of January 1983. No ranking was announced, although in the past a first deputy prime minister has been designated. The prime minister and his deputies coordinate questions of primary importance on a supraministerial level, such as foreign trade, investment, energy, and health and welfare. The chairman of the Planning Commission and other officials with ministerial-level responsibilities, such as the head of the Office for Religious Affairs, are also generally members of the council. Most of the ministries function as purely administrative organs and are not in themselves centers of power. It had previously been common practice for members of the PZPR Politburo and other ranking party figures to serve on the Council of Ministers, although in recent years most ministers held high—but not the highest—party posts and were not members of the Sejm. The PZPR congress of mid-1981 resolved that joint occupancy of high party and government positions was undesirable. As of early 1983 only the prime minister, the minister of foreign affairs, and the acting minister of national defense were members of the Politburo.

The other two recognized parties are usually accorded nominal representation on the Council of Ministers. After the Sejm election of 1980, the council was made up of 37 members of the PZPR, two from the ZSL, one from the SD, and one nonparty member.

The work of the Council of Ministers can be compared to that of a cabinet in Western-style government, except for the absence of policymaking functions. Its members direct and coordinate the work of all ministries and agencies of state administration, including those of local government. The prime minister appoints regional leaders, and the minister of administration, local economy, and environmental protection exercises day-to-day supervision over local governments. The council provides general guidance in the sphere of foreign relations and defense. Its primary duties, however, center on economic affairs—the drafting of the five-year socioeconomic plan for submission to the Sejm, adoption of the annual socioeconomic plan, and supervision over the execution of the national plan and the state budget. Through the individual ministries responsible for various production sectors, the cabinet concerns itself directly with industrial output and development. The council has authority to issue ordinances, which are detailed regulations that give effect to a law, and resolutions, which are executive acts linked with the attainment of socioeconomic plans. To come into force, all ordinances must be published in the official gazette, *Dziennik Ustaw*; many cabinet resolutions are published in *Monitor Polski*.

Within each ministry, from three to nine undersecretaries of state, generally known as vice ministers, share responsibilities with the minister and form an advisory body known as a collegium. Vice ministers have a more pronounced political role than those in many Western parliamentary systems. Certain of these positions are filled by members of the other two recognized parties in agreed proportions. These are approximately 20 quasi-ministerial bodies, generally headed by presidents and responsible directly to the prime minister. Among these are the Committee for Physical Culture and Tourism, the Central Statistical Office, the Committee for Radio and Television, and the Polish Academy of Science.

Supreme Chamber of Control

The Supreme Chamber of Control, functioning in a watchdog capacity, is enjoined to supervise the central and local organs of administration from the standpoint of "legality, the implementation of the socioeconomic plan, efficient management, expediency, and fair dealing." Originally, its effectiveness sprang from the fact that it was independent from the Council of Ministers; although under nominal control of the Council of State, it was subject to the general jurisdiction of the Sejm, which appointed its chairman. Spearheaded by its bureau of inspection, the chamber could carry out inquiries and make reports directly to the Sejm on the implementation of the state budget and economic plans. Although it was said that the recommendations of the chamber were often too formalized to be of practical use, it had a reputation of being an incorruptible body, acting to a degree as a brake on excesses and exposing gross inefficiency.

For a time the constitutional changes of 1976 subordinated the chamber to the Council of Ministers, granting a supervisory role to the prime minister that included naming its chairman. In October 1980 the Sejm reasserted its authority over the chamber by another constitutional amendment that, in addition, expanded the body's power of supervision over the entire state and economic administration. This action was in response to the public outrage over instances of abuse of authority, corruption, and high living by state and party functionaries. Since then, the chairman of the Supreme Chamber of Control has been considered to have senior rank as a member of the Council of Ministers.

Regional and Local Government

Local administration in Poland underwent far-reaching changes between 1972 and 1975 aimed at introducing a more efficient and modern structure, but resulting at the same time in a system more responsive to the central authorities and more closely bound to the apparatus of the PZPR. The country had previously been divided into 22 voivodships (see Glossary), 391 counties, and 4,671 villages. As a result of the reforms, these three tiers of regional and local government were replaced by a two-tier system of 49 voivodships and nearly 3,000 basic administrative units, consisting in 1979 of 799 towns, 21 urban districts (seven in Warsaw, four in Krakow, five in Lodz, and five in Wroclaw), and 1,533 communes.

Popularly elected people's councils function as the legislative units at both the voivodship and the local levels (see fig. 16). Until 1973 each council elected from its own members a presidium as its executive and administrative organ. As part of the reforms, council

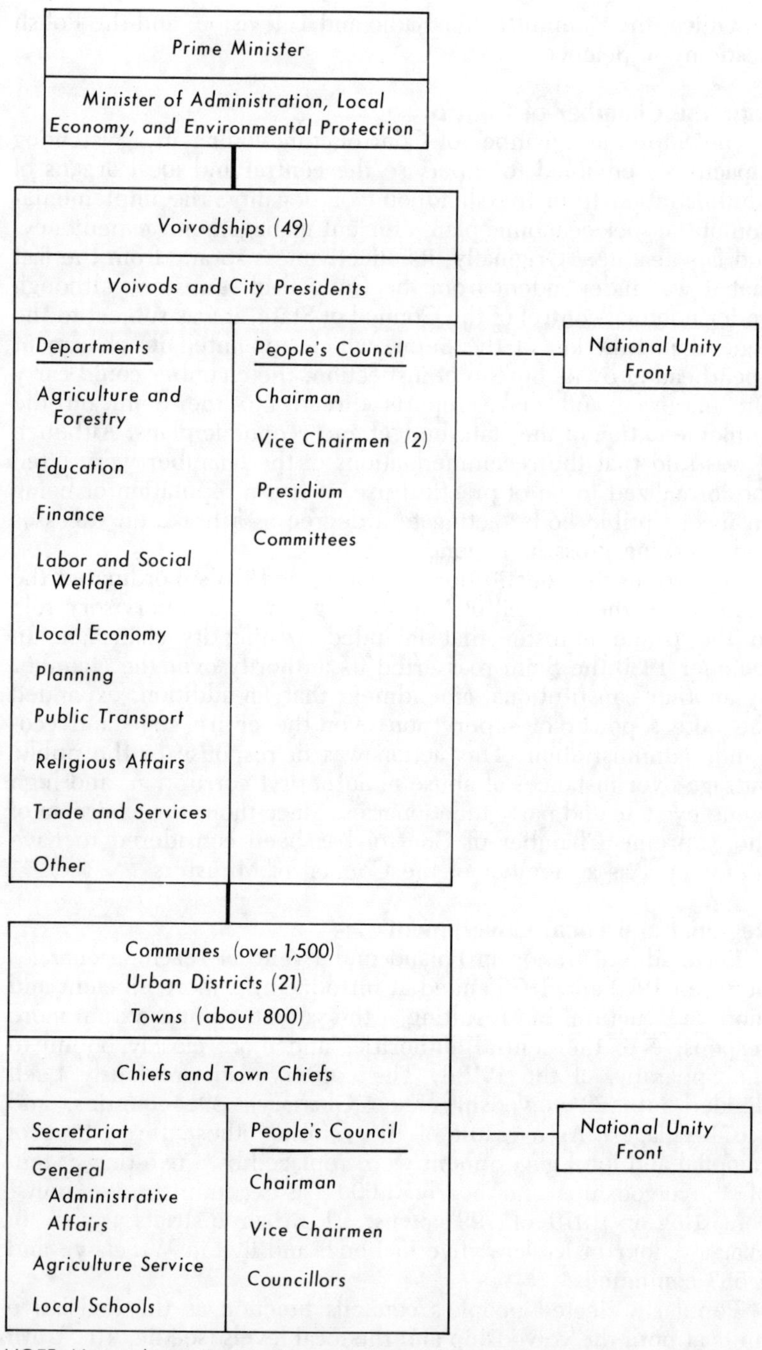

NOTE–National Unity Front selects candidates for people's council.

Figure 16. Local Government Structure, 1982

functions were separated from those of the executive and administrative bodies. At the voivodship level these bodies subsequently have been headed by a voivod (prefect or governor) except for the three municipal voivodships of Warsaw, Krakow, and Lodz, where the highest officials are called city presidents. Other cities having populations of over 50,000 also have presidents. Communities of smaller populations have town chiefs; city districts and the rural communes are headed by chiefs. These local officers are appointed by the supervising voivod or city president in consultation with the local people's council.

Voivods and city presidents and their deputies are appointed by the prime minister. Their terms of office are indefinite, and they are in effect professional administrators who regard themselves as answerable not only to the council but also to the Ministry of Administration, Local Economy, and Environmental Protection in Warsaw. Until the practice was discarded in 1981, people's councils at both the voivodship and the local levels were chaired by the regional or local first secretary of the PZPR; the two deputy chairmen were from the ZSL and the SD. As of 1982, nine of the 49 chairmen of voivodship councils were listed as ZSL members. Commune councils have elected members of other parties and even nonparty members as their chairmen.

Elections to the people's councils for four-year terms are normally held concurrently with elections to the Sejm. A single list of candidates representing the officially recognized parties in predetermined proportions is presented to the voters. Theoretically, the election of an unpopular candidate could be prevented if enough voters scratched his name off the list, but in reality a vast majority of voters return unmarked ballots, ensuring election of the official nominees.

Review over administrative departments is exercised by the people's councils in several ways. They must approve annual budgets and local socioeconomic plans; they adopt guidelines directing activities of the professional management officials; they may review the performance of the administrative apparatus by calling for reports of activities by subsidiary bodies. The voivodship administration is generally composed of 19 administrative departments concerned with matters such as the local economy, agriculture and forestry, finance, trade and services, public transport, labor and social welfare, etc. The plans of locally managed industrial enterprises must be coordinated with regional economic plans. To reduce the possibility of friction, heads of leading industrial enterprises are often co-opted onto commissions of the local administration or are members of people's councils. Centrally directed enterprises (mining, energy, chemicals, heavy industry) and state institutions (universities, scientific bodies, correctional facilities, banks, police) are exempt from voivodship or local control.

At the commune level the administrative structure is simpler. Its secretariat, headed by the second-ranking official of the commune (the commune secretary), supervises departments of general administration and of agriculture and a registrar's office. Communes are responsible for utilities, sanitation, roadbuilding and maintenance, administration of apartment blocks, encouragement of private farming, farm deliveries, and retail trade. In towns they may supervise schools, clinics, cultural clubs, libraries, and theaters.

The administrative reforms of the early and mid-1970s had some progressive features, but the result on balance has been to widen the gap between the community and local organs of administration, to reduce the people's councils to even greater subservience to Warsaw, and to emphasize the role of the PZPR. The earlier village-level unit of government was considered too small to be effective or to attract qualified administrators. PZPR members were generally in a minority on their councils, where ZSL or nonparty members were predominant. The new and larger communes were allotted additional sources of revenue, notably a turnover tax on local industry. Budget surpluses were thus available to be used for locally devised economic or social projects. Moreover, older, poorly educated officials were succeeded by more dynamic state-trained administrators. This improved the effectiveness of local government, but it also reduced popular influence over decisionmaking and brought greater bureaucratization. The distancing of the people's councils from the executive-administrative structure meant, according to some observers, that the councils had become little more than debating societies. The real axis of authority often consisted of the PZPR first secretary, who chaired the people's council, and the chief executive officer buttressed by entrenched administrative departments.

Under the previous system of 22 voivodships (of which five were major cities), the PZPR's first secretaries acted as regional overlords, enjoying a status comparable to that of a member of the Politburo. Gierek, first secretary of the national PZPR during the 1970s and previously a regional first secretary in the industrial heartland of Katowice, was reputed to have governed his voivodship as a semi-independent entity with little regard for directives from Warsaw. By a doubling of the number of voivodships and the introduction of appointive professional administrators as voivods who were also required to carry out the instructions of the central government, the autonomy of the voivodships was considerably curtailed.

Electoral System

Single-slate elections in Poland, as in other communist states, are relatively insignificant features of the political process. In the eyes of the regime, however, they provide a valuable demonstration of its legitimacy and endorsement of its policies by the public. Intense efforts are made to secure a high turnout, and it is regularly claimed that over 95 percent of the eligible voters cast their ballots. The franchise is extended to all Polish citizens over the age of 18.

Candidates for the Sejm and for people's council at the voivodship and commune levels are nominated by political and social organizations that participate in the Front Jednosci Narodu (National Unity Front), a framework body that brings the dominant PZPR together with the two other recognized political parties and mass and social organizations that have been approved as supporting the general policy line of the PZPR. The front draws up a single electoral list, selecting candidates from names submitted by its various member groups on the basis of PZPR directives. Poland is one of several East European countries that allows for satellite parties, but it is somewhat unorthodox in putting forward more candidates than there are seats, creating the illusion that the voter is being presented with an actual choice.

For elections to the Sejm, the country is divided into 72 electoral districts. Of the 49 voivodships, 37 are single constituencies; the remainder are divided into two or more. The number of deputies from each district ranges from three to 10. The electoral list composed by the National Unity Front must contain more names (but not over 50 percent more) than the number of candidates to be elected in a given district. In a four-member constituency, for example, six candidates may appear on the ballot. The officially approved candidates are those at the top of the list. Voters who place unmarked ballots in the polling box are casting their votes for these candidates. Although a voter might retire to a booth to cross out one or more of the approved names, a large majority avoid political risks by casting unmarked ballots. On only one occasion (in 1957) has the striking of a candidate's name caused him to fail in a bid for election. Occasionally, a number of voters will seek to register their dissatisfaction with a prominent party figure by striking his name. In the 1980 election the minister of internal affairs fell from first to sixth place on the list; the prime minister fell from first to fourth place, although he still gained over 90 percent of the votes in his constituency. It is rare for a candidate from the bottom of the list to receive over 5 percent of all votes.

Although the exact procedure has not been revealed, the National Unity Front determines (presumably as directed by the PZPR) the proportion of seats that will go to each group. The number of seats going to each party has scarcely altered since 1957. In the election of March 1980 the PZPR was allocated 261 seats in the Sejm, the ZSL 113 seats, and the SD 37 seats. The remaining 49 seats went to nonparty candidates, including members of approved youth and women's groups and three Roman

Catholic groups (Pax, the Christian Social Association, and Znak), which together were assigned 16 seats. The government announced that the level of participation had involved 98.87 percent of all eligible voters and that, with 646 candidates for the 460 seats, the approved candidates had been endorsed by 24,683,056 voters, against 133,248 ballots rejecting one or more of the front's candidates—an approval rate of 99.52 percent for the official candidates. Some observers found particularly implausible the official data of the 1980 turnout and the percentages of votes in favor of the National Unity Front's list, both of which were claimed to be higher than in 1976. The 1976 election was carried out during a period of relative prosperity, whereas the 1980 elections had been preceded by revelations of grave economic failures traced to shortcomings in the leadership that gave rise to public anger and increasingly bold dissent.

In an analysis of Sejm deputies by British political scientists George Sakwa and Martin Crouch, it was found that between one-half and two-thirds were notables in other party, state, or social organizations at the local or national level. Members of the PZPR Politburo, the ZSL executive committee, or the SD presidium were almost certain to be elected, as were high percentages of PZPR Central Committee members and provincial secretaries of all parties. An unusual development preceding the 1980 election was the presentation of nominees by one of the unrecognized dissident groups, the Confederation for an Independent Poland (Konfederacja Polski Niepodleglej—KPN), before National Unity Front committees in four cities. None was allowed to appear on the ballot.

The Legal System

Polish law is imbued with the philosophical outlook of Marxism-Leninism, but elements of the legal tradition of the Romano-Germanic family of laws still can be found in the legal system. The emphasis is on a systematic grouping of laws, phrased in fairly general terms, in the form of various codes, such as the administrative code, family code, labor code, and so forth. An entirely new penal code was adopted in 1970, and in 1971 a code was passed covering transgressions not to be treated as criminal acts. Judicial decisions are not regarded as a source of law, although Supreme Court decisions are recognized as binding legal rules.

The Judiciary

Justice is administered by a hierarchy of courts headed by the Supreme Court and including voivodship courts, district courts, and special courts. Among the latter are military and labor and social insurance courts.

Misdemeanor boards are part of an informal court system under local organs of administration and headed by laymen. They may administer fines up to 5,000 zlotys (for value of the zloty—see Glossary) and three months' imprisonment for traffic offenses, public disturbances, vagrancy, and drunkeness. It was officially reported that 704,000 offenses were brought before these misdemeanor boards in 1982. Of 1 million cases handled by the courts, nearly 800,000 involved family and civil law, and only 200,000 were criminal violations.

District courts are the courts of first instance for civil and criminal cases. Their jurisdiction generally embraces several towns and communes. As of 1980 there were 261 district courts in Poland, from two to 20 in each voivodship. Judicial hearings take place before a professional judge and two people's assessors who represent the people's interest. The latter, elected by people's councils for four-year terms, have the same rights as judges; findings are reached by a simple majority vote, with the possibility of the judge being in the minority. As in other East European legal systems, a leading role is played by the public prosecutor (procurator), whose purpose is to ensure strict observance of the law, to indict suspects after conducting criminal investigations, and to act as the public accuser at trials. Prosecutor's offices at the voivodship and district levels are units of the prosecutor general's office in Warsaw, which is independent of the Ministry of Justice and responsible directly to the Council of State.

Voivodship courts function as courts of first instance in major civil and criminal cases and as appellate courts in appeals against lower court verdicts. Military courts try individuals, both military and civilian, accused of security offenses. A separate code of criminal procedures applies, and appeals may be addressed only to a military review board.

As the nation's highest judicial body, the Supreme Court supervises activities of all courts. It is composed of four divisions: criminal, civil, labor and social insurance, and military. The first president of the Supreme Court is the chief justice; presidents are in charge of each division. Justices are appointed by the Council of State for five-year renewable terms. In addition to reviewing judgments of other courts, the Supreme Court lays down principles for administration of justice to ensure uniformity of judgments and passes resolutions to clarify regulations over which differences have arisen. When a routine Supreme Court panel of three judges cannot reach agreement on a specific matter, a panel of seven judges may resolve the problem, and the resolution becomes binding on routine panels.

Trials are held in public except in circumstances where an open courtroom could lead to social unrest or would expose facts damaging to national security or other important public interests. Defendants are entitled to counsel, although in the case of misdemeanor boards this rule is apparently not observed; only a close relative is permitted to speak for the accused. Polish attorneys, of whom about 3,700 specialize in court proceedings, are organized into 300 collectives in which profits are partially shared. A successful practice may bring a thriving income in fees.

During a trial the judge enjoys considerable latitude to do what is necessary to reach a just verdict, including direct interrogation of witnesses and experts. The United States Department of State's *Country Reports on Human Rights Practices* for 1980 states that judges appear to protect the rights of the accused in nonpolitical cases and have been known to drop charges or impose substantially lesser sentences against dissidents than were sought by the prosecution. Although judges are ostensibly independent of executive control, decisions having major political overtones are in effect decided by the government even if handed down by the courts. A secret report compiled in 1979 by Experience and the Future, a group consisting of Polish intellectuals, including party members, found that the judiciary was subject to political directives and that people of higher education, status, connections, and money received favorable treatment. The same document (later published in the United States as *Poland Today: The State of the Republic*) added that, in spite of poor pay and an overburden of work, the judiciary strives to perform in a socially worthy manner; judges particularly susceptible to party and government pressure do not enjoy a good name in professional circles.

Several new bodies have been created with the objective of introducing judicial review over those actions by government agencies having the force of law. In January 1980 administrative regulations in 140 laws were standardized, and the central authorities were given power to review the rulings of voivods. The new Supreme Administrative Tribunal in Warsaw enabled appeals to be heard from administrative authorities in areas such as housing construction, taxes, real estate and personal property, education, welfare, employment, and other social matters.

A constitutional amendment passed in March 1982 provides for the Tribunal of State to monitor the official actions of individuals in key posts (except party officials) to ensure compliance with the Constitution and other legal prescriptions. The origin of the new institution can be traced to disclosures during 1980 of large-scale corruption by many high officials. The tribunal is linked to the Sejm by a parliamentary committee on constitutional responsibility, which is to examine proposed suits against officeholders and recommend to the complete Sejm whether the case should be presented to the tribunal. The tribunal consists of a chairman and deputy, 22 regular members, and five deputy members; only half of the tribunal members need have a judicial background. First hearings are before the chairman and six members; the full court sits only for appeals against verdicts of the smaller body.

The same constitutional amendment withdrew from the Council of State the right of review over the constitutionality of laws and stipulated that a constitutional tribunal should be formed to assess all legal acts for conformity with the Constitution. As of early 1983 this new court had not yet been established.

In early 1983, martial law having recently been lifted, it was not possible to forecast whether these new tribunals would become significant features of the judicial scene as guarantors of legality and protection against official misbehavior. The awkward and complex procedure for bringing accused officeholders before the Tribunal of State, not to mention the possibility of its subjection to political pressures, gave rise to doubt that it would be permitted to exercise its functions in an unobstructed and impartial manner. In December 1982 the Sejm's committee on constitutional responsibility was examining charges raised by a group of deputies against a former prime minister and three former vice prime ministers for possible referral to the tribunal.

Civil Rights

The degree of tolerance for dissent and organized opposition in Poland has varied with the political climate. After a brief relaxation of internal controls that coincided with Gomulka's accession to the party leadership in 1956, activities and the expression of views in conflict with the party line were generally curtailed until Solidarity's appearance in 1980. Nevertheless, infringements of personal liberty and constraints on individual rights guaranteed by the Constitution have been less oppressive than in most other countries of Eastern Europe. Outbreaks of dissidence triggered by the bloody suppression of worker riots in 1976 were met with restraint by the Gierek government. Opposition political groups, while subject to periodic harassment, were tolerated; no sustained effort was made to stamp out the underground press, and freer expression of political views was permitted in the Sejm.

In the period preceding the imposition of martial law in December 1981, there were believed to have been for all practical purposes no political prisoners in Poland. The provisions of Polish law permitting detentions of persons under investigation for up to 48 hours were, however, employed by the police to harass dissenters. An unofficial Polish civil rights monitoring group reported in October 1980 that, in addition to often repeated detentions, political dissenters were subjected to dismissal from jobs, surveillance, telephone tapping, and searches of apartments. Misdemeanor charges were commonly brought against individuals on grounds of resisting the militia in the performance of its duties, for circulating unofficial publications, or for making homes available for lectures of the unsanctioned "flying university" (see Popular Political Expression, this ch.). The Polish group documented numerous cases of beatings or intimidation of detained individuals by the militia to secure confessions. Punishment of militia members for use of excessive force was almost unknown. After the emergence of Solidarity in August 1980 until the onset of martial law, flagrant abuses diminished. Except for several instances of deliberate political provocation, the police acted with greater restraint and no longer exercised unbridled authority.

Freedom of assembly, although guaranteed by the Constitution, is conditioned on approval of a meeting or demonstration by the local authorities. After unauthorized demonstrations, organizers were frequently arrested and received fines or one- to three-month jail sentences for disturbing the peace. Before Solidarity, workers who tried to organize trade unions and to strike were often fired on grounds of unauthorized absence from work. This policy was modified after the government accepted Solidarity as an independent labor movement free of state and party control. Most demonstrations organized by Solidarity took place without explicit permission.

The introduction of martial law on December 13, 1981, brought an abrupt end to the liberalizing trends and a suspension of rights delimited in the Constitution, such as personal liberty, inviolability of the home, privacy of correspondence, and freedom of association, speech, publication, and rallies. A punitive campaign was launched against Solidarity, and thousands of it partisans were subjected to internment at 49 detention centers. Summary trials were held under martial law without right of appeal. The *New York Times* of February 5, 1982, described a trial in Gdynia presided over by a naval lieutenant commander in which nine workers were sentenced from three to nine years for offenses such as attending a meeting. The harsh sentences, based on doubtful evidence presented in a hostile court setting, were viewed as politically motivated to crush the spirit of resistance among factory workers. Employees have been forced under threats of dismissal to sign oaths of loyalty and to renounce their allegiance to Solidarity. Peaceful and passive resistance have been quelled by force, and 11 deaths have been acknowledged by the authorities. Detainees were released in groups of several hundred during 1982, but when the suspension of martial law was declared, the government acknowledged that about 1,000 were still in custody, including most senior leaders of Solidarity. In addition, at least 4,000 individuals were under arrest on charges of violating martial law, and another 2,500 had been tried and were serving prison terms.

Political Setting

The political convulsions that engulfed Poland, commencing with the Gdansk Agreement of August 1980 and ending with the imposition of martial law in December 1981, had no parallel since the Soviet Union consolidated its control in Eastern Europe more than three decades earlier (see Solidarity, this ch.). The agreement was only the first of many undertakings extracted from the PZPR at all levels of authority. Discredited officials were dismissed, new economic concessions were promised, and public expression hitherto monopolized by a small group of party elites was being exercised by many segments of Polish society. Professional and regional associations, bona fide trade unions, and Catholic and secular intellectuals could be heard from. Subordinate political parties that had obediently taken their cues from the PZPR voted out their old leaders and adopted more independent policies. Students and faculty struck for university autonomy.

A communist party already battered by economic shocks and revelations of official misconduct was ill prepared to deal confidently with the Solidarity organization, which had enrolled much of the Polish laboring force under its banner. The PZPR's tactics were initial resistance, minimal concessions, and foot-dragging when pressed to fulfill its promises. Solidarity had as its only weapons strikes and the threat of strikes. The result was a tangle of compromises and commitments on which the authorities reneged, implemented in part, or were simply incapable of carrying out under chaotic political and economic conditions.

In an effort to steady the ruling party and create the impression of decisiveness, Poland's top military figure, General Wojciech Jaruzelski, became in February 1981 Poland's fourth prime minister in the space of a year. Some disputes with Solidarity were resolved as Jaruzelski sought a three-month moratorium on strikes. He blundered into renewed confrontation, however, after Solidarity activists were beaten by police in Bydgoszcz. His procrastination over recognition of a parallel Solidarity for farmers stirred further resentment.

By mid-1981, attention had shifted to a special congress of the PZPR. Infected by the new spirit, delegates were for the first time chosen by democratic procedures, and elections to the Central Committee resulted in the exclusion of most party professionals. Stanislaw Kania, a party moderate, was reelected first secretary in what appeared to be a genuinely contested vote. Under blunt pressure from the Communist Party of the Soviet Union, however, policies hardened against Solidarity. Kania, seen as too compliant, was shortly to be replaced by Jaruzelski, who subsequently headed both the government and the PZPR.

The transformation of Solidarity from a free trade union to a mass political and social movement was consummated at its national congress in September and October 1981. The moderate element headed by Lech Walesa, Solidarity's guiding force from its founding, continued in the ascendancy but, in a growing spirit of militancy, the congress concluded with a call for the restructuring of the state and the economy on a democratic basis.

In spite of growing involvement by the Roman Catholic Church seeking to moderate differences, the government was increasingly reluctant to negotiate. Seeing little possibility of reconciling Solidarity's demands with preservation of communist rule and under pressure from the Soviet Union, Jaruzelski's stance hardened. The ensuing deadlock and signs that the government planned to assume extraordinary powers provoked Solidarity leaders to call for a permanent representative body to define the country's economic policies and a referendum on Jaruzelski's rule if this demand were not met.

The introduction of martial law and the extinguishing of civil rights were defended by Jaruzelski as bringing an end to instability while averting economic catastrophe, civil war, and (by implication) Soviet intervention. Harsh measures were invoked. Solidarity militants and moderates alike were interned. Those escaping government roundups and later arrested for continued activity on behalf of Solidarity were given severe jail sentences by summary courts. Academics and journalists were forced to renounce allegiance to the Solidarity movement. Solidarity underground leaders managed to kindle popular demonstrations that revealed deep repugnance for the martial law authority, but tough measures by the government's security forces progressively discouraged protests. In October 1982 the government decreed the dissolution of Solidarity. Jaruzelski had said that he respected a multiplicity of views and that reforms would be preserved and continued. His promises of socialist renewal and the new mechanisms for consultation between the people and the ruling party were, however, greeted with disdain or passivity.

Polish United Workers' Party

Ideological guidance for all forms of state activity in Poland issues from the PZPR directives that define the most important objectives of society, stipulate the pace and methods of attaining them, and dictate the form and composition of administrative structures. Conformity of government actions to party doctrines is ensured through supervision exercised by local party units in the administrative organs themselves and by the Central Committee and local party committees. The ruling party helps ensure correct ideological behavior by putting forward trusted members as candidates for leading positions in the administrative apparatus. The PZPR regards itself as carrying out the aims and interests of the working class in its task of reconstructing society. The working-class character of the PZPR is only partly confirmed by official data which, in 1982, claimed that workers accounted for 41 percent of those on party rolls. Most of the remainder were from the intelligentsia (about 36 percent) and the peasants (9 percent).

Organized opposition to the Marxist-Leninist system or the possibility of any opposition group's taking over political power from the PZPR is inadmissible. This would mean, in the eyes of the PZPR, handing back the hard-won revolutionary victory of the working people to hostile classes of society that had previously brought Poland close to extinction. All political and social activities on a national level are in principle organized, directed, and coordinated through the PZPR. Classified as the auxiliary and mass organizations, they include youth, women's, farmers', and veterans' organizations. The SD and ZSL form part of the system as declared supporters of the communist line. They have not been formally absorbed by the PZPR but are institutionally linked to it through the National Unity Front.

The pre-World War II Communist Party of Poland had failed to attract a sizable following, and its nationalist orientation was viewed with suspicion by Soviet leader Josef Stalin. The party's liquidation was ordained by Stalin in 1938. Its most active members, who had been summoned to the Soviet Union, were executed or died in prison camps as victims of Stalin's purges. After the German invasion of the Soviet Union, a small band of Polish communists in Moscow was permitted to reestablish the party, a step carried out secretly and with great difficulty in Nazi-occupied Warsaw in 1942. Wladyslaw Gomulka, who had survived clandestinely in Poland, emerged in 1943 as first secretary of what was known as the Polish Workers' Party. A majority of the new leaders were, however, Soviet protégés who continued to receive orders from Moscow. Too unpopular to compete openly against the democratic parties that had prewar antecedents, the Polish Workers' Party set out to subdue its opponents through splinter tactics with the help of Soviet-led security organs. A coalition led by the Communists and including the Polish Socialist Party, the Polish Peasant Party, and the Democratic Party won over 80 percent of the votes in the 1947 election, using methods protested by the British and United States governments. The Communists were henceforth in a dominant political position. Consolidating their power in 1948, they combined with the socialist group into a single organization, the Polish United Workers' Party. After a screening process, large numbers of socialist members were purged, leaving the Communists in firm control (see The Sovietization of Poland, ch. 1).

The ultimate source of authority within the PZPR is the party congress, which normally meets every five years. In practice, authority and decisionmaking are concentrated in the top echelons of the party, particularly in the Politburo and the Secretariat of the Central Committee. At the pinnacle of power and policymaking is the party first secretary. Although Jaruzelski has combined this post with that of prime minister, they are generally separate, the prime minister's office being subordinate.

The congress elects the Central Committee, which serves as the supreme party organ between congresses; plenary sessions are held four times annually. The committee oversees the functioning of government agencies and the implementing of policy decisions that have been taken by the congress, exercises control over local and regional party units, and supervises the allocation of party funds (see fig. 17).

Both the Politburo and the secretariat have been "elected" by the Central Committee from its own membership on the basis of recommendations by senior party figures by what has always been announced as a unanimous vote. In practice, the Politburo has been a self-perpetuating body, any changes in its membership or that of the secretariat being prearranged by the party heads.

In order to carry out its administrative tasks, the Central Committee is provided with a bureaucratic structure that functions under the direction of the secretariat. As of 1982 there were 14 main departments, as well as other bureaus, offices, and commissions, operating under direct control of the Central Committee. Two important party organs, the Central Control Commission and the Central Audit Commission, are responsible to the Politburo and the secretariat through the Central Committee. The Central Control Commission is responsible for party discipline and the screening of candidates for party leadership posts, whereas the Central Audit Commission exercises general control over PZPR financial affairs and examines the finances of its various organs. The Central Control Commission has been the instrument through which PZPR leaders have periodically carried out purges of the party membership.

Every PZPR member is a member of a basic organization at his or her place of work. These units numbered about 70,000 in 1980, including 3,500 in the armed forces. They are subordinate to more than 2,000 commune, town, or urban district party committees corresponding to the country's administrative divisions. These are in turn subordinate to the 49 voivodship committees. Each committee holds its own conferences and has a separate secretariat, departments, commissions, and administrative sections. Party units participate in the direction of economic enterprises, train and indoctrinate new members, and transmit and interpret party policies to other bodies, such as labor, youth, and social groups, to ensure that society as a whole is responsive to communist principles and party directives.

According to a leading party figure, the PZPR (which reached a peak membership of 3,092,000 in 1980) had experienced a loss of

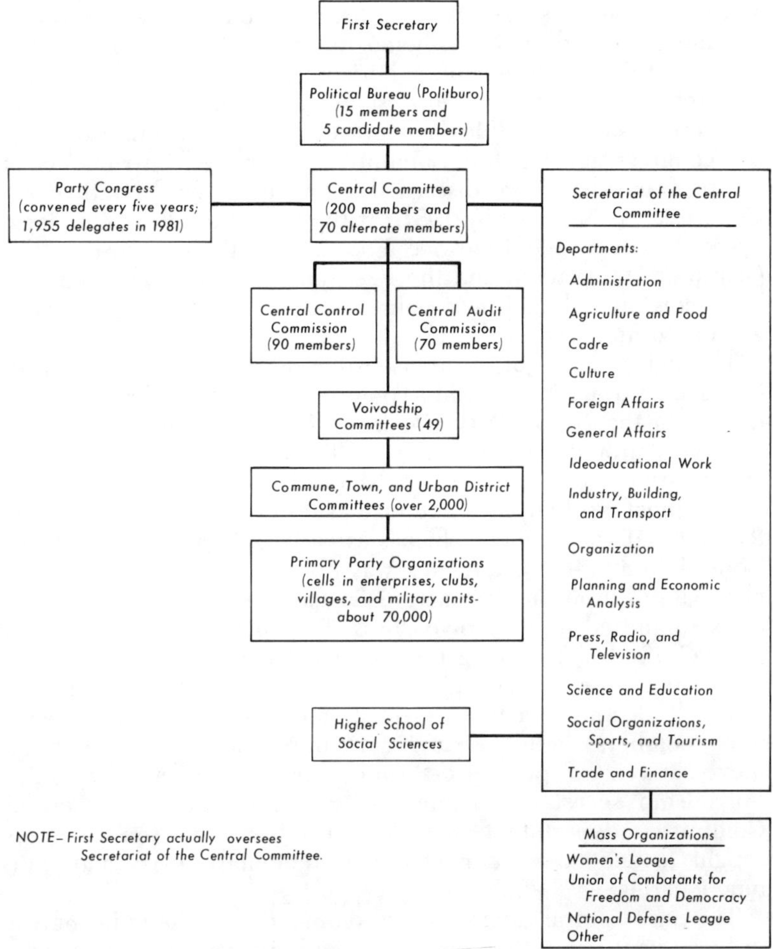

Figure 17. Structure of Polish United Workers' Party, 1982

over 800,000 members by early 1983. Most of the losses came about through mass resignations of more liberal elements after the imposition of martial law. Other members were crossed off the rolls for inactivity or violation of party discipline. Many party units were disbanded in an effort to curb ideological deviation.

Reforms of the 1981 Party Congress

The wave of popular backing for Solidarity, the economic plight attributed to Gierek's blunders, and revelations of official corruption plunged the party rank and file into confusion through most of

1981. Party units in a number of communities, industrial plants, and educational institutions came together to coordinate views on specific issues and to discuss democratization of the PZPR. Unable to curb these unauthorized "horizontal structures," the party hierarchy acquiesced in reformist demands for more democratic election procedures. Rules and practices that had hitherto made the congress and Central Committee disciplined instruments of the party insiders were discarded before the special Ninth Party Congress was held in July 1981. At the same time, hard-line local bodies, such as the Katowice Forum, the Poznan Forum, the Grunwald Association, and the Rzeczywistosc clubs, charged that bourgeois liberal and nationalist (anti-Soviet) tendencies were gaining ground within the PZPR.

Through a series of elections extending from the lower party levels up through voivodship conferences, 1,955 delegates were named to the Ninth Party Congress. Missing were a number of nationally prominent party officials. Their defeat came as a result of new rules, including secret balloting, which overturned the earlier practice of virtually automatic selection of Central Committee and high government officials as party delegates. A list of 275 Central Committee candidates was obtained by combining with nominations from the floor an official slate based on recommendations submitted by the voivodships. By crossing names of candidates off the list, the delegates expressed their preferences for the 200 seats on the committee. The result was a massive repudiation of the leadership. Of those elected, more than 90 percent were new members; industrial and agricultural workers were much more heavily represented than party and state officials. Voivodship secretaries, ministers, vice ministers, and Central Committee department heads were rejected as the congress sought to end domination of the movement by party and state functionaries.

The new Central Committee recommended to the full congress two candidates for first secretary, both representing a centrist position against the extremes of party reformers and hard-liners. Kania (1,311 votes) was reelected over Kazimierz Barcikowski (568 votes) after extensive questioning of both candidates. Two other nominees declined to stand against Kania. This was the only time that the PZPR leader, the paramount authority in the country, had been chosen by secret ballot from a list that contained more than one candidate. The Central Committee then elected Kania's recommendations for the 14 members of the Politburo, two alternates, and the seven secretaries of the Central Committee, defeating candidates nominated from the floor. The prime minister, Jaruzelski, was one of only four full members returned to the Politburo.

In addition to election reforms, the congress overwhelmingly approved new party statutes limiting to two terms the period anyone could serve in executive office, providing for reconvening the congress by petition of half its members, and prescribing other rules to democratize the PZPR and reduce overlapping of state and party functions. The congress finally expelled from the party former first secretary Gierek, former prime minister Edward Babiuch, former deputy prime ministers Jan Szydlak and Tadeusz Pyka, and other leading officials. It seemed that the congress had wrought a permanent transformation, institutionalizing internal party democracy and exposing the process of leadership selection to public view. Yet within three months (on October 18, 1981) Kania had resigned his position as first secretary, and Jaruzelski was chosen to replace him by a nearly unanimous vote of the Central Committee. Kania's withdrawal was said to reflect lack of confidence by other key party figures in his efforts to negotiate with Solidarity and perhaps pressure by the Soviet Union to reimpose the PZPR's authority over the Solidarity movement. A Central Committee meeting at the end of February 1982 was noteworthy for its tone of obedience to Jaruzelski's leadership, fully endorsing the martial law regime, approving by a nearly unanimous vote his nominations to the Politburo, and expressing unqualified condemnation of Solidarity (see table 12, Appendix A).

The party apparatus remained in a debilitated state through 1982, exercising no apparent influence over Jaruzelski in his mildly reformist course plotted with the aid of a small group of trusted generals and technocratic appointees. Moderates like Barcikowski were balanced by more orthodox elements in the Politburo, such as Stefan Olszowski. The Rzezywistosc faction, claiming 60,000 members and advocating more dogmatic policies and a tough attitude in dealing with dissenters, was headed by Tadeusz Grabski, a former Politburo member. When the government disbanded Rzeczywistosc in December 1982, Grabski attacked Jaruzelski's policies in a widely circulated letter in which he criticized economic reforms as detrimental to the workers and charged that the country was threatened by right-wing and counterrevolutionary forces. Grabski was exiled to a post at the Polish embassy in East Berlin. His departure left Albin Siwak, a leader in the official trade union movement elevated to the Politburo in 1981, the most outspoken proponent of hard-line policies. The significance of this faction was that it apparently had the backing of the Soviet Union, which was suspicious of reformist tendencies among some of Jaruzelski's advisers.

As of early 1983 the party was engaged in institutional rebuilding, stressing ideological training, reimposing control over lower level bodies, and allowing some discredited former officials or dissenters to resume their memberships. Party rank and file were directed to concern themselves with economic reforms at the factory level, to become associated with workers' interests, and to help reactivate state-sponsored unions. There remained, however, a considerable degree of passivity among ordinary members, few new recruits, and little evidence that a revitalized party apparatus was a priority goal of the ruling hierarchy.

Other Political Organizations

In addition to the PZPR, two other political parties are legally recognized in Poland—the United Peasant Party (Zjednoczone Stronnictwo Ludowe—ZSL) and the Democratic Party (Stronnictwo Demokratyczne—SD). Acceptance of these two organizations as parties does not mean, however, that they are contenders for political power. They function as auxiliaries of the PZPR and act as transmission belts of party policies to the individual farmers, intellectuals, small businessmen, and artisans whose interests they are designed to represent. Catholic viewpoints are represented in the Sejm by three smaller goups known as circles. The parties and circles were profoundly affected by the upheavals of 1980–81, resulting in leadership shake-ups, internal debate over their role and subservience to the PZPR, and open criticism of government actions. Upon the imposition of martial law, their brief experience of democratization was brought to a halt, although they continued to be represented in the Sejm and figured in new consultative citizens' groups organized by the regime.

United Peasant Party

The ZSL resulted from the 1948 merger of remnants of the former Polish Peasant Party, which had opposed the communists during the early post-World War II period, and the communist-supported Peasant Party. The program of the new party became a replica of that of the PZPR. One of its basic tasks was identified as the mobilization of the peasant masses to fulfill the PZPR's economic plan; a second task was described as that of strengthening peasant solidarity with the working class.

The ZSL undertakes to represent rural interests, mainly of the private farmers, by assisting in organizing peasant economic and cultural activity. Until 1980 there was no question of its acting in opposition to its senior partner, the PZPR, in formulating and carrying out official agricultural policy. As compensation, the ZSL was fairly well represented in senior positions of the government and was allocated one-fourth of the seats in the Sejm. Its leader, Stanislaw Gucwa, enjoyed some prestige by virtue of his position as marshal of the Sejm.

Organized on a basis similar to that of the PZPR, the ZSL has a presidium of 11 members and a seven-member secretariat; there are similar bodies at the voivodship and commune levels. The basic organizational unit is the farmers' circle, of which there were about 28,500 in 1978. Membership in the party was claimed to be 478,000 in 1981, but a decline accompanied the political turmoil of that year. Even earlier, the party, acting without prior PZPR consultation, was demanding greater power over the executive branch by the Sejm. It was also asking that subsidies to inefficient state farms be abolished and that the sale of farmland to private farmers be liberalized to raise productivity. In May 1981 the entire Presidium of the ZSL was forced to resign over rank-and-file dissatisfaction with the leadership's strong opposition to independent farmers' unions (Rural Solidarity). Gucwa was replaced, although he retained his position as marshal of the Sejm. In 1983 the party's chairman, Roman Malinowski, was also one of the deputy prime ministers.

Democratic Party

Much smaller than the ZSL, the SD was founded in 1938 from a group of democratic clubs formed by intellectuals, white-collar workers, and professional people that had opposed successive right-wing, autocratic regimes. After World War II residual non-Marxist political elements were grouped in this party, whose leaders had endorsed communist proposals for land reform and advocated close ties with the Soviet Union.

The highest authority of the SD is the congress that elects the 119-member Central Committee, whose executive bodies are the 12-member Presidium and the General Secretariat. In addition to committees in each voivodship, in 1980 there were 433 municipal committees, 15 city district committees, and seven university committees. The basic unit was the circle, of which 3,400 had been organized. Party membership totaled about 110,000. Its Sejm representation has been set at 38 seats since 1957. The primary purpose of the SD has been to represent the interests of artisans, small business and service industries, and the intelligentsia, while mobilizing these sectors to appropriate political activism in support of the socialist state.

The growing disarray in Polish political life engendered by the rise of Solidarity was echoed by demands within the ranks of the SD that it end its close alignment with the PZPR. In October 1980 its Sejm deputies exercised unaccustomed latitude by voting against a government bill to extend wider powers to the Supreme Chamber of Control at the provincial level. At the SD congress in March 1981, amid calls for greater independence, only three members of the old Central Committee were reelected. The new Presidium chose as its leader Edward Kowalczyk, a deputy chairman of the Supreme Chamber of Control, replacing Tadeusz Mlynczak, who nevertheless retained his government position as a deputy chairman of the Council of State. The SD reaffirmed its support of the three-party alliance but accompanied this by demands for greater adherence to the rule of law and independence of the courts, greater representation of the SD in government agencies, access to the media, and the right to maintain contact with liberal parties in Western Europe. The SD's determination to redefine its role vis-à-vis the PZPR was not acceptable to the authorities and did not survive the onset of military rule. When nine SD deputies in the Sejm abstained or voted against the law abolishing the Solidarity unions in October 1982, they were suspended by their leaders.

Roman Catholic Action Groups

Although not enjoying official standing as political parties, certain Catholic groups exert a degree of political influence and take positions on various social issues. Two of the groups—the ostensibly progressive Pax movement and the Christian Social Association—have generally accommodated themselves with the regime and have advocated Christian support of communist socioeconomic policies short of adopting an atheistic philosophy of materialism. The two groups were awarded 11 seats in the 1980 Sejm election. A more representative Catholic group, Znak, which became known as neo-Znak after its more independent members were purged by the government, was allotted five seats in the Sejm.

Pax was founded in 1952 by Boleslaw Piasecki, who had an unsavory prewar record as leader of a fascist group but later collaborated with the Communists in their efforts to split the ranks of the Catholic opposition. Pax sought to perform a mediating role between the Catholic community and the regime but was never trusted by the church hierarchy. It did attract some Catholic intellectuals and politicians who felt it might help safeguard Catholic values in a state that was officially atheistic. Pax was also allowed to engage in widespread publishing enterprises, which enabled Catholic writings to appear in print. Pax was an ardent supporter of the regime's anti-Semitic campaign in 1967–68.

Upon Piasecki's death in 1980, the new chairman, Ryszard Reiff, presided over a shift in the organization's outlook, calling for political and economic change and associating Pax with many of the popular demands that catapulted Solidarity into the political foreground. Some of the 26,000 adherents of Pax became involved in activity sponsored by the dissidents, and the group's newspaper (*Slowo Powszechne*) campaigned boldly for reforms. Tentative contacts were opened with the church, the episcopate relaxing its previously strict boycott of Pax.

After the suspension of all Pax activity—brought about by the state of emergency in December 1981, which Reiff courageously opposed as a member of the Council of State—the group recanted its brief reformist stance, including Reiff's concept of a "grand coalition" between the PZPR, Solidarity, and the church, and pledged that future Pax activities would follow the political lines laid down by Jaruzelski. Reiff was replaced by Zenon Komender, who joined the government first as minister of domestic trade and services and later as a deputy prime minister.

The Christian Social Association, a group formed by dissident Pax members, has tried to steer a more moderate course while still endorsing the major policies of the regime. Although it has proclaimed loyalty to the church in religious matters, it has stressed its independence from the hierarchy in political affairs and has not been able to win any support from the church for its activities. Its head, Kazimierz Morawski, was named to the Council of State in 1982.

The name of the Znak group derives from the title of its monthly publication, which means "the sign." The five deputies normally allotted to it were at one time regarded as the sole independent voice in the Sejm, representative of politically liberal Catholic intellectuals and those of the church hierarchy who preferred improved relations between church and state rather than continued intransigence. When the Znak delegates spoke out in 1968 against police brutality in dealing with student protestors and the anti-Semitic campaign, the government bitterly attacked the group and drove its most outspoken members from the Sejm. Pursuing its efforts to subvert the Catholic movement, the government supported a more tractable faction organized by Janusz Zablocki. Longtime Znak leader Stanislaw Stomma was dropped from the Sejm when he echoed the church's objections to the constitutional revisions of 1976 and abstained from voting. The neo-Znak element under Zablocki subsequently prevailed. Its subservience to the government was underscored when neo-Znak refrained from joining church leaders and intellectual groups in condemning police reprisals against striking workers in 1976.

In February 1981 the launching of a new national organization, the Polish Catholic Social Union (Polski Zwiazek Katolicko Spoleczny—PZKS), was announced; neo-Znak would henceforth be known as the PZKS parliamentary group. Offering its services as a mediator between the church and the government, PZKS espoused a "historic compromise" involving the PZPR, Solidarity, and the Catholic groups. During the Sejm session called in January 1982 to ratify the marital law decrees, Zablocki, as leader of PZKS, expressed misgivings over the legality of the decrees and proposed the reinstatement of Solidarity. Four of the five members of his group abstained from voting; joined by one nonparty member, they were the only Sejm delegates who ventured to record their dissent from the regime's harsh action.

Popular Political Expression

The communist government in Poland has never succeeded in gaining the allegiance of a substantial proportion of the Polish people. Nevertheless, serious outbursts of discontent—as in 1956, 1970, and 1976—were spontaneous rather than organized; they were normally confined to specific grievances and did not call into question the legitimacy of the party and government. The regime has tolerated a low level of activity by opposition elements as long as they remained segmented and did not provoke the Soviet Union. Criticisms were expressed openly, mainly by intellectuals (educators, writers, and artists) who often were socialist in outlook but democratic in orientation and who managed to mount subtle but effective pressure on the regime in the areas of human rights and artistic freedom. The best organized opposition group was the Roman Catholic Church. Forced at first to fight for its own survival, it was principally concerned with preserving a privileged status until the 1970s. This position gradually gave way to limited involvement in supporting the grievances of embittered workers and in offering to mediate a dialogue with the regime.

The uneasy equilibrium between the communist authorities and the opposition was upset in the mid-1970s. Heartened by the human rights provisions of the 1975 Final Act of the Conference on Security and Cooperation in Europe (CSCE, also know as the Helsinki Agreement) and by activity of dissidents in the Soviet Union in a climate of East-West détente, the adversaries of the regime were emboldened to act more openly. The retreat of the authorities on constitutional amendment issues in 1976, when faced with protests from the church and thousands of intellectuals, further served to encourage the opposition.

The violent suppression of worker demonstrations in June 1976 resulted in the establishment of the Committee for the Defense of the Workers (Komitet Obrony Robotnikow—KOR), after September 1977 known as the Committee for Social Self-Defense-Committee for the Defense of the Workers (Komitet Samoobrony Spolecznej-Komitet Obrony Robotnikow—KSS-KOR). This group included some respected prewar socialists and wartime resistance figures. Among the most prominent of KOR activists were former student leaders who had been imprisoned after the 1968 demonstrations, including historian Adam Michnik and sociologist Jacek Kuron. Initially only 14 strong, the group expanded to 33 members and had perhaps 2,000 active supporters. KOR was formed to circulate underground reports on mistreatment of the demonstrating workers and to solicit funds for their medical and legal bills. Working openly, KOR avoided official restrictions by not adopting a formal structure, although its representatives were active in all major cities. Gradually expanding its goals but adhering to moderate tactics of dialogue with the PZPR, KOR pressed for stronger guarantees of civil rights, free trade unions, an easing of censorship, and an end to religious discrimination. KSS-KOR members were accepted as advisers to the striking workers in August 1980, reinforcing Solidarity's effectiveness through tactical and legal guidance. In spite of its moderate approach, KSS-KOR came under sustained attack from the government as counterrevolutionary and subversive. The committee dissolved itself in October 1981, announcing that it had fulfilled its function and was superfluous in view of Solidarity. The leading KSS-KOR activists were interned when martial law was declared. In early 1983 Kuron, Michnik, and three other KSS-KOR leaders were awaiting trial on charges of violation of martial law.

Other opposition groups and various clandestine organizations—usually associated with underground publications—were inspired by KOR's early success at engaging in political activism without meeting official reprisals. The Movement for the Defense of Human and Civil Rights (Ruch Obrony Praw Czlowieka i Obywatela—ROPCiO), launched in March 1977, was more nationalistic and more antagonistic to the regime than was KOR. Some individuals associated with ROPCiO were involved in the formation of the Confederation for an Independent Poland (Konfederacja Polski Niepodleglej—KPN). KPN was further to the right and more anti-Soviet in its call for a return of Poland's eastern territories, which had become part of the Soviet Union. KPN was subjected to police harassment, and its leaders were brought to trial in April 1981. Another group, the Society for Academic Courses, conducted a regular program of courses and lectures (the so-called flying university) free of communist ideology and distortions in spite of frequent disruptions by the police (see Education and Political Controversy, ch. 2).

Solidarity

During a dramatic interlude between August 1980 and December 1981, Solidarity emerged as an alternative force to the PZPR, which for more than 30 years had monopolized the country's political life. At its peak, the movement embraced 10 million Poles. Like earlier popular uprisings, it was sparked by the government's attempt to deal with the deepening economic crisis by raising meat prices. Remembering the violent worker reaction to previous price increases, the authorities camouflaged their intentions by shifting some better grades of meat from controlled-price to nonregulated outlets. The action nevertheless kindled a series of factory work stoppages throughout Poland, to which the government responded by granting individual wage concessions.

On August 14, 1980, the Free Trade Union, a group of working-class dissidents active in Baltic coast cities, instigated a strike at the huge Lenin Shipyard in Gdansk. The immediate demands were the reinstatement of Anna Walentynowicz, a crane operator who had been dismissed for her activism, and a general cost-of-living increase of 1,000 zlotys a month; the amount was soon raised to 2,000 zlotys—about one-third of the average monthly wage. Workers were in a rebellious mood, and the strike quickly spread to other factories of Gdansk and nearby communities, coordinated by the Inter-Factory Strike Committee. The workers' demands escalated to a 21-point program, the central demand being a government guarantee of free, self-governing trade unions supported by new legislation granting rights to organize and form a single national labor organization. Known as the Gdansk Agreement, this program was accepted by the government on August 31, 1980, after approval by the PZPR Central Committee (see Appendix D). In addition to wide-ranging economic concessions, important political commitments were gained, including curtailment of press censorship and the broadcasting of Roman Catholic services. The strike committee had been augmented by groups of expert advisers—Roman Catholic intellectuals, academics of the "flying university," and members of KSS-KOR and other opposition groups, such as the nationalist Young Poland Movement. The central figure from the outset was, however, Lech Walesa, an electrician who had been dismissed in 1976 from the shipyard for "agitation."

Joined by strikers from Szczecin who had extracted a similar agreement from the PZPR, the Inter-Factory Strike Committee became the nucleus of a countrywide movement soon to become known as Solidarity. Founding committees from various regions of Poland were represented on a provisional national committee; Walesa and other Gdansk activists remained the dominant members. The PZPR found itself divided between reformers and hard-liners over dealing with Solidarity. Relations between the authorities and the new union federation were marked by tensions and confrontation. The struggle stemmed largely from the government's hardening of its position and deliberate procrastination in implementing the Gdansk accord. Threats of strikes were needed to secure legal registration of Solidarity in November 1980 (inscribed as "Independent Self-Governing Trade Union Solidarity") by court acceptance of its internal statutes. A crisis was narrowly averted over work-free Saturdays when a compromise was struck calling for one working Saturday a month. Solidarity was denied uncensored access to the mass media. Localized strikes that sought removal of unpopular community officials or to call attention to social grievances often enabled strike leaders to wring concessions, adding to their sense of confidence and power. In March a vicious police attack against Solidarity representatives in Bydgoszcz resulted in several serious injuries. Solidarity threatened a general strike, which was averted at the last moment when the government agreed to an investigation and punishment of those responsible. Frustration over the government's failure to keep this promise or carry out other commitments contributed to the growing bitterness and distrust. A strong movement arose for factory self-management committees to appoint and recall factory directors, set production goals, and participate in financial decisions for all factory operations. Although not initially advocated by Solidarity, this became a key demand.

The First National Congress of Solidarity was held in two sessions between September 5 and October 7, 1981. Walesa was

Lech Walesa addressing striking workers in August 1980
Courtesy Committee in Support of Solidarity, New York

elected chairman over three other candidates, receiving 55 percent of the 844 ballots. His election connoted the predominance of more moderate elements within Solidarity over militants who were insisting that the government must accept negotiations with the movement on major social and economic issues. The narrowness of Walesa's victory (a minimum of 50 percent was needed) in spite of his popularity and prestige was attributed to widespread dissatisfaction over his neglect in consulting others before making policy decisions. Also elected at the congress were the National Commission, a policymaking body of 107 members (69 elected by the congress and 38 allocated among the six regional chairmen), and the Audit Commission of 21 elected members. The National Commission voted to establish a presidium of 12 permanent members based at the union's Gdansk headquarters and six "commuting" members, chairmen of the regional branches of

Solidarity who would appear for meetings in Gdansk but would remain in close touch with the rank and file. The six geographic areas of the country into which the movement was organized were the Mazowsze region (headquarters in Warsaw), Malopolska region (headquarters in Krakow), Lower Silesia region (headquarters in Wroclaw), Lodz region (headquarters in Lodz), Wielkopolska region (headquarters in Poznan), and Silesia-Dabrowa region (headquarters in Katowice).

The congress, seeing itself as a social movement with the duty of salvaging Polish society from ruin and despondency, adopted far-ranging goals for Solidarity. It called for a restructuring of the state to reinforce democracy and social initiative. A social council for the national economy was proposed for the purpose of subjecting economic reform to public control. Solidarity's effort to reassure the Soviet Union by asserting that the contemplated transformation of society would not violate Poland's international alliances was nullified by its controversial message to working people of the other Warsaw Pact states, expressing support for efforts to form free trade unions in those countries and anticipating meetings to exchange experiences.

Differences between Solidarity and the authorities hardened after the congress. Various actions and statements of the regime, as of October 1981 controlled by Jaruzelski as both prime minister and PZPR first secretary, threatened extraordinary action to block Solidarity in its ambition of becoming a partner in regulating the economy. The government was not prepared to compromise on any major issue, and efforts at negotiation by Solidarity moderates seemed increasingly futile. Kuron later wrote that those arguing for confrontation shouted loudest: "It was usually these voices, frequently young workers from the big industrial plants, which forced Solidarity's leadership to take radical steps, which became increasingly difficult to halt." Kuron said that naive wishful thinking led the workers to hold the authorities and their power in contempt: "Few thought that Polish troops would attack Polish workers or that a military coup was possible."

Under pressure from the radicals, Solidarity escalated its demands, calling for a new trade union law, free elections, an end to harassment, and free access to the media. At a meeting of the national coordinating commission on December 11–12, a national referendum was proposed to obtain a vote of no confidence in the government.

The government's response was to declare martial law on December 13, a measure it had obviously been preparing for some time, banning strikes and public meetings, restricting travel, and suspending activities of major mass organizations, including labor unions. It was admitted officially that over 5,000 individuals were rounded up in the initial wave of detentions, including all of Solidarity's leaders who could be found. The government at first

Lech Walesa en route by bus to gala celebration in Warsaw of official registration of Solidarity, November 1980
Courtesy Committee in Support of Solidarity, New York

indicated that it was prepared to negotiate over the future of Solidarity if the movement would accept greatly diminished powers, limit its right to strike, and abandon its regional structure. The few Solidarity leaders still at large and in hiding rejected any talks as long as their colleagues, particularly Walesa, were interned and could not take part.

In May 1982 Solidarity announced its underground leadership structure, consisting of a provisional coordinating commission of five former leaders who had escaped arrest, representing several regions of the country. It prescribed the formation of secret cells of five members and provisional factory committees. Calls for strikes and demonstrations were at first well heeded, but the government's tactics of swift retribution and displays of police force gradually diminished the effectiveness of the protests. On

October 8, 1982, the Sejm approved in a single session a law sponsored by the government to abolish existing trade unions, including Solidarity. They were to be replaced by a new system based initially on thousands of officially sponsored factory-level unions.

In November 1982 Walesa was released from detention to a warm welcome from Solidarity supporters, but he was forcibly prevented from making public appearances and was ignored by the official media. Walesa was subjected to continual harassment while the police relentlessly tracked down underground Solidarity leaders as well as clandestine radio transmitters and newspapers. The government took the position that, because Solidarity no longer had a legal existence, there was no basis for recognizing its leaders as spokesmen for any segment of Polish society.

In March 1982 the government had announced that internees could apply to leave Poland permanently with their families. It was reported that the regime had brought pressure on political activists to seek exile although, by early 1983, only a few hundred had actually departed.

The Roman Catholic Church

The Roman Catholic Church has for centuries been the spiritual guiding element of the Polish people—entrenched in the national consciousness and imparting its values to cultural and traditional life. To a great extent defining the country's social attitudes, the influence of the church deeply affects the disposition of the people toward political and ideological questions. Its popularity in present-day Poland is heightened by the fact that it is the only national institution privileged to act independently of communist control and, within limits, to make pronouncements on matters of preeminent concern to the people (see Religious Life, ch. 2).

Under the primate, Cardinal Wyszynski, the church pursued an essentially conservative course until the mid-1970s, preoccupying itself with the defense of Catholic religious life and upbringing. The dispute with the government over constitutional changes, which were interpreted as threatening the civil rights of practicing Catholics, widened the area of discord. The workers' food price riots in mid-1976 brought a further decisive shift. Wyszynski swung the authority of the church behind the protest, urging clemency for imprisoned workers and earmarking church offerings to aid those arrested or dismissed. The prestige of the church in Polish internal matters was elevated by the election in 1978 of Karol Cardinal Wojtyla as Pope John Paul II. Opposition forces were heartened by this new source of authority on Polish affairs, unburdened by the obligation to seek conciliation or compromise with the government as Wyszynski's position necessitated.

Upon the launching of Solidarity, the church adjusted its role from that of chief adversary of the regime to become a mediator

Archbishop Jozef Glemp, primate of Poland (elevated to College of Cardinals in January 1983)
Courtesy Reverend Edward Mroczynski, S.Ch.

between the state and the new independent union. Its sympathies clearly rested with Solidarity, and it defended the union's right of free assembly and expression. At the same time, Solidarity was urged to act with reasonableness and to avoid violence. Although Wyszynski had previously been criticized as a conservative whose main interest was to preserve the privileges of the church, he contributed to the resolution of sharp conflicts between the state and Solidarity and insisted on official recognition for Rural Solidarity. Wyszynski was a venerable and strong-willed figure whose death in May 1981 coincided with the political paralysis of the PZPR and Solidarity's mounting insistence to be consulted on national policies.

Wyszynski's successor as primate, Archbishop Jozef Glemp, tried to continue the church's mediating role in spite of the widening crisis. Although he managed to bring Jaruzelski and Walesa together at a negotiating table in early November 1981, by this time it was probably too late to stem the force of events that culminated in the military takeover a month later. After martial law was imposed, Glemp gave little encouragement to worker protests. He counseled against provocative actions that would only delay reconciliation and dialogue with the government. As the regime failed to heed pleas by the church for a release of the detainees and a resumption of negotiations with the suspended union, a breach opened between Glemp and other bishops and priests who felt that more vigorous resistance should be mounted. In December 1982, however, Glemp unexpectedly addressed a protest to the government over the terms of the suspension of martial law, asserting that some of the new legal powers sharpened the rigor and repressive character of the regime.

Mass Associations and Interest Groups

In spite of the absolute exercise of power by the PZPR and state administration, these sources of authority have found it prudent to accept implicit limits in acknowledgement of the influence of other groups in society. The Roman Catholic Church, unique until 1980 in preserving a measure of independence, has been in the foreground of these forces owing to its traditional place in Polish life, its devout following, and its circumspection in leveling demands upon the regime. Other distinct social segments (notably the peasants, the industrial working class, intellectuals, and students) were restrained until the emergence of Solidarity in 1980 from organizing themselves into authentic interest groups free of party and state control. In keeping with Leninist concepts, a number of officially sponsored bodies had been established as a means of mobilizing the population to fulfill party goals and to increase popular identity with the regime. Functioning as auxiliaries of the PZPR, these organizations embraced trade unions; cooperative associations; youth, women's, sports, welfare, and defense organizations; and cultural and scientific societies.

The confusion and demoralization in party ranks that accompanied the enthusiastic response to the Solidarity workers' movement created a brief opportunity for parallel tendencies to manifest themselves among other groups, often in affiliation with Solidarity. A rebellious mood permeated the official mass organizations, leading to demands for greater autonomy and reform. The introduction of martial law resulted in the suspension of the independent groups, while government-sponsored organizations, their spontaneity brought under control, were reduced to their former submissiveness to party direction.

Before Solidarity's rapid transformation into the country's largest and most influential labor organization, most Polish workers were grouped within 23 branch trade unions (so named because they corresponded to the main industrial branches of the economy), represented on the national level by the Central Council of Trade Unions (Centralna Rada Zwiazkow Zawodowych—CRZZ). Ostensibly intended to protect the interests of their members, the unions took part in decisions on wage funds, fringe benefits, work norms, and regulations. The unions could not, however, bargain over pay and were a persistent source of dissatisfaction to workers who recognized that they acted in reality at the behest of the PZPR and state while claiming to speak on behalf of the working people.

After Solidarity materialized, the CRZZ unions were discredited and began to crumble. The CRZZ formally disbanded, and its remnants were reincarnated into a federation called Branch Trade Unions, claiming a membership of 3.5 million. A third labor organization emerged in early 1981 when 25 new independent unions, representing mainly white-collar groups, formed the Confederation of Autonomous Trade Unions, which claimed a membership of 1 million. Rejecting political activism and violence, this smaller federation was close to the Catholic hierarchy in outlook.

The October 1982 legislation disbanding all unions, including Solidarity and the official "branch" unions, had as its primary objectives the limiting of trade union issues to wages and working conditions and the prevention of a workers' movement from ever again emerging to question broad government and party policies. The new law incorporated a framework for the gradual reintroduction of an organized labor system under government supervision. Compulsory official arbitration was forseen; the right to strike was severely restricted, and violators were subject to fine or imprisonment. In many sectors of the economy, unionization would be forbidden.

Initially, all unions were to be constituted at the level of individual factories. At later dates national trade unions and interunion organizations were to be permitted. By December 1982 over 2,000 of the new unions had been registered, generally in smaller enterprises. The official press conceded that most workers were boycotting the unions because of continued bitterness over the suppression of Solidarity and doubts that their interests would be protected.

In spite of the critical importance of the private agricultural sector, Polish farmers had not been permitted up to 1980 to organize on behalf of their interests. Agricultural circles (government-sponsored local bodies) have provided mainly a common pool of farm machinery and a source of selected seeds and fertilizers. They have been viewed suspiciously by farmers as the possible forerunners of collectivized farming. After widespread agitation and strike threats, the authorities eventually permitted the private farmers' counterpart of Solidarity to be officially registered in May 1981 as the Independent Self-Governing Trade Union of Private Farmers-Solidarity. Generally known as Rural Solidarity, it consolidated various farmers' unions that had sprung up since the fall of 1980. The objectives of the new union were to defend the interests of the private farmers with respect to commodity prices, free-market sales, and supplies of fertilizers, fuel, and machinery. It claimed about 2.5 million members, or 70 percent of the private farmers. Rural Solidarity was officially dissolved under the October 1982 trade union law. The discredited Central Council of Agricultural Circles was superseded by the Central Union of Agricultural Circles and Organizations of Private Farmers. Although dismissed by most farmers as an adjunct of the regime, it was nevertheless reported to have joined in some demonstrations.

The leading institution for the mobilization of Polish youth on behalf of party policies and for the education of young people in communist principles has been the Union of Socialist Polish Youth which, in July 1982, claimed to have 2 million members in factories, villages, schools, universities, and the army. Membership was open to individuals between the ages of 16 and 30. While young people were eligible to join the PZPR at age 18, party leaders were said to regard the youth group as a training ground for cadre positions in the PZPR. The Rural Youth Union, which was forced to merge with the larger youth union in 1976 but reappeared as a separate group in 1980, claimed a membership of 200,000. A campaign to reinvigorate the Union of Socialist Polish Youth was undertaken after martial law was imposed. Acknowledging that its socialist ideals were no longer credible to many young people, the leadership of the union turned to a program stressing the material benefits that would be made available to its members in areas such as job retraining and the financing of apartments for young married couples.

The Polish Scout Union for children and youths between 10 and 16 years of age has a lengthy tradition, but it succumbed to communist control after World War II. Official membership figures fell from 3.1 million in 1980 to 1.9 million in 1981. Reportedly, much of the ideological content of the scouting program was discarded at the unit level, and its original purposes were reemphasized during the Solidarity period, but the PZPR-dominated senior leadership remained intact.

The Socialist Union of Polish Students, the weakest of the party-sponsored youth organizations, passed from view after the upheavals of August 1980. The pronounced alienation of postsecondary students precluded its resuscitation. In November 1982 the new Association of Polish Students was formed by the government, ostensibly independent and open to all students regardless of their political outlook but recognizing the leading role of the PZPR. The Independent Students' Union, which was the students' counterpart to the Solidarity movement, claimed that its followers numbered 25 percent of all university students until it was disbanded by the military regime. Those of its leaders not interned or arrested were forced into hiding.

Voluntary associations organized on a national scale enjoy an official status and the right to a monopoly of activity in their specified fields. Fewer than 30 such organizations have been authorized, many of them professional groups. Some, such as the Polish Red Cross, the League for the Preservation of Nature, the Social Antialcoholic Committee, and the Society of the Friends of Children, are regarded as partners of the state and provide services that exceed the state's capacity to supply. The government, however, retains de facto control of the structure, membership, tasks, and activities of these groups and usually assists in their financing. Although the groups may provide government ministries with recommendations and information based on their grass-roots contacts that are useful for policy decisions, as state-dominated entities they cannot be said to function as a voice for particular group interests. While pro forma membership may be very high (in the case of the Polish Red Cross nearly 5 million), most of the membership is passive, having been recruited during campaigns in schools and the workplace.

A few of these organizations are intended to serve the country's political or military purposes. Among them are the Women's League, the National Defense League, and the Polish-Soviet Friendship Society. The Union of Combatants for Freedom and Democracy, a veteran's group, was for long associated with the authoritarian and nationalistic line of Mieczyslaw Moczar, a leading political personality under Gomulka. Scarcely any of these organizations were unaffected by the spirit of independence and assertiveness that marked the Solidarity interlude, but it was not clear to what extent if any this tendency would survive the martial law period.

Martial Law Government

Just after midnight on December 13, 1981, Polish security forces began rounding up Solidarity leaders after cutting communication lines between cities. A few hours later in a broadcast address, Jaruzelski announced that martial law had been imposed and that the country would be governed by the Military Council of National Salvation (Wojskowa Rada Ocalenia Narodowego—WRON). Jaruzelski said that "our country has found itself on the edge of an abyss . . . the structures of the state are ceasing to function. New blows are being struck every day at the dying economy." He accused Solidarity extremists of openly striving to dismantle the socialist Polish state. The existing situation, he declared, would have led to "catastrophe, to complete chaos, to poverty and famine." Jaruzelski promised that reforms would continue under orderly and disciplined conditions and that the idea of a socialist renewal—based on a national accord with a multiplicity of views, including acceptance of "healthy" nonparty trends among the young, the working class, and Solidarity itself—had not been abandoned.

By a decree of the Council of State, citing Article 33, Paragraph 2, of the Constitution, martial law was introduced. Subsequent decrees banned all union activity and all forms of assembly except church services; borders were closed; mail and phone censorship was introduced; and activities of social, professional, and other associations were suspended. The military assumed control of the radio and television stations, and most newspapers were closed down. The employees of about 200 major industrial, mining, and transport enterprises were subjected to military discipline. More than 10,000 individuals were interned for varying periods, and thousands of others were prosecuted for political crimes during the year that martial law remained in effect. Not only were Solidarity activists detained, but also it was announced that a number of discredited former leaders had been interned, including Gierek and his prime minister, Piotr Jaroszewicz. They had been accused of personal responsibility for the economic crises of the late 1970s or of having abused their posts for personal gain. By this gesture, Jaruzelski underscored his position that the workers' protest of 1980 had been justified and that it was the "distortion" that followed that had necessitated military intervention.

WRON's membership consisted of 21 military officers, of whom Jaruzelski served as chairman. Military commissioners or "commissars" headed military operational groups that supervised the daily activities of local administrative bodies. These groups of 10 to 15 military personnel were posted in more than 2,000 cities and towns where, the government claimed, their tasks were to improve operating efficiency, to counter bureaucratic inertia, and to hear citizens' complaints.

WRON was superimposed on the existing civilian organs of government as the highest political authority with proclamations and instructions issued in its name. The Council of Ministers continued to function, and the Sejm passed more than 50 laws during the period. Jaruzelski was at the head of both the civilian and the military structures. Four other WRON generals served at the head of key ministries dealing with internal security, defense, mining and power, and local government. In several places voivods and city presidents were replaced by military officers.

The ostensible exercise of power by WRON was in reality a facade behind which Jaruzelski and a group of close associates assumed control of the instruments of state. The military commissars at the head of many official bodies seemed to be mainly figureheads. The PZPR remained divided and ineffectual while the Politburo and Central Committee provided little more than token endorsement of initiatives stemming from Jaruzelski. The government even avoided committing the army to assist in day-to-day operations against the internal opposition. The army was generally used when a show of force was needed, leaving implementation to the Ministry of Internal Affairs, acting through the security organs.

Three members of WRON were usually identified as among the influential advisers of Jaruzelski—Lieutenant General Czeslaw Kiszczak, Major General Tadeusz Hupalowski, and Major General Wlodzimierz Oliwa. Both Hupalowski and Kiszczak were members of the Council of Ministers as of January 1983, Kiszczak holding the key internal affairs post. The leading civilian advisers included Kazimierz Barcikowski and Jozef Czyrek, both members of the Politburo, and Mieczyslaw Rakowski, a deputy prime minister. The senior economic adviser was chairman of the Planning Commission, Janusz Obodowski. These civilian counselors were generally regarded as holding moderate views.

In the interest of national renewal and conciliation, the martial law authorities launched the Citizens' Committee for National Salvation (Obywatelski Komitet Ocalenia Narodowego—OKON) at the local level and the Patriotic Movement of National Rebirth (Patriotyczny Ruch Odrozenia Narodowego—PRON) at the regional and national level. Under the combined sponsorship of the PZPR, the ZSL, and the SD, many other organizations were represented, including Pax, the Christian Social Association, and PZKS (the former Znak), as well as the revitalized youth, women's, and veterans' organizations. The new associations were declared to be forums in which anyone, regardless of political or religious affiliation, who was not hostile to socialism could participate in political life and debate government policies. There was little evidence that the OKON or PRON had attracted genuine interest. Instead the majority of Poles regarded them as agencies of the regime to foster the illusion of consultation and support.

On December 13, 1982, the first anniversary of military rule, the Sejm approved several laws introduced by the government giving the Council of State power to suspend martial law (and, if necessary, to reintroduce it). Formal action to set aside some aspects of martial law was taken at the end of December, although its most oppressive features were largely left in place. The remaining internees, except for seven Solidarity leaders, were released. Amnesty was not extended to the several thousand individuals serving sentences or awaiting trial on political charges. The requirement for special permits for assemblies and performances was lifted, and an end to postal and telephone censorship was announced.

Other new laws introduced concurrently had the effect of institutionalizing many proscriptions of the martial law period. Military regulations providing jail sentences for the distribution or possession of printed matter that "threatens state security or slanders the state" or for causing a public disturbance were made part of the penal code. Workers or students attempting to organize illegal strikes or "sow disorder" could be dismissed or expelled. While the categories of offenses coming before them were reduced, the military courts would continue to deal with cases involving basic political interests of the state, national security, and public order. Rights of appeal would not extend to certain cases in both military and civil courts. Key enterprises were to be demilitarized, but special rules would continue to apply, including an obligatory 46-hour workweek and restrictions against quitting. Permanent authority was introduced in the penal code for courts or prosecutors to open mail or record phone conversations of individuals. A law against "social parasitism" enabled the state to take action against persons aged 18 to 45 who were not engaged in work or study. The combined effect of these constraints on individual and collective activity was to make many prohibitions of the military regime a continuing feature of Polish life.

Politics and the Information Media

The channels of mass communication are regarded by the communist authorities as the primary instruments of the PZPR and the state to reach large audiences for purposes of propagating the party line. Independent sources of news are available, particularly Western radiobroadcasts, resulting in widespread resentment over distorted and censored official presentation of news events. The highly literate Polish public found the tight controls imposed by the military regime particularly offensive if contrasted with the period between August 1980 and December 1981 when frank and lively examination of issues and even explicit criticism of government actions could be found in the media.

In spite of censorship and sometimes heavy-handed screening of literary and theatrical works, Poland's record in applying restrictions has been relatively less rigid than that of the Soviet Union and the countries of Eastern Europe. The bulk of journalistic production has carried official sponsorship and has been responsive to the PZPR's directives, but small variations in interpretation could be noted. In addition, a number of Roman Catholic periodicals have been tolerated, although they have remained subject to censorship and have usually avoided political topics that did not bear directly on the standing of the church in Poland.

The limited tolerance of the Gierek regime for opposition activity was not matched by any pronounced moderation of press controls. An important counterpart to the dissident movement of the late 1970s was the flowering of underground journalism (*samizdat*). Such publications included KSS-KOR's *Biuletyn Informacyjny*, which provided commentary and collated reports on police searches, brutality, political arrests, trials and sentences; *Zapis*, a literary and political quarterly of censored writers; *Opinia*, the monthly organ of ROPCiO; *Indeks*, a Krakow student journal; *Robotnik*, edited by KSS-KOR members from reports by worker-correspondents on labor conditions, protests, and strikes; and *Spotkania*, produced by young Catholic intellectuals.

Among the demands of Solidarity conceded by the government in the Gdansk Agreement were the reform of press censorship, the access of Solidarity to the mass media, and freedom to publish its own weekly, *Tygodnik Solidarnosc*, the first issue of which appeared in April 1981. Its circulation, fixed by agreement at 500,000, was insufficient to meet the demand, but it was supplemented by 10 regional weeklies and many internal periodicals. All were subject to censorship, which relaxed noticeably during the course of 1981. The Solidarity publications were suppressed after the introduction of martial law; persons continuing to print and distribute materials were subjected to heavy jail sentences. Nevertheless, an underground Solidarity production of flyers and news bulletins continued to appear in almost every part of the country.

Newspapers and Periodicals

As of 1980 over 2,400 newspapers and periodicals were appearing in Poland, including 50 newspapers that were published at least twice a week. All major and most minor organizations published their own journals, scarcely any sponsored activity in Poland failing to be served by at least one publication. The PZPR was the most influential and prolific publisher, although a number of officially sponsored nonparty newspapers had wide distribution (see table 13, Appendix A).

The most important newspaper in the country is the official organ of the PZPR, *Trybuna Ludu*. The authoritative voice of the ruling party, it circulates on a nationwide basis chiefly among party members. As a morning newspaper in the Warsaw area, it competes for readership with the less doctrinaire *Zycie Warszawy*. Provincial party newspapers are patterned on *Trybuna Ludu* in content and format.

Both the ZSL and the SD are permitted to publish national dailies that have smaller press runs. A number of religious publications are sanctioned, among them the daily *Slowo Powszechne* of the Pax group. The respected weekly *Tygodnik Powszechny* and the monthly *Wiez* are affiliated with the Roman Catholic Church. Since they resumed publication under martial law, both have been heavily censored. The weekly *Polityka*, with its relatively sophisticated commentaries, is designed to appeal to both party and nonparty elites. It is generally associated with the views of Mieczyslaw Rakowski, who resigned as its editor in 1982 after being named to Jaruzelski's government. He is counted as one of the reform-minded members of the Council of Ministers.

The national news agency, the Polish Press Agency (Polska Agencja Prasowa—PAP), which has the status of a government department, is the sole supplier of foreign news to the Polish media. It is affiliated with the Soviet press agency, Tass, as well as with Western news agencies, and maintains about 20 of its own bureaus in Western countries. Another specialized agency, Polska Agencja Interpress (known as Interpress), is concerned with promoting Poland abroad and providing liaison services and official briefings for foreign journalists in Poland.

The Gdansk Agreement of August 1980 was followed by an unprecedented period of relaxed control over press content. Dailies such as *Zycie Warszawy* began to criticize openly official failures in coping with the economic situation and to report on strikes and protests. Several of the provincial papers also adopted a more outspoken style, while even *Trybuna Ludu* reprinted highly critical statements made at Central Committee meetings. The Pax daily newspaper joined in reporting on previously taboo matters, such as police excesses. Only the army journal, *Zolnierz Wolnosci*, was unaffected, remaining the leading spokesman of conservative party elements and urging stricter control over worker activism.

Immediately after martial law was introduced, all publications were suspended with the exception of *Trybuna Ludu* and *Zolnierz Wolnosci*. A few weeks later other official newspapers and some weeklies were allowed to appear. The Solidarity publications were closed, and their equipment was confiscated. Journalists were subjected to a "verification" process, including interrogation on their attitudes toward Solidarity, the PZPR, and martial law. It was estimated that 500 to 800 newspaper personnel were victimized by the resulting purge. It was reported that the chief editor and 20 journalists on the staff of *Slowo Powszechne* were dismissed before the newspaper could reappear. The Polish Journalists' Association, which under its outspokenly liberal president, Stefan Bratkowski, had become one of the most reformist organizations of the Solidarity period, was disbanded and replaced by the new Association of Journalists of the Polish People's Republic.

When martial law was suspended in December 1982, the tight controls that had prevailed before Solidarity were again in place. Rigid adherence to prevailing policy lines was demanded. Vague jargon, official slogans, and exhortations were substituted for straightforward news reporting, although some latitude was permitted in discussing economic reform. According to an article in *Polityka* in August 1982, the public was boycotting many journals in protest against repression of the press and the purges of journalists. A new government daily, *Rzeczpospolita*, and the hard-line weekly *Rzeczywistosc* were among those having the largest number of unsold issues.

Radio and Television

In the early 1980s all broadcasting was under the direction of the Committee for Radio and Television, whose members were appointed by the Council of Ministers. Heavy emphasis was assigned to news and information programs, as well as those designed to supplement primary and secondary-school classes. Radiobroadcasts could be heard on four wave bands. Program I consisted largely of lighter music and news commentaries. Program II provided more serious cultural programs and children's fare. Program III combined light entertainment with popularized science and literary programs. Program IV specialized in adult education, including foreign-language classes. The 16 regional stations broadcast daily two to four or more hours of local material and contributed to network programming.

Television was broadcast over two channels principally from Warsaw, although seven regional centers accounted for about one-fourth of all national programming and produced two to three hours of local offerings daily. Linkage with both Intervision (Eastern Europe and the Soviet Union) and Eurovision (Western Europe) permitted certain programs originating elsewhere in Europe to be shown. About 70 percent of all Polish households were equipped with television sets.

Radio and television have been the preferred media for the government's propagation of its views and the shaping of public attitudes toward domestic and international issues. Liberalization of the broadcast media did not proceed as rapidly as that of the press during the Solidarity period, although it did improve, bringing to listeners live broadcasts of Sejm sessions in which Poland's situation was openly debated. After martial law was declared, television programs—initially only commentaries by the military or by journalists in uniform—stressed the return of order and the resumption of normal economic activity, but virulent attacks against Solidarity were also made. It was reported that large numbers of Poles deliberately showed themselves on the streets during news broadcasts to demonstrate their contempt for the omissions and distortions of the official media. According to the head of Polish radio and television, all employees were subjected to ideological screening. As a result, 513 were fired, 134 were downgraded, and 100 younger journalists were required to attend a "reeducation" course to keep their jobs.

Censorship

Freedom of the press is guaranteed by Article 83 of the Constitution, which also promises that "the working people and their organizations shall be given the use of printing shops, stocks of paper . . . and other necessary material means." In practice, the state is the sole supplier of the means of publication. Printing equipment must be registered, and nothing can be printed legally without approval. The government's Chief Office for the Control of Publications and Public Performances oversees operations of the press. In addition to formal censorship, there is an implied censorship that is effective in curbing journalists, who generally sense the extent to which criticism of aspects of the administration will be countenanced. Material that might be questioned by the censors is usually caught by editors who are loyal to the party or conscious of the risks involved in exceeding well-understood limits.

The mass media are prohibited from criticizing the system of government, disclosing state or officials secrets, damaging the republic's international relations (such as any criticism of the

Soviet Union or Poland's alliance with that country), or publishing inaccurate information. Virtually any facts not disseminated through the information department of a ministry or by a high-level official may be regarded as sensitive. Even the most routine matters may thus be inaccessible to Polish and foreign reporters alike. The government prohibited the domestic press and radio from reporting on the strikes that led to the formation of Solidarity in spite of the fact that the Polish public was well aware of the situation from Western radio reports.

In 1977 a Polish employee of the censor's office escaped to the West with copies of its confidential rules and directives. As summarized in an article by Maria Hirszowicz in *Index on Censorship*, these documents gave many examples of forbidden topics, including any information about risks of health arising from use of chemicals in industry and agriculture; reporting on a Katowice mine disaster; mention of Polish meat exports to the Soviet Union; data on coffee and alcohol consumption; commemoration of the anniversary of the Warsaw uprising of 1944; information on the possibility of emigrating to the United States; and criticism of Soviet drilling equipment or suggestions that such equipment be bought from the West. Certain names, mainly those of accused intellectuals, could not be mentioned. Advance guidance was issued on the content of reviews of a film by the well-known director Andrzej Wajda.

In April 1981, after extensive consultations with Solidarity, the Polish Journalists' Association, and other intellectual and social groups, the government submitted a new censorship law to the Sejm in two alternative texts: the "official" version and a more liberal "social" version by the reformist groups. The law represented one of the few tangible concessions to Solidarity pursuant to the Gdansk accord. As eventually approved by the Sejm in July 1981 the government's version largely prevailed, but the new text incorporated a number of innovations. Forbidden topics were specifically spelled out. They were limited to calls for overthrow, ridicule, or denigration of the constitutional system; publication of state, economic, and military secrets (which were not defined in the act); and criticisms of the principles of Poland's foreign policies or those of its allies. Important categories were exempted from censorship: speeches by Sejm deputies and local councillors, court verdicts, legislation and official statistics, textbooks, theses, church publications, and internal publications of labor organizations. Prior guidance on the coverage of events was explicitly prohibited as were lists of people whose work had been banned. Appeals of local censors' decisions could be addressed to the main censorship office and, ultimately, to the Supreme Administrative Tribunal.

Suspension of the censorship law by the military authorities precluded an assessment of the latitude that would have prevailed under its terms. Another law was under preparation by the government in early 1983 covering the rights and obligations of newspaper staffs, to be administered by a press council. The actual situation, however, was that, with the exception of the church periodicals that were forced to contend with rigorous censorship, all legally sanctioned print and electronic media were obliged to follow the official line. In spite of this and the purge of the most respected journalists, some shades of difference could still be detected in editorial treatment in contrast with the total uniformity of the press in most other East European countries and in the Soviet Union.

Foreign Relations

Throughout the entire period of communist control, the determining factor in Polish foreign policy has been its close association with the Soviet Union. This association is cemented by the continuing presence of Soviet troops in Poland, the republic's participation in the military alliance of the Warsaw Pact, and the economic alliance of the Council for Mutual Economic Assistance (Comecon—see Appendix B). The ties with the Soviet Union have reflected both acknowledgement of Soviet hegemony in Eastern Europe and the fact that Poland has regarded the Soviet Union as the main guarantor of its western borders, which incorporate a substantial amount of former German territory. Poland's preoccupation with the border issue and its long-standing suspicion of the Germans were alleviated by the conclusion of a treaty with the Federal Republic of Germany (West Germany) in 1970 and by the provisions of the 1975 Helsinki Agreement.

Poland has aligned itself with the Soviet Union over major international issues, such as Indochina, the Middle East, and Cuba. Warsaw directed an unbridled campaign against the United States for its role in the Vietnam conflict. As one of two communist members of the International Commission of Control and Supervision created under the terms of the Vietnam peace agreement of 1973, Poland blatantly favored the Democratic Republic of Vietnam (North Vietnam), refusing to confirm its massive violations of the agreement. Poland continued to support Vietnam in its dispute with China and its occupation of Kampuchea (Cambodia). After the June 1967 War in the Middle East, Poland strongly defended the Arab cause and launched a sharp propaganda campaign against Israel. Diplomatic relations with Israel were severed and have not been restored. After the Soviet invasion of Afghanistan in December 1979, Poland opposed condemnation of the Soviet Union in the United Nations (UN)

Security Council on the grounds that the Soviets were justified in meeting the request of the Afghan authorities for military assistance to defend against "feudal rebels."

While also following the Soviet lead in all material questions concerning Europe, Poland has taken advantage of opportunities to pursue its own interests in the area. It has sponsored initiatives aimed at reducing tensions between East and West in Central Europe by arms limitations, détente, and economic cooperation in the region. In 1958 it advanced the so-called Rapacki Plan (named for the foreign minister, Adam Rapacki) calling for a nuclear-free zone in Central Europe. In 1963 Gomulka proposed a freeze on production of nuclear weapons and on the transfer of nuclear weapons already deployed in Central Europe. After the rebuff of these plans, which apparently were not endorsed by the Soviet Union, Polish foreign policy became more orthodox and subservient to Moscow. Poland has, nevertheless, continued to treat arms limitation as a prime objective, urging all countries to sign the treaty on the Non-Proliferation of Nuclear Weapons while supporting a general ban on nuclear weapons testing. The Poles have participated in the talks on mutual and balanced force reduction dealing with conventional forces in Europe, which began in Vienna in 1973.

The decade of the 1970s was noteworthy for great intensification of economic links with the West as Gierek sought to stimulate his country's economic performance by borrowing capital and acquiring technology to develop new export products and upgrade domestic living standards. Gierek simultaneously reinforced his economic and political ties with the East, lending almost unquestioning support to Soviet actions in the world arena. Because this period coincided with escalation of the Soviet Union's own economic involvement with the West, Gierek's policies could hardly lead to objections from his senior partner. Poland had acceded to the General Agreement on Tariffs and Trade (GATT) in 1967, enabling it to benefit from tariff reductions by other GATT members in return for a commitment to expand its imports from GATT countries by 7 percent annually. A decision on Poland's application in November 1981 for membership in the International Monetary Fund and the World Bank (see Glossary) was postponed after martial law was invoked.

Poland had long promoted a European security conference, which led to the convening of the 35-nation meeting at Helsinki in 1973. A follow-up conference convened at Madrid in February 1982, was dominated by the issue of martial law in Poland. The Western powers accused the Poles and the Soviets of having violated the Helsinki Agreement of 1975, which had committed all signatories to respect civil rights and promote the free movement of people.

Soviet Union

Relations between Poland and the Soviet Union are founded on two treaties: the 20-year bilateral Treaty of Friendship, Cooperation, and Mutual Aid concluded in April 1965 as a replacement for a similar treaty negotiated in 1945; and a multilateral accord known as the Warsaw Pact, a mutual defense agreement between the Soviet Union and six states of Eastern Europe (see Appendix C).

Of particular significance to Poland is Article 5 of the bilateral treaty, which states that "one of the fundamental factors in European security is the inviolability of the national frontier of the Polish People's Republic on the Odra [Oder] and the Lusatian Nysa [Neisse]," i.e., Poland's postwar Western frontier with the German Democratic Republic (East Germany). The next article names the "West German forces of militarism and revanche" as potential aggressors. The argument that backing from the Soviet Union on the German frontier question is critical to Poland's security and that it justifies alignment with Moscow on all major foreign policy issues lost much of its force after Poland's settlement with West Germany in 1970. Nearly all Polish groups continue to regard it as axiomatic that adoption of a political system or foreign policy inimical to the Soviet Union is to risk Soviet military intervention. This geopolitical reality is generally not made explicit in Poland but is often referred to obliquely by the term *raison d'etat*.

After Gomulka's takeover in 1956, Poland proceeded briefly along a more independent line, sponsoring the Rapacki plan for a nuclear-freeze zone and reaching an economic accommodation with the United States that incorporated a major grain import program. Before long, however, conformity with the Soviet line was restored. Gomulka upheld the Soviet position in the Sino-Soviet conflict, and Polish troops participated in the invasion of Czechoslovakia in 1968. Gierek made numerous gestures to assure Moscow of his allegiance after he replaced Gomulka in 1970. The Soviet leaders responded in turn after the 1976 riots, granting a major loan to ensure needed supplies of foodstuffs and raw materials deliveries to Polish factories.

The political disorder of 1980–81 amid a mounting economic crisis was a source of disquiet to the Soviet leaders, who regarded a submissive and tranquil Poland as indispensable to the security of Soviet forces in East Germany. Moreover, a collapse of the PZPR and capitulation to demands for a more open society could infect the other countries of Eastern Europe. Increasingly shrill warnings in the Soviet press were punctuated by ominous troop movements and higher states of alert near Poland's borders. The PZPR Central Committee received a letter from the Soviet Central Committee in June 1981, accusing the leadership of losing control over the mass media and failing to oppose the enemies of socialism in a determined way with the result that a wave of anticommunism and anti-Sovietism was developing. Fears of Soviet intervention formed a backdrop to successive confrontations between the Polish government and Solidarity. The authorities sought to turn aside demands for radical change by adducing the argument of *raison d'etat*. Solidarity's message to the working people of other communist countries and the demands of Solidarity militants for political power-sharing were construed by the Soviets as open incitement.

Consultations between the Soviet and Polish leaders were frequent throughout 1981. Although there was little evidence of direct Soviet involvement in the military takeover of December 13, 1981, United States Secretary of State Alexander Haig said it was known as early as March 1981 that the Soviets were arguing for the imposition of martial law. Haig stated that the martial law decree itself was printed in the Soviet Union in September 1981 and that the commander of the Warsaw Pact forces, Soviet Marshal Viktor Kulikov, was positioned in Poland before martial law and during its execution.

In spite of the expansion of Poland's economic contacts with the West during the 1970s, the Soviet Union continued to be its largest trading partner, accounting for over 30 percent of Poland's exports and over 40 percent of its imports. Poland receives Soviet oil, natural gas, pig iron, fertilizers, cotton, and other raw materials, exporting in return products of its machine tool, electro-engineering, transport, and shipbuilding industries. Poland's severe economic dislocation has forced Moscow to extend massive credits to compensate for the shortfalls in deliveries. Payments on the Polish debt to the Soviet Union, estimated at the equivalent of more than US$4 billion, have been deferred.

After martial law was implemented, it was reported that Moscow would grant Poland further credits equivalent to about US$3.75 billion at low interest to cover the country's bilateral trade deficit for 1981 and 1982. During a visit to Moscow by Jaruzelski and other leaders of the martial law government in March 1982, Soviet leader Leonid Brezhnev said, "We received with full understanding the news of the national decision taken by our Polish friends to defend the people's power and cool passions and to pull the country out of a protracted and excruciating crisis."

Other Communist Countries

With the exception of Albania and Yugoslavia, relations between Poland and other communist states of Eastern Europe are governed by Comecon and a series of bilateral treaties and agreements. Complementing the bilateral treaty with the Soviet Union, these treaties affirm the inviolability of the Oder-Neisse line as Poland's western boundary.

Of primary consequence to Poland among the countries of Eastern Europe are its neighbors East Germany and Czechoslovakia. These counties rank a distant second and third, respectively, after the Soviet Union, among Poland's trading partners. East Germany obtains most of its oil from the Soviet Union via a pipeline across Polish territory. The Polish rail system is a vital economic and military link between East Germany and the Soviet Union. The bulk of the first-line Soviet armed forces facing the West must be supplied over this route. During the 1970s the obstacles to personal travel by Poles to East Germany and Czechoslovakia were greatly eased, resulting in a heavy two-way flow of visitors, shoppers, and tourists. By 1980 consumer shortages in Poland resulted in complaints that shops were being stripped of their goods in Czechoslovak and East German border communities, necessitating new curbs on currency exchange. East Germany also required Polish visitors to be in possession of written invitations from German hosts.

Because intra-Comecon trade is intricately linked by a series of trade agreements and annual protocols, the economic setbacks that prevented Poland from meeting its commitments with respect to important export commodities, such as coal, sulfur, and copper, had a damaging effect throughout the region. The other Comecon members recognized that mismanagement by the Gierek regime had been largely to blame but had little sympathy with the strikes and slowdowns of the Solidarity period that contributed to the breakdown of the economy. East German and Czechoslovak journals were critical both of the unruliness of the Polish workers and of the indecisiveness of the PZPR, fearing that the political chaos could not be contained within Poland.

Conditioned by negative stereotypes, Poland's neighbors to a large extent held the Polish people responsible for their own dilemma. Residents of other Comecon countries resented having to endure sacrifices for what they saw as a lack of political restraint and work discipline on the part of the Poles. Hungary and Romania were less harsh in their judgments, conceding that inefficiency and corruption in Poland justified in some measure the grievances of the Polish workers. No East European country except Yugoslavia was represented at the first stage of Solidarity's congress in September 1981. Hungary's Central Council of Trade Unions was the only Comecon labor body to acknowledge Solidarity's invitation, but its head reacted with indignation to Solidarity's message addressed to the working people of Europe.

After the introduction of martial law, the East German Socialist Union Party of Germany declared that the new government in Poland had its unlimited support. A well-publicized program of aid and relief shipments of food, medicines, and second-hand clothing was announced. Similar projects were launched in other East European countries. It was estimated that East Germany would have to extend credits equal to US$280 million because of Poland's inability to meet its export commitments in 1982.

Relations with China have been generally antagonistic, as Poland has supported the Soviet Union on issues that have divided the two leading communist powers. Diplomatic representation at embassies in Beijing and Warsaw was reduced to the level of chargés d'affaires during the 1960s, but new ambassadors were named in 1970 during a period of limited reconciliation. The Chinese press initially expressed sympathy for the Solidarity movement, drawing satisfaction from the embarrassment to the Soviet Union, but soon restricted its coverage lest Chinese workers draw undesirable conclusions from the events in Poland. China did not join the Western countries in imposing sanctions against Poland and in fact reached agreement on substantial increases in mutual trade during both 1982 and 1983. The main Chinese exports were tungsten, antimony, and mercury, which were exchanged for Polish machinery, chemicals, and mining equipment.

Western Europe

Poland regards the development of contacts with the Western industrialized states in all fields as a factor contributing to international détente and thus to a principal goal of its foreign policy. Warsaw views the Helsinki Agreement of 1975 as setting the standard for cooperation among the signatories, which include 33 European countries, the United States, and Canada. Poland has regarded France as the West European country with which it enjoys the strongest bonds of cultural affinity and economic and scientific collaboration. Relations with France were reinforced during the early years of Gierek's regime and were highlighted by the Declaration of Friendship and Cooperation signed during Gierek's visit to Paris in 1972. The government of socialist François Mitterand, elected in 1981, was viewed as less sympathetic by Poland owing to its closer association with the Western defense community and its severe condemnation of martial law. Priority has also been attached to enlarging contacts with the Scandinavian countries in the cultural, economic, scientific, and tourism areas. Visa-free travel between Sweden and Poland was one result of an exchange of visits between Gierek and Swedish prime minister Olof Palme in 1972 and 1974. (Poland is linked with both Sweden and Denmark by car ferry.) Polish initiative contributed to the Gdansk convention on fisheries and the protection of live resources of the Baltic Sea in 1973, and a year later an agreement to protect the Baltic against pollution was signed at Helsinki.

A new stage in Poland's postwar foreign relations was reached in December 1970 when a treaty was concluded with West Germany, an event that was virtually the final act of Gomulka's tenure as party leader. The accord provided for the renunciation of force in settling differences, recognition of Poland's existing boundaries, a pledge of no future territorial claims, and the normalization of diplomatic relations between the two countries. (West Germany had previously been represented by a trade mission in Warsaw.) Remaining issues were settled in 1975 by an agreement permitting 125,000 ethnic Germans to emigrate from Poland over a period of five years, the granting of a long-term economic credit to Poland equivalent to US$400 million, and compensation of over US$500 million to Poles who had worked in Germany before 1945 and had contributed to the German social insurance fund. Polish trade with West Germany rose sixfold in value between 1970 and 1980, and a number of joint projects were undertaken, including a coal gasification plant. West Germany ranked fourth among Poland's trade partners, although first among the noncommunist countries.

The imposition of martial law in Poland was greeted with dismay by the nations of Western Europe. A resolution by the European Parliament on December 18, 1981, demanded the release of the interned trade unionists and the restoration of human rights in Poland. A communiqué issued after a meeting of the foreign ministers of the foreign ministers of the European Communities on January 4, 1982, called the actions of the Polish authorities a grave violation of the principles of the Helsinki Agreement and appealed for an end to martial law, release of those arrested, and restoration of the dialogue with the church and Solidarity. A few days later foreign ministers of the North Atlantic Treaty Organization (NATO) denounced the massive violation of human rights in Poland and deplored the sustained campaign of the Soviet Union against efforts of the Polish people for national renewal and reform.

At a meeting of the NATO council on February 3, it was agreed that member nations would enact sanctions against Poland and the Soviet Union in protest over the state of continuing martial law. The actual sanctions finally approved by the European Communities proved to be largely symbolic, consisting for the most part of a minor tightening of travel restrictions against Polish and Soviet officials and restrictions on luxury imports from the Soviet Union. A major difference arose between the United States and its allies over participation in constructing a 5,000-kilometer natural gas pipeline to link up gas fields in northwestern Siberia with the existing Soviet gas network in return for long-term gas supply contracts with Western Europe.

The reaction to martial law among West European communist parties was, with one exception, highly condemnatory. The

Italian Communist Party drew fire from many Warsaw Pact states by resolving that trade unions should be independent even in communist states and that the unitary Soviet model had been proven inapplicable in Eastern Europe. The Spanish and other communist parties similarly rejected the military takeover in vigorous terms. Although the ranks of the French Communist Party were divided on the issue, its leadership under Georges Marchais refrained from criticism of the Polish authorities. The communist trade union federation did not join the other unionists in a massive demonstration in Paris on the grounds that it was "above all the excesses of Solidarity that had ruined the search for a national understanding."

United States

Relations between the governments in Warsaw and Washington have had a distinctive character in testimony to the fact that Poland is the largest and politically most significant of the Soviet-aligned states of Eastern Europe. Actions by the United States pertaining to Poland are followed with close attention by many of the 10 to 12 million Americans of Polish ancestry. The Polish-American community is organized into an estimated 10,000 societies and supports 25 Polish-language newspapers. No single viewpoint prevails, however, on how its concerns should be translated into policies toward the communist regime in Poland.

Liberalizing domestic trends and evidences of a more independent course in foreign policy during the early years of the Gomulka regime (1957–58) brought a corresponding improvement in Polish-American relations. Poland was permitted to purchase surplus agricultural commodities under Title I of United States Public Law 480 on highly favorable terms. After Warsaw's settlement of the claims of American citizens arising from the nationalization of their property in Poland, the United States in 1960 reciprocated by extending most-favored-nation tariff treatment, Poland being the only communist country then enjoying this privilege.

Relations deteriorated during the latter stages of the Gomulka regime, as anticipated internal reforms failed to materialize and Poland reverted to close identification with Soviet policies on the Middle East, Indochina, and Czechoslovakia. Government purges affecting the few surviving Polish Jews in 1968 were found especially distasteful to the United States. Agricultural sales under Title I of Public Law 480 were suspended in 1964, although food donations under Title II of the law continued to be distributed by American relief agencies mainly to schoolchildren and the elderly poor.

The United States responded positively to signs that Gierek aspired to improve relations. Cabinet-level visits preceded President Richard M. Nixon's visit to Warsaw in 1972. President

Poland's First Secretary Edward Gierek (left) accompanies United States President Gerald R. Ford in welcoming ceremony at Warsaw's Okecie International Airport, July 28, 1975.
Courtesy Gerald R. Ford Library

Gerald R. Ford stopped in the Polish capital before attending the concluding session of the Helsinki conference in 1975. This followed a visit by Gierek to Washington in 1974, the first one to the United States by a top Polish leader. Several agreements for joint research in technology and health and an income tax convention were signed in conjunction with the Washington meeting. A joint commercial commission was organized, and the United States Trade Development Center was opened in Warsaw to encourage greater business contacts. Several industrial cooperation projects were negotiated, although most failed to live up to their promise. Perhaps the best known of these was the agreement between the International Harvester Corporation and the Bumar foreign trade organization for the joint manufacture of crawler tractors and loaders.

Cultural and scientific exchanges flourished during the 1970s, financed through Polish currency accounts accumulated from Public Law 480 sales, United States Department of State educational exchange programs, and private foundation grants. These were supplemented by exchanges of performing arts groups, a program to upgrade the teaching of English in Poland, and a wide variety of fellowships and lectureships.

The United States reacted with circumspection to the phenomenal popularity of Solidarity, avoiding measures that could have served as a pretext for Soviet interference. Secretary of State Edmund S. Muskie said that Poland's internal problems "are for the Polish people and the Polish government to settle, and all outside parties should exercise the greatest restraint." New forms of economic assistance were extended to help Poland deal with its food shortage and balance of payments crisis. These included in fiscal year (FY) 1981 US$47.6 million in Title I agricultural sales on concessional credit terms, US$103 million in dairy products sold for local Polish currency, and a US$670 million credit guarantee by the Commodity Credit Corporation for the purchase of agricultural commodities through commercial channels. In addition, the continuing program of food distribution through two American relief agencies (CARE and Catholic Relief Services) amounted to US$30 million in FY 1981.

Martial law brought swift reaction from the United States. President Ronald Reagan expressed Washington's moral revulsion at what he characterized as police-state tactics by Poland's oppressors. On December 23, 1981, he announced the suspension of major elements of economic relations with Poland, including a halt to government-sponsored food shipments, United States Export-Import Bank credit insurance, Polish civil aviation privileges, and Polish fishing rights in United States waters. Allocations of surplus food under Title II for direct distribution by American relief agencies were continued and increased to over US$40 million in FY 1982. Additional restrictions were imposed on the Soviet Union after Reagan announced that Brezhnev had not responded affirmatively to a letter urging the Soviet leader to permit the restoration of basic human rights in Poland. In October 1982, in reaction to the banning of Solidarity, Reagan announced the suspension of most-favored-nation tariff treatment for Poland.

Poland's debt service obligations, amounting to US$11 billion in 1982, were far in excess of its total foreign exchange earnings, leaving the country in danger of being declared in default. To avoid such an eventuality, which could have had a harmful effect on the Western banking system, as well as increased differences within NATO over the West's response to martial law, the United States Department of Agriculture announced that it would reimburse private banks US$71 million in principal and interest on government-guaranteed debts that Poland failed to pay. In negotiations between Poland and Western banks, agreements were reached on restructuring of private debts maturing in 1981 and 1982. The Polish debt payments not backed by government guarantees due in 1981 amounted to US$2.6 billion; the share of United States banks in this was US$400 million.

Jaruzelski reacted to the condemnation and economic blows by accusing Washington of being blinded by "an anti-Polish

Dr. Philip Johnston, executive director of CARE, presents one of the more than 175,000 packages of food and other items of practical value his relief agency has delivered to elderly Poles.
Courtesy CARE Photo

obsession." Charging the United States with impermissible interference in Polish domestic affairs, the prime minister announced on December 3, 1982, that all scientific and cultural contact between the two countries would be reviewed and that all forms of cooperation with the United States Information Agency would be discontinued. Efforts were made to jam Radio Free Europe which had augmented its coverage after the martial law authorities clamped down on the Polish media. Even before this, surveys indicated that 63 percent of all adult Poles were regular listeners of Radio Free Europe and that 33 percent listened to the Voice of America.

The suspension of martial law was not viewed by the United States as constituting sufficient progress to warrant reciprocal actions. Reagan stated that the lifting of sanctions would require meaningful liberalizing measures by Poland, including the end of martial law, the release of political prisoners, and a dialogue with truly representative forces, such as the church and free trade unions.

* * *

Many shorter analyses have appeared dealing with the political upheavals in Poland between 1980 and 1982. A general interpretation is "Poland: The Winter War" by Martin Malia, while more specific aspects are treated in various articles in the journal *Problems of Communism.* A brief history of the conflict between Polish society and the communist movement, followed by a recounting of the events surrounding Solidarity's birth and the first year of its existence, are found in Neal Ascherson's *The Polish August. Solidarity: Poland in the Season of Its Passion* by Lawrence Weschler is a first-hand account of the political and social forces involved in the political drama of 1981 that preceded the imposition of martial law. *Background to Crisis: Policy and Politics in Gierek's Poland*, a collection of articles edited by Maurice D. Simon and Roger H. Kanet, examines the role of various groups in the Polish political process. Although a comprehensive treatment of the martial law period was not available in early 1983, developments could be traced through the commentaries in the periodical *Radio Free Europe Research.*

Concise material on various aspects of Poland's foreign policy—useful primarily as the official viewpoint—is available in *Facts About Poland,* published by an agency of the Polish government. The intermingling of Polish and United States history from the earliest time until 1979 is described in *The United States and Poland* by Piotr S. Wandycz. (For further information and complete citations, see Bibliography.)

Chapter 5. National Security

Syrena, mermaid of Warsaw, legendary protector of the city

POLAND PASSED THROUGH a tumultuous era in the early 1980s when the legitimacy and authority of the ruling communist Polish United Workers' Party (Polska Zjednoczona Partia Robotnicza—PZPR) was challenged by widespread opposition identified with the free trade union Solidarnosc (Solidarity). Poland's internal unrest affected national security by directly threatening the government and also by drawing the attention of the neighboring Soviet Union, which since the end of World War II has demanded that Poland support it in national security matters and, to an extent, emulate it in internal political and economic matters. Popular demonstrations in 1956, 1970, and 1980–81—over economic issues, dissatisfaction with limitations on personal freedoms, and disgust with official corruption—had in each instance led to the replacement of the national leadership and to simultaneous concern about possible Soviet invasion.

During times of domestic ferment, communist regimes in Poland have relied heavily on the Polish People's Army for support. Military units used violence against protesters to quell disturbances and support the leadership on several occasions, most recently in 1970. Soldiers took on an overt political role, however, only during the Solidarity upheaval in 1981 when the discredited, divided, and demoralized PZPR turned to the minister of national defense, General Wojciech Jaruzelski, and named him prime minister and, later, first secretary of the party. In an increasingly unstable political situation in December 1981, Jaruzelski imposed martial law and placed a committee composed of military officers at the head of the government. Jaruzelski's political ascension reflected not only the extent of the PZPR's dissolution and the seriousness of the threat posed by Solidarity but also the scope of military's prestige within the PZPR and the society at large.

Since the early 1970s military leaders have sought to keep their troops separated from civil disturbances in which the army's popularity and the morale of conscripts could be damaged. The Polish People's Army in 1982 included 317,000 men from the "operational army"—ground forces, air forces, and naval units designed to operate in concert with Soviet and other Warsaw Pact forces in time of war—as well as some 85,000 territorial defense troops. Poland's well-developed internal security forces under the Ministry of Internal Affairs were delegated the often unpopular task of maintaining public order. The Security Service (plainclothes secret police) and the Motorized Units of the Citizens' Militia (riot police) were the most prominent in controlling and suppressing dissident activity, while the Citizens' Militia performed more routine police duties.

Jaruzelski's martial law crackdown, spearheaded by the internal security forces, succeeded over a period of months in breaking Solidarity's organization and effectively suppressing overt dissent. By early 1983 martial law had been suspended, but Jaruzelski and the military retained their central roles in the government. It could not be determined at that time if the regime was more than temporarily successful in controlling domestic opposition. Nor was it known if the military's preeminence in the Soviet-styled government of a Warsaw Pact member state was to be more than a temporary aberration.

National Security and the Soviet Union

Poland's security situation has long been shaped by its location between the German and Russian peoples, whose countries have, for several centuries, dominated or partitioned Poland between themselves. Since the end of World War II, when Moscow's Red Army liberated Poland from German occupation and placed a communist-dominated government in Warsaw, the country has been in the Soviet Union's sphere of influence, and its national security concerns and policy have been largely dictated by Soviet security interests.

In keeping with Soviet security and ideological considerations, Poland, like other east European countries in the postwar years, was geographically, economically, politically, and socially restructured to a marked degree by Soviet influence and placed under the control of a communist party, the PZPR. Although direct involvement in Polish internal affairs lessened after the death of Soviet dictator Josef Stalin in 1953, the nature of Moscow's relationship with its East European satellites was demonstrated by the Soviet invasions of Hungary in 1956 and Czechoslovakia in 1968, which were undertaken to suppress movements that challenged the correctness of the socialist path of development or the policy of friendship and cooperation with the Soviet Union. Poland itself was nearly invaded by Soviet forces in 1956 when the PZPR repudiated some of its most staunchly pro-Moscow leaders and during a political crisis in 1970 touched off by workers' riots. According to United States officials and press reports during the Solidarity period of civil disturbances in 1980–81, Soviet forces were poised to intervene on three occasions (December 1980, April 1981, and June 1981), and Solidarity's initial caution was ascribed to its leaders' fear of Soviet intervention. Jaruzelski in fact justified his declaration of martial law in December 1981 as a Polish solution to the country's difficult civil problems (implying that there were also non-Polish solutions).

In this context, official Polish government statements since 1945 have stressed the country's ideological bonds and military alliance with the Soviet Union and the threat posed by the North Atlantic Treaty Organization (NATO) alliance (see Foreign Relations, ch. 4). Through formal and informal coordination between the communist party leadership of Poland and the Soviet Union and through close military cooperation in the Warsaw Pact alliance and joint military exercises, Moscow has played a leading role in defining Polish foreign and military policies (see appendix C). The close ties had been demonstrated in 1968 when the Polish government sent two army divisions to Czechoslovakia to support Soviet forces in suppressing the deviant liberalization experiment undertaken by that country's communist party.

In the early 1980s Poland was an important element in the Soviet security system. Its relatively well-equipped 317,000-man armed forces constituted the largest non-Soviet national component of the Warsaw Pact alliance (see The Armed Forces: Mission, Organization, and Training, this ch.). Polish forces' joint offensive warfare training exercises with Soviet units and Poland's strategic location on the "Northern Tier" between the NATO countries and the Soviet Union made it likely that its 15 operational divisions would play a significant role in any major conflict with West European forces. In the same context Poland served the Warsaw Pact as a major transit, communications, and supply corridor connecting Soviet territory with the large Soviet army stationed in the German Democratic Republic (East Germany).

Poland's alliance with the Soviet Union was ensured by the "temporary" presence (since 1944) of Soviet troops. In 1982 some 25,000 to 35,000 Soviet soldiers, approximately 700 tanks, and 400 aircraft were organized into two tank divisions and a tactical air force. These forces formed the Group of Northern Forces, headquartered at Legnica in southwest Poland. Other Soviet army groups in Eastern Europe included the group of Soviet Forces in Germany (the largest deployment of Soviet forces in Eastern Europe, which in 1982 was composed of 20 divisions and an air army comprising 425,000 troops), the central group of forces based in Czechoslovakia (five divisions totaling 70,000 men), and the Southern Group of Forces in Hungary (four divisions including about 50,000 men), The two Soviet divisions in Poland were headquartered at Szczecin in the northwest near the East German border and at Legnica. They were both of Category I strength, i.e., fully manned and equipped with first-line equipment, but they generally maintained a low profile at their bases.

Domestic Threats to Communist Leadership

The internal security concerns of Poland's communist leaders have evolved since the end of World War II within the basic framework of Soviet hegemony, and some continuity has been evident. In the war's aftermath the major task before the Polish communist leaders was to impose their control over the often-hostile Polish people. Since achieving that goal in the late 1940s, PZPR leaders have sought to preserve their "leading role" in Polish society and have considered any organized dissension, any outbreak of violence, or any significant criticism of the Soviet Union or the concept of socialism to be a security threat. The government has used the security forces at its disposal against Polish workers, intellectuals, the Roman Catholic Church, and party elements who were perceived as threatening the PZPR's monopoly on power (see The People's Republic, ch. 1). Compared with the situation in the Soviet Union and the East European countries, the state of internal security in Poland since 1956 has been relatively turbulent, and popular protests on several occasions have resulted in major political changes—most notably during 1980–81. The year 1981 may have marked a watershed in Polish internal security affairs because in order to stem the coalition of forces aligned against it under the Solidarity banner, the PZPR was forced to call upon the Polish People's Army to play a major role in governing and administering the country.

Immediately after World War II the Soviet-imposed government of Poland faced a serious insurrection that some observers termed a civil war. Considerable opposition arose, particularly in rural areas, in response to the heavy-handed attempts by the communist party (known until 1948 as the Polish Workers' Party) to discredit, co-opt, or destroy sources of political authority independent of its control. Included were rival political parties, the Roman Catholic Church, popular local leaders, and surviving members of the noncommunist anti-German wartime resistance.

As communist control of Poland solidified and opposition groups were crippled or destroyed, new threats to state security were found within the PZPR itself. Stalin, according to historian Norman Davies, "simply did not trust foreign Communists." As the cold war deepened, Soviet authorities and Soviet-led security services moved in 1948 (as they did among communist parties throughout Eastern Europe) to purge the PZPR of "unreliable elements." According to Jozef Swialto, a high-ranking officer in the security service who defected to the West in 1953, paranoia gripped the top levels of the PZPR; its leaders lived in fear of being labeled traitors by their comrades and constantly sought to gather evidence that would compromise possible accusers. But Poland's purges never reached the extremes of those that had occurred in the Soviet Union during the 1930s. Most of the accused party members, including First Secretary Wladyslaw Gomulka, were dismissed from their positions in the PZPR and placed under house arrest.

After Stalin's death and Gomulka's subsequent return to the top echelon of the PZPR, party rivals no longer accused each other of being enemies of the state. In 1971 and 1981, however, former high party officials reportedly were placed under arrest—not, like their predecessors of a generation earlier, on national security grounds but rather for corruption and abuse of official powers. The government interned Gomulka for a short time in 1971, and a decade later Jaruzelski's government arrested former party leader Edward Gierek and former prime minister Piotr Jaroszewicz in response to Polish citizens' disgust over official corruption.

Polish regimes since 1956 have defined as threats "anti-social elements" who "challenged the party's leading role" in the society. The Roman Catholic Church, the only remaining institutional center independent of the PZPR, was viewed with suspicion by party leaders yet was tolerated because of Poland's largely Catholic population. Attempts by the PZPR leadership to weaken the church by confiscating church property, arresting church leaders, and using the splinter tactics that had worked in neutralizing political opposition proved unsuccessful.

By 1956 the authorities had come to accept the social role of the church in a Catholic country but insisted that it stay out of politics. Nevertheless, the church inevitably played an important political role as well (see The Roman Catholic Church, ch. 4). Church-state relations were periodically strained in the 1960s and 1970s when Catholic leaders spoke out on the government's suppression of freedoms, when they addressed an open letter to West German bishops calling for peace between Poland and the Federal Republic of Germany (West Germany), and on other occasions. The power of the church and its potential to threaten the PZPR government was demonstrated after Karol Cardinal Wojtyla became Pope John Paul II in 1978. According to some observers, the popular enthusiasm he generated on his return to his home country psychologically set the stage for the rise of Solidarity in 1980. During the Solidarity period and the year of martial law that followed, government authorities viewed the church as a mediating influence. After martial law was imposed, the primate, Archbishop Jozef Glemp, adopted a relatively conciliatory stance, advising the Poles against dangerous civil disorders. In 1982, however, the authorities condemned the "lower Catholic clergy [for] rekindling old sources of conflict." Most observers did not expect church-state relations to change fundamentally in the near term. However, Soviet condemnation in late 1982 of Pope John Paul II and the Vatican's "subversive" activities in Poland, as well as charges that the church was responsible for creating Solidarity, demonstrated that the church's position was not completely secure.

Whereas the church, despite its opposing world view, was able to reach a modus vivendi with the communist government, dissidence among Poland's small but active intelligentsia was more easily suppressed by the authorities. Intellectuals, virtually all of whom came from the upper classes in prewar Poland, were forced into a subservient role in the decade after World War II and, to a degree, were treated as class enemies by the Stalinist government. In the aftermath of the 1956 "Polish October" there was a flowering of artistic and critical expression throughout the society, a development that officials viewed as too liberal and therefore subversive (see The Gomulka Era, ch. 1). Over the next decade, the government (under the influence of the hard-line Partisans faction then gaining power) increasingly eliminated reformists from its own ranks and shut down virtually all of the intellectuals' journals, confining their activities to discussion groups. The intelligentsia did not constitute an overt threat to the regime, but open criticisms of the leadership threatened it by undermining its legitimacy and authority.

The growing alienation of students and intellectuals from the government was underlined in March 1968 when as many as 10,000 students demonstrated at Warsaw University, calling for autonomous student organizations and protesting official restrictions on freedom of speech. The government reacted by arresting student leaders, encouraging Polish workers to assault the protesters, and instituting a comprehensive purge of Jews from the PZPR and the universities. As a result, according to most observers, virtually all of Poland's intelligentsia—whether Catholic oriented or Marxist reformist—was increasingly estranged from the PZPR and the government.

During the early 1970s intellectuals had little real power or influence, but they continued to press for increased freedom of expression and were perceived by the government as a growing threat. In 1975 many became involved, along with the church, in documenting the government's failure to enforce provisions regarding human rights contained in the Helsinki Agreement of 1975 and in criticizing government plans to amend the Constitution (see The Constitution; Popular Political Expression, ch. 4). The intelligentsia's dissatisfaction coalesced in 1976 when a group of well-known intellectuals, former resistance fighters, and dissident communists sought to support workers who had been laid off or arrested after workers' demonstrations earlier that year. This Committee for the Defense of the Workers (Komitet Obrony Robotnikow—KOR, later known as the Committee for Social Self-Defense-Committee for the Defense of the Workers [Komitet Samoobrony Spolecznej-Komitet Obrony Robotnikow—KSS-KOR]) succeeded in raising funds, attracting attention to its calls for increased freedom of speech, and building ties between the universities and the working class. Over the next four years activist groups proliferated. According to the minister of internal affairs in September 1979, no less than 26 different antisocialist organized groups operating in Poland were engaged in "ideological sabotage."

Intellectuals from these organizations came into their own as a major opposition force in 1980 when many became influential Solidarity advisers. When martial law was declared, the government moved resolutely to eliminate the intelligentsia as a source of opposition. Universities were closed, and intellectuals affiliated with Solidarity were interned. In September 1982 six of the most prominent KSS-KOR members having ties to Solidarity, including longtime activists Jacek Kuron and Adam Michnik, were charged with attempting a violent overthrow of the state, a capital offense. The Jaruzelski regime also sought to split the workers' opposition from the intellectuals, charging that the intelligentsia had "highjacked" a movement that was based on legitimate workers' grievances.

The Polish workers demonstrated by their protests that they were potentially the most dangerous and effective opponents of Polish communist governments. In contrast to the way in which the regime dealt with religious or intellectual dissidents, its ideological rationale was shaken when protesting Polish workers were fired on by government troops. In 1956 and in 1970 when scores of workers were killed by soldiers and internal security troops, fissures in the PZPR widened, incumbents were demoted, and new leaders emerged to deal eventually with renewed workers' protests.

Although the major antigovernment outbreaks among workers were all triggered by government-ordered price increases, the causes of worker dissatisfaction undoubtedly ran deeper. In 1956 striking workers carried signs that proclaimed "Bread and Freedom" and "The Press Lies." In the 1970s observers also noted rising worker dissatisfaction with corruption, which was increasingly prevalent but accepted within the PZPR. According to sociologist Jacques Rupnik, workers also resented their loss of prestige vis-à-vis the more privileged party bureaucrats. Jaruzelski, while rolling back the freedoms won by Solidarity, balanced his actions by appearing to combat more strongly the corruption that was a partial cause of Poles' antigovernment sentiments. Corrupt and incompetent managers were dismissed from their posts and in some cases were arrested along with the discredited former PZPR leaders.

Immediately after martial law was declared, spontaneous strikes broke out at factories and universities. Solidarity leaders who had escaped arrest were able to establish an effective underground organization and coordinate massive demonstrations, most notably in May 1982 (on the first anniversary of the death of former primate Stefan Cardinal Wyszynski) and three months later on the second anniversary of the Gdansk Agreement (see Appendix D). But by autumn the security forces had succeeded in arresting important opposition leaders and blocking other planned demonstrations. The Solidarity underground, which initially appeared to be well organized, was infiltrated by security forces, and tapes of its leaders' secret discussions were broadcast on national radio. The government demonstrated that it was very difficult to carry out a long-term underground dissident movement when the state was mobilized against it.

The crime rate that had increased by 26 percent in 1980 and 40 percent in 1981 fell dramatically in the martial law environment. Most crime involved petty theft and disorderly conduct (according to police in 1982, the last reported armed robbery in Warsaw had occurred in 1964), but steady increases in crime since the mid-1970s had alarmed officials. According to authorities, progress was also made in curbing the activities of corrupt officials who sold public goods on the black market.

The comparative quiescence of opposition allowed the government to suspend martial law at the end of 1982, although restrictions on demonstrations and censorship remained in effect (see Martial Law Government, ch. 4). Whether the calm would evaporate quickly or would persist could not be ascertained in early 1983. In the near term, however, the military establishment and the internal security forces would probably remain prominent in Polish national life.

Armed Forces in National Life

The military had long played a major role in Polish national life, but in 1981–82 its importance was magnified by the participation of army officers at all levels of the government, led by the Military Council of National Salvation (Wojskowa Rada Ocalenia Narodowego—WRON), a group of 21 military officers. Despite its new prominence in national policymaking and the central political role occupied by Jaruzelski, the Polish People's Army between 1944 and 1981 was a closely controlled instrument of the Polish state and the PZPR. Because the vast majority of officers were PZPR members and because of the prevalence of party-oriented institutions within the army, Poland's system of virtually universal military training was seen by party and military leaders as a means of providing Polish youth with discipline and ideological training.

The army of the 1970s had appeared to enjoy a better reputation among the Polish people than did other national institutions, including the PZPR. Military leaders had sought to avoid tarnishing the army's image by keeping the regular military forces from being used in internal repression and by remaining aloof from intraparty conflicts. Even after the military leadership assumed responsibility for the government and imposed martial law, it sought to distance itself from the unpopular policies of former regimes and to ensure that the regular forces were never used to control popular demonstrations. After martial law, however, military prestige became more closely linked to the government's popularity. In early 1983 it appeared that at least for the remainder of Jaruzelski's tenure as party leader, the Polish people's view of the military would depend in large measure on his ability to govern the party and the country effectively.

Military Heritage

The Poles possess remarkably strong military traditions. The noble knight, the lancer, the scythe bearer and, later, the sharpshooter became symbols of their will to resist invasion and foreign occupation. In periods of national travail, they have sought leadership from a pantheon of military heroes—Jan Sobieski, Tadeusz Kosciuszko, Jozef Poniatowski, the young officers of the 1830 rising, Jozef Pilsudski, and Wladyslaw Sikorski.

From the days of the earliest kings, the defense of Polish soil demanded constant vigilance against German encroachment. Throughout succeeding centuries Poland was regarded as the outer bastion of Western Europe, and the Poles, led by an aristocratic military caste, accepted it as their mission to defend the West against intrusions from the East. For several generations before Poland was partitioned among its stronger neighbors in the late eighteenth century, however, its national army serving the king had degenerated into a poorly disciplined, ill-armed garrison force, while the great magnates were able to raise and maintain well-trained and well-equipped armies to wage their private wars. Efforts to revive the royal military establishment had included the founding of a military college that produced the nucleus of a trained officer corps. The army could not prevent the final partition of the country in 1795, but its veterans and graduates of the military college fought alongside the armies of Napoleon and later served in the army retained by Congress Poland after 1815.

The attitudes of Polish officers were inevitably influenced by the practices of the armies of the partitioning powers—Russia, Prussia (Germany), and Austria—into which Polish troops were integrated in the nineteenth century. A number of Poles rose to positions of high command, particularly in Austrian service. During World War I Poles fought on opposite sides. A Polish army was raised in France, and the Polish Legion, formed by Pilsudksi, was allied to the Central Powers against Russia in the hope of eventually winning recognition of Poland's independence.

After independence was achieved in November 1918, the armed forces became an important national institution, partly because of the personality and accomplishments of Pilsudski, who emerged as Poland's dominant political figure during the interwar period. The army was perceived by many Poles as the symbol, as well as the defender of their country's restored unity and independence. When the new republic's civilian government failed to provide stability and prosperity, Pilsudski led a military coup d'etat in 1926 and took over the state. Military officers held prominent posts in the national government, although the officer corps itself was rife with political and personal rivalries. After Pilsudski's death in 1935, his subordinates ruled Poland—poorly by most accounts—in what was called the "Colonels' Government."

Poland was attacked and overrun by Germany and the Soviet Union in September 1939, and most of its large but outgunned army was sent to prisoner of war camps. Underground resistance to German occupation began almost immediately (see World War II, ch. 1). Polish forces were reestablished under British and, in 1943, Soviet command, fighting with great distinction on all fronts of the European theater during World War II. The Polish First Army, serving under Soviet officers with the Red Army, provided the basis for the Polish People's Army.

The Military and the Communist State, 1945–56

In July 1944 the Soviet-backed Polish Committee of National Liberation (Polski Komitet Wyzwolenia Narodoweg—PKWN) was set up in Lublin as a provisional government. One of its first acts was to order the merger of the People's Army (Armia Ludowa—AL), the small communist-led underground military arm in occupied Poland, with the Polish First Army, commanded by General Zygmunt Berling. The Lublin government further authorized the conscription of male inhabitants of liberated areas born between 1921 and 1924, increasing the strength of Berling's command to 400,000 men by the time Germany surrendered in May 1945. The army also took in a few members of the noncommunist underground Home Army (Armia Krajowa—AK), as well as some soldiers transferred from Polish units on the Western front and a large number of Polish prisoners of war released from captivity in German camps. By July 1945 over 40 percent of the officer corps was composed of personnel drawn from this last group.

Until after the end of the war, the Polish army, partly because of its somewhat diverse political makeup and partly because of the necessity of defeating the Germans, was not closely involved in the communist consolidation of power and elimination of opponents, a job left to newly formed security services (see Internal Security Forces, this ch.) After the war the army was involved in repressing anticommunist Polish (and Ukrainian nationalist) elements, particularly in rural areas, but its role remained secondary to that of the internal security forces. In the immediate postwar period the army, unlike other elements of the society, did not suffer any major purges of its noncommunist elements. Communists took control of the top ranks and important positions, however, and the commissar system (officers in uniform, representing the communist party, who taught party principles and ensured the party loyalty of regular soldiers) was dominated by Soviets and officers from the Berling army. In 1949 after the postwar demobilizations, veterans of the Berling army comprised over 63 percent of the officer corps; about 29 percent had been members of the prewar Polish army who had been interned during the war, about 8 percent were Soviet army advisers, and only 0.5 percent had come from other (noncommunist) groups that had fought the Germans during World War II.

In the 1948–53 period the army was subjected, like institutions throughout Eastern Europe, to increased control by the PZPR and the Soviet military. Perhaps the most blatant example of Soviet control was the appointment in 1949 of Soviet Marshal Konstantin Rokossovsky (ethnically Polish) as the minister of defense and commander in chief of Poland's armed forces. At the time the Soviet general was named, the armed forces were being purged of officers not only from the prewar army and other noncommunist armies of the World War II era but also of veterans who had fought in Soviet-sponsored or Soviet-supported groups during the war. Most were tried and sent to prison, but unlike the coinciding situations in Czechoslovakia and Hungary and the purges a decade earlier in the Soviet Union, relatively few were executed. In many cases Soviet soldiers, some of whom had served in the officer cadre of the Berling army during the war, replaced the ousted officers. In addition to Rokossovsky, Soviet officers served as chief of the Polish General Staff, commander of the ground forces, heads of all the service branches, and commanders of the military districts. The Soviet-led Polish army was put on a war footing—conscription was reintroduced in 1949, and the army grew to nearly 400,000 men; new Soviet equipment was introduced to replace stocks from World War II; and the army was completely reorganized along Soviet lines to operate, in fact, as an element of the Soviet army. The military establishment during this period was also thoroughly penetrated by the PZPR and the Stalinist secret police.

As a result of the changes, the military, which had enjoyed considerable prestige among patriotic Poles in the interwar period, was seen as a mere instrument of Soviet policy. Its popularity, already weakened by its inability to protect the country from the ravages of World War II, declined further in the decade after the war. Polish military writings since 1956 have indicated that the operational performance of the armed forces also reached its nadir during this period as a result of disorganization, inadequate equipment, and poor morale.

The military had a major role in the events of 1956 that finally ended the Stalinist era in Poland. In June soldiers refused to follow orders to fire on workers rioting in Poznan for "Bread and Freedom," and the riots were eventually put down after internal security troops inflicted scores of casualties. The Soviets were alarmed when in the resulting political upheaval Poland's political leadership, which had been closely identified with past Stalinist policies, was repudiated in October and Gomulka, who had recently been released after four years of house arrest, rose to become PZPR first secretary (see Internal Politics 1951–56; The Gomulka Era, ch. 1). The Kremlin sent an unannounced, high-level delegation, including Soviet leader Nikita Khrushchev, to Warsaw and dispatched troops and tanks. Several Polish military commanders prepared their troops to fight the invaders, and the internal security forces kept Gomulka informed of Soviet troop movements as he was meeting with the Soviets. Through skillful negotiating backed by the demonstrated willingness to defend itself, Poland averted the fate of Hungary, which was invaded by Soviet troops only two weeks later.

The events of 1956 marked a watershed in postwar Polish history, matched in importance only by the Solidarity experiment and the imposition of martial law in the early 1980s. The armed forces had helped achieve a new internal autonomy for the Polish communist government. For this and because soldiers had refused to fire on Polish workers, the military began to recover some of the prestige it had lost during the Stalin years and reemerged as a political force. Although its direct influence was reduced, Moscow continued to station troops in Poland, train Polish general officers at schools inside the Soviet Union, supply weapons of Soviet design, and include Poland in its defense plans.

Instruments of Party Control

Until 1981, when the party's weakness forced the military into a position of unprecedented prominence in political affairs, the armed forces operated under the unquestioned control and authority of government and party officials. When Gomulka returned to power in 1956, the instruments of party control over the military were in disarray. Soviet officers and the Soviet-influenced security service known as Military Information, which had been prominent in controlling the armed forces, had been thoroughly discredited. After Gomulka attained power, Rokossovsky and the Soviet "advisers" were recalled, and the security service was disbanded. The Gomulka regime and its successors sought to guarantee the "leading role" of the PZPR in all military affairs and came to rely more heavily on other mechanisms of political control, all patterned on the Soviet example.

Ultimate responsibility for Polish military affairs rested with the Council of Ministers and the National Defense Committee attached to it. Although not technically in the chain of command, the PZPR Political Bureau (Politburo) was the source of all important military policy decisions just as it controlled government policymaking generally. The minister of national defense held operational and administrative responsibility for the armed forces and was considered the commander in chief. The position of defense minister under the communist government has always been filled by a general officer who was, except during the

1968–71 period, a full member of the Politburo.

Direct party influence in military affairs was reduced when Jaruzelski occupied the top posts in the army, the PZPR, and the government, but the instrumentalities of party control over the military remained in place during the martial law period. In the early 1980s the PZPR's Central Committee closely supervised military affairs through the Central Committee's Administration Department (which monitored military operations, promotions, spending, and administrative matters) as well as through the Main Political Administration (Glowne Biuro Administacji—generally known in the West as MPA). The MPA was formally a subdivision of the Ministry of National Defense and was headed by a deputy defense minister. But it also functioned with the power and independent authority of a Central Committee department and was directly responsible to the PZPR Secretariat of the Central Committee and Politburo rather than to the minister of national defense. The MPA was the agency responsible for political matters and political indoctrination in the armed forces; it also had a hand in determining personnel policies.

Various party organizations, including communist youth groups directed primarily at young conscripts, also reinforced party control. In early 1983 the most important of these was the Socialist Union of Military Youth, which sought to improve the moral and ideological outlook of service members; before the Solidarity movement was established, this youth group reportedly counted half the conscripts among its membership. After 1956, military membership in the PZPR was also encouraged and became a prerequisite to advancement to the higher officer grades. In 1955 only 53 percent of Polish military officers had been members of the PZPR, but by 1958 the proportion had risen to 67 percent. In 1980 about 85 percent of all Polish officers (and all senior officers) were party members. The Military Counterintelligence Service, a party-controlled police organization that in 1957 took the place of the discredited Military Information, further strengthened the PZPR's power. The new security service operated far more discreetly than had its predecessor in providing political authorities information on military attitudes and activities.

The MPA, which had much in common with like structures in other communist countries, was the PZPR's most extensive and best organized instrument for controlling the military. Headed by a general officer appointed by the Secretariat of the Central Committee, the MPA relied on its own corps of about 1,000 specially trained military officers. Political officers operated alongside line officers of equal rank down to the battalion level. Their power was based on their ability to communicate directly with junior officers and conscripts without regard for the military chain of command and on their system of reporting directly to superiors in the MPA, not the regular force. The lack of professional military competence among political commissars of the MPA had been widely criticized within the armed forces in the late 1950s. As a result, political officers began to be trained at the regular military schools and worked their way up through the ranks in nonpolitical positions. Under this system officers were not usually given political positions (typically, as battalion political officers) until they had attained the grade of major and had graduated from the Academy of Political and Military Sciences. Because of concern that the system might tend to make political officers overempathize with their professional counterparts, the system was further revised in 1975 so that immediately after graduation from military school with a social science degree the political officer was given political responsibilities in addition to military duties. Dale Herspring, an American analyst of Polish affairs, has suggested that the political commissar system will be increasingly strained by the new military technology that demands higher levels of technical training and proficiency, thereby allowing less emphasis on political affairs than in the past. In the early 1980s, however, a more significant constraint on party control of the military—and a stimulus to the military's political prominence—was the PZPR's own disarray and lack of direction.

Party-Military Relations

Beyond rebuilding and strengthening the bureaucratic instruments of political control over the military, Gomulka moved to assert his power vis-à-vis the military by replacing the departed Soviet commanders with Polish officers who had served with him in the wartime communist underground (as opposed to the Soviet-controlled Polish First Army) and with commanders who had prepared their troops to resist a Soviet invasion in 1956. Gomulka and his trusted minister of national defense, General Marian Spychalski, however, proved unwilling or unable to control these strong-willed and politically well-connected military commanders, who soon broke into reformist and conservative factions that disagreed on matters of ideology and policy. Gomulka's tenure was characterized by considerable political conflict and instability at the top grades of the officer corps, generated in part by a group identified as Partisans that emerged as a major force in the military and party leadership. During the 1960s the Partisans, who were nationalist in outlook but against political reform and generally anti-Semitic, sought to remove their rivals from important positions in the military and the party and to replace them with fellow Partisans. Under the leadership of Mieczyslaw Moczar, the Partisans instigated purges of military and party reformists and were behind the 1967–68 anti-Jewish campaign. They were unsuccessful in gaining control of the army, however, because ousted military officers were generally replaced not by

Partisans but by younger professional military officers untainted by factional politics.

This pattern was followed when Spychalski resigned as defense minister in April 1968 and was replaced by Jaruzelski, then a lieutenant general. Few details are known to outsiders about Jaruzelski's past apart from those in his official biography. Born into a landed family and educated by Jesuits, Jaruzelski was either unable or unwilling to join the noncommunist resistance and participated during World War II in the Berling army's campaign against the Germans. He rose rapidly through the ranks and at the age of 33 became the youngest general officer in the army in 1955. Although a line officer, he was appointed to head the MPA in 1960 and later held positions as deputy defense minister and chief of the General Staff. After he became head of the Ministry of National Defense, Jaruzelski moved to place professional officers, rather than those associated with party factions, in important military positions.

The professionalization of the top levels of the officer corps accelerated after the 1970 workers' riots in the Baltic ports of Gdansk and Gdynia that led to Gomulka's fall. The military had backed the militia as it suppressed the dissidents, killing between 44 (official Polish government estimate) and 200 to 300 demonstrators (workers' estimates). But when ordered by Gomulka's deputy to use "overwhelming force" to crush the demonstrations, Jaruzelski and the army refused to act. The national leadership was in turmoil at the time and was giving out conflicting orders; the army indicated that it would not use force against the workers to support Gomulka and his group within the PZPR. In the year after Gierek was appointed party first secretary, the Partisans—who had been associated most strongly with the unpopular violence against the Baltic workers—lost more of their power, and in the military most of them were gradually replaced by professional officers not closely tied to political factionalism.

In 1971 Jaruzelski was made a member of the Politburo, and two years later he was promoted to the rank of general. In the 1970s, however, the military conspicuously stayed apart from ideological and political disputes that were not directly linked to military issues. In June 1976 when workers in Warsaw and Lodz protested against higher food prices, Jaruzelski reportedly stated that "Polish soldiers will not fire on Polish workers" when asked if soldiers could be used to quell the riots. (The price increases were immediately rescinded, and the situation cooled off.)

By appearing to act as a nationalist force and by seeming to stay aloof from politics, the armed forces' prestige in the country increased. According to comprehensive surveys of occupational prestige, Warsaw inhabitants' ranking of the prestige of military officers improved from twentieth of 27 occupations listed in 1958 to thirteenth of 27 in 1975. In the 1975 survey covering all of

Poland, army officers ranked eleventh in a list of 30 occupations. By contrast, as Gierek's ambitious economic schemes foundered and corruption at the top levels of the PZPR became more visible and more repugnant in the 1970s, the party's prestige plummeted. In a poll taken in June 1981 by *Kultura* (Warsaw), the army ranked as the third most respected institution in the country behind the church and Solidarity; the PZPR ranked fourteenth. According to press reports, party members concerned about the negative trends increasingly mentioned Jaruzelski—known as a man of high abilities who lived modestly—as a candidate for top government positions.

When a wave of strikes swept the Baltic ports in the summer of 1980, little serious consideration was given to the use of military force to put down the strikers. In the interparty turmoil that accompanied the government's negotiation of the Gdansk Agreement with the striking shipyard workers, Jaruzelski became an active and influential political force in the moves to replace the discredited Gierek with Stanislaw Kania. The military kept a low public profile, but as the political crisis continued, Jaruzelski emerged as the leading political figure acceptable to most elements of the increasingly divided leadership. On February 11, 1981, Jaruzelski became prime minister, the country's fourth in 12 months. Military participation in the Central Committee had also increased from three regular officers out of 200 members, as was common during most of the Gierek period, to 14 out of 200 in mid-1981. Throughout 1981, statements by military leaders stressing their support thwarted attempts by a doctrinaire faction of the party led by Tadeusz Grabski to oust the Kania-Jaruzelski leadership, which was seen at the time as moderate and open to compromise with Solidarity. Jaruzelski became the most powerful figure in the Polish leadership in October 1981 when, upon Kania's resignation, the Central Committee voted him to the position of first secretary of the PZPR while he continued to hold the premiership and the defense portfolio.

When Jaruzelski declared martial law in December, Solidarity was making increasingly militant demands, economic deterioration was accelerating, and the party was fragmented, demoralized, and seemingly immobilized. During the next year under the leadership of WRON, the government—through a policy of arrests and detentions—managed to extinguish the threat of a civil war, which it said it feared. In early 1983 Jaruzelski and the military remained in control at the top level of government, and military commissars served at the voivodship (see Glossary) and local levels, exercising power that rivaled or surpassed that of the PZPR apparatuses in local communities. Moreover, Jaruzelski had limited the power of party "hard-liners" and other members considered too liberal.

The armed forces emerged from the martial law period relatively more powerful than the PZPR and certainly a stronger political

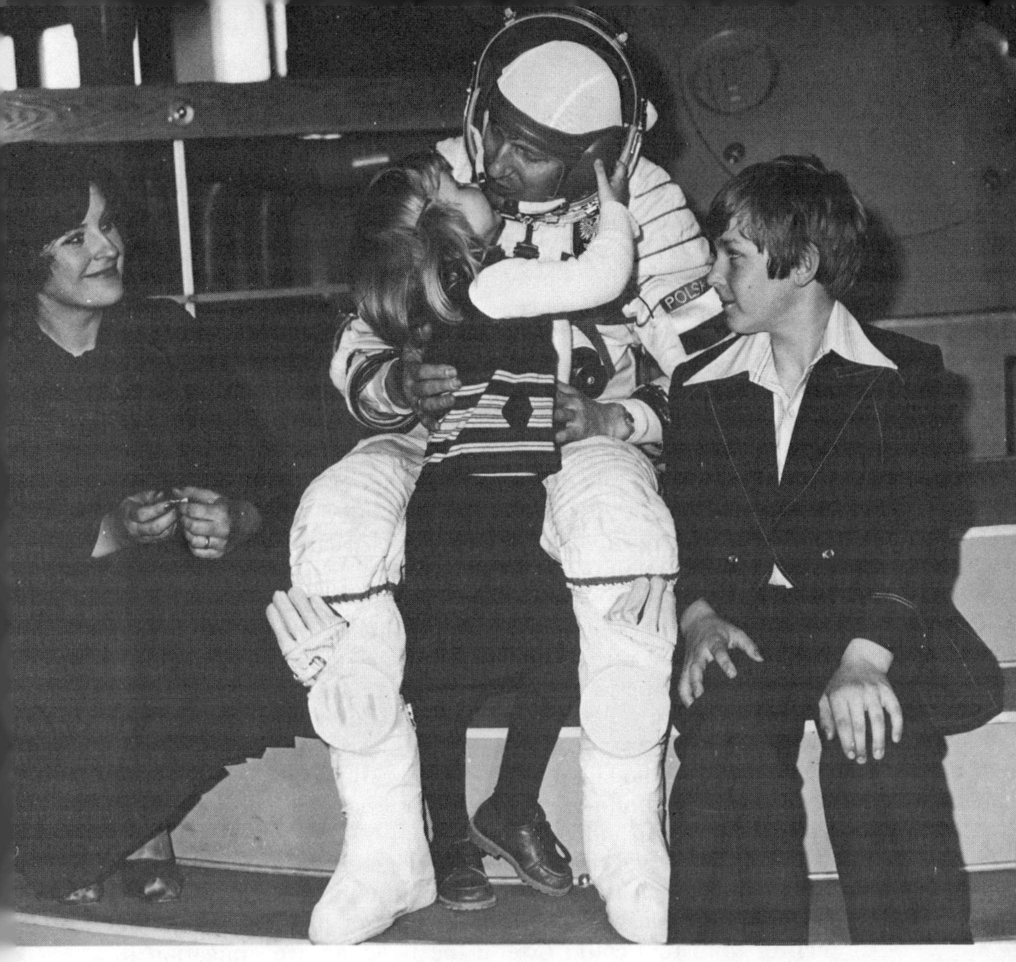

Colonel Miroslaw Hermaszewski, member of Polish air force and Poland's first cosmonaut, with his wife and children. On June 27, 1978, Hermaszewski (then a major) served as flight engineer on Soviet spacecraft Soyuz 30, which docked with Salyut 6 space station for seven days of experiments and research.
Courtesy Consulate General of Polish People's Republic, New York

force than armies in other East European communist countries concerned about "Bonapartism." But unlike the situation in the 1970s when they stood apart from political conflicts, Jaruzelski and the military leadership had made enemies in both the PZPR and the society by using their power. Their continued influence might depend on the ties between Poland's military establishment and the Soviet leadership in Moscow (the strength of which could not be determined), as well as on their ability to govern effectively.

Manpower

According to the constitution "the defense of the Fatherland is the most solemn obligation of every citizen," and since 1949 Polish laws and regulations providing for universal military service for males have helped to ensure that the obligation is met. The Polish armed forces in the early 1980s were able to draw recruits from a manpower pool that included approximately 7.4 million males between the ages of 15 and 50 who were considered fit for military service (about 80 percent of the population in that demographic group). Approximately 60 percent of the operational military establishment (and 75 percent of the ground forces) were composed of conscripts, most of them drafted from among the 256,000 men who reached military age each year. Small numbers of women served voluntarily in the armed forces.

The Military Service Law of 1967 and its subsequent amendments stated that all able-bodied Polish males were required to fulfill their military service obligation after reaching 19 years of age; volunteers for basic military service were accepted at age 17. Those persons who failed to register for conscription within the allotted period were subject to a fine or incarceration up to three months. Draftees who failed to report for duty were liable to serve up to two years in confinement, although it was unclear how many were actually caught and punished.

Basic military service lasted two years except in the technically oriented navy and in rocket and telecommunications units where three years' service was required. In case of national need, the Council of Ministers could extend the basic service obligation to an additional 12 months. After completing basic service, the soldier entered the reserves. Not all Polish conscripts had to undergo basic service. A conscript could perform voluntary alternate service if given permission by the recruitment commandant. Alternate service lasted 24 months and could mean working in health care units, social welfare, or serving with fire-fighting units or the Citizens' Militia (Milicja Obywatelska—MO; see Internal Security Forces, this ch.). Others could fulfill their obligation in civil defense units and be trained to lend assistance in case of national disaster or war. Most Poles who served in civil defense activities were not able or eligible for reasons of health to perform military duties or other alternate service. Like soldiers, those who performed alternate service were usually housed and fed in barracks, subjected to the demands of military discipline, and subsequently they entered the reserves. Their families, like those of soldiers, were also supposed to receive financial compensation if the drafted family member had provided a significant share of family earnings.

Male university students since 1949 have also been required to perform military service, and their service obligations have been steadily increased. During the 1950s all male college students earned an officer's commission in the reserves after taking some military course work and a limited amount of drill with a reserve unit (usually 30 days). Beginning in 1960 students in civilian colleges were supposed to take two to four semesters of military course work (depending on their field of study), drill with regular units during vacations and for three months after graduation, and pass military examinations. If they failed their examinations, the students were liable for basic military service (few failed). If they successfully completed the examinations and other requirements, the students were placed in the reserves with noncommissioned officer (NCO) rank and status as reserve cadet officers. They were generally encouraged to secure a commission by taking a two- to three-month reserve officers' training course. This level of training was thought inadequate to meet military manpower needs; moreover, popular expressions of resentment against the privileged student elite were increasingly heard. As a result, between 1973 and 1979 new laws extended the length and scope of student military service.

In the early 1980s all male students were supposed to perform one year of military service after graduation, although many avoided it. Upon completion of studies (including military courses) and examinations, the graduate was assigned to a reserve officer cadet school where he was given four months of generally technical training before being assigned to a unit for the remaining eight months of what amounted to a military internship. These trainees could be promoted to second lieutenants on the basis of their performance, but most became warrant officers by the end of their terms and were placed in the reserves. Students were given incentives to take their military training seriously. According to a Polish officer involved with the process, "Only those officer cadets who have distinguished themselves will, at the time they are transferred to the reserves, receive a special recommendation that can be very important later in employment, in shortening the waiting time for housing, [and in] receiving a higher position after completing the initial work period."

The bulk of the Polish army's career officers came from the country's 14 higher officer candidate schools (see Education, Training, and Promotion, this ch.). Although statistics were difficult to obtain, there were indications, according to the assistant commander of the naval academy, that in the early 1980s "the military profession has become somewhat less appealing in relation to other professions." As a result, although classes were generally full, Polish officers stated that the military schools were forced to accept applicants with lower educational and physical standards than they had previously.

Because of conscription policies, the military represented a cross section of Polish society. The officer corps, however, was more exclusive as a result of policies implemented since the late

1950s to increase PZPR membership, purge Soviet (in 1956) and Jewish (in 1967–68) officers, and improve officers' educational qualifications. In the first years after the formation of the Polish People's Army, the military operated on the principle that "sheer will" rather than academic degrees made an officer. Officers who entered active duty before the mid-1960s may have come up through the ranks and may or may not have continued their formal education during their military careers. Part of the thrust of regulations enacted since about 1964 was to ensure that as soon as the older group retired, the entire officer corps would have university degrees. By 1980 it was estimated that fully half of the officer corps had degrees, up from 17 percent in 1958 and 40 percent in 1974. Enlisted reserves who had served conscript tours of duty were urged to attend universities and return to the service as officers, but they were not ordinarily granted officer grades unless they had acquired the necessary degrees, usually in an engineering field.

Soldiers discharged from active duty were placed on reserve status until they reached the age of 50 (60 in the case of officers and NCOs). Women without children who had left military service remained on reserve status until age 40 (age 50 if they were officers or NCOs). Reserve training programs were not widely organized and were not extensive enough to keep more than a small percentage of personnel who had completed their service obligations in satisfactory physical condition or up-to-date in the modern weapons technology required in the armed forces. Regulations limited military training during the entire reserve period to 12 months for privates and NCOs who had completed basic service, 18 months for privates and NCOs who had performed alternate service, and 24 months for warrant officers and commissioned officers. The reserves could be called up for duty not exceeding 24 months of the entire reserve period. Although about 100,000 soldiers were discharged from active duty each year—all of whom were obligated to serve in the reserves for nearly 30 more years—only some 605,000 were considered trained reservists in 1982.

The reserves were called up after the declaration of martial law in December 1981. According to unconfirmed Polish press releases, reservists of all ages reported for duty voluntarily, including World War II veterans. The reserves performed a variety of duties under martial law, the most significant of which was auditing and monitoring the activities of the state trading organizations. It was not known how many reservists served during the martial law period, but they were gradually demobilized in early 1982.

Poland, like most other communist countries, has established extensive premilitary training programs for schoolchildren. Most programs have been administered under the auspices of the

National Defense League, a government-sponsored organization with about 200,000 active members in 1982, most of whom were reserve officers. Many Polish secondary schools had programs that would train youths in military and technical subjects. In general, the league's courses were held over a four-month period on nonwork days but, under an agreement with the Ministry of National Defense, in 1980 it began experimenting with premilitary training under a barracks system. The effectiveness of the premilitary programs was indicated by the fact that under certain circumstances a soldier who had completed secondary-school training could have his conscription period shortened by half.

The Polish armed forces have played an important role as a social force in communist Poland. As Jaruzelski pointed out in 1973, "The army is a big school, a school of life through which a major part of our young people pass."

The Military and the Economy

The level of Polish defense spending and the way fiscal resources are used have been largely a function of Poland's security relationship with the Soviet Union and its Warsaw Pact responsibilities. The size and components of the defense budget have been determined by the Polish national leadership in consultations with Soviet leaders and have been based on the military needs of the Warsaw Pact and Poland's ability to pay. Before Jaruzelski attained the premiership and the PZPR leadership, only the party and government leaders—not military officers—were directly involved in formulating the defense budget. According to observers the Polish military thus sought to influence appropriations by building ties with the Soviet military leadership, whose recommendations to Polish leaders usually become policy.

In 1982 military officers were directly involved in the budget process for the first time under the extraordinary situation of martial law, and military spending grew by 156 percent over the previous year's total. Much of the increase could be attributed to inflation as the total national budget increased 68 percent over the 1981 level, but there was evidently substantial real growth.

The 1982 national budget appropriated 183 billion zlotys (for value of the zloty—see Glossary) to the Ministry of National Defense. The officially published defense budget, which in the 1970s and early 1980s varied between 5 and 9 percent of the total state budget, was not thought to be an accurate gauge of defense spending levels. Relative changes in military spending from year to year could be ascertained, but direct comparison with defense spending in Western countries were difficult. It was not known what items were included in the Polish military budget; the costs of goods and services in a centrally planned economy did not necessarily indicate their real value; and the official exchange rate of the zloty had little bearing on its real purchasing power. As a result of these factors, the United States Arms Control and Disarmament Agency estimated that defense spending in Poland accounted for between 15 and 25 percent of the total state budget during the 1970s and early 1980s. Most sources agreed, however, that during this period military spending amounted to between 5 and 8 percent of Poland's gross national product (GNP—see Glossary). Polish military spending was higher than that of all other Warsaw Pact countries except the Soviet Union, but it was thought to be below average when adjusted to Poland's greater population. Economist Thad Alton and others, in a study on East European military spending prepared for the United States Congress in 1981, estimated that the Polish defense budget in the 1970s generally appropriated nearly 80 percent of total military spending to operations, maintenance, and procurement; nearly 20 percent to personnel (military pay and subsistence); and some 3 to 4 percent on research and development costs associated with Poland's arms industry.

Polish industry has long been involved in producing military equipment and items that have both military and civilian uses. Weapons have been of Soviet design or built to Soviet specifications as a means of enhancing standardization and sharing the burden of military production among the members of the Warsaw Pact. In early 1983 the Polish arms industry, which developed in the 15 years after World War II as the second largest in Eastern Europe after that of Czechoslovakia, was capable of producing relatively sophisticated weapons. Polish shipyards were responsible for the production of the widely used Polnochny-class landing ships, and other factories produced T-54 and T-55 tanks (T-72s were reportedly forthcoming), armored personnel carriers, trucks, artillery, and small arms. The Polish aircraft industry also produced a wide variety of aircraft, including, until 1959, MiG-17 jet fighter aircraft (known in Poland as the LiM-5). The importance of weapons production was underscored by former PZPR leader Gierek's negotiation efforts with the Soviet Union in the early 1970s to allow Poland to produce a larger share of Warsaw Pact military equipment. In the early 1980s, however, the country's economic difficulties were reflected in substantially decreased industrial output, including weapons production.

Polish military and political leaders long have stressed that the economic costs of military spending are balanced by the economic benefits provided by the armed forces. Military service is said to make future workers more productive by instilling personal discipline, providing ideological indoctrination and, in many cases, teaching them valuable skills or trades. In addition, given the economy's unemployment pressures and the fact that conscripts have been paid substantially less than most state workers, there appeared in early 1982 to be few economic pressures to reduce military manpower.

The armed forces also have been given tasks that contribute to the national economy. The quartermaster general has supervised crop production and animal husbandry on military reservations, some of which have been self-sufficient in food. The army's transportation units and civil engineers have engaged in a variety of civilian construction projects. Soldiers have extended and repaired roads and railroad tracks and constructed bridges, dams, and flood control projects. In 1981 the army also participated in the harvest. Soldiers helped harvest grain crops and potatoes and sent technicians and mobile repair workshops to agricultural areas to keep farm equipment in repair. In early 1983 the total contribution of the military to the economy could not be determined, but it was believed to be significant.

The Armed Forces: Mission, Organization, and Training

The Polish People's Army was designed to operate offensively in concert with the Soviet Union and other forces in the Warsaw Pact; it was also responsible for defending the nation's borders and could be used to maintain internal security in support of the police. The minister of national defense served as supreme commander of the army and was the chief of operations, but in 1982 and 1983 when Defense Minister Jaruzelski was chiefly concerned with his more pressing duties as head of government and the PZPR, Lieutenant General Florian Siwicki served as acting minister of national defense. The minister was supported by five deputy ministers: the chief of the General Staff, the head of the Main Political Administration, and the commanders of the Main Inspectorate of Training, the Main Inspectorate of National Territorial Defense, and the Inspectorate of National Civil Defense.

The Polish People's Army comprised all of the country's military forces, but it was a nebulous entity from an organizational standpoint. Ground, naval, air, and air defense forces were included within it, but only the chiefs of the naval and air forces reported directly to the minister of national defense. The ground forces, by far the most important of the group, were commanded by the minister through the General Staff and the commanders of Poland's military districts. This apparently remote organizational relationship, however, did not provide an accurate picture of how the system worked. During major maneuvers, for example, the minister might assume direct command of the entire exercise and of the ground forces in particular. The General Staff, which appeared to be related to the ground forces only, made policies and took actions what were binding on the other services as well. (Another source of confusion arose from the common practice—even in some official communications—of regarding the air force and navy as separate elements and using the term *army* to refer to the ground forces rather than to the entire Polish People's Army [see fig. 18].)

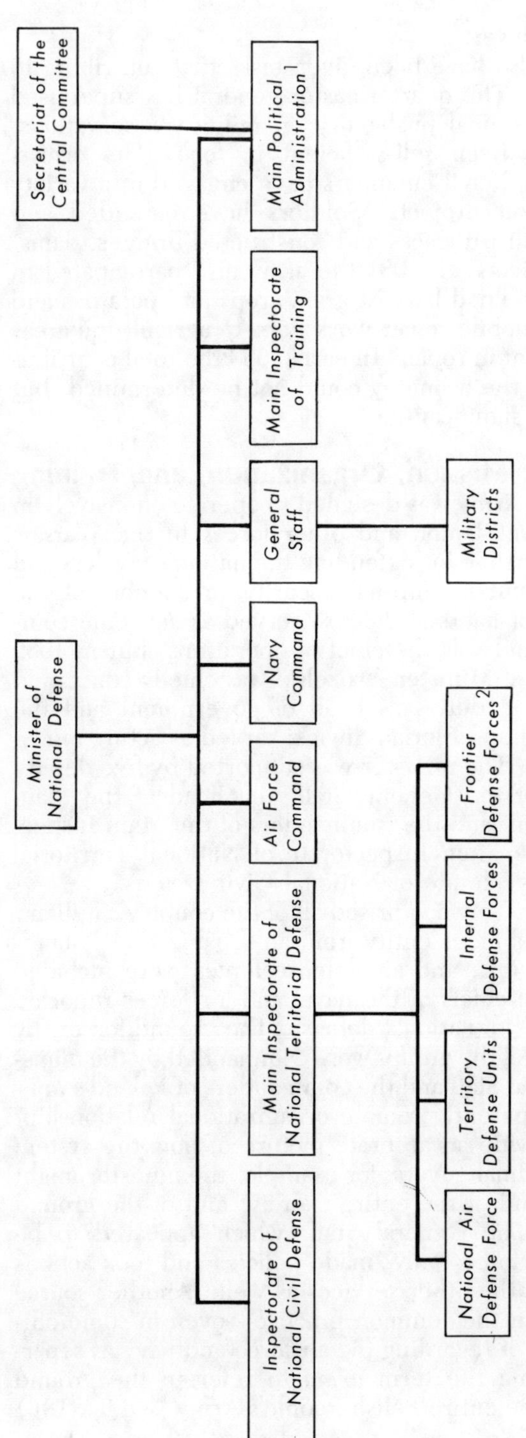

[1]Has dual status as inspectorate of Ministry of National Defense and department of Secretariat of the Central Committee.

[2]Under authority of Ministry of Internal Affairs in peacetime.

Figure 18. Command Structure of Polish People's Army, 1982

The armed forces were also divided into the operational army and the National Territorial Defense (Obrono Terytorium Kraju—OTK) forces. The operational army, manned by 317,000 personnel of the air force, navy, and ground forces divisions, was designed to be used as an integral part of the Joint Armed Forces of the Warsaw Pact. The OTK forces, however, operated only in Poland and were not part of Poland's Warsaw Pact commitments. Included in the Main Inspectorate of National Territorial Defense were the Territory Defense Units, the Internal Defense Forces, and, in wartime, the Frontier Defense Forces. OTK forces also included the National Air Defense Force, but in the event of a war its interceptor aircraft and antiaircraft batteries would come under the authority of the Warsaw Pact's Air Defense Command.

The fighting capabilities of all the services were believed to have declined somewhat during the early 1980s. The higher ranks of the officer corps were preoccupied with controlling the country's political and economic crises, while the weak economy limited the quantity and quality of resources available to the military. Moreover, strains within the society that became more pronounced after August 1980 might have had an adverse effect upon morale, particularly among the large conscript force.

Ground Forces

The ground forces of the Polish People's Army consisted of modern, well-equipped units organized along Soviet lines. These forces were allocated among three military districts, each commanded by a lieutenant general. The Pomeranian and Silesian districts (headquartered at Bydgoszcz and Wroclaw, respectively) occupied the northwestern and southwestern quarters of the country; the Warsaw district (headquartered in the national capital) was larger and included eastern Poland. The 207,000 personnel in the ground forces (154,000 of whom were conscripts) were grouped into combat arms, technical and supporting services, and military specialties.

Poland's 15 ground forces divisions included eight motorized rifle divisions, five tank divisions, one airborne division, and one amphibious assault division. The combined forces could be organized to form one tank and two combined arms armies based on Soviet models. Divisions in the two western military districts were considered Category I units and were usually maintained at no less than 70 percent of their authorized strengths; analysts reported that the airborne, amphibious assault, and selected tank divisions were kept at a particularly high state of readiness. Those in the Warsaw military district were grouped as Category II formations, operating at 50 percent strength or less but ready for a rapid buildup if mobilization was ordered. Authorized manned strength of a motorized rifle division was about 10,800, and each tank division had some 8,700 men. The amphibious assault and airborne divisions were somewhat smaller. All divisions had services and auxiliary arms detachments—maintenance, medical, signals, chemical, transportation, and quartermaster—to provide operational support.

The motorized rifle division, which replaced the World War II infantry division, was redesignated after it had acquired enough motorized equipment to move its entire complement as a unit in an assortment of self-propelled weapons and personnel carriers. Supplementing the greatly increased mobility of the motorized rifle division was the greater firepower of its component artillery regiment, two rocket artillery battalions, one tank regiment, and three motorized rifle regiments (see fig. 19). Motorized rifle divisions usually had 266 tanks, compared with 325 in a tank division, and were supplemented by all-artillery units. These units included three artillery brigades and one artillery regiment equipped with guns of up to 152mm caliber, multiple rocket launchers, and FROG-3 and FROG-7 surface-to-surface missiles. The ground forces also had four brigades equipped with Scud surface-to-surface missiles having a maximum range of 280 kilometers (see table 14, Appendix A).

In early 1983 Poland was the only member of the Warsaw Pact other than the Soviet Union that had airborne and amphibious assault units of division strength. The airborne division, which was composed of three airborne regiments and support units, used lighter weight equipment (and less of it) than other units. All equipment of this elite unit was designed to be carried on transport aircraft, and some of it could be landed by parachute. The amphibious assault division was specially trained and equipped for waterborne operations. In the event of an armed conflict between the Warsaw Pact and NATO, Western analysts expected that this unit would play a major role in military operations in the Baltic region.

Equipment in inventory was not obsolete but was generally a full generation behind the latest Soviet models. Polish armored strength continued to be based on about 3,000 T-54 and T-55 medium tanks that had been a mainstay since the early 1960s. The T-72, which had first appeared in Soviet units in the early 1970s, was beginning to enter service in small numbers; reportedly, it was to be produced in Poland under license. Likewise, the Poles had begun to take delivery of the highly rated Soviet BMP and MT-LB infantry fighting vehicles, but the vast majority of the army's light armored vehicles were of the older SKOT, BDRM, and OT-65/FUG types. Divisional air defense was provided by a variety of antiaircraft guns, including the ZSU-23-4, and by SA-4, SA-6, SA-7, and SA-9 surface-to-air missiles (SAMs). Polish equipment in the ground forces and throughout the defense establishment, although old, was well maintained, and Polish soliders used it competently.

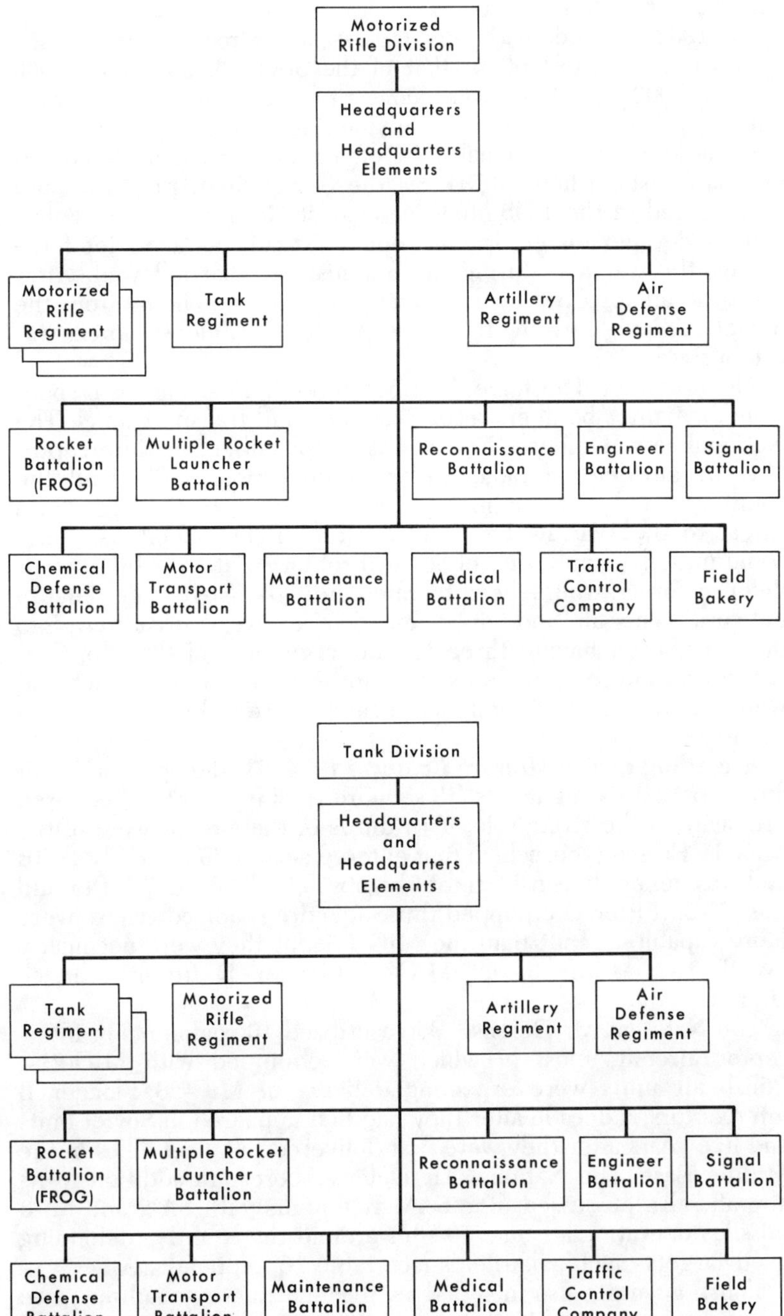

Figure 19. Organization of Representative Motorized Rifle and Tank Divisions, 1983

Air and Air Defense Forces

In 1983 Poland had the largest air force in communist Eastern Europe except for that of the Soviet Union. Its 88,000 men (27,000 of whom were conscripts) and over 700 combat aircraft were organized along Soviet lines under the Air Force Command and the National Air Defense Force. The air force was originally established in 1944 as the Soviet Sixth Air Army and participated in the 1945 offensive against Germany. Using Polish and Soviet personnel, it functioned virtually as a Soviet force during the war and during the Stalinist era that followed. After 1956 the air force won some institutionalized autonomy from the Soviet Union, and in 1962 a separate air defense force was established.

The operational air force, headquartered in Poznan, was responsible for fighter-bomber, reconnaissance, and transport units. The National Air Defense Force was responsible for interceptor aircraft, air defense radar and communications units, and the country's fixed and semimobile SAM systems. In the event of a threat to the Warsaw Pact, the air force fighter-bombers would come under the authority of Soviet Frontal Aviation, while the air defense forces would be integrated into the Soviet air defense network. The air and air defense forces were organized into divisions, each having three to four regiments of three or four squadrons apiece. Squadrons were authorized 12 aircraft each and were based at 35 to 40 military airfields scattered throughout the country.

According to *The Military Balance, 1982–83*, the operational air force utilized six regiments (18 squadrons) of fighter-bombers used primarily in the strike role. Two-thirds of the aircraft were of the MiG-17 Fresco type, which first entered service in the early 1950s and was generally considered to be obsolete. The SU-7 Fitter and the SU-20 Fitter D equipped three squadrons apiece. These were more capable aircraft than the MiG-17, but they were not nearly as effective as the Soviet MiG-27 Flogger D first-line attack aircraft.

The National Air Defense Force utilized 10 regiments of interceptor aircraft, most of which were equipped with MiG-21s. Polish air units were expecting delivery of MiG-23 Flogger B interceptors, a decade after they had first appeared in Soviet units and five years after they were first delivered to Soviet allies in the Middle East. The National Air Defense Force, in addition to its aircraft, also possessed nine SAM regiments with SA-2 and SA-3 missiles operating at some 50 sites around the country, defending fixed targets, such as airfields (see table 15, Appendix A).

Polish air units also included six reconnaissance squadrons, two transport regiments, and three helicopter regiments equipped with a variety of transport helicopters. Soviet-built aircraft that served in a training role included the MiG-21UTI, the MiG-

15UTI, and the SU-7U; Polish-built aircraft included the TS-11 Iskra light jet trainer and the TS-8 Bien primary trainer.

Navy

Polish naval units, consisting of about 150 vessels of various types in early 1983, operated from bases at Gdynia, Hel, Kolobrzeg, Ustka, and Swinoujscie. Personnel included 22,000 officers and ratings, of whom 6,000 were conscripts on three-year tours of duty. The navy was assigned the mission of supporting Warsaw Pact operations in the Baltic and conducting coastal defense, but it was not equipped to perform unassisted in a major naval action.

A former Soviet Kotlin-class destroyer equipped with Goa SAMs was the only major surface unit, but short-range offensive capability, well suited to conditions in the Baltic, was provided by 13 former Soviet OSA I-class fast attack craft (FAC), each armed with four Styx surface-to-surface missiles (SSM). Four Soviet-built Whiskey-class submarines also appeared in the inventory and were geared for deployment in minelaying operations. Nearly one-third of the in-service fleet was composed of minesweepers in 1983, but half of these were considered obsolescent and had been scheduled for decommissioning. Coastal defense craft, including both patrol vessels and smaller FACs mounting torpedo tubes, constituted an additional one-third of total Polish naval units. Some minesweepers and larger patrol craft had an antisubmarine warfare capability. Polish-built tank landing ships and assault landing craft were among the 42 vessels in the inventory designed for amphibious operations (see table 11, Appendix A). Other units included radar pickets, training ships, tankers, and assorted auxiliary craft.

The navy also possessed a naval aviation division of 52 combat aircraft and a contingent of about 1,000 marines trained in amphibious warfare. Three attack squadrons were equipped with MiG-17s, and a single reconnaissance squadron flew refitted Il-28 light bombers. Two squadrons with about 25 helicopters rounded out the division. The naval air arm possessed a limited capability for ground support in amphibious operations as well as for reconnaissance and attacks against lightly armed ships.

National Territorial Defense Forces

Poland's OTK forces were established as a result of developments in military doctrine after 1956. It was assumed that in time of war the operational forces—the ground forces, air force, and navy—would be serving on behalf of the Warsaw Pact, probably outside Polish national territory. The country would therefore lack the resources to defend itself against air attack (including nuclear attack), to stop penetration by enemy airborne and diversionary units, or to quell possible civilian disturbances. Support for the formation of forces dedicated to territorial defense grew among Polish military officers in the early 1960s. Soviet authorities did not object because in wartime, forces dedicated to internal defense could facilitate the transport of Soviet reserve forces and supplies across Polish territory.

In 1962 the air defense force became the first component of the OTK forces to be organized. Three years later the OTK forces were officially established and placed under the command of the newly formed Main Inspectorate of National Territorial Defense, which was headed by a deputy defense minister having authority independent from the General Staff. The OTK forces were composed largely of units shifted from the responsibility of the Ministry of Internal Affairs. The largest of these was the Internal Security Corps (Korpus Beepiecaenstwa Wewnetrznego—KBW), which was renamed the Internal Defense Forces (Wojska Obrony Wewnetrznej—WOW) when it was transferred to the territorial defense inspectorate. The Frontier Defense Forces remained under the authority of the Ministry of Internal Affairs during peacetime, but in time of war they were supposed to be subordinate to the Ministry of National Defense through the OTK inspectorate. The OTK forces also included newly formed Territory Defense Units that operated separately from the WOW.

The combined strength of the WOW and Territory Defense Units was estimated at 65,000 in 1982. The WOW was equipped, like the army, as mechanized infantry and possessed tanks, armored personnel carriers, and antitank weapons. In time of war, component units, which were organized at the voivodship level, were designed to engage and eliminate combat groups infiltrated or parachuted into the interior of the country and to destroy locally organized underground elements intending subversion or sabotage. If the enemy's main forces were advancing into Polish territory, the security agencies under the Ministry of National Defense would join the regular forces in the fight against the invading armies.

Basic training, common services, food, and apparel were supplied by the army and were similar to what the ground forces received. Basic training was similar to that given regular service personnel. Training involved small-unit infantry tactics, riot control, and the use and care of small arms and light equipment. The training stopped short of coordinated exercises involving large formations and did not involve heavy and complex armament or communications equipment. When known as the KBW, the WOW had been prominent in suppressing the Home Army (Armia Krajowa—AK) after World War II and the Poznan workers in 1956; they were not involved in maintaining law and order during the civil disturbances of the early 1980s.

The Frontier Defense Forces, which had a manned strength of 20,000 organized into 12 brigades, were used in peacetime to combat spying, smuggling, and subversive political activities in the country's border areas. The Maritime Frontier Guard, a component of the Frontier Defense Forces, operated 34 coast guard patrol craft in Poland's territorial waters, primarily in efforts to halt smuggling.

National Civil Defense

Although the Inspectorate of National Civil Defense (Obrona Cywilna Kraju—OCK) of the defense ministry was not established until 1979, civil defense preparedness has been a major concern of some Polish authorities since the war scare of the Stalinist era. In the 1950s the National Defense League was primarily responsible for civil defense matters. Civil defense initiative was undertaken primarily at the local level, which allowed great variation in the scope and effectiveness of individual programs. Concurrent with the adoption of OTK doctrine in the 1960s, military interest in civil defense increased, leading in 1979 to the absorption of civil defense responsibilities under the authority of a deputy minister of national defense.

The OCK inspectorate was created in part because many military officers did not feel that civil defense was being taken seriously enough by the public or even by some high party authorities. In 1982, however, the civil defense effort was hampered by the continuing adjustment to the reorganization. Although under military authority, civil defense continued to be implemented at the local level by local authorities. Voivodship civil defense inspectorates had to cooperate with voivods, city presidents, chiefs of communes and towns, directors of plants and factories, and other officials. Moreover, the supply bottlenecks that affected the entire economy also hurt the civil defense effort, and OCK programs continued to be near the bottom of priority lists for equipment and support.

Civil defense personnel also played a role during Poland's martial law period of the early 1980s. They guarded food storehouses as well as industrial plants and other economic sites. Along with active duty and reserve personnel, they also provided relief during severe snowfall in the winter of 1981-82, clearing roads and railroad tracks and participating in flood control activities. They also participated in economic activities to supplement the work force in duties such as loading and unloading trucks and railroad cars.

Education, Training, and Promotion

Military training in the early 1980s was directed by the Main Inspectorate of Training, which was headed by a deputy minister of national defense. (A. Ross Johnson, a noted scholar and analyst of Polish military affairs, believed that the training inspectorate might also serve as the peacetime nucleus and headquarters of a wartime Polish Front.) Individual and unit training were first patterned on the Soviet model when Polish units were formed in the Soviet Union in 1943, and the necessity of standardized training to the success of joint operations was pointed out in 1961 in the first Warsaw Pact maneuvers. Poland's continued use of major weapons designed in the Soviet Union and its participation in joint military exercises with the Soviet Union, East Germany, and Czechoslovakia have not permitted Polish forces to adopt training schedules or tactical practices basically different from those of the Soviet Union or its other northern-tier allies.

Conscript training involved winter programs consisting primarily of individual training, care and use of small arms, work with crew-served weapons or heavy equipment, and drills with small groups. Summer programs were devoted to field training and involved participation in company, battalion, and regimental exercises. The annual program often culminated in Warsaw Pact maneuvers, which were usually held in the early autumn. Training throughout the cycle was rigorous.

Most of the conscripts served out their obligated time as privates or privates first class. A few whose performance stood out during the training program were promoted to higher grades because of leadership abilities, but nearly all who became NCOs were chosen at the time they entered the service and were given specialized schooling. The few conscripts who attained higher ranks either had higher educational qualifications upon entering the service or were selected to attend advanced service schools having longer and more general curricula. After special schooling and promotion to the higher grades that were commensurate with their training, NCOs were usually required to sign on for four years of additional service, warrant officers for six, and officers for 12 years.

Poland operated an extensive system for educating its officers and other ranks, including higher officer candidate schools for career officers, warrant officer candidate schools, military graduate schools, and schools for career NCOs. Ordinarily oriented toward only one specific skill, schools for NCOs accepted qualified candidates from the conscript ranks, as well as volunteers from outside the service, who agreed to sign on for an extended tour of duty. Specialists were trained in all the army combat, support, and service branches and were also prepared to lead small groups of soldiers.

Warrant officer candidate schools trained and educated middle-level technicians beginning in 1967 when a separate career warrant officer cadre was established. In 1981 there were 13 such schools offering one- to three-year training programs in the broad range of military technical subjects. Technical courses were designed to provide expertise within a specialist area but, because warrant officers usually had more leadership responsibilities than

Units of Polish People's Army participated with Soviet and East German forces in major Warsaw Pact maneuver of 1980 ("Comradeship in Arms 80").
Courtesy United Press International

did NCOs, they received more ideological indoctrination in their course work.

Higher officer candidate schools were the major source of career officers for the Polish People's Army, although a few came from civilian schools and stayed on active duty after performing their obligatory military service. Fourteen such institutions were operating in 1982. In addition to the Higher Air Force Officers' School and the Westerplatte Higher Naval School, they included the Higher Officers' School of the Tank Troops, the Higher Officers' School of the Anti-Aircraft Troops, and similar schools for officers assigned to specialties, such as engineering, signals, and supply. Except for the naval school, where the program of study lasted four and one-half years, students were graduated after four years, receiving baccalaureate degrees and commissions as second lieutenants. These schools also had programs for political officers that offered slightly less technical instruction and more ideological training.

Three of the higher officer schools also provided specialized postgraduate programs of study and were considered military graduate schools. Apart from the Westerplatte Higher Naval School, which also served as Poland's naval war college, these included the Technical Military Academy in Warsaw and the Szarecki Medical Military Academy in Lodz, considered among the best of their kind in Poland. The Technical Military Academy trained many Polish scientists and engineers and was center of Polish scientific research efforts. Unlike most of the other higher officers' schools, neither the technical academy nor the medical school suffered from a lack of highly qualified candidates.

The Polish People's Army also maintained two other military graduate schools. The Polish Armed Services General Staff Academy offered course work in advanced military theory to field grade officers; the Academy of Political and Military Sciences was designed specifically to instruct senior political officers. Virtually all Polish general officers had passed through one of these two academies, and many had received further training at Voroshilov Academy in the Soviet Union.

Instruction at Polish military schools, even in the technical schools, has been heavily politicized. Mandatory course work at the higher officer schools and military graduate schools included, among other things, Marxist philosophy, political economy, basics in political activism and teaching, and scientific socialism. The programs at all levels were designed to "instill the socialist outlook among soldiers," but most observers questioned whether students took the ideological training seriously.

Uniforms, Ranks, and Insignia

In addition to the quality of its manpower, equipment, and training, the ability of any military establishment to perform its assigned missions depends to a marked degree on whether it has a sense of institutional solidarity and esprit de corps. In recognition of this principle, the Polish People's Army has fostered allegiance through its distinctive uniforms and system of ranks and insignia.

In 1959 the armed forces began to replace the basic World War II uniform materials and styling supplied to them by the Soviet Union with uniforms of indigenous design. Changes to the 1959 uniforms have been made from time to time. In 1970 and 1971, for example, various alterations were made to improve the appearance and fit of work uniforms, the summer service jacket, and field footwear.

The field-service uniform is normally worn in garrison, on and off duty, for training, and wherever otherwise ordered. Ground forces' uniforms are brown in color; air and air defense forces' uniforms are steel blue; and naval uniforms are the familiar navy blue. Ground forces' field-service uniforms include a single-breasted coat with patch pockets, a shirt, a tie, and trousers tucked into boots. Headgear consists of a service or garrison cap, except in winter when fur caps become an alternative. Distinctive berets are worn by some branches: those of tank crews are black; airborne troops wear red; and marines' berets are blue.

The rank and grade structure is similar to that in most armed forces' organizations, but among the component services there are variations in the number and titles of authorized officer grades and in the titles of enlisted ranks (see fig. 20; fig. 21). Insignia are displayed on shoulder boards and shoulder loops; the Polish eagle and shield emblem is worn on all headgear. Officers' rank is indicated by the number of stars worn and by the kind and amount of braid. A private wears a plain, unadorned shoulder board. Stripes across and borders around the edges of shoulder boards designate the different ranks of NCOs. The arm of service is indicated by distinctive collar insignia.

The Question of Reliability

As an important member of the Warsaw Pact, Poland's operational forces have been closely tied to those of its powerful Soviet neighbor. Despite the stresses in Polish society, there was no indication in early 1983 that the Polish officer corps, whose leading members had cooperated closely with the Soviets in military matters since World War II, were seeking to alter the pattern. But because the Polish military was comfortable with the situation in Eastern Europe, which had brought a measure of political stability to the region, analysts including Soviet analysts, could only speculate on the Polish armed forces' response if ordered into action in a manner that would upset the status quo.

Polish military forces could conceivably be employed in a variety of circumstances. Since 1944 the Polish People's Army has intervened in another Warsaw Pact country in cooperation with

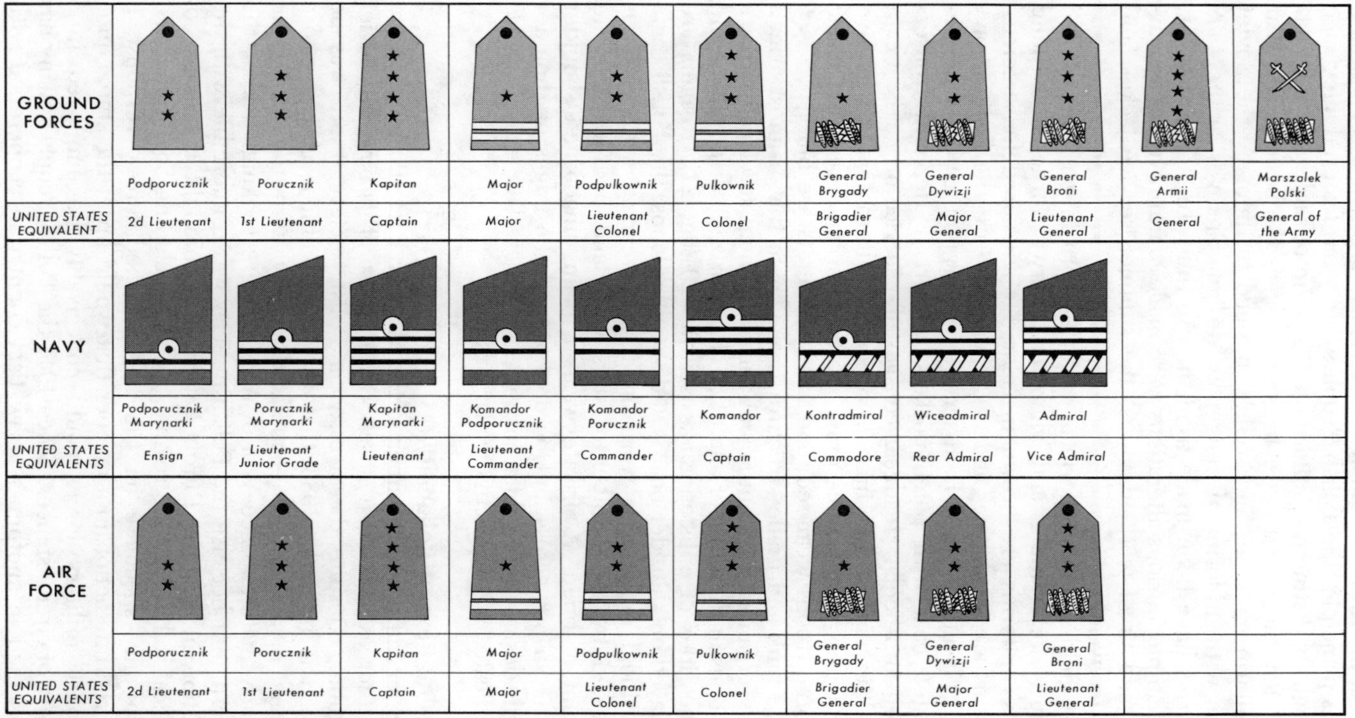

GROUND FORCES										
	Podporucznik	Porucznik	Kapitan	Major	Podpulkownik	Pulkownik	General Brygady	General Dywizji	General Broni	General Armii	Marszalek Polski
UNITED STATES EQUIVALENT	2d Lieutenant	1st Lieutenant	Captain	Major	Lieutenant Colonel	Colonel	Brigadier General	Major General	Lieutenant General	General	General of the Army
NAVY											
	Podporucznik Marynarki	Porucznik Marynarki	Kapitan Marynarki	Komandor Podporucznik	Komandor Porucznik	Komandor	Kontradmiral	Wiceadmiral	Admiral		
UNITED STATES EQUIVALENTS	Ensign	Lieutenant Junior Grade	Lieutenant	Lieutenant Commander	Commander	Captain	Commodore	Rear Admiral	Vice Admiral		
AIR FORCE											
	Podporucznik	Porucznik	Kapitan	Major	Podpulkownik	Pulkownik	General Brygady	General Dywizji	General Broni		
UNITED STATES EQUIVALENTS	2d Lieutenant	1st Lieutenant	Captain	Major	Lieutenant Colonel	Colonel	Brigadier General	Major General	Lieutenant General		

NOTE—There are no ranks above general broni in Air Force and admiral in Navy.

Figure 20. Officer Ranks, Insignia, and United States Equivalents, 1983

GROUND FORCES	Szeregowiec	Starszy Szeregowiec	Kapral	Starszy Kapral	Plutonowy	Sierzant	Starszy Sierzant	Sierzant Sztabowy *	Starszy Sierzant Sztabowy *	Mlodszy Chorazy *	Chorazy *	Starszy Chorazy *	Chorazy Sztabowy *	Starszy Chorazy Sztabowy *
UNITED STATES EQUIVALENTS	Basic Private	Private / Private 1st Class	Corporal	Sergeant	Staff Sergeant	Sergeant 1st Class	Master Sergeant / First Sergeant	Sergeant Major	Command Sergeant Major	Warrant Officer W-1	Chief Warrant Officer W-2	Chief Warrant Officer W-3	Chief Warrant Officer W-4	
NAVY	Marynarz	Starszy Marynarz	Mat	Starszy Mat	Bosmanmat	Bosman	Starszy Bosman	Bosman Sztabowy	Starszy Bosman Sztabowy	Mlodszy Chorazy *	Chorazy *	Starszy Chorazy *	Chorazy Sztabowy *	Starszy Chorazy Sztabowy *
UNITED STATES EQUIVALENTS	Seaman Recruit	Apprentice Seaman / Seaman	Petty Officer 3d Class	Petty Officer 2d Class	Petty Officer 1st Class	Chief Petty Officer	Senior Chief Petty Officer	Master Chief Petty Officer		Warrant Officer W-1	Chief Warrant Officer W-2	Chief Warrant Officer W-3	Chief Warrant Officer W-4	
AIR FORCE	Szeregowiec	Szeregowiec	Kapral	Starszy Kapral	Plutonowy	Sierzant	Starszy Sierzant	Sierzant Sztabowy	Starszy Sierzant Sztabowy	Mlodszy Chorazy *	Chorazy *	Starszy Chorazy *	Chorazy Sztabowy *	Starszy Chorazy Sztabowy *
UNITED STATES EQUIVALENTS	Basic Airman	Airman / Airman 1st Class	Senior Airman / Sergeant	Staff Sergeant	Technical Sergeant	Master Sergeant	Senior Master Sergeant	Chief Master Sergeant		Warrant Officer W-1	Chief Warrant Officer W-2	Chief Warrant Officer W-3	Chief Warrant Officer W-4	

* No direct United States equivalent

Figure 21. Enlisted and Warrant Officer Ranks, Insignia, and United States Equivalents, 1983

the Soviet Union (Czechoslovakia in 1968), has suppressed dissident Polish movements (immediately after World War II, in 1956, and in 1970), and has moved into a prominent position in the government (in 1981–82 when the Military Council of National Salvation [Wojskowa Rada Ocalenia Narodowego—WRON] assumed the reins of government). Elements of the military had also been positioned to repel a possible Soviet invasion in 1956.

As circumstances have changed, the likelihood that the Polish army would be committed to any given action also has varied. For example, it was not at all clear in early 1983 whether the Polish armed forces would be able, or their conscripts willing, to intervene against another East European communist state as they had against Czechoslovakia. This question was probably academic because Poland's internal disorders made it the most likely target of military action by forces of the Soviet Union and other Warsaw Pact countries.

During the Solidarity interlude, speculation focused on whether the Polish People's Army would oppose a Soviet/Warsaw Pact invasion. Most observers and analysts believed that, even if the armed forces as a whole did not oppose an invasion, individual commanders and units might react, as they had been prepared to do in 1956. For this reason it was believed that on several occasions in 1981–82 Warsaw Pact maneuvers moved Polish forces to remote parts of the country from where it would have been difficult (if not impossible) for them to defend important cities and industrial areas. Given the skewed proportion of forces between the Soviet Union and Poland in the early 1980s, any attempted Polish defense against aggressive Soviet military action would likely be futile and extremely costly in political and human terms.

Jaruzelski has stated that it was precisely to avoid the possibility of civil war and of Soviet invasion that the military authorities declared martial law in December 1981. Before the declaration of martial law and the establishment of a military government, most observers who even considered the possibility that an East European army would intervene in the government of a Warsaw Pact member state, thought it a highly unlikely eventuality. But by its action, the Polish People's Army demonstrated that in the right circumstances it would undertake any operation if the costs of proceeding were perceived by the military leaders to be less than the costs of inaction.

In the event of a NATO-initiated military action, there seemed to be little doubt that the Polish armed forces would carry out their Warsaw Pact obligations. But analysts were more circumspect in assessing Polish performance should the Warsaw Pact invade the NATO countries. Dale Herspring and Ivan Volgyes in their 1980 article "Political Reliability in the Eastern European Warsaw Pact Armies" have postulated that Polish participation in

Troops of Polish People's Army marching in ceremonial parade
Courtesy United Press International

such an invasion would be based on perceptions of a West German threat. Moreover, antipathy toward the West Germans (which lessened after Bonn recognized Poland's western borders in 1970) was, according to the authors, counterbalanced by the Polish people's "deep bonds of friendship" with other NATO countries, including France, Britain, and the United States. The authors therefore considered it "questionable at best" that the Poles would be willing to become involved in anything less than a highly successful campaign.

A. Rose Johnson, however, has stated in his 1980 analysis of the Polish military in *East European Military Establishments: The Warsaw Pact Northern Tier* that "the operational army is programmed for massive and rapid offensive actions onto NATO territory in a nuclear environment . . . the commitment of Polish military professionals to this mission, and the corresponding design of Polish forces to serve it, is generally underestimated." Even if NATO posed no immediate threat to Poland and if Polish military and political leaders viewed an invasion of Western Europe as contrary to Polish interests, Johnson noted that a decision to "opt out" would increase the chances of the war's being fought on Polish territory rather than in countries to the west. In these circumstances he felt it was likely that the Poles would go along with an attack by Warsaw Pact forces in order to avoid having their country invaded.

If the Poles did join in an invasion, Johnson claimed that they could make an effective contribution in the early stages of the conflict. He and most observers felt, however, that if success were not immediately forthcoming and if losses were heavy, the reliability of a basically nationalist force made up largely of conscripts would decline significantly.

Internal Security Forces

Polish authorities have charged specialized internal security forces with defending public order and safeguarding the regime and the PZPR. Formation of the security forces was rooted in a July 1944 decree of the Polish Committee of National Liberation (Polski Komitet Wyzwolenia Narodowego—PKWN), which simultaneously dissolved the State Police, which had existed before World War II. Operating under the authority of the Ministry of Internal Affairs (known until 1956 as the Ministry of Public Security), the internal security forces played a central role in suppressing opposition and potential opposition in the years after the war. In early 1982 descendants of all the original forces existed, although the paramilitary units had been transferred in the 1960s to the jurisdiction of the Ministry of National Defense's Main Inspectorate of National Territorial Defense. Minister of Internal Affairs (Lieutenant General) Czeslaw Kiszczak was responsible for the secret service, the regular police, the riot police, and the large national police reserve. These forces were especially visible during the early 1980s as military leaders sought to keep their troops from becoming involved in controversial civilian control actions that could damage military prestige.

Security Service

The Security Service (Sluzba Bezpieczenstwa—SB), formerly known as the Security Bureau (Urzad Bezpieczenstwa—UB), served as the regime's secret police force. It was a plainclothes force, charged with detecting and countering activities that might damage, threaten, or undermine the country covertly, either from within or from outside its borders. Most of its functions related to seeking out subversive elements and investigating actual or potential sabotage. It was the agency specifically concerned with keeping track of foreigners and their activities and monitoring foreign business interests and diplomatic activities in the country.

The UB was established in 1944 with extensive support (and staffing) from the Soviet Union's secret police. In the period immediately after World War II, the UB was the mainstay of the regime and the new communist system. Dominated by the Soviets, it was the instrument that enforced order, guaranteed security, and amassed information on any or all elements of the population. By 1953, however, the UB was widely hated and was unable to erase its terrorist image. It was crippled by the revelations of defectors and mistrusted by the political authorities, who were unable to control "a state within a state." In the liberalizing spirit that arose in the years after Stalin's death, Poles grew less afraid of the once-sinister organization, even ignoring it altogether or treating it with contempt. By 1956 the force was internally disorganized, had no public support, and was virtually impotent and ineffective. The work performed by the UB could not be abandoned entirely, however, and beginning about 1957 the force was gradually rebuilt. In the late 1960s the force again attained a certain notoriety when it was operated by Mieczyslaw Moczar, the politically ambitious interior minister.

Little was known about the SB in early 1983. According to a deputy minister of internal affairs (in 1981), "Over the past 10 years the role of the Security Service [has been a] taboo subject . . . To the extent that anything at all has been published on this subject—apart from internal-use-only publications—it has been confined to a dry and terse communiqué on the unmasking of a spy by the Security Service, the institution of legal proceedings, or the handing down of a sentence by a military court." The size and structure of the SB were thus not publicly known, but the force was generally assumed to be far smaller than it had been during the Stalinist era. Foreign analysts believed that the SB remained the Polish institution most sympathetic to, and most thoroughly penetrated by, Soviet intelligence.

Revelations by dissidents gave some insight into the SB's investigation and interrogation techniques. The SB relied heavily on informers and sometimes sought to use blackmail to widen its network of informants. Unless the police had the special permission of higher authorities, however, their activities were circumscribed by legal constraints adopted in reaction to the unbridled excesses of the police during the Stalinst era. Stories appearing in the Polish media in 1981 glorified the SB's counterintelligence efforts and noted its success in contending with foreign intelligence penetration during the Solidarity period.

Citizens' Militia

The Citizens' Militia (Milicja Obywatelska—MO) was established in 1944 as the country's basic force for policing at the voivodship and local levels. According to regulations that have directed the militia since 1955, the force was charged with safeguarding law and public order, protecting state and private property, controlling traffic, maintaining identification cards and residence locator information, and countering criminal activities. Although the MO was oriented toward local problems and activities, it was nationally organized to ensure uniformity in performance and coordination among all militia units. Local units consulted and coordinated extensively with local government authorities (voivods, mayors, commune heads, and local people's councils), but these units were under the sole authority of the Ministry of Internal Affairs.

In 1983 it was estimated that the MO had a total manned strength of about 110,000 nationwide, or about one policeman per 300 to 400 Poles. Of these some 3,000 were affiliated with the force's criminal investigation sections, and about 4,500 served with traffic control sections. The bulk of the remainder were patrolmen working at local stations. MO officers were often armed but, according to one Warsaw officer, "We have guns for cleaning."

The militia was not directly involved in controlling demonstrations, but it had often acted as a cover for the secret police and was popularly associated with the Ministry of Internal Affairs more than most policemen would like. In the spring of 1981, after Solidarity activists were badly beaten by plainclothes police at Bydgoszcz, many provisional police sought to form their own union and be institutionally separated from the security branch. Police union leaders claimed a membership of 40,000 before the union was disbanded after martial law, but this could not be verified.

The MO always has been a volunteer force. Those applying for a career in the militia must have completed their elementary education, have served their obligatory military tours, be under 35 years of age, and be able to meet prescribed physical and medical standards. Militiamen are grouped into NCO (private through sergeant major) and officer (lieutenant through general) categories. The NCO candidates must spend a year in a special police training program after joining the force. Candidates for officer ranks are ordinarily chosen from among those within the forces who have performed well as NCOs. Young persons eligible for military service can also apply for a tour of duty in the MO. Women in uniform have served on the force, working at the same pay scales and under the same administrative regulations as the men. They have worked more frequently, however, in clerical positions, in traffic control, or with juveniles.

Training in early 1983 was extensive and could last as long as six years. The force was relatively well educated; 70 percent of officers possessed a higher education degree, and 83 percent of NCOs had at least a secondary education. Police personnel could continue their studies at special interior ministry colleges, although the quality of their education as compared with that offered in the civilian universities was difficult to judge.

The MO, like other police services, had difficulty in recruiting personnel in the early 1980s. About 7 percent of the MO personnel left the ranks, and replacements could be found for little more than half of these. Some 700 of those who left in 1980 were dismissed from the force, including 264 for "causing accidents," 76 for "beating citizens," and 71 for committing crimes "for personal gain."

Motorized Units of the Citizens' Militia

Until 1981 few Poles were aware of its existence, but during the year of martial law an organization known as the Motorized Units of the Citizens' Militia (Zmotoryzowane Oddzialy Milicji Obywatelskiej—ZOMO) established itself as the Jaruzelski regime's most active and least popular enforcer of the martial law regulations. ZOMO units were used extensively to control riots and pro-Solidarity demonstrations, to storm factories occupied by workers, and to patrol in tense areas. In carrying out their duties, these police units established a reputation that led to widespread, popular resentment, and ZOMO became the butt of bitter nationwide humor alleging the cruelty and lack of intelligence of its personnel.

ZOMO was established in 1956 after the KBW's brutal handling of the Poznan riots pointed out Poland's need for troops specially trained in riot control. Shortcomings were pointed out when ZOMO was unable to handle the 1970 Gdansk demonstrations, and the force was completely reorganized, retrained, and relieved of several thousand members considered unfit for service. After 1980 ZOMO underwent a major expansion and by 1982 had between 25,000 and 30,000 personnel nationwide. They were equipped with tear gas, water cannon, and other riot control gear as well as light armored vehicles. ZOMO was a mobile force whose units throughout the country were directed from the Ministry of Internal Affairs in Warsaw and could be deployed by air or over land to any trouble spot in Poland within a few hours. In addition to riot control, ZOMO units were also used to control crowds at public events, such as soccer games, and provide support in case of natural disasters.

ZOMO police were accused by their many detractors of being illiterate thugs who were sent into action under the influence of drugs and alcohol. According to government authorities eager to quell the public rumors, all regular ZOMO members were volunteers who had at least a secondary-school education, had completed their military service obligations, were in excellent health, and did not have a police record. ZOMO personnel also included young persons who joined for three-year enlistments in lieu of military conscript service. The average ZOMO member was 26 years old; 92 percent were married, 90 percent came from a peasant or working-class background, and 80 percent were blood donors, according to the authorities. Polish officials admitted, however, that some ZOMO troopers were involved in "incidents of abuse of physical power" but stated that convicted offenders were severely disciplined.

Being a ZOMO officer was a stressful job. In riot situations they were often taunted with shouts of "Gestapo" and "SS," and many were injured by debris hurled by protesters, particularly in the massive demonstrations of May and August 1982. According to official reports, the force had a large turnover rate; most personnel took early retirement or disability, usually for nervous disorders, according to officials. Many others transferred to the regular MO after duty in ZOMO.

Most observers noted that the government offered substantial incentives to induce men to join the unpopular organization, although Polish officials denied this. According to one report, ZOMO personnel earned several times more than regular army conscripts and were given special bonuses if they participated in riot control operations. They reportedly also had access to restricted shops that sold goods usually unavailable or in short supply at regular outlets.

Despite the popular perceptions of their brutality and low abilities, Westerners in Warsaw in 1982 rated ZOMO members as disciplined and effective riot control personnel. Given the experience they accumulated, it appeared that ZOMO would remain an effective force if its members maintained high morale.

Volunteer Reserve of the Citizens' Militia

The Volunteer Reserve of the Citizens' Militia (Ochotnicza Rezerwa Milicji Obywatelskiej—ORMO) was formed during the early 1960s and drew all those it could attract from the former People's Guard (the military arm of the PZPR during the early post-World War II period) and various other industrial guard units. The reserve in 1965 had approximately 250,000 members and grew to nearly 400,000 by the time of the December 1970 riots. In 1982 the force had a manned strength of 461,000. Personnel in the MO's part-time auxiliary far outnumbered those in the regular force, but they served only in emergencies, on special occasions, or for short training periods.

The ORMO volunteers were unpaid, except when they had to be compensated for expenses that arose when their units were called to duty outside the home areas. Most, if not all, members had other full-time employment, and training was accomplished at odd-hour times. Training standards have varied, and some units have complained that they have been restricted by a paucity of training aids and obsolete police and infantry manuals. Most weapons were limited to small arms that were intended to be used, carried, and maintained by the individual volunteer. Because units were organized to augment the MO at major trouble spots, however, they were equipped with vehicles including armored vehicles, to transport personnel; some were armored.

During the civil disturbances in the early 1980s, ORMO units were not generally assigned to handle demonstrations because it

ZOMO units deploying in Warsaw to control antigovernment demonstrators, May 1983
Courtesy United Press International

was felt that their lack of training could put them at risk and because they were only part-time police who might be more sympathetic to protesters. According to the first deputy minister of national defense, who complimented ORMO's contributions in maintaining order during the period of martial law, "the decisive majority of these [ORMO] soldiers were members of Solidarity." In general, they were only assigned to guard duties, but because they wore blue uniforms identical to those of ZOMO, the reserve militia were sometimes attacked by protesters. Despite the ambivalence of many, they proved to be an important component in the government's security forces.

The Prison System

Poland's prison system has operated under national authority, like its police system. Between 1944 and 1955 prison administration was under the Ministry of Public Security, which operated the penal institutions without outside supervision. Serious abuses of law by prison authorities were common in the early 1950s but declined after prison administration was taken over by the Ministry of Justice in 1956. In early 1983 the ministry's Main Bureau of Penal Institutions was responsible for prison administration. Since the 1950s Poland's penal code has permitted free access to prisons by representatives of special penitentiary courts and judges for the purpose of assessing conditions in the facilities, conversing in private with any prisoner, questioning prison authorities, examining prison documents, and investigating inmates' grievances.

According to the United States Department of State's human rights report for 1980, there were about 100,000 prisoners being held in Polish prisons, the vast majority of them on criminal charges. A decade earlier, Polish officials were concerned because roughly 45 percent of the prison population had been recidivist, but in the early 1980s there were not any reliable reports indicating whether this statistic had changed. An extensive parole program in 1981 reduced the prison population by as much as 50 percent to between 50,000 and 60,000. Some observers speculated that the reduction was undertaken to free space in the prisons for the Poles expected to be interned in the crackdown on Solidarity during the martial law period. According to government authorities, however, no more than 5,300 people had been detained for political reasons at any one time (in December 1981 and January 1982).

A prison commission in each institution classified inmates according to their original sentences and their conduct while incarcerated. Prisoners were subjected to one of four regimens—mitigated, basic, intense, and severe—and were moved from more severe to less stringent treatment (or vice versa) depending on their conduct. The severity of the regimen determined the correspondence, visitation, exercise, and other privileges a convict was allowed.

The Main Bureau of Penal Institutions operated several varieties of institutions, all of which were considered rehabilitation centers and economically productive units. Most convicts serving a term of less than five years were placed in semiopen labor centers where only mitigated and basic routines were practiced. Those serving longer sentences—or those convicted of violent crimes—were sent to ordinary penal institutions. Inmates who had served at least two years in other institutions and were nearing the end of their sentences were often sent to transitional prisons. Special institutions were also designed for multiple recidivists, prisoners under the age of 21 who had a relatively short time to serve, and those requiring special medical attention (including psychological care). Women prisoners were separated from the men. Prisoners interned in December 1981 under martial law were housed together, but it was not known which form of treatment was used.

Certain privileges were available to nearly all inmates, regardless of prison regimen. Convicted persons retained their citizenship except in rare instances when it was revoked as part of a severe sentence. As citizens, all had access to legal assistance, including meetings and correspondence with lawyers. An inmate could request revision of a sentence, reopening of the case, conditional release from detention, suspension of penalties, and pardon. Petitions could be submitted to judges, prosecutors, or the prison administration. All prisoners were entitled to sanitary living conditions, medical attention, and access to prison libraries. Since 1956 the church and the government have agreed that prisoners should be allowed to observe the religious practices of their choice or that are expected of them by the church. According to prison rules, inmates could be rewarded for good behavior and, in some case, receive a pass to leave prison for up to five days.

The prison system did not include forced labor camps, but involuntary supervised labor could be included in a court sentence. Prisoners often worked in collectivized establishments where the employer guaranteed adequate safety and hygiene. Women and young people worked only in their usual job categories, a requirement that frustrated many female Solidarity activists who were not interested in traditional women's work. Prison- or court-imposed pay regulations applied to prison labor, and no social security benefits accrued. Business enterprises often used convict labor, and local people's councils employed prisoners in the maintenance of roads and public grounds and during national disasters.

* * *

A variety of English-language sources provide useful information and analysis of Polish national security affairs, although details are often difficult to obtain. *God's Playground: A History of Poland,* an extensive work by Norman Davies, and the more compact *Poland in the Twentieth Century,* by M.K. Dziewanowski, are two of many books that offer a historical picture of Poland's evolving national security situation and the place of the military in Polish society. The emergence of internal security threats that culminated in the Solidarity movement has been traced in a number of works, of which the most thorough English-language treatment is probably Jacques Rupnik's "Dissent in Poland, 1968–78: The End of Revisionism and the Rebirth of the Civil Society."

The development of the Polish People's Army, its organization, and its place in society are viewed in depth by A. Ross Johnson in *East European Military Establishments: The Warsaw Pact Northern Tier* and in his *Poland in Crisis,* which focuses on the role of the military in the government. Dale Herspring and Andrzej Korbonski have each also contributed a number of articles on the issues of military involvement in the political process and army-PZPR ties.

Translations of the PZPR daily, *Trybuna Ludu,* the military newspaper *Zolnierz Polski,* and other publications by the Joint

Publications Research Service and the Foreign Broadcast Information Service are useful in providing information on military and police organization, policies, and official attitudes. The *New York Times*, *Financial Times*, *Washington Post*, *Christian Science Monitor*, and the Western press in general also published considerable material on national security matters in the early 1980s. *The Military Balance*, produced annually by the London-based International Institute for Strategic Studies, provides information on military organization, equipment, and numerical strengths of the armed forces. (For further information and complete citations, see Bibliography.)

Appendix A

Table

Table 1. Metric Conversion Coefficients

When you know	Multiply by	To Find
Millimeters	0.04	inches
Centimeters	0.39	inches
Meters	3.3	feet
Kilometers	0.62	miles
Hectares (10,000 m^2)	2.47	acres
Square kilometers	0.39	square miles
Cubic meters	35.3	cubic feet
Liters	0.26	gallons
Kilograms	2.2	pounds
Metric tons	0.98	long tons
	1.1	short tons
	2,204	pounds
Degrees Celsius (Centigrade)	9 divide by 5 and add 32	degrees Fahrenheit

Table 2. Population Estimates of Principal Cities and Towns, 1981 (in thousands)

City or Town*	Population	City or Town*	Population
Warsaw	1,611.6	Bydgoszcz	352.4
Lodz	843.0	Lublin	308.8
Krakow	722.9	Czestochowa	237.7
Wroclaw	621.9	Bialystok	229.7
Poznan	558.0	Radom	194.4
Gdansk	458.9	Kielce	188.8
Gydnia	237.5	Torun	188.1
Szczecin	389.9	Bielsko Biala	167.8
Katowice	363.5	Olsztyn	140.0
Sosnowiec	251.9	Walbrzych	134.3
Bytom	237.8	Rzeszow	125.8
Gliwice	202.2	Opole	118.2
Zabrze	196.8	Elblag	112.1
Tychy	171.9	Wloclawek	110.0
Ruda Slaska	161.6	Gorzow	109.0
Chorzow	149.6	Tarnow	107.1
Dabrowa Gornicza	148.0	Plock	103.8
Rybnik	126.7	Zielona Gora	103.5
Wodzislaw Slaski	105.9	Kalisz	100.3

*Listed in order of size except for those in the same voivodship, which are listed together.

Source: Based on information from Poland, Central Statistical Office, *Concise Statistical Yearbook of Poland, 1982*, Warsaw, 1982, Table 7, 32.

Table 3. Higher Education: Schools, Enrollment, and Graduates, Selected Years, 1970–71 to 1981–82
(number of students in thousands)

Type of School	Schools 1981–82	Students 1970–71	1975–76	1980–81	1981–82	1981 Graduates
Universities	10	97.5	147.1	131.2	124.1	20.6
Polytechnics	18	124.9	143.6	127.6	114.4	20.1
Agriculture academies	9	33.5	42.0	61.0	57.0	10.0
Economics academies	6	25.0	31.5	34.1	30.5	5.6
Teacher training schools	11	14.8	47.5	36.9	37.0	7.2
Medical academies	10	22.9	29.7	35.1	34.3	5.4
Higher maritime schools	2	0.9	3.5	3.6	3.6	0.6
Physical culture academies	6	5.0	14.2	13.2	11.8	2.7
Higher art schools	17	5.2	7.2	7.7	7.5	1.2
Theological academies	2	1.1	1.8	1.8	1.8	0.2
Centers for teachers' upgrading	—	—	—	1.5	1.5	0.4
TOTAL	91	330.8	468.1	453.7	423.5	74.0

—not applicable.

Source: Based on information from Poland, Central Statistical Office, *Concise Statistical Yearbook of Poland, 1982,* Warsaw, 1982, Table 8 (276), 26.

Table 4. Physicians and Other Health Care Personnel, Selected Years, 1970–81

Occupation	1970	1975	1980	1981
Physicians	46,466	54,461	63,577	65,012
	(14.2)	(15.9)	(17.8)	(18.0)
Dentists	12,966	15,114	16,834	16,962
	(4.0)	(4.4)	(4.7)	(4.7)
Pharmacists	11,775	13,867	15,400	15,619
	(3.6)	(4.1)	(4.3)	(4.3)
Hospital attendants	4,641	4,264	3,747	3,706
	(1.4)	(1.2)	(1.0)	(1.0)
Nurses	98,569	122,600	156,975	162,650
	(30.2)	(35.9)	(43.9)	(45.1)
Midwives	11,553	13,369	16,092	16,810
	(3.5)	(3.9)	(4.5)	(4.7)

Note—Figures in parentheses are number of medical personnel per 10,000 population.

Source: Based on information from Poland, Central Statistical Office, *Concise Statistical Yearbook of Poland, 1982*, Warsaw, 1982, Table II, XXXVIII–XXXIX and Table 1 (293), 274.

Table 5. Reported Illnesses and Selected Diseases, 1975, 1979, and 1980

Disease	1975	1979	1980
Tuberculosis of respiratory system	24,758	25,364	24,408
Tuberculosis, other forms	1,497	1,493	1,399
Syphilis and its sequelae	8,149	5,207	5,362
Gonorrhea	37,134	39,885	37,008
Dysentery	9,220	6,988	2,194
Infantile diarrhea (up to age two)	32,953	37,209	30,803
Whooping cough	1,156	508	232
Scarlet fever	17,055	33,980	68,860
Epidemic meningitis	4,191	6,422	5,100
Measles	146,664	30,653	24,882
Infectious hepatitis	74,559	52,004	48,245
Mumps	138,118	105,072	116,851
Influenza	3,768,054	419,006	1,410,357
Cancer	61,464	64,598	n.a.
Mental and nervous system diseases	148,380	148,382	155,317

n.a.—not available.

Source: Based on information from Poland, Central Statistical Office, *Concise Statistical Yearbook of Poland, 1982,* Warsaw, 1982, Table 11 (303), 278.

Table 6. Employees by Economic Sector, Selected Years, 1970–81[1]
(in thousands)

Sector	1970	1975	1978	1980	1981
Industry	4,453	5,150	5,234	5,245	5,240
Construction	1,075	1,406	1,394	1,337	1,292
Agriculture	5,210	4,860	4,574	4,310	4,315[2]
Forestry	183	156	160	155	153
Transport and communications	940	1,506	1,103	1,119	1,108
Trade	1,046	1,222	1,284	1,305	1,356
Community services	252[3,4]	342	372	401	418
Housing economy and nonmaterial community services	147[3]	155	182	200	205
Science and development of technology[5]	73	151	151	149	144
Education[6]	596	705	721	747	782
Culture and art[6]	83	76	81	83	83
Health service and social welfare[6]	425	523	563	599	632
Physical culture, tourism, and recreation	27	76	101	104	103
State administration and justice	241	224	226	227	227
Finance and insurance	135	160	155	157	160
Not specified	289	310	333	354	330
TOTAL	15,175	16,572	16,634	16,492	16,548

[1]Annual average.
[2]Estimated. Private sector employee number used same as for 1980.
[3]Excluding individuals working as agents paid generally on a commission or contract basis.
[4]Excluding outworkers.
[5]Full-time employees.
[6]Including full-time contract workers.

Source: Based on information from Poland, Central Statistical Office, *Concise Statistical Yearbook of Poland, 1982,* Warsaw, 1982, 41.

Table 7. Production of Major Crops, Selected Years, 1971–81
(in thousands of tons)

Crop	1971–75*	1976–80*	1978	1980	1981
Cereals					
Wheat	5,605	5,089	6,029	4,176	4,203
Rye	7,679	6,474	7,434	6,566	6,731
Barley	3,181	3,560	3,636	3,419	3,540
Oats	3,158	2,434	2,492	2,245	2,730
Subtotal	19,623	17,557	19,591	16,406	17,204
Other	1,310	1,938	1,946	1,930	2,517
Total Cereals	20,933	19,495	21,537	18,336	19,721
Pulses	246	143	151	112	119
Potatoes	47,083	42,742	46,648	26,391	42,562
Sugar beets	13,848	14,149	15,707	10,139	15,867
Oilseeds (chiefly rape)	573	655	714	583	505
Tobacco	78	80	59	56	87

*Annual average production.

Source: Based on information from Poland, *Concise Statistical Yearbook of Poland, 1982*, Warsaw, 1982, 159.

Table 8. Domestic Production of Principal Minerals and Basic Mineral Products, Selected Years, 1960–81
(in thousands of tons)

Mineral or Product	1960	1970	1975	1978	1980	1981
Coal						
Bituminous (hard).	104	140	172	193	193	163
Lignite (brown)	9	33	40	41	37	36
Total coal.........	113	173	212	234	230	199
Petroleum.............	194	424	553	363	329	315
Natural gas[1]...........	549	5,182	5,963	7,991	6,329	6,172
Iron ore................	2,182	2,554	1,192	529	104	105
Steel.....................	6,681	11,795	15,004	19,251	19,485	15,719
Copper ore............	1,760	6,552	16,963	23,307	26,568	22,819
Electrolytic copper...	22	72	249	332	357	327
Zinc-lead ore	2,461	3,583	4,598	5,503	5,510	5,035
Zinc metal.............	176	209	243	222	217	162
Lead....................	40	55	76	87	82	69
Silver[2]..................	35	231	549	680	766	640
Aluminum[3]	26	99	103	100	95	66
Sulfur[4]	26	2,683	4,771	5,051	5,164	4,773
Salt	1,946	2,904	3,524	4,393	4,533	4,271
Cement................	6,600	12,200	18,500	21,700	18,400	14,200
Lime	2,196	3,599	4,791	5,040	4,830	4,105

[1]Million cubic meters.
[2]Tons.
[3]Mostly produced from imported alumina.
[4]100 percent.

Source: Based on information from Poland, Central Statistical Office, *Concise Statistical Yearbook of Poland, 1982*, Warsaw, 1982, 110, 112–13.

Table 9. Imports by Country Economic Grouping, Selected Years, 1970–81 (in millions of foreign exchange zlotys)[1]

Economic Grouping	1970	1975	1978	1980	1981
Socialist countries					
Comecon[2]					
Czechoslovakia	1,241.5	2,248.8	3,169.2	3,345.9	3,189.9
East Germany	1,598.6	3,130.5	4,029.8	3,848.9	3,700.2
Soviet Union	5,445.0	10,556.8	15,227.1	19,323.5	21,664.5
Other	1,217.4	2,321.7	3,987.2	4,542.7	3,881.4
Total Comecon	9,502.5	18,257.8	26,413.3	31,061.0	32,436.0
Other[3]	389.8	829.1	1,165.6	1,348.0	1,358.0
Total socialist countries	9,892.3	19,086.9	27,578.9	32,409.0	33,794.0
Other countries					
Developed countries[4]					
EEC[5]					
Britain	763.6	2,226.7	2,920.8	2,030.7	1,323.6
France	352.1	1,986.9	1,625.8	2,443.0	1,933.7
Italy	293.0	1,388.7	n.a.	1,173.4	811.0
West Germany	572.5	3,359.5	3,479.5	3,933.5	2,937.8
Other	428.2	2,647.9	3,168.0	1,707.4	1,253.9
Total EEC	2,409.4	11,609.7	11,194.1	11,288.0	8,260.0
United States	233.0	1,958.6	2,238.3	2,351.3	2,460.5
Other	1,078.7	6,970.9	7,206.0	6,793.7	4,318.5
Total developed countries	3,721.1	20,539.2	20,638.4	20,433.0	15,039.0
Developing countries	816.7	2,024.6	2,721.1	5,457.0	3,180.0
Total other countries	4,537.8	22,563.8	23,359.5	25,890.0	18,219.0
TOTAL IMPORTS	14,430.1	41,650.7	50,938.4	58,299.0	52,013.0

n.a.—not available.
[1]For value of the zloty—see Glossary.
[2]Council for Mutual Economic Assistance: Albania, Bulgaria, Cuba (since 1972), Czechoslovakia, East Germany, Hungary, Mongolia, Poland, Romania, Soviet Union, and Vietnam (since 1978).
[3]China, North Korea, and Yugoslavia.
[4]All West European countries, Canada, United States, South Africa, Israel, Japan, Australia, and New Zealand.
[5]European Economic Community (also known as the Common Market).

Source: Based on information from Poland, Central Statistical Office, *Concise Statistical Yearbook of Poland, 1982*, Warsaw, 1982, 195,197–98; and Poland, Glowny Urzad Statystyczny (Central Statistical Office), *Rocznik Statystyczny Handlu Zagranicznego, 1980*, Warsaw, 1980, 20–22.

Table 10. Exports by Country Economic Grouping, Selected Years, 1970–81 (in millions of foreign exchange zlotys)[1]

Economic Grouping	1970	1975	1978	1980	1981
Socialist countries					
Comecon[2]					
Czechoslovakia	1,059.0	2,741.6	3,302.4	3,571.5	3,149.7
East Germany	1,313.9	3,151.3	3,684.0	3,572.2	3,196.0
Soviet Union	5,003.3	10,776.3	15,138.6	16,181.3	14,448.9
Other	1,223.5	2,784.1	3,778.9	4,323.0	4,386.4
Total Comecon	8,599.7	19,453.3	25,903.9	27,648.0	25,181.0
Other[3]	464.3	1,018.9	1,405.7	1,369.0	1,045.0
Total socialist countries	9,064.0	20,472.2	27,309.6	29,017.0	26,226.0
Other countries					
Developed countries[4]					
EEC[5]					
Britain	608.7	968.1	1,416.2	1,678.5	1,331.3
France	239.5	1,087.6	1,469.2	1,514.2	966.5
Italy	453.2	994.9	1,144.4	1,519.9	1,022.1
West Germany	723.0	1,777.7	3,037.8	4,220.7	3,499.3
Other	399.0	1,460.9	1,498.8	2,336.7	1,417.8
Total EEC	2,423.4	6,289.2	8,566.4	11,270.0	8,247.0
United States	371.3	777.9	1,463.8	1,298.5	1,106.7
Other	1,232.8	3,700.4	3,953.7	5,294.5	3,782.3
Total developed countries	4,027.5	10,767.5	13,983.9	17,863.0	13,136.0
Developing countries	1,099.0	2,921.0	3,391.5	5,028.0	5,168.0
Total other countries	5,126.5	13,688.5	17,375.4	22,891.0	18,304.0
TOTAL EXPORTS	14,190.5	34,160.7	44,685.0	51,908.0	44,530.0

[1]For value of the zloty—see Glossary.
[2]Council for Mutual Economic Assistance: Albania, Bulgaria, Cuba (since 1972), Czechoslovakia, East Germany, Hungary, Mongolia, Poland, Romania, Soviet Union, and Vietnam (since 1978).
[3]China, North Korea, and Yugoslavia.
[4]All West European countries, Canada, United States, South Africa, Israel, Japan, Australia, and New Zealand.
[5]European Economic Community (also known as the Common Market).

Source: Based on information from Poland, Central Statistical Office, *Concise Statistical Yearbook of Poland, 1982*, Warsaw, 1982, 195, 199–200; and Poland, Glowny Urzad Statystyczny (Central Statistical Office), *Rocznik Statystyczny Handlu Zagranicznego, 1980*, Warsaw, 1980, 23–25.

Table 11. Leading Government Officials, January 1983

COUNCIL OF STATE

Office/Officeholder	Party Affiliation
Chairman	
Henryk Jablonski	PZPR[1]
Deputy Chairmen	
Tadeusz Mlynczak	SD[2]
Kazimierz Secomski	Nonparty
Zdzislaw Tomal	ZSL[3]
Jerzy Zietek	PZPR
Secretary	
Edward Duda	ZSL
Members	
Kazimierz Barcikowski	PZPR
Michal Grendys	SD
Stanislaw Kania	PZPR
Eugenia Kempara	PZPR
Alfons Klafkowski	Pax
Emil Kolodziej	ZSL
Krystyna Marszalek-Mlynczyk	SD
Kazimierz Morawski	CSA[4]
Jozef Ozga-Michalski	ZSL
Mieczyslaw Rog-Swiostek	PZPR
Henryk Szafranski	PZPR
Stanislaw Wronski	PZPR

COUNCIL OF MINISTERS

Office	Officeholder	Party Affiliation
Prime Minister	Wojciech Jaruzelski	PZPR
Deputy Prime Minister	Zbigniew Szalajda	n.a.
Deputy Prime Minister	Zenon Komender	Pax
Deputy Prime Minister	Edward Kowalczyk	SD
Deputy Prime Minister	Zbigniew Madej	n.a.
Deputy Prime Minister	Roman Malinowski	ZSL
Deputy Prime Minister	Janusz Obodowski	PZPR
Deputy Prime Minister	Mieczyslaw Rakowski	PZPR
Ministers		
Administration, Local Economy, and Environmental Protection	Tadeusz Hupalowski	PZPR
Agriculture and Food Economy	Jerzy Wojtecki	n.a.
Chemical and Light Industry	Edward Grzywa	n.a.
Communications	Wladyslaw Majewski	PZPR

Table 11.—Continued

COUNCIL OF MINISTERS *(Continued)*

Office	Officeholder	Party Affiliation
Construction and Construction Materials Industry	Stanislaw Kukuryka	PZPR
Culture and Art	Kazimierz Zygulski	nonparty
Domestic Trade and Services	Zygmunt Lakomiec	n.a.
Education and Upbringing	Boleslaw Faron	PZPR
Finance	Stanislaw Nieckarz	PZPR
Foreign Affairs	Stefan Olszowski	PZPR
Foreign Trade	Tadeusz Nestorowicz	PZPR
Forestry and Timber Industry	Waldemar Kozlowski	ZSL
Health and Social Welfare	Tadeusz Szelachowski	ZSL
Internal Affairs	Czeslaw Kiszczak	PZPR
Justice	Sylwester Zawadski	PZPR
Labor, Wages, and Social Affairs	Vacant	
Maritime Economy	Jerzy Korzonek	n.a.
Materials Management	Jan Antosik	n.a.
Metallurgy and Engineering Industry	Edward Lukosz	PZPR
Mining and Power Industry	Czeslaw Piotrowski	n.a.
National Defense	Wojciech Jaruzelski (Acting: Florian Siwicki)	PZPR
Price Affairs	Zdzislaw Krasinski	n.a.
Science, Higher Education, and Technology	Benon Miskiewicz	n.a.
Trade Union Affairs	Stanislaw Ciosek	PZPR
Transportation	Janusz Kaminski	PZPR
Veterans' Affairs	Vacant	
Without Portfolio	Wladyslaw Jablonski	n.a.
Without Portfolio	Andrzej Ornat	n.a.
Office for Religious Affairs	Adam Lopatka	PZPR
OTHER OFFICIALS		
Chairman, Planning Commission	Janusz Obodowski	PZPR
Chairman, Supreme Chamber of Control	Mieczyslaw Moczar	PZPR
Plenipotentiary for Economic Reform	Wladyslaw Baka	PZPR

n.a.—not available, but career civil servants believed to be members of PZPR.
[1]Polish United Workers' Party.
[2]Democratic Party.
[3]United Peasant Party.
[4]Christian Social Association.

Table 12. Leading Officials of Polish United Workers' Party, January 1983

Political Bureau (Politburo)	Secretariat of the Central Committee
Members	*First Secretary*
Wojciech Jaruzelski	Wojciech Jaruzelski
Kazimierz Barcikowski	
Tadeusz Czechowicz	*Secretaries*
Jozef Czyrek	Kazimierz Barcikowski
Zofia Grzyb	Jozef Czyrek
Stanislaw Kalkus	Jan Glowczyk
Kieronim Kubiak	Manfred Gorywoda
Zbigniew Messner	Zbigniew Michalek
Miroslaw Milewski	Miroslaw Milewski
Stefan Olszowski	Wlodzimierz Mokrzyszczak
Stanislaw Opalko	Marian Orzechowski
Tadeusz Porebski	Waldemar Swirgon
Jerzy Romanik	
Albin Siwak	Central Control Commission
Marian Wozniak	
	Chairman
Candidate Members	Jerzy Urbanski
Stanislaw Bejger	
Jan Glowczyk	Central Audit Commission
Czeslaw Kiszczak	
Wlodzimierz Mokrzyszczak	*Chairman*
Florian Siwicki	Kazimierz Morawski

Source: Based on information from "Supplement to Leadership List," Radio Free Europe Research, 8, No. 1, January 7, 1983, 19–20.

Table 13. Selected Newspapers and Periodicals, 1982

City / Publication	Circulation[1]	Sponsorship or Orientation
Warsaw		
Dziennik Ludowy (d)	172,000	ZSL[2]
Express Wieczorny (d)	568,000	Government tabloid
Gromada Rolnik Polski (d)	450,000	Government; for farmers
Perspektywy (w)	222,000	Illustrated news; PZPR[3]
Polityka (w)	396,000	Liberal wing of PZPR
Rzeczpospolita (d)	130,000	Government
Slowo Powszechne (d)	100,000	Pax
Sztander Mlodych (d)	245,000	Government; for youth
Trybuna Ludu (d)	860,000	PZPR; national circulation
Tygodnik Powszechny (w)	75,000	Independent Catholic
Zolnierz Wolnosci (d)	120,000	Ministry of National Defense; hard-line PZPR
Rzeczywistosc (w)	130,000	Hard-line faction of Politburo
Zycie Warszawy (d)	348,000	Government
Bydgoszcz		
Gazeta Pomorska (d)	282,000	Government
Illustrowany Kurier Polski (d)	102,000	SD[4]
Gdansk		
Glos Wybrzeza (d)	210,000	Government
Katowice		
Dziennik Zachodni (d)	203,000	Government
Trybuna Robotnicza (d)	691,000	Government
Krakow		
Gazeta Poludniowa (d)	199,000	Government
Lodz		
Glos Robotniczy (d)	282,000	PZPR
Poznan		
Gazeta Zachodnia (d)	250,000	Government
Wroclaw		
Gazeta Robotnicza (d)	311,000	PZPR

(d)—daily (w)—weekly

[1]Includes copies returned to publishers during public boycott of press.
[2]United Peasant Party.
[3]Polish United Workers' Party.
[4]Democratic Party.

Source: Based on information from *Editor and Publisher Yearbook*, New York, 1982; and Radio Free Europe Research, 7, No. 38, September 24, 1982, 25–29.

Table 14. Major Ground Forces Weapons, 1982

Type	Estimated Number in Inventory	Country of Manufacture
Tanks		
T-54/T-55 main battle tank	3,000	Soviet Union, Poland
T-72 main battle tank	60	-do-
PT-76 light tank	130	Soviet Union
Light armored vehicles		
OT-65/FUG scout car		Czechoslovakia, Hungary
BDRM-1 scout car	2,800	Soviet Union
BDRM-2 scout car		-do-
BMP-1 armored personnel carrier (APC)		-do-
OT-64 SKOT APC	5,500	Poland, Czechoslovakia
OT-62 TOPAS APC		-do-
MT-LB APC		Soviet Union
Artillery		
100mm gun	600	Soviet Union, Czechoslovakia, and/or Poland
122mm gun (towed/self-propelled)		-do-
152mm gun/howitzer	250	-do-
122mm multiple rocket launcher (MRL)		-do-
130mm MRL	250[1]	-do-
140mm MRL		-do-
240mm MRL		-do-
FROG-3/FROG-7 surface-to-surface missile (SSM)	51	Soviet Union
SS-1 Scud SSM	36	-do-
82mm mortar	650	Soviet Union, Czechoslovakia, and/or Poland
120mm mortar		-do-
Antitank (ATK) weapons		
85mm ATK gun (towed)	450	Soviet Union, Czechoslovakia, and/or Poland
100mm ATK gun (towed)		-do-
73mm recoilless rocket launcher (RCL)	n.a.	-do-
82mm RCL	n.a.	-do-
107mm RCL	n.a.	-do-
AT-1 "Snapper" antitank guided weapon (ATGW)	n.a.	Soviet Union
AT-3 "Sagger" ATGW	n.a.	-do-
AT-4 "Spigot" ATGW	n.a.	-do-

Table 14.—Continued

Type	Estimated Number in Inventory	Country of Manufacture
Antiaircraft (AA) weapons		
23mm AA gun (towed)	750	Soviet Union, Czechoslovakia, and/or Poland
37mm AA gun (towed)		-do-
57mm AA gun (towed)		-do-
85mm AA gun (towed)		-do-
100mm AA gun (towed)		-do-
ZSU-23-4 quad-mounted AA guns (self-propelled)	75	-do-
SA-4 Ganef surface-to-air missile (SAM)	n.a.	Soviet Union
SA-6 Gainful SAM	n.a.	-do-
SA-7 Grail SAM (man portable)	n.a.	-do-
SA-9 Gaskin SAM	n.a.	-do-

n.a.—not available

Source: Based on information from *The Military Balance, 1982–83*, London, 1982.

Table 15. Major Air Force and National Air Defense Force Weapons, 1982

Type	Estimated Number in Inventory	Country of Manufacture
Fighters/fighter-bombers		
SU-7/SU-7U Fitter	35	Soviet Union
SU-20 Fitter C	35	-do-
MiG-17/LiM-5 Fresco	250	Soviet Union, Poland
MiG-21/MiG-21U Fishbed	330	Soviet Union
Reconnaissance aircraft		
MiG-21RF Fishbed	35	-do-
Il-28 Beagle	5	-do-
LiM-6 Fresco	15	Poland
Transports		
An-2 Colt	5	-do-
An-12 Cub	9	Soviet Union
An-26 Curl	12	-do-
Il-14 Crate	12	-do-
Tu-134A Crusty	2	-do-
Yak-40 Codling	5	-do-
Il-18 Coot	1	-do-
Trainers		
TS-8 Bien	300 (TS-8 Bien, TS-Il Iskra, MiG-15UTI/SBLiM-1 Midget, MiG-21UTI Mongol combined)	Poland
TS-Il Iskra		-do-
MiG-15UTI/SBLiM-1 Midget		Soviet Union, Poland
MiG-21UTI Mongol		Soviet Union
Helicopters		
Mi-1/SM-1 Hare	115 (Mi-1/SM-1 Hare and Mi-2 Hoplite combined)	Soviet Union, Poland
Mi-2 Hoplite		Poland
Mi-4 Hound	5	Soviet Union
Mi-8 Hip	26	-do-
Mi-24 Hind	5	-do-
Surface-to-air missiles (SAMs)		
SA-2 Guideline	50 sites; 425 missiles (SA-2 and SA-3 combined)	-do-
SA-3 Goa		-do-

Source: Based on information from *The Military Balance, 1982–83, London, 1982*.

Table 16. Major Naval Weapons, 1982

Type	Estimated Number in Inventory	Country of Manufacture
Large combat vessels		
Whiskey-class submarine (diesel)	4	Soviet Union
Kotline-class destroyer with Goa surface-to-air missiles	1	-do-
Fast attack craft		
OSA I class with 4 Styx surface-to-surface missiles	13	-do-
Wilsa class (torpedo)	10	Poland
Patrol craft		
Obluze-class large patrol craft (LPC)	13	-do-
Oksywie-class LPC	1	-do-
Gdansk-class LPC	9	-do-
Pilica-class coastal patrol craft (CPC), torpedo armed	9	-do-
Wisloca-class CPC	12	-do-
K-8 class CPC	21	-do-
Mine warfare vessels		
Krogulec class	12	-do-
T-43 class	11	Soviet Union
Notec	1	Poland
K-8 class	25	-do-
Amphibious vessels		
Polnochny-class landing ship (medium)	23	-do-
Marabat-class landing craft (medium)	4	-do-
Eichstaden-class assault landing craft	15	-do-
Naval aircraft		
MiG-17/LiM-5 fighter-bomber	42	Soviet Union, Poland
Il-28 light bomber	10	Soviet Union
Mi-2 helicopter	25 (Mi-2, Mi-4, Mi-8 combined)	Poland
Mi-4 helicopter		Soviet Union
Mi-8 helicopter		-do-

n.a.—not available

Source: Based on information from *The Military Balance, 1982–83*, London, 1982; and *Jane's Fighting Ships, 1981–82*, London, 1981.

Appendix B

The Council For Mutual Economic Assistance: A Historical Perspective

THE COUNCIL FOR MUTUAL ECONOMIC ASSISTANCE is customarily referred to as Comecon, CMEA, or simply as the Council. (The Russian wording is also sometimes awkwardly translated as Council for Economic Mutual Assistance, or CEMA.) The primary documents governing the objectives, organization, and functions of Comecon are the Charter of the Council for Mutual Economic Assistance (first adopted in 1959 and subsequently amended; all references herein are to the amended 1974 text) and the Comprehensive Program for the Further Extension and Improvement of Cooperation and the Development of Socialist Economic Integration by the CMEA Member Countries, adopted in 1971.

Membership, Nature, and Scope

It was in Moscow in January 1949 that representatives of Bulgaria, Czechoslovakia, Hungary, Poland, Romania, and the Soviet Union reached the formal decision to establish a Council for Mutual Economic Assistance. The communiqué announcing the event cited the refusal of these countries to "subordinate themselves to the dictates of the Marshall Plan" and the trade "boycott" imposed by "the United States, Britain and certain other countries of Western Europe" as the major factors contributing to the decision "to organize a more broadly based economic cooperation among the countries of the people's democracy and the USSR."

The six original members were joined by Albania in February 1949 and by the German Democratic Republic (East Germany) in 1950. (Albania stopped participating in Comecon activities in 1961.) Mongolia joined the organization in 1962, and membership was expanded in the 1970s to include Cuba (1972) and Vietnam (1978). As of December 1980 there were 10 states represented on the Council: the Soviet Union, the six East European countries, and the three extraregional members (see table A, this Appendix).

Geography, therefore, no longer unites Comecon members. Wide variations in economic size and level of economic development have also tended to generate divergent interests among them. These in turn have given rise to significant differences in their economic organization.

Table A. National Participation in Council for Mutual Economic Assistance, December 1980

Member Countries[1]

Bulgaria (1949)
Czechoslovakia (1949)
Hungary (1949)
Poland (1949)
Romania (1949)
Soviet Union (1949)
East Germany (1950)
Mongolia (1962)
Cuba (1972)
Vietnam (1978)

Nonmember Countries

Which regularly sent observer delegations to annual sessions of the Council in 1976–80:

Afghanistan (from 1979)
Angola
Ethiopia (from 1978)
Laos
Mozambique (from 1979)
North Korea (until 1979)[2]
Yemen (Aden) (from 1979)
Yugoslavia

Which have concluded formal agreements of cooperation with Comecon:

Yugoslavia (1964)
Finland (1973)
Iraq (1975)
Mexico (1975)

[1]Dates of accession in parentheses.
[2]Holding observer status since 1957, North Korea did not attend Council Sessions between 1962 and 1971. More recently, it has been represented at Comecon sessions by its local diplomatic mission chief. It did not, however, send a delegation to the thirtieth anniversary session of Comecon in 1979, nor was it represented at the Thirty-fourth Council Session in 1980.

Unity is provided rather by political and ideological factors. Comecon provides a mechanism through which its leading member, the Soviet Union, has sought to foster economic links with and among its closest political and military allies. All Comecon members are one-party, communist states sharing official (Marxist-Leninist) ideologies and common approaches to economic ownership (state versus private) and management (plan versus market). The ruling parties of the founding states were in 1949 linked internationally through the Cominform, from which Yugoslavia had been expelled the previous year. Although the Cominform was disbanded in 1956, interparty links continue to be strong among Comecon members, and all participate in periodic international conferences of communist parties. The East European members of Comecon are also militarily allied with the Soviet Union in the Warsaw Treaty Organization (see Appendix C).

Official statements stress, however, that Comecon is an open international organization. Its Charter (Article II, Paragraph 2) invites membership from "other countries which share the aims and principles of the Council and have expressed their willingness to assume the obligations contained in the . . . Charter." In the late 1950s a number of other communist-ruled countries were invited to participate as observers in Council sessions: China, the Democratic People's Republic of Korea (North Korea), Mongolia, Vietnam, and Yugoslavia. Although Mongolia and Vietnam later gained full membership, China stopped attending Council sessions after 1961. Yugoslavia, on the other hand, negotiated a form of associate status in the organization, specified in its 1964 agreement with the Council.

In the 1970s the Soviet Union and its Comecon associates sought to use the organization as an instrument for intensifying their collective relations with other, especially developing, countries. Amendments to the Charter adopted in 1974 provide for two basic kinds of relations that may be established between the Council and nonmember countries: participation of a nonmember country in the activities of Comecon organs and Comecon cooperation with a nonmember country "in other forms." The precise nature of the relationship is determined by mutual agreement and can range from observer status to an association close to full-fledged membership. In addition to Yugoslavia, Finland (1973), Iraq (1975), and Mexico (1975) have concluded agreements with the organization. Delegations from Angola, Afghanistan, Ethiopia, Laos, Mozambique, the People's Democratic Republic of Yemen (Yemen [Aden]), and Yugoslavia attended the Thirty-fourth Council Session in June 1980 in Prague as observers.

Comecon is an interstate organization through which the members seek to coordinate economic activities of mutual interest and to develop multilateral economic, scientific, and technical cooperation. The Charter lays down the principle of "the sovereign equality of all the members" as fundamental to the organization and procedures of the Council. Comecon's Comprehensive Program further emphasizes that the processes of integration of members' economies are " completely voluntary and do not involve the creation of supranational bodies."

Hence each country has the right under the provisions of the Charter to equal representation and one vote in all organs of the Council, regardless of its economic size or the size of its contribution to Comecon's budget. The sessions of the Council itself—at which members are represented by delegations that in the 1970s were typically led by heads of governments—are convened at least annually in late June or early July, in one of the member's capitals according to a system of rotation. These "ordinary" annual sessions may be supplemented by "extraordinary" sessions but rarely are. When questions of cooperation arise, the Council makes "recommendations" that are then communicated to member governments for consideration. Recommendations subsequently adopted by the members are implemented through decisions made in accordance with national laws. The Council itself may make decisions only on organizational and procedural matters pertaining to itself and its organs.

The principle of "sovereign equality" is further guaranteed by the "interestedness" provisions of the charter. The Council's recommendations and decisions can be adopted only upon agreement among the interested members, and each has the right to declare its "interest" in any matter under consideration. Furthermore, "recommendations and decisions shall not apply to countries that have declared that they have no interest in a particular matter."

Whereas the principle of unanimity of interested parties is thus established, disinterested parties are not given a veto but rather the right to abstain from participation. A declaration of disinterest cannot block a project unless the disinterested party's participation is vital. Otherwise the Charter implies that the interested parties may proceed without the abstaining member, affirming that a country that has declared a lack of interest "may subsequently adhere to the recommendations and decisions adopted by the remaining members of the Council."

A number of the concrete initiatives taken in the 1960s and 1970s have therefore involved a subgroup of Comecon members. These measures have included the creation of interstate bodies as well as the initiation of joint projects. For example, the establishment in 1964 of an international economic organization for cooperation in the iron and steel industry (known as Intermetal) was accomplished by an agreement initially signed by Czechoslovakia, Hungary, and Poland, with adherence by Bulgaria, East

Germany, and the Soviet Union some months later. Yugoslav and Romanian enterprises have subsequently taken part in the activities of Intermetal through agreements signed in 1968 and 1970, respectively. Romania joined the other Comecon members and adhered to the agreement on the Formation of the International Investment Bank six months after its signing in 1970. Multilateral regional development projects have seldom involved the participation of all Comecon members (see Areas, Forms, and Instruments of Cooperation under the Comprehensive Program, this Appendix).

Some observers suggest that these interstate bodies and joint projects should be regarded as "outside" Comecon because they often do not encompass the full Comecon membership and are not formally organs and activities of the Council. The Comprehensive Program seeks to bring them under the institutional umbrella of the Council, requiring members to coordinate their cooperative activities "primarily" with Comecon. It also requires that the activities of "inter-state organizations established by interested parties" be coordinated with the activities of the Council and directs the latter to take initiatives to this end as necessary. Protocols of cooperation have been concluded with the Council and most such interstate organizations. The Comprehensive Program thus seeks to make the Council the central link in the institutional mechanism of socialist international cooperation.

It is for this reason that the descriptive designator "Comecon" is commonly applied to all multilateral activities involving members of the organization and is not restricted to the direct functions of the Council and its organs. This usage may be extended as well to bilateral relations among members, since in the system of socialist international economic relations, multilateral accords— typically of a general nature—tend to be implemented through a set of more detailed, bilateral agreements. The Comprehensive Program, therefore, also seeks to ensure that bilateral relations among members conform to the recommendations of the Council.

Evolution, 1949–80

During Comecon's early years (through 1955), Council sessions were convened on an ad hoc, irregular basis. The organization lacked clear structure and operated without a charter until a decade after its founding. These loose arrangements were reflective of the limited goals of Comecon at the time and of the character of the Marshall Plan, to which Comecon served as a response.

This was a period, moreover, when the East European members were preoccupied with their first five-year development plans, formulated along the Soviet model. In headlong pursuit of parallel industrialization strategies, their attentions were turned inward. In any case, bilateral ties with the Soviet Union had quickly come to dominate their external relations, and these could be conducted largely through local Soviet missions. Although reparations transfers (extracted by the Soviet Union in the immediate postwar years from those East European states it regarded as former World War II enemies) had been replaced by more normal trade relations, outstanding reparations obligations were not finally forgiven until 1956. In these circumstances there was scarcely need or scope for multilateral policies or institutions.

After Stalin's death in 1953, however, new leaders and new approaches emerged in the countries of the region. The more industrialized and the more trade dependent of the East European countries had belatedly recognized the need to adapt the Soviet autarkic model to their own requirements. New approaches to foreign trade emerged during discussions of economic reform. Given their isolation from the rest of the world and the dominance of intrabloc trade in their external relations, interest in these countries inevitably centered on new forms of regional cooperation. For small, centrally planned economies, this meant the need to develop a mechanism through which to coordinate investment and trade policies.

Instability in Eastern Europe and integration in Western Europe increased the desirability of regularizing intrabloc relations within a more elaborate institutional framework. Politico-military links were formally reinforced by the 1955 Warsaw Treaty and its implementing machinery. On the economic front, Comecon was rediscovered. The example of the 1956 Treaty of Rome, which initiated the processes of West European economic integration, gave impetus and direction to Comecon's revival.

The years 1956–63 witnessed the rapid growth of Comecon institutions and activities, especially after 1959 under the new Charter. The permanent, international secretariat (housed since 1968 in an impressive, specially designed complex of buildings on the bank of the Moscow River) was strengthened and expanded. Standing commissions located in various members' capitals were established to assist the Council in making recommendations pertaining to specific economic sectors or functional areas (see fig. A, this Appendix). An executive committee was created to provide continuity between Council sessions. Efforts to improve the conditions for intra-Comecon trade included programs to unify technical standards, adopt common statistical practices, and improve and regularize procedures for the pricing of traded goods and services. A special bank, the International Bank for Economic Cooperation, was created in 1963 to facilitate financial settlements among members. A program to unify the electrical power systems of the member countries was launched, and a Central Dispatching Board was created in 1962 to manage it; analogous steps were taken to coordinate railroad and river transport. A number of bilateral and multilateral investment projects were also under-

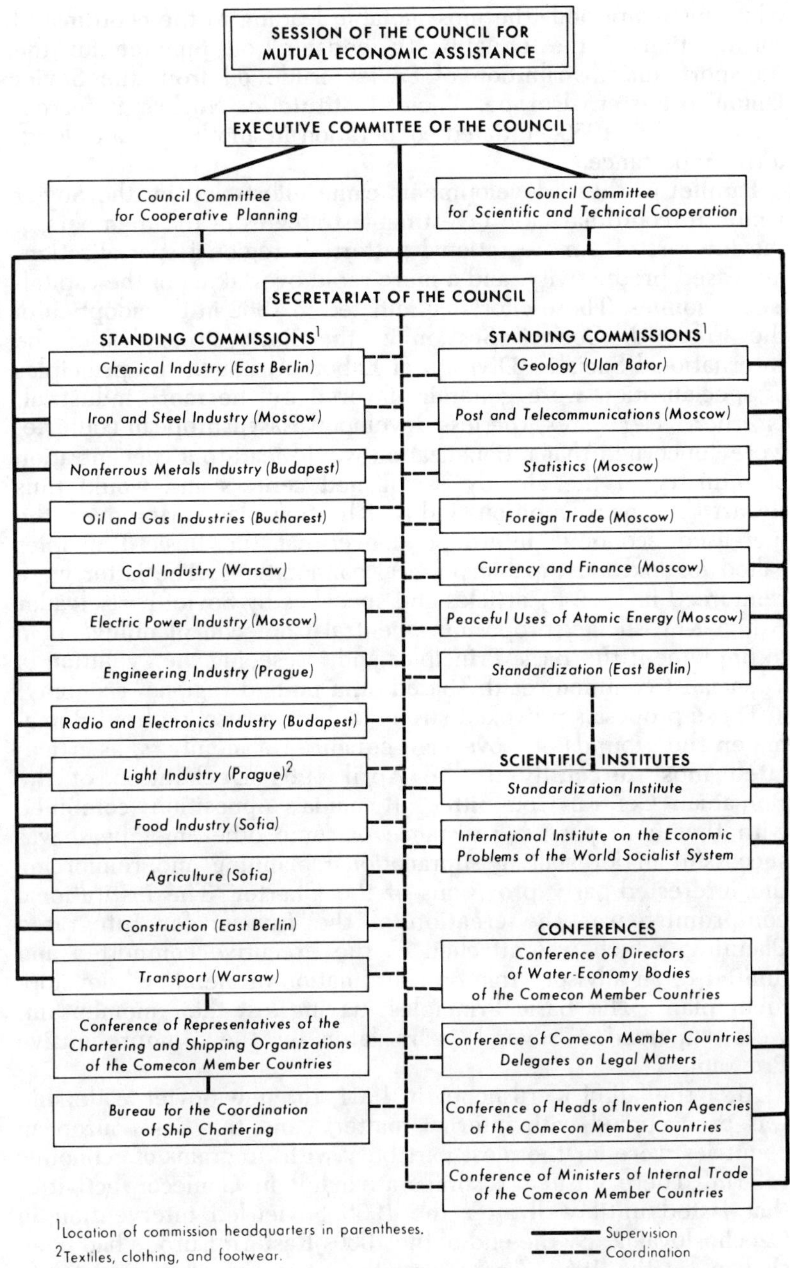

Source: Based on information from *The Multilateral Economic Cooperation of Socialist States: A Collection of Documents*, Moscow, 1977, 290.

Figure A. Structure of the Council for Mutual Economic Assistance, 1980

taken in this period, the most notable leading to the coordinated construction of the Druzhba (Friendship) oil pipeline for the transport and distribution of Soviet crude oil from the Soviet Union to Eastern Europe. A joint Institute for Nuclear Research, established in 1956, initiated cooperation in another area of long-term importance.

Parallel to these developments came efforts led by the Soviet Union to coordinate the investment strategies of the members in the interest of a more rational pattern of regional specialization, increased productivity, and a more rapid overtaking of the capitalist economies. These efforts culminated in 1962 in the adoption of the Fifteenth Council Session of the Basic Principles of the International Socialist Division of Labor. Although the principles of specialization were generally favored by the more industrial, Northern Tier states, the less developed East European countries were concerned that rationalization would lead to a concentration of industry in the already established centers and would thus thwart their own ambitious industrialization plans. Moreover, the increased economic interdependence that the Basic Principles called for had inescapable political connotations. The latter were reinforced in 1962 by articles and speeches by Soviet party leader Nikita Khrushchev proposing a central Comecon planning organ to implement the Basic Principles and foreseeing the evolution of a "socialist commonwealth" based on a unified regional economy.

These proposals provoked strong and open reaction from Romania on the grounds of "sovereign equality" of members, as articulated most forcefully in the April 1964 Declaration of the Romanian Central Committee. Romania's opposition (combined with the more passive resistance of some other members) was successful in forestalling supranational planning and reinforcing the interested-party provisions of the Charter. The institutional compromise was the creation of the Bureau for Integrated Planning, which was attached to the executive committee and limited to an advisory role on coordination of members' development plans. The Basic Principles, having lost their momentum, were superseded several years later by the Comprehensive Program.

After the fall of Khrushchev in 1964, the new Soviet leadership was preoccupied with internal matters, and the East European countries were for the most part busy with programs of economic reform. There ensued a comparative lull in Comecon activities that lasted until well after the 1968 Soviet-led intervention in Czechoslovakia. By the end of the 1960s Eastern Europe had been shaken by the 1968 events, and there was an obvious need to revitalize programs that would strengthen regional cohesion.

Considerable discussion in specialized journals and at international meetings of experts was therefore directed to the question of how to proceed. The reformers, disillusioned by traditional instruments and concerned with the need to decentralize planning and management in their domestic economies, argued for the strengthening of market relations among Comecon states. The conservatives continued to stress the importance of planned approaches. If carried to a logical extreme the latter would involve supranational planning of major aspects of members' economies and thus inevitable loss of national autonomy over domestic investment policy. The old conflict between planned approaches to regional specialization and the principle of sovereign equality could thus not be avoided in any discussion of the mechanism for future cooperation.

What emerged from the controversy was a compromise in the form of the 1971 Comprehensive Program, which laid the guidelines for Comecon activity through 1990. The Comprehensive Program incorporated elements of both the market and the plan approaches. In terms of the former it sought to strengthen the role of money, prices, and exchange rates in intra-Comecon relations and to encourage direct contact among lower level economic entities in the member countries. At the same time, it called for more joint planning on a sectoral basis through interstate bodies that would coordinate members' activities in a given sector. New organs were also envisaged in the form of international associations that would engage in actual operations in a designated sector on behalf of the participating countries. Finally, the Comprehensive Program placed much emphasis on the need for multilateral projects to develop new regional sources of fuels, energy, and raw materials. Such projects were to be jointly planned, financed, and executed.

The Comprehensive Program also introduced a new concept in relations among members: "socialist economic integration." Although never clearly defined, the term was used to suggest a qualitatively new phase in relations to be introduced under the program. Section I, Paragraph 2 of the Comprehensive Program refers to the need "to intensify and improve" cooperation among members and "to develop socialist economic integration." This phrasing, which has since become standard, implies that the latter is a new and higher level of interaction, "a process of the international socialist division of labor, the drawing closer of their economies and the formation of modern, highly effective national economic structures." The Comprehensive Program avoids, however, the suggestion of ultimate fusion of members' economies that had been contained in the 1962 Basic Principles. It sets the limits to the integrative process in the following terms: "Socialist economic integration is completely voluntary and does not involve the creation of supranational bodies."

The term *integration* had formerly been used to designate the activities of Western regional organizations, such as the European Economic Community (EEC). Its new usage in the Comprehensive Program served to suggest a parity of status between Comecon and the EEC. Under subsequent amendments to its Charter the competence of the Comecon to deal with other international organizations and third countries on behalf of its members was made clear. At this time Comecon entered into negotiations to regulate relations with the EEC, but events in Afghanistan and Poland induced the EEC to suspend the talks. In another external initiative Comecon sought to attract the participation of developing countries in Comecon activities. The language of the Comprehensive Program may thus also be regarded as an attempt to revitalize the image of Comecon in order to make association with it an attractive alternative to associated status with the EEC.

The Comprehensive Program was adopted at a time when Comecon members were actively developing economic relations with the rest of the world, especially with the industrialized Western economies. The attempt to intensify regional ties was pursued parallel to the opening up of members' economies to extraregional relations. The two sets of policies were viewed as complementary by the program, which affirmed that "because the international socialist division of labor is effected with due account taken of the world division of labor, the CMEA member countries shall continue to develop economic, scientific, and technological ties with other countries, irrespective of their social and political system."

In the years following the adoption of the Comprehensive Program, some progress was made toward the goals it set for the strengthening of market relations among members. These objectives proved somewhat inconsistent with the predominant trends within the members' economies in the 1970s, which for the most part was a period of recentralization—rather than decentralization—of domestic systems of planning and management. The major exception to this general lack of progress was in the area of intra-Comecon pricing and payment, where the expansion of relations with the West contributed to the adoption of prices and extra-plan settlements closer to international norms.

Achievements under the Comprehensive Program have rather fallen under the heading of planned approaches, especially in the area of joint resource development projects. A second Comecon bank, the International Investment Bank, was established in 1970 to provide a mechanism for the joint financing of such projects. In 1973 Comecon decided to draw up a general plan incorporating these measures. A number of projects formulated in the years immediately following adoption of the Comprehensive Program were hence assembled in a document signed at the Twenty-ninth Council Session in 1975. Entitled the "Concerted Plan for Multilateral Integration Measures," it covered the 1976–80 five-year-plan period and was proclaimed as the first general plan for the Comecon economies. The joint projects included in the plan were largely completed in the course of the plan period.

A second major initiative toward implementation of the Comprehensive Program came in 1976 at the Thirtieth Council Session, when a decision was made to draw up Long-term Target Programs for Cooperation in major economic sectors and subsectors. The session designated a number of objectives to which target programs would be directed: "guarantee of the economically based requirements of CMEA member countries for basic kinds of energy, fuels, and raw materials; the development of the machine-building industries on the basis of intense specialization and cooperation in production; the fulfillment of rational demands for basic foodstuffs and industrial consumer goods; and modernization and development of transport links among member countries." Target programs worked out for cooperation through 1990 in the first two areas and in agriculture and the food industries were approved in 1978 at the Thirty-second Council Session. These programs established the commitments to multilateral cooperation that the member countries were to take into account when drawing up their five-year plans for the 1980s.

Areas, Forms, and Instruments of Cooperation under the Comprehensive Program

The distinction between "market" relations and "planned" relations made in the discussions within Comecon prior to the adoption of the Comprehensive Program remains a useful approach to understanding Comecon activities. This is because Comecon remains in fact a mixed system, combining elements of both plan and market. Although there is much emphasis on regional planning in the official rhetoric, it must be remembered that intra-Comecon relations continue to be conducted among national entities not governed by any supranational authority. They thus interact on a decentralized basis according to terms negotiated in bilateral and multilateral agreements on trade and cooperation.

Market Relations and Instruments

It is not surprising, given the size of the Soviet economy, that intra-Comecon trade has been dominated by exchanges between the Soviet Union and the other members. Exchanges of Soviet fuels and raw materials for capital goods and consumer manufactures have characterized trade, particularly among the original members. Whereas in the late 1970s mutual trade represented from 55 to 60 percent of the foreign trade of Comecon countries as a whole, for individual members it ranged from little more than 40 percent in the case of Romania, to over 70 percent for Cuba and Bulgaria, and over 90 percent for Mongolia. For most members these shares have declined over the long run as opportunities for extra-Comecon trade have increased and been exploited.

Trade among the members is negotiated on an annual basis and in considerable detail at the governmental level and is then followed up by inter-enterprise contracts. Early Comecon efforts to facilitate trade among members were concentrated on the development of uniform technical, legal, and statistical standards and on the encouragement of long-term trade agreements. The Comprehensive Program sought to liberalize the system somewhat by recommending broad limits to "fixed-quota" trade among members (trade subject to quantitative or value targets set by bilateral trade agreements). Section 6, Paragraph 19 of the program affirms that "mutual trade in commodities for which no quotas are established shall be carried on beginning in 1971 with a view to stimulating the development of trade turnover, through expansion of the range and assortment of traded commodities, and to making trade in these commodities more brisk." Later in the same paragraph, the program calls on members to "seek opportunities to develop the export and import of quota-free commodities and to create conditions essential for trade in such commodities." There is no evidence, however, that this appeal has had significant effect or that quota-free trade has grown in importance under the program.

The Comprehensive Program also called for improvement in the Comecon system of foreign trade prices. Under Soviet-style central planning, foreign trade is conducted at prices different from those that obtain in the domestic economy. By 1971 a price system governing exchanges among members had developed, under which prices agreed through negotiation were fixed for five-year periods (corresponding to those of the synchronized, five-year plans of the members). These contract prices were based on adjusted world market prices averaged over the immediately preceding five years; that is, a world-price base was used as the starting point for negotiation. Under the system, however, intra-Comecon prices could—and did—depart substantially from relative prices on world markets.

Although in the 1960s there had been discussion of the possibility of breaking even this tenuous link with world prices and developing an indigenous system of prices for the Comecon market, the evolution of Comecon prices after 1971 was in the opposite direction. Far from a technical or academic matter, the question of prices underlay vital issues of the terms of, and hence gains from, intra-Comecon trade. In particular, relative to actual world prices, intra-Comecon prices in the early 1970s penalized raw materials exporters and benefited exporters of manufactures. After the oil price explosion of 1973, Comecon foreign trade prices swung still further away from world prices to the disadvantage of Comecon suppliers of raw materials, in particular the Soviet Union. In view of the extraregional opportunities opened up by the expansion of East-West trade, this yawning gap between Comecon and world prices could no longer be ignored. Hence in 1975 at Soviet instigation, the system of intra-Comecon pricing was reformed.

The reform involved a substantial modification of existing procedures (known as the "Bucharest formula," from the location of the Ninth Council Session in 1958 at which it was adopted) but not their abandonment. Under the modified Bucharest formula (which did not apply to all transactions), prices were fixed for only one year and were based on a moving average of world prices. The world-price base of the Bucharest formula was thus retained and still represented an average (although now moving) of adjusted world prices for the preceding five years. For 1975 alone, however, the average was for the preceding three years. Under these arrangements intra-Comecon prices were more closely linked with world prices than before and throughout the remainder of the 1970s rose with world prices, although with a lag. Following world-price trends, intra-Comecon prices of raw materials (especially fuels) rose more rapidly than prices of manufactures. As a result, intra-Comecon terms of trade shifted in favor of the Soviet Union, and large deficits emerged in trade between the Soviet Union and its Comecon partners.

It is important to note, however, that under the new price system, Comecon prices of key fuels and raw materials remained substantially below world prices. In the latter half of the 1970s, the Comecon price of petroleum remained at an estimated 25 to 50 percent below the world price. The Soviet Union was therefore essentially subsidizing exports of oil (as well as other fuels and raw materials) to its partners. Comecon sources have placed the amount of the price subsidy on Soviet oil exports in the 1976–80 period at 5 billion rubles (over US$7.5 billion at official exchange rates), but Western estimates range substantially higher.

Basic features of the state trading systems of the Comecon countries are multiple exchange rates and comprehensive exchange controls that severely restrict the convertibility of members' currencies. These features are rooted in the planned character of the members' economies and their systems of administered prices. Currency inconvertibility in turn dictates bilateral balancing of accounts, which has been one of the basic objectives of intergovernmental trade agreements among members. An earlier system of bilateral clearing accounts was replaced as of January 1, 1964, by accounts with the International Bank for Economic Cooperation, using the "transferable ruble" as the unit of account. Although the bank provided a centralized mechanism of trade accounting and swing credits to cover temporary imbalances, it could not establish a system of multilateral clearing, given the centrally planned nature of the members' economies and the inconvertibility of their currencies. In late

1980 the transferable ruble remained an artificial unit of account and was not a common instrument for multilateral settlement. It is for this reason that it continued to be termed "transferable" and not "convertible."

The member countries recognize that the multiplicity and inconsistency of their administered exchange rates, the separation of their domestic prices from foreign prices, and the inconvertibility of their currencies are significant obstacles to multilateral trade and cooperation. Comecon lacks not only a flexible means of payment but also a meaningful, standard unit of account. Both problems vastly complicate the already complex multilateral projects and programs envisaged by the Comprehensive Program. The creation in 1971 of the International Investment Bank provided a mechanism for joint investment financing but, like the International Bank for Economic Cooperation, could not by itself resolve these fundamental monetary problems.

Recognizing that money and credit should play a more active role in the Comecon system, the Comprehensive Program established a timetable for the improvement of monetary relations. According to the timetable, measures would be taken "to strengthen and extend" the functions of the "collective currency" (the transferable ruble), and the conditions would be studied and prepared "to make the transferable ruble convertible into national currencies and to make national currencies mutually convertible." To this end, steps would be undertaken to introduce "economically well-founded and mutually coordinated" rates of exchange between members' currencies and "between 1976 and 1979" to prepare the groundwork for the introduction by 1980 of "a single rate of exchange for the national currency of every country." This timetable was not met; by the end of 1980 only in Hungary were the conditions for convertibility gradually being introduced by reforms intended to link domestic prices more directly to world prices.

If countries are to gain from trade, it must be based on rational production structures reflecting resource scarcities. Since the early 1960s official Comecon documents have stressed the need to promote among member economies a more cost-effective pattern of specialization in production. This "international socialist division of labor" would, especially in the manufacturing sector, involve specialization within major branches of industry. In the absence of significant, decentralized allocation of resources within these economies, however, production specialization can only be brought about through the mechanism of the national plan and the investment decisions incorporated in it. In the absence at the regional level of supranational planning bodies, a rational pattern of production specialization among members' economies requires coordination of national economic plans—a process that is not merely technical but also poses inescapable political problems.

Cooperation in Planning

The coordination of national five-year economic plans is the most traditional form of cooperation among the members in the area of planning. Although the process of consultation underlying plan coordination remains essentially bilateral, Comecon organs are indirectly involved. The standing commissions draw up proposals for consideration by competent, national planning bodies; the Secretariat assembles information on the results of bilateral consultations; and the Committee for Cooperative Planning (created by the Council in 1971 at the same session at which the Comprehensive Program was adopted) reviews the progress of plan coordination by members.

In principle, plan coordination covers all economic sectors. Effective and comprehensive plan coordination had, however, been significantly impeded by the continued momentum of earlier parallel development strategies and the desire of members to minimize the risks of mutual dependence (especially given the uncertainties of supply that are characteristic of the members' economies). Plan coordination in practice, therefore, remained for the most part limited to mutual adjustment, through bilateral consultation, of the foreign trade sectors of national five-year plans. Under the Comprehensive Program there have been renewed efforts to extend plan coordination beyond foreign trade to the spheres of production, investment, science, and technology.

To this end the Comprehensive Program stresses sectoral approaches and introduces a new concept of cooperation in planning—joint planning. The program fails, however, to define the new concept sharply, and its ambiguity is reflected in writings on the subject in the member countries. It is clear, nevertheless, that joint planning is to be applied to "selected branches or lines of production" and is to embrace "preparations for production, production itself, and distribution." Joint planning is to "promote the accelerated development of the most progressive lines of production in industrially less-developed CMEA countries." This suggests that joint planning will be directed to the higher technology manufacturing industries in order to bring them up to international technical standards. Specialization and cooperation in the development of the members' chemical industries is cited as an example of a potential area of joint planning under the Comprehensive Program.

According to the Comprehensive Program, joint planning—multilateral or bilateral—is to be limited to "interested" countries and is "not to interfere with the autonomy of internal planning." Participating countries will, moreover, retain national ownership of the productive capacities and resources jointly planned. But "joint plans worked out by the CMEA member countries will be taken into account by them when drafting their long-term or five-year plans."

The Comprehensive Program does not clearly assign responsibility for joint planning to any single agency. On the one hand, "coordination of work concerned with joint planning shall be carried out by the central planning bodies of CMEA member countries or their authorized representatives." On the other hand, "decisions on joint, multilateral planning of chosen branches and lines of production by interested countries shall be based on proposals by countries or CMEA agencies and shall be made by the CMEA Executive Committee, which also determines the CMEA agencies responsible for the organization of such work." Finally, mutual commitments resulting from joint planning and other aspects of cooperation shall be incorporated in agreements signed by the interested parties.

This seems to constitute supranational planning, albeit on a voluntary, "interested party" basis and limited to designated sectors. Moreover, should joint planning extend to major sectors of the members' economies, it would inevitably constrain national economic planning to a significant degree. The section on joint planning is clearly one of the most politically sensitive in the Comprehensive Program; this no doubt accounts for its ambiguous wording and the many questions, especially on implementation, that it leaves unanswered.

The sensitivity of the issues raised by joint planning, even on a limited, sectoral basis, helps to explain why the Comprehensive Program does not link it more explicitly with another, apparently related, initiative, i.e., the international economic organizations (IEOs). These organizations, to which a separate section of the program is devoted, are instead presented in the more general context of the need to develop "direct links between appropriate bodies and organizations of the CMEA member countries." IEOs function at two levels: a higher level of intergovernmental bodies and a lower level of international associations and enterprises, closer to the operational level of research, production, or trade. Interstate bodies, already traditional Comecon institutions, were to be strengthened in organization and expanded in number under the provisions of the program. The lower level organizations, while not without precedent, were more of an innovation. Both kinds engage in managerial as well as coordinative functions, but the former, linking organizations at a higher level in the member countries, generally deal with a wider range of activities. These include "coordination of production development plans and the joint planning of the appropriate industries, separate lines or types of production." The latter, on the other hand, are more focused in their operations and more commercial in character, taking the form not only of "international economic associations" but also of "institutes, centers, mixed companies, trading or design offices, etc."

The Comprehensive Program stimulated a creative spurt of new international economic associations in the years immediately following its adoption, but the number of joint production enterprises established by Comecon member countries remained sharply limited by the end of the decade (see table B, this Appendix). These new forms of cooperation have, moreover, run into many of the problems that have traditionally impeded Comecon initiatives at the operational level. For example, IEOs, especially of the newer kind, have raised fundamental questions regarding property rights, given the principles of national (state) ownership of the means of production that underlie the members' economic systems. Their activities also pose difficult problems of coordination with national systems of planning and distribution, and their expansion threatens national planning sovereignty. The problems of international calculation, accounting, and settlement that they raise are rendered all the more complex by artificial prices and exchange rates and by inconvertible currencies.

It is extremely difficult to gauge the implementation of plan coordination or joint planning under the Comprehensive Program or to assess the activities of the diverse international economic organizations. There is no single, adequate measure of such cooperation. The only data on activities among the Comecon countries published by the annual Comecon yearbooks refer to merchandise trade, and these trade figures cannot be readily associated with cooperative measures taken under the Comprehensive Program. Occasional official figures are published, however, on the aggregate number of industrial specialization and coproduction agreements signed by members. The number of such agreements signed from the adoption of the Comprehensive Program in 1971 through mid-1980 stood at nearly 800, of which more than 100 were multilateral agreements for cooperation in the production of machinery and equipment for the electric power, extractive, machine-building, electronics, chemical, transport, and agricultural industries. Although such figures suggest a marked increase in numbers of agreements concluded over the level of the 1960s, they reveal little about the economic significance of such activity.

The clearest area of achievement under the Comprehensive Program has been the joint exploitation and development of natural resources for the economies of the member countries. Joint projects ease the investment burden on a single country when expansion of its production capacity is required to satisfy the needs of other members. Particular attention has been given to energy and fuels, forest industries, iron and steel, and various other metals and minerals. Most of this activity has necessarily been carried out in the Soviet Union, the great storehouse of natural resources within Comecon.

Although joint projects predated the Comprehensive Program, those carried out under the program in the 1970s were more

Table B. International Organizations Established by Interested Comecon Member Countries, December 1980 (by kind and in order of year of establishment)[1]

Organization	Headquarters	Year Established
I. *Institutes Attached to Comecon*		
Institute for Standardization	Moscow	1962
International Institute for Economic Problems of the World Socialist System	Moscow	1970
II. *Multilateral Organizations*		
A. *Industry*		
1. Interstate Economic Organizations		
Central Dispatching Board for the Unified Power Grid	Prague	1962
Organization for Cooperation in the Bearings Industry (Interpodshipnik)	Warsaw	1964
Organization for Cooperation in the Iron and Steel Industry (Intermetal)	Budapest	1964
International Society for Cooperation in Fruit and Vegetable Farm Machinery (Agromash)	Budapest	1965
International Branch Organization for Cooperation in Light Chemicals (Interchim)	Halle	1969
Intergovernmental Commission for Cooperation in Computer Technology (Eser)	Moscow	1969
International Organization for Cooperation in Electrical Equipment (Interelectro)	Moscow	1973
International Geological Expedition in the Mongolian People's Republic	Ulan Bator	1975
Joint Organization for Geological Exploration for Oil and Gas in the Baltic Sea on the Continental Shelf and in the Territorial Waters of the Soviet Union, Poland, and East Germany (Petrobaltic)	Gdansk	1975
2. International Economic Associations		
International Economic Association for Nuclear Power Equipment (Interatominstrument)	Warsaw	1972
International Economic Association for Cooperation in the Equipping, Construction, and Installation of Nuclear Power Stations (Interatomenergo)	Moscow	1973
International Economic Association for the Production of Machinery and Equipment for the Textile Industry (Intertextilmash)	Moscow	1973
International Economic Association in the Field of Chemical Fibers (Interchimvolokno)	Bucharest	1974
3. International Economic Partnerships[2]		
Scientific-Production Association for Weighing and Measuring Equipment (Interetalonpribor)	Moscow	1972

Table B.—Continued

Organization	Headquarters	Year Established
International Organization for Cooperation in the Testing of Large Field and High Pressure Electrotechnical Equipment (Interelectrotest)	None fixed	1973
International Service for the Repair of Oil Refining Installations	None fixed	1976
International Organization for Water Pollution Control (Intervodootchistka)	Sofia	1977
International Economic Association for Cooperation in Low Tonnage Oil Products, Additives, and Catalyzers (Internefteproduct)	Sofia	1978
B. *Transport and Communications*		
Organization for Railways Cooperation	Warsaw	1956
Railway Freight Car Pool	Prague	1963
International Association for Maritime Transport (Insa)	Gdynia	1970
Council for Joint Use of Containers in International Traffic	Bucharest	1974
International Economic Association for Cooperation in Barge Transport (Interlighter)	Budapest	1978
International Organization for Cooperation in Post and Telecommunications	None fixed	1957
International Organization for Satellite Telecommunications (Intersputnik)	Moscow	1971
C. *Medical Services*		
International Organization for Cooperation in the Provision of Equipment for Medical Facilities in Third Countries (Medunion)	Budapest	1973
D. *Financing and Credit Operations*		
International Bank for Economic Cooperation (IBEC)	Moscow	1963
International Investment Bank (IIB)	Moscow	1970
E. *Scientific-Technical Organizations*		
Joint Nuclear Research Institute	Dubna	1956
International Strong-Magnetic Fields and Low-Temperatures Laboratory	Wroclaw	1968
International Center for Scientific and Technical Information	Moscow	1969
International Center for Training in Mathematics	Warsaw	1972
International Center of the Academies of Sciences of Member Countries for Specialized Training in Problems of Heat and Mass Exchange	Minsk	1973
International Center for Marine Geology (Intermorgeo)	Riga	1973

Table B.—Continued

Organization	Headquarters	Year Established
International Center of the Academies of Sciences of Member Countries for Specialized Training in the Field of Electronic Microscopy	Halle	1975
International Center for Technical Cooperation in Geology (Intergeotekhnika)	Moscow	1974
International Center for Geological Information (Geoinform)	Prague	1977
III. *Bilateral Organizations*		
A. *Industry*		
Joint Enterprise for Coal Waste Recovery (Haldex)—Hungary-Poland	Katowice	1959
Joint Society for the Development of Mechanized, Intrafactory, Transport, and Storage Systems (Intransmash)—Bulgaria-Hungary	Sofia	1964
Joint Enterprise for Cotton Textiles Production (Friendship)—East Germany-Poland	Zawiercie	1972
International Association for Photochemicals (Assofoto)—East Germany-Soviet Union	Moscow	1973
Joint Organization for Cooperation in Electronic Components (Interkomponent)—Hungary-Poland	Warsaw	1973
Joint Association for Nonferrous Metals Mining and Processing (Mongolsovtsvetmet)—Mongolia-Soviet Union	Ulan Bator	1973
Joint Enterprise for Copper and Molybdenum Mining and Processing (Erdenet)—Mongolia-Soviet Union	Erdenet	1973
International Association for Cooperation in Household Chemicals (Domokhim)—East Germany-Soviet Union	Moscow	1974
Scientific-Production Association for Cooperation in Small Electrical Instruments (Electroinstrument)—Bulgaria-Soviet Union	Moscow	1975
B. *Transport*		
Joint Stock Company (Ulan Bator Railway)—Mongolia-Soviet Union	Ulan Bator	1949
Economic Organization for Cooperation in Port Management (Interport)—East Germany-Poland	Szczecin	1973
Joint Transport Agency (Dunaitrans)—Bulgaria-Soviet Union	Ruse	1976
Joint Agency for the Coordination of Maritime Services in the Black Sea (Intermorput)—Bulgaria-Soviet Union	Varna	1979
Joint Freight and Transport Association (Spedrapid)—Czechoslovakia-Poland	Gdynia	1979

Table B.—Continued

Organization	Headquarters	Year Established
C. *Science and Technology*		
Joint Institute for Cooperation in Computer Programming (Interprogramma)—Bulgaria-Soviet Union	Sofia	1976

[1]Some of these organizations involve all member countries of Comecon; many involve only some countries. Yugoslavia participates in some of these international organizations, as do a few other, nonmember countries.
[2]These are associations without juridical personality. One partner is assigned responsibility for implementation of collective decisions.

ambitious in format. Brief comparison of two multilateral projects in the same sector—the Druzhba oil pipeline project of the 1960s and the Soyuz (Union) natural gas pipeline project of the 1970s—serve to illustrate the major differences. Druzhba was jointly conceived and coordinated for the distribution of Soviet petroleum to Eastern Europe. Each country, however, was responsible for the financing and construction of that section of the pipeline that was planned for its territory. Soyuz, on the other hand, was jointly planned and implemented for the delivery of natural gas from the Soviet fields in Orenburg to Eastern Europe. Located entirely on Soviet territory, it was jointly financed, primarily through the International Investment Bank, and jointly constructed; East European countries were individually responsible for assigned sections of the pipeline. Another important difference was in the degree of Western participation. Whereas Druzhba was delayed because of the difficulty of obtaining the necessary steel pipe in the West, Soyuz was facilitated by an improved East-West political climate that permitted extensive purchase of materials and equipment in the West, much of it on liberal credit terms.

Joint development projects are usually organized on a "compensation" basis, a form of investment "in kind." Participating members advance materials, equipment and, more recently, manpower and are repaid through scheduled deliveries of the output resulting from, or distributed through, the new facility. Repayment includes a modest "fraternal" rate of interest, but the real financial return to the participating countries depends on the value of the output at the time of delivery. Deliveries at contract prices below world prices will provide an important extra return. No doubt the most important advantage from participation in joint projects, however, is the guarantee of long-term access to basic

Table C. Principal Multilateral Development Projects Undertaken by Comecon Members in the 1976–80 Plan Period

Project	Location	Dates[1]	Participation[2]	Volume of Annual Return Deliveries
Pulp mill	Soviet Union (Ust-Ilim, Siberia)	a. 1972 b. 1980	All but Czechoslovakia	205,000 tons
Asbestos combine	Soviet Union (Kiembaev, Urals Region)	a. 1973 b. 1980	All	40,000–50,000 tons
Development of natural gas condensate deposit and construction of transcontinental gas pipeline.	Soviet Union (Orenburg, Urals Region)	a. 1974 b. 1980	All; but limited role for Romania	15.5 billion cubic meters
Expansion of iron ore mining and dressing facilities (five combines)	Soviet Union (various locations, in area of Kursk Magnetic Anomaly and in Ukraine)	a. 1974 b. 1977–80	All but Romania	5.29 million tons
Additional facilities for production of ferro-alloys (seven plants)	Soviet Union (various locations in Ukraine and Kazakhstan)	a. 1974 b. 1979–80	All	n.a.
750-KV Vinnitsa-Albertirsa electric power transmission line[3]	Soviet Ukraine and Hungary (590 of the 860 kilometer length in Soviet Union)	a. 1974 b. 1978	All but Romania	3 billion kwh[4]
Nickel and cobalt production facilities	Cuba (Las Camariocas)	a. 1975 b. n.a.	All	n.a.

n.a.—not available

[1]a. Date agreement signed; b. Date facility operational.

[2]Extent of participation by Comecon members.

[3]Component of Comecon Master Plan for Long-Term Development of United Power Grids.

[4]Estimate.

fuels and raw materials in a world of increasing uncertainty of supply of such products. The multilateral development projects concluded under the Comprehensive Program formed the basis for Comecon's "Concerted Plan" for the 1976–80 period. According to the Communiqué announcing it, the plan (never published) envisaged joint investments in the total amount of some 9 billion rubles (nearly US$12 billion at the 1975 official exchange rate). The major, known projects included in the plan, together with basic details on each, indicated a key role for the Soviet Union (see table C, this Appendix).

Joint development projects are organized on both a multilateral and a bilateral basis. Although the former are generally larger and more significant in terms of the development of Comecon cooperation, the latter are more numerous and, collectively, may even be the more economically significant. Moreover, multilateral projects are typically implemented through bilateral agreements. An important example of a bilateral resource development project between members in the 1970s was the Soviet-Mongolian venture for the exploitation and development of copper and molybdenum deposits at Erdenet in Mongolia.

The Long-term Target Programs for Cooperation previously described provide the framework for joint projects among members in the 1980s. The first program to be implemented covers the area of energy, fuels, and raw materials. Particular priority under this program is given to the development of nuclear power capacity in Comecon countries based on Soviet technology. For example, members are contributing materials and equipment for the construction of a giant nuclear power facility at Khmelnitsky in the western Ukraine and of the line to bring the power it produces to East European industrial centers.

Resource development efforts under the target programs are emerging in a format rather different from the joint projects of the 1976–80 concerted plan. As of late 1982 no major multilateral projects involving joint construction had been announced for the 1981–85 plan period, nor had a new concerted plan been adopted. It appeared that the contribution of the East European countries to further Soviet resource development will take the form primarily of deliveries of specialized machinery and equipment, based on long-term bilateral cooperation agreements. These deliveries are to be repaid, on a current basis, by supplies of Soviet raw materials.

To supplement national efforts to upgrade indigenous technology, the Comprehensive Program lays much emphasis on cooperation in science and technology. The development of new technology is envisaged as a major object of cooperation; collaboration in resource development and specialization in production are to be facilitated by transfers of technology among members. At the 1971 Council session that adopted the program, the decision was taken to establish a special Council Committee for Scientific and Technical Cooperation to ensure the organization and fulfillment of the provisions of the program in this area. Jointly planned and coordinated research programs have extended to the creation of joint research institutes and centers. In terms of number of patents, documents, and other scientific and technical information exchanged, the available data indicate that the Soviet Union has been the dominant source of technology within Comecon. It has, on the whole, provided more technology to its East European partners than it has received from them, although the balance varies considerably from country to country depending upon relative levels of industrial development. Soviet science also forms the base for several high-technology programs for regional specialization and cooperation, such as nuclear power and computers.

Whereas transfers of technology in an earlier period were conducted according to principles that stressed the noncommercial character of Comecon cooperation in technology, the trend from the mid-1960s has been toward commercialization. The need to provide adequate financial incentives to stimulate effective technology transfer was formally recognized by the Comprehensive Program, which states that the "fruits of scientific and technical research shall be passed on . . .free of charge or for a financial compensation in accordance with agreements reached." Increasing links with world markets for industrial technology, as the result of the opening up of members' economies to relations with the Western industrial countries, gave impetus to this trend. Although the number of technology transfers among Comecon members was impressive, their quality generally lagged behind international standards. The inpouring of Western technology that began in the latter half of the 1960s displaced indigenous technology in many sectors. Yet it also provided a competitive stimulus to research and development and the process of technology transfer within Comecon, as did the increased opportunities to commercialize in the West the fruits of domestic research.

If the Comprehensive Program stimulated investment flows and technology transfers among members, there were also increased intra-Comecon flows of another important factor of production—labor. Most of these occurred in connection with joint resource development projects, e.g., Bulgarian workers aiding in the exploitation of Siberian forest resources, or Polish workers assisting in the construction of the Soyuz pipeline. Labor was also transferred in response to labor imbalances in member countries. Hungarian workers, for example, were sent to work in East Germany under a bilateral agreement between the two countries. Such transfers are restricted by the universal scarcity of labor that has emerged with the industrialization of the less developed Comecon countries. Moreover, the presence of foreign workers raises practical and ideological issues on socialist, planned economies. It should be noted, finally, that cooperation in the area of labor is by no means limited to planned exchanges of manpower. Comecon countries exchange information on experience in manpower planning and employment and wage policies through Comecon organs and activities.

Trends and Prospects

Comecon has served for more than three decades as a framework for cooperation among the planned economies. Over the years the Comecon system has grown steadily in scope and experience. It now encompasses a complex and sophisticated set of institutions that represent a striking advance over the state of the organization even at the beginning of the 1960s.

This institutional evolution has reflected changing and expanding goals. Initial, modest objectives of "exchanging experience" and providing "technical assistance" and other forms of "mutual aid" have been extended to the development of an integrated set of economies based on a coordinated international pattern of production and investment. These ambitious goals are pursued through a broad spectrum of cooperative measures extending from monetary to technological relations.

At the same time, the extraregional goals of the organization have expanded; other countries, both geographically distant and systemically different, are being encouraged to participate in Comecon activities. Parallel efforts have sought to develop Comecon as a mechanism through which to coordinate the foreign economic policies of the members as well as their actual relations with nonmember countries and such organizations as the EEC.

Progress toward these goals has been determined by a complex combination of forces, both internal and external to the organization. These forces may also be viewed in terms of their net effect, whether serving to advance or to impede progress toward established goals. In this vein they are sometimes referred to as "centripetal" or "centrifugal" forces.

Common political systems and ideologies have been the most fundamental factors uniting the members. Ironically, external factors have also served to foster Comecon cohesion. In the 1950s the isolation imposed by the Cold War required mutual assistance. Later the formation of a West European common market provided a major stimulus to the strengthening of Comecon goals and institutions. In the period of expanded East-West relations, Western technology and credits served as important elements in Comecon specialization agreements and development projects. After 1975 the international economic crisis and a worsening energy situation gave impetus to new, long-term Comecon programs that emphasized cooperation in resource development, especially in the energy sector.

Asymmetries of size and differences in levels of development among Comecon members have deeply affected the institutional character and evolution of the organization. The overwhelming dominance of the Soviet economy has necessarily meant that the bulk of intra-Comecon relations take the form of bilateral relations between the Soviet Union and the smaller Council members. The metaphor sometimes used to depict the Comecon system is that of a wheel, with the Soviet Union as the hub and the radial spokes representing its bilateral links with the other Comecon countries.

These asymmetries have served in other ways to impede progress toward multilateral trade and cooperation within the organization. The sensitivities of the smaller states have dictated that the sovereign equality of members remain a basic tenet of the organization. Despite inescapable Soviet political and economic dominance, sovereign equality has constituted a very real obstacle to the acquisition of supranational powers by Comecon organs.

The planned nature of the members' economies and the lack of effective market-price mechanisms to facilitate integration have further hindered progress toward Comecon goals. Without the automatic workings of market forces, progress must depend upon conscious acts of policy. This tends to politicize the processes of integration to a greater degree than is the case in market economies.

The more recent course of domestic and international events has produced a situation that may help to overcome these long-standing obstacles. Heightened dependence on Soviet fuels and other raw materials combined with shrinking external options in the 1980s may serve to break down the resistance of the smaller nations to more extensive joint planning. Even Romania, long regarded as the "maverick" among the members, has been forced to reemphasize its Comecon links.

The communiqué of the Thirtieth Council Session, in announcing the decision to work out Long-term Target Programs for Cooperation in key sectors, made significant reference to the surrounding circumstances. It stated that "in the conditions imposed by the present situation," the Council believes it necessary to "take further advantage of the opportunities opened up by the Comprehensive Program . . . to resolve jointly the series of vital economic problems faced by the member countries."

The joint planning instruments established in the late 1970s are now expected to serve as the principal vehicle for integration in the 1980s. The target programs set guidelines for coordinated investments in the longer term. Joint projects within the framework of the target programs are assembled in concerted plans for integration measures covering five-year periods. These commitments are in turn contained in special sections of national five-year plans. These programs and projects are reflected in still greater detail in long-term, bilateral cooperation agreements (through 1990), especially in those concluded at the beginning of the decade between the Soviet Union and the other members.

The strategy behind these programs is to enlist the members in the further development of Soviet raw materials and to concentrate more energy-intensive industrial development in the Soviet Union. The target programs for investments in the machine-building and transport sectors, as well as the central program for cooperation in fuels, energy, and raw materials development, are directed to these ends. For example, the East European members are developing their capacities to produce specialized machinery for the development of facilities for nuclear power generation and transmission, located for the most part in the Soviet Union.

What remains then of the Comprehensive Program? Its measures for integration through reinforcement of the intra-Comecon market-price mechanism appear all but dead. Instead there appears to be more life in its recommendations for joint planning. Joint planning and joint projects as conceived for the 1980s, however, fall short of the goals for broadened multilateral cooperation envisaged in the Comprehensive Program. The increased economic dependence of the smaller nations on the Soviet Union has reinforced traditional bilateral ties. The radial relationships symbolized in the metaphor of the wheel seem destined to dominate Comecon relations to an even greater degree in the 1980s.

* * *

The literature on Comecon in foreign languages, especially Russian, German, and French, is more extensive than that in English. The most recent edition of the principal, general work on the organization in English, Michael Kaser's *Comecon: Integration Problems of the Planned Economies*, was published in 1967. A new English-language book that should help to fill the gap for the intervening period is Giuseppe Schiavone's *The Institutions of Comecon* which, however, emphasizes the legal and institutional rather than the economic aspects of Comecon. Several works in English focus on more specific areas of Comecon activity, such as Edward A. Hewett's *Foreign Trade Prices in the Council for Mutual Economic Assistance* (1974), J. Wilczynski's *Technology in Comecon* (1974), and Jozef M. Van Brabant's *East European Cooperation: The Role of Money and Finance* (1977). The NATO Economic Directorate published the papers presented at a 1977 NATO colloquium in a volume entitled *Comecon: Progress and Prospects*. Another recent conference volume, edited by P. Marer and J.M. Montias, *East European Integration and East-West Trade* (1980), contains papers on Comecon institutions and activities written especially from the perspective of East-West relations.

Several studies by Soviet and East European authors have been translated into English and serve to convey various national perspectives. Among these are Sandor Ausch's *Theory and Practice of CMEA Cooperation* (1972), M. Senin's *Socialist Integration* (1973), and K. Pecsi's *Economic Questions of Production Integration Within the CMEA* (1978).

The Comecon Secretariat publishes a bimonthly bulletin in Russian containing articles and documentary material on the activities of the organization, entitled *Ekonomicheskoe Sotrudnichestvo Stran-Chlenov SEV*, with a table of contents and summary in English. The Secretariat also publishes an annual statistical volume, *Statisticheskii Ezhegodnik Stran-Chlenov SEV*; an English-language edition of the yearbook is published in Britain by Industrial Press. A collection of basic documents translated into English may be found in *The Multilateral Economic Cooperation of Socialist States: A Collection of Documents*.

For further guidance on published materials in English, French, and Russian, the reader may consult Linda Ervin's "The Council for Mutual Economic Assistance: A Selective Bibliography," published in 1975 by the Norman Paterson School of International Affairs, Carleton University, Ottawa. A revised and updated version of this bibliography is included in the volume by Schiavone cited previously. (For further information and complete citations, see Bibliography.)

Appendix C

The Warsaw Pact: Continuity and Change

THE FORMATION OF multilateral economic and political institutions in Eastern Europe was inextricably entwined with developments in East-West relations. It is difficult to avoid the impression that the creation of the Council for Mutual Economic Assistance (CMEA, or Comecon) and the Warsaw Treaty Organization (WTO, or the Warsaw Pact) responded to the dynamics of foreign policy initiatives by the United States and its West European allies. Comecon was created in January 1949 as a way of countering the lure of American economic assistance to Europe provided by the Marshall Plan, which had formally gone into effect the preceding June. In military affairs, the formation of the Warsaw Pact responded not to the creation of the North Atlantic Treaty Organization (NATO) in 1949 but rather to the complex diplomacy by which the Federal Republic of Germany (West Germany) was made a member.

West Germany's inclusion in Western defense arrangements had been formally endorsed by the North Atlantic Council at its February 1952 meeting in Lisbon. West Germany was to be rearmed and integrated into NATO through a series of agreements among Western foreign ministers signed in Bonn and Paris on May 26 and 27, 1952, which created the European Defense Community (EDC) and tied it to the North Atlantic framework. The Bonn and Paris accords were quickly ratified by the United States Senate but met considerable resistance in France. After the American election in 1952, the new administration of President Dwight D. Eisenhower attempted to pressure the French into ratifying the proposed EDC. During his speech to the North Atlantic Council in Paris on December 13, 1953, Secretary of State John Foster Dulles threatened an "agonizing reappraisal" of American policy should the EDC not go into effect.

During these same months, a new leadership began to emerge in Moscow after Stalin's death in March 1953. Nikita Khrushchev, first secretary of the Communist Party of the Soviet Union (CPSU), and Georgiy Malenkov, chairman of the Council of Ministers, vied for power by advancing competitive programs for political and economic change. Beneath these political maneuvers, however, real debates emerged within the Soviet leadership on a wide range of foreign and military policies. In this context the Soviets set forth proposals for alternative security arrangements in Europe; they even held out the bait of "free elections" for an all-German government during the Berlin meeting of French, British, American, and Soviet foreign ministers in January and

February 1954. In August, partly as a result of this Soviet foreign policy, the French National Assembly defeated the EDC, and on October 23 the Allies signed agreements in Paris by which the occupation of West Germany was to be ended. Allied troops were to remain on German soil by invitation of the West German government, and that country was to be admitted to NATO.

The inclusion of West Germany in NATO and its subsequent rearmament were bitter defeats for Soviet diplomacy, which during the preceding five years had placed top priority on preventing that result. In February 1955 Khrushchev emerged victorious in his rivalry with Malenkov and launched a period of dynamic foreign and domestic policy initiatives across a broad front of issues. Khrushchev's signing of the Austrian State Treaty on May 15, 1955, which provided for the withdrawal of Soviet troops from Austrian territory, can be explained partly by continued Soviet efforts to head off West German rearmament. Nonetheless, the Paris agreements bringing West Germany into NATO became operational that same month, and on May 14 the Soviet Union, Poland, Czechoslovakia, Hungary, Romania, Bulgaria, and Albania signed a treaty of friendship, cooperation, and mutual assistance. They also signed a Resolution on the Formation of a Unified Command of the Armed Forces. The Warsaw Pact had been created (see fig. A, this Appendix).

The Early Years, 1955–64

This genesis of the organization explains much of its early history. The Warsaw Pact was created not so much as a defensive military alliance as an exercise in East-West diplomacy. Its purpose from 1955 to 1962 was, first, to signal Soviet displeasure with the integration of West Germany into NATO and, second, to contain the effects on Eastern Europe of political and economic dynamics in the West. The former purpose was underlined in the first meeting of the Warsaw Pact governing body, known as the Political Consultative Committee (PCC), held in Prague during January 1956. The communiqué of that meeting indicated that the German Democratic Republic (East Germany) had been admitted into the Joint Command and reasserted the line of Soviet foreign policy that advocated an all-European collective security system.

Events quickly forced changes in the rudimentary organization of the Warsaw Pact. Khrushchev's ideological innovations at the Twentieth Party Congress of the CPSU in February 1956 represented the most fundamental changes of Soviet policy since 1928. He laid a new basis for peaceful coexistence between the socialist (see Glossary) and capitalist states. More profoundly, he reversed the Stalinist model for relations among socialist states according to which each communist party had carefully based its own political and economic system on the Soviet pattern. Now Khrushchev sanctioned diversity by explicitly condoning "many roads to

Figure A. European Members of the Warsaw Pact, 1983

socialism." This alteration of the Soviet position alone would have had profound effects, but Krushchev also made a "secret speech" in which he detailed the "crimes" of Stalin against the leadership of the CPSU. In many countries of Eastern Europe this de-Stalinization campaign had the effect of undercutting the political leaders who had achieved power during the years of Stalin's rule. Within the year, Wladyslaw Gomulka had replaced his Stalinist rivals as first secretary of the Polish party and, with the explicit sanction of a high-level Soviet delegation, the Stalinist Matyas Rakosi had been forced out of leadership in Budapest. Conditions deteriorated rapidly, and by October a full-scale revolution had developed in Hungary. The Soviet army intervened to suppress the revolt in Budapest, and the Soviet Union found itself under nearly universal opprobrium. Pressed to justify its actions, the Kremlin cited the Warsaw Pact as the legal basis for stationing troops on the soil of its East European allies and for intervening to preserve socialism within the bloc. Thus, out of adversity, a more specific purpose for the Pact had been born. Some evidence suggests that during the crisis of 1956 the Soviet Union actually may have considered making the Warsaw Pact an instrument of genuine collective security based on a form of consensual decisionmaking. But a real effort to broaden participation in security decisions did not come until after the Czechoslovak crisis of 1968.

Three dynamics characterized the Pact during its first decade (1955–64). First, Moscow realized that its post hoc rationalization of the Hungarian intervention by reference to the Warsaw treaties rested on tenuous legal grounds, and in late 1956 and early 1957 it proceeded to sign bilateral agreements with Poland, East Germany, Romania, and Hungary for deployment of Soviet troops in those countries. Second, as Robin Remington argues in her study *The Warsaw Pact: Case Studies in Communist Conflict Resolution*, a pattern developed during these years in which the Soviets used the Pact to gain support for their policy initiatives, although not always with complete success. In 1960 this purpose of the Warsaw Pact took on new meaning. In April the simmering Soviet polemical dispute with the Chinese Communist Party (CCP) broke into the open when Beijing published its sharp attack on Moscow. By summer, the Soviets were clearly attempting to keep Albania (allied with the CCP in this dispute) in line by threatening exclusion from the Warsaw Pact and, finally, by actually forcing the Albanians out of it. Thus, the Pact became an instrument for rallying East European support for Soviet positions in a steadily escalating Sino-Soviet dispute. Third, the Soviet military command began to flesh out the military arm of the Pact by helping its allies build national armies and by providing them military equipment that was being replaced with newer technology in the Soviet armed forces (see table A, this Appendix). This pattern of equipping its allies with weapons one generation behind those used by Soviet forces continued into the 1980s and served as a potential restraint on East European national forces that might contemplate resistance to Soviet interference in crises such as

Table A. Representative Military Equipment in Warsaw Pact Forces, 1982[1]

Equipment—Type	First Appeared in Soviet Forces	Appeared in Other Warsaw Pact Forces
Aircraft		
Tu-22M/26 (Backfire) medium-range bomber	1974	Not in Pact forces, 1982
Tu-22 (Blinder) medium-range bomber	1962	Not in Pact forces, 1982
SU-19/24 (Fencer) ground attack fighter-bomber	1974	Not in Pact forces, 1982
MiG-23/27 (Flogger) fighter-bomber[2]	1971	Bulgaria (1977) East Germany (1980) Hungary (1980) Czechoslovakia (1978) Romania (1981)
SU-7 (Fitter A) ground attack fighter-bomber	1959	Czechoslovakia (before 1970) Poland (before 1970)
SU-20 (Fitter C) ground attack fighter-bomber	1974	Poland (1976) Czechoslovakia (1976)
Missiles		
SS-20 IRBM (3,700- to 5,500-km range)	1977	Not in Pact forces, 1982
SS-5 IRBM (Skean; 3,500-km range)	1961	Not in Pact forces, 1982
SS-4 MRBM (Sandal; 1,800-km range)	1959	Not in Pact forces, 1982
SS-12 SRBM (Scaleboard; 700- to 800-km range; being replaced by SS-23)	1969	Not in Pact forces, 1982
SS-1 (Scud B; 160- to 270-km range; being replaced by SS-22)	1965	Bulgaria (1971) Czechoslovakia (1970) East Germany (1970) Hungary (1973) Poland (1970) Romania (1973)
FROG 3 through 7 (40- to 60-km range; being replaced by SS-21)	1957–65	Bulgaria (1970) Czechoslovakia (1970) East Germany (1970) Hungary (1970) Poland (1970) Romania (1973)
Armor		
T-54/55 medium tank	1954	In all forces before 1970
T-62 medium tank	1962	Bulgaria (1971) Czechoslovakia (before 1970) East Germany (1971) Hungary (1971) Poland (1971) Romania (1971)

Table A.—Continued

Equipment—Type	First Appeared in Soviet Forces	Appeared in Other Warsaw Pact Forces
T-72 medium tank..........................	1972	Bulgaria (1980)
		Czechoslovakia (1980)
		East Germany (1980)
		Hungary (1980)
		Poland (1980)
		Romania (1980)
PT-76 light tank	Before 1969	Bulgaria (1970)
		East Germany (1970)
		Hungary (1970)
		Poland (1970)
		Romania (1974)
BMD infantry combat vehicle (ICV) ...	1974	Not in Pact forces, 1982
BMP infantry combat vehicle (ICV) ...	Before 1973	Bulgaria (1981)
		Czechoslovakia (1976)
		East Germany (1975)
		Hungary (1980)
		Poland (1978)

[1]These data are for illustrative purposes only; caution should be exercised in using them. The missions of aircraft, for example the MiG-21 and MiG-23, vary according to models, and a MiG-21 in one air force may have different capabilities from that in another. Moreover, some data vary according to categories reported by the International Institute for Strategic Studies and do not represent actual dates equipment was introduced into military inventories.
[2]MiG-27 not in Pact forces, 1982.

Source: Based on information from Institute for Strategic Studies, *The Military Balance, 1968–69* (through 1982–83), London, 1968 (through 1982).

occurred in Czechoslovakia in 1968 and Poland in 1980–81.

The organizational structure of the Pact during its first 15 years was quite simple. At the top of the hierarchy was the PCC, which was supposed to meet twice a year—an objective seldom achieved (see table B, this Appendix). In addition, the Pact created a standing commission, probably composed of personnel from the various foreign ministries, and a joint secretariat, but institutional arrangements were secret. The purposes listed previously did not require elaborate machinery for consultation.

A Revitalized Alliance, 1965–69

The role of the Warsaw Pact began to change after the ouster of Khrushchev by a new "collective leadership" (general secretary of the CPSU, Leonid Brezhnev, and chairman of the Council of Ministers, Aleksei Kosygin) in October 1964. Khrushchev had fallen, in part, because his political style had been volatile. The new leadership quickly attempted to contrast that style with a more businesslike approach to public affairs. Their policy stressed

Table B. Political Consultation in the Warsaw Pact, 1969–83

Year	Political Consultative Committee (PCC)	Party and Government Leaders Outside PCC	Foreign Ministers	Defense Ministers
1969	March 17 (Budapest)	December 3–4 (Moscow)	October 30 (Prague)	December 22–23 (Moscow)
1970	August 20 (Moscow) December 2 (East Berlin)	May 8–10 (Prague)	June 21–22 (Budapest)	May 21–22 (Sofia) December 21–23 (Budapest)
1971		March 31–April 9 (Moscow, 24th CPSU[1] Congress August 2 (Crimea) December 8 (Warsaw, 6th PZPR[2] Congress)	February 18–19 (Bucharest) November 30–December (Warsaw)	March 2–3 (Budapest)
1972	January 25–26 (Prague)	July 31 (Crimea) December 20–24 (Moscow, 50th anniversary of Soviet Union)		
1973		July 30–31 (Crimea)	January 15–16 (Moscow)	February 8 (Warsaw)
1974	April 17–18 (Warsaw)			February 6–7 (Bucharest)
1975		March 18 (Budapest, 11th HSWP[3] Congress December 9 (Warsaw, 7th PZPR Congress)	December 15–16 (Moscow)	January 7–8 (Moscow)
1976	November 25–26 (Bucharest)	February 24-March 6 (Moscow, 25th CPSU Congress) June 29–30 (Berlin, conference of European communist parties)		

Table B. Continued.

Year	Political Consultative Committee (PCC)	Party and Government Leaders Outside PCC	Foreign Ministers	Defense Ministers
		August (Crimea)		
1977		July–August (Crimea)	May 25–26 (Moscow)	
1978	November 22–23 (Moscow)		April 25	May 15–20 (Budapest)
1979		July–August (Crimea) October 5 (Berlin, 30th anniversary of East Germany)	May 14–15 (Budapest)	
1980	May 14–15 (Warsaw) December 5 (Moscow)	July–August (Crimea)	July 8–9 October 19–20 (Crimea)	
1981		February 24 (Moscow, 26th CPSU Congress)	December 1–2 (Bucharest)	December 1–4 (Moscow)
1982			October 21–22 (Moscow)	
1983	January 4–5 (Prague)			January 11–13 (Prague)

[1]CPSU—Communist Party of the Soviet Union.
[2]PZPR—Polish United Workers' Party.
[3]HSWP—Hungarian Socialist Workers' Party.

the importance of consultations among the socialist states—on economic matters, within the framework of Comecon, and on military matters, within the framework of the Pact. Meetings of the former in Prague and of the latter in Warsaw during the first months of the Brezhnev-Kosygin leadership were attended by much publicity. The Central Committee of the CPSU and the Soviet Council of Ministers reportedly gave public approval of the actions of the Soviet delegation to the PCC in January 1965. At the Twenty-third Party Congress of the CPSU in March 1966, Brezhnev underlined Soviet determination to upgrade the importance and to improve the framework of the Warsaw Pact.

This campaign to make better use of the Pact framework had its origins in real political issues. First, Moscow needed a mechanism for coping with the complex diversity that had emerged within the socialist bloc. The Sino-Soviet dispute had not abated after the fall of Krushchev; indeed, China had launched its radical political experiment (known as the Great Proletarian Cultural Revolution), and relations between Moscow and Beijing had deteriorated even further. Romania had also emerged during the early and mid-1960s as a source of real challenge to Soviet leadership in the bloc. The new Kremlin leadership was willing to make concessions for shared decisionmaking and to work for consensus within Comecon and the Pact simply because it needed support from other communist parties for its positions in these bloc conflicts.

Second, relations with the United States had been severely strained by escalating American involvement in Vietnam during 1965, and Soviet relations with the West were greatly complicated as a result of a developing mini-rapprochement with President Charles de Gaulle of France. The relationship with Paris offered an alternative to strained relations with Washington and underlined the degree to which the NATO alliance was in disarray. De Gaulle had made known his intention to withdraw French military forces from joint NATO command in March 1966, precisely at the time of the Twenty-third Party Congress when Brezhnev stressed the need for further Pact coordination.

Third, in 1966 West German policy toward the Soviet Union and Eastern Europe began to change profoundly. Bonn sent a dramatic "Peace Note" to most countries of the world on March 25, 1966, and a "Grand Coalition" government formed in the fall of that year by Chancellor Kurt Georg Kiesinger brought the Social Democrats a share of power. Kiesinger made an important speech to the Bundestag on December 13, 1966, in which for the first time he indicated West Germany's willingness to enter into diplomatic relations with the socialist states of Eastern Europe. These West German initiatives were rife with trouble for the Soviet Union and constituted a strong motivation for using the multilateral institutions as mechanisms for holding the members in line. Moscow appeared prepared, for example, to make considerable concessions to Romanian party chief Nicolae Ceausescu at the July 1966 meeting of the Warsaw Pact's PCC in Bucharest because the Kremlin wanted his support for common positions. Nonetheless, Romania established diplomatic relations with West Germany in February 1967. The Soviets then used a meeting of European communist parties at Karlovy Vary (Carlsbad), Czechoslovakia, in April to attempt to build a common line against the threat of West Germany's *Ostpolitik* (Eastern policy).

Finally, throughout most of the 1960s but with special intensity from 1964 to 1969, military cooperation within the Pact was extended. This was accomplished by modernizing weapons and by developing a vigorous program of joint military exercises.

The Alliance Matures, 1969–82

The most serious challenge to Soviet leadership in Eastern Europe came during the Prague Spring. After the pro-Soviet general secretary, Antonin Novotny, had been replaced by Alexander Dubcek in January 1968, irresistible popular demand for reforms provoked rapid liberalization of the Communist Party of Czechoslovakia (Komunisticka strana Ceskoslovenska—KSC) and the governmental system. Inevitably, these developments carried a strong implicit criticism of Soviet interference in Czechoslovakia, but for a time Moscow attempted to restrain the process and to contain its effects within the region. These efforts were mounted explicitly in the context of the Warsaw Pact. A meeting among party chiefs at Dresden on March 23 proclaimed that the unity of the Bulgarian, East German, Polish, Soviet, and Czechoslovak parties revealed the effectiveness of the Warsaw Pact and called for vigilance against "aggressive intentions and subversive action of imperialist forces." The message was a clear warning to the Czechoslovaks even though Dubcek had participated in the meeting. On July 15 the same party leaders (except for Dubcek, who did not attend) sent a letter to Prague warning Czechoslovak party leaders in unmistakable terms, again placing their "fraternal assistance" in the context of their unity within the Pact.

When the invasion came during the night of August 20–21, armed forces from these same countries participated. Thus the Warsaw Pact had developed into a useful tool for Moscow's policy, although the degree to which the other parties also felt threatened by events in Czechoslovakia should not be minimized. The Soviet leadership did not have to rely on coercion to get the support of the communist parties in East Berlin, Warsaw, and Sofia. The Hungarians participated with less enthusiasm, and Ceausescu refused to support either the campaign to coerce the Dubcek leadership or the invasion itself. This, then, was the context within which a remarkable set of changes occurred in East European political and economic institutions.

Two separate campaigns had characterized Soviet relations with Eastern Europe since 1969: economic integration in Comecon and the development of institutional cooperation within the Warsaw Pact framework. The invasion of Czechoslovakia in 1968 created substantial difficulties for Kremlin policies. It divided the Soviet leadership and undermined the very support among other communist parties that they had so carefully cultivated during the 1960s as the Sino-Soviet dispute became more and more exacerbated. Nevertheless, shortly after the invasion of Czechoslovakia—and while several leaders of the KSC were in Moscow as virtual hostages—Brezhnev delivered a speech in which he claimed the right of Warsaw Pact forces to intervene in the affairs of a Pact member. Almost as soon as it was articulated, this so-called Brezhnev Doctrine began to be hedged; by the time violence broke out along the Soviet-Chinese border in March 1969, a considerable retreat had already occurred. By the time of the June 1969 conference of communist and workers' parties, the radical justification for Soviet intervention in other socialist states devised the preceding autumn had already been made a low priority, if not abandoned entirely. These two pressures—the need to repair the damage of the intervention in Czechoslovakia and the eruption of violence in the Sino-Soviet dispute—were, of course, mutually reinforcing. Moreover, the election of Willy Brandt's government in West Germany and its articulation of *Ostpolitik* and the willingness of President Richard M. Nixon to enter SALT I negotiations coincided in the autumn of 1969 to offer a possibility of quite different politics toward the West. As a result the tactics, if not the long-range strategy, of Soviet foreign policy were reconstituted fundamentally. The demands of this détente policy determined Soviet foreign policy, including relations with other socialist countries, at least during the period between 1969 and 1974. Détente clearly altered some of the substantive bases of Soviet foreign policy and may even have altered some aspects of the Kremlin's internal balance of power. This is not to say that détente removed the conflicts between the Soviet Union and its western adversaries but rather that the demands of the bilateral treaties between East and West defining Europe's boundaries, the Berlin agreements, SALT I and II, the Final Act of the Conference on Security and Cooperation in Europe (CSCE—popularly known as the Helsinki Agreement), the negotiations on the Mutual and Balanced Force Reduction (MBFR), and significant increases in East-West trade all required that the tone of Soviet foreign policy be altered. Among other changes, the alterations in relations within the Warsaw Pact and Comecon have been striking. Of course, change has been slow, incremental, and often atmospheric. But the question naturally arises whether gradations of tone and shades of change can, or do, become changes of substance.

Soviet treatment of its relations with the other socialist countries varied in tone during the years of Brezhnev's political leadership in Moscow. It is useful to look at the four Central Committee reports delivered by Brezhnev to the Twenty-third (1966), Twenty-fourth (1971), Twenty-fifth (1976), and Twenty-sixth (1981) party congresses of the CPSU. Brezhnev's report to the Twenty-third Party Congress shared the assessment of the other two that the strength and prestige of the socialist system were increasing, but the emphasis was clearly on bilateral relations between Moscow and the other socialist capitals as evidenced in the treaties of friendship, cooperation, and mutual assistance.

Brezhnev's claims regarding Comecon's success were restricted to its rising trade; the "dovetailing of national-economic plans" was seen as a future development that was necessary if the socialist economies were "to keep up with the turbulent scientific and technological revolution." He also cited military cooperation among the Warsaw Pact armies. The Twenty-third Party Congress set as its goal the further development of cooperation and the strengthening of unity within the socialist bloc; the treatment of Soviet relations with China was strikingly moderate. The Vietnam Conflict and the "military adventures" of the United States were the focus of Soviet policy in 1966.

The contrast with Brezhnev's treatment of these same subjects at the Twenty-fourth Party Congress was unmistakable. Claims with respect to the strengthening of the world socialist system were inflated. The latter had become "a mighty accelerator of historical progress." In 1971 the Warsaw Pact was credited with providing the framework for "coordinating the foreign-policy activity of the fraternal countries," and the emphasis was clearly far more on accommodation of *national* peculiarities among socialist states and communist parties. Brezhnev's report to the Twenty-fourth Party Congress was striking in its candor about "certain difficulties and complications [that] continued to be manifest in the socialist world." He claimed that the "socialist world, with its successes and its prospects, with all its problems, is still a young and growing social organism in which not everything has become stable and in which many things bear the imprint of past historical eras."

Although these trends in the claims of the Soviet leadership continued after the Twenty-fourth Party Congress, subsequent emphasis was on continuity and agreement. References to difficulties became less frequent. Both the Warsaw Pact and Comecon were represented as the basis for a changing system of relations among communist parties and states in which the emphasis was to be on cooperation and coordination. Brezhnev underlined this theme in his report to the Twenty-fifth Party Congress on February 24, 1976. He said that "probably there has not been one meeting of the Politburo at which we did not consider one question or another related to strengthening the unity of the fraternal countries, developing cooperation with them." He argued that the "gradual evening out" of their economic development and gradual political integration "is now very clearly evident as a law-governed pattern." In addition to extolling the virtues of the Warsaw Pact as a forum for political consultation among the socialist states and of Comecon as an instrument of economic integration, he argued that the whole program of closer socialist cooperation had "vast political significance" and that it would create the material basis for a communist international community.

Treatment of the Pact and Comecon at the Twenty-sixth Party Congress in February 1981 differed little from that of five years earlier. The Soviet leadership had, apparently, found its stride in treating relations among the communist states and parties. Brezhnev did note with some pride a "fundamental unity of views on all major problems of social and economic development and international politics." And he attributed that successful coordination of policy to the continued pattern of consultation among the countries of "socialist commonwealth." He singled out the Warsaw Pact committees of defense and foreign ministers for special commendation. He took pride in the Interkosmos program by which cosmonauts from other socialist states had joined their Soviet counterparts in highly publicized joint space missions. On other matters he simply continued themes developed during the 1970s, with the notable exception of Poland. Although he placed the social upheaval in Poland within the context of the "marked exacerbation of the ideological struggle," Brezhnev's remarks also seemed to reflect awareness of the implicit criticism events in Poland held for party rule in general.

On Poland, the Soviet leadership was united. Solidarity and Warsaw's response to it represented a fundamental challenge not only to the fabric of the Warsaw Pact and Comecon but also to the legitimacy of communist elites throughout Eastern Europe. Moscow played the issue within its bloc institutions with some delicacy, and an alteration of policy could not have been expected with Brezhnev's death in November 1982. In fact, the new general secretary, Yuri Andropov, in his first public statement of policy to the Central Committee Plenum on November 22, showed pride in underlining the continuity of foreign policy. In the context of reaffirming the decisions of the previous three party congresses and discussing tensions in the international arena, Andropov stated that "the primary concern of our party will continue to be the strengthening of the socialist community. In unity lies our strength, an earnest of ultimate success even in the most serious trials."

The Parallel Campaign in Comecon

At the Twenty-third Council Session of Comecon in April 1969, the members of that organization endorsed the concept of socialist economic integration. Since that time a major effort has been made within Comecon to put the concept into practice (see Appendix B). In July 1971 the Comecon participants adopted a Comprehensive Program for cooperation and integration that included measures designed to increase intrabloc economic cooperation in the 1971–75 five-year plan period and to begin coordination over a longer time frame as well. This was followed in 1975 by the Coordinated Plan for Multilateral Integration Measures, adopted at the Twenty-ninth Council Session of

Comecon which outlined coordinated activities, such as joint investment and greater production specialization for the 1976–80 five-year plan, and sought to enlarge the scope of the integration effort by making it more multilateral. At the annual session held in Berlin in July 1976, a new form of coordinated planning—called Long-term Target Programs for Cooperation—was adopted in an attempt to facilitate long-term joint projects requiring the coordination of more than one branch of the members' economies.

By the time the Thirty-fourth Council Session of Comecon met in Prague from June 17 to 19, 1980, the emphasis on economic integration had shifted. Although that meeting heard a report on "progress in coordination of Comecon countries' national economic plans for 1981–1985," the emphasis since the 1976 meeting had clearly been on "long-term, specific-purpose, cooperation programs." The latter were agreements among the members to develop five-year plans in specific functional areas. Plans for raw materials supply had received the most attention during the 1976–80 period, but the emphasis seemed to be shifting to developing economic infrastructure in the 1981–85 plans—specifically in the areas of transportation and computers.

At the Twenty-sixth Party Congress in 1981, Brezhnev underlined the need to supplement "the coordination of plans with the coordination of economic policy as a whole." This idea was represented as a program to move beyond "socialist integration on the basis of long-term specific-purpose programs," an objective that would require attention during the "next two five-year plans" (that is, throughout the 1980s). Still, he recognized the greater complexity of international economic relations, a fact underlined by his admission that the Soviet Union had accumulated an 8 billion ruble surplus in trade with its Comecon partners between 1976 and 1981.

But Soviet policy toward Comecon did not develop smoothly after the Twenty-sixth Party Congress. The Polish crisis, and in particular United States sanctions after the imposition of martial law in December 1981, drew international attention to Poland's external hard currency debts. The Soviets responded by attempting to mount a campaign within the socialist bloc to limit trade with capitalist states and to build an economic strategy based on reduced East-West economic cooperation and more self-sufficiency within Comecon. But the Soviet Union's own economic needs compelled it to reduce exports of oil to its bloc partners and to raise prices for energy, causing tensions to rise from late 1981 throughout 1982. These tensions probably surfaced in the Thirty-sixth Council Session of Comecon in Budapest in June 1982 and the 105th meeting of its executive committee in Moscow in January 1983. There were repeated rumors of Soviet efforts to convene a Comecon "summit" at the heads of state level, but other members (including the Hungarians and Romanians) reportedly resisted this idea throughout 1982.

Foreign Policy Coordination in the Warsaw Pact

The picture of institutional adaptation that emerges from an examination of Comecon during the post-1969 period is paralleled within the Warsaw Treaty Organization. Once again the tone and structure of Brezhnev's report to the Twenty-fifth Party Congress are instructive. He first mentioned the Warsaw Pact in a political context, describing it as a framework for "thoroughgoing multifaceted and systematic contacts" among the communist parties of the socialist states. He made it clear that the Soviet leadership conceived the Pact as a mechanism for coordinating policies: "Systematic meetings, both multilateral and bilateral, enable us to consult on all major problems that come up, to share in one another's joys and sorrows, so to speak, and jointly to map out the paths of our future advance."

It is possible that the assumption widely held in the West that the Warsaw Pact is an instrument of Soviet domination and control in Eastern Europe obscures changes in its structure and function. There has been considerable differentiation in the institutions of the Warsaw Pact, and the pattern of consultations among its members' top leaders has been particularly intense in the period since 1969. Meetings of the PCC and the Council of Foreign Ministers (CFM), in particular, have been used to achieve support for various elements of Soviet détente policy. For example, PCC meetings in 1972 and 1974 proposed and endorsed the campaign for the Helsinki Agreement. The CFM met in May 1977 to coordinate policy for the Belgrade review session of the CSCE Final Act (signed in Helsinki in July 1975) and twice in 1980 to prepare for the second review meeting of the Helsinki Agreement that was held in Madrid beginning that November.

Soviet foreign policy shifted to a more defensive posture with respect to NATO in the late 1970s. A consensus gradually had emerged within NATO that the Soviet and Warsaw Pact military buildup represented a threat that required some response. In particular the November 1978 Warsaw Pact proposals were directly intended to counter agreements concluded at the May NATO Council meeting in Washington for a long-term commitment to increase defense spending by 3 percent a year in constant dollars. The May 1980 PCC meeting reiterated Brezhnev's proposals for reduction of military forces in Europe, which had been made the preceding October in an effort to head off the December 1979 NATO agreements to place Pershing II and ground-launch cruise missiles in Europe as a counter to Warsaw Pact theater nuclear forces. This pattern became even more intense under the pressure of the Polish crisis in late 1981. It seemed that Soviet "peace initiatives" were the only thing on which the Warsaw Pact could easily agree, and the CFM met in Bucharest in early December 1981 to support Soviet positions on arms control. Romanian resistance to the Soviet line on these matters caused Soviet Foreign Minister Andrei Gromyko to stay over in Bucharest for what was apparently a tense session with Romanian party chief Ceausescu, who subsequently organized a massive peace march in his capital to underline his independent position on these issues. That Soviet policy within the Warsaw Pact had become reduced to its focus on Moscow's "peace campaign" was underlined again by the meeting of the PCC in Prague in January 1983. It was Andropov's first session as head of the Soviet delegation, and the meeting clearly was orchestrated to give a public boost to arms control initiatives he had enunciated in a major speech in December in Moscow. These public demonstrations of Pact unity on "peace" issues were designed partly to appeal to opposition within NATO regarding the deployment of United States Pershing II missiles and ground-launched cruise missiles.

Thus, one purpose of Warsaw Pact consultations remained constant from the Pact's earliest years until the period after 1969. The Pact had its origins in attempts to prevent (and then to contain) the effects of West German integration into the NATO defense structure. In the late 1960s the Warsaw Pact sought to reduce the impact of West Germany's diplomatic initiatives toward the socialist states. The reactive nature of Soviet policy in the Pact framework has had the effect of making the institution serve dual, and sometimes contradictory, purposes. Looked at in one way, of course, the Warsaw Pact has permitted Moscow to manage its relations with other socialist states. But conversely, the degree to which the Soviet Union has needed the support of its allies has permitted the latter to use the same framework to broaden their own participation in decisionmaking. Not all "consultations" have resulted in the simple adoption of Soviet formulas on policy issues under consideration. The brevity of the March 1969 meeting suggested the Kremlin's appreciation that it could not risk more serious policy discussion in the context of the invasion of Czechoslovakia and the Sino-Soviet border dispute. There is evidence to suggest that the Soviets failed to convince other participants in the November 1976 Bucharest PCC meeting to support fully their position on relations among socialist states as well as considerable evidence that the November 1978 communiqué avoided topics on which Moscow had pressed agreement—namely, the Middle East and the NATO defense increases. Thus, the tensions that surfaced in 1981–82 had precedent in previous controversies.

The Institutional Framework

Paralleling these political uses of the Warsaw Pact, significant changes have taken place in its institutional arrangements. The command structure of the organization has been modified. Arrangements for political consultations have been expanded and, as has been suggested, greater use has been made of them. The quantity and quality of Pact forces have been altered. Along with these alterations, there have been shifts in military doctrine, and there is some evidence that the Pact has coordinated policies toward the Third World.

The crucial issue, of course, is whether such changes have actually transformed, or are transforming, political and military relationships in Eastern Europe in any basic way. The Warsaw Pact is perceived by its members primarily as a military alliance, and military details are the most jealously guarded of all Soviet security secrets. Although the picture that foreign analysts can piece together is sketchy, sufficient details do exist to permit some cautious hypotheses about the character of the changes in the Warsaw Pact. Both the limits of available information and the nature of the changes in institutional structure and forces suggest that the Pact has adjusted to the evolving international situation incrementally and not dramatically. This assessment, however, does not necessarily mean that the changes are insignificant. Although, or perhaps because, the alteration of procedures after 1969 grew out of the turbulence within the Pact during the mid- and late 1960s and followed closely on the Czechoslovak intervention, one might have expected them to bring about a reassertion of Soviet hegemony. But most observers agree that this has not proved to be the case. Instead the changes since 1969 have, if anything, increased the opportunity for East Europeans to assert national control over their components in the Pact's combined forces and have preserved roughly the same balance of forces among national contingents and between Warsaw Pact and NATO forces.

The New Command Structure

The most interesting changes have occurred in the command structure. The decisions of the March 1969 meeting of the Pact probably had less effect on its principal institution (the PCC) than on any other organ, although its membership was changed slightly. Before 1969 the PCC had comprised party first (or general) secretaries, chairmen of the respective councils of ministers, foreign ministers, and defense ministers. But the Budapest meeting established a separate Council of Defense Ministers (CDM), and the defense ministers are apparently no longer included in PCC meetings (see fig. B, this Appendix). At least that has been the case in the six full meetings held since the Budapest reorganization (see table B, this Appendix). The Bucharest meeting of the PCC in November 1976 formally created the Council of Foreign Ministers (CFM). The foreign ministers had been meeting separately and regularly since the early 1970s to coordinate policy on the CSCE and the MBFR; the creation of the CFM made the arrangement official.

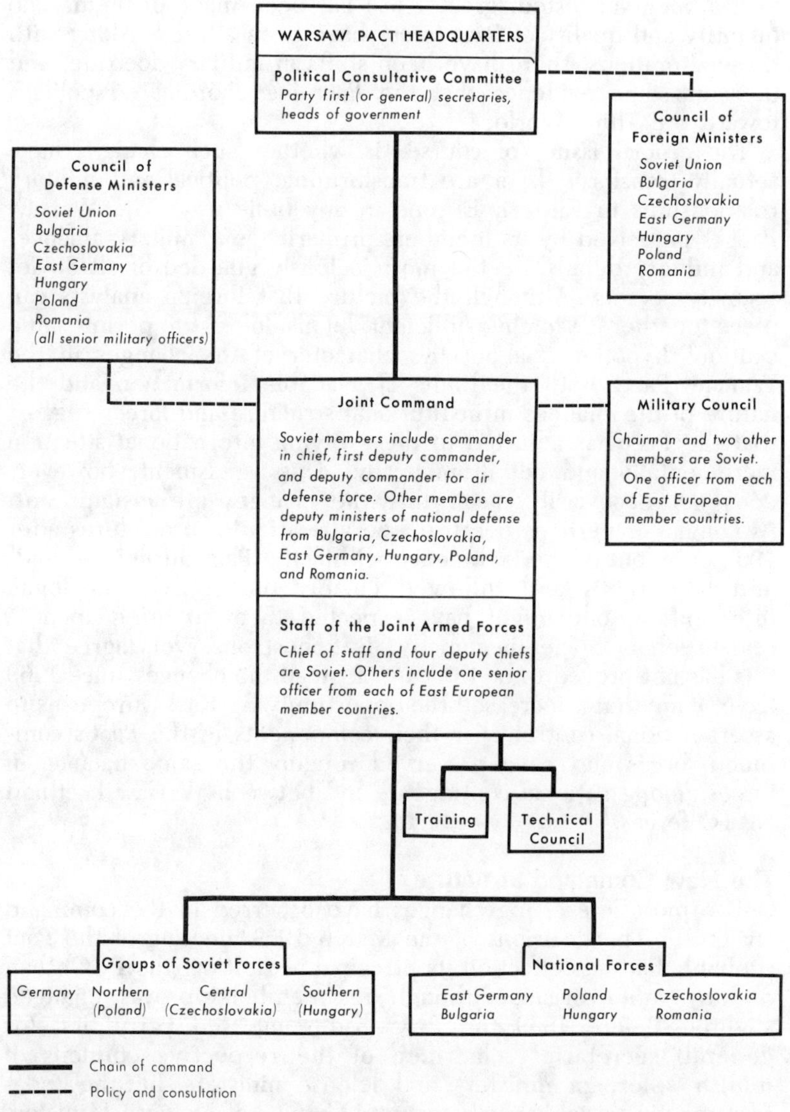

Source: Based on information from *The Military Balance, 1982–83*, London, 1982.

Figure B. Peacetime Structure of the Warsaw Pact, 1982

Although the PCC has retained its status as the preeminent institution of the Pact and apparently continues to provide overall direction to the alliance, it obviously has limited functions as an organ of political consultation; compared with its counterpart in NATO—the NATO Council—it has convened irregularly and infrequently. Apparently, there has been a pattern of biennial meetings. Alternative modes of consultation among the Pact's political leaders have come into being as substitutes for PCC gatherings: principally, annual "vacation" meetings in the Crimea and, of course, regular gatherings of top party, government, and military leaders at various party congresses. The former were singled out by Brezhnev for special mention at the Twenty-sixth Party Congress. He claimed there had been "thirty-seven friendly summit meetings in the Crimea" since 1976.

Of more importance was the creation of the CDM. As a result of this step, the role of the national defense ministers in the Pact underwent a dramatic change. Under the terms of the Warsaw Treaty, the "defense ministers or other military leaders of the signatory states" were to serve as deputy commanders in chief of the Pact armed forces. In practice, this meant that military decisions passed directly from the Pact commander in chief (always a Soviet general) to the national contingents through their defense ministers. The 1969 reforms, by formally assigning a new role to the defense ministers, also made the deputy ministers of defense of the participating states the deputy commanders in chief of the joint forces. Such a modification of relationships tended to strengthen the subordination of military command to national decisionmaking authority, at least in peacetime. Whereas a minister of defense certainly had always been subordinate to his home party and government authority, a deputy minister was probably required not only to report to his national council of ministers and central committee but also to do so through his minister. This additional bureaucratic step within the national decisionmaking process may have afforded national authorities more opportunity to evaluate the decisions transmitted to them. The CDM thus became more of a general policymaking body and was probably less involved in operational decisions.

Another significant innovation made at the Budapest PCC meeting was the establishment of a Military Council. British defense analyst Malcolm Mackintosh has attempted to sketch a picture of this body and has argued that its creation represented the major change of the 1969 reforms. The Military Council apparently includes the commander in chief, a deputy commander in chief, the chief of staff, and representatives of general officer rank from each of the participating states. Although little is known about its actual functions, one might conclude from the timing of some of its meetings—for example, those in Moscow in 1969 and Bucharest in 1972—that the Military Council has the responsibility of advising the CDM. But as table B makes clear, the evidence simply is not satisfactory. On the basis of available information, it appears that the Military Council has not always met prior to sessions of the CDM and that announced meetings of the latter organ have not always followed those of the Military Council. Nonetheless, Mackintosh's judgment that the creation of the

Military Council amounted to a "significant concession" by Moscow—in that it provides increased access to policy discussion for the East Europeans—seems reasonable. The Military Council seems to be responsible for analyzing past operational practices and planning for future ones, especially joint military exercises.

If the Military Council does act in an advisory or staff capacity to the CDM, or if the CDM serves as a meaningful review board for the decisions of the Military Council, such reforms would indeed be important. Whatever the precise relationship between the CDM and the Military Council, the effect of these reforms has been to remove national defense ministers from a position subordinate to the commander in chief and formally to place East European defense ministers on an equal footing with the Soviet minister.

Finally, one further multilateral Pact organ was created in 1969: the Technical Council. In early 1983 little was known about it, although it clearly has responsibility for "modernization of weapons and technology." Its meetings were not announced publicly.

On the operational level, the Budapest PCC meeting created the Staff of the Joint Armed Forces headed by General Anatoliy Gribkov as chief of staff. Analyst A. Ross Johnson believes that this body constitutes the Pact's first permanent joint staff, maintaining that the staff had functioned on an ad hoc basis before 1969. Although the chief of staff, the first deputy chief of staff, and four deputy chiefs of staff are Soviet officers, each other national armed force also contributes a deputy chief of staff of major general or rear admiral rank. As of early 1981 the Staff of the Joint Armed Forces was responsible for conducting training exercises and probably served the Joint Command and the Military Council in an advisory capacity. It is not clear whether the staff is comparable to a theater headquarters that would operate in a fashion similar to NATO and its Supreme Headquarters, Allied Powers in Europe (SHAPE). Reaching a conclusion on this question requires an analysis of the structure of operations during the Czechoslovak intervention in 1968, i.e., before the Budapest reforms. Once combat operations were undertaken at that time, the Joint Command of the Pact relinquished military functions to the commander in chief of the Soviet ground forces, General Ivan Pavlovskiy, who directed the combined forces of the Soviet, Bulgarian, Hungarian, Polish, and East German armies. (Romania refused to participate.)

Eventually, to be sure, the setting up of a permanent joint staff could produce a significant alteration in Warsaw Pact operations. In this connection it is worth noting that the Pact apparently now has a permanent joint staff headquarters at Lvov in the Ukraine. The combination of a permanent joint staff and headquarters would distinctly enhance the Pact's capability to act as a military command in the event of hostilities. Nonetheless, to contend that such a transformation has already taken place seems premature. In any case, logistics, command and control, and air defense would all evidently still be provided primarily by Soviet forces, for the Pact does not possess such capabilities as a separate military organization.

The relationship of the new Staff of the Joint Armed Forces to the older Joint Command is not entirely clear, but it is believed that the command exercises general policy supervision over the staff. Thus, the picture that emerges of the interrelationships within the Pact's new command structure is as follows: the PCC provides broad foreign policy coordination among the Pact states and possibly receives reports from the CDM as well as directly from the commander in chief on military questions. The presence of the commander in chief at PCC meetings when the defense ministers have not been in attendance suggests that the CDM essentially affords a channel of communication with national defense planners; that the CDM has little advisory responsibility outside the roles its members play in national governments; and that the PCC is advised on military considerations fundamentally by the commander in chief. The Military Council, however, probably does report to the defense ministers, either in the CDM or individually within national decisionmaking structures; thus it carries out a communications function. The Joint Command oversees military operations and issues broad policy guidance for the Staff of the Joint Armed Forces. No doubt it functions formally under the Military Council, but the council probably serves merely as a liaison and plays a subordinate role. The staff, then, directs training and implements the policies of the Joint Command.

Implications of the Reform

Two analytical questions are posed by this brief review of the reforms effected in the Pact organization since the PCC's 1969 meeting in Budapest. First, have these modifications in Pact procedures affected the alliance's military capacities? The answer to this question is fairly clear—no. At least, none of the changes is perceived as diminishing the combat capacities of the Warsaw Pact. Perhaps the cumulative adjustments—especially the creation of the Military Council to give East European officers a vehicle for more active participation in the planning process—might be thought to have increased the sense of professional pride and, hence, the combat effectiveness and reliability of the East European contingents. But assessments of the morale and political reliability of non-Soviet Warsaw Pact troops have always been exceedingly difficult, and it might just as plausibly be argued that whatever advantages were gained in this regard were lost through the more cumbersome communication process resulting from the substitution of deputy defense ministers for defense ministers in the Joint Command. In any case, these are judgments based on such slender evidence that their practical military value is highly dubious. It would therefore be prudent to hold that in the event of hostilities the Soviet command structure would in all likelihood prevail just as it did in August 1968 and that the 1969 reforms had no meaningful impact on the military capacities of the Warsaw Pact.

Second, what have been the political effects of the reforms? This question is by far the more interesting of the two. Here the conclusions of Remington and Johnson seem persuasive: the reforms were the outgrowth of agitation by the East Europeans—notably the Romanians and Czechoslovaks (before August 1968)—to expand their role in the military decisionmaking of the Pact; the reforms did in fact set up a somewhat more adequate mechanism through which they could make inputs into the decisionmaking process. Three features of the reforms afford the basis for such an assessment. To begin with, the creation of a permanent joint staff that includes the deputy chiefs of staff from each of the member countries could serve to increase the weight of the national military leaders in the policymaking process. Moreover, the establishment of the permanent staff and the creation of the joint staff headquarters at Lvov enhanced the possibility that at some time in the future the Pact command might be able to retain operational control of its own forces in the event of hostilities rather than becoming subordinate to the national command of the Soviet Union. Secondly, the setting up of the Military Council provided a forum for the East Europeans to make additional substantive inputs into military planning before the CDM or the PCC makes decisions. Thirdly, the shift of the Pact defense ministers out of the line of command reemphasized the subordination of the Pact to national command authorities.

Finally, the pace of joint military exercises clearly increased between 1969 and 1974. Both the number and the nature of the exercises pointed to improved Pact capability for combined action. The slower pace of joint exercises after 1975 undoubtedly partially reflected the political campaign launched at the 1976 Bucharest meeting of the PCC. The political emphasis has been on reducing military tensions in Europe, including the formal but surely propagandistic proposals that neither pact be expanded (to discourage Spanish entry into NATO), that both pacts be disbanded, and that NATO and the Warsaw Pact sign a mutual nonaggression agreement. Dale Herspring, a United States foreign service officer who specializes in Soviet and East European military affairs, has advanced the interesting argument that bilateral cooperation among East European armies, without much Soviet participation, has increased during this same time frame. If this cooperation has established the basis for combined operation, it is indeed significant. But the public evidence on non-Soviet Pact military exercises is not satisfactory to permit more than a tentative observation.

The pattern of exercises also reflects a "stabilization" of Warsaw Pact military institutions. There now tend to be two large, multinational and combined arms exercises each year: a Shield exercise in September and a Druzhba (Friendship) exercise in the spring. For example, Shield-82 took place in Bulgaria from September 25 to October 1, 1982, and involved air, naval, and ground forces from all Pact countries, including observers from Cuba, Vietnam, and Mongolia. Druzhba-82 took place in January with the participation of Soviet, Czech, and Hungarian forces and in March with Polish, East German, and Soviet forces. In addition to bilateral exercises among Pact members and command post exercises, these multinational maneuvers represent a highly developed and rather sophisticated institution with both political and military significance. Overall, the net effect of all the changes probably has been to increase participation by the Soviet Union's East European allies.

Force Structure and Equipment

A major quantitative alteration in Warsaw Pact armed forces came as a result of the invasion of Czechoslovakia in 1968. Before that cooperation, Soviet ground forces in the Pact countries had totaled 26 divisions (20 in East Germany, two in Poland, and four in Hungary). To these were added six divisions in August 1968—one more in Poland (temporarily) and five in Czechoslovakia. In October 1979 General Secretary Brezhnev announced the withdrawal of 20,000 men and 1,000 tanks from the group of Soviet Forces in Germany, and these reductions were completed by the fall of 1980. Although information on the precise strength of the Soviet forces in Eastern Europe is exceedingly difficult to ascertain, Soviet ground troops numbered about 250,0000 before 1968 and slightly over 300,000 afterward (see table C, this Appendix). It should be noted that arriving at comparable data for the years 1968, 1974, and 1980 requires some adjustment of the estimates of the London-based International Institute for Strategic Studies (IISS), from which the table is derived. In particular, the apparent increase in numbers of Soviet forces from 1974 resulted primarily from changes in the institute's methods of calculating the size of Soviet divisions. Nevertheless, the actual components of these divisions probably did increase slightly during the late 1970s. These figures do not include about 10 combat-ready divisions of over 100,000 men stationed in the Western military districts of the Soviet Union that might, in some scenarios, be available for rapid reinforcement of Pact forces.

Manpower figures for ground forces alone, however, give only a rough notion of the increase in Pact capabilities. The additional Soviet divisions after 1968 augmented the number of tanks in Eastern Europe by about 2,000 (see table D, this Appendix). In

Table C. *Warsaw Pact Ground Forces in Combat Formations, 1968, 1974, and 1980*

Armored

Country	Divisions 1968	Divisions 1974	Divisions 1980	Manpower 1968	Manpower 1974	Manpower 1980
Soviet forces in Eastern Europe	13	16	15	133,000	152,000	165,000[1]
East Germany	2	2	2	19,000	19,000	19,000[2]
Poland	5	5	5	47,500	47,500	47,500[2]
Czechoslovakia	5	5	5	47,500	47,500	47,500[2]
Hungary	1	1	1	9,500	9,500	9,500[2]
Romania	2	2	2	19,000	19,000	19,000[2]
Bulgaria	4	1	1	38,000	10,000	10,000[2]
TOTAL	32	32	31	313,500	304,500	317,500

Infantry/Motorized

Country	Divisions 1968	Divisions 1974	Divisions 1980	Manpower 1968	Manpower 1974	Manpower 1980
Soviet forces in Eastern Europe	13	15	15	139,000	175,000	210,000[1]
East Germany	4	4	4	48,000	48,000	48,000[2]
Poland	8[3]	8[3]	8	96,000	96,000	96,000[2]
Czechoslovakia	9	5¼	5	108,000	62,000	68,000[2]
Hungary	5	5	5	60,000	60,000	60,000[2]
Romania	7[4]	8[5]	8	84,000	96,000	96,000[2]
Bulgaria	8	8	8	96,000	96,000	96,000[2]
TOTAL	54	53¼	53	631,000	633,000	674,000

Total Manpower

Country	1968	1974	1980
Soviet forces in Eastern Europe	272,000	327,000	375,000[1]
East Germany	67,000	67,000	67,000[2]
Poland	143,500	143,500	143,500[2]
Czechoslovakia	155,500	109,500	105,500[2]
Hungary	69,500	69,500	69,500[2]
Romania	103,000	115,000	115,000[2]
Bulgaria	134,000	106,000	106,000[2]
TOTAL	944,500	937,500	981,500

[1]In 1975 the International Institute for Strategic Studies changed its calculations for numbers of troops in Soviet divisions, so the resulting increase in manpower should not be understood to constitute increases in actual numbers.
[2]Calculations of manpower totals for East European contingents have not been changed from 1974 to 1980, although there may have been some upgrading as in the Soviet divisions.
[3]Excluded from this figure are one airborne and one amphibious assault division, there being no comparable forces in other national contingents.
[4]Excluded from this figure are some independent mountain units.
[5]Excluded from this figure are two mountain brigades and one airborne regiment, there being no comparable forces in other national contingents.

Source: Based on information from *The Military Balance, 1968–69* (through 1980–1981), London, 1968 (through 1980).

Table D. Warsaw Pact Armor, 1968, 1974, and 1980

Country	Tanks			Type (and number where known) in 1980[4]
	1968[1]	1974[2]	1980[3]	
Soviet Union......	7,020	9,025	9,015	T-10 and T-10M heavy; T-62, T-72, T-54/55 medium; PT-76 light
East Germany....	1,800	2,400	2,600	T-72 and T-54/55 medium (T-34s in storage) PT-76 (about 130)
Poland.............	2,800	3,650	3,600	T-72, T-54/55, and T-34; PT-76 (250) (102 of T-72)
Czechoslovakia ...	2,700	3,500	3,600	T-72, T-62, T-54, and T-34 (100 each of T-72 and T-62)
Hungary	700	1,780	1,410	T-72 and T-54/55; PT-76 (60 of T-72)
Romania...........	1,200	1,970	1,700	T-72, T-54/55 and T-34; PT-76 (1,500 of T-72 and T-54/55)
Bulgaria...........	2,000	2,250	1,900	T-72, T-62, T-54/55, and T-34; PT-76 (100 of T-62 and T-72)
TOTAL....	18,220	24,575	23,825	

[1]Based on information from *The Military Balance, 1968–69*, London, 1968. Figures for the East European countries' inventories taken directly from text. Soviet tanks estimated on basis of 350 per armored division (10 in East Germany, one in Poland, and two in Hungary) and 190 per mechanized infantry division.

[2]Based on information from *The Military Balance, 1974–75*, London, 1974. Figures for East European countries' inventories taken directly from text. Soviet tanks estimated on basis of 325 per armored division (10 in East Germany, two in Poland, two in Hungary, and two in Czechoslovakia) and 255 per mechanized infantry division. (It should be noted that figures provided on pp. 8–14 differ from those given in table on p. 101 of referenced source. However, the former are presumed to be more comparable to data provided in *The Military Balance, 1968–69*.)

[3]Based on infromation from *The Military Balance, 1980–81*, London, 1980. Figures for East European inventories taken directly from text; Soviet inventory estimated on basis of 325 tanks per armored division, 266 per mechanized division.

[4]All T-62 and PT-76 tanks in East European inventories added after 1968, although both types present in Soviet contingents before that date.

part, to be sure, the new Soviet troops and matériel were offset by reductions in Czechoslovakia's forces and equipment. But from NATO's perspective and presumably from that of Pact commanders as well, the substitution of Soviet for Czechoslovak divisions amounted to an upgrading of Pact capabilities, especially in light of the dissatisfactions that surfaced in the Czechoslovak army during the Prague Spring of 1968.

These estimates had not changed appreciably by 1982, although NATO and United States estimates of the quantity of equipment that Pact forces possessed had undergone some revision, and the IISS held that the Soviet Union had withdrawn the additional divisions that it had deployed in Poland in 1968. It should be noted that once the discussions regarding the mutual reduction of forces in Europe began in Vienna in 1973, and once the Western countries had therefore commenced to devote more intelligence resources to "counting" Pact forces, Western estimates of the equipment of these forces were scaled up in some categories and down in others.

On the qualitative side the changes are more difficult to assess, but they have probably been far more important than the quantitative ones. The T-62 tank, which performed very well for the Egyptians during the October 1973 War in the Sinai, constituted a clear improvement over its earlier counterparts (the T-54/55) and was added to the equipment of all member forces of the Pact except Romania; in 1982 Poland and East Germany presumably had greater numbers of them than the other countries. The newer T-72 was added to all Pact armed forces but in small numbers. The IISS estimated that in 1980 there were only 100 each in the Czechoslovak and Polish national armed forces, and it is doubtful that any Pact country had more. (The estimate for Poland was lowered to 60 in 1982.) The institute's estimates also indicate that East Germany, Hungary, and Poland had acquired the PT-76 light tank since 1968. During the October 1973 War the Egyptians used this tank, which has excellent amphibious capabilities (in contrast to the T-62 and T-54/55, which have only some "wading" capabilities), during the initial crossing of the Suez Canal and then operated very effectively with it to open holes in Israel's Bar-Lev Line. Both the T-72 and the PT-76 represent technology at least comparable to front-line NATO armor.

Although tanks have been perhaps the single item of greatest concern to NATO and United States planners (the Soviet Union has been producing about 3,000 a year as compared with about 600 for the United States), the somewhat superior technology of NATO tanks and NATO's higher quality and more widely dispersed antitank capabilities partially offset the numerical advantage of the Pact vis-à-vis NATO (23,825 compared with about 11,000 in NATO). Nonetheless, qualitative improvements not only in tanks but also in the BMD (an infantry combat vehicle) constitute one of the principal upgradings of Warsaw Pact equipment.

But there have been other improvements as well. Since 1968 all Pact national units have received antitank guided weapons (ATGWs)—the Snapper and the Sagger—except for Czechoslovakia, which may have only the latter. Each is optically sighted and wire guided. The Snapper is mounted on armored vehicles, but the Sagger can be carried by an individual. All proved lethal in the October 1973 War in the Sinai. East German ground forces had the newer Spandrel (AT-5), but as of early 1981 none had the Spigot (AT-4) or Spiral (AT-6) used by Soviet forces.

With respect to other missiles, every Pact country has FROG surface-to-surface missiles (SSMs), which have ranges of 40 to 60 kilometers. The FROG is capable of carrying a nuclear warhead. The Soviet Union, however, retains custody of the warheads. All Pact states also deploy small numbers of the Scud, the more modern (1965) variant of which has a range of 160 to 270 kilometers and is capable of carrying either nuclear or conventional warheads. Data suggest that every Pact nation possesses a variety of surface-to-air missiles (SAMs), and considerable modernization in these weapons took place after 1975. These are impressive weapons, but they are not the most modern equipment in Soviet inventories. The Soviets, typically, reserve the most modern generation in each type of weapon for themselves, e.g., the AT-6 (Spiral antitank weapon), the SA-11 antiaircraft weapon, and the SS-12/22 and /23 SSMs.

Air defenses, of course, include interceptor aircraft, as well as missiles, but here again a pattern of Pact dependence on the Soviet Union is evident. All Pact states possess MiGs of the 17 and/or 21 varieties. In addition, Czechoslovakia and Poland have the SU-7 (Fitter A, first introduced in 1959) short-range fighter-bomber. Poland has the SU-20 (Fitter C, introduced in 1974). Bulgaria, Czechoslovakia, East Germany, and Hungary have MiG-23s (Flogger, introduced in 1971). The MiG-23s and SU-20s represent the modernization of the late 1970s. Once again the Soviet Union boasts newer interceptors—the Foxbat (MiG-25), the Flagon EF (SU-15)—and a version of the Flogger (MiG-27). All were first shown after 1967 and went into service in the early 1970s, but as of 1982 none had yet been placed in other national air forces. The Soviet air force also has the Fencer (SU-19), a fighter-bomber with variable-geometry wings. It, too, had been held back from other Pact air forces.

The dependence of other Pact countries on the Soviet Union for air defense is further underlined by the absence of any separate air defense command for the Pact. Instead the Pact relies on the Soviet Air Defense Command, headed by a marshal of aviation.

All the equipment discussed previously, it should be noted, has been created and deployed in accordance with Soviet military doctrine. Doctrine and forces, of course, have a symbiotic relationship. Although much of official Soviet military doctrine is shrouded in great secrecy, discussion in the military press provides some indication of the content of that doctrine. When hardware and forces appear in the field, they constitute a final test of the nature of the official doctrine. Judged by the discussion in the military press, by the disposition of Soviet forces, and by practices in military training exercises, the principal alteration in the doctrine of the Warsaw Pact during the last decade has been preparation for combat operations with tactical nuclear weapons. Whereas public discussion of Soviet doctrine until the mid-1960s largely maintained that any use of tactical nuclear weapons would result in a prompt escalation to general nuclear war, after Khrushchev's fall in 1964 increasing attention was paid to tactical nuclear weapons, and statements began to appear in the military press with a slightly different emphasis. The possibility was entertained that war in Europe might, under some circumstances, be restricted to a tactical nuclear confrontation and not escalate—at least not immediately—into strategic nuclear war. Warsaw Pact joint exercises after 1964 also stressed combat in a nuclear environment. Thus, the indications in the public discussion of military doctrine appear to be confirmed by an examination of Pact training and equipment.

In the view of Soviet military theorists, tactical nuclear war requires seizure of the initiative, highly mobile forces, and widely dispersed formations. These requirements, in turn, dictate not only an emphasis on tanks and armored personnel carriers and the employment of vast quantities of mobile SAMs but also some capabilities at a lower level than those described above, e.g., widely dispersed bridge-crossing matériel and tank units with an in-formation decontamination capability.

Out of this brief description of Soviet and other Pact forces emerges a picture of enhanced military capabilities within the Warsaw Pact. Pact forces have been upgraded quantitatively and, more importantly, qualitatively since the mid-1960s. Yet the pattern of military capabilities of the Pact continues to ensure the military predominance of the Soviet Union and to make the armed forces of the East European states almost wholly dependent on Moscow in two ways. First, the Warsaw Pact lacks any organic capabilities in some critical areas—strategic deterrence and air defense being the most significant. Second, the East European members of the Pact possess few of the most modern generation of Soviet weapons, for the Kremlin has carefully and systematically withheld these weapons from distribution. This is most obvious with respect to fighter-bombers and interceptor aircraft, but it is also true in regard to such items as SAMs, SSMs, and even tanks.

The preceding elements of dependency on the Soviet Union promote alliance cohesion by ensuring that any East European state would have difficulty maintaining an effective defense posture outside the Pact—either against another Pact member or against NATO—and by simplifying command and control problems through absolute integration of forces. At the same time, however, the second element could pose long-term difficulties within the alliance. In the 1970s and early 1980s not only Vietnam but also Egypt, Syria, and Libya received Soviet equipment before it had been integrated into the national armed forces of Pact members. Although one cannot predict whether there might be further manifestations of the kind of resentments that the Romanians have occasionally hinted at and the Czechoslovaks demonstrated in 1968, it would seem that the professional military establishments of loyal allies must find especially galling the contrast between their total dependence on the Soviet Union for current-generation technology and the access of armed forces outside the Pact structure to such technology.

A General Assessment

Three sets of developments, then, have occurred in the Warsaw Pact since 1969: first, Pact institutions were modified in a manner that probably enhanced the national roles of East European states; second, vigorous consultation took place among Pact states on issues of détente, at least until 1973 and thereafter on other European developments; and third, significant quantitative and qualitative modifications were made in Pact military capabilities. The question that remains, however, is what all these changes amount to—whether the fundamental character of the alliance has altered or is in the process of altering.

Judgments on this subject depend to a large degree on the analyst's view of the purpose of the alliance, and this view must be differentiated according to three components: assessments of the role of the Pact in Soviet security calculations, in general Soviet political purposes, and from the standpoint of the East Europeans.

Soviet Security

Regarding the role of the Pact with respect to Soviet security calculations, it is important to realize that since World War II a substantial portion of Western disagreement about détente and East-West relations in general has stemmed from conflicting perspectives on this very issue. One school of analysis has assumed that the primary function of the Warsaw Pact-Comecon structure is to enable the Soviet Union to maintain political control in Eastern Europe, and it has stressed Moscow's use of the Warsaw Pact to suppress the Hungarian uprising in 1956 and the Prague Spring in 1968 as well as its efforts to affect developments in Poland during 1980–81. This perspective has wide currency in Western societies where many analysts, when all other explanations have seemed wanting, have fallen back on the notion that the Pact's apparent preoccupation with preserving a conventional preponderance on the central front in Europe reflects the need to keep allies in a position of political subservience. This conception posits an essentially political role for the Warsaw Pact in terms of Soviet security and does not take very seriously the military contribution made by Pact allies to the defense or achievement of Soviet interests. On the contrary, in this view the need to garrison large forces to maintain political control means that its East European allies constitute a military liability to the Soviet Union.

A second school of analysis, to which many revisionist historians in the United States subscribe, has emphasized "tangential security" as the key element in Soviet thinking about the military function of the Warsaw Pact. According to this school, Eastern Europe constitutes a buffer zone between the Soviet Union and the "imperialist" states (West Germany in particular), and Soviet preoccupation with the Northern Triangle, i.e., the territory embraced by East Germany, Poland, and Czechoslovakia, and with the areas flanking it (Hungary and the Baltic approaches) results directly from Moscow's determination not to permit another invasion of the Soviet Union by this route. Thus, the argument goes, the Warsaw Pact is militarily important to the Soviet Union in two senses: it guarantees the country's defense in forward positions, and it affords a means, through the maintenance of Soviet garrisons in the Pact states, of securing the "rear" of the battlefield, that is, of ensuring safe access to the reserves and matériel that the Soviet Union would provide in the event of a conventional or tactical nuclear war. Although this view upgrades the military value of Eastern Europe to the security of the Soviet Union, it nonetheless pictures the role of East European military forces as largely neutral in terms of that security.

In some representations one or the other of these first two schools of analysis is combined with a sinister evaluation of Soviet intentions. If one judges Soviet intentions to be aggressive, of course, the military reality can be interpreted to fit the political judgment; the need to station troops forward for political control of Eastern Europe or to make a forward defense does place troops nearer to West European targets. Adherents of both schools, however, downgrade the military contribution of East European forces to the achievement of Soviet purposes.

The final school of analysis, which is not often mentioned in Western political writings but receives serious attention among contingency planners in the Western defense ministries and in NATO, holds that the forces of East European Pact members are far more integral to Soviet security calculations than either the "political control" image or the "tangential security" image would suggest. Its proponents point to the positioning of East German, Polish, and Czechoslovak forces and their employment in Warsaw Pact military exercises as evidence that these forces would prove formidable opponents if Western forces should become involved in a conventional or tactical nuclear conflict with them.

Some subscribers to this school share the judgment of those adherents of the other schools who see the Soviet Union as aggressive. Nevertheless, all its proponents have a substantially higher regard for the potential military contribution of the non-Soviet Warsaw Pact forces than do the proponents of the other two schools.

Some aspects of recent developments would tend to lend credence to each of these hypotheses regarding Soviet purpose. The quantitative and qualitative improvements that have been effected in Soviet forces in the last few years, and the continued reluctance of the Kremlin to release the most modern equipment to its allies, might be thought to reinforce the contention that political control of Eastern Europe constitutes the major factor in Soviet judgments about the military worth of the Pact. Moscow's positioning of five ground and two air divisions in Czechoslovakia even after the political situation there had stabilized, and continued Soviet insistence that the Pact's command and staff be dominated by Soviet officers, could be seen as support for the "tangential security" argument. Finally, the qualitative improvements in non-Soviet Pact forces combined with the possible trend toward more genuine sharing of command authority within the Pact might be viewed as corroborating the notion that the Pact is integral to Soviet security.

None of these hypotheses, however, is inherently adequate to explain the pattern of post-1969 changes within the Pact. For example, while the recent quantitative and qualitative upgrading of Soviet forces and Moscow's continued reluctance to release the most modern weapons to its allies can be said to uphold the validity of the "political control" hypothesis, they do not compel that conclusion. It is possible to argue that these developments have simply been designed to maintain the NATO/Pact balance achieved before 1969. NATO has made and continues to make improvements of its own. It is also possible to see Pact developments as being largely the outcome of bureaucratic pressures within the Soviet defense structure. Just as each of the three hypotheses regarding the role that the Pact plays in Soviet security calculations has its vigorous advocates in Western circles, the same is probably true in the Soviet Union, and Soviet purposes probably constitute a composite, or mix, of all three conceptions.

Soviet Political Interests

With respect to Moscow's evaluation of the political utility of the Warsaw Pact to the Soviet Union, two complementary perceptions are current in most Western analyses. The first and most prevalent depicts the Pact as important to the Soviet Union in ideological terms. According to this view the Pact performs a legitimization role. The Soviet political leadership derives legitimacy in international affairs and for its representation of the international environment to the Soviet people by being able to point to the largely sympathetic—cynics would say obedient—stances of other European socialist states. Manifestations of the existence of a "socialist commonwealth," in short, lend weight to the Soviet leadership's political positions and underline the idealistic and international claims of communist ideology.

The second perception has received too little attention in Western scholarship. It, in turn, has interstate and intrastate dimensions. The interstate dimension stresses the value of the Warsaw Pact as a forum for communication and the exchange of views. According to this perception the meetings of the PCC afford an opportunity for all parties to air their concerns and their preoccupations on a fairly regularized basis—just as the biannual meetings of NATO serve as a device for regularized communication among alliance members.

The intrastate dimension reinforces this view of the Warsaw Pact as a political organization that behaves much as political organizations do everywhere. Meetings of the Pact compel East European party and government bureaucracies to perform. Although little is known about the mechanisms whereby the Soviet Union and the East European states prepare for the PCC meetings, Pact meetings provide the calendar targets for the setting of memoranda deadlines and briefings for political leaderships in much the same way as NATO's biannual meetings do for NATO members.

Moreover, the developments of the 1970s tend to reinforce both perceptions. Soviet willingness to accommodate the demands of other Pact members for a larger role in decisionmaking within the Pact may in part reflect the worth that Moscow attaches to the Pact in legitimizing its policy. Certainly, the quantity of Pact consultations has driven the bureaucracies of all the Pact member states, and it has driven them hard. The apparent willingness to use ad hoc forms of consultation, such as the Crimea "vacation" meetings, may indicate a sensitivity to the demands of the post-1969 pace of consultation on party and state bureaucracies.

East European Perspectives

East European attitudes toward the Warsaw Pact no doubt have some similarities to Soviet evaluations; but they probably differ in some respects. By far the most important security-related aspect of East European thinking about the Pact is that it gives concrete form to political, economic, and military reality. Whatever type of social and political system existed in the Soviet Union, the situation of the countries of Eastern Europe would be conditioned by their giant neighbor to the east. No real security would be possible for them without harmonization of their interests with those of the Soviet Union. In other words, the security of the Soviet Union and the security of Eastern Europe are reciprocal—a fact that does not depend on ideological compatibility and one that has long been recognized by Western statesmen. It prompted British prime minister Winston Churchill, for example, to accede to the tentative arrangements he made with Stalin in October 1944, and it motivated the West's tacit acceptance of the status quo in Eastern Europe in the context of the Helsinki Agreement in 1975.

If the security of the East European countries is inseparable from that of the Soviet Union, the political interests of the communist elites in Eastern Europe in the Warsaw Pact also frequently run parallel to those of the Soviet leadership. Not only do the East European rulers, like their Soviet counterparts, derive legitimacy and prestige in the eyes of their own populations from the workings of the Warsaw Pact, but the diplomacy of intra-Pact affairs and of East-West negotiations under Pact sponsorship also provides international political training for East European cadres with leadership potential. In this sense the Pact framework performs a function that requires delicate balancing against national claims—a kind of socialization of cadres by reinforcing values already developed within them by their national political training through exposure to an international system that affirms those same values. Bloc affairs, to be sure, "socialized" East European communist elites in the days of the Comintern and direct Soviet intervention in Eastern Europe. The process is more subtle now, however, and its exact effects will not be known until the careers of junior foreign ministry and defense ministry officials who have participated in the increased intra-Pact and East-West diplomatic contacts have been followed.

In conclusion, it is worth reiterating that the significance attributed to recent developments in the Warsaw Pact depends on three interlocking sets of hypotheses regarding the purposes of the political, military, and economic institutions of the Pact-Comecon framework. These hypotheses offer different evaluations of the utility of that framework to the Soviet Union in security and political terms and of the value that the East European countries place on it. Western perceptions of the framework have consistently tended to attach less importance to its explicit purposes than to its implicit purposes. Thus, the Warsaw Pact and Comecon have been viewed as having the primary functions of exercising political control over a satellite system, rationalizing that control ideologically, and legitimizing the exercise of domestic political power by elites thought not to enjoy adequate popular support to rule. The two organizations have been perceived as having at best only tangential or inconsequential significance for the Soviet Union—in the one case, as merely a geographical buffer and line of forward defense that enables the Soviet army to achieve more tactical flexibility in defending its homeland; in the other case, as a mechanism for the economic domination of Eastern Europe, which could nevertheless still be accomplished (albeit by less camouflaged means) even if that particular institution did not exist.

But these perceptions may contain biases that produce a misrepresentation of present truth and emergent reality. They call for analytical suspicion because they derive essentially from the cold war era. Whether the Pact-Comecon framework has yet acquired concrete substance closer to its explicit purposes than it had previously, and whether it performs functions more integral to the political, military, and economic interests of all the participating states than it did before cannot be determined with certainty, but changes in the Warsaw Pact in the period of détente may point in that direction. Therefore the analytical mind-set to be used in approaching the Warsaw Pact should be receptive to that possibility and alert to the dangers of continuing to view it in terms that have fitted comfortably in the past.

Appendix D

The Gdansk Agreement

[Protocol of Agreement between the Government Commission and the Inter-Factory Strike Committee concluded on August 31, 1980, at Lenin Shipyard, Gdansk]

Having examined the 21 demands submitted by the strikers, the government commission and the Inter-Factory Strike Committee have adopted the following decisions:

With regard to Point One that states: "To accept free trade unions independent from the party and employers as provided for by International Labour Organisation [ILO] Convention 87, which was ratified by the Polish People's Republic and which concerns trade union freedoms," it was agreed:

1. The performance of trade unions in the Polish People's Republic has not fulfilled the hopes and expectations of employees. It is considered expedient to establish new self-governing trade unions that will genuinely represent the working class. No one will have his right to remain in the present trade unions questioned, and it is possible that the two trade unions will establish cooperation in the future.

2. In view of the establishment of new independent and self-governing trade unions, the Inter-Factory Strike Committee declares that they will observe the principles laid down in the Constitution of the Polish People's Republic. The new trade unions will defend the social and material interests of employees and do not intend to play the role of a political party. They endorse the principle that the means of production are social property—a principle that is the foundation of the socialist system in Poland. Recognizing that the Polish United Workers' Party (PZPR) plays the leading role in the state and without undermining the existing system of international alliances, they seek to ensure for the working people suitable means of control, of expressing their opinions, and of defending their interests.

The government commission declares that the government will guarantee and ensure complete respect for the independence and self-management of the new trade unions both as regards their organizational structure and the performance of their functions. The government will ensure for the new trade unions all opportunities for fulfilling their basic functions in defending the interests of employees and implementing their material, social, and cultural needs. At the same time, the government guarantees that the new trade unions will not be subjected to any discrimination.

3. The establishment and activity of the independent, self-governing trade unions are consistent with ILO Convention 87, which concerns trade union freedoms and the defense of trade union rights, and ILO Convention 98, which concerns the right of association and the right to collective bargaining. Both conventions have been ratified by Poland. The diversification of trade unions and employee representations will require suitable legislative amendments. In this connection the government pledges to introduce legislative proposals concerning in particular the law on trade unions, the law on workers' self-government, and the labor code.

4. The established strike committees can, if they want, transform themselves into factory employee representation bodies, such as workers' committees, employees' committees, workers' councils, or the founding committees of the new self-governing trade unions. As the founding committee of those trade unions, the Inter-Factory Strike Committee is free to choose the form of a single union or association within the coastal region. The founding committees will function until new authorities are elected in accordance with the statutes. The government pledges to create conditions for the registration of the new trade unions outside the register of the Central Trade Union Council.

5. The new trade unions should enjoy genuine opportunities for publicly evaluating the key decisions that determine the working people's living conditions: the principles of dividing the national income between consumption and capital investment, the allocation of social welfare funds for various purposes (health, education, culture), the basic principles of pay and wage policy—particularly the principle of automatic cost-of-living adjustments to offset inflation, long-term economic plans, investment policy, and price changes. The government pledges itself to ensure conditions for the exercise of these functions.

6. The Inter-Factory Strike Committee will establish a center for social and labor studies, whose task will be objectively to analyze the employees' situation and living conditions and also methods of representing employees' interests. The center also will prepare expert opinions on the wage and price indexes and will propose compensation plans. It will publish the results of its research. In addition, the new trade unions will have their own publications.

7. The government will ensure that the provisions of Article 1, Paragraph 1, of the 1949 Trade Union Act, which stipulate that workers and employees are guaranteed the right to voluntary association in trade unions, are observed in Poland. The new trade unions will not join the association represented by the Central Trade Union Council. It is agreed that the new law will preserve this principle. Representatives of the Inter-Factory Strike Committee or of the committees that will found the self-governing

trade unions and representatives of other workers' bodies will be ensured participation in formulating this law.

With regard to Point Two that states: "To guarantee the right to strike and to guarantee security for strikers and for persons helping them," it was decided:

The right to strike will be guaranteed in the trade union law now under preparation. The law should define the conditions for initiating and organizing strikes, the methods of settling disputed questions, and responsibility for violating the law. Articles 52, 64, and 65 of the Labor Code cannot be applied to the participants in a strike. Also, the government guarantees for strikers and for the persons helping them personal security and the maintenance of prevailing working conditions until the law is passed.

With regard to Point Three that states: "To observe freedom of speech and the printed word, that is, not to repress independent publications and to make mass media available to representatives of all religions," it was decided:

1. Within three months the government will introduce in the Sejm a draft law on control of the press, publications, and entertainment—based on the following principles. Censorship should protect the interests of the state. This means the protection of state and economic secrets, the extent of which will be more closely defined by legislation, and the protection of the state's security and important international interests. This also means the protection of religious beliefs and, at the same time, of the rights of nonbelievers. It means preventing the dissemination of materials harmful to morals. This draft law will also deal with the right to appeal to the Supreme Administrative Tribunal against the decisions of the agencies responsible for control of the press, publications, and entertainment. This law will be enacted through modifications to the Administrative Procedure Code.

2. The use of the mass media by religious associations for their religious activities will be arranged by agreement between state bodies and the interested religious associations. The government will see to it that the radio will broadcast Sunday Mass under a detailed accord with the episcopate.

3. Radio, television, the press, and publications should express a plurality of ideas, views, and judgments. This use should be subject to control by the public.

4. Like the citizens and their organizations, the press should have access to public documents, especially administrative documents, socioeconomic plans, and so on, issued by the government and its administrative bodies. The exceptions to the principle of the openness of the administration's activities will be defined in the law as stipulated in Paragraph 1 above.

With regard to Point Four that states: "[a] To restore the former rights of persons dismissed from their jobs for the strikes in 1970 and 1976 and the students banned from higher schools for their convictions; [b] To free all political prisoners [including Edmund Zadrozynski, Jan Kozlowski, and Marek Kozlowski]; [c] To abolish repressions for opinions," it was decided:

1. To examine immediately the firing of participants in the strikes of 1970 and 1976. If irregularities are found, to restore immediately the jobs to the people concerned, provided they want to have them back, and to take into account the qualifications they have acquired in the meantime. A similar procedure will be used in the case of the students banned from higher schools.
2. To refer the cases of the persons mentioned in Point Four [b] above to the minister of justice, who will examine them and will within two weeks institute the appropriate proceedings. If the persons mentioned have been deprived of their freedom, their punishment will be discontinued until the new proceedings are completed.
3. To examine whether there is any justification for temporary detention and to release the persons mentioned in the supplement. [The supplement to Point Four, which is omitted here, contains a lengthy list of political prisoners.]
4. To fully observe the freedom to express one's opinions in public and professional life.

With regard to Point Five that states: "To publish in the mass media information about the establishment of the Inter-Factory Strike Committee and its demands," it was decided:

The above demand will be fulfilled by publishing this protocol in the national mass media.

With regard to Point Six that states: "To undertake genuine measures to extricate the country from its state of crisis through: [a] Fully informing the public about the socioeconomic situation; [b] Enabling all social communities and strata to participate in discussions about the program of reforms," it was decided:

We deem it necessary to accelerate greatly the work on economic reform. The authorities will outline and publish the basic tenets of this reform within the next few months. It is necessary to ensure that public discussion of this reform is extensive. In particular, the trade unions should participate in formulating the laws on socialist economic organizations and on workers' self-government. The economic reform should be based on radically increased autonomy for enterprises and on the worker self-government groups' real participation in management. The necessary enactments should guarantee the fulfillment by the trade unions of the functions defined by Point One of this agreement.

Only a nation that is aware of its problems and that has a good knowledge of reality can sponsor and implement a program for streamlining the economy. The government will radically expand the range of the socioeconomic information available to the nation, the trade unions, and economic and social organizations.

In addition, the Inter-Factory Strike Committee demands that lasting prospects be created for the development of peasant family farms, which are the foundation of Polish agriculture; that equal access of all sectors to the means of production, including land, be ensured; and that conditions for the rebirth of rural self-government groups be created.

With regard to Point Seven that states: "To pay from Central Trade Union Council funds all striking employees' wages and annual leave," it was decided:

Employees on strike will receive for the period of the strike an advance payment of 40 percent of their normal remuneration and, after they have resumed work, they will receive up to 100 percent of the difference of their remuneration calculated as annual leave based on an eight-hour day. The Inter-Factory Strike Committee appeals to the workers associated with it that—after the strike has ended and in cooperation with the managements of the factories, business enterprises, and other institutions—they should act to increase productivity, to economize on materials and energy, and to enhance conscientiousness in every job.

With regard to Point Eight that states: "To increase the basic wages of each employee by 2,000 zlotys a month to offset present price hikes," it was decided:

Gradual increases in the wages of all employee groups—above all in the lowest paid groups—will be effected. The principle was agreed that wages will be increased in individual factories and in industries. These increases are being implemented and will be continued in keeping with the specifics of trade, professions, and industries and will seek to upgrade remuneration by a single pay step or by suitably increasing other elements of remuneration or the workers' grade. As for office workers in enterprises, their remuneration will be raised by a single pay step in their wages. These pay raises now under discussion will be completed by the end of September this year in accordance with industry accords. After analyzing all industries, the government, in cooperation with the trade unions, will present by October 31 of this year a program for increasing, as of January 1, 1981, the wages of the lowest paid workers, giving special consideration to families with many children.

With regard to Point Nine that states: "To guarantee an automatic increase in wages to compensate for inflation," it was decided:

Price increases for staple goods must be checked by tighter control of the socialized and private sectors, and in particular by stopping so-called hidden price hikes. In keeping with the government's decision, a study will be made of the cost of living. Similar studies will also be conducted by the trade unions and scientific institutes. By the end of 1980 the government will work out the principles of cost-of-living adjustments in compensation. These principles will be subjected to a public discussion and, when agreed upon, will be implemented. They should take into account the wage needed to maintain a minimum subsistence level.

With regard to Point Ten that states: "To ensure adequate supplies of food for the domestic market and to export exclusively surpluses," and to Point Eleven that states: "To abolish commercial prices and sales for hard currencies under the internal export plan of food sales," and to Point Thirteen that states: "To introduce meat rationing—food coupons—[until the market is under control]," it was decided:

Meat supplies for the population will be improved by December 31 of this year by various measures, including: increased profitability of farm production, restricting meat exports to a necessary minimum, and additional meat imports. By December 31 a program will be presented for improving meat supplies for domestic consumption and for eventual meat rationing by means of coupons.

It was agreed that the Pewex shops [which sell items for hard currencies only] will not sell staple consumer goods produced in Poland that are in short supply. The nation will be informed by the end of the year about the decisions and measures concerning supplies for the domestic market.

The Inter-Factory Strike Committee has asked for the elimination of commercial shops [with unregulated prices] and simplifying and standardizing the pricing structure for meat using average prices.

With regard to Point Twelve that states: "To introduce the principle by which leading and managing cadres are selected by virtue of their qualifications rather than party affiliation and to abolish the privileges of the Citizens' Militia [police], the security service, and the party apparatus by equalizing family allowances, closing special stores, and so on," it was decided:

The demand is accepted that the leading and managing cadres should be consistently selected in keeping with the principle of qualifications and abilities from among members of the recognized political parties and nonparty people. A program to equalize family allowances for all industries will be presented by the government by December 31, 1980. The government commission states that employees' restaurants and canteens in all enterprises and offices are operated on similar principles.

With regard to Point Fourteen that states: "To lower the retirement age of women to 50 and men to 55 or to 30 years worked in the Polish People's Republic by women and 35 years by men regardless of their ages," it was decided:

The government commission regards this demand as impossible to fulfill in view of the country's present economic and demographic situation. The issue can be discussed in the future.

The Inter-Factory Strike Committee has asked that this issue be examined by December 31, 1980, and the possibility be considered of allowing employees doing strenuous work to retire five years early (30 years for women and 35 years for men), and in the case of particularly strenuous work to advance retirement age by at least 15 years. Such early retirement should be at the option of the employee.

With regard to Point Fifteen that states: "To equalize the 'old-plan' pensions and annuities with the present schedule of pensions and annuities," it was decided:

The government commission declares that increases in the lowest pensions and annuities will be effected annually, consistent with the country's economic potential, and will take into account the increases in the minimum wage. The government will present an implementation program by December 31, 1980. The government will propose that the lowest pensions and annuities be raised to the level of the so-called social minimum determined by the research carried out by the appropriate institutes, presented to the public, and controlled by the trade unions. The Inter-Factory Strike Committee stresses the extreme urgency of this issue and maintains its demand that the pensions and annuities of the old and new plans be equalized and that adjustments be made for increases in the cost of living.

With regard to Point Sixteen that states: "To improve health services so as to ensure complete medical care for working persons," it was decided:

It is considered necessary immediately to increase investment in health services, to improve the supply of medicines through additional imports, to increase the wages of all health service workers (to change the wage scale for nurses), and urgently to draw up government and departmental programs for improving the state of the nation's health. Other measures in this field are listed in an annex.

[The annex to Point Sixteen, which is omitted here, contains 30 provisions pertaining to the pay and benefits of doctors, nurses, and other health service employees, as well as provisions on improving health care facilities and services.]

With regard to Point Seventeen that states: "To ensure the necessary vacancies in crèches and kindergartens for working women's children," it was decided:

The government commission fully agrees with the importance of this demand. The voivodship authorities will present the necessary program by November 20, 1980.

With regard to Point Eighteen that states: "To grant maternity leave for three years for infant care," it was decided:

By December 31, 1980, a study will be carried out—in cooperation with the trade unions—of the national economy's potential and length of leave, and the amount of monthly payment will be determined for women on maternity leave (now unpaid). The Inter-Factory Strike Committee demands that such a study consider a payment equivalent to full wages for the first year after the birth and to 50 percent of full wages in the second year, but not less than 2,000 zlotys a month. This demand should be met in stages, beginning with the first half of 1981.

With regard to Point Nineteen that states: "to reduce the waiting period for apartments," it was decided:

By December 31, 1980, the voivodship authorities will present a program for improving the housing situation in order to reduce the waiting time for apartments. This program will be extensively discussed by the people of the voivodship and will be in consultation with the appropriate organizations (the Association of Polish Town Planners, the Association of Architects of the Polish Republic, the Chief Technical Organization, and so on). The program should also consider the utilization of existing plants manufacturing housing components and the further development of the production base of construction trades. Similar measures will be taken nationwide.

With regard to Point Twenty that states: "To raise the per diem from 40 zlotys to 100 zlotys and to increase family separation allowances," it was decided:

As of January 1, 1981, travel and separation allowances will be increased. The government is to present appropriate proposals concerning the matter by October 31, 1980.

With regard to Point Twenty-One that states: "To make all Saturdays work free, with employees working on a shift or under the four-brigade system to be compensated for Saturdays by an increased annual leave allowance or by other paid days off," it was decided:

We will work out and present by December 31, 1980, principles and methods of implementing the program for paid work-free Saturdays as well as other proposals for a shorter workweek. This program will provide for a larger number of paid work-free Saturdays as early as 1981. Other measures in this regard are contained in an annex listing the demands of the Inter-Factory Strike Committee.

[The annex to Point Twenty-One which is omitted here, contains seven provisions pertaining to hours, wages, and benefits for specific categories of workers.]

Having made the aforementioned decisions, the following agreement was reached:

The government pledges to ensure the personal security and observe the working conditions of the participants in the current strike and of the persons assisting them; to examine at the ministerial level the specific problems of different enterprises as submitted by the work force of all the striking factories associated with the Inter-Factory Strike Committee; and to publicize immediately the full text of this protocol in the national mass media (the press, radio, and television).

The Inter-Factory Strike committee pledges to end the strike at 1700 hours on August 31, 1980.

Signed by:

Chairman Lech Walesa and the 17 other members of the presidium
of the Inter-Factory Strike Committee;
Mieczyslaw Jagielski, vice chairman of the Council of Ministers of the Polish People's Republic; and the three other members of the government negotiating commission

Bibliography

Chapter 1

Alton, Thad Paul. *Polish Postwar Economy*. New York: Columbia University Press, 1955.

Anders, Wladyslaw. *An Army in Exile: The Story of the Second Polish Corps*. London: Macmillan, 1949.

Ascherson, Neal. *The Polish August: The Self-Limiting Revolution*. New York: Penguin, 1981.

Backus, Oswald P. "The Problem of Unity in the Polish-Lithuanian State," *Slavic Review*, 22, No. 3, September 1963, 411–41.

Barnett, Clifford R. (ed.). *Poland*. New Haven: Human Relations Area Files Press, 1958.

Bartoszewski, Wladyslaw. *The Blood Shed Unites Us*. Warsaw: Interpress, 1971.

Bartoszewski, Wladyslaw, and Zofia Lewin (eds.). *The Samaritans: Heroes of the Holocaust*. New York: Twayne, 1971.

Belch, Stanislaus F. *Paul Vladimiri and His Doctrine Concerning International Law and Politics*. 2 vols. The Hague: Mouton, 1965.

Bethell, Nicholas. *Gomulka: His Poland, His Communism*. New York: Holt, Rinehart and Winston, 1969.

______ . *The War That Hitler Won*. London: Allen Lane, 1972.

Bialer, Seweryn. "Poland and the Soviet Imperium," *Foreign Affairs*, 59, No. 3, 1981, 522–39.

Bieasiak, Jack (ed.). *Poland Today: The State of the Republic*. New York: Sharpe, 1981.

Blazynski, George. *John Paul II: A Man from Krakow*. London: Weidenfeld and Nicholson, 1979.

Blejwas, Stanislaus A. "The Origins and Practice of 'Organic Work' in Poland; 1795–1863," *Polish Review*, 15, No. 4, Autumn 1970, 23–54.

______ . "Warsaw Positivism—Patriotism Misunderstood," *Polish Review*, 27, No. 1/2, 1982, 47–54.

Bliss-Lane, Arthur. *I Saw Poland Betrayed*. Indianapolis: Bobbs-Merrill, 1948.

Blit, Lucjan. *The Eastern Pretender: Boleslaw Piasecki*. London: Hutchinson, 1965.

______ . *The Origins of Polish Socialism: The History and Ideas of the First Polish Socialist Party, 1876–1886*. New York: Cambridge University Press, 1971.

Bor-Komorowski, Tadeusz. *The Secret Army*. London: Macmillan, 1951.

Boswell, A. Bruce. "Poland." Pages 154–71 in Albert Goodwin (ed.), *The European Nobility in the Eighteenth Century: Studies of the Nobilities of the Major European States in the Pre-Reform Era.* New York: Harper and Row, 1967.

Brandys, Kazimierz. *A Warsaw Diary, 1978–1981.* New York: Random House, 1983.

Bromke, Adam. "Beyond the Gomulka Era," *Foreign Affairs,* 49, No. 3, April 1971, 480–92.

______. *Poland's Politics: Idealism vs. Realism.* Cambridge: Harvard University Press, 1967.

______. "Poland: The Cliff's Edge," *Foreign Policy,* 41, Winter 1980–81, 154–62.

______. "Poland under Gierek: A New Political Style," *Problems of Communism,* 21, September–October 1971, 1–19.

______. "The 'Znak' Group in Poland," (Pt. 1) *East Europe,* 11, No. 1, January 1962, 15–20.

______. "The 'Znak' Group in Poland," (Pt. 2), *East Europe,* 11, No. 2, February 1962, 11–15.

Bromke, Adam (ed.). *The Communist States at the Crossroads.* New York: Praeger, 1965.

Bromke, Adam, and John W. Strong (eds.). *Gierek's Poland.* New York: Praeger, 1973.

Brown, Peter B. " Muscovy, Poland, and the Seventeenth-Century Crisis," *Polish Review,* 27, No. 3/4, 1982, 55–69.

Brumberg, Abraham (ed.). *Poland: Genesis of a Revolution.* New York: Vintage, 1983.

Brzezinski, Zbigniew. *The Soviet Bloc: Unity and Conflict.* New York: Praeger, 1961.

Brzezinski, Zbigniew, et al. "Poland since 1956," *Polish Review,* 4, No. 3, Summer 1959 (entire issue.).

Budurowycz, Bohdan. *Polish-Soviet Relations, 1932–1939.* New York: Columbia University Press, 1963.

Burks, R.V. *The Dynamics of Communism in Eastern Europe.* Princeton: Princeton University Press, 1961.

Ciechanowski, Jan M. *Defeat in Victory.* Garden City, New York: Doubleday, 1947.

______. *The Warsaw Rising of 1944.* Cambridge: Cambridge University Press, 1974.

Cienciala, Anna M. *Poland and the Western Powers, 1438–1939: A Study in the Interdependence of Eastern and Western Europe.* Toronto: University of Toronto Press, 1968.

Cieplak, Tadeusz N. " Some Distinctive Characteristics of the Communist System in the Polish People's Republic," *Polish Review,* 19, No. 1, 1974, 41–66.

Cieplak, Tadeusz N. (ed.). *Poland since 1965.* New York: Twayne, 1972.

Craig, Mary. *Man from a Far Country: A Portrait of Pope John Paul II.* London: Hodder and Stoughton, 1979.

Cynk, Jerzy B. *History of the Polish Air Force, 1918–1968.* Reading, England: Osper, 1972.

Davies, Norman. *God's Playground: A History of Poland.* 2 vols. New York: Columbia University Press, 1982.

______. "Poland." Pages 39–57 in Martin McCauley (ed.), *Communist Power in Europe 1944–1949.* New York: Barnes and Noble, 1977.

______. *White Eagle, Red Star: The Polish-Soviet War, 1919–1920.* New York: St. Martin's Press, 1972.

Debicki, Roman. *Foreign Policy of Poland, 1919–1950.* Ithaca: Cornell University Press, 1962.

Drzewieniecki, Walter M. *The German-Polish Frontier.* Chicago: Polish Western Association, 1959.

______. "The Polish Army on the Eve of World War II," *Polish Review,* 26, No. 3, 1981, 54–64.

Dyboski, Roman. *Poland in World Civilization.* New York: Barnett, 1950.

Dziewanowski, M.K. " The Communist Party of Poland." Pages 245–80 in Stephen Fischer-Galati (ed.), *The Communist Parties of Eastern Europe.* New York: Columbia University Press, 1979.

______. *The Communist Party of Poland: An Outline History,.* (2d. ed.) Cambridge: Harvard University Press, 1976.

______. "Dualism or Trialism? Polish Federal Tradition," *Slavonic and East European Review* [London], 41, No. 97, June 1963, 442–66.

______. "1848 and the Hotel Lamber," *Slavonic and East European Review* [London], 26, No. 67, April 1948, 361–73.

______. "Herzen, Bakunin, and the Polish Insurrection of 1863." *Journal of Central European Affairs,* 8, No. 1, April 1948, 58–78.

______. *Joseph Pilsudski: A European Federalist, 1918–1922.* Stanford: Hoover Institution Press, 1969.

______. "Joseph Pilsudski, the Bolshevik Revolution, and Eastern Europe," *Polish Review,* 14, No. 4, Auturm 1969, 14–31.

______. "King Stanislaw Leszczynski: Some Remarks and Question Marks," *Jahrbücher für Geschichte Osteuropas* [Munich], 16, No. 1, March 1968, 104–16.

______. "Leon Petrazycki: On the Fiftieth Anniversary of His Death," *Polish Review,* 26, No. 3, 1981, 3–19.

______. *Poland in the Twentieth Century.* New York: Columbia University Press, 1977.

______. "Social Democrats versus 'Social Patriots'," *American Slavic and East European Review,* 10, No. 1, February 1951, 14–25.

Fejtö, Francois. *A History of the People's Democracies: Eastern Europe since Stalin.* London: Pall Mall Press, 1971.

Fischman, Joseph. *Revolution and Tradition in the People's Republic of Poland.* Princeton: Princeton University Press, 1972.

Fountain, Alvin M. *Roman Dmowski: Party, Tactics, Ideology,*

1895–1907. Boulder: East European Monographs, 1980.

Friedman, Philip. *Their Brothers' Keepers*. New York: Crown, 1957.

Friedman, Philip (ed.). *Martyrs and Fighters: The Epic of the Warsaw Ghetto*. New York: Praeger, 1954.

Garlinski, Jozef. *Fighting Auschwitz*. Greenwich, Connecticut: Fawcett, 1975.

______ . *Intercept: The Enigma War*. London: Dent, 1979.

Giertych, Jedrzej. *In Defence of My Country*. London: Roman Dmowski Society, 1980.

Gieysztor, Aleksander, et al. *History of Poland*. Warsaw: Polish Scientific Publishers, 1968.

Goldhagen, Erich. "Pragmatism, Function, and Belief in Nazi Anti-Semitism," *Midstream*, 18, No. 10, December 1972, 52–62.

Gromada, T.V. (ed.). *Essays on Poland's Foreign Policy, 1918–1939*. New York: Joseph Pilsudski Institute, 1970.

Haiman, Miecislaus. *Kosciuszko, Leader and Exile*. New York: Kosciuszko Foundation, 1977.

Halecki, Oscar. *Borderlands of Western Civilization: A History of East Central Europe*. New York: Ronald Press, 1952.

______ . *The Crusade of Varna: A Discussion of Controversial Problems*. New York: Polish Institute of Arts and Science in America, 1943.

______ . *From Florence to Brest (1439–1596)*. Hampden, Connecticut: Archon Books, 1968 (reprint.).

______ . *A History of Poland*. (9th ed.) London: Kegan Paul, 1978.

______ . *Poland and Christendom*. Houston: University of St. Thomas Press, 1964.

______ . "Poland's Eastern Frontiers, 981–1939," *Journal of Central European Affairs*, 1, No. 2, July 1941, 191–207.

______ . "The Problem of Federalism in the History of East Central Europe," *Polish Review*, 5, No. 3, Summer 1960, 5–19.

______ . "Problems of Polish Historiography," *Slavonic and East European Review*, (American Series, 2), 21, 1942–43, 223–39.

______ . "The Significance of the Christianization of Poland in European History," *Polish Review*, 6, No. 1–2, Winter-Spring 1961, 3–18.

______ . "Why Was Poland Partitioned?" *Slavic Review*, 22, No. 3, September 1963, 432–41.

Haskins, Charles Homer, and Robert H. Lord. *Some Problems of the Peace Conference*. Cambridge: Harvard University Press, 1920.

Hiscocks, Richard. *Poland: Bridge for the Abyss? An Interpretation of Developments in Post-War Poland*. New York: Oxford

University Press, 1963.

Iranek-Osmecki, Kazimierz. *He Who Saves One Life*. New York: Crown, 1971.

Jedruch, Jacek. *Constitutions, Elections, and Legislatures of Poland, 1493–1977: A Guide to Their History*. Washington: University Press of America, 1982.

Jedrychowski, Stefan. *The Fundamental Principles of Economic Policy in Industry*. Warsaw: Polonia, 1957.

Jedrzejewicz, Waclaw (ed.). *Poland in the British Parliament, 1939–1945*. 3 vols. New York: Joseph Pilsudski Institute, 1946–59.

Jordan, Z. *Oder-Neisse Line: A Study of the Politics, Economics, and European Significance of Poland's Western Frontier*. London: Polish Freedom Movement, Independence and Democracy (NID), 1952.

Kaplan, Herbert H. *The First Partition of Poland*. New York: Columbia University Press, 1962.

Karpinski, Jakub. *Countdown: The Polish Upheavals of 1956, 1968, 1970, 1976, and 1980*. New York: Karz-Cohl, 1982.

Karski, Jan. *Story of a Secret State*. Boston: Houghton Mifflin, 1944.

Kieniewicz, Stefan. *The Emancipation of the Polish Peasantry*. Chicago: University of Chicago Press, 1969.

______. "The Free City of Cracow (1815–1846)," *Slavonic and East European Review* [London], 26, No. 66, November 1947, 69–89.

______. "Polish Society and the Insurrection of 1863," *Past and Present* [London], No. 37, July 1967, 130–48.

Kimche, John *The Unfaught Battle*. London: Weidenfeld and Nicholson, 1968.

Kimmich, Christoph M. *The Free City of Danzig and German Foreign Policy, 1919–34*. New Haven: Yale University Press, 1968.

Kisielewski, Stefan, et al. "Poland from Inside: Part II," *Survey* [London], 25, No. 1, Winter 1980 (entire issue.).

Knoll, Paul W. *The Rise of the Polish Monarchy: Piast Poland in East Central Europe, 1320–70*. Chicago: University of Chicago Press, 1972.

Kobot, Jozef. *The Logic of the Oder-Neisse Frontier*. Poznan: Wydawnictwo Zachodnie, 1959.

Kolakowski, Leszek, and Jan Gross. "Church and Democracy in Poland: Two Views," *Dissent*, 27, Summer 1980, 316–27.

Kolakowski, Leszek, et al. "Poland from Inside: Part I," *Survey* [London], 24, No. 4, Autumn 1979 (entire issue.).

Komarnicki, Tytus. *The Rebirth of the Polish Republic*. London: Heineman, 1957.

Korbel, Joseph. *Poland Between East and West*. Princeton: Princeton University Press, 1963.

Korbonski, Andrzej. "Poland." Pages 37–70 in Teresa Rakowska-Harmstone and Andrew Gyorgy (eds.), *Communism in Eastern Europe*. Bloomington: Indiana University Press, 1979.

______. *Politics of Socialist Agriculture in Poland, 1945–1960*. New York: Columbia University Press, 1964.

Korbonski, Stefan. *Fighting Warsaw*. New York: Minerva Books, 1956.

______. *The Polish Underground State*. New York: Columbia University Press, 1978.

Kruszewski, Anthony Z. *The Oder-Neisse Boundary and Poland's Modernization*. New York: Praeger, 1972.

Kulski, Julian E. *Dying We Live*. New York: Holt, Rinehart and Winston, 1979.

Kulski, W.W. *Germany and Poland*. Syracuse: Syracuse University Press, 1976.

Lane, David, and George Kolankiewicz (eds.). *Social Groups in Polish Society*. New York: Columbia University Press, 1973.

Lednicki, Waclaw. *Henryk Sienkiewicz (1846–1946)*. New York: Polish Institute of Arts and Sciences, 1948.

______. *Life and Culture of Poland*. New York: Roy, 1944.

Leslie, R.F. (ed.). *The History of Poland since 1863*. Cambridge: Cambridge University Press, 1980.

Lewin, Isaac. "Attempts at Rescuing European Jews with the Help of Polish Diplomatic Missions during World War II," (Pt. 1), *Polish Review*, 22, No. 4, 1977, 3–23.

______. "Attempts at Rescuing European Jews with the Help of Polish Diplomatic Missions during World War II," (Pt. 2), *Polish Review*, 24, No. 1, 1979, 46–61.

______."Attempts at Rescuing European Jews with the Help of Polish Diplomatic Missions during World War II," (Pt. 3), *Polish Review*, 27, No. 1–2, 1982, 99–111.

Lewis, Flora. *A Case of Hope: The Story of Poland's Peaceful Revolution*. Garden City, New York: Doubleday, 1958.

Lewitter, Lucjan R. "John III Sobieski: Saviour of Vienna," (Pt. 1), *History Today* [London], 12, No. 3, March 1962, 168–76.

______. "John III Sobieski: Saviour of Vienna," (Pt. 2), *History Today* [London], 12, No. 4, April 1962, 243–52.

______. "The Partitions of Poland," (Pt. 1), *History Today* [London], 8, No. 12, December 1958, 813–20.

______. "The Partitions of Poland," (Pt. 2), *History Today* [London], 9, No. 1, January 1959, 30–39.

______. "Peter the Great and the Polish Election of 1697," *Cambridge Historical Journal* [London], 12, No. 1, 1956, 126–43.

______. "Poland, the Ukraine, and Russia in the 17th Century," (Pt. 1), *Slavonic and East European Review* [London], 27, No. 68, December 1948, 157–71.

______. "Poland, the Ukraine, and Russia in the 17th Century,"

(Pt. 2), *Slavonic and East European Review* [London], 27, No. 69, May 1949, 414–29.

______ . "Russia, Poland, and the Baltic, 1697–1721," *Historical Journal* [London], 11, No. 1, 1968, 3–34.

Lipski, Jozef. *Diplomat in Berlin, 1933–1939: Papers and Memoirs of Jozef Lipski.* (Ed., Waclaw Jedrzejewicz.) New York: Columbia University Press, 1968.

Lukasiewicz, Juliusz. *Diplomat in Paris, 1936–1939: Memoirs of Juliusz Lukasiewicz.* (Ed., Waclaw Jedrzejewicz.) New York: Columbia University Press, 1970.

Lord, Robert H. *The Second Partition of Poland: A Study in Diplomatic History.* Cambridge: Harvard University Press, 1915.

______ . "The Third Partition of Poland," *Slavonic Review* [London], 3, No. 9, March 1925, 481–98.

Lorit, Sergius C. *The Last Days of Maximilian Kolbe.* New York: New City Press, 1982.

Manteuffel, Tadeusz. *The Formation of the Polish State: The Period of Ducal Rule, 963–1194.* Detroit: Wayne State University Press, 1982.

______ . "On Polish Feudalism," *Mediaevalia et Humanistica*, 16, 1964, 94–104.

Mastny, Vojtech. "The Benes-Stalin-Molotov Conversations in December 1943: New Documents," *Jahrbücher für Geschichte Osteuropas* [Munich], 20, No. 3, September 1972, 367–402.

Mickiewicz, Adam. *Pan Tadeusz, or, The Last Foray in Lithuania.* (Trans., Watson Kirkconnell.) New York: Polish Institute of Arts and Sciences of America, 1981.

Mikolajczyk, Stanislaw. *The Rape of Poland: The Pattern of Soviet Domination.* New York: Whitlesey House, 1948.

Milosz, Czeslaw. *The Captive Mind.* (Trans., James Zielonko.) New York: Octagon Books, 1981.

______ . *The History of Polish Literature.* London: Macmillan, 1969.

______ . *Native Realm: A Search for Self-Definition.* (Trans., Catherine S. Leach.) Berkeley and Los Angeles: University of California Press, 1981.

______ . *The Seizure of Power.* (Trans., Celina Wieniewska.) New York: Farrar, Straus, and Giroux, 1982.

Mizwa, Stephen (ed.). *Great Men and Women of Poland.* New York: Macmillan, 1943.

Mocha, Frank (ed.). *Poles in America.* Stevens Point, Wisconsin: Worzalla, 1978.

Montias, J.M. *Central Planning in Poland.* New Haven: Yale University Press, 1952.

Nowak, C.M. *Czechoslovak-Polish Relations, 1918–1938.* Stanford: Hoover Institution Press, 1976.

Nowak, Jan. "The Church in Poland," *Problems of Communism,*

31, No. 1, January/February 1982, 1–16.
______. *Courier from Warsaw.* Detroit: Wayne State University Press, 1982.

Paderewski, Ignacy Jan, and Mary Lawton. *The Paderewski Memoirs.* New York: DeCapo Press, 1980.

Pelczynski, Zbigniew A., et al. "Poland," *Canadian Slavonic Papers* [Ottawa], 15, No. 1/2, Spring/Summer 1973 (entire issue.).

Pelenski, Jaroslaw (ed.). *The American and European Revolutions, 1776–1848.* Iowa City: University of Iowa Press, 1980.

Peszke, Michael Alfred. "The Polish Armed Forces in Exile—Part I: September 1939–July 1941," *Polish Review,* 26, No. 1, 1981, 67–113.

Piekalkiewicz, Jaroslaw. *Communist Local Government: A Study of Poland.* Athens: Ohio University Press, 1975.

Pilsudski, Jozef. *Memoirs of a Polish Revolutionary and Soldier.* (Trans., D.R. Gillie.) London: Faber and Faber, 1931.

Polonsky, Antony. *Politics of Independent Poland, 1921–1939: The Crisis of Constitutional Government.* Oxford: Clarendon Press, 1972.

Polonsky, Anthony (ed.). *The Great Powers and the Polish Question, 1941–45: A Documentary Study in Cold War Origins.* London: Orbis Books for the London School of Economics and Political Science, 1976.

Pragier, Adam. *Polish War Aims.* London: Max Lowe, 1944.

Reddaway, W.F., et al. (eds.). *The Cambridge History of Poland, I (from the Origins to Sobieski).* Cambridge: Cambridge University Press, 1941.

______. *The Cambridge History of Poland, II (from Augustus II to Pilsudski).* Cambridge: Cambridge University Press, 1950.

Reymont, Ladislas. *The Peasants: Autumn, Winter, Spring, Summer. A Tale of Our Own Time.* (Trans., Michael H. Dziewicki.) New York: Knopf, 1937.

Roberts, Henry L. "The Diplomacy of Colonel Beck." Pages 579–614 in Gordon A. Craig and Felix Gilbert (eds.), *The Diplomats, 1919–1939.* Princeton: Princeton University Press, 1953.

Robinson, William F. (ed.). *August 1980: The Strikes in Poland.* Munich: Radio Free Europe Research, 1980.

Roos, Hans. *A History of Modern Poland.* New York: Knopf, 1966.

Rose, William J. *Stanislaw Konarski: Reformer of Education in Eighteenth-Century Poland.* London: Cape, 1929.

Rosenthal, Harry K. *German and Pole: National Conflict and Modern Myth.* Gainesville: University Press of Florida, 1976.

Rothschild, Joseph. *East Central Europe Between the Two World Wars.* Seattle: University of Washington Press, 1977.

______. *Pilsudski's Coup d'Etat.* New York: Columbia University

Press, 1966.
Rozek, Edward. *Allied Wartime Diplomacy*. New York: Wiley, 1958.
Rudnicki, K.S. *The Last of the War Horses*. London: Bachman and Turner, 1974.
Rupnik, Jacques. "Dissent in Poland, 1968–78: The End of Revisionism and the Rebirth of Civil Society." Pages 60–112 in Rudolf L. Tökés (ed.), *Opposition in Eastern Europe*. Baltimore: Johns Hopkins University Press, 1979.
Sancton, Thomas A. "Poland's Lech Walesa: Man of the Year," *Time*, January 4, 1982, 13–20.
Schmitt, Bernadotte E. (ed.). *Poland*. Berkeley and Los Angeles: University of California Press, 1947.
Sharp, Samuel L. *New Constitutions in the Soviet Sphere*. Washington: Foundation for Foreign Affairs, 1950.
Shneiderman, S.L. *The Warsaw Heresy*. New York: Horizon, 1959.
Sienkiewicz, Henryk. *Quo Vadis?* (Trans., C.J. Hogarth.) London: Everyman, 1976.
Simon, Maurice D., and Roger E. Kanet (eds.). *Background to Crisis: Policy and Politics in Gierek's Poland*. Boulder: Westview Press, 1981.
Singer, Daniel. *The Road to Danzig: Poland and the USSR*. New York: Monthly Review Press, 1981.
Spiewak, Pawel. "Polish Reform: A Long Way to Go," *Orbis*, 25, No. 3, Fall 1981, 663–76.
Staar, Richard F. "The Opposition Movement in Poland," *Current History*, 80, No. 465, April 1981, 149–53.
——— . *Poland, 1944–1962*. New Orleans: Louisiana State University Press, 1962.
Stankiewicz, W.J. (ed.). *The Tradition of Polish Ideals: Essays in History and Literature*. London: Orbis Books, 1981.
Stehle, Hansjakob. *The Independent Satellite*. New York: Praeger, 1965.
Steven, Stewart. *The Poles*. New York: Macmillan, 1982.
Stypulkowski, Zbigniew. *Invitation to Moscow*. New York: Walker, 1962.
Suikiennicki, Wiktor. "The Establishment of the Soviet Regime in Eastern Poland in 1939," *Journal of Central European Affairs*, 23, No. 2, July 1963, 191–218.
Syrop, Konrad. *Spring in October*. New York: Praeger, 1957.
Szczepanski, Jan. *Polish Society*. New York: Random House, 1970.
Taylor, Jack J. *The Economic Development of Poland, 1919–1950*. Ithaca: Cornell University Press, 1952.
Tazbir, Janusz. *A State Without Stakes*. New York: Kosciuszko Foundation, 1974.
Tenebaum, Joseph. *Underground*. New York: Philosophical Library,

1952.

Tomsky, Alexander. "Poland's Church on the Road to Gdansk," *Religion in Communist Lands* [Keston, England], No. 1/2, 1981, 28–39.

Ulam, Adam B. *Dangerous Relations: The Soviet Union in World Politics, 1970–1983*. New York: Oxford University Press, 1983.

______. *Titoism and the Cominform*. Cambridge: Harvard University Press, 1952.

Urban, Laszlo K. "Once More with Hindsight: German–Polish Interwar Trade Negotiations," *East European Quarterly*, 17, No. 1, Winter 1983, 89–108.

Wagner, W.J. *The Gentleman from Tennessee Is Wrong*. Notre Dame, Indiana: Balticum, 1957.

Wagner, W.J. (ed.). *Polish Law Throughout the Ages*. Stanford: Hoover Institution Press, 1970.

Wandycz, Damian S. (ed.). *Studies in Polish Civilization*. New York: Institute on East Central Europe, Columbia University, 1971.

Wandycz, Piotr S. *Czechoslovak–Polish Confederation and the Great Powers, 1940–43*, 3. Bloomington: Indiana University Press, 1956.

______. *France and Her Eastern Allies, 1919–1925: French-Czechoslovak-Polish Relations from the Paris Peace Conference to Locarno*. Minneapolis: University of Minnesota Press, 1962.

______. *The Lands of Partitioned Poland, 1975–1918*. Seattle: University of Washington Press, 1974.

______. *Soviet-Polish Relations, 1917–1921*. (Russian Research Center Studies, No. 59.) Cambridge: Harvard University Press, 1969.

______. *The United States and Poland*. Cambridge: Harvard University Press, 1980.

Weinryb, Bernard D. *The Jews of Poland: A Social and Economic History of the Jewish Community in Poland from 1100 to 1800*. Philadelphia: Jewish Publication Society of America, 1973.

Weintraub, Wiktor. "Tolerance and Intolerance in Old Poland," *Canadian Slavonic Papers* [Montreal], 13, No. 1, 1971, 21–43.

Weschler, Lawrence. *Solidarity: Poland in the Season of Its Passion*. New York: Simon and Schuster, 1982.

de Weydenthal, Jan B. "Academic Dissent as a Catalyst for Political Crisis in a Communist System," *Polish Review*, 19, No. 1, 1974, 17–40.

______. *The Communists of Poland*. Stanford: Hoover Institution Press, 1978.

______. "Workers and Party in Poland," *Problems of Communism*, 29, No. 6, November–December 1980, 1–22.

Williams, George H. *The Mind of John Paul II*. New York: Seabury Press, 1981.

Winiewicz, Jozef. *The German–Polish Frontier*. London: Polish Research Centre, 1945.

Wojtyla, Karol. *The Acting Person*. Dordrecht, Netherlands: Reidel, 1974.

Wolodkowicz, Andrzej. *The Polish Contribution to Arts and Sciences in Canada*. Montreal: White Eagle Press, 1964.

Woodall, Jean (ed.). *Policy and Politics in Contemporary Poland: Reform, Failure, Crisis*. New York: St. Martin's Press, 1982.

Wynot, Edward D. *Polish Politics in Transition*. Athens: University of Georgia Press, 1974.

Zawodny, J.K. *Death in the Forest: The Story of the Katyn Forest Massacre*. Notre Dame, Indiana: University of Notre Dame Press, 1971.

Zielinski, J.G. *Economic Reform in Polish Industry*. London: Oxford University Press, 1973.

Ziffer, Bernard. *Poland: History and Historians*. New York: Mid-European Studies Center, 1952.

Zinner, Paul E. (ed.). *National Communism and Popular Revolt: A Selection of Documents of Events in Poland and Hungary, February–November 1956*. New York: Columbia University Press, 1956.

Zweig, Ferdynand. *Poland Between Two Wars*. London: Secker and Warburg, 1944.

Chapter 2

Adamski, Wladyslaw, and Yrjo-Paavo Hayrynen. "Educational Systems." Pages 217–44 in Erik Allardt and Wlodzimierz Wesolowski (eds.), *Social Structure and Change: Finland and Poland Comparative Perspective*. Warsaw: Polish Scientific Publishers, 1978.

Alestalo, Matti, Kazimierz M. Slomczynski, and Wlodzimierz Wesolowski. "Patterns of Social Stratification." Pages 117–46 in Erik Allardt and Wlodzimierz Wesolowski (eds.), *Social Structure and Change: Finland and Poland Comparative Perspective*. Warsaw: Polish Scientific Publishers, 1978.

Alestalo, Matti, et al. " Cultural Participation and Social Structure," Pages 357–85 in Erik Allardt and Wlodzimierz Wesolowski (eds.), *Social Structure and Change: Finland and Poland Comparative Perspective*. Warsaw: Polish Scientific Publishers, 1978.

Allardt, Erik, and Wlodzimierz Wesolowski (eds.). *Social Stucture and Change: Finland and Poland Comparative Perspective*. Warsaw: Polish Scientific Publishers, 1978.

"Alma Mater Autonomous," Foreign Broadcast Information Service, *Daily Report: Eastern Europe*, 2, No. 188 (FBIS–EEU–82–188), September 28, 1982, G–18–G20.

Ascherson, Neal. *The Polish August: The Self-Limiting Revolution*.

New York: Penguin Books, 1981.
"Believers' Complaints," *Survey* [London], 24, No. 4, Autumn 1979, 223–29.
Beskid, Lidia, Antti Karisto, and Hannu Uusitalo. " Income and Consumption." Pages 245–64 in Erik Allardt and Wlodzimierz Wesolowski (eds.), *Social Structure and Change: Finland and Poland Comparative Perspective*. Warsaw: Polish Scientific Publishers, 1978.
Bird, Thomas E., and Mieczyslaw Maneli. "The New Turn in Church-State Relations in Poland," *Journal of Church and State*, 24, No. 1, Winter 1982, 29–51.
Bourne, Eric. "Testing Time for Poland's Academic Reforms," *Christian Science Monitor*, September 20, 1982, 8.
Brandys, Kazimierz. "Diary of Poland's Discontent," *New York Times Magazine*, December 5, 1982, 126–32.
Brumberg, Abraham. "Bleak, Bleak Poland," *New York Times*, September 18, 1982, A23.
Connor, Walter D." Social Change and Stability in Eastern Europe," *Problems of Communism*, 26, No. 6, November-December 1977, 16–32.
______. *Socialism, Politics, and Equality: Hierarchy and Change in Eastern Europe and the USSR*. New York: Columbia University Press, 1979.
Davies, Norman. *God's Playground: A History of Poland*. 2 vols. New York: Columbia University Press, 1982.
Dembinski, Ludwik. "The Catholics and Politics in Poland." Pages 176–83 in Adam Bromke and John W. Strong (eds.), *Gierek's Poland*. New York: Praeger, 1973.
"Der mangler bo/ger, men ikke Fryst" (Shortage of Books, but not of Fear), (Pt. 2), Berlingske Tidende [Copenhagen], July 23, 1982, 1.
Dubet, François, Alain Touraine, and Michel Wieviorka. "Une Intervention sociologique avec Solidarnosc," *Sociologie du travail* [Paris], No. 3/82, July-September 1982, 279–92.
Experience and the Future (comp.). *Poland Today: The State of the Republic*. Armonk, New York: Sharpe, 1981.
Fiszman, Joseph R. "Education and Social Mobility in People's Poland." Pages 83–109 in Bernard Lewis Faber (ed.), *The Social Structure of Eastern Europe*. New York: Praeger, 1976.
"The Flying University," *Survey* [London], 24, No. 4, Autumn 1974, 114–26.
Galeski, Boguslaw. "Determinants of Rural Social Change: Sociological Problems of the Contemporary Polish Village." Pages 229–58 in Bernard Lewis Faber (ed.), *The Social Structure of Eastern Europe*. New York: Praeger, 1976.
Gömöri, George, "The Cultural Intelligentsia in Poland: The Writers." Pages 167–94 in Bernard Lewis Faber (ed.), *The Social Structure of Eastern Europe*. New York: Praeger, 1976.

Griffith, William E. "Is Poland Not Yet Lost? A Self-Limiting Revolution?" *Fletcher Forum,* 6, No. 1, Winter 1982, 112–37.

Gross, Jan Tomasz. "Poland: Society and the State." Pages 303-26 in Milorad M. Drachkovitch (ed.), *East Central Europe: Yesterday, Today, Tomorrow.* Stanford: Hoover Institution Press, 1982.

Haavid-Mannila, Elina, and Magdalena Sokolowska. "Social Position of Women." Pages 183-216 in Erik Allardt and Wlodzimierz Wesolowski (eds.), *Social Structure and Change: Finland and Poland Comparative Perspective.* Warsaw: Polish Scientific Publishers, 1978.

Hirszowicz, Maria. "Intelligentsia versus Bureaucracy? The Revival of a Myth in Poland," *Soviet Studies* [Glasgow], 30 No. 3, July 1978, 336–61.

Huszczo, Adaline. "Public Opinion in Poland." Pages 41-82 in Walter D. Connor and Zvi Y. Gitelman (eds.), *Public Opinion in European Socialist Systems.* New York: Praeger, 1977.

International Yearbook of Education, XXXII. Paris: UNESCO, 1980, 166.

Jaakkola, Magdalena, and Waclaw Makarczyk. "Social Networks." Pages 331–56 inErik Allardt and Wlodzimierz Wesolowski (eds.), *Social Structure and Change: Finland and Poland Comparative Perspective.* Warsaw: Polish Scientific Publishers, 1978.

Janicka, Krystyna. "Intergenerational Mobility in Cities." Pages 81–101 in Kazimierz Slomczynski and Tadeusz Krauze (eds.), *Class Structure and Social Mobility in Poland.* White Plains, New York: Sharpe, 1978.

Joint Publications Research Service–JPRS (Washington). The following items are from the JPRS series:

East Europe Report: Economic and Industrial Affairs.

"Demographic Determinants of the Socio-Economic Processes, 1981–85," *Rada Narodowa Gospodarka Administracja,* Warsaw, June 15, 1982. (JPRS 81670, No. 2310, August 31, 1982.)

East Europe Report: Political, Sociological, and Military Affairs.

"Final Text of [Teacher's] Charter," *Dziennik Ustaw,* Warsaw, February 1, 1982. (JPRS 80534, No. 1997, April 9, 1982.)

Kaminska, Anna. "The Polish Pope and the Polish Catholic Church," *Survey* [London], 24, No. 4, Autumn 1979, 204–22.

Kaser, Michael. *Health Care in the Soviet Union and Eastern Europe.* Boulder: Westview Press, 1976.

Kay, Joseph. "The Polish Opposition," *Survey* [London], 24, No. 4, Autumn 1979, 7–20.

Keefe, Eugene K., et al. *Area Handbook for Poland.* (DA Pam 550–162.) Washington: GPO for Foreign Area Studies, The American University, 1973.

Kifner, John. "Under Martial Law, Polish Economy Slips into Reverse," *New York Times,* September 19, 1982, E3.

Kolakowski, Leszek. "Ideology in Eastern Europe." Pages 43–54 in Milorad M. Drachkovitch (ed.), *East Central Europe: Yesterday, Today, Tomorrow.* Stanford: Hoover Institution Press, 1982.

Kolankiewicz, George. "The New 'Awkward Class': The Peasant-Worker in Poland," *Sociologia Ruralis* [Assen, Netherlands], 20, No. 1, 1980, 28–43.

_____. "The Polish Industrial Manual Working Class." Pages 88–157 in David Land and George Kolankiewicz (eds.), *Social Groups in Polish Society.* New York: Columbia University Press, 1973.

Korbonski, Andrzej. "Social Deviance in Poland: The Case of the Private Sector." Pages 89–112 in Ivan Volgyes (ed.), *Social Deviance in Eastern Europe.* Boulder: Westview Press, 1978.

Krol, Marcin. "A Frozen Image of the Past," *Survey* [London], 25, No. 1 Winter 1980, 100–109.

Lane, David. "Structural and Social Change in Poland." Pages 1–18 in David Lane and George Kolankiewicz (eds.), *Social Groups in Polish Society.* New York: Columbia University Press, 1973.

Lane, David, and George Kolankiewicz (eds.). *Social Groups in Polish Society.* New York: Columbia University Press, 1973.

Lewis, Paul. "The Peasantry." Pages 29–87 in David Lane and George Kolankiewicz (eds.), *Social Groups in Polish Society.* New York: Columbia University Press, 1973.

Lobodzinska, Barbara. "The Education and Employment of Women in Contemporary Poland," *Signs,* 3, No. 3, Spring 1978, 688–97.

Malanowski, Jan. "Relations Between Classes and Perception of Social Class Distance." Pages 125–40 in Kazimierz Slomczynski and Tadeusz Krauze (eds.), *Class Structure and Social Mobility in Poland.* White Plains, New York: Sharpe, 1978.

Malewska-Peyre, H. "Les Recherches sur les modes de pensée égalitaire en Pologne," *Sociologie du travail* [Paris], No. 3/82, July–September 1982, 333–44.

Malia, Martin. "Poland: The Winter War," *New York Review of Books,* 29, No. 4, March 18, 1982, 21–26.

Malinowska, Halina. "Extent and Effects of Alcoholism in People's Poland," *Survey* [London], 25, No. 1, Winter 1980, 53–57.

Matejko, Alexander. *Social Change and Stratification in Eastern Europe: An Interpretive Analysis of Poland and Her Neighbors.* New York: Praeger, 1974.

Meyer, John W., Nancy Brandon Tuma, and Krzystof Zagórski. "Education and Occupational Mobility: A Comparison of Polish and American Men," *American Journal of Sociology,* 84, No. 4, January 1979, 978–86.

Millard, L. Frances. "Health Care In Poland: From Crisis to Crisis," *International Journal of Health Services,* 12, No. 3, 1982, 497–515.

_____."The Health of the Polish Health Service," *Critique* [Glasgow], 8, April 5–8, 1982, 57–91.

Mink, Georges. "La Sociologie polonaise: histoire et tendances," *Sociologie du travail* [Paris], No. 3/82, July–September 1982, 249–61.

Nagengast, Marian C. "Polish Peasants and the State," *Dialectical Anthropology*, 7, No. 1, September 1982, 47–66.

Nowak, Jan. "The Church in Poland," *Problems of Communism*, 31, No. 1, January–February 1982, 1–16.

Nowak, Stefan. "A Decent Person and Higher Necessity," *Survey* [London], 25, No. 1, Winter 1980, 115–17.

______. "A Polish Self-Portrait," *Polish Perspectives* [Warsaw], 24, No. 2, February 1981, 13–29.

______. "Values and Attitudes of the Polish People," *Scientific American*, 245, No. 1, July 1981, 45–53.

Pienkos, Donald E. "Changes in Peasant Political and Religious Attitudes and Behavior in Poland," *Polish Review*, 23, No. 1, 1978, 58–68.

Pine, Frances T., and Przemek T. Bogdanowicz. "Policy Response and Alternative Strategy: The Process of Change in a Polish Highland Village," *Dialectical Anthropology*, 7, No. 1, September 1982, 67–80.

Poland. Central Statistical Office. *Concise Statistical Yearbook of Poland, 1982*, Warsaw, 1982.

Poland. Glowny Urzad Statystyczny (Central Statistical Office). *Narodowy Spis Powszechny Zdnia 7XII 1978*. Warsaw: 1980.

"Poland." Pages 165–67 in *International Yearbook of Education, 1980*, 32. (Ed., Brian Holmes.) Paris: United Nations Educational, Scientific and Cultural Organization, 1980.

"Poland." Pages 227–31 in *Sixth Report on the World Health Situation 1973–1977*. Geneva: World Health Organization, 1980.

"Polish Language." Page 159 in *Encyclopedia Britannica*, 18. Chicago: Encyclopedia Britannica, 1969.

Pospieszalski, Antoni. "Lay Catholic Organizations in Poland," *Survey* [London], 24, No. 4, Autumn 1979, 237–45.

Roemer, Milton I., and Ruth Roemer. *Health Manpower in the Socialist Health Care System of Poland*. (DHEW Publication [HRA] 77–85.) Washington: Department of Health, Education, and Welfare, 1977.

Rothschild, Joseph. *East Central Europe Between the Two World Wars*. Seattle: University of Washington Press, 1977.

Rupnik, Jacques. "Dissent in Poland, 1968–78: The End of Revisionism and the Rebirth of the Civil Society." Pages 60–112 in Rudolf L. Tökés (ed.), *Opposition in Eastern Europe*. Baltimore: Johns Hopkins University Press, 1979.

Sabbat, Anna. "Agreement with Polish Students in Lodz: A Summary Assessment," Radio Free Europe Research, 6, No. 14, March 2–4, 1981, 1–15.

Sabbat-Swidlicka, Anna. "Before the Next Plenum: Is Poland's Youth a Lost Generation?" Radio Free Europe Research,

Background Report, 7, No. 28, July 16, 1982, 1–14.

Sanford, George. "Polish People's Republic." Pages 553–88 in Bogdan Szajkowski (ed.), *Marxist Governments: A World Survey, Volume 3: Mozambique-Yugoslavia*. New York: St. Martin's Press, 1981.

Shoup, Paul S. *The East European and Soviet Data Handbook: Political, Social, and Developmental Indicators, 1945–1975*. New York: Columbia University Press, 1981.

Simon, Maurice D. "A Window on Poland's Social Transformation," *Problems of Communism*, 29, No. 2, March-April 1980, 76–80.

"Situation Report: Poland," Radio Free Europe Research, 6, No. 18, March 12–13, 1981, 1–35.

"Situation Report: Poland," Radio Free Europe Research, 6, No. 35, May 14–15, 1981, 1–37.

"Situation Report: Poland," Radio Free Europe Research, 6, No. 51, July 17–21, 1981, 1–20.

"Situation Report: Poland," (Pt. 2), Radio Free Europe Research, 7, No. 3, January 22,1982, 1–35.

"Situation Report: Poland," (Pt. 3), Radio Free Europe Research, 7, No. 5, February 5, 1982, 1–36.

"Situation Report: Poland," (Pt. 1), Radio Free Europe Research, 7, No. 18, May 7, 1982, 1–21.

"Situation Report: Poland," (Pt. 1), Radio Free Europe Research, 7, No. 20, May 21, 1982, 1–16.

"Situation Report: Poland," (Pt. 1), Radio Free Europe Research, 7, No. 38, September 24, 1982, 1–39.

"Situation Report: Poland," (Pt. 1), Radio Free Europe Research, 7, No. 41, October 15, 1982, 1–36.

Slomczynski, Kazimierz, and Tadeusz Krauze (eds.). *Class Structure and Social Mobility in Poland*. White Plains, New York: Sharpe, 1978.

Staniszkis, Jadwiga. "The Evolution of Forms of Working-Class Protest in Poland: Sociological Reflections on the Gdansk-Szczecin Case, August 1980." *Soviet Studies* [Glasgow], 33, No. 2, April 1981, 204–31.

______. "Polish Peaceful Revolution: An Anatomy of Polarization," *Journal of Peace Research* [Oslo], 19, No. 2, 1982, 181–95.

Staron, Stanislaw. "The State and the Church." Pages 158–75 in Adam Bromke and John W. Strong (eds.), *Gierek's Poland*. New York: Praeger, 1973.

Starski, Stanislaw. *Class Struggle in Classless Poland*. Boston: Southend Press, 1982.

Steven, Stewart. *The Poles*. New York: Macmillan, 1982.

Szafar, Tadeusz. "Contemporary Opposition in Poland," *Survey* [London], 24, No. 4, Autumn 1979, 40–55.

Szczepanski, Jan. "Early Stages of Socialist Industrialization and Changes in Social Class Structure." Pages 11–36 in Kazimierz Slomczynski and Tadeusz Krauze (eds.), *Class Structure and*

Social Mobility in Poland. White Plains, New York: Sharpe, 1978.
———. *Polish Society.* New York: Random House, 1970.
Tarniewski, Marek. "The New Regime," *Survey* [London], 25, No. 1, Winter 1980, 118–34.
Tellenback, Sten. "The Logic of Development in Socialist Poland," *Social Forces,* 57, No. 2, December 1978, 436–56.
Toivonen, Timo, and Stanislaw Widerszpil. "Changes in Socio-Economic and Class Structure." Pages 89–116 in Erik Allardt and Wlodzimierz Wesolowski (eds.), *Social Structure and Change: Finland and Poland Comparative Perspective.* Warsaw: Polish Scientific Publishers, 1978.
Turowicz, Jerzy. "The Changing Catholicism in Poland." Pages 151–57 in Adam Bromke and John W. Strong (eds.), *Gierek's Poland.* New York: Praeger, 1973.
United States. Department of Commerce. Bureau of the Census. *Demographic Estimates for Countries with a Population of 10 Million or More: 1981.* Washington: 1981.
Vaughan, Michalina. "A Multidimensional Approach to Contemporary Polish Stratification," *Survey* [London], 20, No. 1, Winter 1974, 62–74.
Wesolowski, Wlodzimierz. "The Notions of Strata and Class in Socialist Society." Pages 5–28 in Bernard Lewis Faber (ed.), *The Social Structure of Eastern Europe.* New York: Praeger, 1976.
Wesolowski, Wlodzimierz, and Tadeusz Krauze. "Socialist Society and the Meritocratic Principle of Remuneration." Pages 337–49 in Gerald D. Berreman (ed.), *Social Inequality: Comparative and Developmental Approaches.* New York: Academic Press, 1981.
de Weydenthal, Jan B. "The Workers' Dilemma of Polish Politics: A Case Study," *East European Quarterly,* 13, No. 1, Spring 1979, 95–119.
Zagórski, Krzysztof. "Social Mobility in Poland." Pages 71–78 in Bernard Lewis Faber (ed.), *The Social Structure of Eastern Europe.* New York: Praeger, 1976.
———. "Transformation of Social Structure and Social Mobility in Poland." Pages 61–80 in Kazimierz Slomczynski and Tadeusz Krauze (eds.), *Class Structure and Social Mobility in Poland.* White Plains, New York: Sharpe 1958.
———. "Urbanization and Resulting Changes in Class Structure and Education." Pages 48–60 in Kazimierz Slomczynski and Tadeusz Krauze (eds.), *Class Structure and Social Mobility in Poland.* White Plains, New York: Sharpe, 1958.
(Various issues of the following publications were also used in the preparation of this chapter: *Christian Science Monitor,* August 1980–January 1983; Joint Publications Research Service, *East Europe Report: Political, Sociological and Military Affairs,* August 1980–September 1982: *New York Times,* August 1980–January 1982; and *Washington Post,* August 1980–January 1982.)

Chapter 3

Adams, Arthur E. "The Soviet Agricultural Model in Eastern Europe," *East European Quarterly*, 8, No. 4, January 1975, 461–77.

Allen, Gary. "The Bankers and the Crisis in Poland," *American Opinion*, 25, April 1982, 23–25.

Alton, Thad Paul. *Polish Postwar Economy*. New York: Columbia University Press, 1955.

Alton, Thad Paul, et al. *Agricultural Output, Expenses and Depreciation, Gross Product, and Net Product in Eastern Europe, 1965, 1970, and 1975–1980*. (Occasional Papers series, OP–67.) New York: Research Project on National Income in East Central Europe, 1981.

______. *Eastern Europe: Domestic Final Uses of Gross Product, Selected Years, 1965, 1970, and 1975–1980*. (Occasional Papers series, OP–66.) New York: Research Project on National Income in East Central Europe, 1981.

______. *Economic Growth in Eastern Europe, 1965, 1970, and 1975–1980*. (Occasional Papers series, OP–65.) New York: Research Project on National Income in East Central Europe, 1981.

______. *Official and Alternative Consumer Price Indexes in Eastern Europe, Selected Years, 1960–1980*. (Occasional Papers series, OP–68.) New York: Research Project on National Income in East Central Europe, 1981.

______. *The Structure of Gross National Product in Eastern Europe (Derivation of GNP Weights for 1975–1977)*. (Occasional Papers series, OP–64.) New York: Research Project on National Income in East Central Europe, 1981.

Annual Bulletin of Transport Statistics for Europe, 1980, 32. New York: United Nations, Economic Commission for Europe, 1981.

Baird, Jane, and Darrell Delamaide. "The Lessons of Poland," *Institutional Investor*, 16, No. 1, January 1982, 223–26.

Ball, Robert. "Poland's Economic Disaster," *Fortune*, 104, September 7, 1981, 42–45.

Blenkey, Nicholas. "Poland's Shipbuilding: A Study in Success," *Marine Engineering/Log*, 95, August 1980, 49, 52.

Bouren, Eric. "Polish Farmers Get a 'Union'—But Not the Tools They Need," *Christian Science Monitor*, November 24, 1982, 7.

Brumberg, Abraham. "The Workers' Discontented State," *New Republic*, August 30, 1980, 21–23.

Brus, Wlodzimierz. "Aims, Methods, and Political Determinants of the Economic Policy of Poland, 1970–1980. Pages 91–128 in Alec Nove, Hans-Hermann Höhmann, and Gertraud Seidenstecher (eds.), *The East European Economies in the*

1970s. London: Butterworth, 1982.

Bryson, Philip J. *Scarcity and Control in Socialism: Essays on East European Planning*. Lexington, Massachusetts: Lexington Books, 1976.

Burzynski, Andrzej, and Julian Conrad Juergensmeyer. "Poland's New Foreign Investment Regulations: An Added Dimension to East-West Industrial Cooperation," *Vanderbilt Journal of Transnational Law,* 14, No. 1, Winter 1981, 17–49.

Cameron, Juan. "What the Bankers Did to Poland," *Fortune,* 102, September 22, 1980, 125–126.

Colitt, Leslie. "Western Businessmen Find Plenty of Profit in Poland," *Financial Times* [London], January 13, 1983, 5.

"Country Review Paper: Poland," *Land Reform* [Rome], No. 1/2, 1980, 69–78.

"Dairying: Poland's Milk Problems Apply World Wide," *Financial Times* [London], September 21, 1982, 26.

Davies, Norman. *God's Playground: A History of Poland, Volume 2: 1795 to the Present.* New York: Columbia University Press, 1982.

Duymovic, Andrew A. "Poland's Agricultural Policies in the 1970s: Impact on Agricultural Trade with the U.S." Pages 185–97 in Ronald A. Francisco, Betty A. Laird, and Roy D. Laird (eds.), *Agricultural Policies in the USSR and Eastern Europe*. Boulder: Westview Press, 1980.

"Eastern Europe: Seedbed of Capitalism," *Economist* [London], September 25, 1982, 42–43.

East-West (Research and Advisory). *Polish Economic Trends till 1980.* (Research Report No. 10.) Brussels: March 1977.

"The Economic Background to Poland's Difficulties," *International Currency Review* [London], 12, No. 5, 1980 23–28.

Facts about Poland. Warsaw: Interpress, 1980.

Fallenbuchl, Zbigniew M. "Poland: Command Planning in Crisis," *Challenge*, 24, No. 3, July/August 1981, 5–12.

———. "Poland's Economic Crisis," *Problems of Communism*, 31, No. 2, March/April 1982, 1–21.

———. "Poland's Maritime Transport." Pages 43–123 in Bogdan Mieczkowski (ed.), *East European Transport: Regions and Modes.* The Hague: Nijhoff, 1980.

FAO Production Yearbook 1981, 35. Rome: Food and Agriculture Organization, 1982.

Feiwel, George R. "A Socialist Model of Economic Development: The Polish and Bulgarian Experiences," *World Development*, 9, No. 9/10, 1981, 929–50.

Flakierski, Henryk. "Economic Reform and Income Distribution in Poland: The Negative Evidence," *Cambridge Journal of Economics* [London], 5, June 1981, 137–58.

Gabrisch, Hubert. "Economic Reforms in Poland," *Intereconomics* [Hamburg], 16, No. 2, March/April 1981, 70–74.

Galeski, Boguslaw. "Solving the Agrarian Question in Poland," *Sociologia Ruralis* [Assen, Netherlands], 22, No. 2, 1982, 149–66.

Gomulka, Stanislaw. "Growth and the Import of Technology: Poland 1971–1980," *Cambridge Journal of Economics* [London], 2, March 1978, 1–16.

Greene, Robert P., and J. Michael Gallagher (eds.). *Future Coal Prospects: Country and Regional Assessments.* (World Coal Study series.) Cambridge, Massachusetts: Ballinger, 1980.

Hardt, John P., Francis T. Miko, and Victoria L. Engel. "The Polish 'Renewal' and the Debt Problem." (Library of Congress Congressional Research Service, Major Issues System, IB80089.) August 25, 1982.

Hardt, John P., and Kate Tomlinson. "Rescheduling the Polish Debt." (Library of Congress Congressional Research Service, Major Issues System, IB82082.) September 9, 1982.

Jane's World Railways, 1980–81. (Ed., Paul Goldsack.) New York: Jane's, 1980.

Johnson, Paul M. "Lights Out in Poland: The Crackup of Socialist Planning," *Inquiry*, 5, No. 4, February 28, 1982, 22–25.

Joint Publications Research Service—JPRS (Washington). The following items are from the JPRS series:

East Europe Report: Economic and Industrial Affairs.

"Current Situation in Polish Aircraft Industry," *Technika Lotnicza i Astronautyczna*, Warsaw, June 1982. (JPRS 81568, No. 2306, August 18, 15–23.)

"Effectiveness of Individual, Socialized Farming Compared," *Przeglad Techniczny*, Warsaw, October 26, 1980. (JPRS 77105, No. 2078, January 5, 1981, 25–30.)

"Inviolability of Private Farm Ownership Guaranteed," *Slowo Powszechne*, Warsaw, May 7–9, 1982. (JPRS 81124, No. 2285, June 24, 1982, 62–66.)

"Law on Socioeconomic Planning Published," *Gospodarka Planowa*, Warsaw, April 1982. (JPRS 81631, No. 2308, August 25, 1982, 67–82.)

"Long-Range Development of Transportation Outlined." *Przeglad Kommunikacyjny*, Warsaw, April 1981. (JPRS 79313, No. 2193, October 27, 1981, 66–79.)

"Polish Economic Situation, Reform Outlined," *Magyarorszag*, Budapest, September 27, 1981. (JPRS 79465, No. 2201, November 18, 1981, 32–38.)

"Polish Government Report on State of the Economy," *Trybuna Ludu*, Warsaw, July 1981. (JPRS 79144, No. 2183, October 5, 1981, 1–90.)

"Proposals for Basic Solutions to Economic Reform in Poland," *Zycie Gospodarcze*, Warsaw, November 16, 1980. (JPRS 77425, No. 2096, February 20, 1981, 41–105.)

"Proposed Economic Reforms Include Systems, Methods

Changes," *Trybuna Ludu,* Warsaw, July 10, 1981. (JPRS 78785, No. 2161, August 19, 1981, 55–60.)
"Wage Spread, Growth Rate in 1970–1979 Analyzed," *Gospodarka Planowa,* Warsaw, April 1980. (JPRS 76061, No. 2025, July 17, 1980, 65–8.)
"West German Analysis of Polish Indebtedness to the West," *DIW, Vierteljahresheft,* West Berlin, January–March 1981. (JPRS 79096, No. 2180, September 29, 1981, 68–84.)

Jurenas, Remy. "Poland's Food Shortages and the Status of Food Assistance to Poland." (Library of Congress Congressional Research Service, Major Issues System, IB82011.) May 6, 1982.

Kahan, Arcadius. *Agriculture in Eastern Europe: Production Growth and Variability (Final Report to the National Council for Soviet and East European Research.)* Chicago: University of Chicago, February 1982.

Lewis, Paul. "Economic Reforms in Poland Facing a Growing Opposition," *New York Times,* November 22, 1982, Al.

——— . "Output Down as Workers Cut Hours: Poland's Struggle with Coal Production," *New York Times,* October 1, 1981, D1.

——— . "Poland, Hands on Reins, Tries to Spur Economy," *New York Times,* August 2, 1982, A2.

——— . "Poland's Lost Coal Markets," *New York Times,* July 27, 1981, DL.

Marer, Paul, and Eugeniusz Tabaczynski (eds.). *Polish-U.S. Industrial Cooperation in the 1980s: Findings of a Joint Research Project.* Bloomington: Indiana University Press, 1981.

Mellor, Roy E.H. *Eastern Europe: A Geography of the Comecon Countries.* New York: Columbia University Press, 1975.

Mieczkowski, Bogdan. *Transportation in Eastern Europe: Empirical Findings.* Boulder: East European Quarterly, 1978.

Mieczkowski, Bogdan (ed.). *East European Transport: Regions and Modes.* The Hague: Nijoff, 1980.

Minerals Yearbook, 1978–79. Volume III, Area Reports: International. Washington: GPO for United States Department of the Interior, Bureau of Mines, 1981.

Minerals Yearbook, 1980. Volume III, Area Reports: International. Washington: GPO for United States Department of the Interior, Bureau of Mines, 1982.

Mink, Georges, and Anita Tirapolsky. "Pologne: l'économie militarisée à l'épreuve du temps," *Courrier des pays de l'est* [Paris], No. 261, April 1982, 34–49.

Mujzel, Jan. "The Working System of the Economy: Problems with Its Further Development in Poland," *Eastern European Economics,* 20, No. 1, Fall 1981, 20–48.

North Atlantic Treaty Organization. Directorate of Economic Affairs. *Comecon: Progress and Prospects.* (Colloquium held March 16–18, 1977, in Brussels. Series No. 6.) Brussels: n. d.

North Atlantic Treaty Organization. Economics Directorate and

Information Directorate (eds.). *CMEA: Energy, 1980–1990.* Newtonville, Massachusetts: Oriental Research Partners, 1981.

Nove, Alec, Hans-Hermann Höhmann, and Gertraud Seidenstecher (eds.). *The East European Economies in the 1970s.* London: Butterworths, 1982.

Organisation for Economic Co-operation and Development. *Prospects for Agricultural Production and Trade in Eastern Europe. Vol. 1: Poland, German Democratic Republic, Hungary.* Paris: 1981.

Park, Daniel. *Oil and Gas in Comecon Countries.* New York: Nichols, 1979.

Piekalkiewicz, Jaroslaw A. "Kulakization of Polish Agriculture," Pages 86–107 in Ronald A. Francisco, Betty A. Laird, and Roy D. Laird (eds.), *The Political Economy of Collectivized Agriculture: A Comparative Study of Communist and Noncommunist Systems.* New York: Pergamon Press, 1979.

Poland. Central Statistical Office. *Concise Statistical Yearbook of Poland, 1982,* Warsaw: 1982.

Poland. Glowny Urzad Statystyczny (Central Statistical Office). *Rocznik Statystyczny Handlu Zagranicznego, 1980.* Warsaw: 1980.

"Poland," *Financial Times* [London], December 5, 1975, 33–38 (Survey.).

Pounds, Norman J.G. *Eastern Europe.* Chicago: Aldine, 1969.

Price Waterhouse. *Doing Business in Eastern Europe.* n. pl.: October 1982.

Scriven, John G. "Joint Ventures in Poland: A Socialist Approach to Foreign Investment Legislation," *Journal of World Trade Law* [Twickenham, England], 14, No. 5, September/October 1980, 424–38.

Selucky, Radoslav. *Economic Reforms in Eastern Europe: Political Background and Economic Significance.* New York: Praeger, 1972.

Simon, Maurice D., and Roger E. Kanet (eds.). *Background to Crisis: Policy and Politics in Gierek's Poland.* Boulder: Westview Press, 1981.

Steven, Stewart. *The Poles.* New York: Macmillan, 1982.

Szyndler-Glowacki, Wieslaw. "Polish-US Trade," *Polish Perspectives* [Warsaw], 18, No. 3, March 1975, 15–23.

Turnock, David. *Eastern Europe.* (Studies in Industrial Geography series.) Folkestone, England: William Dawson and Sons, 1978.

United Nations. Department of International Economic and Social Affairs. Statistical Office. *Monthly Bulletin of Statistics.* 36, No. 10, 1982 (entire issue.).

United States. Central Intelligence Agency. National Foreign Assessment Center. *Comparing Planned and Actual Growth of Industrial Output in Centrally Planned Economies.* Washington: August 1980.

———. *Energy Supplies in Eastern Europe: A Statistical Compilation*. Washington: December 1979.

———. *Estimating Soviet and East European Hard Currency Debt*. Washington: June 1980.

———. *The Scope of Poland's Economic Dilemma*. Washington: July 1978.

United States Congress. 91st, 2d Session. Joint Economic Committee. Subcommittee on Foreign Economic Policy. *Economic Development in Countries of Eastern Europe: A Compendium of Papers*. Washington: GPO, 1970.

United States Congress. 95th, 1st Session. Joint Economic Committee. *East European Economies Post-Helsinki*. Washington: GPO, 1977.

United States Congress. 97th, 1st Session. Joint Economic Committee. *East European Economic Assessment: Part 1—Country Studies, 1980*. (A compendium of papers submitted to the committee on February 27, 1981.) Washington: GPO, 1981.

———. *East European Economic Assessment: Part 2—Regional Assessments*. (A compendium of papers submitted to the committee on July 10, 1981.) Washington: GPO, 1981.

United States Congress. 97th, 2d Session. Commission on Security and Cooperation in Europe. *Implementation of the Helsinki Accords: Soviet Involvement in the Polish Economy*. Washington: GPO, 1982.

United States. Congress. 97th, 2d session. Joint Economic Committee. *Poland: Performance and Prospects in Trade with the United States and the West*. Washington: GPO, 1982.

United States. Department of Commerce. International Trade Administration. *Foreign Economic Trends and Their Implications for the United States: Poland*. Washington: GPO, October 1982.

United States. Department of State. Bureau of Public Affairs. *Poland: Financial and Economic Situation*. (Special Report No. 96.) Washington: January 27, 1982.

Vankai, Thomas A. "Poland's 5–Year Plan Sets High Food Goals," *Foreign Agriculture*, 15, No. 31, August 1, 1977, 6–8.

Wanless, P.T. "Economic Reform in Poland, 1973–79." *Soviet Studies* [Glasgow], 32, No. 1, January 1980, 28–57.

de Weydenthal, Jan B. "Small-Scale Socialized Industry in Poland: Problems and Prospects," Radio Free Europe Research, *Background Report*, 97, April 30, 1979.

Wilson, Carroll L. *Coal—Bridge to the Future: Report of the World Coal Study*. Cambridge, Massachusetts: Ballinger, 1980.

Wojciechowski, Bronislaw. *Polish Foreign Trade 1976: Facts, Figures, and Problems*. Warsaw: Polish Chamber of Foreign Trade, 1977.

______ . *Prospects in Trade with the Socialist Countries of Eastern Europe. Poland: Policies, Developments, and Institutional Framework.* Geneva: United Nations Conference on Trade and Development, August 6, 1979.

Zwass, Adam. "The Economic Situation in Poland in Light of the Eighth Party Congress," *Eastern European Economics,* 20, No. 1, Fall 1981, 3–19.

(Various issues of the following publication were also used in the preparation of this chapter: Joint Publications Research Service, *East Europe Report: Economic and Industrial Affairs,* May 1980–January 1983.)

Chapter 4

Ascherson, Neal. *The Polish August: The Self-Limiting Revolution.* New York: Penguin Books, 1981.

Bialer, Seweryn. "Poland and the Soviet Imperium," *Foreign Affairs,* 59, No. 3, 1981, 522–39.

Bird, Thomas E., and Mieczyslaw Maneli. "The New Turn in Church-State Relations in Poland," *Journal of Church and State,* 24, No. 1, Winter 1982, 29–51.

Bromke, Adam. "The Opposition in Poland," *Problems of Communism,* 27, No. 5, September–October 1978, 37–51.

______ . "Poland's Upheaval—An Interim Report," *World Today* [London], 37, No. 6, June 1981, 211–18.

Bromke, Adam, and John W. Strong (eds.). *Gierek's Poland.* New York: Praeger, 1973.

"The Church vs. the State," *Newsweek,* February 15, 1982, 8–11.

Darnton, Nina. "The Subtle Power of the Polish Church," *New York Times Magazine,* June 6, 1982, 23.

Davies, Norman. *God's Playground: A History of Poland, Volume 2: 1795 to the Present.* New York: Columbia University Press, 1982.

Day, Alan (ed.). *Political Parties of the World.* Harlow, England: Longman Group, 1980.

Dziewanowski, M.K. "The Communist Party of Poland." Pages 245–80 in Stephen Fischer-Galati (ed.), *The Communist Parties of Eastern Europe.* New York: Columbia University Press, 1979.

Editor and Publisher Yearbook. New York: 1982.

Experience and the Future (comp.). *Poland Today: The State of the Republic.* Armonk, New York: Sharpe, 1981.

Facts about Poland. Warsaw: Interpress, 1980.

Flanz, Gisbert H. "Poland." Pages 1–46 in Albert P. Blaustein and Gisbert H. Flanz (eds.), *Constitutions of the Countries of the World.* Dobbs Ferry, New York: Oceana, 1978.

Frankowski, Stanislaw J. "Polish People's Republic." Pages 175–202 in George F. Cole, Stanislaw J. Frankowski, and Marc G. Gertz (eds.), *Major Criminal Justice Systems.* Beverly Hills: Sage, 1981.

Gati, Charles. "Polish Futures, Western Options," *Foreign Affairs,* 61, No. 2, Winter 1982–83, 292–308.

Gross, Jan Tomasz. "Poland: Society and the State."Pages 303–26 in Milorad M. Drachkovitch (ed.), *East Central Europe: Yesterday, Today, Tomorrow.* Stanford: Hoover Institution Press, 1982.

Haig, Alexander. *Poland and the Future of Europe.* (Current Policy series, No. 362.) Washington: Department of State, Bureau of Public Affairs, January 12, 1982.

Hirszowicz, Maria. "Poland's 'Black Book'," *Index on Censorship* [London], 7, No. 4, July–August 1978, 28–34.

Jedruch, Jacek. *Constitutions, Elections, and Legislatures of Poland, 1493–1977.* Washington: University Press of America, 1982.

Johnson, A. Ross. *Poland in Crisis.* (Rand Note, N–1891–AF.) Santa Monica: Rand, July 1982.

Kaminska, Anna. "The Polish Pope and the Polish Catholic Church," *Survey* [London], 24, No. 4, Autumn 1979, 204–22.

Kanet, Roger E. "Poland, the Socialist Community, and East-West Relations." Pages 371–401 in Maurice D. Simon and Roger E. Kanet (eds.). *Background to Crisis: Policy and Politics in Gierek's Poland.* Boulder: Westview Press, 1981.

Karpinski, Jakub. *Countdown: The Polish Upheavals of 1956, 1968, 1970, 1976, and 1980.* New York: Karz-Cohl, 1982.

Kay, Joseph. "The Polish Opposition," *Survey* [London], 24, No. 4, Autumn 1979, 7–20.

Kolankiewicz, George. "Renewal, Reform, or Retreat: The Polish Communist Party after the Extraordinary Ninth Congress," *World Today* [London], 37, No. 10, October 1981, 369–75.

Korbonski, Andrzej. "Poland." Pages 37–70 in Teresa Rakowska-Harmstone and Andrew Gyorgy (eds.), *Communism in Eastern Europe.* Bloomington: Indiana University Press, 1979.

Lechowicz, Leszek. "The Mass Media under Martial Law," *Poland Watch,* No. 1, Fall 1982, 41–49.

Malia, Martin. "Poland: The Winter War," *New York Review of Books,* 29, No. 4, March 18, 1982, 21–26.

Marer, Paul, and John Michael Montias. *East European Integration and East-West Trade.* Bloomington: Indiana University Press, 1980.

Michnik, Adam. "Poland's Lesson in Freedom," *Index on Censorship* [London], 11, No. 2, April 1982, 16–18.

Nowak, Jan. "The Church in Poland," *Problems of Communism,* 31, No. 1, January–February 1982, 1–16.

Piekalkiewicz, Jaroslaw. *Communist Local Government: A Study of Poland.* Athens: Ohio University Press, 1975.

______ "Polish Local Politics in Flux: Concentration or Deconcentration." Pages 176–90 in Daniel N. Nelson (ed.), *Local Politics in Communist Countries*. Lexington: University Press of Kentucky, 1980.

Pospieszalski, Antoni. "Lay Catholic Organizations in Poland," *Survey* [London]. 24. No. 4, Autumn 1979, 237–45.

Pszenicki, Chris. "Polish Publishing, 1980–81," *Index on Censorship* [London], 11, No. 1, February 1982, 8–11.

Rachwald, Arthur R. "Poland Between the Superpowers: Three Decades of Foreign Policy," *Orbis*, 20, No. 4, Winter 1977, 1055–83.

______ . "Poland: Quo Vadis?" *Current History*, 81, No. 481, November 1982, 371–92.

Raina, Peter. *Political Opposition in Poland*. London: Poets and Painters Press, 1978.

Rakowski, Mieczyslaw F. *The Foreign Policy of the Polish People's Republic*. Warsaw: Interpress, 1975.

Ramet, Pedro. "Poland's 'Other' Parties," *World Today* [London], 37, No. 9, September 1981, 332–38.

Robinson, William F. (ed.). *August 1980: The Strikes in Poland*. Munich: Radio Free Europe Research, 1980.

Rupnik, Jacques. "Dissent in Poland, 1968–78: The End of Revisionism and the Rebirth of the Civil Society." Pages 60–112 in Rudolf L. Tökés (ed.), *Opposition in Eastern Europe*. Baltimore: Johns Hopkins University Press, 1979.

Sabbat-Swidlicka, Anna. "Before the Next Plenum: Is Poland's Youth a Lost Generation?" Radio Free Europe Research, *Background Report*, 7, No. 28, July 16, 1982, 1–14.

______. "General Jaruzelski's Political Prisoners," Radio Free Europe Research, *Background Report*, 8, No. 2, January 14, 1983, 1–22.

______ . "A Profile of Lech Walesa," Radio Free Europe Research, *Background Report*, 7, No. 49, December 10, 1982, 1–11.

Sadowski, Christine M. "Citizen, Voluntary Associations, and the Policy Process." Pages 199–219 in Maurice D. Simon and Roger E. Kanet (eds.), *Background to Crisis: Policy and Politics in Gierek's Poland*. Boulder: Westview Press, 1981.

Sakwa, George, and Martin Crouch. "Sejm Elections in Communist Poland: An Overview and a Reappraisal, *British Journal of Political Science* [London], 8, No. 78, October 1978, 403–24.

Sanford, George. "Polish People's Republic." Pages 553–88 in Bogdan Szajkowski (ed.), *Marxist Governments: A World Survey, Volume 3: Mozambique-Yugoslavia*. New York: St. Martin's Press, 1981.

______ . "The Response of the Polish Communist Leadership to the Continuing Crisis (Summer 1980 to the Ninth Congress, July 1981): Personnel and Policy Changes." Pages 33–44 in Jean Woodall (ed.), *Policy and Politics in Contemporary Poland*.

New York: St. Martin's Press, 1982.

Schöpflin, George. "Poland and Eastern Europe: The Impact of the Crisis." Pages 23–33 in Jean Woodall (ed.), *Policy and Politics in Contemporary Poland.* New York: St. Martin's Press, 1982.

Simes, Dimitri K. "Clash over Poland," *Foreign Policy,* No. 46, Spring 1982, 49–66.

Sokolewicz, Wojciech. "Changes in the Structure and Functions of the Polish Sejm," *East Central Europe,* 11, No. 1, 1975, 78–91.

———. "The System of Administration." Pages 42–94 in Janusz Letowski (ed.), *Administration in People's Poland.* Wroclaw: Polska Akademia Nauk, 1980.

Spiewak, Pawel. "Polish Reform: A Long Way to Go," *Orbis,* 25, No. 3, Fall 1981, 663–76.

"State and Constitutional Tribunals to Monitor Legality," Radio Free Europe Research, *Situation Report,* 7, No. 11, March 18, 1982, 13–19.

Stehle, Hansjakob. "Church and Pope in the Polish Crisis," *World Today* [London], 38, No. 4, April 1982, 139–48.

Steven. Stewart. *The Poles.* New York: Macmillan, 1982.

Swidlicki, Andrew. "The Madrid Report by Social Self-Defense Committee 'KOR'," *Polish Review,* 26, No. 3, 1981, 74–81.

Szafar, Tadeusz. "Brinksmanship in Poland," *Problems of Communism,* 30, No. 3, May–June 1981, 75–81.

Taras, Ray. "Democratic Centralism and Polish Local Government Reforms," *Public Administration* [London], 53, Winter 1975, 403–26.

Terry, Sarah Meiklejohn. "The Sejm as Symbol: Recent Polish Attitudes Toward Political Participation." Pages 27–64 in Maurice D. Simon and Roger E. Kanet (eds.), *Background to Crisis: Policy and Politics in Gierek's Poland.* Boulder: Westview Press, 1981.

"Thirteenth Semiannual Report by the President to the Commission on Security and Cooperation in Europe on the Implementation of the Helsinki Final Act, June 1, 1982–November 30, 1982." Washington: Department of State, 1982.

Underwood, Paul. "Poland." Pages 753–64 in George Thomas Kurian (ed.), *World Press Encyclopedia.* New York: Facts on File, 1981.

United States. Congress. 96th, 1st Session. House of Representatives. Committee on Foreign Affairs. *U.S. Relations with the Countries of Central and Eastern Europe.* Washington: GPO, 1979.

United States. Congress. 97th, 1st Session. Senate, Committee on Foreign Relations. House of Representatives. Committee on Foreign Affairs. *Country Reports on Human Rights Practices.* (Report submitted by the Department of State.) Washington: GPO, February 2, 1981.

United States. Congress. 97th, 2d Session. House of Representatives. Budget Committee. *The United States and Poland: A Report on the Current Situation in Poland after the Declaration of Martial Law.* Washington: GPO, April 1982.

United States. Congress. 97th, 2d Session. Senate. Committee on Foreign Relations. House of Representatives. Committee on Foreign Affairs. *Country Reports on Human Rights Practices for 1981.* (Report submitted by the Department of State.) Washington: GPO, February 1982.

United States. Department of State. Office of Communication. Bureau of Public Affairs. *Background Notes: Poland.* Washington: GPO, November 1979.

Wandycz, Piotr S. *The United States and Poland.* Cambridge: Harvard University Press, 1980.

Weschler, Lawrence. *Solidarity: Poland in the Season of Its Passion.* New York: Simon and Schuster, 1982.

de Weydenthal, Jan B. "Anatomy of the Martial Law Regime: The Institutions," Radio Free Europe Research, *Background Report,* 7, No. 6, February 12, 1982, 1–12.

______. "Poland."" Pages 425–47 in Richard F. Staar (ed.), *Yearbook on International Communist Affairs 1982.* Stanford: Hoover Institution Press, 1982.

______. "Workers and Party in Poland," *Problems of Communism,* 29, No. 6, November–December 1980, 1–22.

Wiatr, Jerzy. "Poland's Party Politics: The Extraordinary Congress of 1981," *Canadian Journal of Political Science* [Waterloo, Ontario], 14, No. 4, December 1981, 813–26.

(Various issues of the following publications were also used in the preparation of this chapter: *Amnesty International Newsletter* [London], December 1981–December 1982; *Christian Science Monitor,* July 1980–January 1983; *Economist* [London], July 1980–January 1983; *Financial Times* [London], July 1980–January 1983; Foreign Broadcast Information Service, *Daily Report: Eastern Europe,* July 1982–January 1983; *Index on Censorship* [London], January 1979–January 1983; *IPI Report* [London], December 1981–December 1982; Joint Publications Research Service, *East Europe Report: Political, Sociological, and Military Affairs,* June 1980–December 1982; *Manchester Guardian Weekly* [London], July 1980–January 1983; *Newsweek,* January 1981–January 1983; *New York Times,* July 1980–January 1983; Radio Free Europe Research, January 1980–January 1983; *Wall Street Journal,* January 1981–January 1983; and *Washington Post,* July 1980–January 1983.)

Chapter 5

Adelman, Jonathan (ed.). *Communist Armies in Politics.* Boulder: Westview Press, 1982.

Alton, Thad Paul, et al. "East European Defense Expenditures, 1965–1978." Pages 409–33 in *East European Economic Assessment: Part 2—Regional Assessments.* (A compendium of papers submitted to the Joint Economic Committee of the Congress of the United States.) Washington: GPO, 1981.

Andelman, David A. "Contempt and Crisis in Poland," *International Security,* 6, No. 3, Winter 1981–82, 90–103.

Anderson, Richard D., Jr., "Soviet Decision-Making and Poland," *Problems of Communism,* 31, No. 2, March–April 1982, 22–36.

Ascherson, Neal. *The Polish August: The Self-Limiting Revolution.* New York: Penguin Books, 1981.

Bailer, Seweryn. "Poland and the Soviet Imperium," *Foreign Affairs,* 59, No. 3, 1981, 522–39.

Bobinski, Christopher, and David Budian. "Jaruzelski Slowly Lifts the Lid," *Financial Times* [London], December 15, 1982, 15.

Bromke, Adam. "The Opposition in Poland," *Problems of Communism,* 27, No. 5, September–October 1978, 37–51.

______. "Poland's Upheaval—An Interim Report," *World Today* [London], 37, No. 6, June 1981, 211–18.

______. "Poland: The Cliff's Edge," *Foreign Policy,* 41, Winter 1980–81, 154–62.

Bromke, Adam, and John W. Strong (eds.). *Gierek's Poland.* New York: Praeger, 1973.

Brumberg, Abraham. "Solidarity Forever," *New Republic,* March 21, 1981, 16–20.

Celt, Ewa. "Wojciech Jaruzelski: A Prime Minister in Uniform," Radio Free Europe Research, *Background Report,* 72, March 13, 1981, 1–4.

Clawson, Robert W., and Lawrence S. Kaplan (eds.). *The Warsaw Pact: Political Purpose and Military Means.* Wilmington, Delaware: Scholarly Resources, 1982.

Cohen, Stephen F. "Sovieticus," *Nation,* 235, No. 17, November 20, 1982, 517.

Darnton, John. "Once Again, to Whom and What Is the Army Loyal?" *New York Times,* February 1, 1981.

______. "The Polish Awakening," *New York Times Magazine,* June 14, 1981, 32–35.

Darnton, Nina. "The Subtle Power of the Polish Church," *New York Times Magazine,* June 6, 1982, 23.

Davies, Norman, *God's Playground: A History of Poland, Volume 2: 1795 to the Present.* New York: Columbia University Press, 1982.

Dobbs, Michael, "Crisis in Communism: The New Poland, Part 1: Unions," *Washington Post,* March 22, 1981, A1.

______. "Crisis in Communism: The New Poland, Part 2: Walesa," *Washington Post,* March 23, 1981, A1.

______. "Crisis in Communism: The New Poland, Part 3: Party

Reform," *Washington Post*, March 24, 1981, A1.

Dziewanowski, M.K. *Poland in the Twentieth Century*. New York: Columbia University Press, 1977.

Erickson, John. *Soviet-Warsaw Pact Force Levels*. (USSI Report 76–2.) Washington: United States Strategic Institute, 1976.

Facts about Poland. Warsaw: Interpress, 1980.

Fallaci, Oriana. "Lech Walesa: The Man Who Drives the Kremlin Crazy" (Interview with Lech Walesa), *Washington Post*, March 8, 1981, C1.

Frankowski, Stanislaw J. "Polish People's Republic." Pages 175–202 in George F. Cole, Stanislaw J. Frankowski, and Marc G. Gertz (eds.), *Major Criminal Justice Systems*. Beverly Hills: Sage, 1981.

Gati, Charles. "Polish Futures, Western Options," *Foreign Affairs*, 61, No. 2, Winter 1982–83, 292–308.

Goldman, Stuart D., and Victoria L. Engel. "Martial Law in Poland." (Library of Congress Congressional Research Service, Major Issues System, IB81181.) July 1, 1982.

"Government Declares Martial Law; Decrees Noted," Foreign Broadcast Information Service, *Daily Report: Eastern Europe*, 2, No. 239 (FBIS–EEU–81–239), December 14, 1981, G13–G17.

Graczyk, Jozef. "Social Promotion in the Polish People's Army." Pages 82–93 in Jacques Van Doorn (ed.), *The Military Profession and Military Regimes*. The Hague: Mouton, 1969.

Hardt, John P., Francis T. Miko, and Victoria L. Engel. "The Polish 'Renewal' and the Debt Problem." (Library of Congress Congressional Research Service, Major Issues System, IB80089.) August 25, 1982.

Herspring, Dale R. "The Polish Military and the Policy Process." Pages 221–38 in Maurice D. Simon and Roger E. Kanet (eds.), *Background to Crisis: Policy and Politics in Gierek's Poland*. Boulder: Westview Press, 1981.

______. "Technology and Civil-Military Relations: The Polish and East German Cases." Pages 123–44 in Dale R. Herspring and Ivan Volgyes (eds.), *Civil-Military Relations in Communist Systems*. Boulder: Westview Press, 1978.

______. "Technology and the Changing Political Officer in the Armed Forces: The Polish and East German Cases," *Studies in Comparative Communism*, 10, No. 4, Winter 1977, 370–94.

______. "The Warsaw Pact at 25," *Problems of Communism*, 29, September–October 1980, 1–15.

Herspring, Dale R., and Ivan Volgyes. "Political Reliability in the Eastern European Warsaw Pact Armies," *Armed Forces and Society*, 6, No. 2, Winter 1980, 270–96.

Jane's Fighting Ships, 1982–83. (Ed., John Moore.) New York: Jane's, 1982.

Johnson, A. Ross. *Poland in Crisis*. (Rand Note, Rand, July 1982.

———. "Soviet-East European Military Relations: An Overview." Pages 243–66 in Dale R. Herspring and Ivan Volgyes (eds.), *Civil-Military Relations in Communist Systems*. Boulder: Westview Press, 1978.

Johnson, A. Ross, Robert W. Dean, and Alexander Alexiev. *East European Military Establishments: The Warsaw Pact Northern Tier*. New York: Crane, Russak, 1982.

Joint Publications Research Service-JPRS (Washington). The following items are from the JPRS series:

East Europe Report: Political, Sociological, and Military Affairs:

"The Air Force: Its Institutions, Schools and Centers, *Skrzydlata Polska*, Warsaw, August 23, 1981. (JPRS 79215, No. 1928, October 15, 1981, 38–44.)

"Civil Defense in the Service of the Defensibility and Security of the Polish People's Republic," *Przeglad Obrony Cywilnej*, Warsaw, February 1981. (JPRS 78096, No. 1880, May 18, 1981, 46–51.

"Decree of the Ministers of National Defense and Internal Affairs," *Dziennik Ustaw*, Warsaw, March 7, 1980. (JPRS 77564, No. 1856, March 11, 1981, 50–58.)

"Dependent Not Only on Ourselves," *Zolnierz Polski*, Warsaw, January 4, 1981. (JPRS 77704, No. 1864, March 30, 1981, 35–38.)

"Fliers, Tankers, Artillerymen and Engineers," *Zolnierz Polski*, Warsaw, April 25, 1981. (JPRS 78162, No. 1883, May 27, 1981, 13–16.)

"It Aids and Rescues," *Czata*, Warsaw, February 22, 1981. (JPRS 78096, No. 1880, May 18, 1981, 51–54.)

"Join the Services!" *Zolnierz Polski*, Warsaw, December 14, 1980. (JPRS 77704, No. 1864, March 30, 1981, 32–35.)

"The Mailed Fist," *Zolnierz Polski*, Warsaw, February 1, 1981. (JPRS 78162, No. 1883, May 27, 1981, 16–19.)

"The Military—An Important Matter," *Zolnierz Polski*, Warsaw, January 11, 1981. (JPRS 77704, No. 1864, March 30, 1981, 38–41.)

"Military Aviation Schools," *Skrzydlata Polska*, Warsaw, January 11, 1981. (JPRS 78430, No. 1894, July 1, 1981, 18–19.)

"National Briefing of Civil Defense Command Personnel," *Przeglad Obrony Cywilnej*, Warsaw, February 1981. (JPRS 78096, No. 1880, May 18, 1981, 44–46.)

"Never Again," *Sztander Mlodych*, Warsaw, September 7, 1981. (JPRS 82114, No. 2069, October 29, 1981, 71–74.)

"On the Maritime Border," *Zolnierz Polski*, Warsaw, February 8, 1981. (JPRS 78162, No. 1883, May 27, 1981, 19–22.)

"The Past and Present of the University of Warsaw Military Department," *Wojsko Ludowe*, Warsaw, October 1980. (JPRS

78430, No. 1894, July 1, 1981, 12–17.)

"Selected Problems of Professional Military Education," *Wojsko Ludowe*, Warsaw, September 1980. (JPRS 78430, No. 1894, July 1, 1981, 7–12.)

"Starting at the Beginning of This School Year—A New System for Military Training of Students" *Trybuna Ludu*, Warsaw, March 4, 1981. (JPRS 78430, No. 1894, July 1, 1981, 19–20.)

"There is No Need to Love the Militia but It Ought to Be Respected," *Zolnierz Polski*, Warsaw, August 15, 1982. (JPRS 82114, No. 2069, October 29, 1982, 63–67.

"ZOMO Behind the Closed Door—They Cry after an Action and Go to Sleep," *Sztandar Ludu*, Lublin, September 3, 4, 5, 1982. (JPRS 82114, No. 2069, October 29, 1982, 67–71.)

Jones, Christopher D. *Soviet Influence in Eastern Europe*. (Studies of Influence in International Relations series.) New York: Praeger, 1981.

______. "The Warsaw Pact: Military Exercises and Military Interventions," *Armed Forces and Society*, 7, No. 1, Fall 1980,. 5–30.

Keefe, Eugene K., et al. *Area Handbook for Poland*. (DA Pam 550–162.) Washington: GPO for Foreign Area Studies, The American University, 1973.

Keegan, John, (ed.). *World Armies*. New York: Facts on File, 1979.

Kolankiewicz, George. "Renewal, Reform, or Retreat: The Polish Communist Party after the Extraordinary Ninth Congress," *World Today* [London], 37, No. 10, October 1981, 369–75.

Kolkowicz, Roman, and Andrzej Korbonski (eds.). *Peasants, Soldiers, and Bureaucrats*. London: Allen and Unwin, 1982.

Korbonski, Andrzej. "The Dilemmas of Civil-Military Relations in Contemporary Poland: 1945–1981," *Armed Forces and Society*, 8, No. 1, Fall 1981, 3–19.

______. "Poland." Pages 37–70 in Teresa Rakowska-Harmstone and Andrew Gyorgy (eds.), *Communism in Eastern Europe*. Bloomington: Indiana University Press, 1979.

______. "The Polish Army." Pages 103–28 in Jonathan R. Adelman (ed.), *Communist Armies in Politics*. Boulder: Westview Press, 1982.

Lange, Peer H. "Poland as a Problem of Soviet Security Policy," *Aussenpolitik* [Hamburg], 32, No. 4, 1981, 332–43.

Larrabee, F. Stephen. "Stability and Change in Eastern Europe," *International Security*, 6, No. 3, Winter 1981–82, 39–64.

Malia, Martin. "Poland: The Winter War," *New York Review of Books*, 29, No. 4, March 18, 1982, 21–26.

The Military Balance, 1982–83. London: International Institute for Strategic Studies, 1982.

Nowak, Jan. "The Church in Poland," *Problems of Communism*, 31, No. 1, January–February 1982, 1–16.

Perlmutter, Amos, and William LeoGrande. "The Party in Uniform: Toward a Theory of Civil-Military Relations in

Communist Systems," *American Political Science Review*, 76, No. 4, December 1982, 778–89.

"Poland from the Inside," *Survey* [London], 24, Autumn 1979 (entire issue.).

"Poland from the Inside," *Survey* [London], 25, Winter 1980 (entire issue.).

Pond, Elizabeth. "Polish Army: How Loyal—and to Whom?" *Christian Science Monitor*, March 10, 1981, 1.

Rachwald, Arthur R. "Poland: Quo Vadis?" *Current History*, 81, No. 481, November 1982, 371–9.

Raina, Peter. *Political Opposition in Poland*. London: Poets and Painters Press, 1978.

Reddaway, Norman. "The Polish Crisis," *Contemporary Review*, 238, February 1981, 57–62.

Remington, Robin Alison. *The Warsaw Pact: Case Studies in Conflict Resolution*. Cambridge: MIT Press, 1971.

Robinson, Anthony. "Dual Authority with a Vengeance: Armed Forces Push Communist Party into Supporting Role," *Financial Times* [London], December 15, 1981, 2.

Robinson, William F. (ed.). *August 1980: The Strikes in Poland*. Munich: Radio Free Europe Research, 1980.

Rupnik, Jacques. "Dissent in Poland, 1968–78: The End of Revisionism and the Rebirth of the Civil Society." Pages 60–112 in Rudolf L. Tökés (ed.), *Opposition in Eastern Europe*. Baltimore: Johns Hopkins University Press, 1979.

Sabbat, Anna. "Reformist Trends in the Polish Police Force," Radio Free Europe Research, *Background Report*, 296, October 27, 1981, 1–11.

Sancton, Thomas A. "Poland's Lech Walesa: Man of the Year," *Time*, January 4, 1982, 13–20.

Sanford, George. "Polish People's Republic." Pages 553–88 in Bogdan Szajkowski (ed.), *Marxist Governments: A World Survey, Volume 3: Mozambique-Yugoslavia*. New York: St. Martin's Press, 1981.

Seegar, Murray. "Poland: A Weakened Communist Party Fights for Survival," *Atlantic Monthly*, December 1980, 6–9.

Spielman, Richard. "Crisis in Poland," *Foreign Policy*, No. 49, Winter 1982–83, 20–36.

Staar, Richard F. "The Opposition Movement in Poland," *Current History*, 80, No. 465, April 1981, 149–53.

———. "Soviet Policies in East Europe," *Current History*, 80, No. 468, October 1981, 317–20.

Stankovic, Slobadan. "Polish Army Will Not Follow Soviet Command, Yugoslav Weekly Claims," Radio Free Europe Research, *Background Report*, 193, September 23, 1982, 1–4.

Stefanowski, Roman, "A Partial List of Martial Law Institutions," Radio Free Europe Research, *Background Report*, 180, September 7, 1982, 1–6.

Steven, Stewart. *The Poles.* New York: Macmillan, 1982.

Swialto, Jozef. "The Swialto Story," *News from Behind the Iron Curtain,* 4, No. 3, March 1955, 3–36.

Szulc, Tad. "A Question of Freedom: An Interview with the Man Who Rules Poland," *Parade,* July 18, 1982, 4–6.

______. "When Poland's Generals Stood Up to Soviet Might," *Parade,* September 20, 1981, 4–9.

Troute, Dennis. "A Diary from Poland: Solidarity's Beginning," *Boston Globe Magazine,* September 13, 1981, 13.

United States. Arms Control and Disarmament Agency. *World Military Expenditures and Arms Transfers, 1970–79.* Washington: GPO, 1982.

United States. Congress. 97th, 1st session. Senate. Committee on Foreign Relations. House of Representatives. Committee on Foreign Affairs. *Country Reports on Human Rights Practices.* (Report submitted by the Department of State.) Washington: GPO, February 2, 1981.

United States. Congress. 97th, 2d Session. Senate. Committee on Foreign Relations. House of Representatives. Committee on Foreign Affairs. *Country Reports on Human Rights Practices for 1981.* (Report submitted by the Department of State.) Washington: GPO, February 1982.

United States. Department of Defense. Defense Intelligence Agency. *Unclassified Communist Naval Orders of Battle.* Washington: November 1982.

______. *Warsaw Pact Ground Forces Equipment Handbook: Armored Fighting Vehicles.* Washington: 1980.

Vego, Milan. "East European Navies," *U.S. Naval Institute Proceedings, March 1982, 43–47.*

______. *"The Polish Navy," Navy International* [Haslemere, Surrey, England], 87, No. 9, September 1982, 1330–36.

______. "The Polish Navy: Part II," *Navy International* [Haslemere, Surrey, England], 87, No. 10, October 1982, 1393–96.

Weschler, Lawrence. *Solidarity: Poland in the Season of Its Passion.* New York: Simon and Schuster, 1982.

Wiatr, Jerzy J. "The Public Image of the Polish Military: Past and Present." Pages 199–208 in Catherine M. Kelleher (ed.), *Political-Military Systems.* Beverly Hills: Sage, 1974.

Woller, Rudolph. *Warsaw Pact Reserve Systems.* Munich: Bernard and Graefe, 1978.

Woodall, Jean. "New Social Factors in the Unrest in Poland," *Government and Opposition* [London], 16, Winter 1981, 37–57.

(Various issues of the following publications were also used in the preparation of this chapter: *Christian Science Monitor,* July 1980–January 1983; *Economist* [London], July 1980–January 1983; *Financial Times* [London], July 1980–January 1983; Foreign Broadcast Information Service, *Daily Report: Eastern Europe,* July 1982–January 1983; Joint Publications Research Service. *East Europe Report: Political, Sociological, and Military Affairs* and *East Europe Report: Economic and Industrial Affairs,* June 1980–December 1982; *Manchester Guardian Weekly* [London], July 1980–January 1983; *Newsweek,* January 1981–January 1983; *New York Times,* July 1980–January 1983; Radio Free Europe Research, January 1980–January 1983; and *Washington Post,* July 1980–January 1983.)

Appendix B

Ausch, Sandor. *Theory and Practice of CMEA Cooperation.* Budapest: Akademiai Kiado, 1972.

Babitchev, Eugene. "The International Bank for Economic Cooperation." Pages 129–52 in Gregory Grossman (ed.), *Money and Plan.* Berkeley and Los Angeles: University of California Press, 1968.

Ervin, Linda. "The Council for Mutual Economic Assistance: A Selective Bibliography." (Bibliography Series, No. 2.) Ottawa: Norman Paterson School of International Affairs, Carleton University, 1975.

Hannigan, John, and Carl McMillan. "Joint Investment in Resource Development: Sectoral Approaches to Socialist Integration." Pages 259–95 in United States Congress, 97th, 1st Session, Joint Economic Committee, *East European Economic Assessment.* Washington: GPO, 1981.

Hewett, Edward A. *Foreign Trade Prices in the Council for Mutual Economic Assistance.* London: Cambridge University Press, 1974.

———. "The Impact of the World Economic Crisis on Intra-CMEA Trade." Pages 323–48 in Egon Neuberger and Laura D'Andrea Tyson (eds.), *The Impact of International Economic Disturbances on the Soviet Union and Eastern Europe.* New York: Pergamon Press, 1980.

Holzman, Franklyn D. "CMEA's Hard Currency Deficits and Ruble Convertibility." Pages 144–63 in Nita G.M. Watts (ed.), *Economic Relations between East and West.* London: Macmillan, 1978.

Karavaev, V.P. *Integratsiia i investitsii: problemy sotrudnichestva stran SEV.* Moscow: Nauka, 1979.

Kaser, Michael. *Comecon: Integration Problems of the Planned Economies.* (2d ed.) London: Oxford University Press, 1967.

Katushev, K. "Sotrudnichestvo vo imya velikih tselei sotsializma i kommunizma," *Ekonomicheskoe sotrudnichestvo stran-chlenov SEV* [Moscow], No. 1, January 1979, 4–11.

Kiss, T. (ed.). *The Market of Socialist Economic Integration.*

Budapest: Akademiai Kiado, 1973.
Kohn, M.J., and N.R. Lang. "The Intra-CMEA Foreign Trade System: Major Price Changes, Little Reform." Pages 135–51 in United States Congress, 95th, 1st Session, Joint Economic Committee, *East European Economies Post-Helsinki.* Washington: GPO, 1977.
Lavigne, M. *Le Comécon: le Programme du Comécon et l'intégration socialiste.* Paris: Editions Cujas, 1973.
Levcik, Friedrich. "Migration and Employment of Foreign Workers in the CMEA Countries and Their Problems." Pages 458–78 in United States Congress, 95th, 1st Session, Joint Economic Committee, *East European Economies Post-Helsinki.* Washington: GPO, 1977.
Marer, P. "The Political Economy of Soviet Relations with Eastern Europe." Pages 231–60 in S. Rosen (ed.), *Testing Theories of Economic Imperialism.* Lexington, Massachusetts: Heath, 1974.
Marer, P., and J.M. Montias (eds.). *East European Integration and East-West Trade.* Bloomington: Indiana University Press, 1980.
Mellor, Roy E.H. "The Genesis of Comecon and the Sovietization of Eastern Europe." Pages 221–48 in Roy E.H. Mellor (ed.), *Eastern Europe: A Geography of the Comecon Countries.* New York: Columbia University Press, 1975.
Montias, J.M. "Background and Origins of the Romanian Dispute with Comecon," *Soviet Studies* [Glasgow], 6, No. 2, October 1964, 125–51.
The Multilateral Economic Cooperation of Socialist States: A Collection of Documents. Moscow: Progress Publishers, 1977.
North Atlantic Treaty Organization. Economic Directorate. *Comecon: Progress and Prospects.* (Colloquium held March 16–18, 1977.) Brussels: 1977.
Pecsi, K. *Economic Questions of Production Integration Within the CMEA.* (Trends in World Economy Series, No. 24.) Budapest: Hungarian Scientific Council for World Economy, 1978.
______ . "Nekotorye problemy ustanovleniia tsen vo vzaimnoi torgovle stran SEV," *Mirovaia ekonomika i mezhdunarodnye otnostheniia* [Moscow], No. 9, September 1979, 93–101.
Schiavone, Giuseppe. *The Institutions of Comecon.* New York: Holmes and Meier, 1980.
Senin, M. *Socialist Integration.* Moscow: Progress Publishers, 1973.
Vais, Tibor. "Cooperation of the CMEA Countries in the Sphere of Employment." (Paper prepared for symposium on "Some Aspects of Employment Policies in the USSR and East European Countries.") Calgary: University of Calgary, 1980.
Van Brabant, Jozef M. *East European Cooperation: The Role of Money and Finance.* (Studies in International Business, Finance and Trade.) New York: Praeger, 1977.

Vanous, Jan. "Eastern European and Soviet Fuel Trade, 1970–1985." Pages 541–60 in United States Congress, 97th, 1st Session, Joint Economic Committee, *East European Economic Assessment*. Washington: GPO, 1981.

Wilczynski, J. *Technology in Comecon*. London: Macmillan, 1974.

Appendix C

Bemis, Samuel Flagg. *A Diplomatic History of the United States*. New York: Holt, Rinehart and Winston, 1959.

Brzezinski, Zbigniew K. *The Soviet Bloc: Unity and Conflict*. New York: Praeger, 1961.

Caldwell, Lawrence T. "The Warsaw Pact: Directions of Change," *Problems of Communism*, September–October 1975, 1–19.

De Conde, Alexander. *A History of American Foreign Policy*. New York: Charles Scribner's Sons, 1978.

Erickson, John, and E.J. Feuchtwanger. *Soviet Military Power and Performance*. New York: Macmillan, 1979.

Gati, Charles (ed.). *The International Politics of Eastern Europe*. New York: Praeger, 1976.

Grechko, Andrey Antonovich. *The Armed Forces of the Soviet State (A Soviet View)*. (Trans. under auspices of United States Air Force, Soviet Military Thought Series, No. 12.) Washington: GPO, 1975.

Herspring, Dale R. "The Warsaw Pact at 25," *Problems of Communism*, September–October 1980, 1–15.

Herspring, Dale R., and Ivan Volgyes (eds.). *Civil-Military Relations: An Overview*. Boulder: Westview Press, 1979.

Johnson, A. Ross. "Has Eastern Europe Become a Liability to the Soviet Union? (II) The Military Aspect." In Charles Gati (ed.), *The International Politics of Eastern Europe*. New York: Praeger, 1976.

———. "Soviet-East European Military Relations: An Overview." Pages 251–64 in Dale R. Herspring and Ivan Volgyes (eds.), *Civil-Military Relations: An Overview*. Boulder: Westview Press, 1979.

Kulikov, V.G. (ed.). *Varshavskiy dogovor—soyuz vo imya mira i sotsializma*. Moscow: Voenizdat, 1980.

La Feber, Walter F. *America, Russia, and the Cold War*. New York: John Wiley and Sons, 1981.

Mackintosh, Malcolm. "The Warsaw Pact Today," *Survival* [London], May–June, 1974, 122–26.

The Military Balance, 1968–69. London: International Institute for Strategic Studies, 1968.

The Military Balance, 1969–70. London: International Institute for Strategic Studies, 1969.

The Military Balance, 1970–71. London: International Institute for

Strategic Studies, 1970.
The Military Balance, 1971–1972. London: International Institute for Strategic Studies, 1971.
The Military Balance, 1972–1973. London: International Institute for Strategic Studies, 1972.
The Military Balance, 1973–1974. London: International Institute for Strategic Studies, 1973.
The Military Balance, 1974–1975. London: International Institute for Strategic Studies, 1974.
The Military Balance, 1975–1976. London: International Institute for Strategic Studies, 1975.
The Military Balance, 1976–1977. London: International Institute for Strategic Studies, 1976.
The Military Balance, 1977–1978. London: International Institute for Strategic Studies, 1977.
The Military Balance, 1978–1979. London: International Institute for Strategic Studies, 1978.
The Military Balance, 1979–1980. London: International Institute for Strategic Studies, 1979.
The Military Balance, 1980–1981. London: International Institute for Strategic Studies, 1980.
The Military Balance, 1981–1982. London: International Institute for Strategic Studies, 1981.
The Military Balance, 1982–1983. London: International Institute for Strategic Studies, 1982.
Remington, Robin Alison (ed.). *The Warsaw Pact: Case Studies in Communist Conflict Resolution*. Cambridge: MIT Press, 1971.
______ . *Winter in Prague: Documents on Czechoslovak Communism in Crisis*. Cambridge: MIT Press, 1969.
Sidorenko, Andrei Alekseevich. *The Offensive (A Soviet View)*. (Trans. under auspices of United States Air Force, Soviet Military Thought Series, No. 7.) Washington: GPO, 1970.
Sokolovskiy, V.D. *Soviet Military Strategy*. (Trans., Harriet F. Scott.) New York: Praeger, 1963.
United States. Department of Defense. *Annual Defense Department Report, Fiscal Year 1975*. Washington: GPO, 1974.
______ . *Annual Defense Department Report, Fiscal Year 1977*. Washington: GPO, 1976.
______ . *Annual Defense Department Report: National Security Strategy of Realistic Deterrence*. Washington: GPO, 1972.
______ . *Annual Report, Fiscal Year 1981*. Washington: GPO, 1981.
Wolfe, Thomas W. *Soviet Power and Europe: 1945–1970*. Baltimore: Johns Hopkins Press, 1970.
Wollina, Paul. "The Strengthening of the Warsaw Military Alliance—An Expression of the Regular Process of Bringing Socialist States Together," *Militärgeschichte* [East Berlin], No. 2, 1980, 152–53.

Glossary

Comecon—Council for Mutual Economic Assistance. Sometimes cited as CMEA or CEMA. Members in early 1983: Bulgaria, Cuba, Czechoslovakia, German Democratic Republic (East Germany), Hungary, Mongolia, Poland, Romania, the Soviet Union, and Vietnam. Purpose is to further economic cooperation among members (see Appendix B).

Comintern—Communist International or Third International. Federation of communist parties founded in Moscow in 1919; dissolved by Stalin in 1943 as a conciliatory gesture to his Western allies.

GDP—Gross domestic product. The total value of goods and services produced within a country's borders during a fixed period, usually one year. Obtained by adding the value contributed by each sector of the economy in the form of compensation of employees, profits, and depreciation (consumption of capital). Subsistence production is included and consists of the imputed value of production by the farm family for its own use and the imputed rental value of owner-occupied dwellings.

GNP—Gross national product. GDP *(q.v.)* plus the income received from abroad by residents, less payments remitted abroad to nonresidents.

International Monetary Fund (IMF)—Established along with the World Bank *(q.v.)* in 1945, the IMF is a specialized agency affiliated with the United Nations and is responsible for stabilizing international exchange rates and payments. The main business of the IMF is the provision of loans to its members (including industrialized and developing countries) when they experience balance of payments difficulties. These loans frequently carry conditions that require substantial internal economic adjustments by the recipients, most of whom are developing countries. In late 1982 the IMF had 146 members.

national income (net material product)—A measurement of national economic activity used by Poland and other Comecon states. Essentially, national income is the sum of the net product contributed by certain sectors of the economy that are classified as engaging in material production. Most of net material product is contributed by industry, construction, agriculture, and forestry. But also contributing are activities defined as productive in transport and communications, trade, community services, and "other branches of material production." Net material product differs substantially from the gross national product (GNP—q.v.) measurements used in the Western economies in that it excludes various service sectors that are included in GNP. In addition, direct comparisons between national economic performances as measured by net material product and GNP are seriously restricted by pricings used in the former that, for political and social reasons, are not necessarily true valuations.

nomenklatura—literally, nomenclature. Refers to the practice whereby the PZPR (*q.v.*) nominates or gives prior approval to persons (usually PZPR members) appointed to key positions in government and other important, e.g., economic and military, institutions. The practice makes political reliability the primary criterion for appointment to the positions on the list (the *nomenklatura,* strictly speaking).

PZPR—Polish United Workers' Party (Polska Zjednoczona Partia Robotnicza). The communist party in Poland, formed in German-occupied Poland during World War II as the Polish Workers' Party. It moved to Poland with advancing Soviet troops and secured total political power during early postwar years; merged with the Polish Socialist Party (Polska Partia Socjalistyczna) in 1948 to become the PZPR.

Ruthenia—Variant of the Ukrainian Russ (or Russia). Term applied historically to East Slavic lands of Polish-Lithuanian Commonwealth that included western Ukraine and part of Byelorussia (White Ruthenia); later restricted to eastern Galicia.

socialism and socialist—In common with the other states that Western writers usually refer to as *communist,* Poland officially describes itself as *socialist* and its economic system as *socialism* and claims that it is working toward communism, which Lenin defined as a higher stage of socialism. Polish socialism bears scant resemblance to the democratic socialism of, for example, Scandinavian countries.

voivodship (*wojewodzstwo;* pl., *wojewodzstwa*)—Largest unit of local Polish government, sometimes referred to in English as province. Before 1975 the next lower level of local government was the *powiat* (pl, *powiaty*), which was equivalent to a district or country; the lowest level was the *gromada* (pl., *gromady*), or village. Since 1975 the only governmental level below the voivodship has been the *gmina* (pl., *gminy*), or commune.

Warsaw Pact—Political and military alliance founded in 1955 in response to the inclusion of the Federal Republic of Germany (West Germany) in the North Atlantic Treaty Organization (NATO). In early 1983 members were Bulgaria, Czechoslovakia, East Germany, Hungary, Poland, Romania, and the Soviet Union. Command and staff headquarters located in Lvov, Soviet Union (see Appendix C).

World Bank—Informal name used to designate a group of three affiliated international institutions: the International Bank for Reconstruction and Development (IBRD), the International Development Association (IDA), and the International Finance

Corporation (IFC). The IBRD, established in 1945, has the primary purpose of providing loans to developing countries for productive projects. The IDA, a legally separate loan fund but administered by the staff of the IBRD, was set up in 1960 to furnish credits to the poorest developing countries on much easier terms than those of conventional IBRD loans. The IFC, founded in 1956, supplements the activities of the IBRD through loans and assistance designed specifically to encourage the growth of productive private enterprises in the less developed countries. The president and certain senior officers of the IBRD hold the same positions in the IFC. The three institutions are owned by the governments of the countries that subscribe their capital. In 1982 the IBRD had over 140 members, the IDA had 130, and the IFC over 120. To participate in the World Bank group, member states must first belong to the International Monetary Fund (IMF—*q.v.*).

zloty—Basic unit of Polish currency (nonconvertible), divided into 100 groszy. Under the officially used exchange rate through 1970, US$1 equaled 24 zlotys; after devaluation by the United States in 1971–73 the rate was set at 20 zlotys to US$1. By 1979 the rate per US$1 had increased to 30 zlotys, and to 35 zlotys in late 1981. A new base rate of 80 zlotys was then introduced; the rate fluctuated during 1982, reaching 86 zlotys to US$1 near the end of the year.

Index

Published Country Studies

(Area Handbook Series)

550-65 Afghanistan
550-98 Albania
550-44 Algeria
550-59 Angola
550-73 Argentina

550-169 Australia
550-176 Austria
550-175 Bangladesh
550-170 Belgium
550-66 Bolivia

550-20 Brazil
550-168 Bulgaria
550-61 Burma
550-83 Burundi
550-50 Cambodia

550-166 Cameroon
550-159 Chad
550-77 Chile
550-60 China
550-63 China, Republic of

550-26 Colombia
550-91 Congo
550-90 Costa Rica
550-152 Cuba
550-22 Cyprus

550-158 Czechoslovakia
550-54 Dominican Republic
550-52 Ecuador
550-43 Egypt
550-150 El Salvador

550-28 Ethiopia
550-167 Finland
550-155 Germany, East
550-173 Germany, Federal Republic of
550-153 Ghana

550-87 Greece
550-78 Guatemala
550-174 Guinea
550-82 Guyana
550-164 Haiti

550-151 Honduras
550-165 Hungary
550-21 India
550-154 Indian Ocean
550-39 Indonesia

550-68 Iran
550-31 Iraq
550-25 Israel
550-182 Italy
550-69 Ivory Coast

550-177 Jamaica
550-30 Japan
550-34 Jordan
550-56 Kenya
550-81 Korea, North

550-41 Korea, South
550-58 Laos
550-24 Lebanon
550-38 Liberia
550-85 Libya

550-172 Malawi
550-45 Malaysia
550-161 Mauritania
550-79 Mexico
550-76 Mongolia

550-49 Morocco
550-64 Mozambique
550-35 Nepal, Bhutan and Sikkim
550-88 Nicaragua
550-157 Nigeria

550-94 Oceania
550-48 Pakistan
550-46 Panama
550-156 Paraguay
550-185 Persian Gulf States

550-42 Peru
550-72 Philippines
550-162 Poland
550-181 Portugal
550-160 Romania

☆ U.S. GOVERNMENT PRINTING OFFICE: 1984 -0- 421-658 (127)

550-84	Rwanda
550-51	Saudi Arabia
550-70	Senegal
550-180	Sierra Leone
550-184	Singapore
550-86	Somalia
550-93	South Africa
550-95	Soviet Union
550-179	Spain
550-96	Sri Lanka (Ceylon)
550-27	Sudan
550-47	Syria
550-62	Tanzania
550-53	Thailand
550-178	Trinidad and Tobago
550-89	Tunisia
550-80	Turkey
550-74	Uganda
550-97	Uruguay
550-71	Venezuela
550-57	Vietnam, North
550-55	Vietnam, South
550-183	Yemens, The
550-99	Yugoslavia
550-67	Zaire
550-75	Zambia
550-171	Zimbabwe